THE COLLECTOR'S HISTORY OF DOLLS' HOUSES, DOLL'S HOUSE DOLLS AND MINIATURES

THE COLLECTOR'S HISTORY OF DOLLS

The Collector's History of

DOLLS' HOUSES,

doll's house dolls and miniatures

CONSTANCE EILEEN KING

St. Martin's Press
New York

Library of Congress Catalog Card Number 83-42930

ISBN 0-312-15028-8

First published in Great Britain by Robert Hale Ltd.

First U.S. Edition

10 9 8 7 6 5 4 3 2 1

CONTENTS

Colour Illustrations

vi

The green silk hung drawing-room from the eighteenth-century Dutch cabinet house that contains dolls of almost certain English origin. The white embroidery is especially fine, with detail such as worked borders of flowers around the doors and well-designed chair seats. On a lacquer table stands the tea equipage. Each doll has its own foot-warmer. (*Museum of Mr Simon van Gijn, Dordrecht*)

The complete lack of scale seems to add to the appeal of Ann Sharp's Baby House. The variety of wax and wooden-headed dolls is also interesting, as they provide a guide to the different types available at this early date. Ann was born in 1691, but most items in the house are very early eighteenth century, though, as in the majority of family houses, some pieces were added later. (*Captain Peter Bulwer-Long*)

The low ceiling of this basement kitchen adds an air of realism, despite the very British lack of scale evidenced in the large plates and the chocolate-making machine. The cook is in remarkably fine original condition. From the Uppark Baby House. (*Uppark, Sussex*)

In the Blackett Baby House kitchen, the British disregard of scale is again seen. Though this kitchen is not as completely original as that at Uppark, it contains a fine jack, and the cooking area is also of interest. *Circa* 1740. (*Museum of London*)

Between pages 294 and 295

One of the finest and most impressive dolls from the Court scenes at Mon Plaisir is this well carved lady with fashionable beauty spots. Despite her large size, she has to be classed as a doll's house figure (*Schlossmuseum, Arnstadt*)

A well-proportioned English Baby House with its original chimneypieces, dresser and spit rack. The contents, including several *papier mâché* dolls, date mainly from the mid-nineteenth century. The house belonged to the Gardner family. *Circa* 1775. (*Author's Collection*)

An unusually well-made wax group, presumably originally created as an almost photographic record of the Seidel family. The high quality of the miniatures and the attention to proportion give an indication of the standard that could be achieved in items for adult enjoyment. The group was the work of Johann Albani. Early nineteenth century. (*Stadtmuseum, Munich*)

'Vittoria Cottage' still retains all its original wallpapers and most of its fabric floor coverings. The furniture is mainly mid-nineteenth century imitation rosewood of the Waltershausen type. In the grate can still be seen the original firewood made from broken-up Grödnertal dolls. Dated on front to 1817. (*Author's Collection*)

A richly furnished middle-class Swiss interior dating to the mid-nineteenth century. Despite the native skill in woodcarving, the furniture remains mainly of German origin. This house is much more reminiscent of the early Continental cabinets than British and American houses of similar date, where the move towards realism of structure is more apparent. Oak grained. 1860–65. (*Historisches Museum, Basel*)

Collector's History of Doll's Houses

Dolls' rooms were much more popular in Germany than dolls' houses, though few structures contain the wealth of ornamentation seen in this example. The bisque-headed dolls are also of German origin. Typical of a Berlin interior of 1880. (*Rheinisches Landesmuseum für Volkskunde, Kommern*)

The model kitchen was among the most popular European toys. This Holstein example was constructed around 1800, though the contents are later. The cook is a porcelain-headed German doll. (*Legoland*)

Despite its mid-nineteenth century origin, this complex house, with its cellars and laundry rooms in the roof, is reminiscent of the early cabinet houses. It was made by Ludwig Adam Kelterborn, a Basel artist, for his daughters. (*Historisches Museum, Basel*)

The front of Hatherlow House, showing the heavy but skilled workmanship of the maker, who seems to have been more used to making furniture than model houses. It is constructed from a mixture of pine and mahogany. The so-called captain's walk on the roof can be unlocked and lifted to reveal a box-like compartment, presumably for the more expensive or fragile items. (*Author's Collection*)

The back view of Hatherlow House. The bricks are painted, and the complete structure pivots on its table-like base. It is one of the most hauntingly curious of houses as the back and front are so completely different in style and decoration. There are inset brass carrying handles at the sides. *Circa 1870.* (*Author's Collection*)

The back interior of Hatherlow House with its strange doors that are much lower than the fireplaces and its narrow, very high rooms. Despite the good workmanship of the staircase and landing rails, the whole model is disconcerting in effect. The porcelain doll is of the pink-tinted 'Berlin type'. (*Author's Collection*)

The front interior of Hatherlow House with its black-painted drawing-room that extends across the complete depth of the model. This room is furnished with tiny, exquisitely embroidered wishbone furniture, dating to around 1865. The metal long-case clock on the landing is German, as is the crockery and ornamental glass. (*Author's Collection*)

Though this photograph shows only one section of Hammond House, which is some eight feet ten inches long, it provides a concept of both its complexity and its vast selection of miniatures. The house takes its title from the name 'Ruby Hammond' that was found on one of its tiny towels. The complete model includes seventy-seven dolls. *Circa 1886.* (*Wallington Hall, Northumberland*)

An exterior view of a Danish doll's house, dating to the second half of the nineteenth century. The steep pitch of the roof gave better protection from the winter snows. The house is known as 'Skottenborge'. (*Legoland*)

Another view of Skottenborge, showing its simple two-roomed interior, made attractive by its variety of furniture. (*Legoland*)

The interior of the Deauville House, showing a variety of lithographed paper on wood furniture of German origin. The pressed cardboard sofa at the back of the room is unusual as, being so very fragile, few have survived. This gilt example is probably French. All late nineteenth century. (*Author's Collection*)

Though the lady dolls are of a basic type, they are made highly collectable by the perfection of their contemporary costumes. The small 'stone bisque' children, including a boy in eighteenth-century-style dress, also date from the 1860s. (*Author's Collection*)

An unusual waxed composition doll's house doll with composition lower limbs and detailed silk Court dress with a train. German. The lady playing the wooden mandolin also wears original dress and is marked 'S & H 1160' for Simon & Halbig. The doll has glass eyes and a bisque head. Both wear mohair wigs. (*Author's Collection*)

A pair of completely original poured wax dolls of English origin, wearing their original muslin frocks and capes. The larger, dressed in pink, has its original box with the label 'To Harriet A. Kinder on her birthday. Jny 12th 1850. From her affectionate brother George.' Such dolls, with small, dark bead-like eyes, were made from the late eighteenth century until 1850. Harriet's doll has painted eyes, but the smaller has glass. (*Author's Collection*)

Few houses contain furniture that was obviously purchased as a complete set. This British-made house contains German furniture decorated with gilt motifs. This furniture was particularly well made, as all the upholstery fabrics were especially printed to scale. *Circa* 1900. (*Author's Collection*)

'The Bay Room', a richly furnished Danish set of rooms including a bedroom and sitting-room and dating to around 1880. (*Legoland*)

An exterior view of the German house of lithographed paper on wood. Similar examples appeared on the catalogues of C. H. Muller Jr., a firm that was established in Olbernhau, Saxony, in 1871. Though the house depends mainly on lithography for its effect, there is also a high standard of carpentry. (*Author's Collection*)

A pair of very rare German porcelain dolls. The bodies are jointed wood with lower arm and leg sections of porcelain. The shoulder heads are attached by a single wooden pin. The sailor, in original costume, has a man's head with moulded hair, and the woman has a moulded, decorated bonnet. *Circa* 1840. (*Author's Collection*)

A *papier mâché* lady in peasant costume. The body is made of pink leather. Sonneberg, *circa* 1835–40. The table is set with a German service known to collectors as the onion pattern type, after the famous Meissen design. The glass and cutlery is also German. From the Gardner Baby House. (*Author's Collection*)

Doll's house pedlars are only occasionally found. This example has a jointed wooden body and a *brotteig*-type head. It was commercially assembled, as larger versions in identical frocks are found. Photographed in the kitchen of the Gardner House. (*Author's Collection*)

During the nineteenth century, great attention was paid to the correct costuming of dolls. This American Family, with waxed composition heads, is unusual as it includes men. The dolls are of German origin but probably costumed in America. *Circa* 1885. (*Margaret Woodbury Strong Museum, New York*)

Black-and-White Illustrations

Collector's History of Doll's Houses

Acknowledgements

Just as a doll's house is an amalgam of the work of various makers, often gathered from several countries, so a book of this kind depends on help, information and co-operation from people, museums and auction rooms in many parts of the world.

I would particularly thank the staff of the Schlossmuseum, Arnstadt, who gave me so much assistance in examining individual items in 'Mon Plaisir'. Also the curator and the librarian of the Toy Museum at Sonneberg who allowed me to study original catalogues and provided an English-speaking guide to explain further some of the exhibits. In West Germany I am indebted to many friends, such as Ursula Driskell, who suggested little known museums and collections to visit. Wicki Schweizer of Munich was also of considerable help as she gave me an old family history describing the beginnings of their production of miniature filigree work. The staff of all the West German museums were unfailingly helpful and often re-arranged lighting and objects so that record photographs could be taken.

In Holland I particularly thank Mevrouw Jetje Roos-Enk who showed me her fascinating collection and talked at length about collecting in Holland. I am also grateful to Hans van der Spaa for his help with the basic translation of the eighteenth-century scroll from Sara Ploos van Amstel's house at the Frans Hals Museum, Haarlem.

In America the staff of the Margaret Woodbury Strong Museum have again been extremely helpful in providing more than adequate information with photographs and in suggesting other pieces which would add to the American history of the subject. I have also relied for much American information on several excellent books on houses and miniatures and gratefully acknowledge my debt in this area. I have discussed miniature and doll's house collecting in America with so many friends, dealers and auction house staff that it is impossible to list them all individually but thank these many people for interesting information.

In much the same way British collectors are always willing to show their collections and discuss acquisitions and to the many people who have shown me their private 'museums' over the years I extend my thanks. Among the public museums I am especially grateful to the staff of the Bethnal Green Museum of Childhood who suffer so many photographers, and the curators of Wallington Hall Museum in Northumberland who were generous with time and help. The London auction rooms, Phillips, Christie's and Sotheby's have also assisted generously with photographs. The Lines family was also extremely kind in allowing me to study and photograph original catalogues. The drawings of houses dating to the turn of the century made it possible to identify many structures previously unattributable. Finally, I thank my husband without whose absolute co-operation in collecting, restoration and photography the book would have been very difficult.

Preface

The subject of European and American dolls' houses might immediately be considered as another aspect of the history of antique toys, but it is rather the development of adult fascination with the miniature that seems, at certain periods, also to have encouraged the toymakers to create good-quality miniatures for children. This curious inter-relation between adult amusement and child's plaything characterizes the entire history of miniatures and their settings so that at the present time, for instance, virtually the only really well-made modern pieces are intended for adult collectors.

In compiling this history, it was necessary to visit all the European houses discussed, as photographs of miniatures are notoriously unreliable, and what appears to be a particularly well-made specimen, often, on close examination, is seen to have been roughly made by a local handyman. Some writers, presumably working from photographs, have described the work of eighteenth-century jobbing carpenters as adult cabinet pieces worthy of the complete preoccupation of an elegant lady, and so it was obviously necessary to re-examine several houses already recorded and survey their construction from the antique-collector's standpoint, rather than that of almost blind enthusiasm. Dolls' houses and their contents, despite the great number of collectors involved, are as yet a lightly researched subject, and I found it necessary to seek much of their history in West and East Germany, Holland and France, which made both the basic travel and the translation from foreign sources a particularly heavy, if fascinating task. American houses and their contents have already been catalogued with great enthusiasm by native collectors, so that it seemed appropriate in the time and finance available to me to study the European aspect in particular depth, rather than repeating work already effected. The tour of the important European houses and centres of toymaking has been both interesting and distressing in its effect –

distressing in that houses were discovered with their valuable textiles displayed in sunlight or having suffered damage even in the few months between visits. Hopefully, the importance of these structures will become more generally recognized by the publication of a further work on the subject.

As I have dealt with the development of dolls' houses and their contents from the historical and social standpoint, my greatest emphasis is on those models whose contents are in virtually original condition, as it is only in these specimens that we are given an even partially correct picture of everyday life in a particular country or specific time. In order to offer a readable book, I have avoided tedious itemizing of the precise details of nineteenth- and early-twentieth-century houses. Some years ago I kept records of such specifications, but it soon became obvious that the only conclusion was that, apart from the obvious commercial models, every carpenter or amateur worked to his own plan, adapting and improvising as the task progressed. From hundreds of precise measurements and descriptions of individual decoration, there was no useful extrapolation, so that my listing and cataloguing was a completely futile operation. All the early houses have to be treated individually, as almost unique structures, because only in the second half of the nineteenth century can lines of comparison be drawn between many houses that exhibit characteristics of the same source.

The subject of dolls' houses is wide, diverse and fascinating, and my own absorption with the subject has steadily increased during the years of research for this book, as interesting and unusual items continually came to light. The whimsical chinoiserie taste for instance, hardly ever revealed in the construction of dolls' houses, was charmingly described in an enchanting country house of massive proportions, complete with stables, that appeared in one of the London salerooms. Eventually, no matter how unusual or strange a particular fashion might be, it is one day manifested in an old miniature. In my first book on toys, I commented that no really effective Art Deco furniture seems to have been made; yet, within a few days of publication, I purchased the well-made set illustrated in these pages. The subject is without end and constantly challenging, so that it is little wonder that the number of collectors seems to increase by the day, despite the growing cost of acquisitions. In particular, many more recent models, especially those of the 1920s and 1930s, are now being rescued and refurbished with contemporary items. To an antique-collector the interest of such late houses is minimal, but from the standpoint of either the sociologist or the historian they are of considerable relevance, suggesting the taste and living-conditions of a particular period as yet too close for sensible evaluation.

Everything one sees on earth
Is dolls' stuff and nothing else.
All that man finds,
He plays with like a child.
Ardently he loves for a short while
What he throws away so easily thereafter.
Thus man is, as one finds,
Not only once but always a child.

A verse handwritten on a scroll that once hung
in the cabinet house assembled by Sara Ploos
van Amstel in the mid-eighteenth century.
The cabinet house is now at the Frans
Hals Museum in Haarlem.

ONE

Introduction

A recurring phenomenon in the history of European and American dolls'
houses is the preoccupation of adults with these fascinating structures, at
certain periods almost to the exclusion of children. In the earliest recorded
stages of their development, it was Court ladies and princes who furnished
and commissioned the decoration of such models, and though the finished
structures were sometimes shown to children, they remained, because of the
value of their contents, completely the province of adults and were displayed
in museum-like curiosity rooms, art chambers or reception areas where their
expensive and unusual plenishments could form a focal-point for discussion.

Like model trains with their accompanying settings, the doll's house
appeals to a common adult absorption with the miniature, apparent in all
advanced civilizations, so that in the seventeenth and eighteenth centuries a
model house or room was as appropriate in the drawing-room, alongside the
specimen cabinets and console tables, as in the nursery. In recent years this
position has been regained, and large numbers of miniature-enthusiasts
display both antique and reproduction models in the setting of their homes.
For many collectors it is the enjoyment of restoration and furnishing that
encourages them in an often long and difficult task, while others delight in an
original model, untouched since the time of its manufacture and in every
respect a fine antique. Some collect because of their affection for the style of
buildings and interiors of the past, while others enjoy creating progressive
modern settings and equipping the rooms with ingenious pieces that they
make with considerable skill. To one collector the doll's house forms a single
object in a wider toy collection, while others concentrate entirely on this one
topic to the exclusion of all other toys and find, within the confines of the
wood and card walls, sufficient interest to engage their attention for many
years.

Whereas a doll has an immediate emotional appeal, often with little

1

relationship to its basic quality, the adult reaction to a model house is far more discriminating, so that the well-made or ingeniously contrived item attracts, whereas the shoddy or badly designed arouses little interest. Consequently, while the history of the doll relates directly and almost exclusively to the lives of children, that of the miniature house is of dual interest, part a mirror of home life and part, at the lowest level, a nursery toy to be roughly handled and treated with scant concern. Between these two extremes lie adult-made models for display under glass shades, expensive toys for very wealthy children who played under adult supervision, and the whole spectrum of toyshop models, ranging from simple cottages costing only a few shillings to great mansions with hot and cold water and electrically operated floors and lifts. Where the doll's house was played with as a nursery toy, it was, until the last quarter of the nineteenth century, almost exclusively a possession of rich and middle-class children, as the most a poor child could have owned would be a simple box-like structure of little lasting interest.

It is because dolls' houses could be directly related to few lives, in comparison with, for instance, dolls or toy horses, that they appear so rarely in autobiographies. Whereas a story or a poem based on the fate of a lost or damaged doll will touch a fleeting element of childhood in all but the most hardened adult, to many, a model house was just a toy that other people owned. Illustrators of children's books seem, until the twentieth century, to have worked on a similar premise, as line-drawings and colourful lithographs showing toys and dolls abound, but the doll's house only occasionally appears. In the course of research into antique toys, I have read through complete volumes of eighteenth- and nineteenth-century periodicals and magazines but have discovered remarkably few mentions of dolls' houses and miniature furniture and just a handful of illustrations. The most I was able to cull from eighteenth-century popular literature was the occasional reference to a loved 'Baby House' or the comparison of an actual building with a toy, and I was made very aware of how minimal was the impact of these expensive toys on the general reading public.

The scene changes completely in the late nineteenth century because of the general increase in prosperity. Life was no longer merely a struggle for survival, so there was a little money to spare for the toys that were displayed so alluringly in shop windows. The doll's house therefore enjoyed a sudden rise in popularity, and games, painting-books, Christmas cards and story books sometimes illustrate attractively dressed children playing with their houses. Even so, the number, in relation to that of dolls, is small, and dolls' houses are usually shown only when there is a positive textual reference, whereas soft toys and mail-carts, for instance, appear in profusion. Artists were obviously aware that a drawing of a doll's house appealed less generally than that of a doll, and, even more importantly, they knew that the large, solid rectangular structure of the house would be difficult to integrate into the

An early nineteenth-century British print, showing a child in the nursery. The simple doll's house is reminiscent of Vittoria Cottage (illustration p.278). Beneath the house stands a model hearth with meat on a spit. Both toys were to teach household skills.

composition of a painting; so at least part of the scarcity of examples can be attributed directly to a wish to avoid an element that would overwhelm the composition. The doll researcher is able to illustrate their development with such evocative renderings as that of Arbella Stuart with her wooden lady doll clasped to her infant chest, but the doll's house historian has to trace their history very completely from the houses themselves, leavened by a few early records of structures of such eccentricity that they aroused widespread interest.

Whereas the large size of dolls' houses discouraged artists from representing them, the doll's house doll suffered, at the opposite extreme, from its very small scale. A 14-inch doll could look most attractive lying in a girl's arms or sitting at a low table, but only the merest suggestion of a 6-inch figure can be attempted, and they rarely appear in illustrations. These miniatures hardly engender the warm love an infant feels for a soft-bodied doll or animal it could take to bed as a companion, and they have inspired few literary excursions in either prose or verse. When the doll's house figure is remembered, it is usually as a miniature adult engaged in every human activity, giving tea- and dinner-parties, having the measles or whooping-cough at the same time as its owner or insisting on purchasing a new frock for a special event. The doll's house doll was never a toy to be cosseted and loved but an object that could be made to dance to the child's own tune and invested with the characteristics of real life. When the child was beaten by her mother or nurse, she in turn vented her anger and frustration on the doll's house children, throwing them angrily into their cigar-box or shutting them in an understairs cupboard as punishment. They rarely arouse the comforting maternal instinct as much as a desire to control and direct life in the way the subservient child finds to be maddeningly impossible. Many people, brought up in poor surroundings, recount how their small dolls regularly attended theatres, night clubs and grand receptions, though their ballgowns were fragments of kitchen aprons and their home a two-roomed box with a torn shawl for a carpet and matchbox furniture. The doll's house family was as much a vehicle for escape and fantasy as a fairy-tale book or an exciting film, and it is the characters with which they were invested, rather than their construction or actual appearance, that is most often remembered. The adult, in reminiscent mood, will often expound on the complete life-story of a doll but, when asked whether its body was jointed or sawdust-filled, will have no positive recollection. The most common memory is the difficulty encountered in making these substitute beings sit and stand realistically, as they invariably slumped sideways or slid to the ground on their insubstantial legs.

The child of today, better fed, more generously entertained and much less likely to be physically chastised, seems to have less need of these substitute beings, and both dolls' houses and miniature dolls are of declining importance. In the early twentieth century, large department-stores could offer the child a wide selection of houses and an unending variety of furniture, but the modern girl is fortunate if she can choose between three or four models, while the blister-packed plastic furniture is depressing in its uniformity. Perhaps we should feel glad that children no longer need to search for substitutes for unhappy homes or frustrated ambitions, but it is impossible not to feel that a society cannot be completely healthy when its young find it tedious to indulge in make-believe.

As a child I played for weeks on end during the warm weather in a disused quarry where, together with my friends, the outline plans of houses, castles, shops and mansions were laid out from the flat stones that lay around. Despite the fact that the walls were not more than a foot high, they were never

Contemporary photographs of children with dolls' houses are rare. This example, *circa* 1895–1900, shows a girl proudly displaying her favourite possessions, including a house probably made by Lines.

climbed over; entrance to any family house was strictly through the front door. Our chairs, tables and beds were all made from rocks, but tattered lace tablecloths, damaged cushions and worn carpets gave prestige to our make-believe existence. Several generations had played the same games in the quarry, and all sorts of rituals and traditions had built up over the years. Our unit of currency was broken china, hidden away at night, as it was often stolen, especially those fragments that showed a printed flower-head or an animal or figure and whose value was twenty times that of a piece of a plain white plate. Our community celebrated weddings, baptisms and funerals, and there were thriving shops for the sale of ivy wreaths and bouquets. Daily life was enacted against a background of frequent threats from bandits and Indians, but oddly, despite the fact that the war years were only shortly past, there was never any concern for a German attack, and even the bogey-man Hitler failed to appear. The imaginary environment belonged to no age and involved no living characters. For a few years other children pursued this activity, but by the mid-1950s and despite a greater number of children, all evidence of this curious miniature civilization was gone, and the stones had returned to their random order, watched over only by the birds and mountain foxes.

The very young children of the 1950s obviously derived little enjoyment in such play but were kept in their own gardens or sat neatly in front of television sets to watch others enjoying the make-believe situations that were beyond their own experience. How rarely do we now see children parading in their dressing-up clothes in the streets or even pushing their dolls in prams: parents feel that a child looks unpresentable or that progress would be too slow if a doll's pram were to be taken around the shops, and the natural imitative elements of play are stunted because of an adult desire to conform and avoid the bother of cleaning dirty children after a day's completely free activity. Little wonder that the girl who can no longer play with ease is less fascinated with the miniature world than her predecessors and, having arranged her doll's house furniture and seated the dolls, quickly shuts the doors and loses interest in a toy that depends so heavily for its success on the element of make-believe.

With great, but too rarely encountered delight, adults watch more fortunate children playing with model houses that were made to satisfy their individual needs by a father or relative. They talk to the dolls, scolding and commending where necessary and at times controlling the figures as on a stage, so that a positive narrative is attempted. Unfortunately, for the majority of children, television supplies their needs adequately, and it seems that in a very few years play of this type will itself have become social history rather than an everyday occurrence.

For adults throughout the centuries the doll's house is an enchanted world in miniature, a substitute home, with a universal appeal. Once arranged,

Lego include miniature houses and furniture in their range of construction toys. The three- to seven-year-old child is encouraged to act out stories concerning such characters as Charlie Cat and Peter Pig. These items are from the Fabuland Story sets.

order is steadfastly maintained: firegrates do not need cleaning, floors sweeping or sinks scouring, so that the chatelaine can stand back from her efforts with satisfaction, knowing that every item will remain in its appointed place behind the locked façade until she chooses to re-arrange the dressing-table or sideboard. Food remains unspoilt in the kitchen to perpetuity, and there is no breathless rush to present a fine dessert before it collapses or to pour a sauce before it congeals. The doll's house is the perfect answer for the inefficient housekeeper as within its rooms can be practised all the virtues which in real life become tedious: the silver tea-set can be used every day and, even if a little tarnished, does not accuse its owner of negligence; Grandma and Grandpa, with their heavily coloured bisque faces, are resolutely healthy and never consider grumbling; the baby, in his perfectly arranged cot, is always satisfied and happy; the dog never bites, and the cat would not

A group of models including a ready-to-assemble *Bauhaus* made in 1979. Bodo Hennig came originally from the Ertzgebirge and still produces toys of natural wood. The houses are made on two scales and have matching furniture. The firm is now based in Allgäu in West Germany.

The well-known Sindy doll was provided with a space-saving house in 1982. There is a lift to all floors and a spiral staircase. The back is decorated as a town house.

consider scratching the legs of an eighteenth-century bureau. The doll's house interior is the perfect household in miniature, and for those who find keeping a full-sized home in reasonable order a constant and losing battle, the model house offers the allure of the unattainable. The interior is a delectable mixture of the charms of Lilliput and Utopia, simultaneously an escape from real life and its mirror.

Perhaps at times the adult collector experiences the sensations and memories of childhood, when every doll had its own personality and history, so that it became more absorbing to play with the doll's house than to play with other children. This lasting impression of a make-believe world is so strong in some cases that the collectors actually regress and create stories and situations around the settings they have created. Even the most sophisticated admit such indulgences to some extent, while those with little concern for their intellectual standing even write simple stories regarding the happenings in 'Jubilee Lodge' or at '3 Regency Terrace'. Children's writers have long realized the potential of this toy above all others as a source of material because the whole spectrum of human life can be enacted with no more effort than the substitution of dolls for people.

The sense of the miniaturization of life is so strong that, peeping through a chink in the curtains or looking into a hall through a half-opened door, one longs to escape from a world of civil wars and terrorism to an age when lace-edged tablecloths were invariably used at tea-time and when the second parlourmaid giggled with her followers outside the kitchen door. Any adult can recreate such a world simply by constructing or purchasing a model house, and the growing number of enthusiasts is proof of the eagerness of modern man to find some transitory escape. Those who find antique houses too shabby in appearance often prefer a reproduction that recreates Georgian elegance or light-hearted Regency Gothick, and there are dozens of furniture, crockery and doll-makers who enthusiastically supply items for their equipping. Others see the construction of the model itself as a challenge and work to their own designs, thus creating completely unique structures.

The collecting of antique houses is a long-established pursuit, and the writer Denton Welch mentions in his letters that even in the 1940s, when many antique items were still considerably undervalued, it was expensive to purchase good miniature furniture. In relation to dolls, antique houses are today relatively cheap, and the greatest expense will be incurred in their furnishing, as a single chair or table can sometimes cost more than its full-sized counterpart. In order to achieve a suitably cluttered effect, it is necessary to purchase a large number of additional decorative items, such as candle-sconces, pictures and rugs, all of which are scarce because they are required in such number. The equipping of such a house, despite expense and difficulty, is an absorbing and pleasant occupation, with the attractiveness of any beautiful but useless item. They have the charm of a lovely functionless

Fabergé mouse or a fine jewelled scent-bottle – items that give pleasure simply because of their lack of any utilitarian purpose.

Enthusiasts often attempt to invest the doll's house with serious historical importance and suggest that the everyday lives of the original owners are mirrored in its contents but the re-arrangement of furniture, redecoration, later additions and basic wear have all contributed to the diminution of the original effect, so that what remains is simply the broadest sketch of nineteenth-century life, which usually fails to substantiate any such claim. Popular journalists are particularly fond of the comment that in a doll's house can be viewed Victorian life in all its detail. In fact the opposite is true. We see of life what Victorian parents thought prudent or desirable for their offspring to view, so that the attractive and romantic was displayed while the sordid or ugly was kept as neatly out of sight as a lady's legs. Even the lavatory, a feature of most middle-class homes by the 1870s, was only very occasionally provided in dolls' houses before 1900, while the dirt, drudgery and sexual tension inherent in daily life were kept firmly out of the picture of comfortable and very perfect family life. In nineteenth-century houses there is none of the realism of beggar or witchcraft, the arrangement of lying-in rooms or the drunken card-playing parties that appear in the seventeenth- and eighteenth-century cabinet houses, made for adult appreciation, as the whole concept was aimed completely at the appreciation and taste of an innocent child. In the few cases where an adult was engaged in creating settings mainly for his own amusement, a greater degree of authenticity is immediately obvious, but the majority of houses made in the last 150 years offer only a light pastiche of the period, and it is much too easy to overrate their importance as documents of social interest.

After 1840, styles, of both decoration and furniture, changed rapidly, and we pass through Biedermeier, neo-Renaissance, Gothic and various revival forms to the light-heartedness of Art Nouveau and the practicality of basic functionalism. While fashionable adults adapted their homes to keep pace with these popular developments, the majority of toy-manufacturers continued to reproduce their traditional designs, and it was not until the advent of Art Nouveau that model furniture sustained any real change. As most furniture was German-made, it mirrored the styles popular in that country, many of which were quite unlike anything seen in a British or American home. It might be thought that some progressive, aesthetic mother would have enjoyed decorating her child's doll's house in the taste she most admired, but it seems that, where children's toys were concerned, the most fashionable retreated into traditional vein and kept the interiors free of any adventurous elements. An up-to-date kitchen range or a curious tin shower-bath sometimes indicates a more progressive selection, but in the main the equipping of the house was left almost exclusively to the manufacturers who had performed the task, with little change, for fifty or sixty years.

Essentially, the doll's house is an extravagant folly, of no practical use to the person who creates or preserves it but offering a romantic shelter from the problems of modern life. Its fascination lies in its amusing, light-hearted qualities and, perhaps because of the extreme functionalism of modern society, it is again casting its spell over otherwise sane and intelligent adults. Many dismiss such pursuits as wasteful of both time and money and comment on the impracticality of hours wasted on the carving of an exquisite cabriole leg or in mending the silk upholstery of a sofa, but the desire for occasional escape is inherent in humanity itself. Perhaps the Thuringian princess who created a miniature town in the eighteenth century sought a similar means of escape from her unhappy marriage and the constant complaints of her husband's family. That the result of such adult escapism frequently reveals a high standard of craftsmanship and artistic expression is an encouraging manifestation of man's ability to create fine work in pursuit of wholly selfish or eccentric impulses.

Early Development

Man's fascination with miniature objects can be traced to the beginning of civilization, though it is unlikely that many of the surviving pieces of furniture were the province of toymakers, as their intention was usually funerary or votive. Various chroniclers of children's toys and dolls' houses have attempted to prove that early Egyptian children played with model rooms and their furnishings, but with such a dearth of proven fact it is possible to make only the broadest suggestions. The problem of differentiating between a child's toy and a miniaturization of an item in everyday use purely for tomb equipment is virtually impossible, as even the most insignificant objects were necessary to ensure that the dead should want for nothing in the after-life. One of the most interesting miniatures that is generally considered to be a toy is a chair measuring $2\frac{1}{2}$ inches and carved from solid wood. As the piece was found among other toy-like items in the grave of a child, it seems likely that these were ordinary playthings, expected to entertain and sustain the spirit after death. This chair, of the most basic shape, can now be seen at the Toy Museum in Sonneberg, but other museums have many basic toys, such as balls and simple animals, that have been discovered in similar settings. It is, of course, impossible to be sure whether these were the actual toys or especially made representations, but they serve to present a satisfactory impression of the types of basic playthings in everyday use.

Egyptian adult love of the miniature was developed to quite a high degree, and model rooms in particular were manufactured in some number. Many of the houses were quite crudely made from clay to act as sheltering-places for the souls of the deceased interred during modest burials of the Middle Kingdom. The British Museum has several examples, including one of the XII Dynasty, *circa* 1900 BC, in which items of food are laid out on the forecourt

12

An Egyptian model house with jars and barrels arranged on a bench. Such houses were made
as sheltering-places for the souls of the dead. XII Dynasty. 1,900 BC.

and jars and barrels arranged on a bench, all these objects being modelled in
position so they could not be moved; in the foreground of this very modest
dwelling is a pool. Wealthier Egyptians were provided with models of much
greater complexity, with removable equipment, such as correctly made lamp-
holders of clay with attractive surface-decoration and even small doll-like
serving figures. The complex model at the Metropolitan Museum of Art in
New York is a particularly fine example of funerary craft of the highest
quality, as it was made for Meket-Rè, an important Court official *circa* 2000
BC. The simple fish pond that was adequate for the man associated with the
British Museum example was not suitable for a man of Meket-Rè's prestige, and
his home was provided with a copper pond that would have held water for a
long period. It stands in a realistic walled garden surrounded by trees and serves
to illustrate the very wide variations in quality dependent on a man's position
and wealth. His house was also correctly made, and the crossbeams of the
rooms are decorated with painted yellow stars on a blue ground, in direct
imitation of the finest interiors of the period. The back of the porch is

Egyptian everyday life is revealed in the many scenes that make up the complex model that was discovered in the tomb of Meket-Rè. In this arrangement cattle are being inspected. The scene is made of wood and dates from 2,000 BC. XI Dynasty.

supported by columns of lotus and papyrus, dominated by a huge slate doorway with a fanlight above, but there are also other tall latticed windows and a side door. A large number of craftsmen, servants and retainers were needed to serve such an important official, and we see these people at work in the weaver's shop, the granary and the bakery. There is also a fleet of boats, one of which is especially equipped for fowling and is reminiscent of the great attention to detail seen later in some of the complex German arrangements.

Much of our knowledge of everyday life in Egypt is derived from the models of people at work, made mainly in earthenware, that were needed in such numbers for tomb use. Other finer materials, such as copper, were sometimes used for model-making, in particular for small altars, while ivory lent itself well to the carving of toys of greater complexity that have also been found in the tombs of children. It is obviously tempting to suggest a whole variety of small items, such as the frequently found Kohl pots, as toys, and several writers have even suggested that the funerary model houses might have fallen into the hands of children and been utilized as playthings, a supposition

Above: An Egyptian wooden chair found in a child's grave. 500 BC.

Right: A decorative miniature lampholder made of clay. Ptolemaic. Egypt. First century BC.

that seems highly unlikely, as historically objects connected with death were held in great esteem. Obviously the Egyptians possessed a deep appreciation of the art of miniature-making, and their children played with toys whose designs are represented in the objects discovered in the tombs of the very young, but there is at present no positive evidence to suggest that these children ever played with model rooms or houses.

The Greek civilization offers the researcher a more varied assortment of miniatures that again have survived because of their preservation in the tombs of children. Although the birth of a female aroused little enthusiasm in a Greek family, she was likely to be adequately supplied with toys and well looked after if she was healthy. Xenophon recounts that a good Greek mother would impress upon her daughters, from their earliest age, that their main aim should be towards fulfilling their eventual role as obedient and submissive wives, and towards this end the mother provided a good selection of toys, mainly of a teaching nature, including models of household equipment. Together with their brothers, the girls would listen in suspense to

15

the ghost and horror stories recounted by their nurse, in which appeared such terrifying bogey figures as Mormo, Gorgo and Alphito.

The miniature wine-jugs that were given as gifts to children at the Athenian festival of Anthesteria, the blossom feast of early spring, are a rich source of information for the toy-historian, as their decoration often includes representations of children at play – though, regrettably, dolls' houses and rooms have not been found on any examples. Some children certainly made models of houses themselves, and there is a reference in *The Frogs* by Aristophanes to a pretty baby who carved himself a barrow of wood and made small model wax houses. Plato believed that children should be allowed to play without restriction until the age of six, after which their games should in some way contribute towards their eventual role in life. The occupation of model-building was obviously quite highly considered, and Strepsiades proudly explained to Socrates that his intelligent son, when only a very small child, had made wooden boats and miniature chariots from scraps of leather, and frog figures from pomegranates, while of particular interest is the fact that he also made houses out of clay. The tyrant Dionysius, during his unhappy childhood, occupied his tedious and lonely hours in making chariots, lamps and small tables and chairs as toys. This type of model-building was very highly commended by Plato, who suggested that prospective architects should accustom themselves from early childhood to the construction of model houses, a concern that was extended to the education of girls, who should become accustomed through play to the tasks they would face as adults.

Despite the high degree of household organization in ancient Greece and the number of servants who could be used to amuse and look after the children, it is obvious that toys were needed in order to distract their attention from troublesome pursuits. Aristotle insisted that children should be kept occupied and suggested a rattle as a suitable diversion for the very young; since so long as the child was busy with this toy, nothing else in the house could be broken: 'As children are incapable of sitting still for two minutes, a rattle is a most suitable toy.' Other children were supplied with toys made of a variety of substances, including ivory, lead and earthenware, which were made on a commercial scale by several manufacturers.

These toys were sold by market traders throughout the year, but the greatest activity took place during the religious festivals in which children could take part and where they were presented with toys or the small jars, decorated with scenes of childhood that were thought to guard against the evil eye, as the pictured children almost invariably wore amulets around their necks. Miniature representations of household objects, needed in order to train a girl for her later role, were produced in some variety, and clay, being cheap, was one of the most popular materials. Surviving earthenware models include a three-legged table and a number of beautifully made lamps, as well

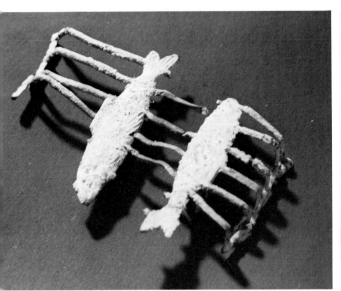 

Above left: A miniature Trojan griddle containing two fish. *Circa* 400 BC. *Above right:* A terracotta figure of a Greek woman in her bath. Made *circa* 450 BC and discovered in a tomb at Camirus.

as working models of craftsmen and traders, such as an activated representation of a woman using a rolling-pin dating to the fifth century BC. One of the most charming models is that of a lady in a bath-tub, dating to 450 BC and found in a tomb at Camirus. The lady was simply modelled in one with the bath, but though it would be tempting to consider her as a toy figure for a miniature room or setting, there is no proof to this effect. At the Sonneberg Museum are several miniature earthenware cooking-pots that were discovered in a grave of the fifth to the fourth century BC, and there is also a charming bowl in which a large fish lies ready for the table, discovered in a Boetian child's grave of the fourth to the third century BC. At the same museum is a Trojan model griddle on which lie two fish, a piece that was personally excavated by the famous Heinrich Schliemann and which is believed to have formed part of a model kitchen. Some of the metal toys to be seen at the British Museum are quite beautifully made, such as a bronze chair with cross-hatching to represent rush and a precisely made tray, and though we cannot be sure that such toys were played with every day by richer children, they serve to indicate the degree of craftsmanship that was lavished on miniatures at this early period.

The survival of such toys is due mainly to the Greek custom of dedicating playthings at the temples of deities, often with an accompanying inscription or dedication, such as 'Augusta, the protectress of children, receive in your temple this doll and this cradle of shining hair. Accept, glorious Ilithiya, this

17

A pair of Greek dolls of the type associated with children. The larger is six inches. Fifth century BC.

gift as a thanks-offering. It is a gift of Tisus.' At the temple of Hera at Olympia was found a small ivory bed thought to have been a toy of Hippodameia, the wife of Pelops, offered to the goddess before marriage. The earthenware dolls that were often included among such offerings range in size from $4\frac{3}{4}$ to 6 inches high, proportions that were later used popularly for doll's house inhabitants, though the leg-jointing of these well-made figures was such as to make it very difficult to persuade them to sit realistically. These Greek dolls have articulated arms and skilful definition of their features, though the hands are given only minimal attention, as they usually carry clappers. The examples with movable limbs were known as *neurospasta* and, judging by the numbers that have survived, were once owned by the majority of children. Finer examples, such as a figure from the third century BC wearing a helmet, or another with ribbon decoration in the hair, indicate that in dolls, as in

18

model furniture, there was considerable variation in quality, probably even more evident at the time of manufacture, when the figures were painted and dressed.

The customs associated with the dedication of toys at puberty extended into the Roman civilization, when children were equally well supplied with model furniture and crockery, though it is impossible at present to be sure whether model rooms were also produced commercially. The Roman historian Suetonius (AD 70–140) describes in his life of Augustus how small children built castles and towers from papyrus and thin sections of wood, a pursuit that is also chronicled by Horace, who describes how children amused themselves by building houses and yoking mice to small carts. It is tempting to think that, in such creative play, these boys were imitating structures of finer quality that were sold commercially, but there is no real evidence to this effect, simply a number of charming anecdotes, such as that supplied by Albius Tibullus in his *Elegiacs*, who describes a scene where children on a feast-day built a small house on the household altar, watched over by their parents.

The majority of surviving Roman miniatures are made of earthenware, one of the most effective items being a portable hearth with carrying-handles and supports for a pot that dates from the first century AD and which is accompanied by a clay model bench that was also made in Italy at the same date. Lead models, in comparison with wood, also stood a greater chance of survival, and a well-made lead chair dating to the fifth century BC has been preserved. An example of the early exportation of commercially made toys is a lead stool that was found in Egypt but which originated in Greece and was a relic of the Roman period. Of the greatest attraction to collectors of miniatures

A portable earthenware hearth with carrying-handles and supports for a pot. First century AD. Roman.

A piece with obvious appeal to collectors of miniatures is this lead tray with food. Roman.

is a group of lead vessels exhibited at the British Museum, which includes a saucepan, a drinking-cup and a bowl, extremely delicate items made with great precision but considered to be toys. Of particular appeal is a lead tray that holds a prawn, a bunch of grapes and a haunch of meat, an early forerunner of similar items in china intended for dolls' houses and dating to the eighteenth and nineteenth centuries.

The fall of the Roman Empire, with its aftermath of a general decline into a more barbaric form of life, is reflected in the dearth of surviving toys. Presumably girls continued to play with dolls and miniature furniture, but the upheaval of the traditional trade-routes and the lack of stable government resulted in a decline in commercial toy-making. The individual items of wood or fabric that were probably made by parents or local craftsmen would have stood little chance of survival in comparison with the much more durable earthenware and metal of the Romans and Greeks. The skills taught by the craftsmen of Rome passed into decline in a relatively short time, so that when Britain, for instance, needed skilled artisans, it was necessary to bring them from Europe. Modern research suggests that some of the traditional beliefs regarding the disastrous state of Britain in the years after the fall of Rome are much exaggerated and that there were in fact quite a large number of craftsmen still in operation, who supplied busy tradespeople, particularly in the areas of household equipment and personal adornment. A great deal of excavation has taken place in Britain during the last ten years that has thrown new light on this period, but no miniatures or basic toys such as model horses have been discovered, only the evidence of games played by adults, such as knucklebones and forms of draughts. As the early Church frowned on what was considered to be the pagan practice of burying a child with its toys, the lack of examples must in part at least be due to this prohibition.

The various European countries did not become isolated from one another during this period of general decline but retained certain of the trade-links, so that glass, for instance, continued to be imported into Britain from the Rhineland. The exchange of goods took place mainly at the great fairs that were a feature of commercial life by the twelfth century, people travelling great distances to purchase goods that were available for only a few days each year. The miniature fighting knights controlled by strings, with which boys played at jousting games, give some idea of the complexity of the better pieces of the period. As girls were very lightly considered, they do not appear in drawings or illuminated manuscripts of the medieval period as often as their important brothers, who are shown flying kites, riding hobbyhorses and playing with whipping-tops. Despite their lack of personal importance, girls were provided with some toys, and in the ruins of Osterburg Castle in the Rhone mountains toy utensils were discovered that can be positively dated between 1200 and 1270. Several medieval German writers also comment on the great beauty of dolls, suggesting that wood and fabric might have been used to create much more alluring examples than the clay figures that were found in the ruins of old Strasbourg.

With the gradual rise of the merchant classes during the late medieval period, there was an accompanying increase in the attention given to the upbringing and education of children. Though girls obviously benefited much less than their brothers, attempts were made to provide them with a greater variety of toys, and by the fourteenth century wax, wood and composition were all used for the manufacture of dolls and miniatures. Sonneberg and Nuremberg became established as toy-making centres in the fourteenth century, while Augsburg and Judenberg were also of some importance. The Nuremberg craftsmen were highly respected throughout the medieval period for the great skill of their work and the enthusiasm of their merchants, who carried the small toys, made mainly of wood, across Europe to the great fairs. An interesting group of pipe-clay dolls, measuring between 3 and 6 inches high and believed to have formed part of a shopkeeper's stock in the fifteenth century, was discovered in Nuremberg and, though they are of rigid design, could have formed part of a room setting, though their true intention is frequently disputed. The *Hortus Sanitatus* of 1491 shows a Nuremberg doll-maker at work on simply jointed wooden dolls which we must regard as the forerunners of the elegantly constructed German dolls of the late eighteenth and nineteenth centuries that were to be found in shops as far apart as New

York and Moscow. Such simple wooden structures could be decorated and costumed to suit the specifications and the pockets of the customer, so that while exquisitely dressed dolls are recorded for sale at the Palais de Justice in France, poor children would have owned the unadorned stick-like objects shown in the *Hortus Sanitatus*.

The names of two doll-makers, Ott and Mess, were recorded in 1465, forming the first known links in a distinguished chain that culminated in the great toy-making families of the nineteenth and early twentieth centuries. In 1578 the Council of Nuremberg authorized pewterers and jewellers to make tin figures as playthings for children, suggesting an acceptance of a trade that was already in operation. The lead mines in the area provided one of the main constituents of pewter and enabled this side of the toy-industry, which was to specialize in particular in the manufacture of doll's house equipment, to expand rapidly. These workers were heavily controlled by strict guild rules, so that for instance a pewterer could make platters and jugs but not supply a cupboard or table for their display. This tight guild control aided the industry in times of high demand, as it discouraged men from leaving their particular trade, but it caused great difficulty when trade was depressed and still men could not seek other work.

Several small dolls which, by their size, might suggest themselves as possible inhabitants of miniature rooms, have survived from this period, including an 8½-inch figure of a lady carved from limewood now displayed at the Germanisches Museum in Nuremberg. The Royal Armoury Collection in Stockholm also has a small lady doll dating to 1590 and reputed to have belonged to one of the daughters of Charles IX, as it is costumed in the height of fashion. The body is built up over a wire armature that is swathed in rose and yellow silk thread in order to create a realistic form, and the face is embroidered. The human hair wig is braided and decorated with a diadem of pearls in accord with the magnificence of the dress, made of uncut velvet and silk taffeta embroidered with pearls. This fabric doll is the only surviving figure of the period in this medium, as the majority would soon have become unsightly and been discarded, and it is also of importance in illustrating the high standard of costuming that was attained in dolls intended for children of noble birth. Wood, *papier mâché* and earthenware were all used as doll-making materials by the sixteenth century, but we can have only the slightest concept of their construction from surviving woodcuts of children at play, as the artists' tendency was always to present a doll that appeared more realistic than was in fact possible, though it is evident that toys were becoming a more generally accepted feature of childhood.

A new concern for the well-being of children was fostered by the publication in 1544 of *The Boke of Chyldren* by Thomas Phaire, the first volume on paediatrics written by an Englishman. His advice was obviously very much in demand, as the book ran to seven editions, suggesting that a

This small fabric doll, made *circa* 1590, is believed to have belonged to a daughter of Charles IX of Sweden. It is the earliest small doll to have survived in such excellent condition. Pink and yellow silk is wound around a wire armature to form the body. The features are embroidered.

much larger group of people was concerned for the sensible upbringing of the young than might be suggested in personal accounts of the period, which often dwell on the unpleasant aspects of life in the nursery. Phaire, solicitor, Member of Parliament and physician, produced the book 'to doo them good that have moste nede, that is to saye, children; and to shewe the remedies that God hath created for the use of man'. Although much of his advice was in the nature of well-tried remedies, such as allowing a teething child to bite on the first tooth of a colt set in silver, he also provides revealing background information regarding the average conditions under which the majority of children lived. He considered, for instance, that the very common ulceration of babies' heads was caused by 'droppyngs of restye bacon and salt beef which commonly hung from hooks in the ceiling', babies at this period being frequently left in the care of the maids in the kitchen areas. In order to amuse the young, who were kept as much as possible out of the way of adults, a few toys were provided, such as hobbyhorses and dolls and cradles, but we have no record of any model houses or rooms available in Britain at this time, though there were pieces of larger-scale toy furniture.

The better-educated parents who read Phaire with concern were anxious that, from the time their children left the cradle, they should be taught to speak the truth and appreciate virtue and goodness, and parents went to great pains in order to ensure that their first sentences should be such phrases as 'God alone saveth me.' Very occasionally a glimpse of a much lighter type of upbringing is provided, but frequently the account has survived only because of its basic moral tone, such as that relating to the childhood of Edward VI, the only son of Henry VIII, who grew up in the care of the Sidney family. On his fifth birthday he was presented with a miniature silver service, with which this delicate and short-lived boy entertained his young friends all day. When they left, with selfless generosity he presented each of them with one of the pieces he liked so much, leaving nothing for himself. This presentation of sets of silver miniatures to the children of royalty was well established in Europe, and a daughter of Henri II of France in 1571 is recorded as ordering a similar set for the children of the Duchess of Bavaria. This group was described in some detail and included 'buffet pots, bowls, plates and other articles such as they make in Paris'. The plate inventory of the mother of Henri IV of France (1553–1610) also records that she owned a 'doll's set of silver table-plenishments set with diamonds'; no indication of scale is provided, but the decoration of diamonds would suggest pieces of very small size, probably intended for display in a cabinet and much more extravagant in design than the basic silver items owned by children. The frequent melting-down of silver and gold has meant that many of these princely toys have perished, and we have to rely completely on contemporary accounts and descriptions that suggest craftsman manufacture on several levels, from cheap pewter to gold. Such costly toys as silver armies were carefully protected during play, and it would appear that similar expensive items were owned by a number of more fortunate children, such as those of Edward Clarke of Chipley, the friend to whom Locke addressed his *Thoughts Concerning Education* written at the end of the seventeenth century. His main concern was to provide parents with advice in order to combat the early corruption of youth that was so prevalent but his comments regarding toys suggest a much greater abundance than might be judged by the very low number of surviving examples. He considered that children should have many playthings of different kinds:

but still to be in the custody of their tutors or somebody else, whereof the child should have in his power but one at once, and should not be suffered to have another but when he restored that. This teaches them to be careful of not losing or spoiling the things they have; whereas plenty and variety in their own keeping, makes them wanton and careless and teaches them from the beginning to be squanderers and wasters. These, I confess are little things, and such as will seem beneath the care of a governor; but nothing that may form children's minds is to be overlooked and neglected, and whatsoever introduces habits and settles customs in them deserves the care and attention of their governors, and is not a small thing in its consequences.

One thing more about children's playthings may be worth their parents' care. Though it be agreed they should have of several sorts, yet, I think, they should have none bought for them. This will hinder that great variety they are often over charged with, which serves only to teach the mind to wander after change and superfluity, to be unquiet and perpetually stretching itself after something more still, though it knows not what, and never to be satisfied with what it hath. The court that is made to people of condition in such kind of presents to their children does the little ones great harm. By it they are taught pride, vanity and covetousness almost before they can speak; and I have known a young child so distracted with the number and variety of his playthings that he tired his mind every day to look them over.

Locke's strictures hardly suggest that children of the late seventeenth century suffered from any shortage of commercially produced toys as the main burden of his advice rests in fact on an over-abundance of lavishly made playthings. Ann Sharp, born in 1691, was presented by her godmother with a splendid doll's house, which she was able to furnish with a variety of items obtained from toyshops but, in some instances, constructed with such care that they were sold for substantial amounts. It is unlikely that this British house was unique, and we have to conclude that, despite the lack of other surviving examples or contemporary accounts, other girls were also provided with similar toys. Some of the very crudely made pieces in the Sharp house still carry their original prices, and as these were not of the quality to satisfy an adult assembler of a curiosity cabinet, it must be assumed that they were the cheapest type of commercial toys intended for the equipping of rooms and houses.

The German and Dutch approach to dolls' houses was far more serious, as any extravagance of either construction or furnishing was compensated by the fact that the model house was much more in the manner of an exercise in the learning of household management, whereas in Britain the doll's house was essentially a frivolous plaything.

TWO

German Cabinet Houses

The craftsmen of Germany were especially skilled in the making of miniature representations of everyday life that were of fascination to both adults and children. When such pieces were brought together as a collection, the problem of their display would almost inevitably suggest the creation of a model house or room. The old German term *Dockenhaus* originally denoted an item in miniature rather than a child's toy, and it is therefore particularly useful for collectors who wish to differentiate between German and Dutch cabinet houses. It is with the development of the *Dockenhaus* that the evolution of the model house as either a toy or an amusement for adults begins.

It is not surprising that the earliest records of dolls' houses and models contained in art chambers relate to pieces made in Germany, as Nuremberg in particular was an international trading centre and obtained a wide variety of craftsman and folk-type toys from the surrounding areas, so that miniature glass was brought from Thuringia and wooden goods from the Bohemian forests. Nuremberg lay across the great trading routes of Europe, the Imperial Roads of the Holy Roman Empire, and merchants could obtain a wide variety of wares in this one town to carry as far as Russia and Britain. Sonneberg, eventually to become the manufacturing centre of the doll trade, grew quickly in importance when Erfurt lost its prime position after the fire of 1472, the merchants from Nuremberg preferring to turn off at Sonneberg for Leipzig,

Opposite above: Despite its cupboard-like structure, the high-quality contents of this Strasbourg house (*circa* 1680) indicate an adult's taste. In the tradition of several German cabinets, part of the ground floor shows an outdoor scene. *Opposite below:* A detail of the Strasbourg house showing the sitting-room on the first floor. This cabinet bears several dates: 1680 on the upstairs door, 1678 on a cupboard and 1681 over a door.

the other great trading centre. The town also gained from its position on a main branch of the Imperial Roads, on which the merchants preferred to travel as they were not liable to Customs duties at the borders of the small states. The Sonnebergers were quick to realize that they could sell their own wares to this constant army of merchants and began to produce the turned and carved pieces for which they became famous. Much of this early production relied heavily for inspiration on Alpine work, particularly that of the Berchtesgaden area, where turners are recorded as having worked since the twelfth century and where there were also artist-carvers in ivory. The woodcarvers of Oberammergau were also fully active by 1520, when their skill was said to be so great that they could carve the Passion of Christ in the shell of a nut. The products of all these areas were copied by the industrious workers of Sonneberg, many of whom were forced into the toy-trade because of economic changes that made mining in the woods around the town unprofitable. There is no evidence of any toy- or miniature-making at the time on a similar scale in any other European country, and the fine toys that were generally available in the seventeenth century originated mainly in this area.

Much of the medieval German work was dependent on the demands of the Church, and it was fortunate for many of the finer craftsmen that, as the demand for religious work declined, the habit of forming collections of curios and miniatures began to fascinate not only courtiers and nobility but also merchants and middle-class burghers who wished to emulate the leaders of fashion. The men who had previously carved saints and crucifixes with enthusiasm now turned to the creation of small decorative items, often copies of everyday equipment that would delight the heart of avid cabinet collectors. Some of the finest pieces for the equipping of the *Dockenhaus* originated in Nuremberg, Furth and the surrounding provinces, but there was also some production at Ulm and Augsburg, and as many as fourteen different guilds are said to have contributed to such work. During the seventeenth century the specialist craftsmen, banded into guilds, were not allowed to work outside their own material, be it copper, silver or wood, which meant that a very large number of people could be involved in the furnishing of a single model room. One exception to this rule involved the carvers of ivory, who were regarded as Free Artists and so highly considered that they were not subject to guild rules. In 1698 Christoph Weigel commented on the industry of the day and stated:

The materials of which these dolls and playthings are made are in part silver and are fashioned by gold- and silversmiths, and in part of wood, which the common carver of images as well as the turner are wont to make; in part of alabaster, such a task being performed by a worker in this material. Others are moulded from wax, in particular many beasts and fowls being made of this and completely true to nature, with their rough skins drawn over them or very prettily bedecked with feathers. Indeed, there is scarce a trade in which that which is usually made big is not also seen copied on a small scale as a toy. This applies especially to dolls' houses, which contain everything necessary for a household's pride and ornament, daintily made and sometimes precious.

One of the illustrations in his book shows the manufacture of small dolls from the gum tragacanth, and the text makes it obvious that the guild workers produced at the same time fine-quality pieces for adults and cheap toys for the young.

The earliest recorded *Dockenhaus* is thought to have been owned by the Duchess Jakobaa, who was born in 1507, and in whose castle, between a panelled room and a large hall, stood a model contained in some form of display case. According to an inventory made in 1581, the house contained a number of dolls and was arranged in the manner of a Court. The Duchess was the mother of Duke Albrecht of Bavaria, who was also absorbed in the fashionable pastime of collecting miniatures. Albrecht V (who reigned from 1550 to 1579) ordered from the master turner Jacob Sandtner scale models that were to represent his five residence towns, Landshut, Munich, Straubing, Ingolstadt and Burghausen. The Munich residence, completed in 1570, was represented in a most accurate and complex form with all the smaller buildings and entrances meticulously copied from the actual building. It was originally displayed in Albrecht's palace but is now at the Bayerisches National Museum in Munich. These model towns are made on a very small scale but are believed to have been accurate miniaturizations and resemble town planners' constructions of today. It is interesting to note that not all the buildings were packed as closely together as is commonly thought but that many of these sixteenth-century town houses had large gardens, made more realistic by artificial trees. Sandtner, who came from Straubing, began the series of scale models with a portrayal of his home town which he completed in 1568. Landshut was offered to the Duke in 1570, Munich in 1572, Ingolstadt in 1573 and Burghausen in 1574. The models, reminiscent of the small houses and churches found in packs of South German wooden toys, were displayed in the Duke's art chamber at Munich. The room must have been large as the towns, still in excellent condition, occupy a substantial amount of floor space. The sand-coloured buildings with their roofs of grey and red, together with the originally bright green foliage of the trees, must formerly have presented a most colourful effect. The model of Straubing is smaller than that of Burghausen and the houses were obviously built much more closely together. On one of the models is an inscription by Sandtner, explaining that the models came completely from his own imagination. He worked mainly, it would seem, in limewood, and though the majority of the buildings were painted, a few were left as bare wood. In the model of Munich, for instance, the town walls and the moat provided him with a very neat edging for his buildings. It is thought by the museum that some alterations were later made to the model of Munich and the Residenz buildings, and the Jesuit College and St Michael's Church were added.

In 1557 Albrecht turned his attention to the creation of a South German princely dwelling that was also intended for display in his museum. Albrecht's brother-in-law, the Archduke Ferdinand of Tyrol, was an enthusiastic collector of a whole variety of curiosities and antiquities, and it is thought that some of his passion was communicated to Albrecht, who was obviously fascinated by the fashionable pursuit. Regrettably, the *Dockenhaus* was destroyed by a fire at the ducal residence in Munich in 1674, but a detailed inventory was fortunately made in 1598 by the ducal chamberlain, Johann Baptist Fickler. In 1879 J. Stockbauer published another description of the house based on the original account, though there is some doubt that the later description was coloured by a knowledge of the Nuremberg collection of *Dockenhäuser*. As this account is not available in English, it seems useful to include it here.

Stockbauer describes a house four storeys high that appears to open in sections, giving separate access to individual rooms, a plan similar to that used in some eighteenth-century British Baby Houses. The number of doors mentioned does not therefore relate to conventional room-entrances but to cupboard-like openings, the third floor for instance having five doors and sixteen windows. In the basement area there was a stable with horses and stable-lads, as well as a cow-stall complete with calves and a milkmaid. Beyond the stall was a dairy where a maid was making butter, surrounded by a variety of wood and copper household equipment that hung from the walls. In the adjoining pantry hung a fine selection of game, while on the table lay a variety of prepared dishes, including a sheep's head and a plate of Westphalian ham. In the wine cellar were six large casks and several silver filigree baskets, as well as a variety of hammered silver flasks and jugs. The coach house was also in the basement area and was supplied with a coach upholstered in black velvet and a smaller version for the ladies, the wheels of which were inlaid with silver.

One of the most interesting features of this early house was the bathing-room, where the mother and her three daughters were engaged in washing themselves, with a bathmaid in attendance. In addition to the bathtub there were copper ewers and two gilded washbasins, as well as two barbers' bowls of gilded brass. In the adjoining dressing-room was a silver washbasin with gilded feet, and an assortment of beautifully embroidered garments such as a shirt and a group of handkerchiefs contained in a velvet purse. On the wall hung two small and ten large gilded brass washbasins and three bathing-hats, possibly for the use of the lady who wore a black silk dress and sat at a table. Such a correctly equipped bathing-area must have been a great novelty at a time when even kings took their occasional bath in the bedroom, and one wonders if the Duke, in this portrayal of a residence similar to his own, was in fact boasting, in the most elegant manner, of his own superior washing-arrangements.

The hot water for the bathroom was supplied from the kitchen conveniently situated next door, where one cook stirred soup and another placed a capon in a copper pot while the chef cut up a pike. The walls were hung with a variety of copper, brass and tin equipment, and on the dresser were eleven tin containers with etched decoration. In the courtyard outside stood a six-sided well, several hen-coops and a lion-house with two occupants who were restrained from wandering in the garden where a stag, deer, a cat and several other creatures of a more equable nature were to be found. The silver fountain, the trees and flowers were all made of a type of wirework.

In the dancing-room on the second floor sat the Prince and Princess under a canopy of brown satin embroidered with silver. As Albrecht was married to Anna of Austria, the ceiling was decorated with the linked Bavarian and Austrian coats-of-arms. On a table with four silver feet is a ball game known as Zum Narren; the balls and board are of silver. This was a popular adult amusement of the period. This room was particularly well supplied with dolls, including four violinists and three pairs of dancing noblemen and their partners dressed in satin and taffeta. The mistress of the Court wore a costume of black velvet, and her three maidens wore frocks of red satin with gold embroidery and girdles of silver gilt. Near the princely couple stood four nobles of the Court service and two pages, all very correctly attired. A gold brocade-hung chamber adjoined the ballroom where the Duke and Duchess were also portrayed, together with the Duchess's household of four, with six servants costumed in black and brown satin. Near the stove, in the warmest place, stood the Court Fool. On a large table in the middle of the room lay a gilded wooden lute and two Indian bells, and above the table hung a silver-gilded cage containing a parrot. On a side table covered with red taffeta stood a silver gilt flask, two jugs, three double goblets, twelve covered shells on feet and several other serving-dishes all made of gilded silver. A small dog made of white Florentine silk lay near the mistress of the house, though several other similarly made dogs stood around the room. The English hound, probably the personal property of the Duke, wore a collar inlaid with silver and decorated with the Austrian and Bavarian coats-of-arms.

The State Bedroom was dominated by the splendid bed draped in red satin with embroidered brocade borders and supplied with pillowcases and sheets that were embroidered with red silk. Near the bed sat the Princess and the mistress of the Court. A linen cloth with decorative embroidery covered a wooden chest of pierced work with gilded inlay. Also displayed on the chest were a nightgown with gold edging, a man's shirt embroidered with black silk and a cap, handkerchief and napkin, all similarly embroidered. At the foot of the bed was an armchair upholstered in red velvet with a matching cushion, and on a wall opposite the bed was a long table on which lay some silver filigree baskets, a face-screen and a washbasin and ewer of silver, etched and parcel gilt, a silver jug, an oval silver box with two gilded rings and a hairbrush with a silver handle.

On the top floor there was a chapel with a carved, painted and gilded altar. The altar-cloth was made of black velvet with the name 'Jesu' and the edges embroidered in silver. On the altar stood a silver gilt crucifix, two candlesticks with gilded decoration, a silver gilt patten with chalice, a silver gilt corporal, two silver cruets with gilded decoration and a silver Mass bell that was similarly patterned. In front of the altar stood the priest, deacon and sub-deacon wearing brocade vestments. A lectern covered with a red taffeta cloth stood in the middle of the chapel, and there was also a virginal with a closing lid. Behind the lectern stood six choristers dressed in long black woollen jackets with velvet edging. On another lectern stood a hymnal for the alto part. In the ante-room near the chapel the Duke and Duchess could hear Mass.

Another bedroom, containing three beds, was situated near the chapel. This room was hung with red damask patterned with gold, and the bed-hangings were made of matching red taffeta, edged with velvet ribbon. A wooden chest was inlaid with enamel plaques and lined with red taffeta, and there was also a turned armchair to seat two people that was upholstered in red velvet. In front of the bed was an ivory chamber-pot.

Next to the bedroom was the sewing-room in which sat two ladies wearing black silk dresses embroidered with gold thread; another woman sat near the stove spinning with a distaff. That this was an apartment set aside for serious female industry was made clear by the presence of a loom, a spinning-wheel and a sewing-box, on the lid of which were displayed the Brandenburg and Württemberg coats-of-arms. This box contained hanks of red and blue thread as well as needles and a thimble. The room, despite its very practical use, was hung with gold silk, and a rectangular table was covered with a cloth of the same material, indicating the interest in matching decorative schemes that ran throughout the structure. This table stood opposite a credenza, also covered in gold silk, on which stood a knife-box, three small slop-basins, two drinking-skulls, a tall-bellied beaker, a glass carved from white chalcedony and a basin and fountain of ivory. There were also two candlesticks, a bowl and eight plates. The skill of contemporary ivory-carvers was evidenced in a well-made ivory-framed mirror.

Curiously, a second kitchen was situated next to this sewing-room, possibly to serve the needs of the day nursery on the same floor. The quantity and type of food in process of preparation, such as a deer roasting on a silver spit, does seem somewhat excessive for the needs of children and their nurses but would have served to keep the children completely separate from the life of the household in general. Near the kitchen fire stood two green glazed pots, and on a shelf were six tin dishes with handles, nine flat tin dishes, six tin platters

In this busy nursery the wide range of children's equipment is shown, including chairs and a baby-walker. A sixteenth-century engraving. Frankfurt.

and seven tin plates. From the walls hung an assortment of copper and brass pans, small tin baths and a whole variety of kitchen gadgets including a water-holder, cooling-pan and water-barrel.

In the day nursery with its red hangings embroidered with silver, stood a woman wearing a silk dress, accompanied by a boy in a velvet jacket and red stockings. Another woman, also wearing a velvet frock, rocked a child in its turned wooden cradle; a baby wearing a shirt sat in a high chair. On a rectangular table behind the cradle was an iron chest painted in gold and tinned on the inside, which contained a variety of clothes made of the finest linen. There were also three baskets of woven silver thread. One of the household pets, covered in Florentine silk, had also crept into the day nursery. Against the wall near the stove stood a credenza covered with red taffeta on which stood a credenza beaker and cover, six court beakers, a nutmeg made into a drinking-glass, in imitation of the popular adult-sized coconut goblets, five dishes, four candlesticks, a ewer and basin, five small candlesticks, three small dishes, two dishes on tripod bases and twelve silver plates. From the wall hung a silver-handled brush and a shovel of the same material. In the night nursery were two beds with hangings of fine linen embroidered with gold thread and decorated with gold fringe.

33

Albrecht V's house, though known only from its contemporary inventory, is of considerable importance, as the names of the different craftsmen involved in the construction are known. The Court cabinet-maker, Wolf Greiss, was responsible for some of the finer pieces of furniture, and the painters Hans Ostendorfer and Hans Schoepfer the elder worked on the decoration of the construction, providing details such as the courtyard and the garden as well as the more obvious framed pictures. Hans Klein and Kaspar Bauer, who were locksmiths, also assisted in the creation of a model whose valuable contents would have needed some protection.

Another house that has survived only in description was that ordered in 1572 by Anna, Electress of Saxony, for her three daughters. The model was to be equipped with a fine variety of kitchenware including seventy-one bowls, forty meat-plates, 106 other plates, thirty-six spoons and twenty-eight egg-cups, all made of pewter that the girls would have been expected to polish and keep as clean and shining as silver. Dolls' furniture of every possible kind was ordered, including cupboards and bathtubs; a poultry yard was also considered necessary, and the commission was undertaken by the *Burgermeister* of Leipzig, Hieronymus Rauscher. The pewter miniatures tablecloths and tableware were purchased in Nuremberg, where the greatest variety was available. This Christmas gift, intended for these important children, forms a direct contrast to the collector's cabinet constructed for Duke Albrecht and suggests that in Germany even in the sixteenth century there were already two standards of manufacture, one the province of artist–craftsmen and the other catering for the instruction of children in basic household management.

Complex miniature houses, gardens and domestic scenes had become popular gifts among the nobility by the early-seventeenth century and were intended purely for the amusement of adults. Duke Wilhelm of Bavaria was particularly fond of model courtyards, and among the recipients of his gifts were the queens of France and Spain. The most complex courtyard was that assembled by the art-dealer Hainhofer for Duke Philipp II of Pomerania-Stettin in 1617, a model that was lost from the Schloss Museum in Berlin during the last war. This structure measured about 7 feet long and was made by Mathias Kager, with the animals provided by Johannes Schwegler of Augsburg, who was a specialist in the creation of such expensive items. In the courtyard could be seen a number of figures going about their daily tasks, such as milking and tending the animals, and in one realistic scene is a maid sitting in a lavatory. In the same year, Hainhofer also supplied the Duke with a house and courtyard known as the Meierhof, and a watercolour dating to around 1640 showed a structure similar to a nineteenth-century toy fort, built on a plinth with the castle on one wall and the buildings for the animals and the various workshops ranged around the sides. In the watercolour the courtyard contained a number of farm and domestic animals, and it was

A scene in a German kitchen showing the cooking area in use. In this illustration the sick are being nursed. Engraved by J. Dryander, Frankfurt, 1537.

considered that these were also Schwegler's work. Several descriptions of the Meierhof still exist, but there is considerable confusion between each account, one suggesting that the courtyard already described was in fact part of this larger model. It seems strange that there are no photographs or recent accounts, as the model disappeared only during the last war, and we have to assume that it was very lightly considered at the time. As the accounts are contradictory, there seems little point in repeating all the details, as the general picture that emerges is of a house similar to, but much less impressive than that owned by Albrecht V, with a well-stocked kitchen, a living-room where a child teased a kitten with a piece of rag and a bedroom containing an impressive bed hung with green taffeta and a small cot in which a baby lay. Within the house itself there were several animals: in a corridor was a dressed monkey on a chain and a caged parrot; in the kitchen a cat attempted to reach a fish out of a tank, and in the master's writing-room stood an English hound.

35

The main reception rooms apparently contained an abundance of velvet- and taffeta-covered furniture as well as several silver items necessary to represent what appears to have been a prosperous household at its daily work.

It is obvious that any important person wishing to purchase a prestige model or a cabinet house found it advisable to consult the art-dealer, collector and connoisseur Philipp Hainhofer, and it was this man whom the town of Augsburg consulted when it was found necessary to purchase an important gift for the Swedish king, Gustavus Adolphus, in 1632. The services of the Augsburg master Johannes Schwegler were again called upon for the construction of the furnishings, but the cabinet was designed by Hainhofer himself and took the form of a room rather than a complete house, though it contained an interesting peep-show and a small falconry. Max von Boehn, in his *Dolls and Puppets*, published in 1929, illustrates two mechanical dolls from this cabinet that were displayed at a museum at Uppsala, a pair of considerable interest as they are the earliest known mechanical pieces constructed for cabinet use. The dolls represented a courtier and his lady, both wearing fashionable costume, though the effect of the lady doll was spoiled by the fact that the head, which once turned as she moved, was lost. The figures stood some $4\frac{1}{4}$ inches high and worked by clockwork. The costume was of a richness that might be expected for such an important gift: the man's consisted of a tunic and silk breeches trimmed with silver braid and a grey wide-brimmed hat, his high boots were correctly made of leather, and a formal sword was carried; the lady wore yellow silk damask with a sash of pink silk, both ornamented with silver braids and fringes. The basic cabinet must have been quite large to have accommodated a peep-show, a falconry and the dancing figures, and the degree of workmanship was evidenced by its cost of 6,500 thalers.

This adult fascination with model houses and rooms in the seventeenth century must be seen not as an isolated fashion, but as a facet of the delight taken in all kinds of novelty items that introduced an element of surprise into lives which must often have become boringly uneventful. The pleasure gardens, with their mechanical devices for squirting water over unsuspecting guests and the sumptuous table-decorations, sometimes incorporating a form of mechanical movement, all contributed to the amusement of the nobility. Complete model towns were sometimes constructed as garden decorations, and Prince Max of Hohenlohe described how Markus Sittichus, a designer thought to have magical powers, planned a garden with streams, grottoes and flowerbeds through which, on stepping into a dark grotto, small strange figures began to move over concealed wells, 'figures of men and animals, of airy spirits and deities, of clumsy goblins and teasing water sprites'. He recounted the wonder which he and other children felt as a metal curtain that screened the view was lifted and before their eyes stood an enchanted and completely strange world.

There stood palaces and houses, strange buildings with high glistening domes and eastern cupolas, narrow streets and wide boulevards, all of them filled with little men and women, motionless certainly, yet deceitfully life-like in their strange, old multicoloured dresses, and near them horses, cats and dogs. Before the town hall stood soldiers all ready to march, commanding officers, and citizens thronging in rich heavy garments; in the marketplace merchants were chaffering and drivers speeding. The most extraordinary thing, however, was that we could see, too, through the walls of houses and watch what was going on within, how the bakers baked, how the washerwomen washed, how the miller prepared the bright golden flour and how the cooks got ready the tasty dishes. One could see here the maids sweeping the floor, here a husband and wife fighting with one another in their room, here the children playing, here the teacher giving his lessons from open books.

Suddenly, at a magic knock, there came strange subterranean music, and the whole town took life. The officers gave their orders, the soldiers marched off and all the various figures set about their various tasks. For the entertainment of these miniature citizens there was also a dancing bear. The spectacle ended as the chimes of the clock on the model town hall died away and the figures slowly ran down and again became still.

This almost incredible model town was displayed at the Hellbrunn Park near Salzburg, but there were several others of a similar nature, such as that in the Castle Park at Heidelberg. A description of such a complex and generously peopled town enables the cabinets and model rooms to fit into a more realistic perspective as part of a contemporary urge to create interesting scenes of everyday life in miniature. At this period there were many wealthy German dukes and princes who were able to indulge their most extravagant whims, and when their acquisitive urge for paintings and sculpture was satiated, they turned for light relief to the creation of amusing models. These structures were not just added to at the whim of the purchaser but envisaged in their entirety by the designers, who themselves employed craftsmen to make the furnishings and figures.

On a much less ambitious scale than the automatic model town or the cabinet created for Gustavus Adolphus was the *Dockenhaus* assembled by a Nuremberg woman, Anna Köferlin, which she displayed to the public in 1631. This widowed lady, both of whose children had died young, sold most of her personal property in order to pay for the model, which she charged the public to view. Our knowledge of this house is derived from a small booklet that was published to accompany the exhibition of her work on the cover of which is seen a typical tall Nuremberg house of the period with projecting roof-gables and metal windows cut with characteristic round panes. The main door was massive and, were it not for the steps on which the house stood, might have been intended, as in other later but similar houses, for a coach to pass into a central courtyard. On the façade was written '*Principio*

Abriß/ Entwerffung vnd

Erzehlung/ was in dem/ von Anna Köferlin zu Nürmberg/

lang zusammen getragenem Kinder-Hauß/ dergleichen nie gesehen noch gemacht/ anzutreffen/ vnd wie
ettlich Hundert Stuck/ alle zum gemeinen Nutz auch dienstlich/ darinn zusehen.

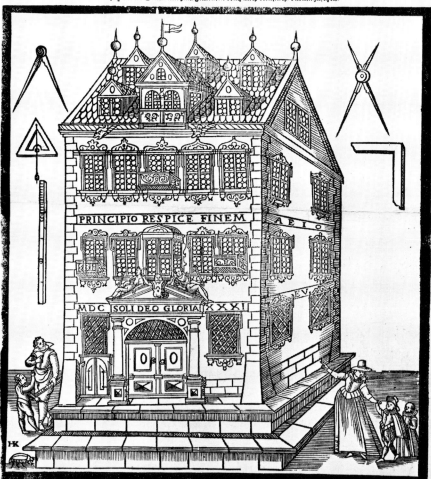

Gleich wie der Vogel zu dem Flug/
Von Gott dem Herrn erkorn:
Als der Mensch/ verständig klug/
Zur Arbeit ist geboren.
Dann sag mir mein/ doch zu was End/
Hat Gott der Herr zwey gegeben/
Ein jedem Menschen gleich zwo Händ/
Dann das bey all sein leben/
Vnd sonderlich wann er Gesund/
Jung Starck an sein Gliedmassen:
Er gang vergeblich keine Stund/
Ohn Arbeit soll hinlassen:
(Ein Christlich Herz das weiß gar wol/
Daß an Sonn: Feyertagen/
Er seine Seel versorgen soll/
Dran am grösten gelegen/)
Die Natur lehrt solchs jederman/
Weil sie selbst nicht ruhet/
Daß vnvernünfftig Vieh zeigt an/
Die Omeiß solchs auch thuet.
Ein Weib ein schwacher Werckzeug ist/
Grosse Arbeit vorzustehen/
Ihr vielmahln mangelt vnd gebrist/
Doch wann wir recht ansehen/
Ihr Hauß-Arbeit vnd grosse Müh/
So sie mit kleinen Kindern
Muß haben/ so wol spat als früh/
Dann werden wir erst finden/
Daß sie niemaln zu feyren hat/
Ich red von arbeitsammen/
Die trägen finden hier kein statt/
Wiewol ihr groß der Stammen.
Weil sie dann bin von Gott dem Herrn/
Zu keiner Hand Werck/
Gewürdiget/ Ich red so fern
Was Gott will haben thut er:)
Jch sie eben drumb wollen richt/
Ganz freyen vnd laß werden/

Sondern was man vor Augen sicht/
Der Jugend ohn beschwerden
Etlich Jahr her zusamm gericht
Mit müh/ vnd allem fleiß/
Der Jugend geben vnterricht/
Daß sie auch gleiche weise/
Von jugend an sich gewehnen soll/
Allzeit etwas zu schaffen/
Weil vnser Leben/ wie man wol
Weiß/ hingeht mehr als halb schlaffen.
Darumb ihr lieben Kinderlein/
Beschaut alles gar Eben/
Wie alles ist geordnet fein/
Soll euch ein gut Lehr geben/
Daß wann ihr dermaleins zu Hauß
Kompt/ vnd euch Gott thut geben/
Eygenen Herd/ daß ihrs vorauß
Bey all eurm Leib vnd Leben/
Ordenlich vnd nach der gebür
Jnn eurem Hauß halten/
Richtet vnd ordnet/ dann wie ihr
Wißt/ daß die lieben Alten
Pflegten zusagen: Jnn ein Hauß/
Wo Anordnung regiret/
So ist es bald mit selben auß/
Vnordnung wenig zieret.
So schaut nun an diß Kinder Hauß/
Ihr Kinder jnn vnd aussen/
Schauts an vnd lernet bevor auß/
Wie ihr einmal solt hausen/
Schaut wies alles ist ordinirt
(Solt anderst recht wol ist geziert)
Jnn Kuch/ Stuben vnd Kammer/
Schaut/ was doch für ein Jammer
Hauß rath/ ein wolbestelltes Hauß
Fordert/ doch mit wenigem
Kompt man zu zeiten auch wol auß/
So man sich gnüge am jengen/

Secht euch wol vmb/ secht hinder sich/
Sechs allenthalben Eben
Wieviel man der hundert stück/
Allhier zusehen geben:
Von Beigen vnd von Kältern schön/
Von Zin Kupffer vnd Messing/
So zugericht/ daß obs schön klein/
Jst doch alls zugerüstet.
Auch zu dem allgemeinen brauch
Ein jedes Stück merckt Eben
Ein jeds bald hie/ bald dort hin taug
Thut einen Nutzen geben.
Es hat Stuben/ Kammer/ Keller Kuch
Darzu seinen Erdboden/
Darinn allzeit vollauff genug/
Ob schon nichts viel gerathen.
Von Septenspiel findt du dergleich/
Zu kurzweiligen Sachen/
Ein Jnstrument/ Lauten vnd Geig
Mit dem man kan auffmachen/
Ein Flöten vnd Zwerg Pfeiff darbey/
Wirst du finden darinnen.
Darmit/ wann man will lustig sey/
Eins zusammen kan stimmen.
Auch hast du dort an einem Eck/
Fein nach der Ordnung stehen/
Die Bücher wie ein Bibliotheck
Nacheinander zusehen.
Ein Rüstkammer auff all Manier/
Rüstung man da anschauet/
Von Büchsen Harnisch/ Wehr Rappier/
Daß ein fast darvor grauet.
Von Kärissen zu Roß vnd Mann/
Von allerhand Kriegswaffen/
Mit verwunderung zusehen an/
Das Maul vergißt/ steht offen/
Also sicht man dort an der Wand/
Gar mancherley gemahlet/

Wie auch zusehen manch Künstlers Hand/
Jnn Stuben Kammer vnd Saale.
Was soll ich sagen von allerley/
Dazu man auch nicht denckt/
Von vielerley vnd mancherley
Jst auffmacht vnd gehenckt/
Die Höch diß Hauses ist neun Schuh/
Fünff Schuh betrifft die breyte/
Die tieffe auch vier Schuh darzu
Ein jed Gmach vnterscheiden:
Der Keller allerley getranck
Von Reinfall Malvasier
Allzeit einen Vorrath herlang
Von Wein/ Roth vnd weiß Biere
So gar/ das was zwölff starcker Mann
Auff zu Zech können trincken
Jch sie darinn versehen kan
Daß sie Taumeln vnd hincken.
Summ alls nach der Proportion
Alles nach dem klein Schuhe
Jsts überal gerichtet an
Durch Weib Arbeit spat frühe/
Das wann Jch solt erzehlen alls
Was darinnen zusehen
Dieses Papier were gleichfalls
Zu wenig/ muß selbst gesehen.
Weil aber dieses nur allein/
O Nur die Form Präsentirt
Werde dir besser gedienet seyn/
Wann sichs wird es geziert/
Drumb hab Jch diß in einer Summ
Hiermit wollen anzeigen
Ders nicht gesehn derselb noch kom
Jhm soll es auch dergleichen
Mit gutem Willn gezeiget werdn
Jch weiß Vnkost/ Zeit/ weile:
Wird jhn nicht rewn/ weil er auff Erdn
Seines Lebens hat ein Theile.

Respice Finem', 'In the beginning I can see the end', and '*Soli Deo Gloria*', 'To God alone the glory'. At the bottom of the woodcut is a monogram 'HK' and a beetle which is thought to be a rebus on the family name. The roof was tiled, and there were two corn-lofts.

In the booklet Anna Köferlin explained her aims and intentions in displaying the house, which she claimed in true showman's style was quite unique. The tract which was used as a form of advertisement for the house, despite its often long-winded style, gives an illuminating description of her educational aims. She explained that what they saw before their eyes was gathered together with diligence and difficulty over several years, so that children could easily study things that would otherwise take them many years to learn.

> Therefore, you dear little children, study everything carefully, how all is well ordered, so that it will provide a good lesson, and when finally you have your own house and God gives you your own hearth, which will become the work of your life and love, you will be able to organize everything in your household in a proper way. Then you will understand what your beloved parents have tried to tell you, that a house that is in disorder reflects the disorder of its housekeeper's mind. Come and look at the *Kinderhaus* children, both inside and out, look and learn how everything should be arranged in a house. See the arrangement of the living-rooms, the kitchen and the bedrooms, so that you will learn lessons for the future. See how complicated a well-ordered house is. Thus, when it comes to the appropriate time, many of you will have learned how to manage each thing. Look around you, look behind things and see how many hundreds of items have been brought together for your instruction, from bedclothes to wardrobes, tin, copper and brass and everything correctly made, so that although very small, it could actually be used for its appropriate purpose. Every single piece that you see is absolutely necessary in a properly run home. It has living-rooms, kitchen and bedrooms and even its cornloft. The stringed instruments, whether lutes or fiddles, can be played, and if you are feeling joyful, you can make them sing. You will find in a corner, arranged in order, such books as would be found in a library, and there is also an armoury where all types of weapons can be seen, pistols, rapiers, daggers and whatever else is needed. There is also armour for men and horses, and every kind of weapon of war, which will be seen with so much wonder that you might forget yourself and stand with your mouth open in amazement. Several different artists have painted the walls of the living-rooms, bedrooms and reception rooms.

She goes on to describe the dimensions of the model, believed to have stood some $102\frac{1}{2}$ inches high and $45\frac{1}{4}$ inches deep. Her concern was directed towards instructing children in the household tasks they would eventually have to perform, as she believed that all intelligent people were born to work

Anna Köferlin's house as shown on the cover of a booklet she published to accompany its exhibition in 1631.

39

and that women who marry have to carry a particularly heavy burden. It appears that the main intention of the model was as a means of raising money, though towards this end she had to sell many of her possessions in order to pay the craftsmen and artists who helped in the project. Regrettably there is no account of the success or otherwise of her venture, though she must have a place in the affections of all collectors who aspire towards one day opening their own museums.

No present-day enthusiast could hope to assemble a group of cabinet houses of the splendour of those on permanent display at the Germanisches National Museum in Nuremberg, where the study of the evolution of European dolls' houses must begin. These cabinet houses have an atmosphere completely of their own, being strange and almost primitive in effect, with nothing of the elegant, mannered appearance of the finest Dutch and English models. The standard both of construction and of furnishing is noticeably lower in comparison, yet they are much more evocative of a period when Germany was considered by both the French and the British as a somewhat barbaric region, where fine manners and the stylish accoutrements of everday life were all too often lacking. The houses have more than adequate furniture, the kitchens are clean and well scrubbed, but we are aware of the animals and horses kept in the cellars and given a strange sensation of the smells, movement and life of actual people in a way that is not communicated by the cool perfection of an English or Dutch house. Though the atmosphere of realism is strong, in no cabinet are we allowed to see the basic realities of the period, the exploitation of servants, the frequent cruelty to children or the enjoyable excesses of both rich and poor; only at Mon Plaisir, for instance, do we encounter a man and woman in bed together, so that what we are offered in these cabinets is not an accurate mirror of life but a glimpse of the surface, rather like a television presentation of a stately home of today. Reality is, nevertheless, close in the *Dockenhäuser,* and though some of their old mystery is lost now that the museum has installed lighting in their rooms, sufficient remains to make their examination a unique experience. The only British model that exudes this sensation of the past as strongly is that once owned by Ann Sharp, a house that is also constructed in a somewhat primitive manner. It seems a pity that, when photographed, the *Dockenhäuser* lose so much of their atmosphere, their endearing imperfections being scaled out of sight and their dark colours heightened. The basic effect of their large size must also be lost, so that even the finest photograph can only suggest the richness of the crowded interiors.

The oldest of the Nuremberg houses carries the date 1611 and despite its very large size is constructed of timber only about half an inch thick,

A large cabinet house bearing the date 1611. Despite its massive proportions it was constructed of half-inch timber.

suggesting that the model was not intended to be moved once it was arranged. Parts of this cabinet were restored in the eighteenth century, such as the living-room, opposite the kitchen that was panelled at this time, so that we no longer see an authentic structure, though sufficient remains to arouse great interest, as no other house has survived from this early period. There are two windows on the roof on either side of a decorative arched centre, and inside the house a staircase and various landings divide the main rooms. Over the doorways on the first floor curious stags are painted in seated positions,

Left: In the kitchen of the 1611 cabinet house some of the shelves are notched to support long-handled pans. *Above:* A scene in the garden of the 1611 cabinet, showing the fine water cistern and one of the painted figures.

with their heads being represented in the round and appearing very realistic. The ceiling of the upper hall is painted to represent tiles, and a flight of stairs leads up to the attic area. The walls are enlivened by painted figures in appropriate positions, so that a lady wearing a ruff is leaving one room and a halberdier carrying a pike stands on guard, and similar armed figures also stand on the other landings of the house. The otherwise plain walls are ornamented with a hunting-frieze that runs around the top, though the bedrooms on either side are more decorative, as the green walls are provided

A room on the ground floor of the 1611 cabinet, with paintings of people hunting and card-playing.

with an attractive white border with painted garlands of flowers and fruit in rich colours. On a plate rail that runs around the room there are a number of pewter pots and plates that also contribute to the richness of the effect. Various pieces of commercially made cabinet-house equipment were added to this room in the eighteenth century, including a baby-walker and a spinning-wheel that both appear to originate in one workshop, as the turning is so similar.

The panelled main living-room has whitewashed walls that are again painted with festooned flowers, fruit and ribbons, and a charming small page boy with black bead-like eyes, probably dating from the eighteenth century, stands at the back of the room. Both the chairs and the settles have the tufted buttoned cushions seen in so many *Dockenhäuser*, and there are two dumb-waiters at hand to hold the food that would be set out ready for the diners. The kitchen, positioned in the centre of the house, is filled with wall shelves, some of which are cut with notches so that long-handled pans can be supported. On one side of the kitchen there are small, individually shaped prestige shelves, for the display of the more important items of equipment, and there is also a particularly fine clockwork spit-rack that probably dates from the eighteenth century.

The ground floor is occupied by a large galleried garden and a smaller eating-area with heavy benches and a table that is dominated by a large painting of a group of people at a feast. This scene, painted on paper and intended to represent a tapestry, is based on an engraving by Jan Sadeler the elder, who in turn was imitating a drawing by Dirck Barendsz (1534–92), the complete scene being somewhat adapted at each stage. It is colourful and lively, as the ladies strive to keep the Court gentlemen from lifting their skirts and fondling their breasts, their table being hidden from the musicians who play on the lawn by a leafy screen that is also hung with a draped curtain. Another amorous scene, most definitely not intended for the moral education of the young, is enacted on the arched gallery overlooking the garden, where a nun is lured away from her companions, engaged in devout pursuits, by a monk who opens her dress to reveal her splendid bosom. Unfortunately a watchman notices their doubtful pursuits, and in the last painting of the series they are both shown doing penance. This *Dockenhaus* abounds with similar lively scenes, and on an outer door, for instance, is seen a barefooted and plainly dressed maid who leads a small naked child by the hand to the bathing-room that was presumably close at hand. Under her arm the maid carries a wooden tub with a tap on the side, and both she and the child wear curious bathing-hats. These paintings give the house, despite the various renovations, a wonderful late-medieval atmosphere and a richness of detail that is quite unique.

One of the most interesting of the seventeenth-century models at the museum contains a room where trading was carried out from a merchant's own home, in a vaulted basement. This house dates from the last quarter of the century and also originated in the town of Nuremberg, always the great centre of South German trade. The basic construction of this model is much less complex than the house with the paintings and represents a very basic rich merchant's town house. The basement area, occupied usually by the garden, stables and store-room, is unusually high in this case, and the constructor of the model appears to have found this section just as interesting as the furnished living-rooms. In the vaulted shop the merchant's wares are neatly arranged on the narrow shelves or packed away in the unlabelled drawers that line one side of the room. On the back wall stands a large cupboard that is painted blue, and on either side are shelves of writing-paper in a variety of different shades, this presumably being the merchant's main

Above: The merchant's selling room with a wax-headed lady doll. From the Nuremberg house dating to the last quarter of the seventeenth century and known as the Bäumler family house.

Opposite: An upper room in the Bäumler cabinet showing the wax dolls with their unusual integral stands. The bottle-glass windows are also very fine.

trade. From the ceiling hangs a carved and gilded swan that was probably the merchant's trade sign. On one side of the vault hangs a neat slate on which both shopkeepers and housewives wrote simple messages, sometimes in picture form, for their servants. Random items such as sponges, an alabaster vase, a stag's head and an effectively painted chest are also found here under the watchful eye of a very fine wax-headed lady, whose hair wig was cleverly plaited in several layers around her face, giving a halo-like effect.

Another very rare group of poured-wax dolls stands in one of the central reception rooms. All have the typical black bead-like eyes, but two have integral moulded-wax bases made in one with the legs, so that these especially made *Dockenhäuser* inhabitants can stand unsupported, rather in the manner of china figurines. They are particularly finely costumed and are intended to represent children, as a larger lady doll supervises their conduct from a high-backed velvet chair. This reception room, with its curious dappled light

caused by the round-paned windows, is decorated with a pair of portraits painted on card and now bent slightly out of shape. Such pictures are found in several of the cabinets and add a primitive, very human touch to the atmosphere. In contrast to these crude paintings are the fine ivory hanging shelves with their tea-bowls, saucers and goblets all carved in position, a type of item common to the Berchtesgaden area. The room is heated by a tall green earthenware stove of massive size, whose presence in a house or model room invariably suggests a German origin. The typical Nuremberg interior is also suggested by the very large number of windows that give the rooms a very identifiable atmosphere. These windows look particularly effective on the side exteriors, as they are arranged symmetrically and terminate in a small attic window at either side. The outside of the house was repainted in a soft grey in 1829, as the original dark red colour was not popular at the time; this colour was recently removed and we again see the original red ground. The windows are surrounded by a stylized painted decoration of leaves and cursive shapes, similar to those that can still be seen on so many old South German houses,

Opposite: The courtyard of the Bäumler house with its fine nineteenth-century coach. Through the arch another painted house is glimpsed.

In the stable of the Bäumler house stand well-carved horses accompanied by grooming brushes and a large haybox with a lid.

though the grey, white and orange are much softer in effect than the brilliant colours that are now used. The base of this model, which stands to adult height, is painted now to represent large stones or tiles. One of the most arresting features of the construction is the very realistically made tin guttering that ends in a crudely made dragon's head. The gabled attic rooms are purely decorative, and the basic house is composed of six main rooms with the central area of the ground floor, next to the vaulted shop, being constructed as an outside courtyard and consequently decorated in the same manner and colours as the original exterior. On a side shelf stands an exquisitely made wooden coach intended to represent a child's toy, as another full-sized nineteenth-century coach is also kept in the yard. Through an arch at the back can be seen a very elegant formal garden leading to a much grander mansion in the distance, giving this model a sense of actual situation not often encountered in *Dockenhäuser*. The stables lie to the left of the main entrance and contain two extremely well-carved and over-fed horses, which stand patiently in stalls supplied with grooming-brushes and a large haybox

49

with a lid. A variety of useful equipment, such as woven baskets, garden tools and tin lanterns, give added realism to the interior.

The reception rooms, in accord with the plan of the other Nuremberg houses, are situated on the first floor, and alongside the drawing-room, in which stand the wax figures with moulded bases, is a hall with a double arch at the rear, from which the stairs lead to the other parts of the house. From the centre of the hall ceiling hangs a large brass chandelier. A considerable quantity of good brassware is also on show in the kitchen, the pride of any burgher's wife, among which is a good set of weights. The cooking-area, with its huge shelved canopy, is the section of most importance, and around the room brown and green earthenware pots, huge rolling-pins, funnels, ladles and plates are displayed. One particularly interesting item is a small pewter table with matching bowls and a tureen, though a spoon-rack, rather like a one-handled metal tray with slits for the wooden spoon-handles to drop through, is also of highly commendable quality.

The main bedroom, at the top of the house, is occupied by two poured-wax lady dolls, one of which carries a tightly swaddled baby. Both have black painted eyes and wear wigs, their bodies appearing to be of the tow-bound type. The baby has a wooden cradle with round carrying-handles, rather like those found on nineteenth-century chests of drawers, on either side. In accordance with the nursery custom of the period, the cradle is piled high with pillows and mattresses, so that the child could lie level with the cradle top. The mother sleeps in a four-poster bed with printed curtains, and the walls of the room are painted in red and white, with the same large, sweeping brush-strokes seen on the exterior. A set of chairs, of highly cursive design, is heavily painted in red and blue with gilt decoration, and there is also a matching table, the whole set seemingly made of cardboard.

A home-made birdcage, constructed of net over a circular card base, hangs from the ceiling of the upper landing from which two arches lead to another part of the house. Also on the top floor is a store-room of generous size, equipped with well-made wooden shelves on which stand jars of wood and metal, strainers, scrubbing-brushes, baskets and colanders: in the foreground stands a beautifully painted chest. The general interior of this model house is greatly improved by the application of strips of wood along all the outer floors and wall edges, which so often have a somewhat rough, unfinished appearance. These decorative strips are further embellished with painted flowers and scrolls, so that a really neat effect was achieved, suitable for the display of the model in a reception area.

Rooms as well as complete houses, were popular in Germany from the mid-seventeenth century, with kitchens and living-rooms being particular favourites, as they offered more scope for the display of the silver, pewter and brass miniatures that were such a delight to collect. At the Nuremberg museum is a two-roomed cabinet dating from the second half of the

In the corner of this typically German kitchen the hens are being fattened in a coop. Late eighteenth century.

A toy kitchen is one of the most traditional German toys. In this eighteenth-century print we see water being heated. From 'Scenes from Children's Life' by J. J. Mettenleiter and D. Theodowiecsi.

Opposite: A very simply constructed cabinet dating to the seventeenth century. The kitchen is particularly well supplied with metal utensils. A mechanical spit carries the date 1550. *Right:* A detail of the fine chandelier in the panelled room of the cabinet dating to the seventeenth century. The plates are decorated in blue and are separated by ornamental devices. *Below:* In the upper chamber of the two-roomed cabinet, a very fine earthenware stove is seen behind the man doll.

seventeenth century that is constructed on a much larger scale than the more conventional *Dockenhaus*. The rooms have an atmosphere that is much less pleasant than the houses,' and the general tone is somewhat gloomy. The upper panelled room, with a bed piled high with mattresses and pillowcases, has an impressive array of blue-painted plates on a shelf, where they are separated by wooden ornamental devices that give the symmetrically arranged pieces additional importance. It seems probable that this was some form of gentleman's apartment, and a man doll still occupies the main seat at the oval table that is set for a meal. This table is a particularly fine miniature, as the four turned legs are separated by an oval stretcher that reflects the main shape of the top. A green earthenware stove is used to heat this very functional chamber, in which the gentleman is able to wash at a cistern that hangs from the wall; a neat towel hangs beneath. The fashionably dressed man, whose head appears to be made of wax over a plaster core, is now accompanied by a small poured-wax child made of this material to waist level only and with her skirts forming a cushion-like base. Her costume is composed almost entirely of gilt braid and lace, and the head is particularly interesting, as some attempt to create a real character was made, with the lips modelled in a petulant, pursed position, quite unlike the much more perfectly composed features of the other waxes. It seems very likely that this tiny figure might originally have been intended as a pin cushion but was so charming that a later owner added her to the setting, perhaps at the same time that a chap book, dated 1725, which hangs from the side of a cupboard, appeared. The lace pillow on the floor and a lady's fan also appear somewhat out of place in this bachelor's apartment but serve to illustrate how successive owners cannot resist adding their own touches to such interiors.

The large downstairs kitchen is of the typical Nuremberg type, with a canopied cooking-area where piles of wood dry beneath the lower arches. The floor is painted in red and white to resemble tiles, and parts of the walls are whitewashed. From one wall hang two boards of the type already encountered in the shop area of the Bäumler family house, in this case showing drawings of various items for the information of the illiterate servants. All these kitchens are supplied with a huge variety of equipment impossible to list individually, but among the finer pieces in this interior is a mechanical spit bearing the date 1550 scratched on its foot. There is also a particularly generous supply of long-handled pans, some with hallmarks, which were so constructed in order that they could be stored on a very high shelf yet the handles could be easily reached as they pointed downwards.

Justifiably, the two most popular houses in the collection are the Kress and Stromer *Dockenhäuser*, which typify all that is rich and evocative in the best of

On its dormer window the Stromer cabinet carries the date 1639. The balustrading is a later replacement. The house takes its name from its last owner, the Baron von Stromer.

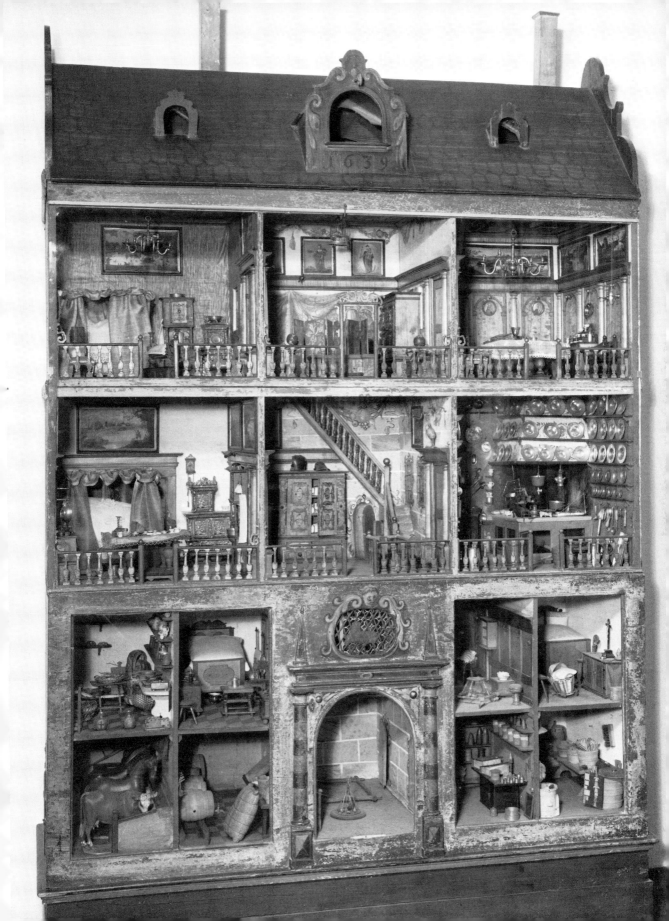

German models. Their rooms are crammed with treasured miniatures, and we are presented with a most effective impresssion of the burghers of the period, with their great love of possessions and pride of ownership. This Stromer house has been in the possession of the museum since 1879, though its original owner is not known, and it now takes its name from that of the Baron von Stromer, its last owner, who died in 1939. He knew something of its history and stated that it was previously in the possession of Emilie Ernstine, Baroness von Haller, who obtained it as a legacy from Karl von Wolckern. Her eldest daughter, Helene Christine, in 1847 married Christoph Gottlieb Friedrich, Baron von Stromer, and the *Dockenhaus* was later inherited by the donor. The Stromer *Dockenhaus* is particularly liked, as it carries its original date, 1639, painted on the decorative front of a dormer attic window and is said to contain over a thousand individual items that never fail to attract the eye, no matter how often the model is viewed.

The house is basically constructed of $\frac{1}{2}$-inch pine, and the side windows are painted with the typical round panes. A touch of unusual realism is provided at ground-floor stable level, where a man is painted in the act of walking through a door to feed the horses. This is the only *Dockenhaus* where any provision for movement of the whole construction has been made, as it was once possible to lift off the roof and the upper floor and then remove the lower section from the base. The other large cabinet houses have no convenient means of transportation, so that the maker of this model was showing unusual forethought. In a photograph, the Stromer cabinet seems completely perfect in detail though on close examination much of the workmanship is found to be rudimentary, and certain effects, such as the balustrading that fronts the upper two floors, are simply painted on flat sections of thin wood, rather than being correctly turned, though it is probable that this indicates the hand of a restorer. The lower section, where we are given an unusually complete view of life below stairs, is constructed on a completely different scale to the reception areas, as the eight box-like compartments are also fitted with furniture and equipment of a small size. Here we see the stable with an exquisitely carved pair of horses and the cow which provided milk for the household. At the back is the stableboy's bed, so that he can guard his animals throughout the night and also keep a watchful eye on the kegs of wine and beer and the sacks of provisions stored in the rooms alongside. In another small store-room above are kept the more perishable items, such as bread and vegetables, and in this section sleeps another, more important servant, who has left his razor on the table of his more comfortable room. The other half of the lower section is separated by the wide stone hall, in which stands a cage of chickens to be fattened for the table. Once again there are four small rooms, but these are much less spartan and their contents more colourful. Here we discover the night nursery, with its carved baby-walker, obviously a quite indispensable item of equipment, as it is found in almost all the early

In the Stromer nursery is a safety bed with doors and a cradle tied with decorative ribbons.

houses. There is also a chair for the nurse and a cupboard bed at the back. These infant beds, with grid-like wooden doors, were made especially for the protection of children who had grown too big for cradles but could not be relied upon to sleep safely in a conventional bed. (Several other examples are to be found in the nurseries of Mon Plaisir in Arnstadt.) Presumably the child who slept in this bed once occupied the cradle that stands close by, with all its blankets and covers decoratively ribboned in position, until the arrival of another baby. The infant who used this room was well provided for, as there is a table and bench intended for a child's use and a water-cistern hanging from the wall.

There is another nursery apartment next door, with a large uncurtained

The effectively decorated upper hall with its large linen press filled with the items so necessary in the German woman's dowry. The Stromer House.

Opposite: The kitchen of the Stromer cabinet, with its painted canopy over the cooking area. It is unrivalled among *Dockenhäuser* for its mass of equipment. The clockwork jack is a superb piece, and the room perfectly exhibits the skill of the many craftsmen whose work was combined in these models.

bed in which the nurse would sleep; during the day, in her quiet moments, she was expected to work at a spinning-wheel. In a very small filigree cradle lies a small wax baby doll with painted eyes, and there is also a particularly interesting dappled rocking-horse of the very early type of construction, with board sides. The few large versions of this type of horse to have survived have lost their paint, so this miniature is of considerable importance as it establishes their original appearance: we find, for example, that the mane was painted, while the tail was made of hair. In the centre of the nursery is a wicker cradle on wheels, an early forerunner of the perambulator and, though most probably of eighteenth-century origin, again of interest, as full-sized examples are not known because of the fragility of the material.

The main section of the cabinet is not provided with any doll inhabitants, though the contents are so closely packed that perhaps it was decided that there was simply no room for their addition. An impressive staircase rises from the main hall at the centre of the house, and on a half landing a small dog is painted on the wall, forever in the act of bounding up the stairs of this lonely house. The walls are painted to resemble stones and decorated by great

58

swags of painted fruit and leaves, while the windows at the back of the landings have their curtains also painted in position. For the decoration of a very large cupboard the maker achieved the effect of a carved piece by glueing sections of fretwork in suitable positions. Painted arches are represented in perspective, so we are given a *trompe l'œil* effect of other passages leading off.

The kitchen, unrivalled among *Dockenhäuser* for its wealth of pewter, brass and copper, is hung from floor to ceiling with the neatly arranged equipment that delighted collectors of miniatures. There are some particularly fine pierced-work graters and a good wooden plate-rack with an exactly fitting set of wooden plates. The large canopy over the cooking-area, intended for the display of more important plates, is effectively decorated with painted flowers, which gives added realism. Instead of the usual painted arches under the cooking-area, there are actual doors in this instance, so that wood could be stacked to dry. The clockwork jack is also extremely fine, the most perfectly made example yet encountered, and we are given the impression that at any moment the cook might appear and all the equipment be brought into immediate use. This kitchen is particularly memorable, as it combines the

In a man's bedroom in the Stromer cabinet, a barber's bowl hangs from a peg. On the bed lie his finely stitched nightshirt and cap.

warm effects of the various metals with wood, painted decoration and the multiplicity of cooking-devices, all reflected in the red and black tiled floor, exhibiting some of the most interesting work of the many craftsmen who combined their specialities in such expensive exhibition pieces.

On the opposite side of the hall is a man's bedroom with a nicely made water-cistern that pivots into a bowl beneath and accompanied by a sponge and brushes for his toilet. From brass pegs on the opposite wall hang a bowl and a barber's bowl, as well as a small mirror set in an embroidered frame. On the bed lies his exquisitely stitched nightshirt, together with a lace nightcap. On a side table lies a letter. The simply constructed four-poster bed is hung with green silk, and near at hand is a carved close-stool, still with its original earthenware chamber-pot. Above the panelling, the walls are hung with

60

paintings of river scenes, and on a table lie blue and white tea-bowls and saucers, candlesticks and cutlery with ivory handles.

The stairs lead to an upper landing with the ceiling painted to resemble panelling and the back wall painted with curtains in red and grey. There is a six-fold screen to act as an additional protection from draughts, one side being covered with floral paper and the other decorated with embossed figures. There is also a very simply made working spinet that has unfortunately lost its legs. The adjoining main bedroom also relies heavily on painted decoration for effect, the ceiling being treated with strips of grey with stylized flowers. On the floor, painted to resemble tiles, stands a good model of a swinging cradle, whose heavy base contains drawers. The end poles, from which the cradle is suspended, are heavily carved in a typically South German manner. Like the man's room, this bedchamber has a very lived-in atmosphere, and brushes and toothcombs, a cistern and a washstand all stand in readiness for the mistress of the house, obviously literate, as she is supplied with several leather-bound, brass-clasped books.

The other reception room on the top floor also contains several books, including one with a printed cover. Though the situation of one of the main rooms at the top of the house might now seem strange, it was quite common at the time, as the more important rooms were thus kept away from the smell of cooking and the activity of the basement section. In town houses, where street noise and stench were often very unpleasant, a drawing-room far removed from sordid reality was doubly welcome. A large table stands in this room on huge bulbous turned legs and is spread with a white cloth, which shows to advantage a particularly beautiful parcel-gilt goblet, slightly out of scale, but of superb quality. Card-playing is obviously a favourite pursuit, and a pack lies on this table. On the panelled walls hangs a brass platter decorated with a scene of the Crucifixion, and there is also one of the common green earthenware stoves. The panelling of the room is discontinued around this stove area, presumably because the heat would cause it to crack. There are several large paintings of a town, possibly Nuremberg itself, in all seasons, filling the space above the main panelling. This room was given additional light from mica windows set into the wall of the central hall.

Despite the abundance of equipment and the attractive decorative painting, the Stromer house is fairly basic in lay-out and construction, whereas the other famous *Dockenhaus*, that which originally belonged to the Kress family, is much more complex. The Kress house, dating from the second half of the seventeenth century, has the added attraction of containing its dolls, which are of particularly high quality. In a high chair sits an all-wax baby with bent limbs, similar to the figures of the Infant Jesus made at Oberammergau, with small black bead-like eyes and painted hair. Another wax baby is carried by a very beautiful wax lady with painted features. Her body is of an interesting construction as the arms are fabric with the fingers represented by delicate

61

Above: In the nursery of the Kress house, a lady carries her swaddled child, while an older, bent-limb wax infant sits in a high chair. *Opposite:* The superb *Dockenhaus* once owned by the Kress von Kressenstein family. This model retains its original balustrading and decorated arches.

rolls of fine linen, sewn very neatly. Another, differently constructed, rather patrician wax lady stands in an upper hall. This example, wearing a pink and silver bonnet, has an unusual wig of flocked wool, similar to the method later used by dollmakers such as the Gebrüder Heubach in the late nineteenth century. The body-construction differs from that of the other lady as the legs are made of wood, including her painted shoes. The most attractive of the dolls is obviously the lady who is seated in her underclothes, with the garments she is about to wear set out around her to show their fine workmanship, and including a pink skirt and corset and a muff. The lady doll in undress is seated in a panelled but quite simply furnished room decorated with paintings and a good mirror. There is an empty cradle and a close-stool, also with its green-glazed earthenware chamber-pot.

The basic plan of the Kress von Kressenstein cabinet is very complex,

In the lowest hall of the Kress house, the door leading to the stable is decorated with a painting of a horse. The servants ate in this area.

especially that of the basement area, where there are several flights of stairs and landings to give complete realism to the interior. Unlike the Stromer *Dockenhaus*, all the balustrading, which is such an important feature, is correctly turned and assembled, and the room and hall fronts are further enhanced by arches at ceiling level, which give a particularly well-finished effect. The two upper floors, which are occupied by the family, are set out in the conventional way, though the steep, very realistic staircases contribute to the atmosphere of a real town house of the period.

In the street-level area of the model the lay-out becomes completely asymmetrical, with a corridor balcony connecting the various sections. In the stable is a horse carved with the assurance of that seen in the Stromer cabinet, but this example is provided with a magnificent saddle made with the precision of a craftsman's miniature from fabric and leather and properly studded. The ostler is also given better accommodation and sleeps in a simply

64

The fine kitchen of the Kress cabinet, with a coarse-faced cook made of wax. The room is packed with plates and moulds of blue-and-white earthenware and pewter.

furnished room reached by his own staircase. The central area is occupied by the servants' hall, with a large wooden water-trough at the rear for the supply of the whole household, and in the foreground a group of very basic furniture. A door, painted with a horse, leads from this section into the stable, whereas in the Stromer house the only entrance to the section where the animals were kept was through a door painted on the outer wall where a stable boy was represented in movement as he walked in to feed the horses. On the right-hand side of the servants' hall are two very simple rooms (quite unlike the well-equipped nursery in the other house), in one of which sleeps a servant to guard the provisions stored beneath in kegs and barrels and wicker baskets.

The rooms of the family section of the model are much more spacious. In the large kitchen stands a coarsely modelled cook, preserving the tradition that domestic servants were invariably ugly and rough-featured, while only the merchants and their children were fair, a convention that was also

In a reception room of the Kress house a stylishly dressed wax-headed man stands at a table inlaid with ivory. On a wall hangs a sundial with the later date of 1785.

maintained in English Baby Houses of the eighteenth century, where the menials were often made of carved wood, whereas the family was of good poured wax. The wax cook in the Kress house presides over a kitchen that is packed from floor to ceiling with plates and moulds made of pewter and blue-and-white earthenware. In the foreground there is a dough-bin and a very pleasing rolling-pin carved with decorative motifs that created patterns in the pastry when it was rolled. The kitchen is separated from the dining-room by a narrow hall, in which stands a simply made long-case clock.

The colours of the dining-room are still quite rich especially the tapestry-covered high-backed chairs and the rich blue coat of the man who stands at a round table inlaid with bone or ivory. This room is again panelled, with a painting, plates and jars displayed on the shelf above. On one wall is a painted

66

wooden sundial bearing the date 1785, another example of the frequent addition of attractive items at a later time. In this chamber the continuity of the wooden panelling is not broken for the large earthenware stove that must have made the room stiflingly hot when all the diners were seated. On the table stands a group of early blown-glass decanters in clear glass, a splendid silver-lidded tankard and some blue-and-white plates. The door of this reception room has a very well-made frame, and its construction is repeated in the upper hall, where two doors lead into the bedrooms that are simply furnished but enlivened by the fine dolls already discussed.

Part of the effectiveness of the Kress house depends on two very tall gables which, on various occasions, have been placed in different positions on the roof, though the way they are now arranged would seem more logical. This *Dockenhaus*, like the others at Nuremberg, is obviously constructed for the appreciation of adults, as the rooms of importance are all arranged at a level completely suitable for easy adult viewing, and it is only the lower, working areas that have to be viewed from a kneeling or stooping position. They still retain the power to demand attention, yet, curiously, seem much less popular with the public of today than the early houses in Holland, as there is rarely any problem of viewing them in peace. There are at present no guide-books to the houses and few photographs available to the general public, and the visitor cannot help but wonder why native interest is so minimal in a town that was the traditional centre of the toy trade, especially as the houses are well displayed in a most splendidly designed museum.

Far from home, in the Bethnal Green Museum in London, is displayed another Nuremberg *Dockenhaus* of much more modest proportions, one which was possibly once a genuine child's plaything as the basic scale is in accord with a girl's height. The house is a four-roomed, almost box-like construction, given some importance by its well-made roof and interesting metal stars that were apparently typical of a fashion that was unique to Nuremberg. These metal stars were obviously something of a danger in high winds if insecurely fixed, and their use was consequently prohibited at the end of the seventeenth century, so that this model with the date 1673 on one of the chimneys was probably among the last to be so decorated. This quite modest house is also unusual in that the original two-door front is still retained, whereas the splendid examples at Nuremberg either have lost their façades or were made as plain cabinets. The pine structure is painted to represent stone, and there are seven small square front windows with the main arched door leading somewhat strangely into the kitchen. The roof is painted in dark red with the outlines of tiles rendered in black.

The main bedroom has a typically German pine four-poster bed piled high with mattresses, in front of which stands a child's high chair of polished wood and an extremely well-detailed turned-wood baby-walker, still holding the original child doll with a wax-mask face. Two other figures of the same

The exterior of the Nuremberg house showing the interesting metal stars on the roof.

Opposite: This is one of the smallest surviving Nuremberg cabinet houses and was probably originally a child's toy. The date 1673 is carried on a chimney.

construction are seen in the room, one seeming to represent an adult though it stands only as high as the children. In the adjoining room is another wax-mask faced figure representing a lady in Court dress carrying a fan and costumed in gold lace over silk. She seems strangely out of place in this artisan's dwelling and, together with the figures in the main bedroom, probably originated in another cabinet house of the period, as the scale was usually much more closely observed. The chamber in which the Court lady stands is similar in arrangement to several encountered in Nuremberg, as it is intended both for sleeping and as a sitting-room. The walls are panelled and finished at the upper edge with a plate-rail for the pewter and earthenware in which the women took such pride, though in this instance they have been lost. The bed, which is built into the corner, has curtains and an unusual wooden stocking-shaper which hangs from a convenient hook. The room is heated by a large green-painted stove, made in imitation of those in earthenware and standing on turned legs. The outer wall of the *Dockenhaus*

is provided with opening outlets for this stove, again indicating the degree of
realism that was considered necessary even in a model that was intended for a
child or a cabinet assembler of fairly modest means.

The ground-floor kitchen contains the usual abundance of shelves and
cupboards, where the impressive array of cookery utensils could be displayed,
and there is also the conventional large corner cooking-area with stands for
cooking over charcoal on the surface. In a line along a side wall stand a group
of unusual wooden casks, quite different in construction from any
encountered in the Nuremberg Museum models, though obviously original
and made of the fine chip wood that bends so easily and was used to such effect
by box-makers in the Berchtesgaden area. The kitchen floor is painted in dark
red and outlined in a darker colour to represent tiles, a device that is also
resorted to in the main bedroom and the dining-room. The copper and
brassware in the kitchen have been cleaned during the last few years, and the
very dark gloomy effect once transmitted by the model is now banished, and

The interior of a Nuremberg-type cabinet house dating to the first half of the seventeenth century. This house was photographed before the last war at the Schloss Museum, Berlin.

we can again see the interior as it was originally intended, with the soft gleam of the moulds, buckets, pans and large scales and weights. A simple door leads from the kitchen to the main living- or dining-room, which is also plentifully supplied with copper and brass, which, when not in use, was stored away in a large cupboard at the rear, over which is an open, paled platform. In the other corner is a neat cupboard containing a privy, an unusual touch as, though lavatories were often supplied in early Dutch cabinets, they seem to have been considered unnecessary in German constructions.

It is likely that smaller models of this type were originally made in some number, both for the household instruction of wealthy children and for the amusement of cabinet collectors, but unfortunately their very modesty of basic construction resulted in their destruction, whereas the large and impressive models were obviously items of great social importance and were consequently preserved in German museums. It is fortunate that this single example was acquired by an English museum to represent the craftsmanship of the *Dockenhaus*.

Another Nuremberg house, believed to date to the first half of the seventeenth century, was illustrated in a 1933 edition of the *Studio*. The model stood some 5 feet 6 inches high and was then at the Schloss Museum in Berlin. Unfortunately this museum, now in East Germany, was badly bombed during the last war, and the house has disappeared, only to be recorded in a few poor-quality photographs where it appears to be much broader in construction than the more conventional early German cabinets and much more akin to the English Baby Houses in proportion. The rooms all had well-carved or moulded ceilings, and the heavy carved furniture is typical of the early cabinets. On the top floor three rooms were situated. In a bedroom, a four-poster bed was filled to canopy level with pillows and mattresses and hung with checked fabric. This bed canopy rose to a point in the centre, a design also encountered in the Kress house. The room was papered in a very large-scale design, and there was a changing-screen and a cabinet for clothes. In the room alongside, there was a large earthenware stove situated in a corner and several high-backed chairs. On the table stood several bottles. Three landscape paintings fitted perfectly above the moulded picture rail. In the third room a simple meal was set out on a carved table, and the walls are hung with still-life scenes.

The middle floor was composed of four rooms, in one of which stood a splendid day-bed, comfortably positioned against the stove, and an alabaster table with matching bowls that must have been added early in the eighteenth century. In the background was a painted cupboard containing linen that was neatly tied into bundles with ribbon. In the ladies' work-room a spinning-wheel and a cradle were found, and in the store-room were discovered the usual labelled jars, barrels and tubs. In the kitchen was the usual assortment of metal utensils. The ground floor represented some type of hall, set around with arched windows containing Nuremberg-type pierced metal panes. A very large table, presumably for banquets, stood in this area.

The *Studio* also illustrated another South German house dating to around 1700, but of the typical tall, Nuremberg type with an integral courtyard, where a maid stands. In the stables a large coach was housed, and in the small room above slept the servants. The dining-room was panelled and provided with a large dresser and an earthenware stove. The dining-table had huge baluster legs and stood on a massive rectangular platform. The windows were curtained. The kitchen was of conventional appearance, with a large canopied cooking-area and many shelves with the usual assortment of metal equipment. In the bedroom above, two ladies and a gentleman prepared to descend to their meal, one of the ladies possibly a maid, being represented as she opened a wardrobe door. In the other room a visiting man talked to a

71

lady wearing a fashionable hat and carrying a bag. The earthenware stove in this apartment was of a more ornate shape than usual, and there was an effective writing-desk with cabriole legs. A bird in a crudely made cage was set on a bobbin-turned single-pillar table.

Projects such as the furnishing of complete houses, or even small towns such as Mon Plaisir, were aided by the rapid development of the German toy-industry. During the seventeenth century Nuremberg and Fürth had found little competition, but by the eighteenth century the toy-makers of several regions, such as Seiffen and Groden, were making their own contribution, and there is evidence of direct trading, for instance, between the Sonneberg merchants and Britain as early as 1735. By the mid-eighteenth century the Sonnebergers had gained the same rights as the sellers of Nuremberg at all the big fairs, so that the almost complete monopoly was broken.

From the beginning of the Sonneberg toy industry, its success depended on the merchants' and distributors' willingness to exploit their workers, so that the living-conditions of these people were traditionally lower than in other parts of Germany. *Papier mâché* dolls, with which this area became particularly associated, were made under the most bitter conditions, which is why they were able to sell such vast quantities over a long period, continually undercutting the work of other regions. A small group of makers and merchants found it possible to manipulate the economic policy of the ducal government of Meiningen and so obtain complete control of the toy-makers, who were dependent on them for the sale and distribution of their work. Their difficulties were exacerbated by the sanction of a local ruler who in 1789 decreed that production should be completely separated from marketing, thus dealing a severe blow to the workers in this folk-based industry, as it placed all their work in the hands of the frequently ruthless merchants, an act known as '*Grosse Handelsprivileg*'.

Many Sonneberg wares in the eighteenth century were still of the turned and carved wooden type that had been in production since the previous century and which were stained with natural colours, such as bilberry juice. Items made for model kitchens were, however, frequently left plain for greater realism. In the eighteenth century it became necessary to make the work more attractive in order to compete with the effective work from other regions, such as Oberammergau, and at this time the decoration of toys passed into the hands of the bismuth painters, so called because they applied a waterproof layer of that substance to chests. The dolls supplied by these Sonneberg carvers were intended mainly as children's playthings and were of simple turned construction, similar to those seen in nineteenth-century Noah's Arks, where they represent the women of the family. The eighteenth-century examples are characterized by the slimness of their construction, so that from the waist downwards the figures contrast with the almost bell-like shape favoured in the Alpine regions.

The industry began to move away from this traditional turned-wooden production in the eighteenth century and began to manufacture figures made of rye flour, plaster and sand in some quantity, dolls with heads of this dough-like material, referred to as *Brotteig*, being among the main products. The new material was fairly economical to use, and very realistic figures could be cast from moulds that could be used several times. Though basic *papier mâché* was used for dolls' heads in Britain and France at this time, it appears, from popular belief, that the technique was not introduced to the Sonneberg area until the early nineteenth century, after which it became the most popular technique until the general introduction of porcelain.

A similar range of turned wooden kitchen pieces for dolls' rooms and houses was also made at Berchtesgaden and Oberammergau, both areas of Germany where agriculture was not in itself sufficient for the adequate support of a family. The Oberammergau industry is thought to date from the Middle Ages, probably due to the encouragement of the monks at Rottenbuch and Ettal. The local woodcarvers received their guild constitution in 1563, and it was revived in 1681. The guild system operated particularly heavily in this region, and consequently, to a far greater degree than in the less isolated Sonneberg, skills were retained within particular families, some of which are still in existence today, practising artistic carving of a decorative type, as well as the traditional religious pieces. The original production was also mainly religious, but toys became one of the most important products during the eighteenth century, aided by the fact that a period of peace was enjoyed in the region, so that the merchants were able to set up several wholesale trading firms on the lines of those already established by the Nurembergers. Unfortunately the majority of these early toys, intended for children, are lost, and we find only occasional examples of this work in the store-rooms, kitchens and stables of the *Dockenhäuser*. Though these models are now associated mainly with adult collectors (such as the Count von Nadasdy, who in 1671 was recorded as the owner of a black-stained Nuremberg doll's cabinet with seventeen partly panelled rooms), they were also owned by children. The example in the Bethnal Green Museum in London seems at present to be the only piece which might originally have been a genuine toy, presumably the others, thought of little worth, being discarded. The Augsburg historian Paul von Stetten the younger, writing in 1765, described many of the customs of the previous century and seems to be in no doubt that many houses were especially made for children. In his book *Comments on the Town of Augsburg illustrated with Copper Engravings*, he pursues the subject further:

With regard to the education of girls, I must refer to the toys with which many play until they become brides, namely the so-called *Dockenhäuser*. Therein was everything that belonged to a house and the household, in miniature, and several of these models carried the luxury so far that such a toy could cost up to a thousand guilder and more. On the other hand, allow a young lady to have nothing in her room but holy books and a calendar, and even these are bad enough, and one would have no difficulty in preventing her from learning anything other than her household duties, and her conversation and manners would hardly be different from the empty phrases of your maids.

The German woman's traditional role was completely linked to her household and family, and all her training was towards making her a good housewife when she married. Von Stetten's condemnation of an education that hardly raised a woman's conversation and knowledge above that of her maids was therefore heartening, though it was many generations before the education of girls was to change significantly. His reference to the cost of toy houses is now frequently found questionable, as the amount would seem to relate more to models especially made for adults, though the basic tenet of his observation was obviously true. From an inventory relating to the estate of a well-to-do Nuremberg merchant, Leonie von Wilckens comments that a *Dockenhaus* with all its furnishings was valued at only 25 guilders, but Johann Christoph von Lemp of Ebenreuth owned a walnut wardrobe valued at 24 guilders, suggesting either that the house was intended for the children of the family or that it was valued only according to the basic value of the raw materials used, which would seem a strange form of assessment.

The construction of a model room also engaged the attention of both adults and children in the seventeenth and eighteenth centuries, and as the project involved considerably less expense than a complete house, it could be indulged in by a much wider social group. Some were arranged in glass-fronted box-like cases, while others were almost peepshow-like in effect. The quality of the items in such settings varies considerably, some being home-made from paper, tinsel and card, while others contain individual pieces of finely made miniature furniture. A photograph taken in 1933 showed a particularly fine group of this type that was then exhibited at the Maximilians Museum at Augsburg. The room was set out in a shallow box, and the centre of interest was a gilded console table above which hung a small mirror. On either side of the table is a chair. The dolls give the tableau interest, as they are made of wax with moulded hair and costumed in the style of the 1740s. A serving man is seen as he carries a decanter to the table. Similar settings in glazed cases are seen in several German museums showing not only simple household interiors but also shops and outdoor arrangements. In the Museum of Folk Art in Erfurt is a model that shows an elderly gentleman visiting the barber's shop, a model constructed on a scale that could easily have formed part of a larger setting in a curiosity cabinet or art chamber and almost identical in style to the figures contained in that lavish construction Mon Plaisir, situated only a few miles away at Arnstadt.

74

The inspiration and planning behind all other eighteenth-century *Dockenhäuser* and Baby Houses pales into insignificance beside the awesome detail that was lavished on the collecting project of the Princess Augusta Dorothea von Schwarzburg-Arnstadt. This acquisitive lady was not to be satisfied with a conventional structure of a mere twelve or fifteen rooms but found it necessary to construct a model of the town in which she lived, represented complete with its inhabitants engaged in their daily life. It was described as '*Mon Plaisir*' ('My Pleasure') as French was, of course, the Court language of the period. It is doubtful whether the Princess ever considered the wax figures as any more than a necessary feature of the complete scene, but to the viewer of today it is the dolls that seem to dominate, so that when the town is seen for the first time, the initial impression is one of a breathtaking selection of fine figures in fairly rudimentary settings. This feeling of slight anticlimax is engendered largely by the very dull plain white cases in which the settings are displayed and which themselves seem out of place in the elegant rooms of the Castle Museum, where the dolls have been kept since 1930. The problems involved in the display of such a complex model with its eighty-two rooms must be very great, as it was originally made to fit in a gallery, especially constructed for the purpose, in the Augustenburg Palace, where a much more integrated effect was achieved, with the centre of the princely residence rising to some five storeys. The town buildings, taverns and small shops were originally linked by stairs and alley-ways on which stood various characters, so that the effect of an actual town at work was achieved. It seems possible that the Princess might have been encouraged in her work by such superb mechanical settings as that at the Hellbrunn Park near Salzburg, though her town was never automated in any way.

Unfortunately, though this model has always been considered an object of considerable historical importance, it was moved and packed away several times with the inevitable accompanying damage to the more fragile sections, so that all that now remains are the actual buildings, while all the clever linking, doors, archways and passages that were necessary to present a complete model, are lost or were blocked up or nailed down with each reconstruction. As there are no original plans or later engravings of Mon Plaisir, it is not possible to reinstate these sections except by the widest play of the imagination, so that it was eventually decided to separate the buildings and display them either individually or in small groups, so that the visitors could inspect each in detail. Originally the model stood too high to have been viewed in entirety without the use of library steps, and though this would be in accord, for instance, with certain of the Dutch cabinets, its re-arrangement is probably to the advantage of the viewer, who now sees a group of tableaux.

The exteriors of the shops, rooms, houses and church are very simply made and have no relationship to the effectively decorated walls of the Nuremberg cabinets, and we are presented with an almost amateurish effect, with mediocre carpentry and unimaginative finish. In a few instances, where the cases are in relatively original condition, as in the Deer Hunt, there is an elegant archway over the scene with appropriate painted decoration giving a well-finished effect. Perhaps originally more of these arches were used, though it would now be pointless to attempt a reconstruction. In any case the Princess's main interest seems to have lain with the many characters and the interiors, so that the buildings were mere sketches against which she assembled her extravagant tableaux.

There is no other early cabinet house whose creator's life is so well documented or whose character can be judged so closely, and it is this aspect of the ambitious enterprise that brings it so vividly to life and evokes so completely the atmosphere of eighteenth-century Arnstadt so carefully documented by the Princess.

Augusta Dorothea's father was Duke Anton Ulrich II of Braunschweig-Wolfenbüttel, who owned a very famous art collection and who was probably responsible for the arrangement of her marriage to Anton Gunther II, who also grew up in his Court. The eighteen-year-old Dorothea came to Arnstadt as a bride in 1684, and at first there is evidence of her husband's affection, such as a gift to his 'well-beloved consort' of a plot of land next to a recently built pheasant-house on which she intended to build a small palace. There is often confusion regarding Dorothea's title, as she had come to Arnstadt as a duchess but the state was raised to a principality in 1697 and after that time she was known as a princess. Taking the title of prince caused difficulties for Anton Gunther with the Elector and the Dukes of Saxony to whom he was subservient, and it became necessary for him to sell his very large collection of coins in order to meet his debts. It was perhaps unfortunate that at the same period Augusta Dorothea, who shared her husband's collecting enthusiasm, should have embarked upon her own Pleasure Palace, and it is from this point that the relationship between husband and wife seems to have deteriorated, as he was constantly upbraiding her for a lack of restraint and a preoccupation with her own projects, such as the Augustenburg which she built in the shadow of the Schwarzburgers' ancestral home, Kafernburg. She ensured by deeds that after her death this property should revert to her own family, together with other estates she obtained in 1710.

Like the model Mon Plaisir, the Augustenburg was provided with a fairly simple exterior, but the Princess threw all her energy into furnishing the rooms with costly items, and it was described in 1711 as containing expensive furniture, paintings and mirrors and having an especially captivating porcelain room, with an impressive collection of Chinese, Persian and Japanese wares as well as audience chambers and French rooms also distinguished by their fine contents. Nothing that the Augustenburg contained was adequate to assuage Dorothea's passion for collecting, and her long-suffering husband was constantly forced to pay off her creditors. Perhaps the Princess's acquisitive tendencies would have been less strong if there had been children of the marriage to engage her attention, but by 1711, at the age of forty-five, she was still spending very freely on the furnishing of the Augustenburg, despite her husband's complaints. The model town, Mon Plaisir, formed an attractive display-feature in the Palace and was begun around 1704. Though the equipping of the model was necessarily expensive, it formed only a small fragment of the great expense of the complete house which by 1710 even Dorothea was beginning to see as a liability. Her conversion to the Roman Catholic Church in 1715 worsened her relationship with her Protestant husband, though he gave permission for Mass to be said at the Augustenburg for the Princess and her servants. Her new catholic connexions, shared by her niece, the wife of the Emperor Karl VI, offered another source of income, and she was to borrow heavily from the Ursuline convent at Erfurt while she attempted to persuade her relatives to pay off her debts. After the death of Anton Gunther in 1716, her in-laws remained quite deaf to her pleas and threats and intervened in her affairs only at the most critical times.

It was against this background of continual financial crisis, followed by a lonely widowhood of thirty-five years, that the construction of Mon Plaisir progressed, perhaps at times forming a cheaper substitute for the collection of works of art that she had once enjoyed so much. The character of the Princess and the life-style she enjoyed are important elements in the study of Mon Plaisir, as an understanding of the tremendous acquisitive urge from which she suffered and a desire to complete everything, down to the smallest detail, helps in the understanding of the breadth of vision that engendered a complete town rather than a mere art cabinet. Her basic reason for embarking on the construction of her model is not known, and unfortunately no bills or letters concerning the project have survived, with the exception of an order for 'a quarter loth of dolls' things' bought at the Leipzig Easter Fair in 1697, objects that have only a possible connexion though they were somewhat expensive for children's playthings. While she was working on the project, it is possible that it was regarded with tolerant amusement as an eccentricity of a woman, separated from her husband even while he lived, who spent too much time alone. This possibly accounts for the lack of contemporary interest, as such a large project would have aroused great curiosity in Britain at the time and attracted many visitors. In comparison, Germany in the early eighteenth century was still feudal in atmosphere, and there was little of the stability that characterized social life in Britain, so that even during her lifetime many of the treasures of the Augustenburg were stolen by robbers. The merchants of the town journeying to Sonneberg were constantly attacked by bands of robber knights, who lay in wait in the Thuringian mountains. Life outside the boundary of the city state was highly dangerous, and in comparison the people living in the town felt relatively secure. It was the event of one day in the life of the town she knew so well that Dorothea sought to portray.

As the settings are now arranged, the time of day varies from group to group, and it seems probable that the original sequence would have made the tableaux more logical in effect. The scale of the buildings and the figures also differs, and it is probable that the smaller pieces once formed the background, rather in the manner of German and Italian crèche settings, where the main figures are very large and those we are intended to assume are some distance away much smaller. The quality of the furniture and plenishments of the rooms and shops also vary, some being fine miniatures of art-cabinet standard and others seeming more in the nature of children's playthings.

For the collector of antique toys, it is the dolls in the palace settings that are the most striking feature of the model. These are not made on the usual fairly small scale of doll's house figures but stand some 12 inches high in many cases, and were they not contained in Mon Plaisir would unhesitatingly be classed as basic play-dolls of the period. With very few exceptions, the heads are modelled in wax, and there is a strong local tradition that the characters familiar at Court were completely recognizable: certainly the Princess herself, who appears in several scenes, is immediately identifiable. Most of the dolls have painted eyes, and the hair is frequently made of tufts of lamb's-wool quite roughly inserted into the wax scalps. The actual modelling of the faces is highly skilled and finer in quality than that usually associated with playthings, and though less delicate, they are more in the form of portrait waxes than the somewhat stylized characters seen in the Dutch and English houses. Some of the women seen playing cards or attending a Court levée have round faces with substantial rolls of fat around their chins, while others have the most patrician features. The hands and, usually, the feet are moulded in wax, though one lady with a wax head has the original legs and feet carved in wood. In most cases the bodies are made of fabric, but in a few a wooden construction was used, and one particularly fine example, with black-painted patches on her face, was made completely of wood and is a typical but fine quality play-doll of the period.

It is obvious, from their modelling, that the dolls were made by several people, and the inclusion of the child's doll raises the question as to whether some of the other figures might also have come from toy-sellers rather than being especially commissioned. It is, however, indisputable that the majority of the inhabitants of this extensive model were especially made, mainly, it is believed, by two monks, one of whom left a plaster mould and a wax copy of an oval plaque of the Princess inscribed 'P. Einhorn *fecit* 1751': the modelling of dolls would certainly have been well within his capability. Many monks were skilled in the wax modelling that was necessary for the manufacture of statuettes, crèche figures and religious figures for children, and it seems probable that the construction of most of the dolls was organized by the two monks from Erfurt, who are recorded as living at the Augustenburg as the

Princess Augusta Dorothea, wearing the light brocade dress, takes tea with a Court lady dressed in velvet.

Princess's confessors. A few of the menial characters are carved of wood and given only basic characterization, and a few other examples, particularly the actors on the stage, are constructed of composition and probably originated in Sonneberg.

The costuming of this large quantity of dolls must have involved considerable effort, as, for instance, all the stockings are correctly made in miniature and knitted on pin-like needles. Though most of the costumes are very correct in general effect, many have their garments sewn in position, as fastenings on such a small scale distort the general shape of the figures. The dolls were dressed over a period of several years so that the fashion detail varies from around 1700 to 1730. While some of the garments worn by the dolls are correct in effect rather than detail, those seen hanging in the tailor's shop and awaiting attention in a maid's room are correct in every particular.

One maid is working on a pink shirt that is laid out on a table and is decorated with ribbed green silk ribbon arranged in a pattern down the front. On the wall of her room hangs another very correctly embroidered skirt, and on the floor is a straw hat and a chest, also made in the straw-work that was a typical craft-technique of the area. It was customary in the early eighteenth century for servants to sleep in the rooms where they worked in order to guard their employers' possessions at all times, a practice that is encountered in many of the rooms and storage-areas in the town.

The quality of the ladies of the Court is superb, but other characters are, at times, of a noticeably lower standard, such as a group of monks, made in the smaller scale, who stand in consultation around a table in an ante-room. Some of the less important men are also of a very basic standard. The quality of costuming varies much less, and the impression is given of the Princess, a stern taskmaster, standing severely over her sewing-women, the ladies of the Court and the nuns, ensuring that the work they offered her was of the very best.

One of the most memorable rooms at the Court shows an early-morning scene where a barber shaves an elderly courtier, wearing a dressing-gown of rose-coloured silk damask with a matching pink nightcap that lies on a table. The barber's assistant stands in attendance carrying a large faience barber's bowl and a clean towel, neatly folded over one arm. The Court barber and his assistant themselves wear fashionable coats and have covered their customer with a barber's wrap that is edged with lace, and placed his wig on a stand, so that he sits in the chair with his bald head revealed. Among the barber's equipment is a small silver spoon that was used in the mouths of old men to push out the wrinkles in their cheeks so that they could be shaved more easily, a practice which gave rise to the German proverb 'Don't let yourself be shaved over a spoon.'

In another early-morning Court scene we find the maids at work in the laundry, surrounded by well-made wooden equipment, as well as the press and box-mangle that are seen in all the eighteenth-century Continental houses. The maids are of the basic wax shoulder-headed construction but are very well dressed, especially in comparison with many of the women in the street scenes, and it is obvious that it was beneficial at the time to be in service. The laundry-maids are in the process of tying up the Princess's linen, each item embroidered with her monogram under a crown. On the floor lies a wicker basket, similar to those seen in the laundry rooms of Dutch houses and very necessary for the storage of dirty linen when many important households washed their linen only twice a year.

The kitchen is a scene of great activity, with a male cook, wearing a tall white hat, supervising the proceedings. The height of the kitchen is surprising, as it seems so out of scale with the other rooms and was probably made necessary by the scale of the copper and pewter miniatures many of which appear to be commercially made. The painting, set into a panel over the open hearth, illustrates how the kitchens of this period were also prestige rooms and considered as showpieces, to display the housewife's love of order to the whole world. The basic construction of the kitchen is fairly rough, the tiles, for instance, being very crudely painted on the walls and chimneyback, but the general effect is fascinating because of the large number of beautiful miniatures, such as a spoon-rack and several fine funnels, pudding-moulds and a pestle and mortar which give a tremendously vivid impression of completeness and colour. The servants appear diminutive beside the towering shelves, and though it was the practice to remove items from the high shelves with a hook on a long-handled pole, their comparative scale is amusingly improbable. In contrast, the wine cellar, which can be viewed beneath the kitchen through an arch, is fairly truthful in scale, and we see the tasting of a new cask of wine which the cellarer appears to be commending. The costumes of these male servants are not as accurate as those of the ladies, but the atmosphere of the cool, dark cellar is cleverly contrived. Each of the many bottles standing on the floor and table has to be sealed with wax after the wine is poured through a funnel from the stoneware pitchers. On a table a group of particularly fine glasses stand in readiness for the serious drinking that will take place at Court in the evening. The activity of the kitchen area and all the ordering of provisions was in the hands of the Clerk, who is seen in the store-room sitting at a table with an important-looking pile of papers laid out before him. He is in the process of bargaining for provisions with an unfashionably dressed shepherd and two farmers. Once secured, the provisions were stored in labelled drawers at the back of the room and in several meat-safes, where they were given added protection from rodents by a large rectangular mousetrap, in this instance complete with four captives.

In the Princess's bedroom two maids are at work spreading out the monogrammed silk coverlet with its extravagant laid-work embroidery. The general scale in this apartment is again hardly accurate, and the size of a brass warming-pan and a knitted nightcap are both highly improbable. Out of doors the gardeners have to be early at their work in the Albertine garden that is laid out in formal French style, with a painted backdrop of trees and an arched building. In the foreground is seen an ornamental pool, several statues and urns in earthenware and porcelain and a gazebo. The gardeners fit perfectly into this elegant Baroque setting as they are all very well dressed and seem intended to form part of the general ornamental effect. The gardeners have to work quickly in the early morning, for everything has to be perfect before the Court ladies take their walks after completing their toilets.

In one bedroom sits a lady wearing an open robe of cream silk and brocade with a wig of sheep's hair inserted into her wax head. Unusually, she wears yellow wooden shoes with red heels over her wax feet and is attended by an equally well-costumed maid with a large red silk bow tied around her neck and a neat lace cap over her brown, unpowdered hair. The maid's frock is made of damask, in attractive shades of orange and red, and she wears an ornamental apron of yellow silk edged with cream and red striped ribbon. Her mistress sits before a dressing-table of simple rectangular construction, covered with red fabric and decorated with a layer of net with lace edging and a cream silk quilted cloth on which lies a tray made of card covered with silk and decorated with glued-on artificial flowers. The room itself is hung with a striped silk that is as rich in effect as the yellow brocade-draped bed on which lie further items of dress. The windows are represented now by sheets of mirror, though Princess Dorothea would hardly have been satisfied with such a basic solution, and we have to imagine painted outdoor scenes or even groups of smaller figures seen in tableaux.

Two wax-headed Court ladies stand in conversation in another room, which is crudely constructed but made effective by its wall-covering of red silk, onto which hand-coloured prints of figures of huntsmen and country scenes were glued. Though hardly polished in effect such work is completely in character with the period, as many ladies derived considerable pleasure from print rooms that were assembled in a similar way. The dolls in this room are particularly effective, as their scale was so large that the modeller was able to create their patrician features with great realism, and the costumier combined brocade and gold lace to achieve very impressive results. Another room with brown silk walls was also decorated with cut-out prints, and in this setting we find three well-made wax ladies sitting around a table. Every character is completely different, and it seems as though the modeller was instructed to create actual portraits of women with whom the Princess was familiar. At the back of the room stands a particularly fine wooden doll, whose head is carved with great realism and decorated with fashionable black patches. This figure, most probably an ordinary play-doll of the period whose quality attracted the Princess, wears a powdered white Court wig. Two wax ladies play at dice in another upper room, in which the cream silk walls are decorated with glued-on prints of chinoiserie style.

The formal aspect of Court life is exemplified by a scene in which the Princess gives an audience to one of her counsellors, who stands, book in hand, while he advises her on her many problems. At her feet sit her dogs, made completely of wax. The canopied chair, rather like a foreshortened half-tester bed, on which she rests, is provided with lavish pale orange embroidered hangings, while the very opulent effect of the room is heightened by the oriental prints with which the walls are papered. While the Princess is involved in the organization of her affairs, the courtiers sit around in small groups playing cards, drinking or sipping tea. A sick lady, obviously in some danger of her life, lies in a quiet room on a yellow damask hung bed and is read to by another woman. A priest in a brown habit stands praying in the centre of this room, having already listened to her confession.

In this Court scene a priest has heard the confession of a very sick noblewoman. Another wax-headed Court lady reads to her.

Oblivious to such dramatic scenes, two children's maids and a wet-nurse care for the young Prince in his light and airy nursery, which is equipped with a particularly well-carved cradle. His finely dressed mother sits at a table waiting for the wet-nurse to hand the swaddled child to her. The nursery is now one of the best constructed rooms of the Court, and an arched alcove, surmounted by Cupids, shows off a four-poster bed most effectively.

Few men are seen in the Palace during the day, as they would have been engaged in some form of hunting or in supervising their own estates. One very elegantly dressed group of men is seen out in the country hunting with their dogs, and already one deer has been slain, while another group fishes on a somewhat ornamental lake. Within the walls of the Court an artist works on a portrait of Dorothea, and a professor wearing a knitted cap and a dressing-gown sits at a table surrounded by large volumes in which he is writing a Court history that begins 'From the beginning of the generations of mankind to the times of the most noble and blessed Anton Gunther'. Watching over his progress is a realistic skeleton.

The professor probably advised the Princess regarding suitable acquisitions for her own art chamber, and it is in a representation of this room that he is seen in her model. Here we discover a crucifix, whose main support rests on a skull and crossbones, and in equally Germanic style is a figure of the crucified Christ and yet another very elongated crucifix. In these 'wonder chambers' were displayed all sorts of strange items ranging from natural objects of little financial value to expensive paintings and sculpture, and in this example there is a somewhat miscellaneous collection of pots, busts and statuettes. It was in a curiosity chamber such as this that Mon Plaisir itself was eventually to be displayed when it was given to the nuns at Erfurt.

A similar affectation to a wonder or curiosity chamber was a porcelain room, in which could be displayed the fine oriental work that was beginning to be imported to Europe in some quantity. At Mon Plaisir the porcelain is shown in a fine baroque interior with five large mirrors set among robust gilded carving. On a japanned table stand several pieces of Chinese blue-and-white china, while other smaller vases stand on especially made individual brackets. Such miniature pieces were not of course especially made for the Princess but were originally intended for cabinet display, being marked with the K'ang Hsi reign mark (1662–1722).

Before the Princess could appear at a Court levee, it was necessary that she should change her costume, and we find her much later in the day seated again at her dressing-table but now wearing an orange dressing-robe, edged with green ruching, and an orange cap. Soon she is joined by her husband, and in one of the most lively Court scenes we witness their arrival at an important reception. All the ladies and gentlemen are seen in formal dress with powdered wigs, and the men wear their ribbons of honour and carry their swords and hats. Most of the gentlemen wear woollen coats decorated with braid, and their wax faces are all modelled with serious regard for their actual characters, some having pale, thin faces and others being florid and heavily coloured. The well-made leather boots are a memorable feature of their costumes. One group of courtiers sit at a card-table in another scene, while others begin to dance. The Prince himself is very plainly dressed and does not even wear the usual Court wig, in complete contrast to the very worldly Dorothea. The ballroom is most impressive, as it is papered in yellow and has a particularly fine carved chimneypiece and impressive doors at

A corner of the Court Porcelain Room decorated with mirrors and rococo carving. The blue-and-white porcelain carries the K'ang Hsi reign marks.

A group of wax-headed courtiers sit in an ante-room during a Court function. They wear red coats.

A pale Court lady wearing a lace and gauze dress sings at a Court reception. Note the difference in tone on the men's faces. All the heads are made of wax.

either side, architectural detail of a type that seems to have been lost from the other main rooms. The glass chandeliers with their glass chains are also very fine and were possibly obtained, like many of the other good glass miniatures included, from the many glasshouses that worked in the area around the Augustenburg.

In an adjoining room with white walls, decorated with figures and trees, is found the Court orchestra, and in other small rooms we see vignettes of evening activities, such as perfectly dressed groups of card-players, groups of priests in solemn discussion and two gawky youths with carved wooden heads who sprawl in their seats with full steins of blue-and-white faience set before them. One lady occupies herself at an embroidery frame, and a particularly fine man doll with implanted black whiskers sits at the gaming-table, obviously the most popular activity. A wax-headed lady with a particularly pale complexion sings to entertain her friends and looks very beautiful in a lace and gauze frock that is very rich in effect because of its silver underskirt. (Paleness in a woman was highly commended, and all sorts of devices were used in order to achieve a sufficient degree of pallor, such as eating arsenic, though most resorted simply to very heavy powdering.) This pale-faced lady is attended by three gentlemen wearing wigs and red-braided coats, who sit on particularly fine chairs with well-carved barley-twist legs. These men, with their natural appearance, look almost over-coloured in comparison with the white-faced women, and it appears that German courtiers, unlike the French of the period, declined to powder their faces.

The game of Nine Man's Morris, played on a correctly marked board, is enjoyed in another ante-room, and in the dining-room we find repeated the practice of tying the tablecloth to the table legs so that it could not be accidentally pulled off during boisterous activity and was kept free of the dirt on the floor. Two wax servants with napkins folded over their arms await the arrival of the courtiers. All these interesting scenes rely for their effect mainly on the quality of the dolls and the very fine glass, porcelain and faience, rather than on the construction of the rooms or the furniture, though it must be remembered that both furniture and architectural detail were probably lost to some extent during the frequent reconstructions.

The miniature faience found in so many of the settings was once believed to have been the reason for the establishment of the Dorotheentaler-Fayence-Manufaktur and was thought to have been another example of the Princess's great extravagance. Though this attractive story is now discredited, it does serve to illustrate Dorothea's character, as the factory was actually established to supply the Augustenburg with decorative pieces but had a more lasting importance as the earliest pottery in Thuringia to make faience; any surviving examples of its production are of considerable importance. Mon Plaisir contains a large number of plates, apothecary jars, jugs and tazzas that are sometimes marked 'AB', derived from the word Augustenburg. The painter's initials, 'Al', 'f' and 'H' are also discovered on some of the items which Wolfgang Leber believes to refer to Johann Christof Alex, Johann Theobald Frantz, Heinrich Hegelmann or Johann Erhard Herbst, who were all working at the factory in the 1720s when production was at its height. Few dolls' houses contain any pieces that are so completely attributable, and Mon Plaisir is, in this respect, again highly unusual.

The Princess's conversion to Catholicism in 1715 meant that she was both to aid and be aided by the nuns of the Ursuline convent at Erfurt, and the life of the convent became woven into the structure of Mon Plaisir, as the activity of the Church in teaching, counselling, almsgiving and nursing was as important in the life of the town as were the craftsmen and the Court. A church forms the most complex of the religious scenes, and the viewer looks through the main doors at the back of the building at the Court, burghers and common people all attending Mass. Among the religious orders represented in the church are Franciscans, Premonstratensians, Augustinians and Carmelites, all identifiable by their habits. The pillars of the chapel are painted to resemble marble, and the curtains behind the high altar are also painted. The side of the church is removable for access, but the effect is greatest when the figures are viewed through the many windows. The very direct contact between Church and people is seen in the way that the Ursuline nuns taught the children of the burghers, and though the instruction appears to have been mainly in womanly skills such as sewing and knitting, their civilizing influence was considerable. The room in which the children work is austere, but the colourful costumes of the girls, one of whom works at a lace pillow, add a splash of cheerful colour. Another nun is seen giving alms to one of the lowest members of society, a beggar, who is offered bread from a flat basket. It would appear, from the presence of a swivelling alms-window behind her, that it was more usual for the nun to place the gift on a ledge and swing the wooden partition around, so that she would have no physical or visual contact with the person being aided, but the scene is probably more understandable in the way in which it is now presented. Something of the austerity of convent life is seen in the cell of a young nun who kneels at prayer with her scourging-whip close at hand.

While they eat, the nuns listen to a reading by one of the monks, their food being prepared in the very simply equipped convent kitchen with its miscellany of out-of-scale equipment. Most of the nuns seem well fed and expensively dressed, as many were, of course, members of important families who had taken the veil, often because they had remained unmarried. One well-to-do nun is seen in her cell before a Baroque private altar with a painted inset that is surmounted by gilded decoration. At her side hangs a huge crucifix and a whip of twigs in preparation for scourging. The monks are seen in several of the Court settings engaged in their work of giving advice and absolution, while the nuns remained in the seclusion of the convent.

Providing the Court and the people of Arnstadt with their worldly needs were the weavers, tailors, dressmakers and apothecaries, whose daily life we are able to examine in detail. Possibly the most effective of the shops is that of the apothecary, as the wooden counter with its nine drawers and a stand for the display of glass jars has remained in fine condition and offers an exact representation of a chemist's shop. In the Museum of Thuringian Folk Art at Erfurt, a full-sized shop of this type, dating from an early period, can be seen, and it is obvious that Dorothea's craftsmen were making careful copies of actual structures, as the miniature mirrors the genuine shop. The apothecary at Mon Plaisir holds a Royal Warrant and is seen in the process of making up a heart powder on his scales, while his apprentice grates up another substance. All his bottles and potions are correctly labelled, and while he can frequently

The accuracy of the scenes in 'Mon Plaisir' is confirmed in this engraving where children are learning to embroider, as in the convent at Arnstadt. Engraved by E. Porzelius, Nuremberg, 1687.

offer no more effective a remedy than peppermint water, purging pills or aqua-vitae for the stomach, a visit to the mysterious interior of such a shop with its retorts, leather-covered jars and strange powders and herbs must have provided the sufferer with some hope of healing through almost magical sources.

The much lighter needs of the Court ladies are served by a visit to the draper's shop, where a lady in a red saq-backed gown and powdered wig is seen examining a roll of silk brocade. On shoulder-high, turned wooden stands are displayed a number of fashionable caps and bonnets, though most of the stock consists of carefully rolled fabrics with the price-tickets hanging from the central cores. There is also a number of white-paper packages and oval pink boxes with white cut-paperwork decoration whose contents are unspecified. The saleswoman, dressed in sprigged muslin and holding a roll of pink tape, is constructed on a much smaller scale than the Court lady she attends, and it seems probable that these figures were once in different situations.

The tailor's shop must prove to be of even greater interest to costume enthusiasts, as here the fabrics purchased from the draper would be assembled. The tailor sits in the middle of his shop in the characteristic cross-legged position with his legs pushed through a hole in the form of a half cross especially cut for his ease in the table top. In the basket beside him paper and rulers stand ready for his next pattern-making session. The walls of his shop are decorated with large prints of potted plants that appear to have been cut from books, and among these hang several perfectly constructed women's gowns that he is in the process of completing. One of the Court women discusses her order with him, though he continues to work as she talks. Through a small door at the back of the shop we can see the narrow, dark room in which he sleeps. His work is obviously mainly for the Court, as his room is directly beneath the elegant apartment in which the Princess, accompanied by her dogs, is giving an audience.

The joiner is also fairly obviously engaged in manufacturing furniture for the richer citizens, as he is seen at work on a fine set of baluster-legged high backed chairs. He is also well dressed and wears a red silk waistcoat under his traditional green apron. This setting is fascinating to craftsmen of today because of the number of tools that can be seen hanging from a very strangely shaped panel at the back of the room. Next door is the weaver's workshop, which contains two looms that are both perfect and accurate copies. One represents a normal basic loom of the period, but the other is a particularly fine miniature of a shank loom. The family lives and works together with the machinery in this room, and the women are seen winding the shuttles soon to be used by the men. Both the weavers and the joiner's rooms are above the shop of the apothecary that has to be at street level. The turner, in even less advantageous accommodation, works on the second floor at a pole lathe. In the

The well-dressed baker and his wife work in their shop. The small sweep came originally from another setting. The big bread oven is behind the baker.

foreground we see a number of the items he has already made, including some very beautiful ivory spinning-wheels. His wife, dressed in a cheap checked peasant's apron, examines carefully the pieces he has made, in order to point out any defects, and among these completed wares are a jug, a barrel, and cups and saucers, all in fact made from ivory, as the very small scale would have made their representation in wood almost impossible.

No tradesman or farmer could have survived at this time without the services of the cooper who forced wooden or metal bands around barrels and tubs that were used for storage. In his workshop some idea of the very large variety of vessels that were commonly used is gained, including the special conical barrels that were used for the storage of sauerkraut or pickled meats.

The baker's shop was also fairly obviously a family concern, as his wife stands nursing a small child while she awaits a customer. The huge bread-oven at the back of the shop was heated by wood, and the long fork that was used for lifting the logs into position is visible, as are the bellows that were so necessary for keeping the oven at the right temperature. Bread-shovels, tins and waffle-irons lie around the shop, and the cooked produce, represented in plaster, lies appetizingly on plates that are arranged on a table with its cloth folded to a point on one side. Both the baker and his family are well dressed and obviously prosperous, and we are reminded that this area of Germany was at the time in an affluent period. In realistic vein, outside the baker's shop, we see a delivery-wagon with sacks of flour. Nearby is the butcher, dressed in a blue jacket and a white apron accompanied by an assistant. His wife is about to be approached by a poor beggar woman who carries a bag for alms and a pot in which she cooks her soup. This interchange between rich and poor, Church and Court is continually presented in such scenes and serves to bring alive the atmosphere of the period in a way no print or painting could hope to do.

Scenes from Court life portray not exclusively the higher nobility but also a number of Court officials. Of particular interest in this sphere is the life-style of the Court Moors. Though it was a fashionable conceit all over Europe in the eighteenth century for the wealthy to own an almost ornamental blackamoor as a servant, only rarely could a complete family have served in this way. The Moor attended the Court levee and was obviously a necessary feature of the scene. The family nursery is an effective room peopled with wax-headed dolls with glass eyes. The mother sits nursing her swaddled youngest child, while another baby lies in a carved cradle. There is also an upholstered high chair in which the children can sit during the day. The curtains of the Moor's bed are gaudily patterned, and we are obviously intended to appreciate the fact that they enjoyed bold colours and designs.

The infants of the courtiers and burghers are seen in their own especially planned apartments, and we are given a very informative picture of child life of the time. Frequently it is suggested that children in the early eighteenth century were provided with the most meagre accommodation and few especially made pieces of nursery furniture, but the four nurseries at Mon Plaisir completely disprove this assertion and suggest that especially planned rooms were more common than often suggested. In one nursery, provided for the child of a rich merchant, an old-fashioned cage-like cot is seen. This box-like construction was locked once the child lay on the mattress so that a night nurse was not needed in order to stop him falling from his bed. At a table sits a small child in a high chair with a fringed and upholstered seat, playing with a group of carved wooden toy animals. In the foreground, watched over by a nurse, lies a younger baby in a rocking wicker cradle. Their mother, wearing a white gauze apron, smiles benevolently at the scene.

The princely nursery is much more splendid in effect, though a wickerwork

The well-furnished nursery of a rich merchant's child with its large safety cot and interesting group of miniature playthings on the table.

cradle is still used, but this superior example is embellished with carving on the hood and the rockers. An older child lies at night in a small-scale version of an adult four-poster with green silk hangings. This noble nursery is also supplied with a baby-walker to assist the young Prince in his first steps. The babies and the young children in this room are all made completely of wax, the youngest being tightly swaddled. The baby-clothes and equipment are stored away in several baskets, one of which stands on an elegant pedestal table. As Dorothea was the only princess of the short-lived line of Schwarzburg-Arnstadt, it is curious that she included a princely nursery in the setting. Perhaps this was an imaginary child that she delighted in supplying with all the items she would have enjoyed purchasing for the heir, or possibly she felt that such a nursery was necessary to give an impression of

Court life in more usual circumstances. The most likely possibility, however, would seem to be that her children died in infancy and were consequently unrecorded. Anna Köferlin, for instance, was for several centuries described as childless, and it is only recently that the fact that her children actually died young has been discovered. Perhaps Dorothea was also the mother of such short-lived offspring: she certainly appears to have derived enjoyment from the equipping of the model children's rooms.

Dorothea's vision of presenting a perfect and complete picture of Court life was not restricted to comfortable domestic scenes: she also found it necessary to show the manner in which various social groups in the town amused themselves. Evening entertainment was provided for the courtiers by a visit to the Court theatre, a colourful and well-made model with the proscenium painted to resemble carved marble and the safety curtain painted with the coat-of-arms of the Prince. From their boxes at the sides of the stage, the courtiers encourage the actors, who are all cleverly modelled in a grotesque manner to represent large-headed dwarfs. Their heads are made of *papier mâché*, and their costumes are highly coloured and exceptionally decorative, being assembled from stones, feathers, foil and wool in the traditional stage manner.

The passing of the hours during a day in the life of the town is very clearly presented in the outdoor scenes, where the common people are seen at work. In an interesting variety of sets every stage of the day is depicted, though we see a somewhat idealized commentary on life, as there are few scenes of cruelty, no slaughter of animals, except in the picturesque hunting-scene, and no extreme poverty in the homes. The Princess very obviously wished to present a happy day in the life of the town she had grown to love, and this air of delight pervades the numerous tableaux. She chose to represent her town on its annual market day, when the townspeople thronged into the galleried marketplace, where tradesmen from great distances came to sell their wares. Officers, burghers, children and peasants all mingle in the crowds that stand around the posting-inn or by the traders' booths, as this was the most important trading-day of the year and offered Dorothea a wonderful assortment of character and incident.

The earliest scene of the day is set at the manorial farm, where the shepherd is about to drive the sheep from their small pen. While the cows are being milked, the farmer chops wood, and we see a fine selection of the agricultural tools of the period. These farm scenes are enacted under two large arches, and through an upper window a farm worker can be seen in the hayloft. In the third arch of this setting a young farmer and his wife can be seen at breakfast, with their baby lying alongside the table in a carved wooden cradle. Their home is simply furnished with a trestle table and a large earthenware stove with a heavy iron door. Their hope for a bountiful harvest lies in the harvest crown of the previous year that hangs above a cow byre. All the various

94

The arrival of the coach at the Post House in Arnstadt. Despite its realism, the sedan chair is made of painted card.

animals are made with some skill, the chickens being constructed from actual feathers and the cows from fur.

Early in the day, the stage-coach arrives at the post house in Arnstadt, and it is possible to see how really large numbers of boxes and barrels were able to be secured for transportation. Two coaches are also waiting to depart with a number of passengers and a dispatch rider in a yellow uniform. In the foreground is a sedan chair made of painted card but appearing quite realistic; inside sits a fashionable woman who is handed a letter by a Court footman. Several of the other passengers are also receiving last-minute notes and letters, and a group of dogs and villagers stands watching the busy scene. In the market square a soldier and an officer circulate among the crowds in order to ensure that no one is misbehaving, though the excessive noise has already

A burgher and his wife lie in their correctly draped bed. Both figures have wax heads.

Opposite: In the second-hand shop lie plates, pictures and perfectly made costumes. The scale of the figures suggests that some came originally from other groups.

awakened some of the citizens who glower crossly out of their windows still dressed in their night clothes. In one room, not too disturbed by the commotion outside, a burgher and his wife lie together in their bed, a scene of conjugal bliss not encountered elsewhere in the somewhat prudish world of dolls.

The copper- and tinsmiths are situated, in accordance with the town ordinances, next to one another in the market and offer enough kitchen equipment to furnish several dolls' houses. The well-established dealers sell their goods from properly constructed booths, and beyond a group of travelling musicians who entertain the shoppers from their simply made stage, we find a well-stocked hat-stand and a draper's where a woman haggles over the price of a length of cloth. In the foreground is seen a Thuringian forest balsam-seller, who walks about offering his wares to the townspeople. Other traders with baskets or portable small stands sell engravings and baskets. The knife-grinder is also seen to be working busily. The curiosity-dealer carries his wide assortment of items in a box slung around his neck and sells such items as bag-handles, mirrors and bottles. The

96

candlemaker's shop is of particular interest, as we find both twisted tape candles and large straight waxes hanging in bundles from their long wicks that are tied together. Near this trader, under an arch, sits a pot-seller surrounded by her crudely made peasant wares; a shoemaker stands proudly amid his extensive selection of boots and shoes, most of which seem somewhat large for the townspeople but again provide the student of costume with valuable detail, some being made of leather but others, intended for the Court ladies, exquisitely embroidered. All the booths are made in the same way, with two horizontal flaps, so that when open the upper section forms a canopy to shelter the wares and the lower, supported by swinging brackets, provides the counter.

A group of musicians is seen in the beargarden entertaining the crowd who have assembled to watch a sad and dutiful bear perform, while at the same time a group of peasants arrive from the country in a horse-drawn cart for a wedding. The whole of the market is alive with activity, and the goods offered for sale are of a wide variety and good individual quality, a sad contrast to the Arnstadt market place of today, with its depressing array of cabbages and

97

root vegetables illustrating the austerity of a Communist state for whose citizens shopping must have been a much more rewarding occupation over two hundred years ago.

After the death of Augusta Dorothea in 1751, the governors of the orphanage at Erfurt asked the Duke of Brunswick for the model town, which they felt would add to the attraction of their own curiosity chamber. It would appear that their request was not granted as in 1762 the historian Iohanz Stephan Putter saw the model still in its old position at the Augustenburg and commented that it was an important object in the manner of the old art cabinets. Perhaps because of some general interest in the model, it was offered for sale by public auction in 1765, but it did not reach the required price of 100 thalers. The Court kitchen and the Ursuline convent seem to have become separated from the main structure at this period, as they were sent to Brunswick to be displayed in an art chamber for the young ladies and gentlemen of the Duke's family, who presumably were uninterested in the remainder of the model, as he instructed that it should be sold in the auction. A little later in the same year, the Duke having been persuaded to keep Mon Plaisir, it was loaned to the orphanage at Arnstadt and went on display in their curiosity chamber in 1766, where it could be seen by the public for a small fee.

The model remained at the orphanage until 1850, when the board of governors was wound up and their possessions became the property of Arnstadt town council, who put it on public view in 1855, despite the problems of ownership that had arisen. In 1881 Princess Marie von Schwartzburg-Sondershausen claimed the model and insisted that it should be kept at her palace in Arnstadt so she could protect it from damage, several items having been stolen or lost over the years. Before her death in 1930, the Princess transferred Mon Plaisir to the collection of the Arnstadt Museum, where experts attempted to undo much of the bad restoration that had taken place during the nineteenth century. During the last war, the town was again packed away and stored in villages around Arnstadt, so that it was not until the 1950s that it went on permanent display at the Schloss Museum.

Augusta Dorothea's project is without doubt the most ambitious to be included in the development of dolls' houses, yet despite its obvious merit and great importance, the structure has a melancholy atmosphere engendered by the character of the Princess herself. The model, with its colour and activity, has, despite its fragile construction, withstood constant movement and change, while the Augustenburg, on which Dorothea lavished so much time and money, has long since fallen into ruin. All that now remains is a tower, a few crumbling walls and part of an ornamental pond, where a crumbling satyr grins at the folly of the individual.

THREE

Dutch Cabinet Houses

The German traveller Zacharias Konrad von Uffenbach, visiting Holland in 1711, described with some amazement the passion with which a Dutch collector of curiosities regarded her acquisitions. She showed the travellers her blue-and-white porcelain, carved stones and shells and a great collection of broken bits and pieces of all kinds and sizes. Her enthusiasm extended to the acquisition of stones, ivory, coral and medallions, on which she had expended vast sums and which were displayed in especially constructed cabinets. Among the series of display cases was one containing dolls' rooms, not the centrepiece but simply a single exhibit in her widely selected assembly of interesting objects. The practice of arranging collections in cabinets encouraged Dutch craftsmen to create some particularly fine pieces of furniture especially for this purpose with small drawers and niches for specimens that were sometimes concealed behind an almost architectural structure. Such detail was not often attempted by the doll's house assemblers, who seem to have been content to arrange the rooms within quite basic walnut or lacquered cabinets with no attempt, except in the case of the model at Haarlem, to represent a façade. The houses are therefore true collectors' cabinets, designed by and intended for the appreciation of adults who sometimes purchased the contents of older important models to augment their own acquisitions.

The Dutch cabinets are much more refined in general atmosphere than those made with such enthusiasm in Germany and appear to have no taint of any discernible education purpose. Though they were once fashionable amusements for the rich, few complete specimens have survived, and it seems that their importance was appreciated by only a few families. The basic arrangement of these cabinets is completely different to that of the German houses, and in the attic area we find the store-rooms and, usually, a splendidly

A curious Dutch mechanical house with the words '*De Vogelensang*', 'The Bird Song', written on the façade. The toy was clockwork operated, and the mirrored windows lift to reveal carved wooden figures. A monkey eating a nut appears from the roof between the chimneys. The doors and windows also open to reveal activity. An eighteenth-century adult toy. 22 inches wide.

Opposite: A splendid model kitchen, probably of Dutch origin and dating to the seventeenth century. Some of the contents are much later additions, but there is some sound eighteenth-century pewter and silver. The cabinet is oak. The doll in the foreground is modern.

equipped laundry. In the German houses, these practical rooms are usually at street level, and there is much less interest in the processes of washing and ironing clothes, as the cooking of food demanded prime importance. Whereas the German cabinet-makers created tall, narrow dwellings, those made in Holland are much wider and lower and have more in common with the proportions of the English Baby Houses. They also differ from those made in England in that gardens and courtyards are sometimes found in the cabinets, whereas the viewer was expected to imagine that the Baby Houses were set in fine parkland or in their own town gardens. The stables, store-rooms and servants' quarters that make the basement sections of the German cabinets so interesting are not represented in the much more hygienic atmosphere of the Dutch houses, which seem to be pervaded by the sweet smell of freshly laundered linen and well-scrubbed floors.

The Dutch dolls' houses are usually quite literally contained in commercially produced cabinets of the type that would be used for the storage of clothes or papers, and they are consequently acceptable items of decorative furniture, completely in accord with the most elegant of apartments. The height of these structures was useful, as the base was frequently in the form of several drawers, while at other times the cupboard section stood on graceful cabriole legs, so that when the doors were opened, the rooms were set out at adult eye-level with no necessity for the visitor to crawl about the floor in order to appreciate the lower sections, as in the German houses, where the rooms continue almost to floor level. Apart from these collectors' cabinets in the form of houses, the Dutch also displayed their treasures in shallow, bow-fronted cabinets with glazed doors, which could be hung from the wall and often contained two or three shallow shelves. This great fascination with miniature items is a very definite trait in the Dutch character, and even today collectors' cabinets of simple construction are sold in great number for the display of the silver, porcelain, brass and pewter items that are offered in greater profusion in Amsterdam than in any other city in Europe.

The best-documented of the cabinet houses is that found at the Centraal Museum in Utrecht, where an inlaid olive-wood cabinet, standing on a walnut pedestal, can be viewed in an actual room of the correct period with the appropriate furnishings. This museum creates perfectly the atmosphere of the model's original environment and is one of the most pleasant to visit. Frequently dolls' houses, despite their adult intention, are displayed in halls or small side rooms, but here we have the correct situation of a main reception room where the rich collector would have proudly discussed and examined the contents with his friends. The construction and furnishing of the cabinet dates from the last quarter of the seventeenth century and have remained, with a few additions, as they were left by their original owner, Petronella de la Court, who was born in Leiden. The initials 'AO', carved on the back of a settle in the cabinet are believed by museum researchers to be those of Adam

Princess Augusta Dorothea seated on the throne in the audience room of Mon Plaisir, created between 1704 and 1751

Opposite: Princess Augusta Dorothea at supper

Above: Bed-making at Mon Plaisir

Above: The Silver Room of Sara Ploos van Amstel's doll's house, mid-eighteenth century

Right: The Music Room in the Dutch cabinet house assembled by Petronella de la Court, late seventeenth century

The Yellow Drawing Room at Nostell Priory, *c.* 1735–40

The drawing-room of an eighteenth-century Dutch cabinet house

Ann Sharp's Baby House, *c.* 1700

The basement kitchen of the Uppark Baby House, *c.* 1730–40

The kitchen of the Blackett Baby House, *c.* 1740

Petronella de la Court assembled this cabinet in the late seventeenth century.

Oortman, an Amsterdam brewer whom Petronella married. The extravagance of the contents, which include a painting by Gerard Hoet in the art chamber dated to 1674, makes it quite obvious that this model was an adult's treasure-chest rather than an educational aid to assist children in learning to run a home. With its air of utter sophistication, it is in complete contrast with the robust Nuremberg cabinets.

In 1707 a list was compiled of the possessions of Petronella de la Court which is now to be found in the council archives in Amsterdam. It includes her collection of paintings and drawings and a number of 'curiosities'. This assembling of pieces of random interest was a fashion that extended over the whole of Europe to some degree and was manifested in Holland and Germany in the 'art chambers' with the almost inevitable skeleton and chests of fossils

103

and ores. This aspect of the cabinet doll's house is well brought out at the Centraal Museum, as a conventional curiosity cabinet of the same period stands next to the house and contains items such as snakes and butterflies. Petronella obviously delighted in her collections, and the largest and most impressive of her belongings was 'an excellent doll's chest, with eleven rooms richly furnished with all the appropriate belongings', which appeared in the inventory before the smaller cabinets for items such as stone reliefs and objects of mother-of-pearl and cut paper.

This cabinet offers the viewer an exact model of a Dutch curiosity chamber of the period, among its other rooms, and, as in Mon Plaisir, the walls of this room are whitewashed to provide a sharper background for the display of paintings. As in the Princess Dorothea's model, there is again a generous use of hand-coloured engravings to create effects such as the 'painted ceiling' which symbolizes the four elements. The symmetry of the ceiling is echoed on the floor, which is inlaid with woods of different colours in imitation of the parquet that was so popular at the time. Instead of the chimneyboards that are used to suggest summertime in other houses, an ivory relief portraying Mercury is here used to represent a piece of sculpture. The mantelshelf is supported by heavy barley-twist pillars and further decorated with fringe. Among the works of art adorning the chimneybreast are a carved ivory relief in an amber frame and a portrait of Cornelia Esther Slob (1748–76), who was the wife of an Amsterdam medallist and a sister of a later owner of the cabinet, again indicating how frequently items were added when they seemed suitable in scale. High on the walls on either side of the chimneypiece are impressive paintings in heavy gilded frames painted by Gerard Hoet in 1674. It is considered that several artists who were commissioned by Petronella were also asked to paint miniatures for her cabinet: this man was certainly of some importance, as he was also responsible for the murals at Slangenberg Castle in Gelderland. Among the other painters who, in addition to working for her on the conventional scale, also supplied miniatures for the doll's house, are Willem van Mieris (1662–1747), Herman Saftleven (1609–85) and Jan van Hughtenburgh (1647–1733). Even these miniatures were therefore costly items. Though Petronella de la Court was herself the assembler of an art chamber, she did not represent herself in the room but chose to place there three wax men, one wearing a dressing-gown who talks to a farmer or peasant wearing the costume of the Waterlands. On a ruffled cushion sits a pet dog.

The great contemporary interest in geography, exploration and foreign trade, on which the owner's wealth depended, is suggested by two globes. In a glass-fronted cabinet is a fine collection of porcelain, and on the other side of the chimneypiece is an inlaid specimen-cabinet decorated with the popular ivory star motif. This case contains a selection of ivory cutlery similar to that seen in Ann Sharp's house in Britain, also silver, drawings, prints and a number of coins dating from the Roman Empire to the nineteenth century. This art chamber is much more elegantly furnished than that at Mon Plaisir, and there are upholstered chairs for visitors and a very lovely amber table inlaid with ivory. It was in the surroundings of such a room that Petronella de la Court employed the hours in furnishing the doll's house after her marriage in 1649. The cabinet was probably kept in the family house on the Achterburgwaal, though their brewery, the Swan, was on the Singel in Amsterdam. After her husband's death in 1684, she ran the firm herself with the assistance of her children and is in great contrast to the spendthrift Princess Dorothea. After Petronella's death in 1707, the cabinet passed to her daughter, Petronella Oortman, who was born in 1654. It was at this time that it was examined by the German traveller Zacharias von Uffenbach, who was initially interested in younger Petronella's collection of *objets d'art*, assembled after her marriage to the merchant Abraham du Pré in 1677. She obviously added several items to her mother's cabinet, and it is extremely fortunate that, after her death in 1727, an inventory of her estate was made, which describes the cabinet which was then standing in an ante-room at the Swan brewery – a strange situation for the storage of such a valuable item, possibly suggesting that her interest had waned as she grew older. The inventory mentions that the house contained eleven rooms, the compiler presumably including the two small rooms in the centre and the garden area. There is no mention of the presence of closing cupboard doors to protect the contents, though presumably they were originally present. On top of the cabinet stood several pieces of ornamental porcelain, as at the Hague house.

After the death of Petronella Oortman's husband in 1728, the family obviously lost interest in the old-fashioned cabinet, and in 1730 an advertisement appeared in the *Amsterdamse Courant* offering a 'Royal Cabinet, namely a doll's chest'. In 1736 the same advertisement again appeared, but the house remained unsold and seems to have remained in the du Pré family until it was purchased by an Amsterdam tobacco-merchant in 1744 as a gift for his wife, Maria Sophia Heykoop. After her death in 1754, the cabinet again appeared in the 'For Sale' columns, now described as 'the well-known Royal Cabinet, namely a doll chest consisting of eleven rooms, all being very artistically and expensively furnished'. It seems that the cabinet was sold to a foreigner, but the Dutch then regained possession as it was soon owned by Pieter van der Beek's daughter, Margareta. Sadly, at this juncture the house left Amsterdam, as Margareta married Dirk Slob of Aalsmeer. She appears to have taken considerable interest in the house and printed a catalogue of its contents which survives in the municipal archives at Utrecht, a catalogue that was probably used when the house was displayed to the visitors whom she encouraged. It is because of this very specific list that the museum is now able to arrange the rooms as they were when the model was in her ownership. This most efficient custodian bequeathed the cabinet to her daughter, and it was eventually taken to a house on the Janskerkhof in Utrecht, where it was again seen by many. General interest in the model remained constant, and in 1866 Petronella Hendrik Pipersberg (née Slob) gave the cabinet to the Municipality of Utrecht, who placed it in the Centraal Museum in 1921.

The long history of this cabinet is remarkable not only because of its precise documentation but also because it remained a source of almost constant interest. From the time of its construction it was visited by collectors and artists as well as by the general public. Few people interested in art and antiques would today visit Utrecht without looking at this venerable cabinet in the beautifully arranged museum.

Many of the fine pieces of furniture which the house contains were obviously especially commissioned, but others were available from specialist shops, such as the carved pieces of ivory and amber that were intended for rarity cabinets. The wax dolls which occupy the house in some number are very similar to those found in the Petronella Dunois house in the Rijksmuseum but are much more elaborately costumed. The basic figures are obviously commercially produced, though modelled with much more characterization than is common, and were obviously costumed by the owner of the cabinet or her maids and sewing-women, who seem to have taken great pleasure in the work, as the costumes, though not removable, convey with exactitude the fashionable dress of the period. It seems that the ladies dressed the dolls over several years, as there are some differences of basic style, but all are stitched and decorated with a true eye for detail.

In the late sixteenth and early seventeenth centuries, the Amsterdam merchants had lived and worked in the same buildings, which included store-rooms for their goods, but by the time of the construction of this model, their increasing wealth inspired much grander ideas, and all that remains of this householder's daily work is the small counting-house in the centre of the building. This is an entirely masculine room with its simply hewn table and rudimentary bookcases. In one respect it contains more detail than other apartments in the cabinet, as the interconnecting doors are represented, whereas the other chambers are completely without entrances. The wax-headed master of the house wears a flowered silk chamber-gown, and it is obviously late in the day, as he has settled down to read his books. His outdoor shoes, beautifully made of leather, with buckles at the sides, lie behind his simple rush-seated chair, and he wears his indoor mules. Before him, on a sloping writing-top, lie papers addressed to 'Mijn Heer Constantius Popperyus' and 'Mijn Heer Constantius Pouperys int Poppehuis', one letter being dated 10th June 1678 (1670?). The fact that this is the counting-house of a tobacco-merchant is indicated by the basket of clay pipes from Gouda that lie behind his chair and the rolls of tobacco on the shelves. His trade is also underlined by an Amsterdam receipt dated 1743 listing six casks of tobacco for 600 florins from Jan Daams, a detail that was obviously added by the

The wax-headed child's nurse wears Waterlands costume and helps her charge to walk with the aid of leading-strings.

tobacco-merchant's wife, who was given the model in 1744. Presumably the room was originally filled with similar details from a brewer's counting-house. To sustain the merchant during his hours of solitary work, there is a well-stocked liquor-chest. His spiritual needs are served by a prayer-book dated 1683 and several song books and miniature home-made books of prints cut down from larger engravings. It is cautionary to realize that all the wealth of this rich house depended on the work carried out in this small, simply furnished room.

Below the counting-house is the main entrance hall, as we have to imagine that the middle floor of the structure is at street level, with the rooms below represented as a half basement leading out to a garden. As the hall is very low, the children's nurse in her Waterlands costume towers nearly to ceiling level. The detail and the furnishing of this area are very fine, of particular note being an exquisite tortoiseshell long-case clock made in Britain in the seventeenth century by Theodore Arnaud. Against the whitewashed wall stands the carved wooden bench bearing the initials 'AO' that serve as a clue to the name

Above: In the lying-in room a splendid cradle holds the new baby, while the older children use the room as a nursery. To the right is one of the large earthenware stoves, the pride of every rich household. In Holland, as in Germany, the lying-in room was of great importance. From a seventeenth-century Nuremberg broadsheet.

Opposite: In the lying-in room of the de la Court cabinet a fashionably dressed woman visits the new-born baby and its mother. All the dolls have wax heads.

of the original owner. The hall is almost filled by the maid and a toddler who is held up by her leading-strings and carries a tiny carved wooden doll held against her heavily decorated frock. A small-scale boy doll, possibly intended to represent an older son or even a personal servant, is also present. He carries a basket but is very richly costumed. Though no well-to-do woman of the period in Britain would have gone marketing herself, this was quite common in Holland, so it would perhaps not have seemed inappropriate for her son also to carry a basket. The finely detailed costume of the children's maid indicates the standard of the other dolls, as all her undergarments are sewn in detail, and her apron shows the double rows of strings at the back which kept it, though stiffly starched, in neat alignment with her skirt.

The contemporary affection for mythologically inspired decoration is seen on the ceiling, where the four winds are depicted. On the walls are carved ivory reliefs of tales such as those of Pyramus and Thisbe, and Diana and Endymion, added in the eighteenth century. The completely different scale and structure of this section of the house suggest that the hall might have been

divided horizontally as late as the eighteenth century, to allow space for the counting-house, as so much of the decoration was added later, and, of course, the dolls themselves would have fitted more appropriately into a room of more conventional height—a suggestion that would, of course, weaken the claim that this is the cabinet referred to in the 1707 inventory, though it is possible that the adaptation had already taken place. Two white busts of Mercury and Minerva, the gods of Science and Trade, watch over the fortunes of the household. On either side of the household deities stand four ivory carvings representing the four seasons as children at play, figures that contrast well with the rich wood of the panelling beneath. The hall is lit by a single candle in a sconce in the form of an arm holding a silver candlestick, which is made on a much larger scale. A silver cistern with a porcelain bowl was also provided so that visitors could wash their hands before being announced.

In the lying-in room at basement level, we find the merchant's wife, who wears a silk dress and a very heavy cape and apron. She seems completely out of tone with the delicacy and precision that characterize the dress of the other characters and was obviously finished by less skilful hands. The swaddled wax baby is about to be fed by the wet-nurse, who has uncovered one plump breast in readiness and is of great interest as the only doll in a lying-in room that displays such intimate detail. The dry-nurse or children's maid is also in attendance and wears a black silk frock. As married women of the period inevitably spent a good deal of their childbearing years in these rooms, the latter were often furnished with great care. The great childbirth bed stands in an alcove in the panelling at the rear of the room, and as the arrangement of the blankets would have been difficult in such a small space, a bedstick is provided for the smoothing of the crocheted bedspread and linen. The lying-in room is given a warm appearance by its red silk walls and a rug with a matching fringe. The linen is contained in a fine chest with barley-twist legs decorated with ivory reliefs of Hope and Faith on the doors. There is also a painting by Gerard de Lairesse (1641–1711), which shows two women floating in the clouds accompanied by an angel, a particularly generous supply of figures of Fortune and Trust, suggesting that both mother and child were in need of as much heavenly assistance as could be mustered. As many visitors called to see the new mother, the room is well supplied with carved ivory chairs with silk-upholstered seats. We find one such visitor, dressed in the height of fashion, taking tea with the mother. On the table is a Kandeel bowl that would have contained a drink made of eggs, sugar, Rhine wine and spices, which would have been served to the mother after the birth.

While recovering from her confinement, she could sit in the small garden which in Amsterdam town houses was always at the rear and of a comparatively small size. In this section, we are asked to imagine that we are in fact behind the house itself. This formal garden is very charming because of the arrangement of trelliswork and the pots of flowers that are set against walls painted to imitate the sky, against which a very stylized peacock is represented. The garden is dominated by four ivory statues illustrating the elements, and on a table in an arbour a game of tric-trac is set out. Various finely made gardening tools lie around, and there is a very well-made wooden wheelbarrow. In the foreground is a set of skittles, and it is recorded that the girl doll once carried a kite in her arms, indicating how the garden, despite its small size, was used by the whole family.

When not playing along the sanded paths of the formal garden, the children spent their hours in the nursery, a somewhat dark and forbidding room with red silk hung walls situated on the top floor, close to the laundry. An open fire was considered dangerous in this room, so it was heated by a silver stove decorated with scenes that include Abraham with the angels. The nursery is quite well furnished and contains a very impressive bed with a round baldachin suspended from the ceiling and draped with the same patterned silk that was used for the cushion of the day-bed and the mantelshelf frill. Several good oriental porcelain vases stand on chests and on the mantelpiece. On the floor there is a baby-walker and a child's high chair as well as the lace pillow and thread-winder at which the maids were expected to work when the children were quiet. In the high chair sits a small doll being visited by a very elegantly dressed doctor who is about to take a sample in the urine bottle which he holds. In order to encourage the boys in manly pursuits, the walls are hung with drawings of cavalry battles in tortoiseshell frames, a lighter note being given by a print of spring, glued to the ceiling and intended to represent a painting. On the tripod table a warm drink stands ready for the doctor.

Food for both the lying-in room and the nursery was supplied from the kitchen situated in the basement, remarkable for its unusually precise scale. All the Dutch houses contain kitchens that are much more sophisticated than those of the *Dockenhäuser*, and this example is given additional attraction by its green-painted beams and woodblock floor. Two doors with eighteenth-century-style fanlights lead from the main kitchen to a hall and another small room that contains a copper water-cistern, known as the barrel-house, as tubs and containers were left here near the tap. There was also a lavatory in this room with a two-holed seat, a particularly unhygienic arrangement that obviously encouraged the spread of diseases such as cholera that decimated whole populations until the end of the nineteenth century. There is a further room at the back which we have to suppose leads to the cellar, and there are several barrels of beer.

It seems that the cooking-area of the fireplace in the kitchen is missing, as the maid is about to cook over a small fire-basket. In other respects this room is particularly well equipped for both cooking and cleaning, and there is a fine knife-sharpener and a beautiful collection of drinking-glasses, including some Venetian pieces that are displayed on a hanging shelf. On a much finer carved set of shelves is a display of good porcelain, mainly of Chinese origin. An unusual plate-rack hangs on the wall, beneath which plates were allowed to dry after washing. In a chest is concealed a collection of silver, dating mainly from the nineteenth century. The kitchenmaid, who was expected to work at a spinning-wheel when not cooking, wears much rougher clothes than those worn by the personal servants, and her costume consists of a red laced bodice, a checked skirt and a blue over-jacket. Unlike the inhabitants of the British Baby Houses, the maids, even of the lowest orders, are also made of wax.

The kitchen was kept free of storage-cupboards for provisions: these were kept either in the beer cellar or in the small store-room at the top of house, which was of course suitable only for dry goods. The store-room, with its typical Dutch wooden palings, is supervised by a simply costumed maid wearing a purple jacket and carrying a basket of cleaning-equipment; among the brushes and dusters are several birds' wings that were used for cleaning delicate objects. This room is obviously a repository for things no longer needed, such as a spinning-wheel and the skates that hang from the wall.

Barrels containing basic foods, such as pearl barley, groats, white beans and grey peas, stand on simple wooden shelves, and there is an egg-rack of proportions suitable for such a large household. In the foreground is a barbaric rat-trap of guillotine-like construction, hygienically supplied with a small basket for the severed heads.

The maid was expected to guard the food, peat and firewood at all times and her bed lies behind the wooden palings. Like maids of the period all over Europe, she was supplied with only the most basic necessities of a bed, chair, table and chamber-pot. The domestic work was also undertaken in the laundry room at the top of the house, where better-dressed maids with coarse linen aprons are seen. In this room is a splendid linen-press that we see in operation, while a second maid works with an iron, containing hot coal, at a table. There are many linen-baskets and trays, and on the table is a bowl of water for sprinkling on the starched clothes.

Petronella de la Court's cabinet house contains only one bedroom, and even this is of modest size though extravagantly decorated, as in Holland the bedroom was used occasionally for the reception of guests. The floor is covered with green-and-white checked silk, and the walls are also hung in silk and decorated with a number of paintings by artists such as C. Wilt, W. van Mieris and D. Vertangen, whose subjects included Bathsheba bathing, a country scene and bathing nymphs. A much later painting of a vase of flowers by P. V. Slingeland was added in the nineteenth century. This room is occupied by a particularly beautiful lady doll wearing a *fontage* and many rows of pearls at her neck and wrists. She is one of the first occupants of the cabinet, as the style of her open robe dates the doll between 1680 and 1690. The face is modelled with great expression, as though the woman is just about to speak, and the complete pose of the figure with its hint of imperiousness is very cleverly contrived. The richness of her dress accords well with the furnishings of the room with its fringed upholstery and extravagantly tasselled dressing-table cover. There was once a blue porcelain bowl in this room, but it is one of the items that have been lost over the years. As in all the Dutch houses, there are a number of foot-warmers. On the toilet table is a group of very oversized brushes, and a piece of miniature silver is also placed against the boarded fireplace. The ceiling decoration is again effective, being assembled from a painted engraving of the coronation of the Emperor Leopold I (1640–1705).

Undoubtedly the most impressive of the reception rooms is the salon, as it was fashionable in the late seventeenth century to give such apartments added importance by painting the whole of the walls and, occasionally, the ceiling with a landscape, which must have given visitors a sensation of escape

The fashionably dressed wax-headed lady stands admiring herself in a mirror in the bedroom. The costume dates to between 1680 and 1690.

from the close confines and noise of life in Amsterdam. One of the walls carries the signature of Frederick de Moucheron (1633–86), who decorated the salon with a South Italian landscape. While the art cabinet was in the possession of Mevrouw Pipersberg, the house was raided, and the silver chandelier that hung originally in this room was stolen, to be replaced in 1831 by one made of glass. Additional lighting was provided by candles that stood in silver sconces, and we are asked to imagine that the company has been playing cards and drinking from the glasses that stand on the table. The ladies are seen ready to enjoy the gentlemen's music, and a cello, violin, clavichord and several flutes all lie awaiting the start of the informal concert. They are about to play fashionable dances from their handwritten music, including '*La Lacquoquellé*' and '*La Bourée de Basque*'. Just as they are about to enjoy French music, so French fashion is appreciated, and all the company is dressed in French style, with the women wearing the very low necklines not commonly seen in Holland. All these dolls are exquisitely costumed with fabrics and decoration especially selected to suggest the adult figure beneath the clothes. Against one wall stands a very good console table, with the base in the form of an eagle with outstretched wings. This baroque-style piece has a marble top and dates to around 1660. In fact the room contains less furniture than the other, less prestigious apartments and relies for effect mainly on the rich costumes of the characters and the splendid wall-paintings.

The recorded theft of the silver chandelier from the house is a further indication of the Dutch appreciation of miniatures, especially those of precious metals which were created in some number not only for cabinet houses but also simply as display items in their own right. Consequently, the various cabinet houses contain a much greater display of silver than is found in British Baby Houses, as the Continental silversmiths were much more adventurous in their basic designs and created ornate filigree screens, Boulle cabinets, cradles, a breathtaking variety of furniture and a most comprehensive amount of kitchenware, including coffee-grinders, wafer-tongs and that indispensable item of dolls' house equipment, the mousetrap. The silversmiths of Leeuwarden in Friesland were producing miniatures even in the fifteenth century, and production was well under way by the seventeenth century in Haarlem and Amsterdam and at The Hague. The very early items are somewhat restrained in design, but there is usually some decoration of the borders and edgings, the popular filigree work being a characteristic of the Leeuwarden area. Among the main Amsterdam producers of toy pieces for cabinet use were Willem van Straut, Roelof Helwig, Reynier Brandt and Arnoldus van Geffen. The makers at The Hague including Reynier de Haan, F. M. Simons and Cornelis de Haan.

There is a particularly long tradition of silver toy making in Holland as the collecting of such pieces never went out of fashion as it did in Britain, and the production is even more extensive today. During the seventeenth and eighteenth centuries a considerable amount of the Dutch production was exported to Britain, so that the British toymen described themselves as 'sellers of Dutch and English wares'. Pieces made especially for export to Britain were necessarily of the higher silver standard, 93·4 per cent pure as opposed to the 83·3 per cent standard, permitted since 1663 in Holland but which would have been described only as 'white metal' across the Channel. Much of the Dutch silver, like that made in Britain, was unmarked because of its very small size, but a few specialist makers are recorded, such as Arnoldus van Geffen of Amsterdam and, the most prolific producer, Fredrik van Strant and his son, who worked between 1725 and 1750.

The oldest cabinet house in the Rijksmuseum at Amsterdam contains a particularly fine variety of miniature silver, including some good-quality firebacks as well as the more usual candle-sconces and drinking-vessels. This model, which was once thought to have belonged to Margaretha de Ruyter, stands on a massive walnut base with barley-twist legs and was obviously the pastime of a wealthy lady, though she did not put as much detail into the furnishings as Petronella de la Court. Fortunately fewer items have been added over the years, so that the house remains in virtually original condition. For many years it was thought that this model was once owned by the daughter of Michiel Adriaenszoon, who married the clergyman Bernardus Somer in 1673. It was thought that Margaretha Somer worked on the house until her death in 1689 when the inventory of her possessions was taken, which included a 'walnut doll's house standing on an oak table'. This description has long given some cause for doubt, as the existing model has its own, very obviously original, walnut stand. The traditional attribution to the great Admiral de Ruyter's daughter depended largely on the fact that the art cabinet was in the possession of David Willem Elias and his wife Catherina Susanna van de Poll in the early nineteenth century, David Willem being a descendant, through the female line, of Margaretha herself, and the presence of a horseman on several of the hearth plates also supported the theory, as the Dutch word for horseman is *ruyter*.

Current research, reported by C. W. Fock in the Rijksmuseum Bulletin, suggests that in fact the cabinet house originally belonged to Petronella Dunois, a well-known art collector and an ancestor of Catharina van de Poll, rather than to her husband, David Willem. Petronella Dunois and her husband were important Leiden citizens, and the house was apparently brought by Petronella as a dowry on her marriage in 1677. It is considered probable that the construction was the work of Amsterdam cabinet-makers as she had lived there before her marriage. The initials that are found on a pin-cushion in the house carrying the date 1676 thus fall neatly into place, not as a record of the death of Margaretha de Ruyter's father but probably the actual date of the furnishing of the cabinet by Petronella Dunois.

The history of the house is clearly documented in Wills and inventories in the female line of Catherina Susanna van de Poll up to the time when it passed to her mother. How it actually passed to Susanna herself is, however, not recorded, though the museum suggests that the fact that the house was willed to her grand-daughter, unlike her other possessions, which she left to her husband's daughter by his first marriage, is a firm indication that it was an heirloom in her own family rather than that of her husband, a theory that obviously suggests that the house once owned by Margaretha de Ruyter was lost by her descendants.

Among the finest features of the walnut cabinet are the inlaid floors that give the effect of parquet and tiles and contribute to an effect of perfect unity, as a similar type of inlay is seen on the exterior. As in the Utrecht house, the laundry room is situated on the top floor, and its walls are covered with whitewashed paper. From the raftered ceiling hangs a clothes-line, complete with several beautifully stitched garments of completely accurate miniature construction. A maid works at a simple pine trestle-table covered with a heavy ironing-pad. She wears a simple grey dress and a white starched apron and cuffs. At the back of the room are several low benches, on which are piled folded blankets bound with silk ribbon; on the table is stacked the starched and ironed linen; other laundered garments are stored away in cane baskets. These baskets are a particular feature of the Dutch laundry rooms and were made in a wide variety of shapes and sizes, from deep-lidded versions to others that resemble trays. This considerable amount of storage-space for both soiled and laundered items was very necessary, as the main household washing of rich families was carried out only once a year, when hired laundry-women were brought in to assist in the work. Because of this custom, almost a form of exhibitionism, the linen supply necessary for a household of average size was huge, as hundreds of sheets, tablecloths and shirts were needed, all of which were monogrammed and proved to the world that the mistress of the house was so well supplied that a yearly laundry was all that was required. The cane baskets were therefore very necessary for the storage of the soiled as well as the clean items and in themselves formed proof of the affluence of the establishment.

Similar baskets are also found in the nursery, which, as in Petronella de la Court's house, is situated near the laundry. This room, however, is much more simply furnished and has whitewashed walls and fewer objects. Among the basketwork is a wicker cradle decorated with braid and a flat, tray-like carrier on which a young baby in his swaddling-bands could be laid. Cane was also used for a charming model baby-walker that was wound around with pink silk and gold thread, giving an unusually bright appearance to this functional item of equipment. Alongside this colourful home-made piece

A cabinet house on a walnut stand that is thought to have been assembled by Petronella Dunois. Late seventeenth century.

stands a child doll who resembles an adult, as she wears a scaled-down version of adult dress. The nursery chimneypiece is quite crudely made of thin wood and sections of moulding painted to resemble marble. The Delft tiles on the chimney wall are also simply achieved by painting on paper. The mantelpiece is decorated with a fringe, a device also seen in several of the rooms in the Utrecht cabinet. The small four-poster bed is extremely effective as it is hung with silk and surmounted with a huge tassel-like pineapple, a device used frequently on furniture well into the eighteenth century, as it was accepted as a symbol of hospitality. The basic bed is very roughly made from sections of dowel, thin wood and card that has been painted in black and yellow, though little of this framework can be seen. This bed is not as high as the other in the main bedroom and was possibly intended for an older child. The children, all wearing expensive patrician costume, are being visited by a lady, probably their mother, who is also dressed in the height of fashion.

The dolls in this cabinet are made of wax and are similar in construction to those found in the Utrecht house, with detailed characterization and finely modelled hands. These figures vary in size from 12 to 20 centimetres and were costumed with very particular attention to detail. The mistress of the house wears her hair drawn up into a huge bun at the back of her head with two loosely curled ringlets falling to her shoulders in front. Her silk open robe reveals a gold lace petticoat, and the rich general effect is heightened by her pearl necklace and bracelet. There are small bows, known as *faveurs*, attached to her costume, a detail also worn by the men on shoulders, shoes and breeches. The faces of the men dolls, some of whom wear moustaches, again exhibit great character, and it seems very possible that they were made by the same craftsmen as those found at Utrecht. In this case almost all these wax figures are modelled with one hand in an open position and one clenched, with a hole running through so that delicate items such as sticks could be carried or other objects easily sewn in place. The wrinkled old man wearing a smock and a shabby hat who is found in the store-room at the top of the house is a perfect example of this excellent wax characterization.

The two most richly furnished apartments, the salon and the main bedroom, are found in the centre of the house. The represented family is not intended to be as wealthy as that at Utrecht, and there is no separate lying-in room, though the mother's needs, providing she was of small stature, might have been served by a brief sojourn in the nursery. In the main bedroom, which in this instance is being used as the lying-in room, the walls are hung with a somewhat overpowering red-and-gold printed fabric that is also used for the bed-hangings and counterpane. Even this heavy decoration is not sufficient, and the ceiling is also painted. The nurse sits by the fire nursing the newly born baby, who lies, firmly swaddled, on a flat board and is so heavily decorated that he resembles a small silk-and-ribbon-tied ornament rather than a living child. The mother lies in bed and is supplied with a silver

118

The wax-headed mistress of Petronella Dunois's house wears a silk open robe with a gold lace petticoat.

chamber-pot. The bed itself is again made in a very rudimentary manner and decorated with tassels, though in this case the bed-linen and pillows are finely stitched. Most of the furniture with barley-twist legs and fringed and upholstered seats is typical of the period, but of particular note is a cupboard with one of the large brass locks that characterize so much very early miniature furniture and a fine inlaid oystershell pattern to the doors.

The drawing-room walls are also hung with silk, neatened with braid along the edges. At the back of this pale green room is a large, well-stocked linen-cupboard, on which stand several oriental porcelain vases. The ivory chairs with upholstered seats and fringing are also very fine, and this good-quality ivory carving is also used for the supports of a set of shelves. On the table lies the pin-cushion carrying the date of the furnishing of the model in 1676. Nearby stands the mistress of the house. Her drawing-room is well supplied with silver, such as a firebasket and a shovel, as well as a large plate that hangs on a wall. Other pieces lie on a table, and there is a good glass decanter and goblets.

Another chamber, designated for the use of the men of the household, is at ground-floor level. The masculine atmosphere of this smoking-room is accentuated by its exquisite barbers' bowls with red, blue and gilt decoration. At the rear of the apartment stands a large cupboard stocked with cream and clear glasses and decanters, some with gilded tops. On the central table stands a fine red stoneware teapot some $\frac{3}{4}$ inch high, together with several glass tea-bowls: the gentlemen's pipes also lie close at hand. On one wall hangs a beaded set of shelves, and there are also a few paintings. Upholstered stools stand ready for other visitors. As in several of the Dutch houses, the carpet is skilfully painted, though in this case the technique is rather less successful, as it was used on paper rather than the more usual canvas. If the room became too draughty for the topers, a folding Japanese screen could be brought forward.

The kitchen is decorated with a yellow wash over thin paper and is quite simply furnished, though the general effect is more welcoming than that in the Utrecht model. There is the usual large fireplace with a fringed mantelshelf, and on a Delft rack there are wooden or *papier mâché* plates that are painted to resemble porcelain. On the floor lie a pair of heavy wooden clogs that would have been taken off as soon as their owner entered the house and which were usually left outside the door. (In certain areas of Holland, the presence of these clogs on the doorstep was an indication that the inhabitant was at home and willing to receive visitors.) The housekeeper wears a clean apron and is seen carrying a basket of bread towards a table on which lie plaster food and a large chopping-board. The housekeeper's comfort is aided by the wooden foot-warmers that were a particular feature of Dutch interiors and which are found in some number in this house in both the domestic and the reception areas. In full scale, these were square oak boxes that were covered with chip carving which disguised the holes in the top from which the heat came. The fronts opened to reveal earthenware containers with a handle so they could be filled with hot charcoal. The earliest examples are thought to have originated in Friesland. A few were also provided with brass handles so they could be transported easily, some people even taking them to church, where they were concealed from the clergyman's eyes by the women's long skirts. The majority of the cabinet-house models have long since lost their charcoal-containers, which were made of bone, ivory or, more correctly, earthenware, but a few rare examples have survived intact.

There is no separate barrel-room in this house, as there is at Utrecht, and instead, in one corner stands a copper with a turned wooden bowl on top. There is also a neat lavatory situated in a cupboard-like area and provided with a wooden seat. This curious mixing of oddly insanitary arrangements within the spotlessly clean and otherwise unusually hygienic kitchens was a constant source of wonder to travellers, especially those of British origin. A Mr Holcroft published an account of his travels in Holland in the late-eighteenth century in a British ladies' magazine and commented on the lifestyle of the housewife: 'She has two kitchens, even in an inn; one for use and one for ornament. She wishes only the latter to be seen. Go into it and you are surprised at the order, neatness and cleanliness of its contents; cast your eyes upward and you smile at the row of chamber utensils hanging over her clean dishes, bright copper pots and unsoiled saucepans. It is a combination which could only have been made by a Dutch woman.'

It is obvious from the presence of a lavatory in this kitchen, and in the

The kitchen of Petronella Dunois's house showing several wooden foot-warmers. As there is no separate barrel-room, a copper stands in one corner.

barrel-room in the Utrecht cabinet that this was quite a normal situation, and presumably the chambermaids cleaned and emptied the silver chamber-pots from the bedrooms in these areas where cooking was taking place, giving a very precise picture of the actual conditions of the period. In this house, the store-room is situated much more conveniently for the kitchen and contains, instead of the ferocious guillotine rat-trap, one for mice. On the shelves are stored the provisions which the careful housewife has laid down for the winter and covered with leather, tied tightly in place to stop the contents drying out. Various items intended for the table can also be found here, such as a boar's head and a chicken. From the palings which divide the provision-room from the cellar hang bunches of grapes and dried fish. Firewood and various sweeping-brushes are also arranged around this section of the house, and the whole area exudes an atmosphere of complete order and tranquillity, heightened by the low, peaceful dimensions of the model itself, which compares well with the tall and much more nervous proportions of the cabinets at Nuremberg.

Another even more impressively massive cabinet can be seen at the Rijksmuseum and is believed to have been made for Petronella Oortman, born in 1656, who married Johannes Brandt in 1686. Dolls' houses have rarely formed an attractive subject for artists, so that the portrait which accompanies this example gives it an immediate air of superiority. It is unlikely that the artist, Jacob Appel (1680–1751), was greatly inspired by the house itself, and it seems more probable that he was asked to represent the model accurately after furnishing, as the painting, with complete disregard for perspective, is very obviously intended as a record rather than as a work of art. It is, however, of great interest, as it shows how, originally, the model was peopled with a family of dolls wearing the costumes and hairstyles of 1690–1700. It is, of course, possible that these figures were mere artistic licence, but the accuracy of the presentation in all other respects would suggest otherwise. Their poses are, it must be admitted, far too realistic ever to have been achieved by the figures of wax and wire that were available, and as these original figures are lost, it is probable that it will never be possible to be absolutely sure. The model, after many years without inhabitants, is now supplied with another group of the right period similar to those in the walnut cabinet.

The painting shows that the valuable contents of the house were originally protected from dust by six panelled glazed doors that opened, cupboard-like, at centre front. As sunlight would have faded the contents, there were curtains which could be drawn across when the house was not on display, a device which more museums might well use, as it is so distressing to see old houses set out in brilliant daylight. The painting also shows all the rooms with their own numbers, which again underlines the probable use of the picture as some form of guide.

Apart from the distinction of having its own portrait, the *poppenhuis* is also highly impressive for the pure quality of fine cabinet-makers' work which it exhibits. While the walnut house has something of the amateur touch in its smaller detail, this is completely the work of highly accomplished master craftsmen who never economize. It is little wonder that such credence was given to the story that in fact this house was the one recorded as having been commissioned by Peter the Great of Russia but never delivered, as he eventually considered that the asking price was too high. This story, of nineteenth-century origin, is not now seriously regarded, but it does indicate that the model was traditionally considered an item of truly magnificent craftsmanship.

The only cabinet house to be accompanied by a contemporary portrait is that owned by Petronella Oortman. It was painted by Jacob Appel (1680–1751).

The interior of Petronella Oortman's cabinet showing the complex arrangement with access to rooms at the rear. The 'Best Kitchen' on the ground floor shows the crockery that formed part of a Dutch bride's dowry.

On the splendid exterior the very costly device of tortoiseshell veneer was used, a technique normally reserved for much smaller items of furniture. A similar extravagance of finish and basic materials is also seen in the other rooms, where superb chimneypieces, panelling and ceilings all testify to the most lavish and princely of commissions. Perhaps it is this very perfection of the most minute detail that gives this cabinet house such a remote atmosphere and, despite its superb quality, makes it one of the least alive of the early Dutch houses. The Utrecht house has its many doll inhabitants to give life, and the walnut house contains much evidence of the personal needlework and decorative skill of the owner, but here all is perfection, with little of the wayward human touch.

124

As in the Utrecht cabinet, the most important room in the Oortman *poppenhuis* is decorated with landscape paintings of Arcadian scenes, the work of Nicolaas Piedmont (1644–1709). The fine chimneypiece supports an integral painting of a strutting cockerel surrounded by admiring hens, in a park setting, by W. van Rooyen. In the fireplace beneath, there is a chimneyboard with a painting of an urn of flowers, illustrating the more conventional method of dealing with the sooty open fireplace during the summer months. The absolute correctness everywhere apparent in this model is seen in the way that the peat-buckets and the firedogs are stored away in the attic until the autumn. The fine rosewood furniture with green velvet fringed seats and delicately carved legs is accompanied by a reading-stand on which lies a brass-bound Bible. On a small ivory table, obviously intended for the gentlemen smokers, lie several ivory pipes and a tea-bowl.

The visitor must imagine he is entering the house through the main hall, which is also situated on the middle floor of the model and which is given importance by the exceptionally fine carving which immediately attracts the viewer's eye. The richness of the detail on the hall seats forms a good contrast with the marble floor and two windows which, when opened, reveal another inaccessible area, again suggesting the great skill involved in the basic construction of this model. In the early painting of the cabinet this section looks quite different, as the heavy carving at ceiling level is missing and, at the rear, instead of the additional rooms, there was a view of the garden. Perhaps a sometime owner of the model felt that this section lacked detail and requested the use of much more woodwork, as even the fine seats are not seen in the painting.

To the right of this perfectly constructed hall is the main bedroom, with

A silver spirit kettle and urn marked 'CW' for Christiaan Waarenberg of Amsterdam. It stands in the bedroom of the Oortman house.

The red draped bed that stands in an alcove in the main bedroom of the Oortman cabinet.

walls completely panelled in rosewood. The bed exactly fits an alcove and is draped with red velvet decorated with fringes and tassels. On either side of this bed, tall linen-cupboards are built in, giving a look of complete unity that would not be amiss in a twentieth-century setting. Inside these large cupboards are piles of monogrammed linen. All the furniture is upholstered in red silk, and the chair seats are neatly buttoned and fringed, which gives the room a look of perfect, if precisely contrived unity. A fine embroidered linen cover decorates the plain toilet-table on which stand a few tea-bowls. The babies of the house are obviously accommodated in this room, and there is a rocking-cradle and a child's chair, both made of wicker. The chimneypiece again contains a painted panel, in this case by J. Voorhout, and near the fire is a silver equipage bearing the initials 'CW', indicating the work of Christiaan Waarenberg of Amsterdam. The ceiling painting, depicting Moses with the tablets of the Law, was the work of Jan Voorhout (1647–1723).

The basement reception room, usually referred to as 'the tapestry room' because of its overwhelming patterned walls, is not as masculine in effect as

A black and gold lacquer curiosity cabinet from the tapestry room of Petronella Oortman's house. Height 11 inches.

the art chamber that is found in a similar position in the Utrecht house, though it does contain the inevitable curiosity cabinet holding a collection of shells, an item of furniture that is made in the chinoiserie style. Through a door left ajar, we are offered a glimpse of the well-stocked library. It is obvious that the women of the household also make use of this apartment, as a lace-pillow, scissors and workbox lie on a draped table. The blue silk covered day-bed also seems to be designed for female taste.

The basement hall, from which the tapestry room is approached, has a pink marble floor and a corner chimneypiece, a space-saving device that is sometimes encountered in Baby Houses. The large built-in china-cupboard contains a wide assortment of porcelain, and over the door is a rack from which hang bottles and a small wire figure. At the side of the hall is a sink with splendid brass taps, above which hang several baskets and a knife- and spoon-rack. Food is already prepared for serving and is laid out on a long shelf. The cabinet-maker at this juncture gives us another exhibition of his considerable skill as, through a door at the back, we catch a glimpse of a cellar that appears to be accommodated beneath the main house.

The 'Best Kitchen' in a Dutch home was the province not of the servants but of the mistress herself and was traditionally furnished with pieces that formed part of her dowry. The twice-married Petronella's cabinet contains the finest surviving example of such a room, much of whose effect depends on the skilfully painted tiles, some of which were divided by lines into four sections to give an even more realistic scale effect. The large glass-fronted cabinet at the rear is a highly decorative piece, with its flower-painted panels and attractive border designs. Inside, on shelves especially shaped for the display of porcelain, stand rummers, tea-caddies, blue-and-white porcelain and a few pieces of transfer-printed ware that were added much later. The physical comfort of the mistress of the house was given some attention in the Best Kitchen, and the rush-seated chairs were provided with velvet cushions and foot-warmers. To protect the child of the house from damaging himself on the white marble floor, his chair was fitted with a bar. This particular example is unusual, in that a bell for the amusement of the occupant was also provided. The child and his mother could also be entertained by the singing of a bird in a cage. The absolute order of this kitchen, with its attractive furnishings and plenishments, is enhanced by the chinoiserie windows situated just above the dresser. A row of carefully selected Chinese vases stands in front of these decorative windows and again indicates the way in which every item was especially selected for this prestige room.

Very similar windows also decorate the nursery, which is situated at the top of the cabinet and whose furnishings are considerably less perfect than those of the main rooms. The walls are simply whitewashed and hung with gilt-framed mirrors and paintings. The rather crudely made bed is draped with cream silk, edged with blue braid; the drapery on the baby's cradle is also made in a less than satisfactory manner, and one feels that very definite economy was used in the furnishing of this area, which obviously held little appeal for the decorator, who did not bother even to provide a carpet. Presumably, the fabrics which now give the room a somewhat bedraggled air were, when fresh, carefully arranged as we see them in the painting, causing them to harmonize more effectively with the complete order of the rest of the model, an order that can again be seen exhibited in the well-organized laundry, with its massive linen-press and cane storage-baskets. On the ironing-table are two brass charcoal-heated smoothing-irons, and from the clothes-line hang perfectly sewn garments and correctly knitted stockings. At the back of the room and lit, when the doors are closed, by two extremely effective oval fanlights, are the maids' bedrooms, each equipped with a crudely constructed four-poster bed hung with printed chintz, a rush-seated chair, in this instance without cushions, and a chamber-pot. Between the

This small thoroughfare room adjoins the Best Kitchen. It contains a sink with large brass taps and was used partly for the preparation of food. Petronella Oortman's house.

laundry and the nursery is a hall that leads to the storage-area, supplied with the usual sweeping-brushes and bundles of wood. The disused spinning-wheel and mousetrap also seem essential features of this section of a cabinet house.

The strength of these fine Dutch models lies in the makers' absolute control of all the detail and furnishing so that an almost completely correct effect could be achieved. Every chair and table, every carpet and painting was especially selected and designed for particular situations and then augmented with carefully chosen incidental items, such as imported Chinese porcelain,

commercially made dolls and the miniature silver that could be obtained from many sources.

The problems that arise when such a correctly planned model is found without its costly craftsman-made plenishments is illustrated by a very beautifully proportioned eighteenth-century model also found at the Rijksmuseum. This model conforms much more closely to the accepted doll's house plan, as it is provided with an opening façade with a main entrance approached by a *piano nobile*. The furniture with which it is now equipped, though antique, serves only to show the impossibility of matching such a perfect craftsman-made interior with pieces discovered at random, which give the rooms an atmosphere of only partial occupation.

The interior of this model, known affectionately by the Dutch as 'the Canal

The chimneypieces in the 'Canal House' are particularly fine, as in the decorative detail of this room on the first floor.

Opposite: The so-called 'Canal House' with its *piano nobile* is reminiscent of eighteenth-century British houses and has a classical perfection of detail.

House' from its resemblance to the fine patrician houses in Amsterdam, was given greater realism by its exquisitely formed staircase that rises up through the centre of the house with complete accuracy. On the top floor are several laundry rooms, probably with their original correctly scaled fittings. In the low-ceilinged basement are the storage rooms and kitchens. The main reception rooms are given considerable importance by the very lovely chimneypieces in rococo style, the heavy simulated decorative plasterwork and the decorated ceilings. All the basic interior detail is effected with absolute correctness, and this model must have once been one of the finest eighteenth-century examples, as it is so much a representation of a real house. The supposition that it was intended originally for an adult's collection of miniatures is supported by the fact that the fronts of the central section were made to lock. This model has a special attraction for British visitors, as it has such affinity with the Baby Houses with which we are so familiar, though few surviving dolls' houses could rival the cabinet-maker's work seen here.

The massive walnut cabinet house at the Gemeente Museum at The Hague has the attraction of a model with almost complete documentation that assists our understanding of how similar projects were developed. This impressive cabinet, standing on bun feet and containing three large locking drawers in the base, was purchased on 28th October 1743 by Sara Ploos van Amstel and made to her very specific requirements, as she wished it to contain a number of miniatures and room-settings which she had purchased on 10th April of the same year. On that day Sara had attended an auction at the Keizerskroon in Amsterdam and returned home the proud possessor of 'three cabinets with all pertaining thereto'. These cabinets, one painted and two lacquered, were originally owned by the widow Rachel Wijnershoff and were obviously items of some interest, as the two smaller models, which held five and six rooms respectively, were owned in the late seventeenth century by the painter David van der Plaes. The other, larger house that was artistically furnished with pieces from the Wijnershoff family, noted silversmiths, contained some eight rooms and had obviously taken this early cabinet collector some time to equip. Van der Plaes had apparently purchased the cabinets he furnished in 1700 and 1703, but it seems unlikely that he changed the contents very much, as he died in 1704, after which they passed into the Widow Wijnershoff's keeping.

Sara Rothé, later Ploos van Amstel, has bequeathed to the chronicler of dolls' houses one of the richest possible sources of information in the records, bills and inventories which she kept so carefully. She was, it seems, a most genial woman whose most noticeable feature was her extreme stoutness. Her obesity was eventually to cause her death, as it was impossible for rescuers to lift her from a coach that had overturned and thrown its occupants into a canal near Halfweg. Council archives and records, which the Dutch seem to have kept much more assiduously than the British, provide further information: she was christened in New Church in Amsterdam in 1699 and was the daughter of a banker who lived on the Keizersgracht; her husband, Jacob, was a well-educated merchant who married her in February 1721. They were comparatively wealthy and lived in a house some three times the width of a normal canal house that was also situated on the Keizersgracht and which is now an auction room. As no children were born, it seems that she was able to devote much of her time and money to collecting, and at her death she was the owner of 'two large art cabinets with other small household goods' and yet another 'little doll's house that stood before the fireplace in the main room'. In addition there was a variety of dolls' items, extra furniture and plenishments from the dolls' chests as well as a number of silver miniatures. She was also the possessor of a dressed doll and a box of dresses. As her

Sara Ploos van Amstel incorporated sections of earlier houses into this massive walnut cabinet made by Jan Meijjer.

husband's income was 8,000 florins a year, at a time when a well-to-do citizen earned some 600 florins, it was possible for Sara to collect on an extensive scale and to employ the most skilled craftsmen on her projects. Like many other wealthy Amsterdam merchants, they owned a house in Haarlem for the summer months, and it was on a journey to meet her husband who was returning there from Amsterdam that she was eventually drowned.

A few months after purchasing the three old cabinets at auction, Sara began assembling the first of her houses, the model that can now be seen at The Hague. While the purist grieves for these seventeenth-century pieces taken apart by an enthusiastic collector, we should perhaps console ourselves with her invaluable documentation, which lists in many cases not only the place of purchase but also the names of the craftsmen. The two houses she assembled were displayed in the main reception rooms of her house, 'one with all its belongings in complete order', which was in the new outer chamber and another 'with all that small household equipment' situated in the inner chamber. The model at The Hague is accompanied by two notebooks, only the first of which is in her own handwriting, the second being merely an inventory. Sara informs us that the massive walnut cabinet in which she arranged her miniatures was constructed by Jan Meijjer, and she also found it useful to itemize 'all that which cabinet number three hath cost to alter'. From the pages of this thrifty Dutchwoman's journal we discover that it was necessary to provide some of the dolls with replacement heads and that several pieces of furniture, though completely British in style, were in fact the work of Dutch craftsmen. Such information is without parallel in the development of dolls' houses until the late nineteenth and early twentieth centuries, providing a completely unique account of the construction of a Dutch cabinet.

Incorporated in The Hague model are the eleven rooms from the David van der Plaes cabinets, as in this structure Sara was not attempting the realism she was later to achieve in the Haarlem model. All the contracts with workmen and the supervision of their work was her own responsibility, and as so many were employed, it is her own personality and taste that were reflected in the finished work. Much of the copper and brass for the kitchens was supplied by J. ten Ham, and the Widow Bronkhorst, who ran a pewter workshop, also made a number of items which carry her mark. Most of the work in marble was effected by Christoffel Hortung. All Sara's costs were carefully recorded, and we learn that the work on the model at The Hague cost her 608 florins. The positioning of the cabinet house in a main reception room indicates that there was no special art chamber in her home, some of the merchants having such extensive collections of natural objects and artificialia that they supplied visitors with catalogues of the contents. (Jacob Ploos van Amstel was among the most modest of collectors, as he owned only a few medals, some sixty paintings and a folio of prints.)

Like the assembler of the Utrecht cabinet, Sara decided it was necessary to install a garden at basement level, 'between the lying-in room and the kitchen. At the back there is a painting of a garden in perspective, which cost 18 florins. In the middle of the garden, towards the back, stands a carved bench that was previously in cabinet number three.' This garden is much more formal in arrangement than that at Utrecht and has considerably less charm, as the rows of plants and gardening-tools lying around give Petronella de la Court's house a feeling of reality which the formal painted urns and rigid balustrading cannot rival, especially as the basic painting of this section left much to be desired. In order to create this outdoor scene, the skills of Jan Meijjer, her carpenter, and Jurriaan Buttener were employed. Buttener, who carried out much of the decorative work both on this model and on that at Haarlem, came to Amsterdam from Kiel in 1743 and specialized in portraits, though he seems to have been able to devote a great deal of time to the cabinets. Sara explains that 'For the painting of the porch which is in the front of the cupboard and for the garden, views and perspective and the sky, being altogether seven pieces for the which to be paid 18 florins, and also the same for the painting of the ground in this garden and for that laid with pebbles has been paid 6 florins.' This positioning of the garden within the house itself was a purely imaginary exercise, and other apartments, such as the lying-in room which is situated on the ground floor, would also rarely have been found in this position in real life. It is this curious mixture of absolute reality and an exercise of the imagination that gives her work such charm. The rather poor background painting is enlivened by the presence of the finely carved bench and the extremely effective parterre that stands in the centre. In Sara's journal we read: 'To the making of a marble parterre and a pedestal with the colour inlaid, 24 florins. On the pedestal there is a cupid which was made by Mijnheer Sluys and gilded by Mijnheer Buttener.'

The cabinet's interior also follows the typical seventeenth- and early-eighteenth-century Dutch convention, with the inevitable lying-in room and art chamber, both indicating a household of some standing. As in the Utrecht cabinet, the lying-in room is next to the garden, and again we see the mother sitting in her chair to receive a visitor. This apartment is of particular note, as it once formed part of cabinet number three but was fitted into the larger structure by Jan Meijjer. In the process of this reconstruction, the original wall-coverings of imitation tooled gold leather were removed and replaced with rose-red moiré which is somewhat out of place with seventeenth-century carvings and furniture but which probably appeared to Sara as a much more fashionable setting. The mother doll wears a blue dress and a shoulder-cape made by her cousin Nigt Hoogehuyse and herself. 'The lady with a pink sac and lace sleeves was dressed by Jr Castang and has fine stones in her ears. These dolls have new hands and heads.' Like many of the German crèche figures, it is obvious that doll's house inhabitants of wax were sometimes provided with new shoulder-heads either to suit their character or environment more correctly or, perhaps more usually, because of damage.

The bed, situated in an alcove at the back of the chamber, is hung with silk that matches that on the walls, and the counterpane was effectively embroidered by Sara, who also, with the help of her seamstress Johanna, sewed all the flounces on the bedstead. In her description of the furniture, she informs the reader that some of the contents were purchased from shops, such as a table and a doll dressed in white lace and chintz. The heavy furnishings of the room are to some extent relieved by the fine costumes of the dolls and the rich hangings, combined with the gleam of the dressing-table silver, which was provided in some abundance and dates from the mid-seventeenth century. The rich, heavy atmosphere of the lying-in room, created more for its effect on visitors than for the comfort of the mother, is encapsulated in this

The lying-in room of Sara Ploos van Amstel's cabinet was always sumptuous in effect so that visitors would be impressed by the wealth of the family.

miniature room with its marbled walls and tall eighteenth-century-style linen-cupboard, very similar in manner to that in which the model is accommodated. Such cupboards were very popular in Holland at this time and were used for the almost ceremonial display of the vast quantities of linen and woollen blankets by which the mistress of the household proclaimed her social status. Generous refreshments have been laid out for the elegant visiting lady wearing a pink sac dress, who was no doubt expected to notice the great number of closely folded linen items in the cupboard.

The kitchen, again at basement level, is a little disappointing, as it is without the complete and very Dutch order that is seen in those made by Petronella Oortman and Petronella de la Court, and it might appear that the contents of the three cabinets did not mix particularly well in this instance, as we are presented with an assortment of scale and effect with more affinity to a child's play-house than an adult's display-piece. The basic construction of the

136

The basic section of this kitchen came from Sara Ploos van Amstel's third cabinet, though the equipment, as can be seen from the complete lack of scale, came from several sources.

kitchen was originally in the third cabinet, Jan Meijjer earning 1.10 florins for its installation. For the painting of the ceiling and the varnishing of the tiles, Mijnheer ten Osselaar earned 12 florins. The kitchen, with its built-in cupboards and painted doors, is presided over by a white-aproned housekeeper, her status denoted by the chatelaine worn at her belt. She is accompanied by two other dolls with wax heads, hands and feet which both wear small shawls over their shoulders and neat household caps. 'In the middle of the kitchen stands a cabinet in which I have placed all sorts of pewter ware'; pewter that is, in fact, wildly out of scale with the dolls but includes a barber's bowl, a strainer and a teapot. Such pewter services had formed an essential feature of every Dutch kitchen in the seventeenth century and, though generally replaced by Delft ware by the time that Sara was assembling her cabinet, were still retained in some homes. The grey-bodied earthenware pots that stand around the room were also a little old-fashioned

137

but again served to represent a well-stocked, if somewhat outdated interior. On a side wall hangs a Delft rack containing blue-and-white plates, and in a similar position on the opposite side of the room, another rack is used for the display of a red-and-grey painted *papier mâché* set. On another shelf is a set of oriental porcelain described in the inventory as the 'Japanese dolls' tea-ware which I had as a wedding gift'; these are also very out of scale and were probably included for their sentimental associations. The remaining kitchen equipment is an assortment of commercially produced miniatures in a variety of sizes that are interesting individually but which hardly contribute to the ordered atmosphere of perfection, the hallmark of a Dutch model kitchen. There is a large pestle and mortar, a small egg-rack and, on the table, a small waffle-iron and a box containing ivory-handled knives. The foot-warmer is a good example, as it still retains its ivory or bone charcoal-holder. The kitchen of the old cabinet was originally equipped with silver utensils, but Sara chose to replace these with items made of iron, including a chain for the chimney, a brazier, a coal-shovel and a spittoon, all of which she obtained from her nephew, Theodorus Ploos van Amstel, for 12 guilders and 12 stivers. Little cooking seems to take place in this kitchen, as the fireplace is occupied by a large wicker fuel-basket, and the general effect is one of comfortable but completely un-Dutch confusion.

Complete order returns on the ground floor, entered through the centrally positioned hall, with its impressive hanging lantern which cost Sara 4 guilders and whose partner is seen in the Haarlem house. This hall, with its imitation grey marble walls, was 'made by Mijnheer Buttener, as was the plaster and the five doors in polished wood. The walls are marbled and the floor painted as white marble, and the cost thereof was 25 florins.' A clever effect of added depth was given by an archway situated near the back, a device which she repeated in her other, more realistic model. The doors, painted to represent polished wood and given painted mouldings, were supplied with actual knobs. This painted detail is extremely effective and appears completely realistic in photographs, though we do notice that the doors do not open. The stucco work on the ceiling and walls was also achieved in this way. The mat in the hall is somewhat reminiscent of the kitchen, with its complete lack of scale, and it is surprising to discover that, despite its inappropriate size, it was especially woven in yellow and black from the Brettehenweberei, a German tapestry-works, and also has a partner in the Haarlem model. The long-case clock is simple but very effective and was the work of Meijjer, who was also responsible for its copperwork. 'In the case there is a small gold pocket-watch with a gold chain, for which my husband paid Thr. Burrius the sum of 28 florins.' Several later doll's house enthusiasts were to sacrifice good items of jewellery for their hobby, but this gesture appears to be the first of the kind.

Dutch order is also complete in the music room, where the walls are completely covered with landscape scenes. One of these paintings was the

The walnut long-case clock of the Ploos van Amstel cabinet was made by Jan Meijjer, who incorporated a small gold pocket-watch to form the face. The clock case cost 4 florins 16 stivers.

work of David van der Plaes, who was the original owner of the cabinet from which this apartment was taken. To the modern viewer, the mirrors, candle-sconces and chandeliers that seem to hang from the painted sky seem sadly inappropriate, but it was a convention that was followed regularly in full-scale rooms of the type. Sara was particularly proud of the contents of this area: 'In this room hang from white silk cords silver sconces of which four were in cabinet No 2 and the others I had made later at a cost of 1.18 florins.' The original pieces all carry Haarlem silver-marks. Painted rooms of this type were somewhat outdated at the time, but having such a finely decorated example at her disposal, she was obviously unable to resist its temptations, despite its somewhat outdated effect in combination with the furniture that is mainly eighteenth century.

In this painted room stands a clavier which previously stood in cabinet No 3 and has been restored and repainted by Buttener, for which I paid him one florin. On

139

The music room of the Ploos van Amstel cabinet, with its painted walls, one of which was the work of the original owner of the cabinet house from which this section was taken.

the clavier music-rest there is a music book, and in the drawer of a little table in the room there are three similar books and two flutes. Also in that room there is a viol da gamba. The instruments and books came from cabinet No. 3. [This very organized collector continues:] On two of these little chairs sit two wax dolls which I had made and with the clothing cost me 3 florins. These dolls were dressed as gentlemen by Meinheer Castang.

The two gentlemen in the setting have obviously put their instruments aside and are relaxing with their pipes and a drink. One wax-headed man wears a chamber-gown of red damask, and the museum guide to the cabinet points out that a similar full-scale garment can be seen in the costume department. The other man wears a striped red silk waistcoat and jacket decorated with gold; his leather gloves, beautifully made tricorn hat and sword lie on a chair, indicating that he is paying only a short visit. Some of the furniture in the music room is mid-eighteenth century, as Sara records an order for 'a polished table in the latest style with a drawer therein, six English chairs with red velvet seats for 13 guilden and 10 stiver and two ivory gueridons painted to resemble wood'. This convention of painting ivory to imitate other substances is seen in several other eighteenth-century houses, as this was the only material that could be carved in really minute detail to represent the smallest household effects.

Many of the most impressive items in the room came from the older cabinet, such as the clavichord that was probably repainted by one of her and a silver tray. Also on the table was a pretty wine-cistern which is gilded on the inside and a green glass flask with a gold stopper.' The room contains several examples of fine seventeenth-century Dutch glass, including rummers, beer and liqueur glasses in both green and other coloured glass; other green flasks stand in the wine-cooler. A few of the music-room furnishings are below the standard of the items from the seventeenth-century cabinet, such as the clavichord that was probably repainted by one of her craftsmen, though the general effect of the chamber remains very good. The modern doll's house assembler will find the carpet of interest, as it is painted on canvas in a Turkish design, creating a most effective substitute for needlepoint, which often looks rather too rough. On a cupboard in a corner stands one of the finest items in the room, a Nevers glass blackamoor, and on a table in the foreground is another treasure, a fine inkwell and sander in gold.

Another apartment designed almost purely for dramatic visual effect is the 'Porcelain Room', one of the most frequently photographed sections of this important cabinet. Again we find a painted canvas carpet, but in this instance the paint was applied in small spots to give an even more realistic effect, a similar technique being used in the late nineteenth century by the constructor of Titania's Palace in Britain. Sara again made use of sections from the old cabinets: 'There was a small half-round chest that was previously in cabinet No 2 and a large cabinet made by Jan Meijjer which is approached by a step and has a small cabinet in the middle. On the walls are eighteen brackets and four large mirrors in frames which, together with the woodwork, cost 10 florins.' The effect of this porcelain room with its vast collection of blue and white is breathtaking and gives a very accurate impression of the fervour with which the Dutch merchants pursued their assemblies of fine items, whether in a wall cabinet or in a complete section of a room. The majority of the 'porcelain' in this cabinet is in fact made of glass, as it would have been extremely difficult to represent some of the smaller shapes in a ceramic substance, especially those displayed in the central section. On the decorative brackets, designed to hold single pieces, is displayed some very fine *blanc de chine*, in all some fourteen pieces that were originally in Cabinet No 2, and again actually made of glass.

The Porcelain Room of Sara Ploos van Amstel's house was especially constructed to incorporate sections of the earlier cabinets. The chairs were made in the fashionable 'English' style. Such displays of porcelain were quite common among wealthy merchants.

Opposite: Some of this *blanc de chine* was originally in the second cabinet. Like much of the blue and white 'porcelain', it was made of glass.

'In the middle of the half-round room stands a very pretty cabinet made of tortoiseshell with small drawers in which there are stones and shells' – in fact, a typical collector's chest of the period. 'In this room stand four English chairs with satin seats.' Sara and her group of craftsmen obviously put a great deal of effort into combining the old and new elements in this room to create a really unified effect. The china-cabinet section, for instance, which came from one of the older houses, was 'framed' within a carved rococo shape by Jan Meijjer, and the tall mirrors on either side were made more effective by new painted frames. This somewhat ostentatious display of good porcelain was necessary in every rich Dutch family in the eighteenth century, as its collection was highly competitive. It was known as 'Kraak' porcelain as it was carried to Holland in Portuguese *caraques* in the early seventeenth century, many large houses having shelves especially made so that as great a collection as possible could be put on display. This room of the cabinet house perfectly illustrates this feature of Dutch merchant life that was continued until the end of the eighteenth century.

With the porcelain room, we leave the most prestigious areas of the cabinet and climb to the attic rooms with their difficult curved ceilings, caused by the shaping of the cabinet itself. It seems that these ceilings defeated even the ingenious Sara, as we see in this section little of her verve, and even her account books were left incomplete, providing no further details of work or purchases. In another hand, in a second book, a person who seems to have taken more interest in the curiosity room on the top floor continues. This room is situated on the left of the attic area and contained 'two paintings, a mirror, a table, two books, four chairs, a cabinet with medals, a ditto with books, a cabinet with shells, a settee with all the things relating to it'. The room was hung with gilded paper, but its general effect is spoiled by the number of objects that are so completely out of scale within the context of Dutch cabinets that relied so much on accuracy. The fringed, upholstered velvet furniture is in itself both rich and impressive, as is the day-bed, both of which probably originated in the seventeenth-century cabinet. The large bookcase was made of walnut, and on the lower shelf are eight red morocco-bound books containing prints from the Old and New Testaments. On the top shelves are twenty similarly bound volumes with the title *The Wanderings of Ulysses* in twenty-four volumes, which were written in 1744. Some eighteen volumes in this miniature size were necessary to cover one book of the *Odyssey*. A painting in the art chamber is the work of the one-time owner of the earlier cabinet, David van der Plaes. The shell-cabinet is inlaid with palm wood and has ebony feet, while the medal-cabinet is made of inlaid walnut and has pink-satin lined drawers containing items such as a 'Friendship Penny' of 1746, a 1662 quarter ducat from the archbishopric of Sattsburg and a George III Maundy penny. The chamber was heated by a German-style stove, providing a much more comfortable curiosity room than was usual.

Above left: A detail of the laundry room in the Ploos van Amstel cabinet with its huge box mangle. *Above right:* This painted child's chair now stands in the laundry room and was obviously decorated by the same hand that repainted the clavichord.

The laundry room is completely conventional, though it occupies a much smaller area than usual, and we are expected to imagine that most of the work is carried out beyond the paling screen. There is the usual abundance of wicker baskets and several wooden boxes into which the washing was laid before it was drawn through the great mangle. The nursery is again situated near the laundry, and in its many baskets we find examples of the fine needlework that occupied so much of the women's time. The room contains an effective painted child's chair, decorated in blue and gold by the same hand that repainted the clavichord. This fine miniature has a padded back, and a bell hangs at the front to amuse the child. The four-poster bed with its lavish hangings came from one of the earlier houses and contributes to the rich effect, though its basic construction, like those in the other houses, is quite crude.

Few model houses proclaim the zeal of a collector as joyfully as that of Sara Ploos van Amstel, who was prepared to purchase, commission, adapt and even butcher earlier cabinets to satisfy her own concept of a richly stocked model, contained within a completely acceptable piece of household

145

furniture, in the lower drawers of which she was able to store her gloves, bedcaps and jewellery. Many modern collectors, sometimes reluctant to reveal their acquisitions to the uninitiated, make use of a similar device and set out model rooms or display their dolls inside wardrobes or cupboards that both protect the contents and offer the delight of a fresh visual feast on each occasion that the doors are opened. Perhaps it was the thrill of renewed surprise that encouraged the Dutch to assemble their miniature rooms within these huge cabinets, though there are exceptions of a much more conventional form with integral façades, such as the other model assembled by Sara Ploos van Amstel which is now displayed at the Frans Hals Museum in Haarlem, where a doll's house seems somewhat out of place in a building devoted almost exclusively to the work of painters, even though the model is shown in a room setting.

This model also has an unusually complete pedigree, as it passed, on the

146

Opposite: This realistic façade now hangs beside the cabinet of miniatures assembled by Sara Ploos van Amstel.

The complex fanlight monogram incorporates the initials of Sara Rothé, later Ploos van Amstel, and that of her husband.

death of Jacob van Amstel, to his niece Anna Margaretha Ploos van Amstel, wife of Jan Stadlander. Her daughter Cornelia married Gerrit Blaauw, and the house was auctioned by their direct descendant in 1939 when it was purchased by an art-dealer. Its last owner, Mevrouw Rienstra van Stuyvesant, sold it to the museum in 1958. The structure is immediately impressive as its generously proportioned rooms contain detail that is both intricate and true. The inventories suggest that Sara worked on this cabinet after that at The Hague, and her enthusiasm seems to have grown during the period so that this model is much more ambitious. Her initials, sometimes combined with those of her husband, are found in several places, particularly on the fanlight over the front door where a most complex monogram was used. It also appears in the painted arched vestibule and on several pieces of silver. In a manuscript book relating to the couple's silver wedding is included a special verse that relates to the dolls' houses she collected so eagerly.

This large cabinet is also remarkable for its basic complexity of construction, as Sara wished it to look completely realistic when the large black-lacquered oak doors, decorated with classical scenes in rococo style, were opened. Instead of a group of rooms arranged on virtual shelves, her visitors were offered a house with a perfectly constructed façade, something in the manner of the important double patrician houses made of sandstone found in the richer areas of Amsterdam and standing three storeys high. The main door is obviously the most important exterior feature, as the fanlight displays the family monogram, and the ornamental door case is richly carved with leaves and shells. This façade is now mounted on a wall alongside the house, and the viewer can examine the complex detail, such as the windows, each with some fifty-two neat panes painted on the glass. The detail on the façade, probably the work of Buttener, is so skilfully executed that the eye is completely deceived, and we can only admire the perfectly contrived symmetry of the building, with its ornamented central windows and complex cornicing. The skill of the assembler was revealed not only in the fine painting and furnishing but also in the mechanical structure. When the doors representing the façade were closed, they were locked neatly together by a bolt concealed behind a pillar, so that the external lacquered doors could in turn be closed to protect the windowed front. Even more complex arrangements are soon discovered as, at the top of the heavy front legs, we discover ratchets so that the complete massive cabinet could be lifted in order that the visitor could see with ease into the rooms contained in the lower section. A few small rooms, such as the kitchen and storage-cellars, were situated in this lower section of the most complex and perfectly recorded of houses.

In a small parchment-bound book that accompanies the cabinet, Sara begins with an inventory of the silver found in the earlier cabinets, and there is also a description of her work that explains how she used the eight rooms from the larger cabinet she bought at auction for this structure. She also made use of much of the old silver, such as a pair of compasses, a trowel, a pair of skates and a set of scales. Some of the fine ivory, often painted to resemble other substances, came from the earlier cabinets, as did the majority of the dolls, though both these and those at The Hague were re-dressed by a Frenchman, Jac Castang. The source of some of the furniture is not clear from the inventories, and it is obvious that she mixed them all together as she felt most appropriate, though she seems to have separated the glass and silver, placing the glass in the model at The Hague and the fine silver in the more realistic house.

When studying the interior, the eye is immediately drawn to the large central room, which has an arched vestibule in the foreground, painted in shades of blue which form a sympathetic background for the carved settle in mildly rococo form and the superb chandelier, which both came from the

The interior of Sara Ploos van Amstel's cabinet reflects the lifestyle of wealthy Dutch merchants. The silver room is of especial interest.

artist's houses. Behind the attractive arch is a 'marble' floored area with mirrored walls which are also decorated with monochrome paintings of classical figures that stand in painted niches. Gilded ornaments stand elegantly around this apartment on *torchières*, creating an impressive atmosphere for a chamber that was probably used for small functions such as musical evenings or simply as an ante-chamber for visitors. Curiously, this vestibule, though completely secular in decoration, with its classical figures and rococo murals, was described in one of the eighteenth-century inventory books as a chapel. It is now thought probable that this was due to a mistake in copying the word '*koepel*', meaning 'arched' or 'domed', as *kapel*, which means 'chapel', and certainly the room seems to have little religiosity in its atmosphere. The problem of equating the decoration of the chamber with the word 'chapel' was curiously solved for a short period during the ownership of the Stuyvesants by converting it into a masonic hall and placing one of the dolls in the centre of the room seated on a chair to represent the Grand Master. He was surrounded by a number of masonic devices and curious objects, all of which were swept away when the house came into the museum's care so that we again see the chamber as Sara, with no masonic associations, intended. One of the room's most interesting details is the painting of the initials 'SR' surmounted by a cherub, which in fact can be seen only by looking into one of the mirrors, as it is situated on a wall that curves out of sight.

Adjoining this important reception area, where the furniture was kept to a minimum so that visitors could move around easily, is the music room or painted chamber, containing a very imposing gilded mirror with shell decoration, in front of which stands a console table with a gilded base. The walls are painted with semi-classical romantic Italianate scenes incorporating columns, pedestals and various birds, while the ceiling represents children and flowers in an oval device. As at Mon Plaisir, the windows are made of mirror to give an illusion of depth. The carpet, in typical Dutch cabinet-house tradition, is painted in reds and blues to imitate a Smyrna product, while the skirtings and all the woodwork are wood-grained. The large chimneypiece is also painted, but to resemble marble. The fine furniture, supplied with delicately carved barley-twist legs, includes a table, a stool, an armchair and several basic chairs. On a lacquered side-table stands an imitation porcelain set made of glass including blue-and-white tea-bowls and saucers, and there is also an elegant silver teapot. In the centre of the room stands a particularly fine cabriole-legged clavichord, made in the height of fashion, which looks particularly effective in combination with the richness of the painted walls, the candle-sconces with their light-reflecting mirrored backs and the green silk curtains (a very unusual feature in a Dutch cabinet) that are held in position with tasselled cords. The pelmets are also beautifully embroidered and embellished at the centre with additional tassels. The silver sconces are of particular interest in this room, as only one came from the old cabinets, the

150

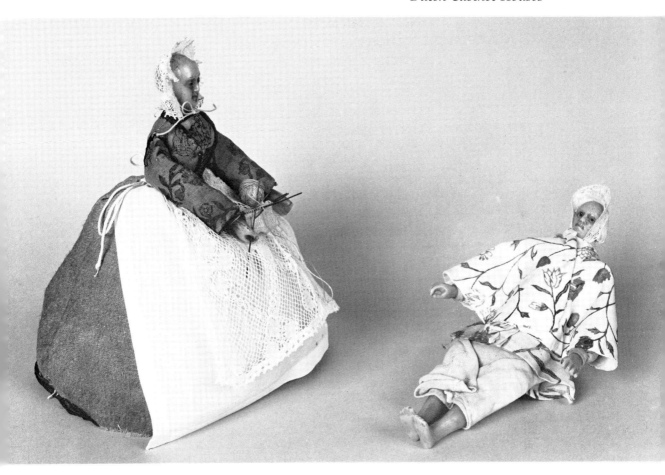

The wax-headed dolls from the lying-in room showing the detail of the mother's short bedjacket.

design being carefully reproduced by Arnoldus van Geffen and Willem Kunst, their work carrying contemporary marks dating to the 1740s.

At the opposite side of the house to the mirrored area is the lying-in room, the walls of which are hung with cinnamon-coloured ribbed silk. This room, in which the mother spent six to eight weeks after the birth of her child, was partially repainted in 1871, and there is a note to this effect on a door panel. The door frame is cleverly painted in imitation of marble and surmounted by a grisaille panel, signed Jacob de Wit, which exactly echoes the curved top of the door. The large and important bed was hung with green-lined saffron silk and covered with a decorative canopy that Sara embroidered herself. Supported by high pillows is a wax-headed and somewhat elderly-looking mother, who wears a short chintz bedjacket over a nightdress and is also

151

The lying-in room from the cabinet of Sara Ploos van Amstel. The massive cabinets held the abundance of linen necessary to impress visitors.

covered with a chintz counterpane. A wicker cradle once contained a baby that is now lost, and there is also a matching basket with a cover for the baby-equipment. Both these wicker pieces are covered with silk that matches the bed-hangings and tones most effectively with the colour of the walls. Alongside the bed is a good serpentine-front cupboard with drawers in the lower section. Some idea of the workmanship of the piece is indicated by the additional minute drawers that are contained in the upper section and which were quite invisible when the doors were closed on the linen. This breathtaking piece of the miniaturist's craft is further enhanced by the oriental vases that stand on the specially shaped display platforms on the top. The toilet-table has a draped base, decorated with satin-stitch embroidery and is equipped with silver toiletware and a mirror, some of which carries the mark of Arnoldus van Geffen. The wax-headed nurse, wearing a chintz frock, sits knitting, with her beaded and silk-decorated workbag lying alongside. It

152

seems that several items from this room have been lost since Sara listed the contents, including an engraved glass with a good-luck slogan that was used by guests who came to greet the mother and which was known as a 'birth glass'.

As in other Dutch cabinets, the low-ceilinged upper floor is used mainly for storage, and in the centre is the usual laundry room with wooden palings, in front of which stands a ladder leading to an imaginary loft. A Japanese-style screen bearing the mark of an Augsburg publisher of prints, seems ill at ease among the practical ironing-equipment, storage-baskets and large polished chest that contains valances for the lying-in room and a bedspread for the nursery. There is also an additional bedroom on this floor, though originally it was intended as a provisions area with the usual palings and a number of jars and barrels. It now contains a crudely made bed, and the chamber seems intended for a man, as there is a fine gun in the wall rack, and a number of large books are stored in a chest. It is otherwise very sparsely furnished, though the nineteenth-century improver did add a painted ceiling.

The nursery is also somewhat depleted, as the original inventory lists two children with their toys that are now lost, so that the room seems more in the nature of an ordinary but plainly furnished bedroom. Some of the household ironing, which came from one of the earlier houses, lies on a table, though the maid who was originally working here is also lost. Socks, presumably awaiting mending, lie realistically in a basket. The fireplace is of the simplest type, but there is a comfortable buttoned and upholstered armchair known as a 'sick chair', in which an invalid would sit. In the painted panelling at the rear are two built-in cupboard beds, with a storage cupboard situated

Left: The deep-buttoned 'sick chair' stands in the nursery.

Right: The tow-seated chair dating from the seventeenth century stands in the attic.

This ebony art cabinet inlaid with copper comes from the doctor's room and contains shells and fragments of coral. Late seventeenth century.

Opposite: The doctor's room with its wax-headed inhabitant and a selection of impressive paintings.

between. These beds were very cleverly designed, as the fronts were hung with frills and curtains so that, when closed, the structure resembled additional windows. In this eminently practical room stand several exquisitely made ladder-back chairs, presumably from the earlier cabinets, and a somewhat out-of-place good rococo mirror.

The most absorbing rooms of this cabinet are situated on the ground floor and separated by a marble hall that is laid out similarly to that at The Hague. A pair of *blanc du chine* vases from the antique cabinets add interest to the area, and there is a heavily carved almost Chippendale-style seat, also from the earlier cabinets, on which originally sat a maid 'with a urinal in the hand'. A single, somewhat small-scale maid wearing a white cap is now the only occupant of a section of a merchant's home that was often used for business. The hall is given great effect because of the splendid lantern that cost 4 florins and which is reflected in the mirror of the door at the rear.

The somewhat mysterious study now referred to as that of the astronomer Ludemann, is completely masculine in effect and is hung with heavily framed paintings by Buttener, illustrating scenes from a doctor's life, including such subjects as a man painting with a brush between his toes. In a chair sits the

doctor, wearing a silk chamber-gown and indoor cap over his breeches and knee-boots. He has a wax head and hands that are particularly realistic and modelled in an open position. Ludemann, whose name is now associated with this chamber, was a well-known astrologer and quack doctor in Amsterdam, who began life as a shoemaker and was so successful among his patients, especially women of hysterical disposition, that when he died he left a large fortune. It is thought unlikely that Sara intended to represent this well known figure, though the room is obviously intended for a doctor, and there were originally two men and women engaged in conversation. The largest of the early cabinets contained a doctor's chamber, and the majority of the pieces in this section came from this model and are much more old-fashioned in style than the lighter mid-eighteenth-century furniture and plenishments that she commissioned herself. The *memento mori* of silver and crystal was an inevitable feature of a doctor's consulting-room; a medicine chest stands on the floor, and several books contain prescriptions for medicines, all underlining her intention to create another doctor's study. Beside the doctor, on a table, stands a tobacco-box, a bottle and a good games compendium, one of the smallest examples encountered, which contains cards and draughts-pieces. The high-backed chairs are silk upholstered and were once neatened with braid; a foot-warmer provided some additional comfort. On the white wall hang silver seals, and various curious items lie around, such as a small carved monkey and silver animals; on a black curiosity cabinet stand several Chinese pots. One of the most interesting items is an ivory tilt-top table painted in chinoiserie style and most probably the work of the turner Hilgert Laenssom. At the back of the chamber is a well-made wall arch with sliding doors which, when pushed aside, reveal a central chest made partly of metal painted to resemble wood, containing a selection of books, some of which feature cut-out prints dated 1745 and 1746. On one particularly large volume lies a silver compass and set-square. In various niches are coloured bottles, many of which came from the seventeenth-century cabinets, as well as a number of Chinese jars. This chamber, with its mellow tones and curiosity-type objects is useful in correctly illustrating a working doctor's room of the period that would only very rarely have survived in full size.

One of the main reception rooms, which in the nineteenth century was converted into a dining-room, is hung with red moiré and provided with a red-and-blue painted turkey carpet. Though somewhat sparsely furnished, this room is very elegant, with basic detail so precise that actual furniture was not much needed. Around the walls hang heavily framed portraits of the kings and queens of England, and in the centre of the room is a small tripod table with an embroidered top that was especially designed for card-playing and sewn by Sara herself. On a small side-table stand a number of silver-stoppered bottles in a silver basket, and on the sides of the chimneypiece, painted to resemble marble, hang silver brushes. The apartment's great focus of interest is the stupendous collection of silver, including two trays marked with the monograms of Sara and Jacob. This fine collection of silver, displayed on brackets, is revealed when the large doors at the rear are pushed back to reveal a cabinet-type area similar to that of the porcelain room in her other model. The pieces originated mainly in the earlier cabinets, but she continued to add items until the time of her death, and some dated 1769 were added later by her niece. On all the specially designed shelves stand coffee-pots, porringers, coolers, candlesticks and trays all contributing to a wonderfully rich effect, especially as all the shelf-supports are embellished with gilding. This arrangement was not a miniaturization of that effected in full size in Dutch houses, for though it was usual to display porcelain in this way, silver was kept in much smaller cabinets, so that obviously Sara was simply devising an interesting method of displaying the good collection of silver she had acquired at auction and later purchased and commissioned separately. In the room are four pieces marked 1743, five pieces 1745 and two pieces 1746. The notebook refers to two trays which she ordered from Gijsbert Sas, as well as a chandelier. One of the coffee-pots was made by Cornelis Coutrier, and two octagonal candlesticks were by Jan Bordwr. Arnoldus van Geffen, a noted

Above left: A card table whose embroidered top was the work of Sara Ploos van Amstel. It stands in the red moiré silver room. *Above right:* A superb cruet made by Arnoldus van Geffen and dated Amsterdam 1769. It stands in the silver room on a side table.

specialist maker of miniature silver, made several items, including a cruet set and a chocolate-pot. The great skill which the Dutch showed in the manufacture of miniature silver might have inspired other assemblers of cabinets to put especial emphasis on this feature, but it is only in the models arranged by Sara that we discover these collecting-areas that she obviously took such delight in equipping.

In the corner of the room containing the silver display is an especially made stand for oriental china, though this collection is of modest proportions as the majority was put into the Hague cabinet. The walnut chairs with loose seats are in Queen Anne style and look effective against the Smyrna carpet painted by Buttener, who was also responsible for most of the decoration of the room except for the painted ceiling by Jacob de Wit.

The domestic areas of her cabinet are contained in the lower section which is almost separate and forms part of the base. It can today be examined only by peering in through the lower windows that can be left in position when the main façade is removed. The plain stairs lead down in the centre, and on one

157

A collection of beautiful seventeenth-century glass that hangs in the kitchen.

Opposite: In the basement dining-room the lavatory door is open to show the basic toilet arrangements.

side is a door leading to a store-room where jars and pots are kept. To the left is a kitchen, very much a working rather than 'best' room and made in eighteenth-century style with a marble-effect floor. This room contains some 250 separate items, as all the cupboards and shelves are particularly well stocked. The kitchen, painted in brown and yellow, has the usual prestige cupboard at the rear filled with the pewter dishes that were purchased from the Widow Bronkhorst. In the foreground is a sink with well-made brass taps, and there is also a splendid pump with brass handles. The maid and a boy in livery who once stood here are lost, as is a bird on a spit, but otherwise the kitchen is very much as Sara intended. The large fireplace is decorated with a frill, and the room exudes a feeling of warmth because of the glow of the brass pots and the silver and pewter items. Two very unusual copper ovens stand near the fire, containing an upper and lower chamber. In the lower section were put hot coals so that food could be cooked in the enclosed area above. On the top of this cylindrical arrangement pots could be stood to heat. The main fire was heated by peat, and a chest for this substance also stands in the hearth. On a very delicately constructed hanging shelf is a group of exquisitely fine seventeenth-century glass and on a Delft rack are plates made in ivory by Hilgert Laurenssom which were painted to resemble china. Much of the copper and brass was made by J.ten Ham and the earthenware by the potter Cornelis Sluis; the ironwork was provided by Sara's nephew Theodorus

Ploos van Amstel. The kitchen is now occupied only by the household cat, which looks longingly at a mouse caught in a round cage trap.

The main dining-room is situated in this basement section, a position not thought suitable in the nineteenth century but now restored. The walls were painted in rococo style by Buttener, and in a large glass-fronted cabinet there is a good collection of ivory and blue-and-white porcelain that was mainly added in the nineteenth century. The table is laid with a good assortment of silver, and tall fluted glasses stand on a side-table. In a corner display-unit there is a further collection of the seventeenth-century blue-and-white glass that represents porcelain. It is obviously summer, and in the empty hearth stands a large dish for decoration. With a touch of completely Dutch basic functionalism, the lavatory is situated in a cupboard in the corner of the dining-room. It is in touches of realism such as this that the Haarlem model reflects daily life at the time so well. In other rooms, Sara sometimes imitated aspects of her own household, so that, for instance, in this house, as in her home on the Keizersgracht, the dining-room is situated next to the kitchen in the basement rather than in the *bel étage*, which was more common. Curiously, though the house at The Hague is frequently recorded in both guide-books and publications on toys, this model, one of the most carefully documented and historically important, is rarely mentioned in English and German books. The cabinet is also unusual in that it has the good fortune to possess its own inscription, in verse, that once hung in the lying-in room.

> Everything one sees on earth
> Is doll's stuff and nothing else.
> All that man finds,
> He plays with like a child.
> Ardently he loves for a short while
> What he throws away so easily thereafter.
> Thus man is, as one finds,
> Not only once but always a child.

Few houses of any period can boast such a revealing and timely comment, and something of the atmosphere of the verse, so typical of the eighteenth century, seems to pervade the whole construction.

It is fortunate that the considerable importance and value of this cabinet were always recognized by the family and that, despite its eventual sale at auction, it remained in Holland. In comparison, a few houses travelled far from their original settings as, being objects of interest, they were inherited by relatives who had left the country. The Gontard house, now at the Historical Museum at Frankfurt am Main, is believed to have gone to Germany in the mid-eighteenth century, and certainly the appearance of the cabinet supports this claim, as it is completely in the manner of those seen at the Rijksmuseum, Utrecht and The Hague, though made in a much cruder and more economical style, suggesting to some experts that it was reconstructed in the nineteenth century though incorporating the original rooms. The black lacquered structure stands to the conventional height of the cabinet houses so that a standing adult could not see over the top, and there were probably originally front-opening japanned wooden doors, long since replaced by a glass panel. The lacquering of the cabriole-legged cabinet, with its carved frieze, is not of a particularly high quality, and the gold lining of the exterior is more florid than might be immediately associated with a Dutch craftsman of the period, though the complete effect is completely in the manner of the models already mentioned. Some of the painting in the Sara Ploos van Amstel cabinets, for instance, is not particularly commendable, and it is likely that many other structures such as this, made with rather more economy, have been lost simply because they are not as immediately eye-catching with regard to craftsmanship.

The cabinet was originally given to Susanne Maria Gontard by a friend who lived in Holland, and it was obviously considered a family treasure, being passed down through the generations, so that by 1857 there had been six owners who all added pieces but had fortunately protected the structure. A certain Mrs Belli-Gontard eventually restored the model to what she believed was its original eighteenth-century appearance, though her knowledge was quite obviously based mainly on German interiors, as the rooms now appear

The scroll now hangs in the lying-in room of Sara Ploos van Amstel's house.

almost completely German and give a slight odd effect, especially as several are hung with the soft, sprigged doll's house paper seen in many small commercially made toy houses of the mid-nineteenth century. Perhaps to some extent this imposition of the hands of several generations humanizes the structure: it is no longer perfect, like the finest of the Dutch museum cabinets, but it is now much more in the nature of a child's plaything, despite its extravagant size.

Rather strangely for a Dutch house, the kitchen is placed upstairs, in *Dockenhaus* tradition, and it is completely German in appearance, with its

161

large canopied cooking-area decorated with rows of plates and tankards, all displayed for maximum effect against a large-patterned wallpaper much earlier than the others in the house and possibly original. The painted ceiling in reception room idiom suggests that this apartment was not originally intended as the kitchen and again indicates the number of changes to which the house has been subjected. A wooden doll, dating to around 1835, acts as a cook and sits surveying a wicker basket in which unplucked ducks lie ready for the table. Next door is a small room with what is believed to be a miniature fruit-press dominating the other furnishings. In the centre of the single bedroom stands a large black German stove with a wicker cradle placed near for warmth and supervised by a wax-headed nurse with the round face and bead-like eyes that denote an eighteenth-century origin. On a wall hangs a particularly fine silver water-stoop that would have been completely in character with a Dutch house of the period.

There is only one downstairs reception room, in which stand a group of dolls awaiting a meal at a round table. These dolls are again a mixture of the original and later additions, as there are eighteenth-century waxes in original costumes alongside *papier mâché* ladies of the 1820s wearing dress of vaguely eighteenth-century style. The dolls of *papier mâché* have the unvarnished rounded faces associated in particular with Sonneberg; over their moulded and painted hair they wear additional, but original, plaited wigs.

The hall is nicely laid out with a carved staircase and a large hanging lantern. A servant stands on the lower flight of stairs welcoming two much smaller-scale wax visitors. One cannot help but wonder whether the store-room was originally intended as some kind of garden, as there is a landscape painted on the section behind the gallery, and a coach and horses would seem to fit more happily into this section than the provisions with which it is now equipped. A door leads to this section from a landing on the stairs, which would again serve to support the theory that the storage-area was once a courtyard, as the doll inhabitants would have been unlikely to wish to survey their winter provisions from the elegant balcony. A section of paling divides what is now the storage-room in two, and a servant sits in perpetual guard over the sacks of dried pulse vegetables, breadbaskets, hams and the inevitable German sausages. Were it not for the fact that the exterior of this cabinet is somewhat Dutch in style, it would immediately be considered purely German, but its known pedigree, combined with its elegantly shaped construction, suggests that it should be dealt with in the context of its original fellows.

Another Dutch cabinet that exhibits the very considerable influence of a foreign country can now be seen at Dordrecht in the charming waterfront museum of Mr Simon van Gijn. This very simply constructed model came from the estate of Schaep en Burgh and was acquired by the museum in 1971. The interior is composed of three separate cases that were placed on top of one another to give a completely cabinet-like effect. On the top floor are a bedroom and sitting-room and on the middle floor a long drawing-room. In the basement is a kitchen and a storage-area. Of paramount importance in this unusual model are the dolls, which are of the typically British 'Queen Anne' type with characteristic fork-like hands. Some have very highly coloured cheeks and in construction are typical of many such figures found in British houses. Did the family perhaps purchase them in Britain, or were they possibly sold in a Dutch toyshop? Perhaps they originally came from a completely different setting and were re-used by this assembler. It is even possible that some enterprising toymaker from Britain set up in business in Holland. It is probable that their true origin will never be discovered, though no doubt there will be considerable speculation, as these British ladies seem so out of place in the very Dutch setting, though it should of course be remembered that silver, furniture and dress moved easily between the two countries because of their particularly close association, and perhaps the dolls formed part of this constant exchange of objects and fashions.

The cabinet has a curious atmosphere, with something of the mystery associated with Ann Sharp's Baby House, its simple construction being very reminiscent of that structure. On the ground floor is the typical Dutch kitchen with the walls papered and painted with small Delft tiles. The floor is also papered and then painted with black and white tiles. On the frilled mantelshelf, a row of good pewter plates is displayed, and on a corner rack are several brass skimmers. In a large cupboard stands a cream dinner-service very reminiscent of Leeds ware and possibly obtained at the same time as the wooden dolls; it is on a scale that is much too large for the model and is similar to that found in Ann Sharp's Baby House. On the floor lie the pattens that will keep the housekeeper's feet dry when she next visits the muddy marketplace. In one corner of the kitchen stands a wooden pump with a bucket. The housekeeper, wearing a printed frock in reds and blues with white lower sleeves and a stomacher, sits in a chair. She is a typical eighteenth-century wooden doll with unusually large black eyes. The maid wears an apron over a black dress and has a kerchief over her hair. In the adjoining store-room with the usual Dutch separating palings, there is an assortment of brass pans and buckets.

The impressive drawing-room spreads across the whole width of the cabinet and is remarkable for the range and quality of the very fine needlework and embroidery which are revealed. All the walls are hung with green silk that was especially embroidered in panels, with small motifs in the centre, the needlework all carried out in white silk. This detailed work gives the room an unusually complete appearance, as there are even especially worked borders of flowers around the door frames, a very difficult task, as even the slightest stretching of the basic silk during the working process would have meant that it would not fit neatly around the door. The wall

panels of silk were then completed with an edging of gilded moulding. At ceiling-level a mock dentilled cornice made of gilded cardboard was added to give an even richer effect. The furniture is equally fine and upholstered in the especially embroidered silk also used on the walls. On the chairs an even smaller border pattern was worked around all the edges, a wearisome if rewarding task, as there are four dining-chairs, two armchairs and a three-seater sofa. The cream silk curtains are edged with blue braid and also completed with an embroidered border, with further tucks, braid and embroidery added to the lower edge. The needlewoman concerned with the furnishing of this model obviously delighted in her work, as she also created extravagant pelmets cut at a deep angle so that they fell low on one side.

On a lacquer table stands a tea-equippage, including a caddy, all decorated with blue painting. In the corner of the chamber a kettle stands ready on an ornamental stand. Chinese porcelain vases on either side of the chimneypiece are displayed on tall *torchières*, though the interior is somewhat overwhelmed by a large, beautifully constructed walnut clock with ormolu mounts. All the furniture, including an unusual goldfish-bowl on a stand, is effective, and the room is also provided with a smoothly embroidered carpet. On the walls are small ivory pictures, and each doll is given a foot-warmer. On the elegant sofa sits a lady, with the panniers of her skirts spread wide. This is a particularly fine doll, and the wig is piled high and decorated with ribbons and net; her dress is made of pink silk edged with white lace, and white leather gloves and white silk shoes complete the ensemble. The gentleman wears his sword, and on the table in front of him lie several ivory pipes and a low candlestick with a handle, intended for the lighting of pipes; he is also provided with a silver tobacco-jar and a bowl in which the warm pipes can rest. This doll wears a lace-trimmed hat and a pink muslin coat trimmed with white lace over a simple white knee-length garment, suspiciously resembling night attire. A visiting lady sports a large black hat lined with grey silk and decorated with a grey bow. Her frock is made of a dark-brown and white striped fabric, and a white stomacher with an attached peplum is worn. The other gentleman wears a green jacket lined with white and a brown-edged waistcoat with black silk breeches and shoes of the same fabric with knitted socks. His pale face is effectively set off against a lace jabot.

In the once-separate top section of this model, there is a bedroom with a chintz-hung four-poster bed and a painted wooden chimneypiece decorated with painted swags; the carpet is worked in red and blue cross-stitch. A small wax-headed baby lies in a cradle covered with a counterpane of the same

A simply constructed eighteenth-century model made in three box-like sections. The drawing-room is remarkable for the quality of the needlework and embroidery. The walls are hung with silk.

In the bedroom, the baby lying in the cradle has a wax head and is typical of the dolls found in other Dutch cabinets.

fabric as the bed-hangings. This small doll is of the typical Dutch cabinet-house type, with small bead-like black eyes set in a very pale wax face. A maid, wearing a striped skirt and a neat white cap, is looking after the baby. Her jacket is made of sprigged cotton, and she wears a neat brown fichu. The baby is supplied with an arched basket, and among the other good miniatures is an oriental chamber-pot and a candleholder with an unusually long handle, somewhat resembling a frying-pan in form. A print-hung boudoir adjoins the lying-in room and is decorated with early nineteenth-century-style prints enlivened by a red-bordered paper spread along the top of each wall and down the sides. The chairs and footstool again have embroidered seats, and the lady sitting in the room wears a pale green ribbed striped silk open robe with a stomacher. Her white fabric shoes, with correctly made leather soles, are exquisite miniatures. She sits knitting, while a fine silver kettle boils on its stand. At the back of the apartment is a glass-panelled *bombé* cabinet with shell carving at the top, and there are also several pieces of the much-collected blue-and-white china.

This virtually unknown model at the museum of Mr Simon van Gijn has the dual interest of exhibiting particularly fine needlework and miniature costume as well as the curious group of British doll's house dolls. A similar use of a very cheap and simple construction must have seemed attractive to other, less affluent Dutch collectors, but they have probably failed to survive as they were not impressive items of furniture, making this piece especially fascinating as a specimen of a much less splendid type of house, relying for its effect mainly on skilful needlework and ingenious decoration.

A visit to the museum itself, on the New Harbour, is interesting, as it occupies an eighteenth-century patrician building, in the popular late Louis XIV style which was the home of a wealthy merchant family. This house, with its properly set out and traditionally blue-painted kitchen, together with the many collections which the various owners assembled, gives a very accurate impression of the type of Dutch home that would once have displayed the popular cabinet models.

FOUR

Eighteenth-Century Baby Houses in Britain and America

The development of the doll's house in eighteenth-century Britain closely reflects the order and stability of a society that is perhaps most perfectly mirrored in the controlled and splendid architecture that almost casually asserted Britain's worldwide importance. Ann Sharp's Baby House, created in the opening years of the century, suggests the confusion of thought that had been evident in the previous century, and in its rooms a portrait of a witch shares pride of place with prints of the Old Testament. An air of muddle and confusion, delightful in pure atmosphere, pervades the house, and the viewer is aware that people who inhabited such a setting would exhibit similar contradictory emotions in their personalities. The contrast between this rather primitive house and a later example based on the architecture of the period, such as that at Uppark, is complete. In the later model we see the absolute order and precise reasoning that underlies British decoration, building and thought in the eighteenth century, a discipline so strongly established that both architects and decorators worked to set orders of design.

Girls of the period were expected to be trained and educated for the eventual management of their own homes in a similarly controlled manner. There was no excuse for a badly run establishment, and even the richest woman was expected to participate in the basic organization of her household. It was not uncommon for gentlewomen to work with their servants in the dairy or kitchen, and there were frequent complaints in the Press regarding the difficulty of telling mistresses and servants apart, as the employees did not wear special uniforms and were often dressed in their mistresses' cast-offs. Even in dolls' houses, it is not always clear whether some of the more plainly garbed figures are family or servants. It was difficult for the mistress to set herself completely apart while she shared in wine-making, pickling, preserving and the preparation of medicine with her servants, and in the rooms of dolls' houses we see this relaxed mingling of the social classes that was to end in the nineteenth century, when servants were banished to basement kitchens and kept very firmly in their place.

Hannah Moore, writing in her strict authoritarian manner, set out the role of a lady in society. Her work held great appeal for the more rigid eighteenth-century parents, and we have to assume that the character of many young Georgian women was in some part moulded by her strictures set out in *Female Education*, written in 1799, which gave the girl little excuse for a casually managed home, no matter how rich or how superior a being she might consider herself.

> Economy, such as a woman of fortune is called on to practise, is not merely the petty detail of small daily expenses, the shabby curtailments and stinted parsimony of a little mind, operating on little concerns, but is the exercise of a sound judgement exerted in the comprehensive outline of order, of arrangement, of distribution, of regulations by which alone well-governed societies, great and small, submit. She who has the best regulated mind will, other things being equal, have the best regulated family . . . as in the visible works of Providence, that which goes on with such beautiful regularity is the result not of chance but design; so that management which seems the most easy is commonly the consequence of the best concerted plan.

The respected educationalist then proceeded to emphasize her belief that a sound household economy is simply sound understanding brought into action, calculation realized and the doctrine of proportion reduced to practice. This complete order was insisted upon in all spheres of a girl's daily life, from the clothes she wore to her lessons, and it is little wonder that the Englishwoman of the late eighteenth century was regarded not as some pretty ornament but as a partner in the running of country estates.

Despite woman's lack of political weight and her poor legal status during the eighteenth century, there was a curious basic divergence of aspiration between the sexes, made very clear in the pages of contemporary magazines. While females insisted on basic order and good sense, they were remarkably indulgent towards the excesses and foolishness of men, and we are left with the very strong impression that women aspired to standards far higher than would seem necessary for the general tone of society and were obviously working towards very real improvement. It was with obvious irritation that the writer of an 'Essay on the Education of Young Ladies', which appeared in the *Ladies' Magazine* for 1775, commented on the short-sightedness of men who considered their daughters of little importance. She attributed this foolishness 'in part to that evident levity and injudiciousness that appears in men when selecting objects for Hymeneal attachments, by their being more engaged in general by exterior and transient charms than by intrinsic and valuable ones. . . . Parents should consider that, though external graces enkindle affection, they are very unlikely to maintain it immutable and inviolate.' That such advice could have held any appeal for a young man ensnared by a shapely breast and sparkling eye is unlikely, but the woman's sound good sense is undeniable, and similar thinking was to underlie all facets of society. When studying household arrangements or the disposition of furniture in a room, we are constantly aware of the basic belief in rational thought, organization and foresight that was basic to the lifestyle of eighteenth-century Britain, a style that is mirrored perfectly in the finest of model houses.

There is virtually no evidence to suggest that dolls' houses were used as teaching-toys for the regulation of a household as they were in Germany at the time, though few nursemaids and mothers could have resisted suggestions and advice while the children played. Cheap houses were available throughout the century from toyshops, and many were also made by local craftsmen. In comparison with the number of dolls that were sold, the doll's house was a much more unusual toy, and one searches in vain through the pages of contemporary magazines and novels for interesting references. Presumably the writers were aware that dolls' houses were owned by so small a section of the public that their readers would not relate to them as they would to that much more universal toy, the doll. In general, the study of the eighteenth-century Baby House has therefore to be undertaken from observation of the models themselves rather than from written references. There are no known manufacturers' catalogues or price lists, no carefully documented firms, simply a few references on trade-cards of the period regarding the stocking of furniture for Baby Houses and occasionally to the selling of them, sometimes fully equipped. The manufacturers, the craftsmen, the decorators, all are unknown, and their work has now to be assessed purely on its quality rather than by attribution to any named source.

There had been some commercial manufacture of miniature furniture during the seventeenth century, though it is often difficult to be sure of the maker's intention. In 1666 Macaulay referred to the manufacture of miniature pieces in the Tunbridge area, in particular mentioning miniature tea-sets made of local yew-wood. Early references to British wooden toy furniture all seem to relate to this particular area, and Celia Fiennes, visiting Tunbridge Wells in 1697, describes 'shopps full of all sorts of toys, silver, china and all sorts of wooden ware'. She also commented that the craftsmen of the town were famous for the delicate wooden wares in white lignum vitae. These particular miniatures remained popular throughout the eighteenth century, being found in several Baby Houses, as the wood was believed to have medicinal qualities. There was also an established, if small, industry concerned with the manufacture of dolls in sizes small enough both for model houses and for use with miniature furniture. Both wood and wax were used, presumably in a manner similar to that used for small religious figures, where the body was frequently modelled to waist-level only and relied heavily on the costuming for effect.

The term 'Baby House' was in general use in both Britain and America during the eighteenth century and lingered, as an outdated expression, until the middle years of Victoria's reign. A bill relating to purchases for her children, and dated to 1846, mentions a certain Daniel Miller who supplied a 'Baby House with furnishings and figures', thus emphasizing the fact that the term was not strictly confined to the eighteenth century. The word 'baby' was in common use instead of the term 'doll', making the title 'Baby House' self-explanatory. Collectors have continued to make use of this eighteenth-century title, as it forms a useful distinction between these finely made houses that aroused the interest of adults and those of the nineteenth century that were intended purely as toys for small children. Despite the fact that houses of this early period have survived in some number, very few still retain their original contents, as many were passed down in families, each generation cheerfully adding to and replacing the furnishings and repapering and painting the structure. Many Baby Houses now in private collections are consequently left completely bare, refurnished with Victorian pieces or, the less desirable solution, filled with modern reproductions in eighteenth-century style. Although several dozen Baby Houses are known, there are only six that are almost completely original: Ann Sharp's, the Westbrook, Nostell, Uppark, and the Blackett and Tate houses. Of this list the last mentioned has suffered from nineteenth-century additions and redecoration, and the Blackett house has also lost much of its original furniture. The Westbrook Baby House and Ann Sharp's house are still in private ownership, but the remainder can be viewed either in museums or in houses owned by the National Trust.

In the contents of these six classic houses can be seen the eighteenth-century trend away from individual craftsman-made pieces to commercial toys, though obviously these were of the finest type, often intended as adult amusements. Included in Ann Sharp's house, for instance, there are expensive trinkets such as might have been brought back by a husband on a visit to London for his wife's curiosity cabinet, mixed with roughly made pieces that were obviously intended as playthings for children of very modest means. The standard of furnishing in the houses at Uppark and Nostell, made later in the century, is generally of a much higher quality, and the hand of a fine craftsman is felt to have worked on the highly finished interiors. Even so, in houses obviously of adult intention, a few genuine playthings are encountered, such as the alabaster tea-table and crockery at Uppark and the cheap wooden cradle at Nostell. In complete contrast to these simply made, inexpensive items are the good silver miniatures that were added, despite the fact that their scale often left much to be desired.

The history of English Baby Houses is made particularly fascinating because

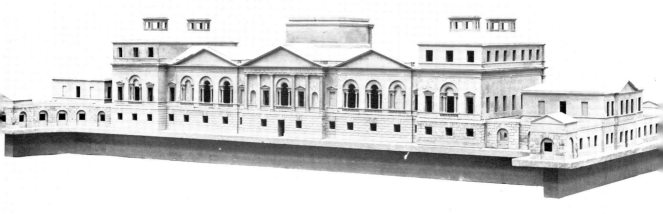

The true architect's model needed much greater detail than that found in the most complex of Baby Houses. Some idea of this workmanship is provided by this palace designed by William Kent (1685–1748).

of the large number of completely unsupported traditions that surround them. The great favourite is that a particular example was made as a model of an actual house by an architect, either for the approval of his patron or as a charming toy for the children. Other traditions link Baby Houses with great designers such as Vanbrugh, Chippendale and Adam. Though such traditions add great interest to a general discussion of the models, the actual evidence that supports them is extremely vague and based on hearsay and on charming but unsupported family tales. Despite the lack of substance, they continue to be repeated in the popular Press and even in museum and house guides, a further instance of how a pleasing but unsubstantiated story will continue to be retold despite a lack of positive fact. Perhaps everyone feels that objects of such great craftsmanship *should* have been made or at least designed by a Chippendale or Adam.

The cost of constructing a good model house was high, even in the eighteenth century, and the sheer value of the object was probably largely instrumental in ensuring survival. Nostell and Uppark were both made as fine models of houses of the period and provided with panelling, correctly made chimneypieces and architecturally correct façades. When a carpenter was employed to create a model of the Radcliffe Camera to the projected design of Nicholas Hawksmoor, he charged the substantial sum of £87 11 shillings for his work. The model was made of oak and constructed with precision, but it does not approach the wonders of the finest Baby Houses, which must have cost very much more. It is little wonder that the people who commissioned the models guarded them and treated them as respected items of furniture.

Nicholas Hawksmoor charged £87. 11s for this oak model of the Radcliffe Camera in 1734.

It seems very possible that the British affection for Baby Houses might have sprung from visiting Continental collections of miniatures while on the Grand Tours that were used to complete a young person's education. There is little evidence to suggest that the collecting craze ever reached Dutch proportions in Britain, however, and the prestige cabinet type of house was the conceit of a very limited number. In general, the Baby Houses were made as toys for children of quite wealthy parents, and it is examples of this lesser type that come into the hands of collectors today.

The collection of miniatures for a Baby House frequently continued to fascinate its owner into adult life, so that Ann Sharp, for instance, continued to add curious items to her cabinet for many years, and Lady Winn and her sister Miss Henshaw worked on the fine model at Nostell long after Lady Winn's marriage. This adult interest was encouraged by the fact that the sellers of adult *bijouterie* also stocked 'fine Babies and Baby Houses with all sorts of furniture', so that the woman who might have visited a shop to select a fan or a purse was often beguiled by some miniature household object. One of the most popular shops was that run by Mrs Chenevix, from whom Horace Walpole purchased his full-scale play-house, Strawberry Hill. Enraptured by his new and absorbing passion, he described the house in Twickenham as 'a little plaything house that I got out of Mrs Chenevix's shop, and it is the prettiest bauble you ever saw'. Another shop frequently mentioned as a source of amusing miniatures was 'Bellamy at the Green Parrot near Chancery Lane', where a good variety of English and Dutch toys could be purchased. The seriousness with which the assemblers and furnishers of dolls'

This eighteenth-century model gives rise to much controversy among experts regarding its original intention. Was it once part of a model house that could be disassembled, or was it once fitted onto some specific position in a cabinet? The contents are certainly of the finest quality, and the wooden dolls are very interesting as they represent part of a family. They stand some 15 inches high.

houses regarded their projects is emphasized for instance by a bill issued by Thomas Bromwich of the Golden Lyon, Ludgate Hill, which includes a charge for 'lining a Baby House with various fine papers'. Bromwich was a reputable dealer who supplied Walpole with many of the furnishings for Strawberry Hill and whose services were in this instance considered necessary for the effective decoration of a good model.

Unpeopled Baby Houses were obviously unsatisfactory, and the beautifully costumed dolls that have survived indicate a well-established craft, as so many exhibit striking similarities. The woodens in particular, with their flat dark-brown or black glass eyes and highly coloured cheeks are obviously of commercial manufacture, as they are found in so many sizes from almost child-high play-dolls to small figures from 5 to 10 or 11 inches, intended for miniature rooms or cabinets. They have simply turned bodies with sharply jutting hips that helped support wide skirts, and very crudely carved legs and

174

An exquisitely preserved pair of mid eighteenth-century woodens of German origin. The lady wears maroon and cream silk and the man a purple coat. Though the visible parts are well finished, the bodies are rough wood. They were almost certainly costumed for a small Baby House.

arms, jointed at shoulder and hip. In some cases the actual limbs are made in one piece with only minimal shaping, but other craftsmen attempted realism and rounded the calves and jointed the arms at the elbows also. The finer examples have fork-shaped hands that are well defined with correct separation between the fingers, but occasionally a similar effect was obtained by substituting card hands that were just cut in outline and coloured to match the face. In a few cases the arms were made of fabric, though it is difficult to be sure whether these were old substitutes because of damage or were perhaps used for greater realism, as they are frequently covered with the dress material.

The servants at Nostell and in Ann Sharp's house are, however, quite idiosyncratic, as the faces are both carved and painted in a manner that is much more realistic than the stylized rendering with which the collector is more familiar. Both of these houses originated in the north of England, and the possibility of a particular maker, perhaps in the York area, is interesting. These very realistic woodens are not found in larger sizes, being completely different from those seen in Europe, and were possibly made especially for Baby Houses, as their rustic, highly coloured faces are particularly at home in the large kitchens.

Wax was the traditional substance for the manufacture of noble families, as a very high degree of realism could be attained and the faces given proper characterization. Those found in eighteenth-century British houses are very much in the manner of the dolls encountered in the Dutch cabinets, though it is at present impossible to be sure of their origin. Wax modelling as a craft was practised widely in the eighteenth century, and as there was a great deal of movement between Britain and Holland, it is not unlikely that skills and techniques were common to the craftsmen of both countries. With their wax shoes and slightly turned heads, they can be found, in larger versions, at the Princess Dorothea's Court, suggesting that the manufacture of figures in the *genre* was even then well established, the makers of those in the Arnstadt town being, of course, recorded. Strangely, there is much more similarity between British and Continental wax modelling than there is between the wooden dolls made at the time, probably because wax was a much more fashionable medium with workers who moved from town to town. The influence of the Church craftsmen who created the Arnstadt figures has also to be considered, as techniques used for the making of crèche scenes or figures of saints were obviously occasionally applied to secular projects.

With such a wide variety of dolls to choose from, it is little wonder that the wealthy assemblers of Baby Houses selected the most beautiful figures for the drawing-rooms and bedrooms. The range of sizes offered was also wide, so that a large room or a complete house on a more modest scale could be occupied by figures in correct proportion. It would appear probable that, in general, the dolls were costumed after purchase by the ladies of the house, as I have been able to discern no similarities of dress, fabric or device on the examples I have handled. The standard of needlework is frequently high, and it is obvious that the better dolls were made intentionally as items to be studied by adults rather than to present to a child, who desired only a rapidly created effect. This fine needlework often extended into the hangings, carpets, bed-covers and linen, so that the Baby House stood testament to hours of painstaking, if enjoyable effort. After the lavishing of such patient care, it was inevitable that the contents should be protected from harm, usually by some type of lock, though all kinds of ingenious methods were used, from the straightforward cupboard-door-type fitting to ornamental drop bolts. Several houses have a central panel at the front that fits tightly against its neighbours and can be pegged in position. Others have sections that lock individually, so that particular rooms could be protected. Very basic houses of obvious play intention frequently have no means of secure fastening, so that the presence of a lock often indicates a house of some original interest. Often, with the original contents dispersed, a locking house is of only minimal interest, as some are simply cupboards with dividers across the shelves. The presence of carrying-handles was also once thought to indicate a quality house, but the examination of a number of eighteenth-century models proves that little relevance can be attached to them: sometimes quite beautiful brass handles are found on crudely made structures, while another finely finished house has none. In fact, their presence often seems a completely random addition, as very heavy houses that might seem to require handles are often without, while cheap versions, possibly because the carpenter just happened to have an old drawer with fine handles lying around, were embellished with splendid hand-made carriers.

Far better, as guides to age and quality, are fine miniature locks and doorknobs on the interior, correctly carved chimneypieces, detailed chair rails, cornicing and skirtings all indicating the work of a good craftsman creating a correctly equipped house of his period. Exterior quality is usually made obvious by a lavish use of specially made mouldings and well-seasoned timber, in combination with such details as opening doors and sash windows that can be lowered. When the original stand has survived, this will also be some indication of quality, as some, such as that on the Westbrook Baby House, are really made to the standard of fine pieces of furniture.

It seems likely that the assemblers of curiosity cabinets and Baby Houses, in imitation of a Continental fashion, also obtained some of the finest pieces from Holland, as there was a very thriving import of Dutch furniture, particularly during William III's reign (1688–1702), and miniatures were most probably included. Some of the finest pieces in the important Baby Houses were almost certainly made to order for specific positions, but children and less affluent furnishers obtained items from the wood-turners, who often ran a profitable sideline in the construction of trinkets and toys. Despite the great skill of the craftsmen, there are no attributable items, and we are made very much aware of the anonymity of these people, who often worked in small groups away from the main showrooms. Early American furniture was made by craftsmen such as Elfe Thomas who worked in Charleston, South Carolina, from 1751 to 1771 and who employed many Negro slaves who were highly trained craftsmen. Various London sellers are also known through their trade-cards, such as Gough, who worked at Wharton's Court in 1772 and who created 'mahogany toys such as chairs, buroes, commodes, basin-stands, looking-glasses, chests of drawers', and Willerton & Roberts who advertised in 1768 as 'turners to their Royal Highness ye Duke of Gloster . . . and toymakers to his Royal Highness ye Prince of Wales'. John Marshall in the 1770s was also offering 'toy looking-glasses in oval, square and ornamental frames' that could be finished in purple and gold, white, or green and white.

177

Warmly coloured mahogany of the early type was used at the beginning of the century for miniature items, but this was steadily replaced by the more easily obtained Spanish mahogany that is much darker and has a slight grain. This was in very widespread use by 1730 and was augmented in the second half of the century by Honduras mahogany or baywood, which faded to a much lighter shade. These eighteenth-century mahogany items can be differentiated easily from the red nineteenth-century mahoganies that were sometimes made in eighteenth-century styles. Walnut was an expensive wood, and even in miniature pieces, made at the end of the century, it was often veneered. The finest pieces were made of satinwood, which reached its height of popularity in the 1760s, though the majority of customers were well content with cheap pine that was frequently painted or lacquered. In America, the main woods were ash, oak, elm, maple, walnut and red cedar, though, again, pine was the cheapest and most frequently used. The main areas of production were western Pennsylvania, the Connecticut Valley and Philadelphia, though there were obviously many joiners and furniture-makers in towns such as Boston and New York.

The particularly fine surface of the early miniature pieces was achieved by long continuous rubbing with oil and tripoli powder, though less costly furnishings were treated with linseed oil and beeswax. While it is romantic to consider that all these pieces were hand-made, it should be remembered that mechanical drills and saws were used in the seventeenth century and that Samuel Bentham set up his first factory for the manufacture of moulding, rebating, grooving and sawing machines in 1791. Fortunately, the scale of the smallest pieces made it uneconomical to use mechanical equipment, so that doll's house furniture frequently continued to be made by hand when full-sized items were mechanized.

It is highly probable that much of the furniture and wooden equipment for British Baby Houses originated in the Tunbridge area. In 1776 Benge Burr, in his *History of Tunbridge Wells* commented on the number of people employed in the manufacture of amusing woodwork. Holly was the most popular material as it 'furnishes a prodigious variety of the prettiest ornamental inlays that can be imagined'. Cherry, plum, sycamore and yew were also used for these toy items, which were mainly of the turned type. A few finer pieces involved inlay and cabinet work, but in general eighteenth-century Tunbridge ware was quite different from the colourful inlays that we associate with the area in the nineteenth century. The Tunbridge wares were sold by toyshops all over Britain, while other craftsmen, trained in the area, set up their own establishments. In London, at the 'Elephant and Coffee Mill in Crooked Lane' between 1776 and 1793 worked 'John Alexander Ivory and Hardwood Turner' who sold 'Tunbridge toys'. Another turner, Gerard Crawly, worked at Cornhill and advertised 'Tunbridge and other Turnery Wares'. That the turners worked not only in wood but also in ivory and bone

Some idea of the fine quality of eighteenth-century British carving is provided by these elegant chairs from a bedroom in the Nostell Priory Baby House.

A pair of Tunbridge ware tables showing the characteristic inlaid decoration.

is therefore very evident. There is a great temptation to attribute many items of this type found in British houses to a German source, but these traders' cards make it obvious that a substantial quantity was made in Britain at the time by craftsmen such as Thomas Jaques of Leather Lane who, in 1790, was making 'Ivory, Hardwoods, bone and Tunbridge ware'. A large number of makers remained in the Tunbridge area, one of the oldest families, named Wise, working from 1685 to 1899. Though much of the woodwork was finished by polishing, there were other techniques, all of which are sometimes encountered in Baby Houses, such as painted scenes on dark backgrounds, red and black lacquer and even a painted tortoiseshell effect. Firms such as Fenner & Nye, Jordan and Barton & Burrows all contributed to the creation of a variety of pieces, such as the lignum vitae urns and cellarettes with their lavish stock of ivory miniatures that are found in the greatest houses, such as that owned by Ann Sharp.

Princess Anne, later to become Queen, thoughtfully presented her goddaughter Ann Sharp with a Baby House that was preserved with great care because of its royal connexion and which now survives as the earliest recorded British doll's house. Ann Sharp was born in 1691, one of the fourteen children of John, Archbishop of York – the high mortality rate of the period is chillingly illustrated by the fact that only four of these children survived their parents. It is paradoxical that this crudely made, box-like house with its very basic furniture should be the only model that can be positively associated with the monarch whose name is so often used in conjunction with any well-made house in the style sloppily termed 'Queen Anne'.

The first impression of this house is immediately reminiscent of the Nuremberg cabinets, as the basic construction exhibits nothing of the skilled carpentry associated with the better Baby Houses: the box-like rooms have no skirting-boards or picture-rails, and the cornicing is of the most basic type. The chimneypieces were utilized from sections of cheap picture-moulding, some being positioned on the back walls and others in corners. The firebaskets also show casual improvisation, as they are made with backs of playing-cards and roughly cut tin bars. The model stands 5 feet 10 inches high, so that an adult cannot see over the top, and this size also reminds the viewer of the German models. The rooms themselves are also deep and dark, and as it is unlikely that this was the only house made at the time, it seems possible that very early houses were constructed in a similar way in both Britain and Germany.

The survival of the house from Ann's childhood is due largely to the fact that she retained her interest long after her marriage, at the age of twenty-one, to Heneage Dering, Dean of Ripon. Its connexion with Queen Anne could not be forgotten, as her portrait, painted on the back of a playing-card, hangs in the house, a constant reminder of the royal origin. Generations of the family have treasured the house, and it is now seen surrounded by the metal

This contemporary portrait of Ann Sharp attributed to J. Richardson now hangs in the same room as her Baby House.

and plastic toys of the new generation but overlooked by a portrait of Ann Sharp attributed to Jonathan Richardson. Though she was a lady of substance, her claim to fame rests only on this portrait and her Baby House, as she appears, according to family papers, to have led an uneventful life. Like many women of the period she took her housekeeping seriously and wrote down several of her favourite recipes for use by her family and servants.

Her Baby House was one of the few that were highly regarded in the nineteenth century, and one of the earliest published descriptions appeared in an issue of *Aunt Judy's Magazine* in 1870. Just after the First World War, the *Connoisseur* found the house worthy of mention, publishing two articles by Mrs Willoughby Hodgson that were particularly helpful with regard to the dating of the miniature silver. Since that time the model has stood as the starting-point for any investigation of the Baby House, as it contrasts so interestingly with the more sophisticated versions.

A particularly fine example of the alabaster sets that are found in different sizes and designs in several early European houses.

Opposite: In the dismal atmosphere of an upper room in Ann Sharp's Baby House hangs a portrait of Mother Shipton, the Yorkshire witch.

In atmosphere, its rooms are strangely disturbing, and somehow the effect is given of interiors far earlier than those at Nuremberg. This misleading impression is created partly by the rustic simplicity of the construction and some of the furniture but is emphasized by particular scenes, such as that in an upstairs parlour or boudoir, where a large wax-relief portrait of Mother Shipton, the Yorkshire witch, dominates the gloomy setting. Mother Shipton was born in 1486 and made many prophecies concerning figures such as Cardinal Wolsey. She was greatly feared, and her influence in the area was to be felt as late as 1881. Her face, in the wax portrait, was once coloured but has now faded in an eerie manner, and the short gipsy pipe which she anachronistically smokes, in combination with the large scale of the picture, overwhelms the room. The effect is heightened by what at first appears to be a large witch-ball hanging from the ceiling by a turned walnut holder. That on closer inspection the 'witch-ball' is seen to be merely an adult toy of the period, in the form of an intricately carved cedar or limewood chandelier with sconces for eighteen candles, hardly detracts from that first impression of evil pervading the room. The apartment was obviously intended as the boudoir for the mistress, and the pet monkey sitting on a chair is typical of the period, as they were popular amusements. In an arched cupboard stands a wire birdcage whose spider-like outline adds to the air of mystery. William Rochett, 'Ye heir', stands uneasily in this gloomy room waiting for his mother, with whom he will take tea at a low alabaster table with matching tea-bowls and saucers painted with a leaf-like decoration. These sets are found in a wide variety of sizes all over Europe and were obviously very popular gifts. The

183

large brass candle-sconces that originally lit the room are also commercially made toy pieces of interest to both adults and children of the time.

Small dolls, such as William Rochett, were supplied in great number and variety by Ann Sharp, who carefully pinned the names of most of the characters to their costumes and consequently created a unique model, as in no other early house do we know exactly who the dolls were intended to represent. The boy doll who stands in the room dominated by Mother Shipton is among the most interesting, as his head is very unusual for the period, being modelled with an open-closed mouth with a slightly protruding tongue. His eyes are blue and quite realistic, creating an interesting divergence from the majority of play-dolls of the period, which have dark, expressionless eyes. The shoulder-head is made of poured wax, and the hands, of the same material, are modelled to the wrist only. The feet are constructed in a similar way; only from the ankle down was wax used. William was costumed in a jacket, waistcoat and trousers of pale blue silk with moulded red shoes with buckles. He wears a lambswool wig and a large silk hat and appears completely unaffected by the curious atmosphere of his mother's room.

The younger children are to be found in the adjoining nursery where 'Fanny Lang' (or Long), 'Ye child's maid', presides. This doll, in complete contrast, is made of carved and painted wood with simply painted eyes and bright red lips. The head is of the finest quality for the type, as it is carved in real detail, which contrasts strangely with her arms, which are simply cut in outline from thin card. She wears a robe of sprigged linen, whose skirt is lined with a playing-card, and a sensible apron. She looks after a small wax child costumed in pale saffron. This child doll is modelled to the waist only, and in one piece, so that the head, arms and torso are made of wax, and the face has painted features. The half figure is mounted on a skirt that is stiffly lined with card to make it stand safely. This construction is also seen in a few figures in the early German cabinets and was an obvious solution at a time when a woman's legs and feet were rarely seen. The oak cradle, dominating the nursery, is well made and ornamented with an ivory fret border. The original curtains are still in place in the hood, and inside is a very roughly shaped wooden baby wearing a frilled cap and more than adequately supplied with warm coverings. Its food is contained in a silver saucepan that stands on a walnut stool. The apartment is given importance by the splendid four-poster bed, with its lined green silk curtains that are exquisitely embroidered on the borders with pink and dark green. All the bed-hangings are in fact fine miniature pieces of English embroidery of the period and made with correct detail, rather than (as is often the case) being odd lengths of fabric suitable for utilization. Even the inside of the canopy is embroidered with a formal design, though it could only rarely be seen, and the curtains, two to each side, run on rings from brass rods. The headboard is attractively arched and is set against the flower-embroidered, formal back hanging. Great attention was often

The card house that was made after 1750 for Ann Sharp's Baby House and which now stands in the 'attic' room.

given to this part of a bed, as its great height was so dominant. William Kent is particularly associated with some of the finest designs of this type, as at Houghton Hall in Norfolk, just a few miles away from Ann Sharp's Baby House.

The most important bed was placed in the nursery or lying-in room, as it was there that a mother would receive her guests after the birth of her child. In this Sharp house, it seems clear that the room became the nursery after the mother returned to her own bedchamber, though in other cases its use was specific. In this room, the children were supplied with a model doll's house of their own, constructed from playing-cards. Its style and furniture suggest that it was added by Ann Sharp many years after she had ceased playing with the house as a girl's toy.

A Baby House doll's house is a concept that appeals greatly to the modern collector, as they are seen in so many reconstructions, though they were in fact extremely rare in antique examples. This structure, though now bent out of shape, is extremely interesting as it still contains the original furnishings, including some roughly painted pictures of country houses, one of which is believed to represent Bishopthorpe, the home of the Archbishop of York. Several pieces of furniture, in the whimsical Gothick taste, give a useful indication of period, particularly the drawing-room long-case clock suggesting a date after 1750. The painted cardboard furniture includes a four-poster bed with silk hangings sewn in place, while in the kitchen the dresser has plates that are painted on the shelves. The inside walls of the house are green, and the drawing-room carpet and the brick floor of the kitchen are also painted. A large medieval-style fireplace in the kitchen has a complex hanging device attached to which hangs a pathetically small kettle. The complete effect of this very miniature Baby House is charming, as it reflects the mixture of traditional and Gothick furnishings that were seen in so many fashionable houses of the time and also serves to indicate the length of time in which Ann Sharp continued to add interesting items to her cabinet.

The remaining bedroom belongs to 'Lady Rochett', the mistress of the plainly dressed maid with a wooden head, who stands in front of a bed hung with striped pink satin and decorated with braid and fringe. There is a simple lace-draped toilet-table with its pin-cushion, such as is almost invariably found in houses of Dutch, German or English origin. On another table, several small ivory boxes holding miniature brushes are set out. These beauty-aids bear a suspicious resemblance to scrubbing-brushes and were probably originally from some kind of kitchen set. A face-screen made of cut-out figures glued to card is effective and reminiscent of so much work in this manner at Mon Plaisir.

In the drawing-room beneath, overlooked by the portrait of Queen Anne, sits the family under the eye of the decidedly cross-faced 'Lady Jemima Johnson', an elderly lady whose head is made of cleverly carved wood. This doll is also of the half-figure structure and has arms of card. Her wig is made of human hair, and she wears a lace trimmed cap; at her breast a flower droops. Another *grande dame*, constructed in an identical manner, is dressed in a faded blue silk open robe that looks quite plain beside Lord Rochett's costume of pale rose silk, trimmed with now tarnished silver lace. In order to represent his shapely legs correctly, they were made of card. His head was also carved, and a bag wig made of wool adds to the convincing effect. The drawing-room was given added richness by the splendid gilded wallpaper that is marked with a barely decipherable 'AMC P S c m', probably an excise mark and indicating that the paper was hung after 1714, when such marking became law. Over the chimneypiece hangs a very worn-looking glass, and the remaining furniture is of the most basic type. Of much greater interest are the lignum vitae items that are placed in the main hall that is alongside.

This central room, into which the roughly made staircase leads, is intended

The drawing-room of Ann Sharp's cabinet was hung with a richly gilded paper that still carries its excise mark. The dolls have heads of both wax and wood.

to represent the old Great Hall where both servants and employers ate, as it was of large proportions and usually the main chamber. Here, with disregard for scale, this is the same size as the lesser rooms. Actual eating with the servants had gone out of fashion long before this model was constructed, but the central room was soon adapted as a more private dining-room, or sometimes used by the servants. The main table is of a size that was suitable only for the main family, while the remainder of the furniture is unexceptional and was added much later than Ann's childhood. The floor is papered and painted to resemble marble tiles, with a compass-type motif in the centre. A particularly good corner cupboard is painted in red and gold to imitate the popular lacquered furniture of the period, and there is a similarly made clock in another room. These are of interest as they are so obviously toy Baby House furnishings made quite crudely and not even well sanded. The clock is the better and has an embossed, gilded face and hands that move as one, a typical device of toy pieces throughout the ages. On the face we discover the name 'Beesley', who is recorded as having worked in Dean Street in 1725 and who quite possibly made some toys as a sideline to his main craft. Another very obviously commercial piece is a small brown table decorated with a painting of a young woman's meeting with a soldier. These pieces still carry the original prices, and a similarly made red lacquer table cost 5 shillings 5 pence, a substantial price for so rudimentary an item with virtually no work on the parts not immediately visible.

The lignum vitae urns in the Great Hall were even more expensive, the cutlery-box for instance being marked 20 shillings 9 pence, which must have formed quite a substantial gift for a lady. The cellarette, with its bottles of turned wood with ivory stoppers, a large cruet with ivory detail and the round cutlery-box are so similar in construction that it is fairly obvious that they came from the same source; they indicate a very positive taste for miniatures among the British as well as the Europeans. Of superb craftsmanship is an ivory-embellished urn filled with a vast assortment of tiny ivory and lignum vitae cooking-utensils, cutlery and crockery in such astonishing variety that one wonders how they were all safely accommodated in the one container. It must have made a delightful gift, rather in the manner of the *petit ménage* so often referred to among French princely gifts.

The dining-table is attended by 'Roger ye Butler', an interesting figure as the head is carved with a beard. On the table we find a good set of creamware plates with the characteristic Leeds feather edging, together with a serving-plate from another set, as the borders do not match. A large creamware dish holds moulded oysters in shells. This piece is of a much heavier body than the plates and would not usually be described as Leeds, though the visual similarity is great. Another plate has a good pierced-work edge and probably once held moulded and coloured wax food that included the inevitable boar's head. This Leeds service, dating to around 1760, is augmented with turned wooden plates and a fine assortment of glass, including a quite spectacular delicate yellow and clear glass goblet with a spiral twist in the stem. The amber glass candlestick with its white candle with a red flame, the delicate milk-glass spoons and flasks and the blue and purple pieces, popularly ascribed to the Bristol area, all contribute to the air of richness.

A cook, whose wooden face is carved with some realism, presides over a kitchen with built-in shelves along one side and a simple seat in the corner. The cook wears a frock with a pink and brown printed leaf pattern that is again supported on a card base, though in this case a black and white striped petticoat is worn under the ornamental pink silk that shows beneath the open robe. This very well-made outfit is largely hidden by the apron but serves to underline the fact that in Britain there was no great distinction of costume between menials and the ladies of the house – a fact that many historians suggest was largely instrumental in avoiding the class-hatred that engendered revolution in other countries.

In the large kitchen fireplace is a mock inglenook with two seats, though the effect is spoiled by the later book end-papers that were glued on because they resembled marble. Scale was completely abandoned in this room: the fire-tongs tower halfway up a wall, and the bellows, of red lacquer, are of a size to have daunted the small cook. From the ceiling is suspended a pair of hanging scales, and in front of the fire stands a fine miniature revolving plate-warmer, stacked with creamware plates. The busy toy ivory- and bone-turners supplied several amusing miniatures, such as a mop with a good bone handle and an ivory axe and meat-hammer. Some of the cooking obviously takes place in the scullery, beneath the kitchen, where a pig roasts on a tin spit and a pudding boils in a pot. This room was of doubtful intention but now contains a charming wheeled horse with a coat of ruched linen and a rocking wooden toy of a man standing on a pair of galloping horses. Next door is a servants' hall, in which a footman, wearing a red woollen coat, stands near a table on which lies a pack of cards. This man's body differs from that of the other inhabitants, as his limbs are made by cutting a rough outline from flat, stick-like pieces, though the head is well shaped. The playing-cards in the servants' hall were sold by the Grotto Toy Shop in St Paul's Churchyard and cost one shilling. The shop offered to engrave and print visiting-cards and sold a good selection of children's toys. From the same supplier could be obtained sets such as 'The Impenetrable Secret', 'Cries of London' and 'The Emblems of Love', though we are not informed whether these were also in miniature. On the back wall a huntsman was painted, again reminding the viewer of the decoration of the Nuremberg houses. The furnishing of the hall is very simple, but there is a large pair of tin candlesticks to provide illumination.

'Mrs Hannah ye housekeeper', has her much more comfortable apartment in the room off the hall. There is a four-poster bed, and a large-scale toilet glass does duty, on the floor, as a dressing-table. The housekeeper is interesting, as her eyes are painted in a downward-slanting position. The arms and legs are of the straight wooden type, and a red flannel petticoat is worn. The eighteenth-century housekeeper was a highly respected person, as she was usually left in complete charge of the home when the family was away, and her status is suggested by the furnishings of her room.

Ann Sharp's house itself, made of tongued and grooved pine boards and with crudely panelled sides, is completely in the cabinet idiom and has a special shelf at the top that is intended purely for display. At this level is arranged a miscellany of items that either fascinated Ann herself or were later thought suitable and which include prints, children's toys, a pair of embroidered shoes, straw-work boxes, an ivory spinning-wheel and a tiny model theatre. Records in connexion with the house suggest that there was never a conventional façade but merely glazed doors, so that the model was truly of cabinet intention. It seems unlikely that the house was unique, and it would be fascinating to discover any other very early British models in the Continental manner.

Like many of the Dutch houses, the Sharp Baby House contains some fine miniature silver, such as a pair of candlesticks dated 1703, a tankard dated 1717 and a beautiful pair of candle-snuffers on a tray marked 1686. One coffee-pot is marked with the maker's initials 'MD' and a teapot 'AC'. Items of popular shellwork, small oriental vases and the wealth of ivory and lignum vitae all suggest that many friends supplied extravagant and amusing gifts for the cabinet.

I first examined the contents of Ann Sharp's house when they were packed away in boxes in a museum store-room, with the huge husk standing forlornly in another area, so that it was highly rewarding to revisit the model when it was returned to its own family and the contents re-assembled. Several items that can be seen in very early photographs of the house seem to have disappeared over the years, but it is delightful to see this shambling single example of late seventeenth-century Baby House set out as its original owner intended, proving that the collection of miniatures by adults was not a purely European pastime.

It is difficult to imagine the cabinet ever standing in the muddled interior of a nursery, as it fits more suitably in the imagination on a landing or even in a large central hall. Of purely nursery intention are the unusual model houses apparently made by 'Mr Joy' expressly as children's storage-cupboards and containing shelves, drawers and hanging-space. A more delightful method of nursery storage can hardly be imagined. One of the houses, standing 5 feet 4 inches high, bears the inscription 'Edmund Joy 1709' and was illustrated in Vivien Greene's *English Dolls' Houses* written in 1955. I visited what appeared to be the same model in the mid 1960s, though it had by then passed into ownership other than that attributed in *English Dolls' Houses*. The new owners seemed convinced that either the house itself or the room it was displayed in was haunted, as odd noises were heard and their dog reacted strangely to the atmosphere of the dark room dominated by the curious structure, part doll's house, part nursery cupboard.

Another house, apparently made by the same hands, now stands in the cool, rational environment of the Bethnal Green Museum and holds little menace, being purely a delightful and useful toy. This model has a lantern in the roof and exhibits both strong similarities and differences, indicating that the maker was quite happy to adapt his design, though the basic size was similar, the museum house measuring 6 feet 6 inches to the lantern top. These cupboard storage houses are extremely interesting, as they were presumably made for very favoured children who could hang their clothes in the centre section and keep their books and small treasures in the drawers, and the thought that Baby Houses might also have been created by this maker is extremely attractive. The Bethnal Green exhibit has three dormer windows in the roof and a central lantern, while that illustrated in Vivien Greene's book has a roughly turned balustrade on the roof and the remains of a cupola. The doors are very similar, with arched pediments and three semicircular steps leading up. The museum version has the strange arrangement of a window that disappears behind the mouldings of the door. On the inside the windows are papered over, presumably to represent curtains, and the model stands on a base that contains a long drawer. The small, fitted drawers on the right-hand side of the interior are japanned, in an amateurish representation of fashionable chinoiserie. The houses both carry the same lock guards, though that in the museum seems in better general condition. I once felt that the name, painted on the back in large letters was that of the original owner, but the appearance of two models signed in a similar way makes it more likely that in fact Mr Joy was actually the maker who used the same basic mouldings, locks and door furniture on his work and painted the models in a rich brownish red to imitate brick. The one exterior shows a two-storey house with attics, while the other has three main floors, but they are completely at one in general effect. Were it not for the hanging-space in the centre which appears designed for child-length clothes, these houses might well have been extravagant curiosity cabinets for adults, in which could be stored the shells, flowers and other minutiae that so fascinated eighteenth-century society. We can only conclude that their original place was most probably in the nursery, where they were used for the inculcation of neat and tidy habits, a further indication of how good order and discipline were instilled at the earliest time.

Perhaps this was due to the influence of Locke, who, in *Some Thoughts Concerning Education*, answered the questions of parents of the late seventeenth century who had found themselves without any good advice on how to educate and breed their children. His ideas were basically very sound, and he established a foundation of educational theory that was to be followed, in somewhat modified form, by many of the more advanced families in Europe. Toys, which children should own in good number, should 'be in the custody of their tutors or somebody else, whereof the child should have in his power but one at once and should not be suffered to have another but when he restored that', a rule that would teach them to be careful of not losing or spoiling the things they have, 'whereas plenty and variety in their own keeping, makes them wanton and careless and teaches them from the beginning to be squanderers and wasters'.

Many of the children of nobles and men of importance were showered with expensive playthings by people paying court to their parents, such as the Baby House that was given to Elizabeth Westbrook by the tradesmen of the Isle of Dogs when her father moved from the area. This comparatively small model,

Very elegant Georgian-style houses in the Baby House manner continued to be made in the early nineteenth century, as in this example, 'May 1830'. The back opens in three sections to reveal one upper and two lower rooms.

Opposite above: A heavily constructed Baby House (*circa* 1730) with a painted blind storey. The house opens at each side and can be locked. The opening front door has two brass plaques. One is illegible, but the other reads 'Mackie'.

Opposite: The first-floor parlour of the Mackie Baby House showing the heavy, almost crude finish that is also found in Ann Sharp's house. This was almost certainly a child's toy.

still in private ownership, has a beautifully proportioned arched, integral stand, and the complete house is made of polished oak, which gives a particularly mellow effect. As in many early dolls' houses, the central section is fixed, and the side fronts open to reveal the main rooms, which contain a rich variety of the original fittings including, as in the Sharp house, several instances of the crafts of the period, such as a rolled-paperwork picture frame and a good walnut drop-leaf table. In addition, there is a correctly costumed family of wooden dolls and a magnificent group of silver miniatures, mainly of London origin. Such gifts were frowned upon by Locke, as he felt that they served only to confuse and unsettle a child's mind, teaching him or her 'pride, vanity, covetousness, almost before they can speak'. He had known children so distracted by the number and variety of their toys that they tired their minds each day in looking them over. One boy was 'so accustomed to abundance that he never thought he had enough but was always asking "What more? What more? What new things shall I have?" A good introduction to moderate desires and the ready way to make a contented, happy man!'

Locke's complaints regarding the abundance of toys in richer households are illuminating, as a picture of the seventeenth- and early eighteenth-century child owning very few toys is often presented. His book developed from a series of private letters addressed to his friend Edward Clarke of Chipley, a man of means but no rich prince, yet the educationalist obviously expects an abundance of extravagant toys to be commonplace in his friend's home. He suggests, however, that they should be avoided, as 'a smooth pebble, a piece of paper, the mother's bunch of keys' will divert a small child just as much as the expensive and curious toys that could be obtained from the shops and were soon 'put out of order and broken'. He felt that it was far more useful to encourage children to make things for themselves, 'whereby they will be taught moderation in their desires, application, industry, thought and contrivance'. Both the play and the diversions of children were to be directed towards good, useful habits 'or else they will introduce ill ones. Whatever they do leaves some impression at that tender age and from thence they receive a tendency to good or evil; and whatever hath such an influence ought not to be neglected.'

With such strictures in mind, parents encouraged their young to help in the dressing of dolls and in the making of items for their Baby Houses, which must often, when first purchased, have resembled nothing more than a simple box. Heslington Hall, now at the Castle Museum, York, is strongly reminiscent of the simple model owned by Ann Sharp, as the arrangement of the rooms is similar, and we are shown a model obviously originally intended for play rather than as an exhibit for adults. That Ann Sharp continued to interest herself in the doll's house long after her childhood makes it now resemble a typical cabinet of the period, whereas the house at York stayed within the

The interior of the Yarburgh Baby House still retains some good detail, such as the fireplaces and much of the kitchen equipment. On the top floor are the original hand-blocked wallpapers.

The Yarburgh Baby House, made *circa* 1715 for the children who lived at Heslington Hall. Each room has its own opening front. The front door is glazed. The quality of the house is much better in a photograph than when actually examined.

196

nursery environment for well over a century.

In construction, Heslington Hall is basically a divided box with only a minimal attempt at embellishment and architectural detail. It provides yet another example of the way in which early British houses differed from those of much more complex structure in Europe. Here is no adult preoccupation but a gloriously robust toy designed to withstand years of rough-and-tumble in the nursery.

The Baby House was originally made around 1715 for the Yarburgh children, who lived at Heslington Hall, by a local furniture-maker or a worker on the estate. It has a flat roof, and each room has its own opening door, rather in the manner of the much more splendid model at Uppark, each fastening with a simple latch. The general effect is heavy and brooding, which underlines its affinity with the Sharp house, but this model has more attempted realism, as there are glazed windows made with correct, if somewhat large-scale mouldings. The front door is also glazed and has an interesting arched top that must have been especially made, though its large scale is in accordance with the commercial-type mouldings used for the windows. This arched door, in combination with the fact that Henrietta, the eldest of the Yarburgh girls, married the architect Sir John Vanbrugh in 1719, has given rise to an often-repeated story regarding its construction: as Vanbrugh was working at Castle Howard, Yorkshire, between 1702 and 1726, a tradition has lingered that he might also have designed or even built the Baby House for his wife's younger sisters.

Vanbrugh's architectural designs were in the nature of splendid continuous vistas, so that from one impressive setting the eye was persuaded to explore the next and even beyond towards buildings or scenes in the gardens. Wherever the eye rests, all is perfection and delight, a technique which he exploited to its utmost at Blenheim Palace. That the great exponent of the English baroque should have designed this Baby House seems not only improbable but laughable. It is very easy to connect superb models such as Nostell Priory or even the Westbrook house with the leading architects of the day, as they were so obviously designed to please both the eye and the senses, whereas Heslington Hall is a model of absolutely basic workmanship, and even a planned design is virtually non-existent.

Vanbrugh's style has been optimistically detected in the arched door, a favourite device, and used to perfect effect in the Orangery at Kensington Palace, and also in the shape of a shallow display-niche in the dining-room, but these designs were so basic to hundreds of country craftsmen, usually making only the most primitive furniture, that they can hardly be used as proof of the master's hand. One can only imagine the chagrin of an architect as fastidious as Vanbrugh at having such a clumsily structured edifice linked with his name.

This lack of high architectural connexion does not diminish the Baby

House in any way but forces us to examine it in basic reality rather than with emotions cluttered with the wisps of a suggested pedigree. What we are therefore presented with is a substantially made model that stands on a hefty base. The interior woodwork is of the simplest kind, and all the doors are fixed in a closed position. Despite their lack of ornamentation, some of the rooms are very effective, such as the kitchen with arches over the fire, spit-racks and clockwork jack. On one wall hangs a large-scale plate-shelf that is excellent for the display of the sizeable items of pewter and tin that were common. Several of the other plenishments are of a much later date, but the early eighteenth-century atmosphere is perfectly set by the arched fireplace with its huge ovens.

In the adjoining hall, which is tiled in black and white, stand a lacquered clock and a pair of wax-headed figurines of the type made in eighteenth-century Holland and not originally intended as play-dolls. There is also a nineteenth-century Waltershausen-type hall table, with a top in high-Victorian Gothic, an unusual piece and worthy of interest. One of the better-constructed interiors now represents a small dining-room with arched display alcoves and correctly shaped open shelves. The walls are finished with long rectangular panels, probably originally intended for the display of special paintings or hangings but now left unadorned. In other houses of the period a room in this position might have been used for the housekeeper or even, in Continental cabinets, as a lying-in apartment, the reception rooms usually being upstairs.

The centre floors, which would originally have held the finest items, are not of such great interest, as they were refurbished and papered in the nineteenth century, but there is an eye-catching and original red lacquer cupboard of such obvious similarity to that in Ann Sharp's house that one wonders whether they originated at the same shop. The fireplaces are also fine, as their perfectly made steel and brass firebaskets are still in position. The top floor, which would originally have held heavy canopied beds, is now of interest as the block-printed papers are still in place. The scale of the pattern makes their original intention as ordinary domestic wallpapers evident but also serves to underline the improbability of Vanbrugh's association, as such a perfectionist would surely have chosen a correctly proportioned decoration. The constant desire among doll's house enthusiasts to link the names of great architects to the models is almost always unfortunate. The houses are charming objects in their own right and hold just as much historical interest when they stand without improbable attributions such as Vanbrugh.

Eighteenth-century England's cool elegance is most popularly represented by the two beautiful houses at Uppark and Nostell Priory, where they have been treasured and considered as items of great interest for over two hundred years. Collectors frequently disagree as to which is the more perfect or richly equipped, but suffice it to say that in these Baby Houses we reach the sublime

Probably the finest of Baby Houses, Nostell Priory was constructed between 1735 and 1740. The exterior is completely original and has faded to a lovely soft green-brown. The carpentry is of the highest quality. Note how the fronts slide apart. Height without stand 66 inches.

heights of construction and furnishing to adult specifications. The pristine condition of the contents makes it obvious that few children could ever have examined the furnishings without supervision, and they were probably restricted to much simpler nursery models in the manner of Heslington Hall.

Nostell Priory, near Wakefield in Yorkshire, is now owned by the National Trust, and the Baby House stands at the end of a long, vaulted lower hall. The doll's house dates from between 1735 and 1740 and is an extremely pleasing antique object, as the exterior has never been repainted and has faded to an inimitable soft green-brown. The carpentry is of the highest quality, as the

199

sash windows open individually and the detail of the large pillars is correctly carved. In construction, the house is unusually heavy, as inch-thick pine was used for the exterior walls, which are given added realism by the side windows. Sash windows were a fashionable addition to older houses at the time, as they were considered particularly progressive, and by 1725 quite small houses in country towns were so provided. The makers of dolls' houses were very much aware of the newly found importance of sash windows, and very small, mean play-houses frequently have a disproportionate concentration on this feature.

It is thought that the Nostell Baby House was made for the children of the fourth baronet, Sir Rowland Winn, who in 1729 had married Susanna Henshaw, daughter and heiress of a Lord Mayor of London. In one of the upper rooms there is an original label which states that the furnishings were supervised by Lady Winn and her sister Miss Henshaw, and it seems very likely that the two women derived such enjoyment from the project that the children were allowed to approach only with care and wonder. Sir Rowland Winn might well have seen similar adult-intentioned cabinets on his Grand Tour, which had taken him five years, and would consequently not be averse to this Continental affectation.

Comparisons are inevitably drawn between this façade and that of Nostell Priory itself, as they are both of Palladian inspiration. Regrettably, there are almost as many differences as similarities between the two, partly because the design of the house itself developed slowly, though both have Ionic pilasters and a pediment decorated with the Winn coat-of-arms that was designed by Paine in 1743; both also have a basement. The Baby House once resembled the actual more closely, as the raised terrace and the two curving flights of steps that considerably altered the appearance of the actual house were added by Robert Adam some thirty years later. The general effect of the miniature is, nevertheless, sufficiently in accord with the main house plan to constitute an acceptable doll's house artist's impression, and this similarity adds greatly to its interest.

Several eighteenth-century dolls' houses are claimed by their owners to be architect's models, though in fact this theory is rarely supportable, as the play-houses are so simply arranged inside. Though the façade might well present an adequate sketch of the completed building, the rooms are obviously in a completely divergent idiom. The practice of building architect's models of a much more accurate type was fairly general practice, as it gave the patron some idea of the finished appearance of the structure. In 1792, when Richmond House caught fire and there was a great struggle to preserve its valuable contents, the *Ladies' Magazine* of 6th December commented that the books in the library were saved, as well as 'the model of the new house intended to be built by the Duke at Goodwood, and all the valuable busts were also saved'. It is perhaps curious, as the architect's models were so highly

The family of the architect and decorator Thomas Hope, showing a model house in the background. Painted by Benjamin West in 1802.

regarded, that a greater number has not survived. Perhaps others, beside Hawksmoor's model, now at the Bodleian, were taken over by the children of the house and utilized as dolls' houses – an expensive plaything, as Mr Waitwell (Smallwell?) was paid £87 11 shillings for his work. Another working model was constructed by Thomas Hope and can be seen in the background of a picture painted in 1802 by Benjamin West entitled *The Hope Family*. The house, in a modified Greek revival style which he considered at the time to be the only architecture of the past worthy of imitation, stands on a properly constructed base, so that the ground floor was at adult eye-level when standing and is completely in the idiom of a studio display-feature. Another, much smaller model that I recently examined was properly divided on the inside, but access was from above, a method which few children would feel to be adequate.

The design of Nostell Priory itself has been variously attributed, but it is now thought to be the work of Colonel James Moyser, a popular but amateur gentleman architect and one of Lord Burlington's circle. It is thought probable that the design was later executed and professionally adapted by James Paine, who would have been only fifteen when it was first conceived. Moyser's complete intention was never realized, and even several of the state rooms were incomplete when Sir Rowland died in 1765. Fortunately, the equipping of the Baby House took a much shorter period, and we see it today just as the original designer, probably Paine, intended. Though his design for the Winn coat-of-arms was not engraved until 1743, that on the doll's house is a simplified version, and the charming possibility of the device being first tried out on the doll's house presents itself. As no positive records exist, we are very much in the land of conjecture regarding the miniature, but the very names of the designers associated with Nostell are so great that they inevitably arouse discussion.

Family tradition connects Chippendale with some of the furniture in the model, as he was born only some 30 miles away, at Otley. It is claimed that Chippendale began his career by working at the great house, as he was seventeen in 1735 and Paine just one year older. What is certain is that Sir Rowland's son purchased a great deal of furniture from Chippendale's London showrooms in later years, though this was naturally of full rather than miniature size. It is obviously very romantic to imagine these two young men of genius working together in the miniature scale, but regrettably, at present, nothing can be proved or substantiated, and we have to consider how frequently tradition is completely unreliable.

The Baby House treasures compare well with the rich interiors of the house itself, and Miss Henshaw and Lady Winn must have insisted that they should be in accord. Access is obtained by sliding apart the heavy front, which means that a very wide area was originally devoted to the display of the model, so that it is a method too wasteful of space to be often encountered. Inside, all is rich wood, with well-polished floors and colourful textiles in almost perfect condition. The upper two floors are evenly divided into three rooms on each level, but on the ground floor the hall is much wider, and there are smaller rooms on either side. Though there are basement windows, there are no doors to this part, and the attic section seems also to be sealed.

As in the Sharp house, the family dines in the oak-panelled hall, in this instance with an impressive staircase that is just a little spoiled by the over-large stairs. Over the white marble chimneypiece hangs a painting of a King Charles spaniel, while other, more finely executed paintings of game, painted in blue and grey tones, are also displayed. On the unadorned but well-made table stands a group of silver miniatures of the type avidly collected by adults.

The brass-faced long-case clock has additional finials which also makes it a very desirable miniature. Near the table stands a wooden servant with a real hair wig drawn into a pigtail. This doll is constructed in a different manner to those in the Sharp house, as the lower legs are carved in the round to represent high-heeled black boots.

Another extremely interesting doll of the period stands in the lying-in room. The wax face has the usual plain dark eyes, but the characterization is particularly fine and the face alert and expressive. The lying-in room walls are painted in a lovely shade of green that has faded to a colour immediately evocative of the period and quite impossible to recreate, and the door is supplied with a beautiful brass lock that actually works properly. (These good locks are a particular feature of this model, as even at Uppark they are only representations.) The chimneypiece fits across a corner of the room, and a neatly fitted cupboard utilizes the space above, with flowers painted on the door. The large four-poster bed has a finely stitched quilt and matching pillow in white, though the bed-hangings are much less exquisitely made. The canopy is effective, despite the household chintz in a large pattern that was also utilized for the matching curtains. The other occupant of the room is a wax-headed nurse with black moulded hair and painted eyes, who is obviously deemed to be a person of some standing, as the other servants were provided only with wooden heads. Wet-nurses, employed to save mothers the bother of feeding, were treated with extreme caution and respect, as it was known that any small upsets could affect their milk, and it was obviously not always easy to find a strong, healthy young woman of sound morals at the right time. Since the medieval period, animal milk had been used only as a last resort, as it was believed that the child was likely to partake something of the beast's nature, so that women were comparatively well paid for this service, Mary Verney offering 4 shillings a week and two loads of wood to a strong young matron in the mid-seventeenth century.

In the lying-in room at Nostell, a quilted baby-basket that once accompanied a cradle lies on the floor. The carved ivory chairs are particularly fine, and very similar pieces are found in the Uppark Baby House, suggesting that they probably both came from the same source, possibly a popular London *bijouterie* shop that would also have stocked silver miniatures. This room is invariably well appointed in models of the period, as the visitors to the baptism of the child sat and took refreshments in the lying-in room and presented the wet-nurse with gifts of money after paying their respects to the mother.

Another bedroom is more sparsely furnished but made effective by the bed-hangings of watered ribbed taffeta enriched by braids. The same deep shade of yellow is also used for the expensive upholstery of the chairs, which would have been carefully protected in an actual house. (Susanna Whatman, in her contemporary instructions to servants, is constantly advising extreme caution with regard to the sun's rays, which could be avoided only by lowering the blinds in the various rooms as the sun moved around.) At Nostell, the usual draped dressing-table was abandoned, and we find a mirror hung over a knee-hole desk fulfilling this function. The rich yellow taffeta was used again in the boudoir which, in accord with eighteenth-century English taste, is sparsely furnished but given presence by the fine grey marble chimneypiece, with fire-irons made of carved ivory, which is complemented by an especially painted landscape that fits perfectly in the panelling. The fire-basket, quite unlike the exquisite examples at Heslington Hall, is fairly obviously home-made from odds and ends of ivory. The occupant of the room is a wax lady with a long patrician face and elegant hands, dressed in striped silk and satin and wearing a lace cap and lappets. Her skirts are short enough to reveal her ankles and feet, which are also wax and modelled to represent high-heeled shoes.

In the room beneath stands another fine lady, whose features again exhibit some characterization, this time creating a woman of a Mediterranean background. Her hands are modelled in a slightly open position, and her white dress is meticulously embroidered in red, to create an absolutely perfect miniature pattern. The doll also wears a fashionable short, decorative apron and a lace cap. The chimneypiece in this room is made of black marble, and a gilded mirror hangs above, surmounted by a landscape painting, both especially made and enclosed in the same framing. It is this sort of precise detail that makes the Nostell Baby House so remarkable, as it is obviously created by a designer who was used to such perfectly balanced interiors in actual houses. The Chippendale-style chairs still retain the original leather upholstery, and there is also a bureau bookcase, made with great accuracy. Between the windows hangs a long mirror with a frame that exactly echoes that of the painting over the fire and adds to the ordered effect.

The main central bedroom on this floor is somewhat overpowering in decoration, as the walls are hung with crimson velvet that almost matches the oppressive crimson of the bed-hangings. There is a marble hearthstone set into the floor, a precise type of detail that is hardly ever found in a model. A particularly lovely tallboy, made of walnut and provided with minute brass lock-covers and handles, again indicates the maker's attention to detail. Another senior servant, this time the ladies' maid, wearing a grey frock and provided with a wax head, stands in this very perfect apartment, surrounded by alabaster miniatures and an effective group of china monkeys, as well as a silver porringer and jug that were probably added much later.

The sumptuous effect of the drawing-room is created largely by the wallpaper, which is made up from contemporary French prints, painted predominantly in a rich yellow and representing pastoral scenes. The grey marble chimneypiece, surely the finest in any doll's house, is surmounted by a gilded bust, meticulously foiled by the arch of the gilded and carved

A wax-headed lady doll from the Nostell Priory Baby House. The good-quality figure wears a dark pink and cream striped frock and the fashionable short apron favoured by ladies. The shoes are moulded in wax.

The sumptuous drawing-room at Nostell Priory contains some of the most perfect architectural detail, such as the door-case, the ornate cornicing and the splendid marble chimneypieces. The walls are hung with contemporary French prints.

overmantel mirror, a shape that is itself reflected in an ornate continuation carving of scrolls and flowers that rises to cornice level. Susanna Whatman, in her housekeeping book, constantly advises her maids to place their hands behind the furniture when standing it against a wall, in order to avoid damaging the decoration. In this room, a fashionable chair-rail serves to protect the paper from the furniture that was pushed back against the wall when not in use. This is also one of the few rooms provided with a carpet, embroidered in reds and browns in *petit point*, a rich touch for even the royal family had some uncarpeted rooms in the eighteenth century, as their use was often considered effete. When they were used, they were often nailed in place, so that a nailed carpet in a Baby House would be absolutely correct. Not only are the massive doors leading to the main room panelled but the well-carved detail is further accentuated by gilding. The crimson velvet, so

In the kitchen at Nostell stands a carved wooden cook similar to those in Ann Sharp's house. The kitchen has a wonderfully realistic atmosphere as so much of the original equipment is intact.

oppressive in the bedroom, is completely right in this detailed ornamented interior. The furniture, though fine, is almost unobtrusive in effect, but there are two double settees and several chairs made in Chippendale style, of beautifully polished rich wood, which contrast well with a pair of Italianate chests with matching small boxes decorated with powdered glass. The floor is highly polished and reflects the colours and textures of this splendid room.

The kitchens in most eighteenth-century houses were quite large, but in this model it is insignificant and not over-generously equipped. Perhaps the two ladies, living some distance from a large and fashionable town, found it difficult to obtain the much cheaper items that are frequently genuine children's toys rather than adult gifts. The walls are painted to represent stone, and there is a varnished wooden spit-rack with its spits still in position. The huge arched fireplace is equipped with a steel basket and fireguard, and

207

there is a particularly fine floor-standing plate-rack. A built-in dresser with a pot-shelf, well stacked with silver plates and other base-metal miniatures, follows the regular pattern for Baby House kitchens. One of the most useful pieces of kitchen furniture was a large cutting-block, and at Nostell we find not only the doll's house example but also the full-sized version designed by Chippendale himself. The cook, being a menial, has a carved wooden face, and a great similarity can be detected between this example and that in Ann Sharp's house, suggesting a possible local commercial manufacture. One hand is carved with a neat hole running through the clenched fist so that a spoon or brush could be carried, a manufacturing method that is also seen in Continental waxes. His feet are carved to represent high-heeled boots, and he is accompanied by a fabric-covered dog, provided with amusingly over-large feet for balance. Several fine pieces of porcelain, including an exquisite tea-caddy that must originally have belonged in the drawing-room, have been relegated to the kitchen, as has a nicely made side-table that also started life as a reception-room piece in more elegant surroundings.

This most exquisite of English Baby Houses at Nostell Priory compares favourably with the Dutch cabinets, as it so perfectly mirrors domestic life of the time. A model that is as perfectly preserved is sometimes of more use in studying domestic life of the period than the great houses themselves, which were adapted and modernized in the nineteenth century, so that the lying-in room, for instance, is not found, and the paintings that were especially commissioned to fit the appropriate sections in the panelling have often been moved to more secure positions or even sold. Few Baby Houses have survived to present such an accurate picture, so that familiarity with this model is of supreme importance to anyone with a serious interest in the subject.

The silver miniatures that are so generously supplied in the Baby Houses were manufactured as a sideline by the silversmiths, though there were a few craftsmen who specialized in the work. Although tankards, cruets, tea-canisters, salvers, table baskets, kettles, goblets and candlesticks are the items most frequently found, larger pieces such as firebacks, girandoles, mirror-frames, tables and chairs were also produced. Occasionally, an unusual and rare piece such as a salt-box, a pair of snuffers on the original tray or even a complete toilet-set will appear, made by a craftsman such as John Deard of Fleet Street, who died in 1731 and who created several of the fine miniatures in the Westbrook House, including a grate with an attached fireback.

There is often confusion regarding the initials found on this early silver, and collectors frequently disagree in the case of incomplete marks as to whether some refer to the seller or importer rather than to the craftsman himself, though it is a great temptation to link any initials discovered with the recorded names of men working at certain periods. British silversmiths were more prosaic in their approach than the Dutch, and we find none of the extravagant filigree birdcages, coaches and scenes made with such obvious enjoyment in Europe but, instead, simple scaled-down versions of objects in everyday use, relying for their effect on careful craftsmanship and the use of high-quality metal.

Very early miniatures were shaped from flat plate, and the detail of spouts, handles and purely decorative devices was formed from small castings that were soldered in position, the most frequently used technique, however, being that of casting and then giving a hand-tooled finish. By the late eighteenth century, hollow ware was often lathe-spun rather than hand-raised with a hammer, a technique that is particularly evident in Dutch work. The finest British silver showed the figure of Britannia stamped on the miniature, which indicated a high degree of pure silver never approached by the Dutch. The earliest recorded British miniature is a small silver bowl decorated with a rose and provided with wire scroll handles that carries a London hallmark for 1653, while the snuffer on a tray found in Ann Sharp's house and dated 1686 is also a highly desirable piece, as at that time those interested in this type of collecting obtained their acquisitions mainly from Holland.

As the fashion for collecting spread over Europe, more silversmiths became interested in their manufacture, though in Sir Ambrose Heal's *London Goldsmiths*, which lists some seven thousand names, only thirty are recorded as toymen, and it is obvious that only a few of these marked their work in an attributable manner. The small sizes meant that Assay Office requirements for full marking were often waived, but after the 1790 Act the law was considerably tightened. Unfortunately, by this time the great popularity of miniatures was in decline. This lowering of general interest began as early as 1740, and though many items were obviously made long after that date, the main vogue was past. Today vast quantities in traditional designs are still created, as the items have great appeal, and it is a type of collecting that has never gone completely out of fashion.

Among the more prolific manufacturers was George Mountjoy, who worked between 1684 and 1710 and made pieces of furniture such as chairs and day-beds with the silver chased and worked to imitate turned uprights and with back panels often pierced to resemble cane. He appears to have been the first London silversmith to specialize in toys, among which he included complete fireplace sets composed of dogs, firebacks, andirons, fenders, tongs, shovels and pokers that were eminently suitable for Baby Houses. Among his finest pieces is a charming silver spoon-rack, complete with its two rows of spoons. Fireplace equipment of a somewhat similar type is found in the Westbrook house, though this was made by John Clifton. In the same house, so magnificently supplied with silver, are two chairs by Matthew Maddon of Lombard Street and a three-legged pot made in 1713 by Thomas Evesdon of St Martin's-le-Grand.

Another specialist producer of miniature silver was Augustin Courtauld, whose mark was registered in 1708 and who worked in St Mark's Lane. One of his craftsmen worked full time on the manufacture of these trifles, rather than as a sideline for quiet periods, as was so often the case. Courtauld's marked work included tea-equipages, porringers, warming-pans, coffee-pots and conventional furniture. Isaac Malyn of Gutter Lane produced some particularly fine work between 1699 and 1720, though his products are so similar to those made by Mountjoy that experts consider it very probable that he was at one time apprenticed to him. Other recorded manufacturers include Joseph Daniel, John East, John Cann and James Slater. At the Golden Head in the Strand worked Thomas Clark, who advertised himself as a jeweller and toyman producing 'all sorts of toys in gold, silver and other metals'. At the Golden Door against Suffolk Street, Paul Daniel Chevenix, who provided fine miniatures and specialized in silver toys for Baby Houses, was established in the shop by 1730. The Deards were another great toy-making family that worked from various addresses in the Haymarket and Fleet Street between 1720 and the end of the century. Many of these toymen sold a variety of *bijouterie*, such as John Sotro of the Acorn, St Paul's Churchyard, who was 'a goldsmith and toyman making all sorts of children's toys, wholesale and retail at reasonable rates'; he also proudly claimed to be an agent for Bow china.

Possibly the most prolific London maker was David Clayton, who registered his first mark in 1697 and worked until the mid-eighteenth century. In the earlier Higher Standard period, which extended to 1740, he marked his work with a large 'C' enclosing a smaller 'L' and manufactured warming-pans, tripod tables and other crockery-type items. In a doll's house popularly known as Scadbury Manor, believed to date to the eighteenth century, is a fine plate-warmer holding twelve silver plates marked by Clayton.

It was inevitable, as silver miniatures were very much the conceit of the more wealthy, that the main producers worked in London, making provincial pieces extremely rare. One of the few provincial makers was Matthew Boulton (1728–1809) of Soho, Birmingham, who was in partnership with John Fothergill from 1762 to 1782 and who later worked from the Matthew Boulton Plate Company. There was a substantial production of miniatures in this city, and factory silversmiths were established there in the last quarter of the eighteenth century. Silver toys were also made in Sheffield, with which town the name of Sarah Bowman, who created many fine items, is particularly associated.

In America, as in the British provinces, there were no specialist makers of miniature silver, though toy pieces were made as a sideline. The Yale University Art Gallery possesses a collection of silver toys made in the late seventeenth century, and it is obvious that, even at this early date, in an insecure environment, silversmiths found a ready sale for these frivolous items. The Yale pieces are unmarked but are considered to be of American origin as they originally belonged to Bethiah Shrimpton who bequeathed them to her sister's children as 'silver Baby things'. The group includes sugar-

A collection of silver toys made in the late seventeenth century. Unmarked but believed to be of American origin.

casters, goblets and a pair of snuffers on a tray.

Main American production appears to have centred on New York and Boston. Some particularly desirable pieces, including tankards, were made by Peter Oliver of Boston (1682–1712), while good caudle cups are known to have been produced by John Coney (1656–1722), of the same town. At the end of the eighteenth century, Robert Evans was also producing fine wares, including some attractive teapots. In New York, Pieter de Riemer (1738–1814), made some highly effective fireplace furniture, and surviving examples include pairs of andirons. The earliest recorded American miniature spoons originated in Portsmouth, New Hampshire, and were made by William Whittemore.

American production was obviously only slight when compared with that of European countries, as people were more concerned with the basic problems of survival than with stocking collectors' cabinets. The rarity of the examples has meant that any early pieces of American miniature work command prices far higher than would be expected for comparable European examples. These early pieces differ from the British in that there was no

211

requirement to mark work with an assay stamp, and it was left to the individual maker to ensure that the quality did not fall short of the sterling standard of 0·925 fine silver. Fortunately, it was customary for the maker to stamp his wares with his own punch, which obviously helps considerably in attribution. Many of the first silversmiths who settled in New England were of British origin, whereas in New York, where silversmithing began a generation later, the Dutch influence is very strong.

Marked American pieces of the early dates are obviously rare, but by the mid eighteenth century makers such as Edward Lang of Salem, Massachusetts (1742–1820), were producing complete tea-services with scallop-shell decoration in some number. The Minneapolis Institute of Arts has a particularly good miniature basket, made by Zachariah Brigden of Boston who died in 1787. Miniature spoons, presumably because they were produced so generously, have stood the best chance of survival and can still be found, though only rarely in the miniature size small enough for Baby Houses. Despite the fact that the silver miniatures are so highly desirable, the very quality of the metal gives a timeless effect, so that it needs a very active imagination to conjure an impression of the past from even the most sympathetic grouping of such minutiae.

For a realistic portrayal of eighteenth-century life, we have to turn instead to the Baby Houses themselves, in which is to be found a confusion of all the crafts of a particular period. The only British house that compares with the model at Nostell is that at Uppark, which also dates between 1730 and 1740. Once again, the lying-in room has great importance, but in this structure a decidedly weary wax-headed mother still lies beneath a quilted counterpane while her wax twins sleep in a wicker rocking-cradle. The dressing-table, conventionally draped with net, is well equipped, and the room was lit by candles held in brass sconces. Even before the baptism of the baby, this room was important as it was here that the mother, with her newly born, received her guests and their good wishes. A contemporary, Mrs Papendiek, comments that on the birth of her children, the caudle, chocolate and cake of the very best quality, were always ready to please her visitors. In return they placed 2 shillings and 6 pence in a saucer as a *douceur* for the nurse. The mother also received gifts, and Mrs Papendiek relates how, on one caudle visit her father presented her with six nankeen double-handled cups and saucers. In the Uppark lying-in room two well-carved ivory chairs with cabriole legs and high, shaped backs, stand ready on either side of the cradle for the admiring guests, while an English-made wooden-headed nurse with a shaped face and typical wooden fork-like hands sits in attendance.

The Baby House came to Uppark in Sussex, now owned by the National Trust, through the marriage of Sarah Lethieullier to Sir John Matthew Fetherstonhaugh, who had purchased the estate on succeeding to the vast fortune of a distant relative. Sarah, an attractive girl, whose portrait by

The Uppark Baby House (1730–40) has a most impressive façade though the statues on the parapet strike a note of discord. On the decorated pediment is the Lethieullier coat of arms.

Pompeo Batoni still hangs in the drawing-room, was the only daughter of Christopher Lethieullier of Middlesex, and it was the coat-of-arms of his family that was on the pediment of her doll's house. In order to meet the stipulations in his relative's Will Sir Matthew was instructed to purchase a baronetcy and a country estate in the south, a transaction which he completed by a suitable marriage to an innocent girl. Sarah presumably brought the Baby House to Uppark among her other possessions, though its actual origin is unrecorded. It now stands in a service lobby, though it once occupied a more important position near the head of a staircase on the first-floor corridor.

The exterior is painted in a soft grey, though obviously several fresh coats of paint have been applied through two centuries. The Georgians were particularly fond of light-painted effects both inside and outside their houses, so that there was a very general use of white paint, and even the exteriors of brick buildings were frequently stucco-coated to give this pale tone. This Baby House is much larger than that at Nostell but occupies less display-space, as all the rooms, like those of Heslington Hall, have separately opening fronts. In quality, however, this workmanship is much superior, as all the sections fit perfectly together when the model is closed, and the inner surfaces are correctly panelled to match that in the rooms, a feature that could only really be appreciated by the doll inhabitants. The tympanum of the pediment carries the coat-of-arms, and the roof parapet is surmounted by classical figures. The sash windows also reveal a minute attention to detail, as they open by means of a pin concealed in the panelling. The integral base is probably one of the most immediately effective aspects, as it is assembled to imitate the stables, so that the unreality of a table-like stand was avoided. It is believed that this section was modelled on the arcade of the Covent Garden piazza and that there were originally carriages and horses, as in the German cabinets.

The façade of the Baby House is Palladian, and even if the perilously perched white-painted statues are over-large, they add to the particularly distinctive charm of this most elegant construction. As in the Nostell model, the main construction is of pine and has carved detail on the pillars. All the rooms are correctly panelled and provided with especially painted pictures to fit the main sections. The chimneypieces, in contrast, are much more simply made in Sarah Lethieullier's house, though the same particularly eighteenth-century atmosphere of established order, combined with quiet richness, pervades the two models.

At Uppark, the dining-room is on the first floor, in accordance with the gradually progressing segregation of the family unit away from the servants and the working-areas. Two well-dressed serving-men of the wooden so-called Queen Anne type await the diners. The dolls are good examples of the more superior carving that was reserved for the better-quality versions, as they have properly shaped chins and expressively carved wooden hands. They stand behind a well-made extending table, generously equipped with silver, which, though out of scale, contributes to the expensive effect of the room, further enhanced by a chinoiserie-style Georgian display-cabinet, the shining brass of the candle sconces and the glitter of the glass set out on a side table. Like the silver, which includes a good George III tankard, the glass is of the fine quality associated with pieces intended for an adult's curiosity cabinet rather than a child's toy, the beautiful *blanc de chine* monkey in the wall cabinet further accentuating this intention. These deviations from accurate scale are often highly attractive and give the Baby Houses more life than the perfection that is seen in the more recent models, such as Queen Mary's doll's house. In the centre of the dining-room floor stands a very obviously adult-sized salt-cellar, doing duty as a wine-cooler, again with more interest in

The interior of the Baby House at Uppark with a central staircase that is glimpsed through the doors on the first and second floors. Note the fine selection of contemporary dolls.

usefulness than in accuracy. As at Nostell, the chimneypiece has its own fitting mirror, and a painting hangs over this. The chairs are superbly made and the finest encountered, as they have elegant cabriole legs with additional carving on the knees and finely caned seats.

The well-made stairs rise, as at Nostell, from the main hall, though at Uppark the scale is more accurate. This lower hall appears to be the servants' dining-room, and the furniture, though well made, is much simpler, and there is no purely ornamental decoration. The table equipage is also of a much baser type and is composed of an alabaster tea-set similar to that encountered in Ann Sharp's house. A wooden-headed porter stands on the stairs, ready to answer the ringing of a bell. The adjoining housekeeper's room is also very

The fine quality alabaster tea-table with its bowls, saucers and an unusually good caddy. Seen in the housekeeper's room at Uppark.

low ceilinged but more comfortably decorated, and there is a good side-table on which stand some of the heavy glass rummers particularly associated with the period. The wooden doll wears a red and white sprigged frock and sits at an alabaster tea-table that is of the pedestal type and quite delicately painted in blue and purple. This is by far the most complete set of the type I have seen either in a doll's house or displayed in a museum as a single exhibit, as it consists of a tea-caddy, sugar-bowl and tazza, as well as the more common bowls and saucers. Another flat-topped alabaster piece matches the table and was possibly originally intended to represent a wine-cooler or a similar low table.

The kitchen at Uppark is far superior in equipment to any of the other Baby Houses, which is appropriate, as the full-sized house was itself to become

216

renowned for the cooking of the famous chef Moget, whose dishes were so fine that the owners of other houses in the county preferred visitors to stay with them *on their way* to Uppark, as any food they could offer would seem poor after his splendid meals. The miniature kitchen reveals generous rows of pewter plates, a candle-box, the inevitable mousetrap and a really generous supply of ivory cutlery. A somewhat over-large smoothing-iron still holds its heating-brick, and there is a fine Leeds-type coffee-pot. As in the dining-room, many of the items are out of scale, but the general visual effect of the shining pewter and copper is much warmer and more inviting than in the very spartan work-room at Nostell. On the floor stands a very unusual miniature chocolate-machine, again in the genre of a somewhat larger-scale adult gift. Sarah and her husband were obviously very fond of chocolate, as family records show how, on a visit to Goodwood, he spent £2 14s on this commodity, but only 7 shillings at the races themselves. Perhaps this affection for chocolate also inspired the purchase of the miniature. A wooden cook wearing a cap and apron over a blue sprigged frock tends a chicken that lies on a Leeds plate on the large table.

The three bedrooms are situated at the top of the house, and each has its own beautifully polished door, supplied with a shining brass lock. Such doors were a mark of a fine house at the time, as a painted door was not approved of in an elegant apartment, though painted and grained doors were quite common in smaller houses. This eighteenth-century affection for doors almost as decorative additions is particularly notable in this Baby House but extended in real houses to the extreme of adding splendid doors complete with architraves to shallow cupboards or minute store-rooms. Victorian and Edwardian children were much more familiar with painted doll's house doors, and almost invariably, when a model has been played with down the years, the lovely rich wood disappeared as the model was brought up to date. It is only in such perfectly preserved Baby Houses as Uppark and Nostell that we are really made aware of their true effect.

The four-poster beds with their original hangings occupy most of the space in each room. The hangings do not approach the finely stitched perfect miniatures seen in Ann Sharp's house and at Nostell, but this lack of detail is compensated for by the exceptionally fine needlework on the quilts that are also very correctly made. (The doll's house fabrics are cleaned regularly at Uppark with a mixture of soapwort and springwater that is believed to be particularly effective.) The bedrooms are simply furnished with ivory chairs and draped toilet-tables, but present a satisfactory effect because of the beautifully made panelling and the correctly structured extended chimneypieces with their brass candle-brackets and rare glass 'smoke-consumers'. The central apartment has less depth than the others, to accommodate the passageway and staircase. The bedrooms are completely uninhabited, as the family sits below, taking tea in the parlour, which is lit by candles in the most

Few dolls' public houses are found, and the 'George III' is in itself interesting as a fine eighteenth-century house. The central panel remains fixed. Dating to about 1790, it is constructed of pine.

The interior of the 'George III' retains its original paintwork, panelling in the rooms and panelled doors. The door furniture is correctly made to work. There is a fine staircase that can only be glimpsed through the front door.

elegant silver sconces, which carry, as does the silver fireback, the Lethieullier coat-of-arms.

The main family, in accord with its station, is made of wax and to a particularly high standard, as all the ladies' heads are modelled in a slightly turned position which gives added realism. The man is also notable, as his elegant legs are modelled in wax to knee-level with his dark blue high-heeled shoes included in the mould. Like the ladies, he is given dark bead-like eyes that to some extent lessen the realism. According to the custom of the day, the gentleman wears his sword at his side even in his own home, where he sits, elegantly dressed and wearing a powdered wig. Because of their wide-panniered taffeta skirts, the lady dolls are propped against chairs while they take tea at a beautiful silver table with a matching tea-set, including a spirit kettle. A long, gilded mirror hangs on the back wall, though it seems probable that paintings were originally intended for at least a few of these long panels. In the shallower central dining-room, part of this section is occupied by the chinoiserie-style wall shelves, which the gilded mirror in the next room helps balance.

The elegance of this Palladian house, though much less meticulous than that at Nostell, is highly memorable, as so much of the atmosphere of Uppark itself seems to pervade the model. It is remarkable that this adult plaything survived, as Sarah's only child was a son, the spendthrift but tasteful Sir Harry, under whose ownership the house became the 'rendezvous of all that is gay and fashionable in the county' (*The Craftsman*, July 1785). It was frequently visited by the Prince Regent, who shared Sir Harry's fascination with women beneath his station, encouraging him first to become the lover of Emma, later Nelson's mistress, and eventually to undermine all his father's social aspirations by marrying his head dairymaid. The Baby House was therefore not protected by an inheritance along the female line as is so often the case but must, even in the next decade, have been considered a work of great interest and even value.

Eighteenth-century taste is particularly suggested by the simple lines of the furniture and by the uncluttered atmosphere of interiors that seem to rely on minimal content for an elegant effect. It seems almost odd that such practical people should have preserved any of the dolls' houses that contained such light-hearted and almost casually selected items, but alongside their rationalism lurked a small affection for the curious, the novel, the cleverly contrived or the visual surprise. Many writers in the late eighteenth century complained bitterly at this counter-taste that was founded on surprise and curiosity. In an essay on 'False Taste', written in 1784, Mr Shenstone grumbles at 'the fondness of some persons for a knife shaft made from the Royal Oak or a tobacco stopper from a mulberry tree of Shakespeare's own planting. It gratifies an empty curiosity.' He criticizes 'dogs expressed in feathers, woodcocks in mohair, pictures made of shells: In all such cases difficulty should not be allowed to give a casting weight; nor a needle to be considered as a painter's instrument when he is so much better furnished with a pencil.'

Examples of items made in accord with all that Shenstone criticizes can be discovered in profusion in the Baby Houses already discussed, which were intended not so much for play as for adult curiosity cabinets. Small rooms and scenes in shellwork and needlework that were framed and glazed to protect the craft were also popular, though many were of such a fragile nature that they were eventually discarded. Sometimes commercially produced miniature wax-headed dolls were used as part of these scenes, and the toy-collector is often distressed to find a very fine early wooden doll set firmly in a bocage of shells and dried seaweed. Other, much more complex models were sometimes attempted, such as a 'magical palace' described in Dr Hooper's *Rational Recreations* published in 1775:

> On a hexagonal or six-sided plane six semi-diameters are placed. In each of these six triangular spaces, contained between two mirrors, place little figures of pasteboard, in relief, representing such objects as, when seen in an hexagonal form, will produce an agreeable effect. To these add small figures of enamel, and take particular care to conceal, by some object that has no relation to the subject, the place where the mirrors join, which all meet in the common centre.
>
> When you look into any one of the six openings of this magical palace, the objects there contained, being repeated six times, will seem entirely to fill up the whole of the building. This illusion will appear very remarkable, especially if the objects made use of are properly adapted to the effect that is to be produced by the mirrors. . . . If you place part of a ballroom, ornamented with chandeliers and figures in enamel, all these objects being here multiplied will afford a very pleasing effect.

The late eighteenth-century woman obviously found more available leisure than her ancestors and was eager to employ the time in creating amusing small pieces purely for the delight of the basic work rather than for any useful end. Some of the model rooms contrived of pasteboard and scraps of fabric now appear gloomy and rather pointless, but when freshly constructed with beads, shells, wax and bright paint, they probably satisfied the enthusiastic creator. Such models have little appeal for the doll's house collector but perhaps deserve much more serious consideration, as they are exactly in accord with the motivation behind the great Baby Houses themselves.

The quality of fine models such as that at Uppark should not blind us to the fact that these houses were in fact splendid exceptions among the dolls' houses constructed at the time. Although these houses were owned originally by the women who worked on them, when they were children, the contents display adult interest and an adult's concern with correctness, particularly with regard to the soft furnishings and the costume of the dolls. Many of the miniatures are also quite costly, such as the ivory chairs and silver and especially made side-tables and mirrors. The obviously play-items, such as some of the crude tables and chairs in Ann Sharp's house, give us some idea of the contents of an ordinary girl's Baby House. Later in the century, the choice and the quality of children's miniatures improved, and the alabaster sets, the lacquered cabinets and clocks, the pine kitchen dressers and a wealth of copper, tin and brassware for the kitchen were available. There is little to suggest that the Baby Houses were ever used as a vehicle for domestic instruction as in Germany, and they are invariably spoken of lightly in writings of the period. When a model was required for some form of learning, it took a very different form, to suit the professed rationalism of parents who instructed their young according to Rousseau's principles.

In *Adelaide and Theodore, or Letters on Education*, published as a series in the *Ladies' Magazine* in 1785, the writer stresses the idea that all sorts of play should be useful and adds,

> I have substituted also, instead of any other favourite amusement of children, that of building castles of cards, a play that gives them some idea of architecture. I also had two houses and two palaces of pasteboard constructed in miniature, which may be taken asunder; all ornaments of architecture are to be found in them; all the pieces are numbered, and on each is written the name of the subject represented. My son has likewise several fortified castles.

None of the letters mentions playing with either conventional Baby Houses or model rooms as a method of instruction, and the rational educationalist fairly obviously thought of these as purely time-wasting pursuits. These eighteenth-century toys apparently pleased girls, if not the educators, as they were sold and have survived in some number. Unfortunately the very simplest models had little lasting appeal and were soon broken up, but those with some pretensions to architectural realism survived, because their fine craftsmanship made adults hesitate before reducing them to firewood. In this context one thinks particularly of models such as the Norwich Baby House, with its well-proportioned, typically Georgian façade, and the elegant structure made for Mary Foster of Liverpool, *circa* 1800, with a façade equal in effect to any of the classic examples already discussed. Neither of these houses has a particularly grand interior, though the Foster house has well-made doors and chimneypieces, and the Norwich model has an effective kitchen. It is obvious that in such models we are approaching actual playthings of the period that have been repapered and lost their original furnishings, as they were passed from child to child. They are also becoming more modest in scale, and though

The 'Norwich Baby House', though perfectly proportioned, was of a size suitable for a child.

The Blackett Baby House with its impressive *piano nobile* and fine detailed carpentry. Mid-eighteenth century.

the Foster house, for instance, is fairly wide in proportion, it is not as overpoweringly high as that at Uppark.

Few eighteenth-century houses are as perfectly scaled exactly to suit the height of a small girl as was the Blackett Baby House, now in the Museum of London and dating from the mid century. This particularly well-constructed model is formed with a *piano nobile* that forms a highly effective stand. A child could have stood comfortably in front and re-arranged the rooms, which are also of an accessible depth, without the need of a stool or library steps, indicating a toy rather than a cabinet of the period. The façade is extremely impressive for its amount of very detailed carpentry, the fanlight over the door for instance being one of the finest discovered on a miniature. Around the main door the brickwork is carved to give a realistic effect, realism that is furthered by such details as opening sash windows. Fortunately, the original

224

In the small parlour of the Blackett Baby House sit two wax lady dolls in contemporary costume. The hand-coloured wallpaper is rich blue.

polished door has escaped without being painted and augments the external effect of complete originality. The house is now painted cream, not apparently the first coat but of sufficient age to give a satisfactory effect. In the attic and basement there are small doors on each side, presumably so that these sections could be used for storage of extra items, though they were high enough for occupation by the house servants.

The workmanship of the stand is much lower in quality than that of the main section, possibly because the carpenter was aware that it would be subjected to kicks and scuffs from the child's feet. The hand-rail, running up the steps, is surely a replacement because of such damage, for how else could the hands that created the fine roof balustrading have countenanced such primitive work?

The festooned curtains, still with the original cords threaded through the

225

upper part of the window-frames, are one of the most interesting of the original features, as it is so rare for curtains to be made with such exactitude. Those upstairs are of a soft, beautifully faded green silk, while those in the dining-room are cream. The three main rooms are all correctly supplied with cornices, skirting-boards and chair-rails, though their delicate formal effect was spoiled by a later 'improver' who added lengths of gilded cup-and-ball moulding which spoils both the balance and the period atmosphere of the rooms. This particular moulding is excellent in Edwardian and Victorian models, as its rather florid effect is completely in character with the massive furniture and bold colours, but applied beneath a relatively delicate eighteenth-century cornice, it is discordant. This clumsy 'improver' even added sections around the lovely door-frames and contrived to draw even more attention to a device that was really being used to neaten the edges of the wallpaper, by painting it gold.

The papers with which the house is decorated are hand-painted and extremely effective, though it is difficult to be precise regarding the date when they were hung. In the dining-room a series of classical scenes is painted in grisaille, a basic style that is a problem to date, as similar decoration was even used in houses made in the 1920s. In the upstairs drawing-room is another hand-coloured wallpaper in a rich brilliant blue, with a chintz-type design that is exactly right for the period. In each room there is a deep chimneybreast, though, rather surprisingly, the maker dispensed with the mantelshelves that would have been a great help to anyone furnishing the rooms. The kitchen has not only a large fireplace for cooking but also two large coppers. Fortunately, the original wooden spit-racks and a most impressive mechanical jack have survived, as the furniture is now a mixture of original and late nineteenth-century pieces.

It is perhaps appropriate that one of the items to have survived is the draped four-poster bed, which, in an actual house, would have been one of the most expensive and important pieces, not only because of its impressive effect but because the quality of the bed was not discounted as a help in the begetting of healthy children. At Dr James Graham's Temple of Health, opened in the Adelphi in 1778, the Celestial Beds, claimed to cure all sorts of ailments, were also said to be excellent for the begetting of children of matching celestial charm. In 1781 one of his electro-medical beds was available to the public in Pall Mall and offered 'a sweet undulating tittulating, vibratory, soul-dissolving, marrow-melting motion', the fee for the use of this bed, with one's own partner, being a very substantial £100 a night. The Baby House bed, though an important item of furniture, was hardly as exciting and in fact is quite crudely made, though it is embellished with somewhat tentative pineapples suggesting hospitality.

In the rooms, the hand-worked carpets seem to be nineteenth-century additions, though the draped dressing-chest in the bedroom and a number of

The kitchen of the Blackett Baby House still retains its original fitted furniture and spit rack, and there is also an impressive mechanical jack.

chairs are almost certainly original. There is also a fine chest with brass handles and a tiered, round-shaped dumb-waiter. Fortunately much of the kitchen detail was built in place, so that the dresser, the shelving and the arch over the brick copper are still intact. Around the kitchen stands a miscellany of kettles, pots, moulds and some finely woven baskets of the type seen in Continental houses mainly for the storage of laundry. These were not needed in such profusion in British houses, as the washing was usually carried out in a wash-house that was built separately from the main house as a type of outbuilding or was even a small cottage-like structure some distance from the house itself, so that the lines of drying clothes should not be seen by the owner's family. The washing and laundry equipment that forms such an important feature of European houses is therefore barely represented in British eighteenth-century interiors.

The greatest delight of the Blackett house (so described as it was presented to the museum by a lady of this name) is the fact that, almost miraculously, the original dolls have survived. Fortunately, the hand that added the gilded moulding forbore replacing the plain old figures with a more fashionable family. This group is much less finely made than the Uppark family, and the hands in particular are far more coarse. As at Uppark, the lower legs are moulded in wax to represent shoes, but the faces are much flatter in appearance, though given an attractive expression by their painted dark eyes. The costumes are not in the height of fashion but represent those of the upper-middle classes. The two ladies seated in the drawing-room are protected from draughts by a screen made from contemporary playing-cards, and there are several good pieces of oriental blue-and-white porcelain of adult cabinet rather than toy size. A considerable quantity of miniature china, silver and glass that was stored in the basement rooms used to stand in front of the model in the old London Museum at Kensington Palace. Unfortunately, this is no longer on view, and the Baby House stands alone, but very impressive, in its own large glass case.

The Tate Baby House at the Bethnal Green Museum is probably the best known of all British eighteenth-century houses and is so impressive with regard to both size and style that it remains the most arresting item in a superb collection. The museum has several houses dating to this period on permanent display, including a particularly charming, very small house that could have been accommodated in the smallest town home, though made with the architectural detail associated with eighteenth-century craftsmen. The doll's house section of the museum was replanned and set out much more interestingly in 1979, and there are many ideas that an ordinary collector could well copy.

The Tate house, like the Blackett, contains a number of pieces that have been added, and the Edwardian half-figures, often made up as pin-cushions, are particularly distressing in this context. Collectors and museums are often faced with the problem of whether to leave all the items that have gradually accumulated to the date of acquisition or to remove the more discordant in the interests of authenticity. In some instances, so little remains of the authentic that to remove all the later pieces would present the viewer with an empty shell, and one is therefore forced into offering a house that has remained a genuine toy, with the additions of each generation. In contrast, where there are relatively few later items, it would seen preferable to remove them so that the casual visitor does not gain the impression that, for instance, delicate porcelain-headed ladies are usually to be found in eighteenth-century models.

This large Baby House was made in Dorset *circa* 1760 and reflects a fashionable home of the period with an impressive *piano nobile* and a central lantern on the roof to light the staircase.

229

A detail of the Tate Baby House showing the opening Venetian window. Note the detailed carpentry and attention to architectural detail.

In this central side window of the Tate House the true period effect is given. It seems a pity that the other later sash windows could not be restored to their original condition.

The complex structure of the Tate Baby House can be appreciated only in this series of photographs. Note the pin at the back which links to the next section.

The Tate House was presumably made in three separate sections so that the massive house could be moved. It required considerable skill to be sure that the secret of the construction was not visible on the exterior when fully assembled.

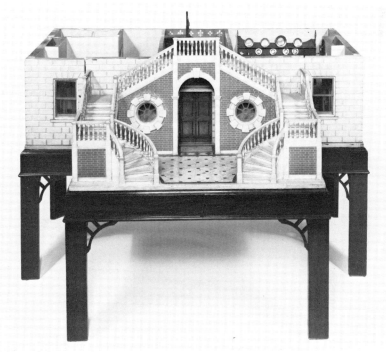

General interior of the Tate House.

Perhaps the perfection of Nostell clouds the approach to all other houses of the period, as, despite its shortcomings, the Tate Baby House has features impossible to better, such as the superbly constructed façade and the quite beautiful central Venetian window and central main door, both with complementary pediments. The balustrading of the *piano nobile* is both elegantly designed and finely constructed, and the whole of this ground-floor level is made in a completely convincing manner, quite different from that section of the Blackett house. The lantern on the roof is another feature of convincing realism as it served to illumine the main central staircase and, also from a purely aesthetic angle, balances the two tall but completely correct chimneys. The exterior presents a disconcerting, almost Edwardian effect,

232

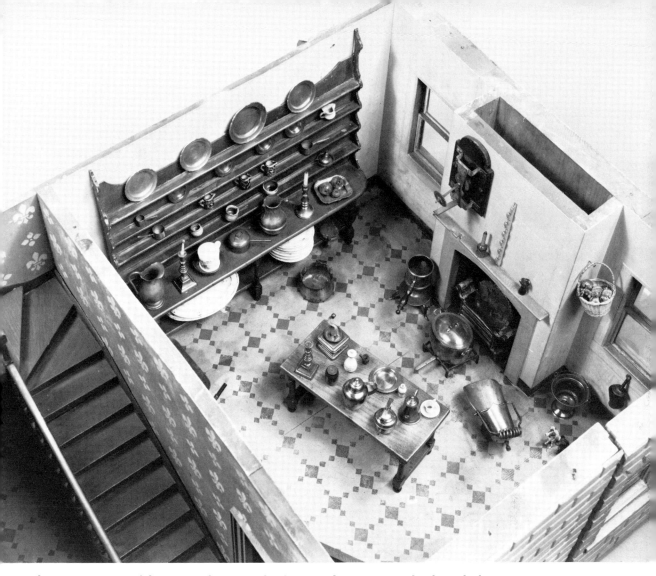

The arrangement of the Tate Baby House kitchen can be seen very clearly with the upper section removed. The dresser is one of the finest encountered in an English Baby House.

because the opening sash windows have lost their glazing-bars which give the traditional twelve-paned Georgian effect. These bars were sometimes properly made of wood, but in other cases very well-made houses have only card or even painted bars, which were of course lost if the original glass was broken. The windows show no structural damage along the sides, but it seems probable that this essential feature was removed at some time during restoration, possibly that of the 1830s, as these two-paned windows were then highly fashionable. Draw in the missing glazing-bars on a postcard of the house, and it is at once transformed into a model of truly splendid effect, as the whole atmosphere of the façade is improved and pulled together to present a correct eighteenth-century appearance.

The originally intended effect of this model is now perhaps best seen at the sides, where the central 'blind' windows are painted to resemble glass and provided with the conventionally Georgian twelve panes. Above the top-floor windows is an extremely fine decorative carving representing swagged fabric and flowers, which, in combination with the heavy cornicing and convincing balustrading, provides the viewer with that tightly constructed, completely finished effect that is typical of the better Baby Houses and which seems impossible for a modern maker to emulate. The cabinet-maker who worked on the Tate house was obviously a complete perfectionist, as even the chimneys were provided with decorative scrollwork on the bases in representation of ornate masonry. The mouldings used over the upper front windows are also of a superior type with additional carved detail, the window-frames themselves also being given carved decoration. The central Venetian window, beautiful in its general construction, is somewhat depleted by the fact that all the smaller glazing-bars have been lost, and it seems a pity that some minimal restoration could not be effected to bring the house back to its original splendour.

The superb cabinet-making extends into the rooms, where particularly good carved mouldings are used for the door-cases and the cornicing, the

234

Opposite: The façade of the Gardner Baby House with a pegged central panel that holds the fronts in position. There is a window in the back wall that lights the stairs. The original paintwork is a mellow grey-brown.

Detail of the Venetian window of the Gardner Baby House.

chimneypieces also exhibiting the unmistakably Georgian sureness of touch. Unfortunately the remainder of the interior was restored in the 1830s, when new wallpapers and several new pieces of furniture were added. A later restoration also appears to have taken place in the early part of this century, possibly when the pin-cushion-type half-dolls were added, as the arrangement of the furniture in several of the rooms gives the effect more of a family home of this period rather than of the eighteenth century. The late-Victorian and Edwardian earthenware jugs, the cheap oriental snuff-jars and the late pots of flowers all contribute to this curiously early twentieth-century effect, which is heightened by the unusually small scale of some of the main furnishings, especially in the dining-room. One thinks particularly of the heavy blacksmith-type brass fender that is now in this room, ruining the effect of the fine chimneypiece. Such cottage fenders were popular until the 1920s in the homes of poorer people, though in middle-class houses they were sometimes used in the kitchen or in a bedroom or nursery of little importance. In one of the main reception rooms of such an impressive household it is both out of place and out of scale. Similarly discordant items are found in other rooms, such as the fitted carpet of very late design in one of the bedchambers, so that it becomes impossible to find the interior of this most beautiful model

235

Above left: A group of fireplace items made of brass, iron and silver in the late eighteenth century. Possibly American. *Above right:* Miniature pewter candlesticks, probably American, though it is possible that they were imported from England in the eighteenth century.

anything other than a series of questions and discordant notes, such as a metal dog by courtesy of William Britains Ltd. Perhaps at some time, purely as an intellectual exercise, the museum will remove from the rooms all the pieces made after 1800, so that, perhaps just in a photograph, the really concerned could be given an impression of the interior in its original state. Until that time, we must gaze in wonder at the beauty of the exterior and admire the extravagance of an age when such an exquisite model could be made as a toy.

During the eighteenth century, dolls' houses, miniature dolls and furniture formed part of regular shipments from Britain to America, and Baby Houses of the period discovered in museums or private collections tend to be described as of British origin. Early settlers, living in the so-called 'English Houses' that contained one large ground-floor room with a huge fireplace and simple sleeping-quarters above reached by ladder-type stairs, and forced for the sake of economy to extinguish candles for family prayers, could provide their children with only the most basic of toys, such as balls and simple wooden or rag dolls, but as standards improved, the children began to be offered almost as fine a selection as their relatives in Europe. In 1725 Mr William Price, print- and map-seller, advertised 'a great variety of fine looking-glasses, tea-tables and sconces, toys and small pictures for children'. In 1743 William Price was more specific regarding the origin of his stock and described them as 'English and Dutch toys', though it seems probable that many of these were of the adult type.

A substantial amount of eighteenth-century American miniature furniture must have been made at home with the simplest of tools, and it seems unlikely that model houses were ignored. These primitive items always fare badly as, lacking the immediate attraction of fine carpentry, they rarely survive the childhood of their owners. Even the British Baby Houses shipped to America would usually have been of the smaller and less pretentious size, and there are no examples that can be positively attributed to these early shipments. In 1785 an advertisement in the *Philadelphia Gazetteer* offered 'dressed dolls, naked dolls and Lilliputian dolls, besides two new houses with gardens'. These were available from John Mason, who described himself as an upholsterer.

Native production of furnishings for dolls' houses seems to have begun with the development of the tinware industry in the mid eighteenth century. The most important family to be connected with this development was that headed by Edward Patterson, who had emigrated from Ireland between 1730 and 1760. At first they made use of imported tinplate and carried their work around the country in baskets, but they soon prospered so that the very name of the family became synonymous with tinware.

Regrettably, the only American doll's house to have survived from the eighteenth century is the model that is now in the Van Cortlandt Museum in New York. This effective house carries its original date, 1744, and was made for a member of the Homans family of Boston. Despite the fact that the original furniture is lost, this Baby House is the American equivalent of Ann Sharp's house in England and retains a very similar atmosphere. The date 1774 also appears just below the line of the roof of an ornamental pillar and is thought to relate to the date of birth of the second owner, though there is no positive documentation relating to this theory. The model stands over 4 feet high and is built with two integral drawers that form a sturdy base. It contains four rooms, the upper pair segregated by palings, a device frequently used in cellars, kitchens and attics of Dutch and German cabinets. The Dutch influence on this Baby House is particularly strong, as the narrow section represents the front, as in the canal houses of Holland. There is a pedimented front door with steps leading up to it, and in the roof is a small window through which goods could be hauled up from street-level. The sides of the house are left open, and it is thought that this is original and planned to allow the children complete ease of access. The kitchen, with its hooded fireplace and long shelves running right around the room, is reminiscent of model Nuremberg kitchens, and the carpenter who constructed this was obviously familiar with Continental methods. In many American homes of this period, economy necessitated that floors should be painted to resemble rugs and carpets, and towards this end local skills were developed in the technique. The Van Cortlandt House offers the visitor a charming period touch, as these painted rugs are still visible.

It seems highly probable that the lack of eighteenth-century American houses is due at least partly to the heavy Puritanism of the British settlers, who treated their children, both at home and at school, with much greater

The Homans cabinet house which carries the dates 1744 and 1774.

Opposite: Though not strictly a doll's house, Ann Anthony's Pavilion is of great interest as it is the earliest recorded American example of its type.

severity than did the Dutch. Much of the literature was of a moral tone and was imported mainly from Britain, but by the middle years of the century there was some adaptation of these very serious books for the Colonial audience. In much the same way, it is thought that most of the imported Baby Houses would have resembled the houses of Britain rather than the mainly wooden American structures. A much greater basic freedom regarding toys began to appear in the middle years of the century, and in 1750 Benjamin Franklin, editor of the *Pennsylvania Gazette*, claimed to be 'importing parcels of entertaining books for children', most probably those of Newbery. To the child who was constantly provided with British moral tales only occasionally interspersed with Newbery humour, there was little that seemed strange in playing with a Baby House in British style peopled with small wax or wooden dolls whose costumes also reflected those of fashionable Englishwomen. Also in European vein were arrangements in glazed cases such as a charming pavilion of cardboard, mica, paper, shells and wax created by Ann Anthony in 1769 at the age of fourteen.

The education of girls was at first no more seriously regarded than in Britain: in most homes they simply aided their mothers in housewifely duties. Even in wealthy houses they were expected to assist in such necessary tasks as candle-dipping and soap-making, and their assistance in the basic running of the home was even more commonplace than in Britain. James Nelson, in his essay on the 'Government of Children', published in New York in 1753, suggests only the most superficial education for girls, who should learn to cast simple accounts, exercise of the needle and some household management, so they would be acquainted with the right times for the storage of provisions; they should also be taught how to select good food at market, how to carve a joint efficiently and how to deport themselves at the table. Their main purpose in life should be to please others, and all their personal fulfilment would come, like that of their British contemporaries, from the cheerful pursuit of their duties.

Despite the fact that a lighter element was appearing in the lives of Colonial children in the second half of the eighteenth century, play was still generally considered to be a waste of time. In *A Present to Children*, published in New London in 1783, the tone of the general advice differed only a little from that handed out to previous generations: 'Improve your time. When you play, do it because God gives you leave. Learn to get good and do good in your plays.' Such idle pursuits as playing with painted toys and Baby Houses was severely reprimanded in a *Song for Little Miss*, and her delight in 'glittering shelves, tiny tables, plates and chairs of her Baby Room' is claimed to be the very foolish folly of a young mind. Even the dolls she clasped to her breast were not free from the taint of idleness. Sadly, to our ears, but with the ring of morality and absolute truth triumphing over childish natural desires, the poet declaims:

> Fain would I guard this prattling voice,
> These haughty airs surprise;
> No more shall Baubles be my choice
> Nor plays nor idleness.

Despite such Puritanical strictures, the American nursery gradually acquired a character distinctively its own, aided by publishers who, in a variety of books, encouraged the children of the new republic to develop their own nationalistic elements. One of the first American history books was Noah Webster's *Elements of Useful Knowledge, containing an Historical Geographical Account of the United States.* Biographies of important national figures such as George Washington also began to appear from 1794. Although the nursery was not immune from the inculcation of nationalism, the majority of games and books continued, until the end of the first quarter of the nineteenth century, to be mainly British in inspiration, so, amusingly, we find that American children were instructed regarding the flora and fauna of Britain as well as British traditions and culture long after the foundation of the republic.

Much of the severity with which Colonial children were treated was caused by the insecurity of adult life. The ambitious father, brutally chastising his young, saw in the child's wilfulness the awful possibility of his hard-won civilization regressing into barbarism. The American father of this period was an almost God-like figure, who believed that his iron hand had scriptural commendation. In comparison, the woman's role was even more subservient than in Britain, as she had virtually no rights. Fortunately there were a few more liberal parents, such as William Penn, who advised his own married children against being too dogmatic about obtaining complete obedience and added, 'If God give you children, love them with wisdom, correct them with affection; never strike in passion, and suit their correction to their age as well as the fault.' Despite advice of such sterling worth, which is still appropriate in the twentieth century, the literature of the period serves only to make us aware that girls were considered suitable only for domestic work. In *Memoirs of a Peg Top* by Mary Jane Kilner, published in Worcester, Massachusetts, in 1788, the small girl is firmly instructed:

> A top my dear girl is ill chosen for you.
> So take up your doll, to your Baby House go,
> And there your attention much better bestow!
> Leave the peg top behind, and behave like a Miss,
> And I'll give you this picture, these nuts and a kiss.

Obviously whipping-tops were considered quite inappropriate for a girl, but American manufacturers were themselves becoming able to offer her a much wider range of toys of impeccable domestic character, so that the New York pewterer Robert Boyle in 1781 was advertising 'doll dishes, plates and platters', and the Philadelphia Museum of Art has an American-made miniature fireplace with andirons and tongs and a candlestick and candlemould, all of miniature size, dating to 1731. The last ten years of the eighteenth century saw the establishment of tin-toy manufacture at Stevens Plains, Maine, and Berlin, Connecticut. These domestic miniatures were originally produced as sidelines by workmen concerned mainly with full-sized utilitarian objects, but the potential of the children's market was soon appreciated, and a whole variety of toys, including complete tin kitchens, was made. Similar, but even smaller-scale manufacture of toys was undertaken by carpenters who, as in Britain, sometimes produced particular items to special order, though the really significant American production did not get under way until the early years of the nineteenth century and in fact was not to reach its peak until after 1910.

Illustrations of contemporary dolls' houses are rare. Here a large-scale model is played with, and though there is no kitchen, the other rooms are well supplied with furniture. In the dining-room the chairs are set back against the wall in eighteenth-century style.

FIVE

Nineteenth-Century British Dolls' Houses

British nursery life in the first half of the nineteenth century was greatly influenced by Maria Edgeworth's *Practical Education*, in which parents and those entrusted with the upbringing of children were given sensible, if somewhat sombre advice. Her almost obsessive dislike of many of the more romantic and imaginative playthings is rarely concealed, and collectors of today can only rejoice in the fact that many of her strictures were not taken too seriously, or we should have lost some of the most visually attractive antique toys. In the sensible, logical mind of Miss Edgeworth, toys and learning-activity were completely united, and she would have regarded a beautifully costumed doll's house doll or a model room furnished with gilded chairs as an object of derision. She had little regard for the needs of sensitive, imaginative children, for whom a well-set-out tableau or exquisitely made miniature could be an object of wonder and an exciting adventure of the senses: everything had to have a purpose and a measurable result.

The child's basic inquisitiveness with regard to the construction of toys was to be encouraged, and the unceasing reproof of a governess was not appropriate to a situation where, in search of knowledge, the child had broken his toy to pieces. Children need toys 'which continually exercise their senses or their imagination, their imitative and inventive powers. The glaring colours or the gilding of toys may catch the eye and please for a few minutes, but unless some use can be made of them, they will, and ought to be, soon discarded.' As long as the intelligent individual child retained the courage to investigate and even destroy his toys, Edgeworth feels he could come to little harm, but unfortunately,

> In general he is taught to set a value on them totally independent of all ideas of utility or any regard to his own real feelings. Either he is conjured to take real care

243

of them because they cost a great deal of money; or else he is taught to admire them as miniatures on which fine people pride themselves.

A little girl, presiding at her baby tea-table is pleased with the notion that she is like her mama; and before she can have any idea of the real pleasures of conversation and society, she is confirmed in the persuasion that tattling and visiting are some of the most enviable privileges of grown people; a set of beings whom she believes to be in possession of all the sweets of happiness.

When discussing dolls, Miss Edgeworth treads very warily, conscious of the fact that Rousseau had occasionally commended these nursery companions as a means of introducing some dress-sense to girls at the earliest opportunity. Just in case any parent should feel that dolls were completely safe toys and allow over-much indulgence in their costuming, she adds rather grimly, that, 'A watchful eye should be kept upon the child to mark the first symptoms of a love of finery and fashion.'

She is even less generous to children who enjoyed playing with dolls' houses, as the influence of Rousseau was here much less oppressive.

Our objections to dolls are offered with great submission and due hesitation. With more confidence we may venture to attack Baby Houses; an unfinished Baby House might be a good toy, as it would employ little carpenters and seamstresses to fit it up; but a completely furnished Baby House proves as tiresome to a child as a furnished seat is to a young nobleman. After peeping, for in general only a peep may be had into each apartment, after being thoroughly satisfied that nothing is wanting, and that consequently there is nothing to be done, the young lady lies her doll upon the state bed, if the doll be not twice as large as the bed, and falls fast asleep in the midst of her felicity.

Quite obviously the writer had never watched a child playing with a model house with that complete concentration engendered only by the most successful of toys; each doll has its own character, the house has its own situation, and the girl manipulates the interior as a playwright his actors, deriving, in her infantile manner, comparable satisfaction in the solving of domestic problems.

Edgeworth's comments regarding children's ability to construct their own toys appears much more accurately observed, and one cannot but wish that more late-Victorian fathers had followed her advice. She considered it most unwise to inspire a child with high-flown ideas about the perfect things he could make if he owned, for instance, a carpentry set. The boy would obviously dream of perfectly constructed model bureaux, chests of drawers and tables. All such imaginings were doomed to disappointment when the boy realized that, at the age of ten, he had neither the basic ability nor the range of tools needed to complete a project he had visualized. All such problems could be solved if only the child could be taken to a Rational

Toyshop where all manner of carpentry tools and suitable wood could be correctly selected. Younger children might well fare better with paste and cardboard, and 'Models of common furniture should be made as toys, which may be taken to pieces, so that all the parts and the manner in which they are put together might be seen distinctly, the names of the different parts should be written or stamped upon them . . . From models of furniture we may go on to models of architecture; pillars of different orders, the roofs of houses, the manner of slating etc.' If a child was employed in the building of a model, the opportunity should be taken to 'Teach him how bricks are made, how the arches over the windows and doors are made, the nature of the key stone and the butments of an arch.'

That the advice of educationalists, even those speaking with such clear good sense as Maria Edgeworth, has rarely had any lasting influence on toy-manufacturers is evidenced by the fact that the doll's house gradually became more popular as the nineteenth century progressed. Despite dire warnings regarding the unsuitability of dolls' houses as learning-aids, children from an ever-widening social group began to enjoy the fascination of equipping and caring for a miniature home. This affection for the doll's house, enjoyed, by the end of the century, by working-class children as well, was engendered at least partly by the pride that ordinary people were able, because of increased prosperity, to take in their own homes. The artisans, who in the eighteenth century were only slowly moving towards some standing in society, were straining by the mid-nineteenth century towards a middle-class type of respectability that was centred in a pleasant, comfortable and well-run home. A letter from Mayhew's *Morning Chronicle* series describes a cabinet-maker's house in the 1850s: 'You have the warm red glow of mahogany furniture; a clean carpet covers the floor; a few engravings in neat frames hang against the papered wall; and bookshelves or a bookcase have their appropriate furniture. Very white and bright-coloured pot ornaments, with sometimes a few roses in a small vase, are reflected in a mirror over the mantelpiece.' Comfortable, attractive interiors, such as that described by this avid social commentator, are mirrored in many small dolls' houses, and the hard-working parents, almost as much as their eager children, must have enjoyed setting the model to rights and making the small rooms comfortable and snug. The doll's house is rarely the toy of the socially deprived but, by its very presence, suggests a home with a degree of stability and parents or nurses with the time to help the child achieve the maximum enjoyment from a toy that was often both large and, in relation to others, quite costly.

The importance of warmth and comfort in domestic interiors is frequently remarked upon in nineteenth-century literature, and the dolls' houses seem to follow this new mood, with much smaller rooms than those of the previous century and a much more lavish use of wallpaper and carpets. Those models made at the beginning of the century retain a strong aura of the classical houses with wide rooms and long, low, façades, but, as the century progresses, so the more cheaply constructed dolls' houses become taller and narrower, so that the rooms, in proportion, seem much higher. These less generous proportions were not echoed by the furnishings that were now imported, mainly from Germany, in great abundance. The girl could pack her toy parlour with beadwork, ormolu, overmantels, china and glass of all colours and quality, in imitation of the cluttered full-scale interiors with which she was so familiar. In a single apartment are often found miniatures from France, Germany, Britain and even India, and it is this mixing of items, some long out of fashion, that makes the precise dating of individual interiors so very difficult.

Doll's house furniture often continued to be made to well-established popular designs for as long as fifty years, so that items in the Biedermeier style were sometimes sold at the end of the century alongside pale Art Nouveau pot-stands and writing-desks that were also of German origin. Biedermeier never became a popular style in Britain, yet, judging by the miniature interiors, one could be forgiven for thinking that every family possessed an elegant sofa or a set of dining-chairs in this style. Similarly, very few British kitchens contained the wealth of equipment that a German or French housewife would have felt necessary and which the toymakers such as Märklin produced in such quantity, so that in the doll's house a girl encountered an assortment of gadgetry she would probably never use in her adult life. In peopling the house, it was sometimes necessary to utilize a man doll in splendid Prussian Guard uniform, while a visiting uncle might unexpectedly appear as an admiral in the German Navy, all this being enacted in an architectural setting reminiscent of the backwaters of an English cathedral town. It is therefore meaningless to comment that a nineteenth-century doll's house perfectly presents the viewer with a picture of British domestic life in miniature. The furnishings and their disposition might be charming, but they have little social relevance when compared with a painting or print, and their historical exactitude is also questionable as there was usually no full-scale counterpart. The doll's house is purely an evocation of nineteenth-century Europe, highlighted with small touches such as a newspaper, a particular form of dress, a curious arrangement of furniture or a nationalistic print that suggests a particular country or the character of the original owner.

It might be expected that some particularly artistic parents would have decorated their child's house in the aesthetic taste, to accord with the clothes she wore, or for some sturdy follower of William Morris to have created a Brotherhood interior in miniature, but we discover no such treasures. In general, the doll's house was obviously considered purely an amusing plaything to be equipped and furnished with little exactitude but much enthusiasm, so that it is now possible to date the contents only in the broadest

A most unusual Art Nouveau house, *circa* 1912, designed by Jessie M. King, a member of the Glasgow school. The house, which measures $27\frac{1}{4}$ inches by $10\frac{1}{2}$ inches, is painted in blue and grey.

manner. Very occasionally, a house is accompanied by some form of pedigree which enables the collector to establish the date of its basic construction, though the contents provide evidence of only the most general kind. I have found eighteenth-century kitchen equipment in Edwardian houses, twentieth-century tables in an early-Victorian dining-room and pieces, home-made during the last war, all in houses which the families who own them claim to be completely untouched since a particular ancestor's death. There is usually no conscious wish to deceive in such statements, but the layman hardly notices small additions, and if a parent for fifty years has insisted that the contents date to a particular year, there is often little family inclination to dispute or question the fact. The collector needs to study such

247

models with great caution, as it is very easy to abandon the critical faculty when confronted by an object of immediate attractiveness, made even more alluring by its reported history.

The doll's house dolls are often of much more use in dating a model than the furniture, as women's fashion was so much more volatile, and a girl was unlikely to want a family dressed in the style of her mother's generation. Even within the family, considerable variations of date are often found, as individual characters were added and others redressed for special occasions. Despite such problems, the dolls' costumes do provide a much more precise guide than the furniture, though there are many reservations. Despite the allure of dolls' houses and miniature furniture, we must therefore be cautious in attributing qualities to them which they patently do not possess. British nineteenth-century houses are fascinating, but they provide us with little evidence of contemporary life-style in the manner of the earlier Baby Houses. Their importance is therefore not less but completely different in quality.

In the nineteenth-century interiors, a tangible expression of the richness of British life is given, the number of servants, the well-filled nursery, the vast quantity of food and the often garish colours of wallpapers and fabrics, all combining to present a picture of the prosperous family life that was the goal of every sensible citizen. Maria Edgeworth was possibly right to condemn dolls' houses as frivolous and time-wasting, but it is the decorative rather than the most sensible items from the past that collectors most revere. Many parents in the nineteenth century found the ideas of such educationalists attractive, though the results of the child's rational play were rarely preserved, and we have to rely on a few autobiographies, such as that written by E. Stevenson when she was an elderly woman in 1871. Her miniature dolls were kept in the bottom drawer of a large chest that stood in her nursery:

> When I had plenty of time to spare, I used to arrange them in smaller drawers of another empty chest, four storeys high, which made a capital doll's house, quite as neat and commodious as any of the 'family mansions, replete with every requisite convenience' which one sees advertised so abundantly in the morning papers.
>
> I never had a proper doll's house bought for me. Mama always liked me to invent my own playthings, and then she said they both lasted longer and I enjoyed them more. I believe she was quite right, for I had the fun of inventing and the still greater fun of seeing how the invention turned out. I don't think the girls of today, with their miniature dinner-parties and real moulds of blancmange, and soups and open tarts which have been made specially for them in the kitchen by a proper cook, have any idea how Lucy and I enjoyed keeping house upon two lumps of sugar and a piece of seedcake in that dear old oriel window, with pieces of writing-paper, turned up at the corners for dishes and nut-shells for cups and saucers. . . . I'm sure we got a lot more satisfaction, real, lasting, solid satisfaction, out of our four-storey chest of drawers with papa's old cigar-boxes for beds and acorn cups for toilet-services and half-a-dozen empty pillboxes for stools and square pieces of

wood supported on cotton-reels for tables, and little round bits of cardboard for plates and dishes, than children get now from their toyshop dining-rooms and drawing-rooms and bedrooms with real furniture and sets of proper crockery and things that are always getting broken and spoilt.

Some of my dolls were babies. They used to sleep in lozenge-box cradles . . . they were just like little real cradles, frilled around with white muslin and something over the top for curtains.

It is noticeable from this account that, although mama thought it better for her daughter to construct her own houses and furniture, the dolls were commercial, possibly because of the great difficulty a child would encounter in modelling a realistic figure on such a small scale. In the early years of the nineteenth century, the old-style wooden dolls with their somewhat overlarge heads and simply made bodies continued to attract customers for some time, as did the basic waxes, but the much more revealing costume of fashionable women soon made it necessary for the manufacturers to pay more attention to the body-shape of even the smallest doll. Gradually better-shaped breasts, lower legs and arms emerged from the woodcarvers' workshops to create a small doll with much greater realism that could be costumed in delicate muslin. These figures, which have survived in such number in early nineteenth-century houses, were produced mainly in the Grödnertal, though similar figures were also made in Berchtesgaden, but in a smaller quantity. Princess Victoria's German mother and governess were obviously familiar with similar dolls from their own childhood, and the future Queen was encouraged to play both with dolls of this type and with a doll's house. It is fortunate that her playthings have been preserved and can still be seen at the Museum of London.

The large group of Grödnertals which the Princess costumed, with the help of her governess, is surely the most photographed assembly of doll's house dolls yet recorded. They were of considerable public interest during the Queen's own lifetime, and in 1894 Frances Low satisfied public curiosity by the publication of *Queen Victoria's Dolls*, a volume that carried Her Majesty's approval. The book was apparently inspired by the very general attention that was given to an article in the *Strand Magazine* which provided a general description. Frances Low approached her task with the lowly mien of a worshipping subject, and consequently many of her statements are obvious eulogies. Her account is, nevertheless, completely fascinating, especially as the Queen corrected any small points upon which she disagreed.

Miss Low describes how the lonely young Princess played with her small dolls until she was nearly fourteen years old: 'The little one, now pursuing her kind vocation of mother, now reprimanding, now caressing, reveals in a thousand ways the same thoughts, feelings and passions which will one day bring happiness, or the reverse, to those who are watching her'. Sir Henry Ponsonby also commented that, 'Her favourites were small dolls, small

A group of Grödnertals that were costumed by Queen Victoria and her governess, Baroness Lehzen, between 1831 and 1833.

wooden dolls, which she would occupy herself with dressing; and they had a house in which they could be placed.' These figures are now of great fascination to collectors, as they were documented by the young Victoria in a faded copybook entitled *List of my Dolls*. With precision, the girl inscribed the name of the doll, its costumier and the character represented. Ballet and opera performers were also identified by the name of the show in which they appeared, and it is obvious that the Princess was a great follower of the London stage. Out of 132 dolls, the Queen herself costumed only thirty-two, leaving the remainder to her industrious governess. Out of the whole collection only seven are dressed as men, and the Princess obviously most enjoyed the costuming of the Court and theatrical ladies, though she also sewed some of the small rag babies that the Grödnertals carried or which were laid in cradles. Slight variations in decoration, always to be found in hand-finished dolls of this type, were developed by the two costumiers, who chose the plump-faced dolls for certain ladies of their acquaintance and the very delicate-featured to represent the dancers. In the hours of patient work expended on these figures, with their drawn threadwork, initialled handkerchiefs and fine bead jewellery, we are instructed to see 'the scenes that affected her, the stories that enchanted her, the characters that caught her fancy and left an impression on her imagination; and we see also in these childish achievements the same qualities of self-control, patience, steadfastness of purpose and womanliness which have been constantly achieved by Queen Victoria'.

The Court ladies are distinguished by their longer skirts and also by their much closer adherence to the dictates of fashion, with low pointed bodices and large puff sleeves. Victoria must have been especially fond of Lady Arnold, as she is separately costumed in five different outfits, ranging from a sombre dark green velvet to a much more youthful yellow crêpe trimmed with mauve ribbon. Miss Low allows herself a delicate complaint regarding one of this lady's costumes of white lawn, which she compares 'to a nightgown with a flounce at the bottom: Over it there is a sort of paletot reaching below the knees, which fastens in front and has a frill around the bottom. . . . It is curious and quaint and has an old-world air, but it must be confessed it belongs to the kingdom of dowdyism.' Her daughter wears a typical girl's outfit of the period, of a pale lilac sash on a simple muslin frock; from her shoulders a lace fichu hangs to floor level. With her dark coal-scuttle bonnet, this doll is typical of many seen in quite basic dolls' houses of the period. The majority of the Court ladies can be distinguished by the colours they wear, as the basic costumes are very similarly constructed but given variation by lace or jewellery. The Duchess of Worcester wears yellow silk, the Countess of Deptford mauve. Princess Collorowsky was personally dressed by the future Queen, and her frock was embroidered with silver tinsel on a buff-coloured ground. Alice, Countess of Rothesay, was costumed in two different outfits and probably attracted much attention at Court as she was the mother of twins. These babies were carefully constructed from fabric, one being costumed in satin and the other in lawn, while their mother, in this tableau, wears a simple white satin dress. The twins are also shown lying in a cardboard cradle covered with pink satin and trimmed with ribbons. Mary, Lady Roxburgh, sports a frilled, white lace bonnet which is tied under her chin, but she seems weighed down by the exceptionally large sleeves of her yellow silk dress trimmed with lace.

Characters from the theatrical world were obviously as important to the Princess as the grand Court ladies, and an equal degree of attention was lavished on their costumes, which can be differentiated from those of the Court by the shorter skirts. The number and variety of these stage figures led Frances Low to speculate whether Victoria had once owned some sort of stage for their display. Mlle Sylvie Leconte, said to have been second only to Taglioni in the art of dancing, appears, as does Mlle Porphyrin Brocard, a lady who married into the aristocracy. She is shown in two outfits, and the more interesting represents the condemned heroine she played in *The Maid of Palaiseau*. The child actress Miss Poole is represented by a particularly tiny doll without a carved comb, probably intended to represent the character she played in *Old and Young*. One of the few men is M. Albert, a ballet master at the King's Theatre, who wears an eye-catching shirt of fine linen trimmed at the hem with rows of blue ribbon. One of the most dazzling outfits was that worn by Miss Cawse as 'Fatima, Lady Brighton'; this was composed of a brilliant yellow silk frock edged with white fur, worn with a scarlet satin pannier and a huge matching hat. She was intended to represent the elder sister in an updated version of 'Beauty and the Beast', the character who asked her father to bring her back costly robes from his travels. Her other outfit is also fur-trimmed, but this time the colour combination is blue and black. The frock worn by Mlle Leontine Heberle, of white Spanish net over satin, was the work of Victoria herself and is particularly charming in effect, with its decoration of white satin piping, bunches of pink roses and bows of pink ribbon.

The Court ladies have few attendants, probably because the costumes of servants would have proved tedious to sew, and Mrs Martha the housekeeper seems to be in sole charge. This doll, larger than the others and having an even rounder face, was obviously a good candidate for domestic work and is dressed in a white lawn gown with simple, long sleeves and a purple apron. Her cap, in comparison, is completely frivolous, composed of white net and a generous allowance of pink ribbon. In general, the figures costumed by the Princess are simpler in effect and without much of the textural decoration achieved by the use of embroidery, pearls and braid by the Baroness Lehzen.

The variety with which the decorators painted the basic wooden heads is very obvious in this group, as no two are completely alike; about half the total number wear carved combs in their hair, while the others have simple, short hairstyles, with individuality given by the twist of a forehead curl or a loose tendril of hair on the cheek. Most of the dolls wear carved, red-painted slippers, but a few wear green or yellow. In no other museum is it possible to see such a wide selection of Grödnertals, and these are especially worthy of study because of their complete originality. The figures costumed in outdoor dress are particularly memorable, as few of these small dolls were dressed in anything other than the simplest of frocks, so that the dress of fashionable women as well as the variety of doll's house dolls available at the time can be studied.

The Queen's doll's house is, in comparison with her splendid dolls, a surprisingly unpretentious structure and somewhat disappointing, as Victoria might have been expected to own a model in the Baby House tradition, with some extravagance of construction and fittings. Instead we find a very simple house of the period, exactly mirroring that simplicity of life-style that was eventually to endear her to her subjects in later life. She was a queen who preferred a bonnet to a crown and, when on an important state visit to France, aroused the affection of her people by insisting on carrying a handbag embroidered with a parrot and made by one of her children, while the grand French ladies who escorted her were dressed in the height of fashion. This doll's house of her childhood is completely in this manner and also serves to indicate how, as a child, Victoria was encouraged in her modest tastes by her mother and governess.

The doll's house has now lost most of its furniture but was described in the *Girls' Realm* of 1899 in some detail:

> The kitchen is filled with everything necessary to the most fastidious housekeeper. An ample dresser shows rows of shining pewter plates, and there are frying-pans, saucepans and other culinary utensils placed neatly upon the walls or shelves. There is a capacious knife-box filled with iron spoons and forks and wooden-handled knives. There are flat-irons, an iron-stand, a warming-pan, a coffee-mill and a clock. The grate is one of the old-fashioned kind, and an iron kettle is on the hob. On each side of the fireplace stand doll servants. I grieve to state they are neither clean nor trim. 'Biddy' in a daintily striped cotton bodice and a red petticoat, looks a regular marchioness, while James the cook does not look as if he was a servant belonging to the 'quality'. There is a tea-service of common ware, obviously intended for kitchen use. As there is no staircase, you must reach the drawing-room by an imaginary flight. The furniture is not sumptuous. The square wooden table has some pretty little china cups and saucers on it. A kind of cabinet of plain wood stands in one corner, and a birdcage with a parrot on it hangs from the ceiling. The chairs are all small and apparently do not belong to the same suite.

The doll's house, judging from this late nineteenth-century account, was obviously somewhat bare and neglected even during the Queen's lifetime, and it has suffered further depletion over the years, so that many of the pieces mentioned in the kitchen, for instance, are no longer in place. One of the most attractive features of this flat-fronted house is the painted fanlight over the door, with its additional side windows, quite a common feature of actual houses of the time but extremely rare in a doll's house. This red-brick, flat-fronted construction is a particularly British style of doll's house building and, with minor alterations, mainly to the shape of the front door, continued in popular use until the Great War, making well-constructed models that have lost their original wallpapers extremely difficult to date precisely.

If only a quarter of the dolls' houses and doll's house dolls said to have been presented by Queen Victoria to various children were to have survived, the number would still seem improbable. Almost every other British family claims to own some toy said to have been presented by the Queen on a christening, birthday or official visit. Though the majority of these statements are generally regarded with scepticism, it has to be admitted that she was particularly fond of giving dolls as gifts. Houses seem to have been sent only occasionally, and among the lucky recipients was the Princess Charlotte of Belgium, who wrote a thank-you letter from Laeken on 18th July 1848: 'My dearest cousin – I have received the beautiful doll's house you have been so kind to send me, and I thank you very much for it. I am delighted with it; every morning I dress my doll and give her a good breakfast; and the day after her arrival she gave a great rout at which all my dolls were invited. Sometimes she plays at drafts [*sic*] on her pretty little draft-board, and every evening I undress her and put her to bed.' There is no further description of the toys, though it seems doubtful that a very large house was sent, as toys in the nineteenth century were only very rarely prestige gifts sent to impress the Court. The playthings of the Queen's own children were in the main such as might have been owned by any middle-class child, so that there is no longer the complete divergence of standard encountered in the eighteenth century, when adult interest was so strong.

Despite the change of emphasis, early nineteenth-century adults were slow to relinquish completely an interest in model houses and interiors, though, for propriety, their construction often appears in the guise of a three-dimensional setting in a glazed frame or as a tableau under a glass shade. Manufacturers were also aware of the comfortable appearance of a small model home and created, in particular, many needlework boxes with exteriors carved or decorated with marquetry to resemble town houses of the period. Small drawers were often concealed in the sides, and the roofs opened to reveal the sewing-compartment. In better examples, there were neat rows of containers for the mother-of-pearl cotton-reels, needle-holders and stilettos that were so

Two doll's house cabinets that served as containers for Fry's chocolates and carry the firm's label, *circa* 1905.

In the early nineteenth century a number of houses were made in the large scale associated with Baby Houses. This most effective example is an unusual chinoiserie style and opens at the front to reveal a panelled hall with a staircase on either side. The detail of the room is less impressive than the exterior. The two small wings are curious additions. One is fitted as a kitchen and the other as a stable with four stalls and grooms and tack-room behind. Width 95 inches.

loved by the Victorians. Grace Foakes, in her book *Between High Walls*, describes a similar box owned by her mother: 'On opening the front door, two drawers were exposed. The side doors revealed more drawers. Father always kept this model locked.' The craftsmanship expended on these functional models was invariably high, and they were always kept in a place of safety, though this did not stop many children from regarding them almost as toys rather than as adult equipment. Even finer work is sometimes seen on the tea-caddies that often formed an important gift, such as that made by William Potter of Cornhill in 1786 in the form of a small group of town houses; this model can now be seen at the London Museum. A large caddy forms the central house, and two smaller, separate containers form a smaller, complementary house on either side, with the detail beautifully inlaid. Simpler versions were to be found in many middle-class homes, the very shape of the container suggesting comfort and stability. In the early twentieth century, complete tea-sets were made in the form of small cottages and probably served to bring the comfort of neat, well-appointed homes to people broken-hearted as a result of the Great War.

Money-boxes, chocolate-containers, ornaments and tea-cosies all utilized

A charming model made (*circa* 1870) almost entirely of glass with ground shell and sand forming the paths. The curtains are fabric. The glass forming the sides of the house is in shades of red and green. There are additional windows at the sides and back. It is a good example of the glassmaker's art combined with that of a modeller. Height 14 inches.

the basic model house shape, and many items that were originally purely ornamental became, with only a few changes, children's toys. One thinks particularly of the attractive houses made purely as ornaments for display in glass cases that were decorated with dry flowers and plasterwork. These were not always the work of adults, as the *Girl's Own Toymaker* in 1859 includes several sets of instructions for model houses and cottages that 'will make a very neat embellishment for the drawing-room'. These models were made from folded cardboard and included a cottage with a projecting front section and a hipped roof, surrounded by a fence and a rustic Swiss Cottage that was further ornamented with split, dried twigs, glued in position to give the effect of a log cabin. 'The ground may be filled up with moss, pieces of wood and small stones, and if the whole is perfectly made, it will make a very complete chimneypiece ornament.' The more adventurous girls could then progress to constructing arbours, chairs and tables, all in rustic style, from dried wood.

Drawing-room embellishments of this type are still frequently discovered,

A cottage from the
Girl's Own Toymaker
published in 1859.

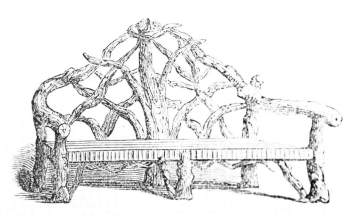

A rustic chair whose
design was suggested
in the *Girl's Own
Toymaker* in 1859.

as they have often survived because of their protective glass. The workmanship and ingenuity expended on the better examples is extremely high, and sometimes the interiors were furnished and peopled with as much care. Doll's house collectors often avoid purchasing such items, despite the fact that the craftsmanship involved is often of a much higher quality than usually seen on a child's toy, and it seems a pity that so many become the props of interior decorators rather than forming links in the development of model houses. These structures are the nineteenth-century equivalent of the Baby Houses that were furnished by adults and deserve much more serious attention.

The Victorian love of novelty encouraged the use of materials other than wood and card for the construction of the most remarkable pieces, such as a cake that is lit by electricity from within, and prestige exercises, such as that shown at the Crystal Palace Co-Operative Festival in 1888 and described as a very uncommon and exquisite piece of work:

A whole variety of unlikely objects were made in the shape of buildings, such as the wedding cake made for Princess Mary in 1922. On removing a piece from the bottom layer with a ribbon, all the cake was lit with some fifty bulbs.

Opposite far right: Such albums were correctly made miniatures with brass clasps and tooled leather binding. *Right:* The album open. It contains pictures of the royal family, *circa* 1865.

It represents a summerhouse and covers less than a foot of space. It is made entirely of brass. Every plank was formed separately and then fastened together with tiny nails in true carpenter's fashion. There are trelliswork windows and a table within, laden with pipes and refreshments. On either side, nesting over the roof, are two grapevines, each leaf and tendril most delicately worked in silver. At the back of the house there is a collection of garden tools, roller, wheelbarrow etc, all in working order. The gravel walk outside is studded with little brass flowerpots, just about the right size to hang on a watch-chain, and in these are garden flowers, each one perfectly recognizable by its own peculiarities.

This exhibit, only one example from a number of similar works of great craftsmanship that were shown at displays throughout the nineteenth century, was the work of an elderly man, H. J. Davies. Very fine quality miniature furniture was also a popular subject for exhibition pieces, though it was usually of a larger size than would fit conveniently into a conventional doll's house. The makers of chairs, in particular, did not confine themselves to the most obvious medium but used brass, copper, silver and a wide variety of more amenable substances such as paper and composition. Particularly fine models, sometimes small enough for inclusion in a doll's house, were made on a commercial scale by several manufacturers and were originally intended as

258

containers. Small chairs, stools and sofas made of metal or wood were supplied with well-upholstered seats so they could be used as pincushions. From Whitby came carved jet miniature tables and stools, and a variety of engaging household furnishings originated in Tunbridge. During the eighteenth century exquisite mahogany spinet workboxes had formed particularly elegant additions for a large Baby House. Inside were silver sewing-sets, and there was often a musical movement in the base. Miniature knife-boxes, made usually of tortoiseshell, were produced throughout the nineteenth century and look splendid on the larger-scale sideboards, though their original intention was as étuis. Gilt photograph-frames are often found in the form of an artist's display-easel of doll's house size, and many a needlecase in the form of a parasol has finished its days in a miniature umbrella-stand. A host of similar items of dual intention are found in model houses, their correctness disputed only by the strictest purists.

Despite the fact that fine items of adult intention, especially those connected with needlework, continued to be made in Britain, there was no substantial manufacture of doll's house furniture, as it could be obtained so cheaply from Germany. Instead, a number of small craftsmen, often working alone or as outworkers for a wholesaler or shop, specialized in particular lines. This work was never marked in any way, and as the most popular wood, in both Britain and Germany, was pine, it is at present impossible to identify the British-made production, which, judging by contemporary accounts, was of a reasonable size. In 1852 a whitewood toy-maker was interviewed by *Hogg's Instructor*; he made a variety of cheap items, none of which cost more than a penny: 'In sawed and planed pinewood, I manufacture penny and halfpenny toy bellows, penny and halfpenny toy tables, penny wash-hand stands, chiefly for Baby Houses, penny dressers with drawers for the same purpose, penny bedsteads. The toy bellows now have no run. Six or seven years ago there was a great rage for them. Then I made about twelve thousand in one year, but you see they were dangerous and induced the children to play with fire, so they soon went out of fashion.'

Nine years later, Mayhew visited a small toy-maker who lived in a cottage at the back of Bethnal Green Road in London: 'The little railed space in front of the humble dwelling was littered with sundry evidences of the maker's ingenuity.... I found the cripple himself in bed but still sitting up, with a small desk-like bench before him.' The man described himself as a small-time whitewood toy-maker, specializing in items to be sold for less than a penny. His production was made for the warehouses in Sheffield and Birmingham, and he was paid 7 pence a dozen for the items that were to be sold for a penny each. He was helped in his work by his whole family and was particularly proud of his daughter's skill. Interestingly, despite their poverty, the whole family could read, and the young son was sent to school.

According to Mayhew's *Occupation Abstract*, there were 407 toy-makers and 146 toy-merchants and dealers in London in 1841, while in the whole of Britain he estimated that there were 1,866. The London toy-makers were divided into several classes, such as the turners, the Bristol or greenwood toy-makers, the whitewood toy-makers, the fancy toy-maker or modeller and the doll-maker, of which there are two grand branches, 'the makers of the wooden and the sewed dolls. Then there are the tin toy-makers, the lead and pewter toy-maker.' The so-called Bristol toys were apparently originally made in that area, but the term was in general use in the nineteenth century to describe common toys, made for the children of the poor, to retail at a penny. This type of toy had been made, particularly in London, for some fifty years.

Many of the makers of such toys worked in complete isolation and were obviously not even aware of other producers in their speciality. It should be remembered that the great flood of German imports really got under way in the second half of the nineteenth century, as their economical production of metal toys could not be approached by the British makers. Sadly, many of the items discussed by Mayhew were of the cheapest and most ephemeral type and probably survived for only a few weeks after purchase, leaving us very few examples, while the German arks, wooden animals and dolls were attractively decorated and were consequently treated with respect. In all the various accounts of the British 'Bristol Toy' or whitewood toy-makers there is little reference to painting of high quality, whereas in Germany this aspect of toy-production was particularly emphasized. It is little wonder that these very basic items were soon lost.

In *The Cricket on the Hearth*, by Dickens, the poor toy-maker, Caleb, worked for Tackleton, who hated toys so much that he delighted in making them as ugly as possible. It seems very probable that this was a sarcastic reference to much of the British toy-trade of the time. Caleb himself was much more conscious of the need to please the children who were to receive his models, as he specialized in the making of dolls' houses and rooms. Dickens, with his meticulous attention to detail, describes a typical maker of the mid-nineteenth century who is concentrating on the larger toys that were traditionally well made, as they were too expensive to import.

> Caleb and his daughter were at work together in their usual working room, which served them for their ordinary living room as well; and a strange place it was. There were houses in it, finished and unfinished, for dolls of all stations in life. Suburban tenements for dolls of moderate means; kitchens and single apartments for dolls of the lower classes; capital town residences for dolls of high estate. Some of these establishments were already furnished according to estimate, with a view to the convenience of dolls of limited income; others could be filled on the most expensive scale, at a moment's notice, from whole shelves of chairs and tables, sofas, bedsteads and upholstery. The nobility and gentry and public in general, for whose accommodation these tenements were designed, lay, here and there, in baskets, staring straight up at the ceiling; but in denoting their degree of society and confining them to their respective stations (which experience shows to be lamentably difficult in real life), the makers of the dolls had far improved on nature, which is often forward and perverse; for they, not resting on such arbitrary marks as satin, cotton, print and bits of rag, had superadded striking personal differences which allowed of no mistake. Thus, the doll-lady of distinction had wax limbs of perfect symmetry; but only she and her compeers. The next grade in the social scale being made of leather, and the next of coarse linen stuff. As to the common people, they had just as many matches out of tinderboxes for their arms and legs, and there they were – established in their sphere at once, beyond the possibility of getting out of it.

Caleb did not work exclusively on dolls' houses but also made other toys, while his daughter dressed the dolls and put in their eyes. Dickens was obviously using great artistic licence in his account, and it also seems doubtful, judging by the number of surviving examples, that arks were often made in Britain, but dolls' houses were certainly made in this type of atmosphere, and it is obvious, by the description, that a very wide range of models was commonly available in the 1840s.

Despite the fact that the production of wooden miniatures was of the most rudimentary kind, there was a traditional manufacture, especially in the Midlands, of heavy metal items, particularly of brass. Many of these toys had provided chimney ornaments for the poorer people since the eighteenth century, and though many were too large in scale for use in dolls' houses, some, such as the tilt-top tables and small fenders, were useful as furnishings. Wheelbarrows, cradles, chairs and fireplaces have survived in some number and were precision-made in the brass foundries. The chimneypieces were often included in the larger-scale houses, but great care has to be taken in purchase, as so many are now reproduced. The fireplaces, sometimes even protected by glass for display purposes, were very perfect copies of contemporary designs and were supplied with fenders and fire-irons. Models in a similar vein continued in production well into the Edwardian period, and as these are often in the smaller scale, they are particularly useful to the collector. They are sometimes accompanied by brass kettles that were also made in the Midlands, though it is sometimes difficult to give a provenance to those of lighter quality, as there is obviously little difference in construction from those made in Germany. Those chimneypieces made from a combination of cast iron and brass are extremely attractive, and though some are as large as 14 inches, the smallest are eminently suitable for dolls' houses.

Mayhew, in 1849, visited a copper toy-maker who worked in a small ground-floor workshop and specialized in better-quality pieces that might well have accompanied the model fireplaces. The man explained that he had worked in the trade from the age of five, when he used to help his father in cleaning the toys and punching holes.

At present I make chiefly copper tea-kettles, coffee-pots, coal-scuttles, warming-pans and brass scales (toy scales), these are the most run on, but I make besides brass and copper hammers, saucepans, fish-kettles and other things. I am now, you see, making copper tea-kettles and saucepans. There are sixteen pieces in one copper tea-kettle – first the handle, which has three pieces, seven pieces in the top and cover, one piece in the side, two in the spout, one for the bottom, and two rivets to fix the handle, in all, sixteen. That's the portion of the trade requiring the most art. Copper toys are the hardest work, I consider, of any toy work. The copper is this dull sheet of copper here, 8 feet square in the sheet of it. I use generally a 4-pound sheet costing 13 pence a pound. I make six dozen tea-kettles out of one sheet. The copper must be planished to make it bright.

I make in the average for the year eight dozen tea-kettles every week. I make all that is made in London, yes, in the world. Here's the world's shop sir, this little place, for copper toys. . . . I make as many scuttles in a week as I do tea-kettles, for I'm always at it, and as many coffee-pots. . . . They're all fit to boil water in, cook anything you like, every one of them. They are made on exactly the same principle as the large kettles except that they are brazed together and mine are soft soldered. . . . All my toys are retailed at 6 pence each.

He estimated that, over the whole year, he earned 15 shillings a week.

That's little to keep a wife and two children on. It's little to earn for making all the copper toys, as far as I know, in the world. I think I could do well in New York, where my trade is not known at all. I have the art of the trade all to myself. It was very good once, but now it's come down very bad in this country, and I would like to try another. People here haven't the money for toys; besides, mine last too long; they ought to break quicker. What my father once had 20 shillings for, I now get 5 shillings. When these toys first came up, an Irishman cleared £1,400 in five years by selling them in the streets. That's twenty years ago, and he's now thriving in America.

262

This very obvious isolation of the individual makers was probably one of the main reasons for Britain's lack of success in mass-producing toys on the folk-type basis that established the German industry. Despite substantial manufacture of very similar items in the Midlands for instance, the hard-working Londoner was completely unaware of the type or the quality of their work and was even blissfully unaware of any possible competition.

A substantial quantity of tin and pewter doll's house equipment was also made in Britain, though it is again impossible to differentiate between the origin of different items, and many doll's house kitchens probably contain more covers, skimmers and coal-scuttles of British origin than we might immediately think. In 1883 C. L. Mateaux, discussing toy-making in his *Wonderland of Work*, commented that the old tea and pewter coffee-pots, lead spoons and candlesticks that were thrown away when broken became the raw material of the London and Birmingham toymakers, who transformed it into thousands of miniatures. 'Pewter knives, forks, spoons, stoves, irons, gridirons, birdcages, fenders, fire-irons and, more especially, delightful little tea, coffee and dinner sets with which our children love to furnish their dolls' houses, hang upon their Christmas trees or hold imaginary banquets . . . such toys can be used and broken and bent and replaced at the low rate of a farthing or little more.'

The metal used for the miniatures was apparently difficult to work, as it was an uncertain mixture of old tin and lead, and the worker was forced to mix in new lead until the substance was perfect for individual hand-casting. One London factory alone was reputed to use a ton of this material every month, and the writer visited the establishment to watch the process, which began in the simmering iron vessels full of boiling pewter. For the manufacture of miniatures, three completely different methods were used: 'First those that are cast and poured out; secondly those that are cast complete in a four-piece mould, and thirdly those that are cast in one solid piece in a single mould and look very like silver basketwork or filigree when finished.' This reference to filigree furniture is interesting, as it is usual to attribute virtually any doll's house items of this type to Germany. Mateaux noticed that more tea-sets were made at the factory than sets for dinner or coffee, and he describes how they were made: 'The worker carefully fixes the parts of a four-piece mould made of hard gun-metal and, holding it in his well-padded left hand, quickly fills it from a ladle full of the liquid pewter, then he pours back into the ladle as much of the hot metal as he can. This leaves a thin coating of the pewter which has been cooled in the mould and now appears a neat little teapot.' These four-piece moulds were used for making round items such as teacups, basins and lids, women workers being particularly skilled in the technique. These women worked at great speed, dipping the moulds into cold water so that the toys fell out, and they could make 2,200 cups in a single day. Each week the factory produced eighty-five gross teasets, each consisting of twenty-two pieces. The 'silver' cutlery was, of course, cast in groups of half a dozen, and the metal joins were cut apart while still soft. Frequently, the makers failed to rub down the edges and joins adequately, so that the construction-method can still be seen clearly.

One-piece-mould toys were cast in a flat block of metal which the writer compared with a butter-mould engraved with the design. On the top of the solid mould a drainage-channel was cut down to the pattern, and through this the molten metal was poured. A sheet of blotting-paper was placed on the stone bench at which the women worked so that the piece could be lifted swiftly from the stone. These were the cheapest of the toys and had to be produced at great speed and then daubed with green, blue or yellow naphtha lacquer which dried almost instantly on the small sofas, fenders and farthing chairs, 'which now lie, all flat and shining, like so many wirework ornaments which will be bent into shape and hooked together with all those little catches by the dealers of the retail shops'. Vast quantities of these 'one-mould' toys were sold at Christmas, as they made excellent gifts on the tree and were also of help to the manufacturers in that they survived in the nursery for only a very short time. E. Nesbit was born in 1858 and owned 'a very complete set of pewter tea-things in a cardboard box' which she took with her to school in Brighton in 1865. An aggressive fellow-pupil to whom she refers by the pattern of her dress, 'Stuart Plaid', quickly purloined her new toy and spitefully 'bit every cup and saucer and plate into a formless lump'.

British manufacture of these helpfully fragile items continued, despite German competition, into the twentieth century, when firms such as James Norris of Sherbourne Road, Birmingham, were still making dolls' kitchen utensils, miniature candlesticks, scoops, frying-pans and toy scales. The Reka Company of Wimbourne Street, London, also made a very large variety of penny toys, including saucepans and toilet-jugs and basins. In 1908 their 'New Stove Kettle' was described as a fine model and was available in imitation tin or copper, tin top with a coppered bottom and, even more realistically, tin top with a black bottom. The company specialized in light, hollow and solid castings in metal, which were plain cast or finished in colour or gilded.

Though the production of factories such as those mentioned was substantial, their wares formed only a small part of the furnishings sold by the toy-shops, and it was not until the Great War that British manufacturers were forced into creating more work for the home market. During the war, there was obviously little metal to spare for the toymen, but the impetus to create such objects lasted long afterwards, as it was felt unwise to rely too heavily on foreign manufacturers. Firms such as Cartwright, who specialized partic- ularly in the model mangles that are found in so many dolls' houses, and Chad Valley, are among the well-known names of this period. Cartwright was eventually to become a subsidiary of Chad Valley and was to make the

'Gwenda' play-sets in the 1930s. Their furniture was made of steel and coloured in pastel blue, red, pink or green. These sets were very fashionable and were sold in strong boxes, complete with carpets, so that a complete room could be furnished. The dining-room set contained a very large and impressive wireless, six chairs, a table, sideboard and carpet. A few years later the firm was selling wire and tin furniture of the most functional style, with the flat tin sections painted in bright red or blue enamel. In basic design, the Cartwright mangles hardly changed from the early years of the century until the 1930s, when they were marketed as the Holdfast Series. They cost between 3 pence and one shilling each and were individually boxed. Like most of the metal toys, they were produced in sizes ranging from those suitable for the smallest-scale doll's house to others which could be played with on the floor or table.

The firm of William Britain, though more usually associated with model soldiers, also made a range of doll's house equipment, such as the boxed kitchen sets which they advertised in 1905. In comparison with the firm's meticulous attention to detail and scale in other models, these sets were highly improbable, as the coffee-pot was as large as the kitchen steps. Their well-made black-enamelled saucepans with metal lids are to be found in a large number of dolls' houses and are recognizable by their heavy weight in contrast with their size. They were, in the tradition of the better British toys, made to last, unlike the much flimsier German counterparts. The coal-scuttles were originally sold with a clawed tongs, but these are almost invariably lost, whereas the scuttles frequently appear. The baby's chair that could be adapted into a rocker and their very Edwardian-style pushchairs are only occasionally found and are among the items most liked by enthusiasts. With the typical toymaker's versatility, Britains turned their production lines to the making of shrapnel during the First World War and later bought it back to melt down and make more toys.

Surviving dolls' houses that date to the first half of the nineteenth century usually exhibit the endeavours of workmen producing toys in almost complete isolation, as the designs and the standard of workmanship are so varied, some of the finer models being the pride of good cabinet-makers while others display an almost total lack of even basic skill.

One of the most beautiful houses that very closely follows the Baby House tradition is that once owned by Mary Foster of Liverpool, whose initials appear over the front door. This model has all the elegance associated with fine eighteenth-century models and was made around 1800, though by this date its architecture would not have been in the height of fashion. The interior has the spaciousness associated with the eighteenth century, and the low-ceilinged bedrooms are also completely in the idiom. The furnishings are of less interest than the house itself, but there are a few good items, such as a set of dining-chairs and a plate-warmer. In completely different vein is the crudely constructed house now at Audley End, with its box-like partitioned rooms, obviously made as a nursery toy. Fortunately the interior was furnished with enthusiasm and remains virtually untouched since the 1840s, suggesting that it was in almost continuous nursery use from 1820. In some cases, these furnishings reflect an earlier taste, with the chintz-hung four-poster beds and the massive mirrors over the fireplaces. Among the rarest of the furnishings is a delicately patterned harp played by one of the Grödnertals. The dolls still wear their original costumes, though it seems likely that the original number was much greater. The pressed-tin furniture, often thought to be of French origin and made in the style of the mid-1830s, is quite apt for the wooden dolls and helps in the creation of some evocative interiors, such as that of the dining-room in the centre section of the ground floor. The drawing-room sofas are very obviously home-made, those with chintz covers being a later addition, as the original furnisher intended all the chairs and sofas to match the gold-braided curtains which would have presented a most elegant effect.

Though the basic construction of the Audley End house is typical of the majority of play-houses of the period, well-made models continued to appear, such as the Rigg house, now at the Tunbridge Wells Museum, which was made around 1840. The exterior is of a most impressive appearance, with a columned porch approached by a double row of steps. This precise attention to detail was continued inside the house, as all the furnishings were craftsman-made and the carpets especially supplied from Brussels.

The concept of a cabinet house was also maintained in the nineteenth century, and several interesting interiors were created in completely basic cupboards. Perhaps the finest example is that in the Bethnal Green Museum, which was equipped between 1835 and 1838 by the wife and daughter of a Manchester doctor, John Egerton Killer. The cabinet contains a particularly impressive number of Grödnertals, including children in the nursery and primly dressed maids in the kitchen. In general, the furnishings are quite sparse, creating a fairly accurate picture of actual rooms of the period. Some commercial toy furniture was used, despite the fact that its scale was too small, but the four-poster bed, of exactly the right proportion, was obviously home-made, as ordinary gilded picture-moulding was used for the cornice. Like many nineteenth-century houses, the cabinet contains only four rooms, so that the decorators were forced to decide which essential apartments to represent. Mrs Killer decided on a kitchen, morning-room, drawing-room and lying-in room, omitting bedrooms of the more basic type. Very few people

Large cupboard-like houses of this type are often difficult to furnish because of the large scale of the rooms. This model (*circa* 1850) contains six rooms and has semicircular steps leading to the impressive front door. Height approximately 52 inches.

abandoned a kitchen when making their selection, possibly because the easily available range of equipment was so great.

Many early nineteenth-century houses retain eighteenth-century characteristics, such as large arched fireplaces with spit-racks and massive built-in dressers, often creating an impression of an earlier date. The collector is therefore advised to familiarize himself with architecture of the period, though again this can only be an additional guide, as several models were made in the earlier style. The plan of the rooms, their proportions, the wallpapers, mouldings and types of wood used and, above all, the fireplace designs, have to be carefully assessed in order to establish a tentative date. In general, the Regency makers preserved the long, low lines so favoured by the Georgians, but the twelve-paned windows have generally been replaced by two or four panes because of the advances in the manufacture of large pieces of glass. Regency houses were also much shallower than those of the previous century, so that a doll's house could fit more easily on a small table. The rooms of many town houses were themselves of modest proportion, and a very large toy would have become a burden; in country houses, however, a large house was still welcome, and several were constructed with integral stands, one being made with arched supports reminiscent of Uppark. Despite the variations in style and proportion, the construction of the majority of models made before 1845 is comparatively heavy, and inch-thick timber was frequently used on models of a small size, a feature that has aided their survival.

Though most houses are inhabited by Grödnertals, a few reveal small poured waxes with dark bead-like glass or painted eyes that are of British manufacture. The construction is very basic, as the heads and shoulders are modelled in one, and the lower arms and lower legs, also made of poured wax, are sometimes sewn but more frequently glued to the fabric sawdust-filled body. The hair, almost invariably blonde, is roughly implanted in several large tufts but carefully arranged to give the correct effect. The original costumes exhibit particularly fine needlework, as dress was again becoming much more detailed and women obviously enjoyed sewing the large hats and wide-skirted frocks. White pantalettes were, by 1840, an essential feature of every girl's costume and are almost invariably found on dolls of this type. These delicate, round-faced poured waxes were made in several sizes, though the variety is nothing like as great as that of the Grödnertals.

The designs of British dolls' houses of the first half of the nineteenth century vary as much as the architecture of the period, and while the Gothick taste that seems so particularly suitable had little real impact, there is a small and very charming example at Wallington Hall and a much more simply constructed model, in a more tentative expression of the taste, at the Bethnal Green Museum. These charming models, with their arched doors and windows, sometimes assume the pure Gothick form of a castle or include a

A mid-nineteenth-century Norfolk house believed to have been one of a specially made pair. The almost Baby House proportions of the exterior accord strangely with the very basic interior with its narrow staircase completely in nineteenth-century style.

This substantial family house (*circa* 1840–50) painted in a soft yellow is typical of many mid-nineteenth-century South London houses.

small tower to create the mystery of 'Gothick gloomth'. A number of drawing-room models in this style, intended for display, were also produced, as the romantic and historical association of the Gothick taste was aided by a model surrounded by towering dark trees or a suitably dramatic rocky landscape.

The Gothick house at the Bethnal Green Museum opens, cupboard-like, at centre front and is painted to represent slabs of sand-coloured stone. As in many actual houses of the period, the central window is 'blind', being simply painted on the wall. Blind windows were used extensively by eighteenth-century architects as an aid in creating a completely symmetrical appearance. My own home, built in 1723, has a blind storey running along the roof parapet, behind which one can walk, and similar blind windows were also added to one complete side to give the many-windowed effect, so often impractical from the interior but giving exactly the right balance from the outside. Originally, the majority of blind windows were painted black with white glazing-bars, and this original colouring has survived on the dolls' houses, whereas it is often painted over on Georgian and Regency houses, giving a curious, walled-up effect.

270

The interior of the Bethnal Green Gothick cottage is disappointingly simple, and there is neither appropriate wallpaper, chimneypieces nor furniture in the taste. Perhaps because of the difficulty of finding miniature items in the style, very few pieces in the genre are found in these dolls' houses, and the interiors are completely mundane. This example contains some German *papier mâché* inhabitants. German-made dolls and furniture become increasingly obvious in British dolls' houses as the century progresses, though Mayhew's comments regarding a substantial manufacture of metal and whitewood items would suggest that at least some of the furniture in houses, such as that assembled by the Killer family, was of British origin. In that house, the small tables and *chaise-longue* are almost certainly British made. That the standard of locally made miniature furniture was acceptable is evidenced by the high quality of many of the basic fittings, such as kitchen dressers and chimneypieces. It was not lack of skill but the inability to produce toys very cheaply that inhibited British manufacturers.

Mortimer House, dating from the first half of the century, is of particular interest, as it was documented by its original owner so that her daughters should fully appreciate the history of their toy. In February 1875 Emma Brigstock dedicated 'This little fragment of a story' to her

> Dearest daughter, with whom I connect so many loving memories of the dear old Baby House. It was actually mine when I was eleven years old (at least the centre building!), and about eleven years afterwards I fitted it up for my dearest eldest daughter, then some years later I had the two wings added again for my two youngest darlings. Some few articles of the original furniture are still in the hall. Its name is exchanged to that of the family supposed to reside in it (the Mortimers). The whole story has often been in my mind, and I write it down for any who may take an interest in this old Baby House.

This dedication and the story accompanied the house when it appeared in a London saleroom: the handwriting was extremely difficult to decipher, but the story basically concerned the history of an imaginary family after the death of Mr Mortimer, 'a true type of the good old Englishman'. All his descendants appear to have been much favoured by the gods, as they are well provided for, cheerful and amiable. The eldest son, who inherited the family house, married a baronet's daughter who 'had been carefully educated by an admirable mother and early taught every feminine duty as well as accomplishment'.

Various generations had obviously augmented the contents of this house, which is of particular interest as it shows so clearly how extra sections and floors were often added to a basis structure, either to accommodate extra furniture or to allow space for more children to play. Only the central, roofed section of Mortimer House is original, as it was once a two-floored construction. When the wings were added on either side of the main bedroom

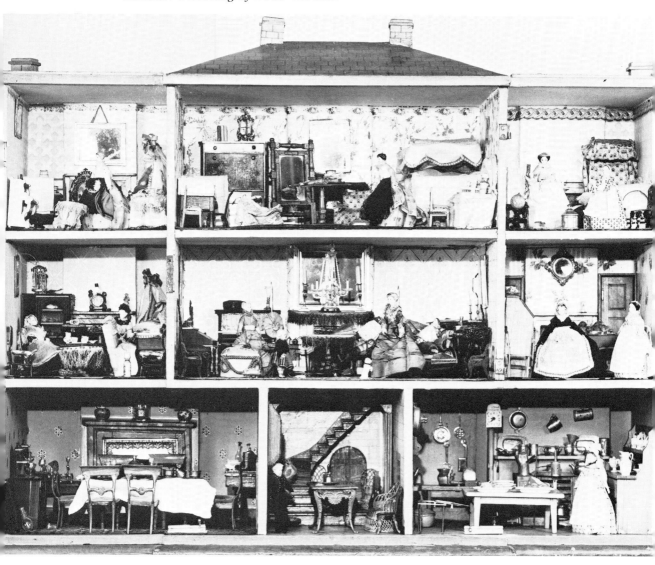

Above: 'Mortimer House', painted to simulate stone and with a tiled roof. The house was given to Emma Margaret Glass early in the nineteenth century. The later addition of wings and basement can be seen here.

Opposite and following pages: A closer look at the rooms of Mortimer House.

Opposite, top: The lower hall of Mortimer House was a later addition and made in a curiously old-fashioned style. The table is metal.

Opposite, below: Detail of the dining-room in Mortimer House, showing the metal chairs.

Above: A bedroom in Mortimer House, with the abundance of drapery typical of the late nineteenth century.

and drawing-room, a wide basement was also added with a well-made flight of stairs in the central section. Subsequent owners kept the house well stocked with dolls and also replaced faded wallpapers. The atmosphere of the house is now very much that of the 1880s, with a clutter of attractive objects, and any evidence of the early origin is almost completely submerged. The model is nevertheless of great interest as it exemplifies the way in which so many houses are adapted and extended and because of its known history and amusing story, which conjure up the age of middle-class respectability so perfectly.

Mortimer House is just a single example among an increasing number of named houses encountered in the nineteenth century. Any named or dated model has a great appeal to collectors, as such a small percentage have

The simplicity of Vittoria Cottage is typical of many early nineteenth-century houses. The name and date, 1817, are written over the door. Front opening in one section.

retained this useful information. The name sometimes appears on a brass plaque on the door or is occasionally simply pencilled on some convenient surface, as in my own Vittoria Cottage. The naming and dating was a feature of many actual houses during the last century, and many small cottages and houses carry their original date in the plaster or on a decorative stone. The commemoration of the whole spectrum of British life became popular as the pride of the nation both in its own achievements and in its queen increased, encouraging ordinary people to take pleasure in remembering special events in their own circle. Plates, silver, samplers and even patchwork quilts were all made as commemorative items, and it is little wonder that model houses were also named after important national events or after the name of a home of which the family was particularly proud.

The methods of opening nineteenth-century houses vary even more than in the eighteenth century, though there is now less concern to protect the contents. The complete front of Vittoria Cottage swings open in one piece and simply hooks shut at the side, whereas 'Dollette' is much more complex, as a brass peg passes into the centre panel of the front which holds the two sides in position. Others have opening sections for each room, as at Uppark, or pegs which hold the front sections in position. The exteriors range in quality from fine examples with individual bricks carved into the surface for complete realism to others that are papered, with the stones or bricks painted: some are left as plain wood, others stained and polished according to the taste of the individual maker who, in general, worked towards a realistic effect.

Right: A heavy and well-made doll's house, believed to be of Irish origin, with a brass plaque on the door with the name 'Blessley', while above is another of painted wood, with the house-name 'Dollette' and the date 1838. The brass peg in the centre of the pediment holds the centre panel in place.
Below: Interior of the Blessley house. Particularly interesting is the bathroom, the earliest yet recorded in a British doll's house, with its primitive tap. All the original papers are still in place.

The *Girl's Own Toymaker* published in 1859 included this design for a card and fabric half-tester.

This striving towards a realistic interpretation was continued into the middle years of the century, though a few models that relied much more on the imagination were also available. In 'Polly's Doll's House', an illustration in the 1859 edition of the *Child's Own Picture Book*, we see very simple rooms which the child has placed on low tables. These rooms are quite large in scale, almost half the girl's height, and they represent a parlour and a kitchen. There was also a great interest in the educational value of teaching children to make their own houses and furniture, a need which E. Landells and his daughter attempted to fulfil in their *Girl's Own Toymaker and Book of Recreation*, published in 1859. This volume was one of a series produced because 'The method of teaching by toys has been proved in our infant and national schools to be so productive of the best results that the system has daily become more universal.'

In the introduction, the authors explain the problems that mothers faced in keeping children out of mischief and directing their energy into the right channels, as 'A habit of destructiveness, carefully engineered, may have a pernicious effect on the future of the child.' Like Maria Edgeworth, the Landells felt that a toy would be valued more highly if it was made by the child himself. The eighteenth-century concept of play as a serious preparation for adult life is again suggested, since:

The child who is instructed to make its own doll's clothes, toy furniture, bedding etc. will soon take a pride in making them properly and will thus be acquiring knowledge of the most useful and practical character. Girls, a little older, will find much to entertain and amuse themselves. Nothing is more becoming than to see a home neatly and tastefully embellished by the handwork of its inmates: while the formation of habits of industry and usefulness are not only satisfactory in enabling young ladies to decorate their own homes by employing their leisure hours profitably, but also in furnishing the means of making suitable presents for their friends.

The instructions for making the dolls' houses and furniture were completely the work of Alice Landells, and she began her course by making the child create a cottage in the simplest manner, from folded paper. There was a central front door and a window on each side, but the effect was improved by a neat gate and railing made simply from strips of gummed paper. Inside was a chair, fireplace, table and bed, each item being cut in one piece. A pretty fender could be made in pinwork. Cardboard was obviously more suitable for models where some strength was needed, and the writer urged the child to experiment so that she could create her own patterns. The designs she provided were of the most up-to-date type, including armchairs and a turned-leg couch. Several exercises in the construction of geometric shapes served as preparation for the construction of a set of bed-steps, fixed at the back with small strips of paper. The washstand was of a generous size, with two bowl-holders, and the bed was provided with a canopy and a cornice; the hangings were to be painted. Some curiously progressive advice is given regarding the finishing of pieces, to the effect that, if kept clean, the cardboard can be left plain as it is completely satisfactory in its own right.

Items of furniture where folded card and paperwork were combined with needlework were also suggested by the ingenious Alice Landells, the very formal half-tester bed being a particularly attractive example. After glueing together the basic construction, the girl was advised to

> Take some pink glazed calico and cut a covering for the inside of the canopy. Cut out, the same size and form, a piece of lace, and put it over the pink and tack them together inside the top of the bed. The same must be done for the lining and the covering for the inside of the shape for the back of the bed. Cut out another piece of glazed calico for the curtains, cover this with lace, the same as the top, put down one side and at the bottom a piece of lace, frilled on; this will make one curtain. Make another exactly the same . . . for the valances round the bottom, take a piece of white dimity . . . hem it round neatly at the foot and sides, gather it up at the top and sew it upon one side of the bed; the other side must be done in the same manner. For the foot of the bed cut out in the same material, gather it in at the sides and tack it inside the foot of the bed.

The mattress was to be made of strong calico, as was the round-ended bolster, and both were to be filled with feathers. The pillows were made of much finer calico and had three buttons and buttonholes added. 'Then take a piece of lawn and frill it all round the case.' The sheets were linen, and the blankets flannel. 'Buttonhole them at each end with red worsted, then, with dark blue, run in and out to form stripes.' The counterpane was to be made of soft marcella: 'To imitate other counterpanes, sew over with embroidery cotton to form a star pattern and bind it neatly around with braid.'

Another useful piece was a draped rocking-cradle described as a bassinette and completely made of cardboard, including the arched hood and the rockers:

> Take a piece of light blue or pink glazed lining, cut this to the shape of the inside, and cover the ribs with the same; put over this the lace, then a frill of lining around the outside, and also cover these with a frill of lace, not further than the ribs, and put a piece of quilled ribbon around the edge. Then cut a small half-circle of net for the top, cutting out the same figure in glazed calico, putting it under the lace; tack the straight edge round the first rib . . . the ribs must be covered with quilled ribbon. For the curtains, take a rather broad piece of lace and catch it up in the middle with a bow.

Other bows were added to the sides and to the foot. The bedding was again made of calico and feather-filled, as was the pillow, which, despite its very small size, was provided with buttons. The sheets were made of fine calico, the top edge of the upper being decorated with a frill of fine lawn. A fine-patterned marcella was to be used for the counterpane.

Similar instructions were included in girls' magazines and annuals in the second half of the century, some of which must have required great feats of imagination. Despite many of the shortcomings in the designs, such instructions formed appropriate occupations for wet afternoons when children were forced to play in the nursery. Large round tables draped with thick plush tablecloths in red or green were an essential feature of nursery life in the nineteenth century. With their lunch cleared away, the children would gather round the table with scissors and flour-and-water paste to make new furnishings for the doll's house. A description of the Lyttleton nursery in the 1840s tells how the walls were hung with old prints of foreign men and women, a picture of the Queen and her mother, the Duchess of Kent, and a large map, decorated with birds, beasts and fishes.

With an eye to the amusing of children indoors, several firms produced sets of bricks and sectional buildings from which a variety of different houses could be made. A set at the Bethnal Green Museum, 'Building Cards and Pretty Pictures', dates to the 1850s, and the printed slide-topped box contains twenty cards to create a brick house. The people who live in the model are printed at windows and at doors, giving a lively and realistic effect. One talks to a servant-girl, another is just going out walking, creating an interesting scene which children must have enjoyed building. The variety of con-structional toys was matched by an increasing abundance of miniature

Though the interior of this house made for Mrs Bryant in 1860 is extremely sophisticated, the brick-painted exterior is completely in the idiom of a child's toy.

furniture, so that even the poorest children were able to own a few items, though an actual house was beyond their dreams. The eight-year-old watercress girl who was interviewed by Mayhew worked at a Jewish house on Saturday nights, where she snuffed the candles and poked the fire while they kept the sabbath. They were very kind to their little servant and gave her 'a fireplace and a box of toys, and a knife and a fork and two little chairs'. This girl had no dolls or a doll's house, though other children from humble families were occasionally given a house made by one of their relatives. Such models are often of the most basic type but are occasionally enlivened by some unusual feature.

In complete contrast to the home-made toy houses is the very accurately constructed house made for Mrs Bryant in 1860, with its fine furniture that was especially commissioned from a crippled craftsman. This model is almost eighteenth-century in atmosphere, as it is constructed on a very large scale and is very obviously the interest of an adult. The upholstered mahogany

The kitchen of 'Mrs Bryant's Pleasure' with its curious lack of scale. The Doulton water filter in the foreground is an effective piece.

Opposite: One of the largest houses in the museum collection was furnished by Laurence and Isaac Currie in the 1870s. Amongst the plethora of interesting rooms is a Roman Catholic chapel. The model is known as Dingley Hall.

furniture, with its correctly sewn deep buttoning, is perfectly made and was obviously extremely expensive to produce. The kitchen is much more in the idiom of a play-house, but the reception rooms and bedrooms are in the nature of adult miniatures. It is fascinating to notice how, in dolls' houses, bedrooms were frequently provided with fitted carpets, whereas in actual homes such luxury was rare. The half-tester beds, marble-topped washstands and huge wardrobes with mirrors in the doors accurately represent furniture that was in popular use at the time, making this model one of the most important of the period, as it displays completely British workmanship of the highest quality and exactly typifies the period. The only strange touch is in the ground-floor dining-room, where the guests seem to be intended to eat from low-seated armchairs, though a visiting child is correctly provided with a nicely made high chair. During the years it would seem that the dining-chairs were elevated to the bedrooms, as these echo the turning on the legs of the dining-table, and it seems a pity they have not been reinstated. Presumably

Mrs Bryant intended some of the armchairs now in the dining-room for other situations. She obviously took great delight in stitching the carpets and in finding small items such as oriental vases for the drawing-room and attractive pictures.

Dingley Hall, dating to 1874, is another impressive model, but the real interest of this example lies in the fact that it is completely equipped with genuine toy items such as were available to the general public. With its Catholic chapel and seemingly unending rooms, this house is one of the most extravagantly equipped of the period, and the enthusiast can visit the house time and time again at the Bethnal Green Museum and still feel it impossible to remember all the room settings. This model disproves the assumption that dolls' houses are a girl's toy, as it is the creation of two brothers, Laurence and Isaac Currie. The house was begun when Laurence was fourteen, and he continued to add pieces throughout his life that he found when travelling, such as the splendid variety of ornaments and the many German items, including a fine assortment of dolls with moulded moustaches and whiskers. The model is

The marbled pillars give this house great prestige. It dates to the middle of the nineteenth century and was once owned by Mary Gregg, who presented the museum with many fine pieces from her extensive collection. The front door bell is wired to interior rooms.

of additional interest as some of the contents were recorded by the boys, for example: 'A pair of gilt candlesticks, bought 1879 at the Lowther Arcade, 3 shillings. One undressed doll (priest) bought 1879 at the Lowther Arcade, 1s 6d. Set of vestments, the gift of Mrs Currie. One dressed chef, bought 1879.' The most surprising entry is for the Venetian glass chandelier, the gift of B. W. Currie Esq, which was bought in 1882, 'made to order at Salviati's in Venice, £25. 0. 0d'.

The extravagance of the Curries' purchases for the house was matched by its size, and the front opens in five separate vertical sections to expose the almost claustrophobic interior that is dominated by the atmosphere of the incense-filled chapel. This is a house where intrigue and mystery are always to the fore, and we regard the lavish contents with curiosity, wondering how much of the atmosphere is engendered by the lingering presence of situations created for the characters by the two boys.

Alice Corkran, writing about her childhood in the *Girl's Realm* in 1901, was in no doubt regarding the play value of her doll's house, which lured her away from tedious history and geography into the realms of its own especial enchantment:

It was the residence of the Princess Amanda, whose placid face, surrounded by a halo of flaxen hair, carried a cheery smile and who, alone of a retinue of dolls,

The exterior of this doll's house was probably reconstructed in the mid-nineteenth century to allow more light into rooms and now accords strangely with the original dentilled cornice. The house was owned by the Thornton Smith family.

The interior of the house that once belonged to the Thornton Smith family is still in a relatively unspoiled state. The Gothick alcoves are particularly effective, though the effect is spoiled by the very small furniture of a much later date. The house appears to date to *circa* 1820 though the quality of the detail is completely in the Baby House idiom.

retained her proper number of limbs. The principal role of Amanda and her ladies was to sit in the drawing-room of the mansion in what we could not deny to ourselves were stolidly stiff attitudes, awaiting the arrival of Amanda's suitors; or with these to assemble around the dining-room table on which was spread a tempting repast of painted cardboard dainties. They were not particular, however, as to the part we wanted them to play, and as events in their home were the faithful mirror of what happened in ours, they cheerfully adapted themselves to its various conditions. Thus, when illness prevailed at home, they all retired to bed, took medicine cheerfully and unanimously received the doctor's visit. They even allowed their drawing-room to be littered with evidence of study when we became distracted with lessons. Our supreme delight, however, the magic of which never paled, was preparing the house for one of Amanda's great receptions or one of her dinner-parties. A delicious sense of hurry scurry would then prevail from kitchen to parlour; no wonder the frying-pan was occasionally found repositing on the drawing-room sofa; and the housemaid's broom lying among the delicacies in the dining-room. Sometimes we felt we had too many persons at table, and by way of relieving the pressure we removed one or two to the kitchen to take service with the cook. But it was troublesome, for they had to be dressed over again for their new part, and their heads, which fared well enough in the dining-room, had a tendency to make a hole in the ceiling of the scullery. Ah, dear house of enchantment, where everything happened exactly as we wished it to happen, your spell still draws me, as it drew my truant thoughts away from the old schoolroom and other places depressingly devoted to learning.

The Corkran doll's house was obviously a place that reflected the activity and the emotions of its child owners, and the dolls were necessarily much more interesting than the furniture, which was incidental to the central drama, whereas the Currie boys obviously found greatest delight in acquiring furniture and interesting accessories for their much more accurate model. Many of these mid-nineteenth-century houses were of an impressive size, as many nurseries were themselves spacious, and it was in this room that the doll's house was most likely to be stored. Eleanor Ackland, writing of her Westmorland childhood between 1878 and 1888, commented that her drawing-room toys were few in number as she wanted no toys when she had the company of her mother. In comparison the doll's house was large and impressive and stood in the nursery.

I cannot rid myself of the notion that it was built on a grander scale than any such house I meet with nowadays – because I always have to stoop to look into their rooms, whereas the top floor of our house was just nicely on the level of our eyes. It had eight rooms and three storeys: downstairs on the left was the kitchen, on the right the dining-room, with the staircase hall in between; upstairs, two bedrooms and a room which was sometimes used as a nursery, sometimes as the drawing-room, and, above these again, two attics. This mansion always seemed to promise a good spell of play. One of us would say 'Hurrah, it's a real wet day. Let's play the whole morning with the doll's house.' There had to be a definite decision because the windowed front of the house was kept locked, and a grown-up had to come and unlock it and unlatch it back against the wall and tell us to mind and not go breaking the glass. Then, somehow, when we had straightened up the fallen bits of furniture and tidied the beds, and had a roll-call of the doll inhabitants, we generally failed to develop any really amusing game. There stood the eight rooms, three walled, like those of a theatre stage; but whether we set out to produce the tragedy of how all the doll's house children died of the measles, or the comedy of how nurse fell into the bath, the drama would hang fire. The doll actors, moved by our Brobdignagian hands, thrust in often at cross purposes, from the auditorium, failed to play their roles at all convincingly; they were of flagrantly ill-assorted sizes, the baby of the family being much larger than the mother, and they had a way of flopping limply over the furniture at tense moments. So the game was disappointing, and that produced vexation of spirit and squabbling, upon which the windowed front would be peremptorily shut and locked up.

That unsupervised play with a doll's house often led to quarrels and bitterness is made clear by Eleanor Ackland and is an aspect of this toy that is frequently commented upon by adults remembering their childhood. In order to lessen such tensions, a number of two-sided models were constructed so that the children could play without disturbance on either side. Such models were, in fact, much more realistic, as the ground-plan of a genuine house could be imitated, but they are, of necessity, large and consequently hold less appeal for collectors, who prefer narrow houses that stand neatly against a wall and can be opened from the front. One double house in my own collection is made in a completely different style on each side, one having complex bay windows and a balcony and the other being in a flat-fronted, almost Gothic style. Even the surface treatment is different, the bay-windowed side being stained and varnished in a dark colour and the other red-painted to represent bricks. This model is one of the most curious I have ever examined, as the complete house swivels on its integral base so that either façade can be seen, and there is also a locking compartment in the roof, presumably for the storage of the toy silver or the best china. Inside the eccentricity is heightened by the strange proportions of the small rooms, with fireplaces as high as the doors and a bannister rail of massive proportion. There is also a black-painted, high-ceilinged room where surely some occult events were witnessed. I purchased the house unfurnished, and it has proved most difficult to equip, as the towering rooms still appear empty when the floors are filled with furniture, and there are very few dolls that seem to suit the scale, which is almost more in the nature of a cabinet-maker's model yet made very specifically to be played with by two children.

Dolls' houses were, by the late nineteenth century, at the peak of their success as toys, and it is from this period that the collectors of today find the majority of their acquisitions. Parents who had longed for fine toys in their

A brick-painted house (*circa* 1865) with two blind windows and an arched fanlight over a non-opening door. The central section remains in position when the side fronts are opened. There are six large rooms decorated with the original large-scale wallpapers of roses-on-a-trellis background. Probably home-made. Height 66 inches.

Opposite: A most meticulously made model house constructed purely for display but exhibiting the maker's skill to advantage. It does not open, but the curtains in the windows give realism. The date 1899 is carried on the porch. Width 22½ inches.

own childhood, often passed in less fortunate circumstances, ensured that their children should enjoy the things they had missed, and dolls' houses came well to the fore. The toy-factories, unable to compete with the Germans in the manufacture of small, cheap items, were without any real competition in this sphere, and together with a number of outworkers, they created dozens of models in imitation of popular architecture. Town houses, sometimes several storeys high, were the best sellers, as they mirrored the designs of the girls' homes; country cottages are comparatively rare, indicating the great increase in the town-bred middle classes. These town houses, with their rows of neatly curtained windows and brass door-knockers, are still very popular, as their shallow depth can be accommodated in most homes. Their general construction was also much lighter, and from the mid-1880s fretwork was often added to the façades. Much of the inspiration for decorative fretwork was American, and Charles Churchill & Co of Finsbury was one of the main importers of such tools and machines. Plywood also began to be used in the

1890s and, though prone to attack by woodworm, made the production of model houses even more economical.

Though the area of commercial production is of paramount importance in this period, the home-made model continued to interest, and the constructor was now provided with a number of readily available accessories and tools. In 1889 *Little Folks* announced that the winner of a competition they had held in the previous year was a doll's house made by a child. It was 'made of a box enamelled outside and divided within into two storeys. The walls were papered, the floors varnished around the edge and carpeted in the middle. Most of the furniture was made by hand. Two of the dolls were downstairs at tea, and others were upstairs with the baby and the cat. All was complete even to the fans on the wall and the table of books, the candlestick on the bracket, the bellrope hanging by the mantelpiece.' Competitions of this kind, which involved the dressing of a doll or the furnishing of a model room, were very popular until the First World War, and photographs of bazaars and fêtes

Above: A fanciful villa, *circa* 1910, that was almost certainly home-made using generally available mouldings. The front opens in three sections. There are low attic rooms and six large rooms with side windows. Height 47 inches.

Opposite above: A most substantially made house, *circa* 1910, painted to resemble stone and brick, the painting of the stone being particularly skilful. The integral stand is also stone-painted. The side fronts open with neat brass bolts, and the opening front door is wood-grained. Though the exterior is particularly fine, the interior with four large rooms has been redecorated, and the general standard of carpentry is also disappointing, as though the maker ran out of enthusiasm. Height without stand 43 inches.

Opposite below: A neatly planned house (*circa* 1910) with components similar to those used by Lines, and it seems possible that this was one of the special designs as the actual model does not appear in any surviving catalogues. Height approximately 40 inches.

often reveal examples of the ingenuity of both adults and children.

Little Folks was particularly anxious to educate its readers in simple handicrafts and in 1894 provided instructions for making the cork-and-pin furniture that is found in so many houses. Sometimes horse chestnuts of a suitably flat shape were substituted for cork, but the method remained the same:

> You must first of all get some ordinary-sized cork and some red or other bright-coloured material, not very thick; you will also need a good supply of pins and some crochet cotton which should be the same colour as your cloth. . . . Take some pins and push them carefully into the cork, arranging them to have the heads all even and as close together as possible . . . take the crochet cotton and wind it in and out of the pins, first securing the end to one of them. Have your rows of cotton close together and, of course, begin at the bottom and work upwards.

Larger items could be made of cork, whereas chestnut furniture was limited to stools and tables: for a cork bed a rectangle was cut, covered with fabric and provided with a row of pins at each side. If an adult was available to give some assistance, more adventurous pieces made from wishbones decorated with silk and embroidery could be attempted, though these were much less popular than the simple pin items. Instructions were given in several ladies' and children's magazines in the 1890s for the making of a doll's house cradle from an eggshell decorated with ribbon and lace, and for beds and cradles made from boxes with the lids stood upright at one end to form the bedhead and suitably decorated and embroidered. Such items are still encountered in some number and have to be assessed on their condition and quality, though their value is slight in comparison with the commercial items that were made with so little effort.

In *Frontpiece*, Marion Howard Spring recalled how in the 1890s her doll's house was kept in a deep recess on a landing. It was made from a large wooden stores-box and papered with pieces left over by the house decorators. The house was the creation of her brother who, on leaving school, bought a fretwork machine and made some really beautiful furniture for the old house from patterns in *Hobbies*, which he took every month, no doubt regretting the lack of equipment that had limited his initial construction. She had originally supplied the house with a family and furniture cut out of magazines and pasted on to card, but, out of her penny a week pocket money, she was also able to buy one doll about 6 inches high or two smaller ones.

A much more economical house made of printed cardboard had been available since September 1888, when Hinde's 'Doll's House for One Shilling' was advertised. The model, judging from the advertisement, was very effective, with a bay window on either side of the front porch and three neat upper windows. This manufacturer had first offered a paper dressing doll,

One of the finest of the Mon Plaisir dolls

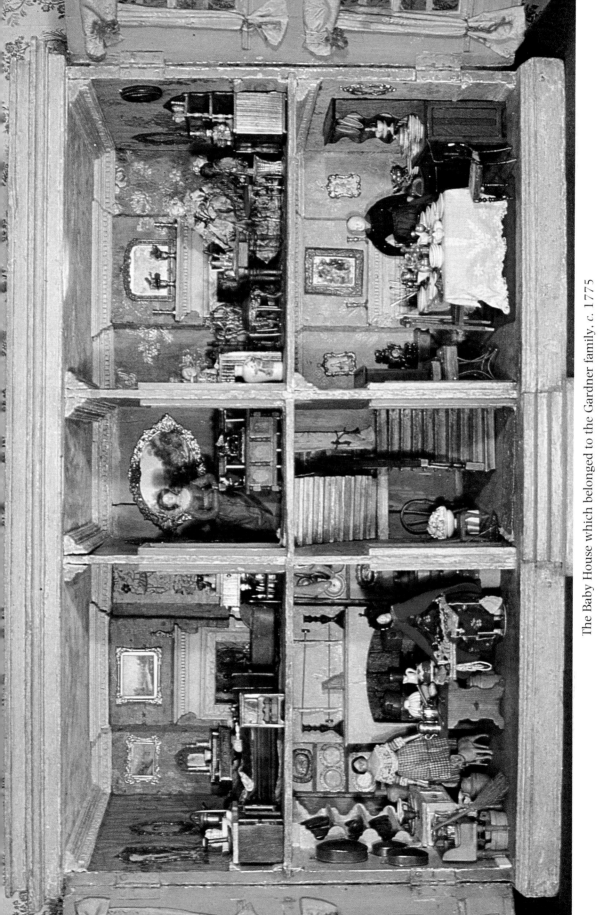

The Baby House which belonged to the Gardner family. *c.* 1775

Right: A wax group, presumably originally created as an almost photographic record of the Seidel family: the work of Johann Albani, early nineteenth century

Below: Vittoria Cottage, 1817

A mid-nineteenth-century Swiss interior

A doll's room typical of Berlin interiors of 1880

A model kitchen from Holstein, *c.* 1800

The cabinet house made by L. A. Kelterborn, Basel; of mid-nineteenth-century origin
but reminiscent of the early cabinet houses

Hatherlow House, *c.* 1870. *Above*: front and back views. *Below*: front and back interiors

Hammond House, *c.* 1886

The Skottenborge house, from Denmark, dating to the second half of the nineteenth century

Hinde's doll's house
first advertised in
September 1888.

'Dollie Daisie Dimple', which was followed by a 'Sailor Boy Doll' with his sea-chest. The popularity of these figures encouraged the production of the much more ambitious house, though all were marketed for one shilling. It was claimed that, with care, the model would last for a year and was offered under 'Her Majesty's Royal Letters Patent'. Dimple Villa measured $16 \times 11 \times 8$ inches and contained several rooms including an 8×10-inch drawing-room. It could be taken to pieces and packed flat for transit and storage but could be rebuilt in a few seconds. From an inset photograph it would appear that the interiors were also printed, making this British house particularly progressive for the 1880s.

The energetic marketing of this toy is just a single example of the

295

Above: Though several of the babies in this nursery date after 1910, the basic furniture and decoration date to 1900. The nursery was no longer a repository for discarded furniture but was especially decorated and made attractive. Note the fine telephone.

Opposite above: The atmosphere of this many-roomed London-type house is completely feminine with its pale colours and silk-decorated walls. It dates to the 1890s and is inhabited by fashionably dressed women. Known as Miss Miles's House.

Opposite below: The billiard-room of Miss Miles's House contrasts with the very feminine atmosphere of the other rooms. One of the bisque-headed men, of German manufacture, reads an *Illustrated London News*. The *Graphic* lies on a chair.

promotional efforts of retailers of the period, who set out to attract custom by frequent advertisement. This energetic marketing seems largely to have died out after the Great War, and women's and household magazines of the 1920s carry virtually no toy-trade advertisements. This decline in marketing activity was possibly because the profit margin on toys was low, but there is also the feeling that adults themselves regarded toys with less interest. The pages of *The Lady*, for instance, in the 1890s contain many references to the Christmas toy displays in the big stores and new advances in the types of mechanical toys that were available, indicating that the women themselves found the subject of interest and probably derived as much enjoyment from selection and purchase as their children. During and after the war there was a noticeable decline in interest, which did not re-awaken until the 1930s, and then in a much diminished form. The Victorians and Edwardians seem genuinely to have enjoyed their children's toys, and this adult involvement must have spurred the manufacturers on to even greater effort in producing miniature suites and needlework cabinets which beguiled mothers as well as girls. It was for adults that *cosaques* in the form of wardrobes with glass doors were made, though they also made capital doll's house furniture. Easter eggs, intended for women, sometimes contained boy and girl dolls or tea- or dinner-services of wood or china. Sets of wooden furniture, glass and metalware for the kitchen were also attractively packaged for children in containers that assumed a wide variety of shapes, from animals to simple boxes, and given allure by the lavish lithography of the printed label. Such fine-quality packaging was possible only when labour was extremely cheap, and once the sweat-shops and the employment of under-age children disappeared, after the First World War, so the mass-produced box replaced the delights of the Victorian age.

Baby Toilers, published in 1907 and written by Olive Christian Malvery, describes the conditions under which the fancy box makers still worked.

> Three young children stand busily engaged spreading glue on the paper and handing it to mother and sister. The room is half filled with a bed which is piled with some rags, and on these are cast some pasted boxes. See how quickly they work! Great skill is necessary, extreme accuracy and such sureness and certainty of touch that, though the workers' fingers are filthy to look at and sticky with glue, no mark appears on the boxes, and the tissue paper is spotless. Think what it would mean to have these dainty boxes spotted with tears.
>
> The persons visiting these homes casually flee from them in despair, and the memory of the children haunts them ... children who live in foul odours, labouring with tired hands to make pretty boxes to hold sweets and presents for good and happy children.

Such children had little time for learning, so that their reminiscences are rarely available, and when their plight was discussed in popular magazines, it

A group of children making doll's house furniture at the Girls' Ragged School in Grays Yard, James Street, Oxford Street, London, in 1854. They worked for two hours, four days a week. The project was inspired by the 'Tudor Villa' model that was exhibited at the Great Exhibition of 1851. The furniture was made of wire and decorated with composition castings made to imitate cast iron and carving.

was sentimentalized into unreality. Perhaps it is as well that we are not too intimately aware of their working-conditions or we should perhaps look less with nostalgia than aversion at the beautiful things they created to give brief pleasure.

The toy-makers of the garret type fared little better, and one boy, John Bench, who lived in Paradise Street, spent his whole life sitting at a workbench. His back was humped, and his legs were so twisted and thin that they could support him for only a few moments. Despite his matted hair and decayed teeth, his face was redeemed by his beautiful eyes. 'John Bench sat all the livelong day with three pots of paint before him, daubing over with skill and swiftness rough animals and men made from whitewood which his father carved.' The situation of this family was disastrous because of a drunken father who could work for only two days each week, so that his wife was forced to tramp the streets with the baskets of cheap wooden toys.

Garret workers made doll's house furniture, costumed and sometimes assembled dolls and sometimes made complete houses to special order from a retailer. In the *Girl's Realm* for 1901 the life of a typical doll's house maker was investigated.

> He has to work very hard to make both ends meet. The winter is his busiest and most profitable time; during the other months of the year he just continues to rub along. If he is a married man, his wife and family are all engaged in the business. He is a little masterman with a masterman's worries about a Saturday night. He is chiefly to be found in the East End and manufactures dolls' houses of the appropriate English pattern for the large wholesale toymakers who supply the retail toy shops with the wares that he turns out. He is the architect as well as the builder and decorator, paper-hanger and fitter of the miniature cottages, villas and mansions that he makes. And he has the credit of turning out stronger work than the foreigner, whose tasteful and more fanciful work is brought to him to mend, for it soon goes to pieces. I know such a maker. With evident pleasure he will point to a dilapidated Swiss Château that has been sent to him for repair. His home and workshop are situated in a busy place in Essex, a short ride from Liverpool Street Station, facing a large open green space . . . the front shop is the main workroom, and it contains English-made dolls' houses in all stages of progress, together with some foreign ones under repair. On the day we called to see him, there were two large mansions especially, at which the doll's house maker and members of his family, with some assistants, were at work. Heaps of shavings littered the floor. The benches were loaded with tools and bits of dolls' houses. And these were bewilderingly mixed up with pots of size and pots of paint. There were some small circular saws and a lathe going, making the queerest industrial music . . . piled up on shelves and almost reaching the ceiling were no end of carcasses of houses all coloured red outside and awaiting the finishing touches.
>
> 'All my work,' said the doll's house man. And he explained how he did it. 'We put the houses together first, then we fix in the staircases which are already made,' and he showed me a lot all finished and varnished up just so, and he clapped in one with a landing, then the doors and the windows and so on and 'finally we paint and decorate the outside.' He had begun life as a carpenter and drifted into doll's house making seven years before.
>
> 'I tried at first to make dolls' houses and take them about for sale, but I could not sell any; so at last I went to the firm I work for now and they gave me employment. And they have ever since found me plenty to do. I work from about six in the morning until about eleven at night most months, but the others leave at about six-thirty. I keep on after they have gone, getting things ready for the morning – there's always something to employ me. In the winter time, when we are busy, I work all night. You must stick to it if you want to get along,' he added with much determination in his rather sad eyes.

The illustration of the workshop that accompanied the article shows town houses with box-like interiors similar to those made by G. & J. Lines until 1910, and it seems very probable that this man was in fact one of their outworkers.

The connected firms G. & J. Lines and Triang were so prolific that the great majority of houses discovered by British collectors are to be found in the pages of their catalogues. I had long suspected that a whole variety of sturdily constructed models with a generous use of obviously standard mouldings and turnings were in fact the work of one manufacturer, but I was not sure of the actual source until I was able to examine the early G. & J. Lines catalogues, where so many models that I had known to be connected were set out. The excitement of discovering an actual maker, either by finding a single marked example or by relating an item to a catalogue drawing, is very great. The Lines catalogues at last gave a manufacturer to models previously described as 'Kits Coty' or 'Kensington Style'. These houses are substantially made to withstand really rough play, and it is little wonder that collectors often thought they were individually made by local carpenters. Apart from these heavily constructed typical G. & J. Lines houses, it was also surprising to discover that so many of the flat-fronted models with brick-and-tile paper-finished façades were also produced by this firm. It was also disturbing, from the dating angle, to discover that many, completely in late-Victorian style, were still manufactured in the 1920s.

The Lines family, without doubt the most important of the British toy-makers, began work in the last quarter of the nineteenth century, when the Thistle trademark was used. It is thought that some toys and baby-carriages were first made at Bagnidge Wells, near King's Cross, London, in 1858, and that a few rocking-horses were also made at that time. The family is uncertain regarding the detail of this early period, but Joseph Lines, in an official document of 1877, was already describing himself as a toy-maker. The exact date of the appearance of the characteristic Thistle Mark is also uncertain, but the 1931 catalogue mentioned the fact that 'Thistle Brand Toys' had been 'world renowned for over fifty years' suggesting the year 1879. At this time the firm was organized mainly by Joseph Lines, a clever and far-thinking businessman who possessed a particular flair for marketing. George is believed to have been the more artistic of the brothers, with a flair for design, but, presumably because of his lack of business sense, he allowed Joseph to buy him out, and he disappears completely from the scene, though his initial continued to be used.

Joseph employed his four sons, William, Walter, George and Arthur, in the factory as soon as they left school, in the manner of many heavy-handed fathers of the time. Though a professed Liberal who regularly marched his sons to Tory meetings in order to heckle and be ejected, he was, in fact, a very true-blue Tory. He is accepted by his descendants as a typical despotic Victorian father, whose sons were forced to live exactly as he dictated, and they were not spared the unpleasant side of the factory work, such as cleaning raw cows' tails before they were cured for rocking-horses. In order that the family concern should not suffer in any way from the boys being set to work so early, they were sent to evening classes at Camden School of Art and also attended building, carpentry and cabinet-making classes at the Northern Polytechnic so that they could develop as all-round toy-makers and businessmen. Joseph himself supervised all that occurred in the factory and, in real Victorian style, paid out the weekly wages from a small pigeonhole, examining each with care to see that no man was overpaid. Anyone earning more than 30 shillings was the subject of an immediate investigation. When all the wages were paid, he put the money that remained into his left-hand pocket; this belonged to the firm.

By 1895 G. & J. Lines owned several small factories in North London and were already marketing a wide variety of dolls' houses alongside their popular rocking-horses, carts and prams. The dolls' houses ranged in price from 1s 3d to 65 shillings, all those costing over 8s 6d being provided with curtains. The better houses, valued in excess of 35 shillings, contained staircases that were obviously quite time-consuming to make. It would appear that the majority of the toys were designed by the family rather than the workmen, a feature that contrasted with the practice of the leading German makers, who had little actual involvement in the articles. British manufacturers of this period laid great emphasis on the strength of their work, and the whole range of Lines products that have survived are themselves a testimony to this claim.

The 1909–10 catalogue still lists many of the items described in 1895, a lack of change that is very typical of the attitude of Joseph. Having trained his workmen to plane particular mouldings and having found a cheap supply of curtain fabric and wallpapers, he continued to use them, unchanged and with little regard for fashion, for many years. The 1909 list is Number 42, and it is considered by the family that one was issued each year, suggesting that the first catalogue might have appeared as early as 1867. In 1909 the main address is given as Electric Works, Caledonian Road, with other factories at North Road and Roman Road. Their designs were now copyrighted because of the degree of unscrupulous imitating that had taken place. Now, apart from the conventional dolls' houses, they were offering large Wendy House structures in which four children 'can sit and take tea – it folds up when not in use and then is only 6 inches wide. Lock and latch key, knocker, letter-slot and windows to open'. This structure closely resembles an ornamental garden-shed and was made over a long period, as were screen dolls' houses, in this particular catalogue being described as 'improved'. The drawing showed a screen containing a door and a window that could be placed across the corner of a room; the outside was finished in red and white brick, and the inside was papered. It was still described as 'new' after the Great War.

These very functional play-houses were completely overshadowed by their

A simple four-roomed Lines Brothers house with printed paper brickwork, *circa* 1900.

exciting range of actual dolls' houses, most of which were made in the heavy, substantial manner of the majority of Lines toys. One of their long-popular models was the type known to British collectors as 'Kits Coty' but described by the firm as 'a really splendid mansion, elaborately fitted up, inside and out. Staircase, doors to rooms, French window, curtains, beautiful paper on walls. 33 inches high. 32 inches wide. Priced at 75 shillings'. Another fine model was described as 'a country residence with motor garage attached and beautiful garden laid out with flowers. Fine staircase and finely decorated throughout'. It is obvious from the house with a garage that G. & J. Lines were not always old-fashioned, as few families of the time owned a car. The garage and garden seem to have been simply laid in place and not attached in any way, and I have never located a complete example.

More traditional in style were the flat-fronted houses that were always provided with fitted fireplaces. The porches and balconies gave these models some importance, despite their economical construction. They contained four

303

Lines houses of this basic type were made from around 1910 until 1925. This model with delicate pillars is of the earlier period. The windows have metal frames. These models were made in several sizes.

rooms, but only the more expensive boasted staircases. Priced at around £2 10s, they were obviously much more popular than the houses with a garage that retailed at £5. It was fascinating to discover one of the larger houses in this catalogue in my own collection. It was described as 'a high-class town house, six rooms on three floors, fine staircase (or lift), brass-fronted fireplaces, bay windows, fine porch, lock and key to door. Opens in centre. Price 130 shillings.' The illustration showed a house with white-tiled paper to first-floor level, though my own house has lost this at some stage and been repainted. I had originally felt that the sloping roof had been added to cover the transformer and wiring of the house but discovered from the catalogue that this feature was in fact quite original. It was described as 'a lift-

Windows became simpler and the balustrading more rudimentary in Lines houses made *circa* 1920.

up gable roof with two attic windows and two chimneystacks. The house is a very suitable one to fit with a bathroom as the tank can be hidden under the roof.' This model was more expensive, at 150 shillings. With a two-tap working bath, it would cost an extra pound. Most of these basic designs seem to have been produced from the 1890s until the First World War, though there is no other surviving catalogue from the pre-war period.

A much smaller range of houses was also manufactured from the same basic sections. It was claimed that these economical models contained real staircases rather than dummies. Joseph Lines obviously felt he had to make some concessions towards the new movement in toy-manufacture that encouraged learning-activities rather than pure amusement. Towards this end he introduced his 'Clock House', expected to appeal to mothers from the instructional as well as the recreational point of view. 'The little girl can learn how to tell the time from her doll's house clock, which is a thoroughly good time-keeper.' In fact, the clock, fixed to a gable, appears to have hands that never moved an inch! The model was provided with 'four nicely papered rooms with hygienic parquet floors and latest pattern fireplaces'. It is very advanced for its time and has half-timbering on one side of the opening front somewhat similar to the Stockbroker Tudor villas that were to become so popular in the 1920s. Most collectors, finding an example of the Clock House, would, I am sure, date it at least fifteen years after its actual date of manufacture, one of the rare instances of a house seeming more recent than its actual date. In general the Lines models of this period are all retrospective and seem completely Victorian, with their Captain's Walk balustrading and ornate porches and balconies. Several of the larger town houses were offered with lifts instead of the more usual staircases, but the company needed at least two weeks' notice for the fitting of this modern device. The very personal attention that was given to the firm's individual customers is indicated by the fact that they were prepared to repair and redecorate houses to look like new. The company policy was outlined in this 1909 catalogue:

> All our dolls' houses are improved from time to time. The papers used for decorating the rooms have been specially printed and are delightful miniatures of some beautiful designs used by high-class decorators. The decorative woodwork is, in all cases, beautifully white enamelled and gold lined. The construction of our model houses is, above all, strong and artistic. Designs call forth praise from all who see them. We cordially invite buyers to inspect their manufacture in all processes. We put curtains in all houses and fitted fireplaces in all except '00'. All houses with gable roofs nicely red tiled. All work executed in our own works.

The variety of extra fittings that were available is surprisingly large for a period when few actual houses were supplied with bathrooms and kitchens with heated water and is an indication of the fact that, even in the early-twentieth century, larger houses remained the province of the richer child. A house with a bathroom with water laid on through metal pipes from a tank in the roof would cost 15 shillings, if the bath had only one tap, or 20 shillings for two. Water could also be supplied to the kitchen, and this was cheaper if a bathroom was also fitted. For a kitchen when there was no bathroom in the house, the additional cost was 15 shillings. Electricity was obviously a necessity in all these large houses, and each bulb was supplied with a silk shade. Up to nine lights could be fitted, so the landings and staircases were left without. For an extra 8 shillings any model could be fitted with an electric doorbell. If a customer required some other type of special fitting, G. & J. Lines would quote a price and were also 'pleased to give estimates for houses to be made to any specification, but it must be understood that to make only one of a pattern is very much more expensive than using usual stock designs'. The astonishing fact is that they were even prepared to consider such projects.

Despite the mouth-watering selection of well-made houses, the firm did not manufacture any furniture, a convention completely in accord with the British Strong Toy tradition, where any small items that could be cheaply imported from Germany were ignored in order to concentrate on the large, heavy items. It says much for the construction of these early Thistle-Mark houses that so many have survived generations of play and redecoration and yet remain completely recognizable. The wallpapers, of which Joseph Lines was so proud, are, in general, unexciting, as a simple striped paper in soft browns, green and blue was the most popular. Blue and cream tiles were often used in the kitchens, and a red and gold design was liked in dining-rooms. Decorative borders were not originally used.

Joseph's four sons succeeded in persuading him to establish a new factory at Tottenham, and in 1914 the company moved its main production centre to the Thistle Works at Down Lane with its own railway sidings and a floor-space of some 40,000 square feet, all set out according to a wooden model made by Walter Lines. Pride in the new achievement did not last long, as three sons were soon involved in the war, leaving only the eldest, William, to work with his father. The changes engendered by the war made Joseph's sons impatient for a more adventurous factory policy, but their father, fixed in his Victorian ways, would have none of their new schemes, and they eventually felt it necessary to break away and set up their own factory. George Lines remained at G. & J. with the father, and their production of well-made, substantial items continued until Joseph's death in 1931, after which the company was absorbed into the newer Lines Brothers.

William, Walter and Arthur, the three Lines that created a triangle, decided to use this device as their brand name 'Triang Toies' (*sic*). They found an old factory in the Old Kent Road where they proceeded to make wooden toys with gas power until they could afford to install electricity. The brothers designed their first range of toys and turned out the prototypes, which they showed to leading retailers such as Harrods. When the workers had left for home, the brothers would remain to do the office work. Despite the fact that Joseph's sons had broken away, they all appear to have remained on good terms, and G. & J. Lines purchased many items from Lines Brothers and added them to their own catalogue.

Though Joseph, at the Thistle Works, objected to change, there are some very positive differences in the catalogue numbered 79 and thought to date to 1929. The child-sized play-houses, for instance, are now augmented by a folding play-shop, and the dolls' houses are also quite different in design. Though some of the cheaper flat-fronted versions with balconies were still made, the main interest was now in the Tudor style. A few models in somewhat retrospective idiom with a veranda and metal windows provided with paper Venetian blinds were available, but these were probably old stock, left over from the early 1920s. The use of a rough-cast finish was very popular in the late 1920s and was frequently used in combination with imitation thatch to create models in the Olde Worlde idiom so liked at the time. Among the new models was 'Ye Village Stores', which stood 25 inches high and was described as 'a novel departure in dolls' houses, combining the facilities for playing at houses and shops with a fascinating letter-box in which notes can be posted. Each shop has a counter. Finished in Old World style, boarded and roughcast. This line will prove irresistible to boys and girls.' The model had twin gables and a barge-boarded front. The shop, with decorative shutters, was completely retrospective, and at the side of the window was a 'GR' postbox. 'Ye Village Stores' was still made in 1931, one section of the shop being modified and used as a small post office.

The 1929 catalogue shows several old designs brought up to date by the addition of mock timbers and rough-cast brick. They were described as 'Elizabethan', and the fronts and backs of several models could be separately opened. A 27-inch model was given a thatched roof and an integral garage in true pseudo style. One of the houses was provided with a wall sundial. This particular device was a feature of Lines Brothers work at Triang, and it seems probable that this model was purchased or marketed for his sons. A large Tudor mansion included 'a fitted bathroom and kitchen, eight rooms, serving-hatch, French windows from drawing-room and side entrance. Attic opens. Castors fitted for easy moving. Back and fronts made to open.' The Villa Garage was made in two sizes to be purchased separately from the house.

As early as 1900, G. & J. Lines had sold charmingly made Gipsy Caravans supplied with brushes and pots and pans as part of their range of horse-drawn toys, but in the 1929 catalogue we also find a somewhat old-fashioned Motor Caravan, still furnished with buckets and brooms. As the model was 35 inches long, it was obviously meant to be furnished.

The 1931 Thistle Mark catalogue showed contemporary interest in stockbroker Tudor, but there is also a new range of very cheap bungalows, retailed from 3 shillings, an indication of the much wider social group now catered for. One was described as 'a delightful little house with one large, useful room. Includes porch with seats, chimney and fireplace and rainwater barrel, nicely decorated in cream, green and red with realistic flowerbed transfer on front and side.' Another, more classically proportioned house was given a porch with shrubs, a dresser, a kitchen stove and windowboxes for flowers. Until the 1930s there was little interest in marketing furniture, but in the last G. & J. catalogue issued before Joseph's death these items appeared in the rooms. The houses hold little appeal in comparison with the early work, but they are still well made and produced for children at all social levels.

Lines Brothers were able to obtain many important orders in their first years as an independent company as they were already well known in the toy trade, and their father seems to have been quite prepared to help the new venture. The earliest surviving catalogue of Lines 'Triang Toies' is a supplementary list dating from 1921–2, when they were operating from the Hatcham Works on the Old Kent Road and also owned a shop at 9 Fore Street. Their dolls' houses were, at first, very simplified models of the old Thistle Mark toys, and many contained only a single room up and down. The designer, probably Walter Lines, was very fond of long, low upper windows. He was the main driving-force of the partnership and is still vividly remembered in the toy-trade. He was a small, rotund figure, inordinately fond of his own family and with a genuine liking for children in general. His dislike of any kind of waste was extreme, and remaining pieces of old models were often used up on new projects; other outdated stock was often adapted. He was particularly concerned about the really efficient organization of the factories, and his grandson remembers his habit of sending around small notes regarding the shortcomings he had noticed. He was a very clever designer and a brilliant businessman who was skilled in entrepreneurial quick deals and the use of frequently doubtful advertising. When the famous Regent Street toyshop, Hamley's, was put on the market because of money problems, Triang was quick to see the advantages of such a good trade outlet, though the shop was never under any obligation to buy the Lines Brothers toys. Possibly Walter's most famous invention was the Fairy Cycle. So great was his involvement with toys that after his retirement he made wooden toys at a wooden crate factory the firm had taken over.

It is thought by the Lines family that most of the designs in the Triang catalogues were Walter's work, and they show little of the retrospection of the Thistle Mark work. After the First World War, there was great difficulty in housing many of the returning soldiers, and Triang commented: 'The house shortage has been just as acute in the doll world as elsewhere, but that has not forced prices up, in fact prices are very much down, and though the ones illustrated are only for sale and not to rent, they are within the range of most people. . . . Kitchens are fitted with metal cooking-ranges. Front doors are panelled in bright green and with fitted brass knockers and letter-flaps. Curtains to all windows. Green shutters as shown.' Lines Brothers were much more interested in fitting their houses well, and each model had a metal range in the kitchen and fireplaces in the other rooms. Their small 'Summer Cottages', though too small for staircases, were given optional electricity.

A 'Devonshire Country Cottage', with six rooms, a large hall and a staircase, was much more expensive. It was rough-cast finished, and the roof could be tiled or thatched. 'This dainty cottage will be the pride of her little ladyship. It can be run quite easily by two doll maids and is therefore suitable for modern conditions.'

The distasteful and decidedly sickly advertising material regarding children's toys that was popular in the 1920s and 1930s is reflected, though only for a short time, in the Triang Lines Brothers Catalogue particularly in the promotion of their 'Country House':

> When Dolly Heather and Dolly Jim get engaged, they will be looking around for a house just like this. They will be lucky to get one at such a moderate price. The very big room and nice, bright, modern style will help them to keep young and cheerful. Besides, it's fitted with curtains to all rooms and Period fireplaces with nice imitation coal fires and real brass fenders, also the kitchen will enable Heather to 'Feed the brute' because the modern range is included in the price. The exterior is half cast, rough timbered and old red brick with a tiled roof.

A similar but larger house was also built from the same component parts and has the same arched porch over the front door. Another version was provided with a folding stand and was described as a perfect doll's country house. This model contained eight rooms, and the kitchen was equipped with a range, a housemaid's sink and a table. It had a thatched roof and exposed timbers and is more typical of the period than those previously mentioned. It could be supplied with a sun veranda all round the ground floor 'for American and Colonial markets'.

The most interesting development of Lines Brothers Triang was their introduction of doll's house furniture. It seems doubtful whether these sets were ever very profitable, as German imports in the 1920s were again strong. British firms had changed their attitudes, however, and were no longer willing to allow the foreigners complete monopoly and were prepared to make a real effort to establish a supply that would be superior to the imports. Triang furniture was of very good quality and was sold under the registered trademark of 'Period Dolls Furniture'. The sets were attractively boxed, and the covers pictured the four settings that were available, so that the child would soon be encouraged to demand another group. 'Up to now doll's house furniture has been made down to a price. Period furniture is made up to quality only. All the famous old masters are represented in a scale of one inch equals a foot. This is a size which suits admirably the average doll's house. Ladies will love it and find a place for "specimens" on their bric-à-brac tables. It will help to educate the kiddies to love good furniture'.

A dining-room and bedroom suite were made in Jacobean style, somewhat reminiscent of the pieces made recently by Barton's but with much more detail to the panelling of the fronts of coffers and the backs of chairs and settles. The Jacobean dining-room set was augmented by a matching fireplace with an overmantel with carved shields and a club fender with rails. Very similar furniture was made at this time by Elgin of Enfield, who are known to have supplied Triang, and it seems possible that much of this miniature work was undertaken by smaller firms and then packed and marketed by Triang.

The 'Empire Bedroom Suite', painted in white or cream, has a typically Edwardian-style bed wth mattress and pillows and a wardrobe with an arched mirror in the door. It is completed by a washstand, two chairs and a dressing-table. The 'Chippendale Dining-Room Suite' was in much more elegant style, and the box contained delicate cabriole-legged chairs, a sideboard with a metal rail and a fireplace with a brass fender. This set was matched in style to a bedroom suite with a four-poster bed, with delicately turned posts, a chest of drawers, a wardrobe and chest with a toilet-mirror. The 'Adam Drawing-Room Suite' was finished in white and again sold with a matching chimneypiece and a brass grate. Two cushions and a large round cushion, termed a 'Humpty Cushion', were also provided. This Humpty Cushion was also sold with the 'Queen Anne Drawing-Room Suite', again with cabriole legs but including a particularly effective glass-fronted display cabinet. The retailers obviously pointed out that the houses also needed kitchen equipment, and this was also sold, boxed, by 1924. The kitchen set comprised a metal range, a table and two chairs, enamelled sink, towel rail, pastry-board and roller and a dresser. Though hardly rivalling the wealth of German kitchen equipment, it probably sold well, as it was so much better packed. It seems possible that the Period Furniture was too expensive for retailers in poor districts, so a much cheaper, but well-made line was also introduced that included a very functional dining-room set. The firm claimed that nothing but 'real furniture wood' was built into the sets, which should 'fascinate and educate'.

Many of the 1930s Triang houses were very simple, though a few were given thatched roofs. One of the more interesting models dating to 1924 was 'The Queen's Doll's House', 26 inches wide and 19 inches high. 'This house is an excellent reproduction of the design made famous by Her Majesty the Queen, who furnished the first model and gave it to the London Hospital in aid of their funds. It was bought at the sale for over £300.' The illustration shows an idealized country cottage with shuttered casement windows and a thatched roof. Triang were now also making a range of somewhat Colonial-style mansions with Georgian-style doors with pillars on either side that appear much older than their actual date of manufacture. All were finished in red brick and white enamel and contained staircases. Some of their larger houses measured over 70 inches long and were intended either for hospitals or for very rich children.

The Triang company grew rapidly, and a new factory at Merton was occupied in 1924, as the Old Kent Road premises became too small. Factories in the British Dominions were also established, and as the output became vast, the three brothers passed over the designing of toys to an Experimental Design Department, where Tom Rathbone was responsible for the wooden section. It is disappointing from the point of view of the researcher to discover that there are no drawings or modification designs attached to these early

DOLL'S HOUSES

Attractive Models
in Realistic Colours

DOLL'S HOUSE No. 50
(6510)

Pressed metal front, hinged at sides, with opening door. Four large rooms, embossed tiled roof with rough-cast chimney. Complete with trees in tubs. Length 16½" (42 cms.).

DOLL'S HOUSE No. 60
(6511)

A well-made two-roomed house at a popular price. Opening, metal-framed windows, tiled sun porch and front steps. Pleasing floral front and Red tiled roof. Length 13¾" (35 cms.).

DOLL'S HOUSE No. 61
(6512)

A larger house with two large rooms and built-in garage. Metal-framed windows with curtains, tiled sun-porch and steps. Red tiled roof. Length 19" (48 cms.).

DOLL'S HOUSE No. 62 (6513)

(Not illustrated.) Large double-fronted model with four rooms, staircase, built-in garage, steps and Red tiled roof. Nicely flowered front and Tudor-styled timbered gables. Length 26½" (68 cms.).

TRI-ANG " QUEEN ANNE " DOLL'S HOUSE (7530)

Designed by our resident architect in that lovely style so often seen in the English country-side. Heavy board construction with exterior coloured as shown in illustration. The house contains 4 large rooms, bathroom, hall and staircase. Opening walls at rear. Measures 24" (61 cms.) long.

A page from the Tri-ang 1953 catalogue showing the Queen Anne house.

models, as they were simply constructed, improved and then hung up in the factory to act as a guide. A photograph of the Merton factory, taken in 1958, shows the doll's house assembly room with a range of mock-Tudor houses not unlike those popular in the 1930s, illustrating the lack of adventure in the construction of houses that has contributed to their decline in popularity as toys.

Despite the over-conservatism that made Triang's later years in the production of dolls' houses somewhat repetitive, the Lines family produced so many models that there is at least one example in almost every collection,

DOLLS' HOUSES
in distinctive
Country Styles

DOLL'S HOUSE No. 76 (6514)

DOLL'S HOUSE No. 77 (6515)

"PRINCESS" DOLL'S HOUSE (6518)

DOLL'S HOUSE No. 93 (6516)

DOLL'S HOUSE No. 76 (6514)

A fine house with a hinged front for access to the two large rooms. Curtains fitted to opening, metal-framed windows. Sun-porch and seat with tiled floor. Complete with built-in garage fitted with opening doors. Red tiled roof. Length 24" (61 cms.).

"PRINCESS" DOLL'S HOUSE (6518)

A distinctive model with thatched roof and stuccoed exterior. The four rooms, hall, staircase and landing are tastefully decorated and have imitation linoleum floor covering. Electric lights are installed in the main rooms. (Batteries not supplied.) Front hinged in two parts. Colourful print curtains at opening metal windows. Length 30" (76 cms.).

DOLL'S HOUSE No. 93 (6516)

A full-sized house of fashionable Tudor design. Built-in garage. Two bedrooms, dining room, fitted bathroom and kitchen, hall, staircase and landing, all tastefully decorated with wallpaper and imitation lino on floors. Opening metal windows draped with curtains. Front opens in four places. Side entrance with porch and seat. Electric lights in all rooms. (Batteries excluded.) Length 47¼" (120 cms.).

DOLL'S HOUSE No. 77 (6515)

Double-fronted house opening at two places to reveal four large rooms. Front door opens, showing staircase to bedrooms. Tudor style timbered front with neat floral effect. Red tiled roof. Length 33¾" (86 cms.).

A page from the Tri-ang 1953 catalogue showing the 'Princess Doll's House'.

though obviously it is those constructed by G. & J. Lines under the Thistle Mark that are the most popular.

Several Lines houses appear in the Wallington Hall collection in Northumberland, one of the most interesting displays to be found outside London. With the exception of the mansion-like construction known as Hammond House, the exhibits have the endearing air of the attainable and are of the type found in personal collections all over the country. There are a few charming curiosities, such as a Gothick villa, reminiscent of Louden's drawings for lodges and farm cottages, but the overwhelming impression is

313

'The Long House' is especially attractive as it is so well made and retains its original pale cream paintwork. It dates to *circa* 1870 and is 40 inches high by 56 inches long.

that of an average collection with the lucky finds and somewhat doubtful inclusions of every individual assembler.

The main part of the Wallington Hall collection was presented to the National Trust by the family of Mrs Graham Angus of Corbride on her death in 1973. Twelve houses and their contents were included, as well as a number of toys and several good sets of miniature china. Few of the models contained any original furniture, so the assemblers decided to put the finest pieces in one of the oldest and most impressive, known as 'The Long House' and dating to

The interior of the 'Long House', *circa* 1870. The chimneypieces are original, but only a few fragments of the original wallpapers remain. The furniture is mainly of the imitation rosewood type. The carpets were hand-made for the house.

1870. This model is one of those basic, pleasantly proportioned, late-Victorian homes seen in every suburb and known as 'The Hollies' or 'Wisteria Lodge'. This model, with its low façade and original paintwork, has great appeal, as the general standard of carpentry is so satisfactory. It was necessary to re-paper most of the rooms, and the carpets were also specially made replacements, but the atmosphere of a home of the period has been carefully maintained. The proportions of the façade and the interior are somewhat at variance, and it seems possible that the staircase hall was added

'The Joiner's House', *circa* 1830, a charming and rare example of a country carpenter's work. It is cream-painted with a green roof and window frames. The sides open to reveal very low, small rooms. $18\frac{1}{2}$ inches high by 20 inches wide.

at some stage to what was originally intended as a six-roomed construction. The designer obviously loved symmetry, and a flight of steps, leading so unsatisfactorily to the side of the hall, would surely have caused him grief. Possibly the original owner, on being shown the house, demanded a staircase, so that the irate carpenter was forced hastily to adapt his original concept.

The small and mysterious 'Joiner's House' in country Gothick, with its original faded cream and green paintwork, is to me the most interesting of the Angus collection. The model is crudely but effectively made and has the allure

'Red Gables', a painted red-brick house that carries its original date on the façade. The front opens in three sections. With its battlemented bays and arched door, it is typical of much late-Victorian suburban Gothic building. Height 34 inches.

of the complete curiosity: though hundreds of lodge and labourers' cottages were erected by fashionable or romantically minded landowners in the eighteenth and nineteenth centuries, few were copied as toys, making this one of the rarest items. Despite the very small scale of the model, there is a central landing and stairs, as well as four low rooms to which access is gained from the sides.

'Red Gables', dating to 1886, illustrates the progression of the Gothic style from its light, imaginative Regency idiom to the much more staid

A brick-painted house known as 'Claremont', with its original date, 1867. The opening room fronts are fixed in position with ivory hooks. The sides of the house are painted in plain red. The slates are also painted. This house is unusual not only because of the sectional front opening but also because of the integral garden. Height 33 inches.

Opposite: The interior of 'Claremont' with its narrow, realistic staircase. The six rooms have the original wallpapers, and the sink and the copper are also original. The furniture dates mainly from the late nineteenth century.

interpretations of the late Victorians. The winsome Gothick of the Joiner's House has now disappeared, and we find the almost ecclesiastical detail so admired by the followers of Pugin. 'Red Gables', with a date plaque on the central panel, has an arched front door and the battlemented bay windows always considered so suitable for town vicarages. Similar models were owned by many children, as they were made by local carpenters or skilful fathers, but this is exceptional because the paintwork is so completely original.

The most precisely constructed house is surely 'Claremont', dating to the 1860s. Not only are the bricks and slates carefully painted but each section is hinged separately so access can be gained to the nine individual sections. Each door is held by well-made bone stays, which contribute to the air of absolutely perfect control. In front of the house is a neat garden which, together with the stand, forms an integral part of the construction. The original wallpapers are still in place, and the general condition of the model is perfect. Frequently

318

A room decorated with French commercially made furniture. The wallpaper is modern. The house (*circa* 1895) is vaguely Continental in appearance but is probably an early G. & J. Lines model.

Opposite: This curious house is included to illustrate the degree of adaptation and extension to which a doll's house is often subjected. The lower half was commercially made by G. & J. Lines in 1925 and has typical metal windows and doors. The upper part was carpenter-made in imitation of the style of the lower section. It is known as Sir Walter Gilbey's House. Height 57½ inches.

dolls' houses with a garden are unwieldy, but 'Claremont' was planned so well that this aspect is completely satisfactory.

Lines houses appear in several forms in this representative collection. The most attractive model used to be described as 'the French house' because of its ornate window-mouldings with brass upholstery-tack decoration. In fact this structure is very obviously an 1890s Thistle-Mark model, as it reveals the mouldings and general construction methods so liked by the firm at this time. The simple interior staircase is of the type that G. & J. Lines continued to use well into the 1920s, though it was first used some thirty years earlier. A particularly French atmosphere is created by the gilded, ornate furnishings, the painted set in the bedroom being particularly effective. One of the strangest models in the collection also originated at the Lines factory and is known as 'Sir Walter Gilbey's House'. This house is at present catalogued as *circa* 1900, but in fact its date cannot be earlier than 1925, as the lower section was first made by Lines in that year. The model was purchased at a

This curious but substantially made house dating to around 1905 has the unusual addition of a massive brass central chimney which gives the structure great prestige.

Opposite above: A section of Hammond House, constructed in the late nineteenth century, showing the servants' bedrooms. In the centre of the middle floor is the governess's bedroom. On its right a drawing-room. Height 37 inches. *Opposite below:* Another section of Hammond House showing the children's rooms on the top floor. Note the realism of the staircase which links to a long central corridor. On the bottom left is the library.

sale where it was described as belonging to Sir Walter Gilbey of the wine family, but it seemed worthy of inclusion as it illustrates how a basic model was often adapted and added to over the years to create a complete nonsuch. The lower part is typically commercial, with the metal-framed windows and printed-metal doors which Lines used until the 1930s, with standard chimneypieces and the stock staircase seen also in the 'French House'; the second and third floors have completely different chimneypieces, but the exterior has obviously been made by a carpenter who copied the lower metal windows very carefully in plywood but added a parapet and a balcony to give the structure some unity. Despite his efforts, the finished effect is strange but indicates the degree of adaptation which children often demanded.

All the Wallington Hall houses pale into insignificance beside the breathtaking Hammond House, whose magnificence can only be hinted at in a photograph, as, to do full justice to the detail of the rooms, each would need to be separately illustrated and described. The visitor, perhaps familiar already with a photograph, is hardly prepared for either the size or the colour of the interior, and a personal visit is a necessity for any enthusiast. The exterior, with its distressing modern pink brick paper, is not worth illustrating, as it is so horribly reminiscent of bad municipal housing. This part was restored because the original state was so bad, but one longs to see a

A section of Hammond House showing the maids' bedrooms on the top floor. In the centre is the housekeeper's room. Bottom left is the butler's pantry with a stillroom next door. Note the number of bells in the boot-room on the right.

photograph or description of what remained before 'restoration', as we now have a façade completely in the style of the 1920s and 1930s. Inside, with a schizophrenic shock, we encounter the atmosphere of the late nineteenth century. The actual date of the structure is unknown, as it was presented to the National Trust in 1970, but on a small trowel and on a miniature copybook is the name 'Ruby Hammond'. The date seems to be a little optimistically put at 1886, though the disposition and the atmosphere of the rooms seem much more Edwardian. Despite some doubt regarding the date of construction, nothing can detract from the magnificence of this interior, with its thirty-six rooms, long service-corridors, two staircases and lift. The service-corridors run the whole length of the house and are almost worryingly realistic, as one expects to see housemaids flattening themselves against the walls as guests move between the rooms.

When Hammond House first came into the possession of the Trust, an eager team of restorers set to work, and a detailed list was kept of each person's

324

A detail of the housekeeper's room in Hammond House, showing the interesting variety of metal furniture including an unusual 'conversation' in the foreground.

contribution. The interior certainly repaid this effort, which must at first have seemed daunting, as they were faced with dozens of boxes of furniture and dolls. Under one room was an original label, 'Footman's bedroom', so the restorers set about organizing a perfectly run household in which the many servants are provided with excellent accommodation. In this aspect, Hammond House is supreme among models, as in no other are the servants so well provided for. Fortunately, the floor and wallcoverings were in unspoilt condition, so that the interior retains its original character. It seems strange that such a large model should have remained unknown and unrecorded in a York attic for so many years when other, much less impressive models were given extensive publicity, and we have to be grateful that one of the National Trust workers, Sheila Petit, was able to acquire it complete. One has a nightmare vision of the contents of each room being sold separately at auction and dispersed all over the world by eager dealers.

The scale of the model and its contents is so carefully maintained that it seems very much an adult preoccupation, perhaps of the same person who carefully painted the photograph album and stitched the linen. In the many rooms can be found examples of almost every piece of furniture, crockery and equipment made between the 1870s and 1920, all carefully selected to form convincing settings. The dolls are beautifully costumed to represent all the household characters and include men with side-whiskers and small children and babies, the nursery being among the most effectively arranged of the apartments. Dating of such adult-assembled models is invariably difficult, as owners so often embarked on such an exercise in retrospective mood, whereas children preferred houses in the modern idiom. I once owned a house constructed and furnished in the late 1920s but provided with dolls in their original 1890s costumes. The atmosphere, the furniture and even the china were completely nineteenth-century, as the lady who arranged the rooms was deliberately creating an old-fashioned interior, perhaps to remind her of her own childhood. The question of the date of Hammond House remains one for debate, but nothing can detract from the pure enjoyment of finding so many fascinating miniatures assembled in a single structure.

No such problems surround the very simple house displayed in the nursery at Wallington. This brick-painted model was the plaything of several generations of the Trevellyan family, who occupied Wallington Hall from 1777. The house is of the tall, narrow, three-storeyed type without a staircase and has been opened so frequently by small children that the hinges have fallen apart. It forms such a complete contrast to the perfection of Hammond House that the visitor must end by questioning his own preferences for models or children's toys.

In furnishing and equipping Hammond House, few problems would have been encountered, as the variety of miniatures available in the toyshops at the end of the century was very great. Almost every nursery contained a doll's house and rocking-horse, but whereas the horse could be forgotten by the parents, the house constantly required furniture and inhabitants, much of which was imported from Germany. From Spence & Co 'a little housemaid's box, containing twelve articles for 1s 5d' could be obtained, while at Peter Robinsons in 1897 sets of doll's house furniture were sold boxed from 1s 11½d. These were 'artistic and perfect little models of sideboards, wardrobes and other pieces. Among these are sets for bedrooms, drawing-rooms, dining-rooms and kitchens, and there are also separate bathrooms at moderate prices. There are pumps that pump real water at 1s 11½d and lovely sets of baths and cans complete.'

The Trevellyan House stands in the nursery at Wallington Hall and was played with by the children of the family who owned the estate. It is painted brick and dates to between 1850 and 1860. Height 44 inches.

The Gorie House made in the early twentieth century, the garage section with its upper bathroom being a later addition. The upper and lower sections open separately at the front, and the roof with painted slates lifts off. Height $27\frac{1}{2}$ inches.

The variety of dolls' houses had also increased significantly by the end of the century, as children demanded much more fashionable models than the simple box-like structures that had satisfied their ancestors. Garrould's Bazaar in 1892 displayed a doll's house 'that resembles a modern villa instead of the red-brick, many-windowed William and Mary houses of our youth', commented a reporter from *The Lady*, admiring a house with a Dutch gable, a tall porch with pillars and the inevitable bay window. At Hamley's in Regent Street were displayed dolls' houses of all kinds in 1893,

from the modest cottage or bijou residence to spacious mansions furnished most sumptuously and oh! Wonder of Wonders! fitted with electric light in every apartment. Accessories to well-appointed houses to dolls of every degree appear

328

Flat-fronted houses were very popular in Britain between 1890 and 1910. The bright red and yellow decoration must have appealed to children.

on every side; here are toilet-tables with drawers crammed with toilet-requisites; miniature perfume-bottles etc; a lovely little wardrobe offers five changes of apparel; a linen-chest is stored with dainty linen, and there are fitted kitchens, laundries and shops.

Many writers expressed concern in the 1890s regarding the extravagance of children's toys, and there was a very definite movement towards the old belief in useful rational pursuits and in encouraging the young to construct their own playthings. If it could be suggested that some higher motivation than pure amusement was integral to a particular toy, the manufacturers were eager to capitalize on this aspect. A reporter visiting Peter Robinson's in November 1894 remarked that

Few doll's house size pieces of good quality were made in Britain in the second half of the nineteenth century. This washstand set by Goss is an exception. The set was sold with several different designs, including one with rabbits.

Most children are naturally domesticated to begin with, and playing at cooking may be turned into a very useful educational process. All we have to do is provide the small people with the proper paraphernalia, and so strong is the miniature faculty that they will learn many household arts in the course of unconscious play. Thus a well-fitted doll's house – they have electric bells now – often teaches more valuable lessons than half a dozen books . . . mater and pater familias who desire their daughters to grow up useful women can hardly do better than invest in toys of this useful kind.

Houses with working bathrooms were obviously a great novelty in the 1890s, and for those unable to afford a completely plumbed villa, there were small sets sometimes accompanied by a tank. Though model rooms were never as popular in Britain as on the Continent, the novelty of running water encouraged the sale of a number of working kitchens and bathrooms. At Spence's in St Paul's Churchyard in 1896, a fitted bathroom with taps that ran water cost from 4s 11d to 6s 11d, 'but it is doubtful whether the nurse would obtain as much satisfaction from them as the children would. A pretty little stand with various brushes and brooms necessary for keeping the doll's house clean can be had from 6½d to 4s 6½d. A pair of toy scales in the smallest size costs only 6½d.' Their wide range of well-made furniture included a canopied four-poster bed, button-back dining-chairs, a dressing-table with an oval mirror and an unusual washstand with a curtained mirror. From F. Aldis, Belgrave Mansions, drawing-room furniture upholstered in pale colours could be obtained in sets or set out in elegant little drawing-rooms, while the selection of dressed dolls of German and French origin was overwhelming to any small visitor.

The quality of these late nineteenth-century miniatures was obvious to

Poorer children's houses have only rarely survived. This Norfolk example, despite its primitive construction, contains some good pieces and an effective kitchen range.

adults, and many tables set with china and glass, dolls in attractively gilded chairs and dressing-tables fully equipped with tapersticks and powderbowls, were displayed in parlour cabinets or set out under glass shades. When Beatrix Potter was writing *The Tale of Two Bad Mice*, she preferred to use doll's house items as models rather than simply imagining ordinary furniture on a small scale. Norman Warne, the youngest son of her publisher, was an enthusiastic toy-maker, working at dolls' houses in his basement workroom; among these models was a house for his niece, Winifred Warne. The story of Hunca Munca and Tom Thumb was already planned, and Norman helped by borrowing a flaxen-haired doll and another dressed as a policeman from the

The robustly constructed house dating between 1865 and 1875 that was owned by Beatrix Potter.

family children. He also obtained a wooden 'Dutch Doll', to act as cook, and some doll's house food. Some of the pieces were sent from Hamley's, and Beatrix Potter commented in a letter that the appearance of the hams would surely be enough to cause indigestion. The actual house on which the story was based was kept in the nursery of Fruing Warne's house, where Beatrix Potter had hoped to work, but, as usual, her strict parents disapproved, though she was nearly forty, and she was forced to work from interior and exterior photographs, which Norman supplied in some number. The interior was wonderfully cluttered and reminded her of rooms in which it was impossible to move without knocking something over. When the book was published in 1904, it was dedicated to Winifred Warne, 'the little girl who had the doll's house'.

The doll's house at Hilltop, now owned by the National Trust, though often thought to have been the inspiration for the well-known story, was in fact obtained at a much later date. It seems likely that the well-made battlemented house in the style of the 1860–70s was bought locally, as it appealed to Beatrix Potter's fascination with miniature objects and made a suitable repository for the food she had made for *The Tale of Two Bad Mice*. Perhaps it also aroused fond memories of Warne, who had died suddenly in 1905, shortly after they had decided to marry.

Reminiscences and contemporary accounts suggest that Hamley's was the main supplier of dolls' houses and furniture, and in 1901 they offered such additions as a greenhouse complete with plants on a sill and arranged in pots around the base. A reporter from *Girl's Realm* photographed one of their larger houses, which represented a modern mansion, built half of brick and half of painted stone. The nine rooms and staircase were elegantly carpeted, and the model was fitted with every modern improvement. 'Baths, bells and the newest of kitchen ranges, a model scullery – even the water is laid down in this magnificent toy.' In the following year another journal commented on their fine dolls' houses 'specially arranged with a view to the easy manipulation of furniture, and possessing a staircase as well as an ingeniously arranged side that folds back in sections! Has a double bay on one side and a large window on the first floor and has an integral stand' – a model that again sounds very similar to those produced by G. & J. Lines. From a rival supplier of toys, Schoolbred's, on the Tottenham Court Road, a wide selection of houses was also available in 1901, 'veritable Lilliputian mansions some of them, others suitable residences for dolls of moderate means, costing from 6s 6d each if they are English make or 2s 6d if foreign manufacture, though, without any national prejudice, one may assert that the superiority of the houses made in the home country is greater than the few shillings in price might warrant'. Maple's, in less patriotic style, was marketing folding printed cardboard models that closely resembled the American products and which were probably imported. 'It can be built up or taken to pieces at will and fits into a neat box. The rooms have pictures, fireplaces and windows with draped curtains printed in place.' The line-drawing shows a simple gabled construction with a single room upstairs and down and no front, though the interior looks attractive because of the arched and pillared finish. Gamage's was also offering some foreign houses among the British models, such as a Swiss-type chalet with the very unusual addition of cattle in a barn on the ground floor. In order to help small boys provide well-made furniture for their sisters' houses, there was 'The Little Joiner's Set', containing all the tools, wooden slats, nails etc for making furniture without the use of glue.

There were many complaints in Edwardian magazines concerning the over-indulgence of children: they were given too many toys of an expensive nature; their education was becoming too easy as the theory of learning

THE HALL OF THE GUILDS

through play was becoming more widely used, and spoiled infants were consequently becoming more common. In 1913 it was commented that the toys available were marvels of ingenuity and workmanship but doubted if they were as much appreciated as the old-fashioned dolls and wooden toys of a few generations before. Many, it was felt, were almost too fine for common nursery use and tended to fall to pieces when so used. That most extravagant of toys, the doll's house, was subjected to frequent criticism as it was so popular. Alice Corkran commented in 1901 that dolls' houses were never before so frequently found.

> Our mansions, our suburban villas, our country cottages, our shops, are all represented in miniature. Some modest edifices cost a few shillings, some elaborate dwellings fetch very high prices. When the King of Siam paid a visit to Edinburgh a year or two ago, he visited the Royal Hospital for Children and was so moved by the sight of so many little ones in pain and lassitude that he ordered a doll's house to be made and sent to the children to play with. The house is an ordinary middle-class dwelling but is a marvel of solid construction and finished workmanship; upon his gift the King spent £50.

The model was indeed substantial and stood on a low, turned-leg base. It was completely conventional in design, with steps that led to a pillared front door, five neat windows and three dormer windows in the attic. Sadly, like so many hospital gifts, the house, despite its substantial construction, could have survived for only a few years in the hands of children who had scant respect for a toy they did not personally own.

One of the finest examples of a parent's indulgence of his child is the world-famous Titania's Palace, which transcends the sphere of ordinary dolls' houses, as it is at once both a toy and an artistic expression of the period, conjuring up for the modern visitor both the atmosphere and the literature of the idyllic pre-First World War years. One of the more unusual manifestations of this curiously dream-like period was the fascination of many intelligent and creative adults with the subject of fairies. Trees with sinuous animated roots from which appear fairy-like figures were characteristic of early-twentieth-century British illustration, even in connexion with subjects of adult intention. The romantic but substantial figures created by Rossetti and Burne Jones had, by 1900, become stylized into linear creatures of the waves and air, with more affinity to the characters in *A Midsummer Night's Dream* than to the very human creations of the Pre-Raphaelites. A delicate and somewhat wistful literary interpretation of the Fairy World was attempted, but even when such characters were unspecified by the writer, the illustrator

The Hall of the Guilds from Titania's Palace with steps leading to the Throne Room. The upper walls are painted with panels of winged maids holding the arms of the medieval Florentine guilds and the arms of Sir Neville as Ulster King of Arms.

335

frequently added spirits of his own invention to give added life to the seasons or the elements. Despite the fact that many books and poems of the period have titles that would now suggest an association with childhood, their presentation and idiom makes it clear that they were intended for adult appreciation. This preoccupation with the Fairy World was to be a fairly short-lived phenomenon, extending from around 1900 to 1920, its images lending themselves well to the late Art Nouveau idiom with its long-tressed females, sylphs and elf-like forms.

The nineteenth-century illustrator, when seeking an air of sublimity, relied on religious devices such as wistful angels, and it seems likely that, as the intellectual and middle-class following of the Church became less strong, the desire for a supernatural element was supplied by the creatures of fairyland. It became very evident, from the wide Press coverage when Titania's Palace was sold at Christie's in 1978, that Sir Neville Wilkinson's preoccupation with the theme of fairies was considered more than a little strange. Here was a professional soldier, Harrow, Sandhurst and the Coldstream Guards, at the age of thirty-eight and having served with distinction in South Africa, bewitched by the Queen of the Fairies! Viewed in context, against the fascination with fairyland that was so prevalent, the project appears less an eccentric indulgence than a model completely in line with the preoccupations of artistic people of his generation.

It is impossible to avoid comparison between the life of Wilkinson and that of another explorer of the enchanted world of make-believe, Arthur Rackham, who was only two years older and whose artistic development must have been subject to comparable stimulus. The two men both appear to have made their escape into make-believe when the settled, slowly evolving order of the world in which they had matured was shaken by the ferocity of the Great War, though in neither case was man's current barbarity allowed to enter into their creations. Many of Rackham's books, despite their fairy themes, were highly expensive productions aimed almost purely at the adult market and presented in lavish investment-type form. To a great extent, the atmosphere of the Palace is similar, as few children could have appreciated the rarity of the objects which were introduced, though an adult is filled with wonder. In one of Rackham's illustrations for *Peter Pan in Kensington Gardens*, published in 1906, a fairy is shown emerging from the roots of a tree, and the great interest taken in this story must have formed part of the almost explosive artistic absorption with fairyland that engendered the building of the Palace. Its very inspiration could lead easily from this single illustration, though Sir Neville tells that, while he was drawing a sycamore tree, his daughter Guendolen, then aged three, claimed to have seen a fairy disappearing between the roots. This incident took place at their Irish home, Mount Merrion, near Dublin, aided no doubt, by the old-established Irish affection for the Little Folk.

Superficially for the amusement of his daughter but obviously mainly for his own diversion, an intricate story of the Court of the Fairies (who of course lived under the tree) was developed on this enchanted day in 1907. How might this Queen of the Fairies and her Court respond to a palace that a mortal might build with the help of the finest craftsmen of the time decorated with treasures worthy of her kingdom? Perhaps Her Iridescence Queen Titania, her Consort Oberon and the Prince and Princesses might be persuaded to take up residence. It was towards this end that work began.

Sir Neville Wilkinson had served with distinction in the army, but his main interest soon became heraldry and art, and he studied etching at what is now the Royal College of Art. In 1908 he was appointed Ulster King of Arms. The background and basic motivation of this soldier turned artist are important, as there is no other doll's house that is so completely one man's inspiration and that so accurately epitomizes the literary as well as the art movements of the time. Though the Palace was begun in 1907, it was not put on display until 1922, and even then it was in an unfinished state, as Sir Neville wished the public to see his work before the house being assembled for Queen Mary could be compared with it.

When seeing the Palace for the first time, the impact of the rather squat construction is somewhat disappointing, the main section being only some 30 inches high but 116 inches long, with some added height given by a dome and cupola which rise over the chapel. The building was constructed by James Hicks of Lower Pembrook Street, Dublin, who worked to the specific instructions of Sir Neville. It is the very correct architectural construction that creates the somewhat unfortunate low effect, as doll's house manufacturers tend to exaggerate height to give a more pleasing shape. The original drawings for the model are still in existence and show how precisely the work was envisaged, all the decorative woods, for instance, being deliberately specified. The main construction was in old mahogany which has developed a rich, dark patination which is very effective. His care for detail is particularly shown in the chapel window, with the instruction that the semicircle over it was to have walnut moulding and a satinwood centre. He took an obvious pleasure in these drawings and signed the sheets, thereby giving the model added interest, as such a degree of documentation is unique.

The construction of the Palace was made more difficult because of Sir Neville's intention to move it from place to place when complete, in order to give delight to children of all kinds and, in the process, raise money for those who were handicapped or deprived. It was eventually to travel as far as the United States and Canada and was to be viewed by over two million people. In order to make it completely transportable, it was made in eight sections that could be individually lowered into a protective container. Each section was provided with a removable façade, and the interiors were glazed for protection during exhibition. The pine base was curtained and surrounded by a brass handrail that was also intended to act as a seat for very young children. It must have seemed very necessary to make the structure of an impressive size in order to attract visitors and provide them with the impression of moving from room to room in an actual building. The realism of many of the apartments is heightened by views through the rear windows of a courtyard with a central fountain. The carpentry of the exterior is very fine and surpasses that usually found in eighteenth-century houses, though it still remains incomplete as Sir Neville died before completing his project, and only two short façades were made, flanked by pavilions. The State Front has five bays and is built in what a Christie's cataloguer described as 'Wrenaissance Style', the designer believing that there are no styles or periods which must be copied in fairy architecture. Sir Neville was prepared to adapt all that he considered good, and he created a surprisingly well integrated structure with its three-bay pavilions with columns of the Doric and Corinthian orders, the lower windows having heavy keystones under a mezzanine storey. The capitals of the main section are made of gilt bronze, and the original intention was to decorate the walls also with bronze ornaments. A touch of added prestige was given by the elegant belfry, designed by Sir Edwin Lutyens.

The interior decoration is completely in late nineteenth- and early twentieth-century style, though the source of inspiration is obviously Renaissance Italy. Every wall and surface is given lavish and colourful treatment, so that an abundance of tone and texture is created, rather in the manner of some of the churches of the period, such as All Saints', Margaret Street. The richness of the furnishings, set against the painted walls, brings the work of William Burges immediately to mind, and some of the red-painted cabinets decorated with medieval-style figures are completely in his manner. It is this complete period atmosphere that gives the Palace its unique appeal and raises it far above the realms of adult whimsy. Wilkinson was very consciously creating as splendid a home as any sublime creature of his period could possibly desire, and we find that strange mixture of Victorian and contemporary design that is so much a feature of early twentieth-century interiors. There are of course, no dolls in the Palace, as the intention was to leave it free so that Titania and her retinue could move in at any time, though the viewer dreams of occupants as delicious as the gold leaf and mother-of-pearl creations of such artists as Frederick Marriott, whose Oberon springs immediately to mind.

The State Rooms, obviously Sir Neville's main interest, occupy the complete height of the building, the living-accommodation being set out on two floors. Despite the fact that the scale was well maintained, this plan does unfortunately give these lower apartments a somewhat stunted effect. Their furnishings are also, though good, on a lesser plane and have much more in common with ordinary dolls' houses, though the miniature treasures that lie so casually around can be found only in a few. The State Rooms are quite unique and are veritable treasure-houses of rare and valuable miniatures, many of which were acquired by Sir Neville on his travels in Italy, and around which some of his children's stories were woven.

Additional interest and colour luminosity were given to the walls and ceilings of the State Rooms by a technique Wilkinson described as 'mosaic painting', involving the application of as many as one thousand or more carefully planned dabs of paint to the square inch. This breaking up of colour succeeds in giving the decoration a truly miniaturized effect and works particularly well on the ceilings and walls but less effectively on floors, such as that in the Throne Room. This apartment is one of the most splendid in the Palace, with its fine ceiling depicting Oberon surrounded by the names of the great writers of fairy stories. The windows, overlooking the central courtyard, are framed by mother-of-pearl, and the throne is approached by steps of the same material. The throne itself is a very unsatisfactory piece, with little beauty of design, and was obviously contrived to display the valuable gem-encrusted peacock, originally, and, much more satisfactorily, a brooch, made by M. Baugrand, Napoleon III's Court jeweller, for the Paris Exposition of 1856, and later believed to have been given to the Empress Eugénie. The outspread tail of the bird is set with diamonds, rubies, emeralds and sapphires, while the throne itself is made of ebony, inlaid with ivory and tortoiseshell. On either side, ivory pillars display a pair of golden figures of boys attributed to Benvenuto Cellini. A pair of malachite models of Buddhist lions, of Chinese origin, stand rather uneasily on either side of the throne but, as they were presented to the Palace by Queen Mary, it was necessary that they should be accommodated. The Throne Room also contains one of the most painstaking sections of Sir Neville's work, in the form of a 4-inch frieze above the canopy and windows, inspired by a visit to the tomb of Galla Placidia in Ravenna. Each inch of this 5-foot frieze took a day to complete, and its creation is typical of the energy and time he was prepared to expend in order to achieve the desired effect. In the centre of the 'mosaic' floor is a Greek inscription, 'Silver and gold I have none but what I have I give thee', forming the dedication to the crippled children who were to be helped by its display. This room is now, in common with some of the others, too full of potted plants and vases of flowers. The realistic painted brass flowers were the work of Beatrice Hindley of London and, though extremely effective in themselves, now detract from the proportional realism of the room and could be wished elsewhere. A pair of splendid doors, leading into the garden, was the work of a Sheffield craftsman, Joseph Barker.

The Throne Room is approached through the Hall of the Guilds, considered by Sir Neville 'the Entrance to Fairyland'. The doors of the Hall stand open, so that from a child's eye-level a vista of great opulence leading to the throne can be seen. The coffered ceiling, encrusted with sea-shells, acts as a foil for the banners that hang from the frieze, and the upper walls are painted with panels

The Hall of the Fairy Kiss from Titania's Palace with its impressive walnut screen and gallery in late Renaissance style. A silver door-case leads to the chapel.

of winged maidens who carry the arms of the medieval Florentine guilds as well as those of Sir Neville as Ulster King of Arms. The lower walls are made of Connemara marble. The black and white marble tiles of the floor act as a foil to the appropriately valuable furnishings, which include a fine Nuremberg gilt copper casket with an elaborate lock, dating to *circa* 1600, a pair of bronze Italian figures of prancing horses and a fascinating late eighteenth-century Swiss mechanical fountain, mounted with three gold and enamel putti. This clockwork fountain, set with diamonds, is a splendid miniature and was known in the fairy lore of Titania's Palace as 'the Golden Fountain of Youth'. One of the most valuable miniatures is also found in the Hall of the Guilds and takes the form of a gilt brass cannon and carriage, made *circa* 1600 and attributed to the armourer Michael Mann of Nuremberg. The creator's intention in placing the weapon in this position was to 'keep the spotted

'The Order of the Fairy Kiss' that forms the centrepiece of the large hall in Titania's Palace.

snakes with double tongues and thorny hedgehogs out of fairyland'.

The Hall of the Fairy Kiss, Chancery of the Most Industrious Order of the Fairy Kiss, to which only members of the Most Industrious Order were admitted, is again somewhat spoiled in appearance by an over-abundance of potted plants. Nevertheless, the room, with its central feature of a walnut screen with a gallery, made by Thomas Lennon in late-Renaissance style, is splendidly effective and richly embellished with silver and bronze figures. The decoration is augmented by dozens of miniatures, such as small ivory statues, a bronze frieze of putti and a 3-inch agate seal in the form of a blackamoor on a faceted rock-crystal plinth. Paintings of Queen Alexandra and Queen Mary, both the work of Sir Neville, hang in this area, which was intended originally for assemblies of the Chapters of the Order and for dancing, though the royal sleigh, with a toy-compartment, was also kept here, to be borrowed each year

The staircase that leads from the Hall of the Fairy Kiss, with a portrait of Queen Alexandra.

by Santa Claus. From the Hall of the Fairy Kiss, the Chapel is entered through a door with a frame of very lovely hand-wrought silver, the work of Joseph Barker.

The Chapel, so completely in the manner of contemporary church decoration, is Titania's private oratory and is furnished with a particularly fine reredos with a reduction of the Assumption of the Virgin by Murillo which apparently earned for Sir Neville the Vice-Presidency of the Society of Miniature Painters. The design of the ceiling was inspired by the Book of Kells, and in the spandrels are the four archangels standing on crystal spheres. The stained-glass windows were the work of Kathleen Quigly, and the chamber organ, with its Doric columns, is a copy of the famous original by James Watt. The organ can be blown through the bellows under the platform and the keys played, somewhat unromantically, with a matchstick. The Chapel's furnishings are appropriately generous and include an eighteenth-century German ivory group, a Flemish boxwood Virgin and Child with St Anne and St John, made in the eighteenth century also, and a pair of silver gilt and rock-crystal altar candlesticks made in the seventeenth century. On the lectern is a particularly lovely French illuminated Book of the Hours, *circa* 1450, which was especially rebound in white vellum for the Palace. There are a few welcome touches of human weakness in all the splendour, such as the rather sad shells that were used to frame the painted panels on the upper walls and which present a somewhat Arts-and-Craft effect that is discordant.

The Chapel is by far the most splendidly constructed in any cabinet house and reflects a period when even Anglican churches were liberally covered in dense, bright decoration in the late style of the Arts and Crafts movement. With the alteration and even demolition of so many of these churches in what was, until recently, a maligned taste, this miniature has an importance of its own, being a record of an almost Renaissance flowering of a delight in pattern and design.

Titania entered the Chapel through a secret panel from her boudoir, which is a charming but quite ordinary living-room, in complete contrast to the State Apartments. It is again a room completely in period and is the boudoir of any wealthy, artistic woman of the time, being equipped with an eighteenth-century-style toilet-table supplied with painting-materials for her occupation during leisure hours. In these domestic apartments the visitor returns to the atmosphere of a much more conventional house of the period, though the amount of precise detail is still very great, such as the intarsia floor, inlaid with mother-of-pearl, the work of Colonel Gillespie, and the coffered ceiling, inlaid with various woods and decorated with intricate mouldings by Thomas Lennon, based on the Holbein ceiling at St James's Palace. The mirror, hanging over the chimneypiece in the boudoir, was carved by Pierre Metge of Skerries who also made many of the chairs in the Palace. This room also contains an elaborate *bonheur de jour* by George Swindell and a semicircular

THE ROYAL
BEDCHAMBER

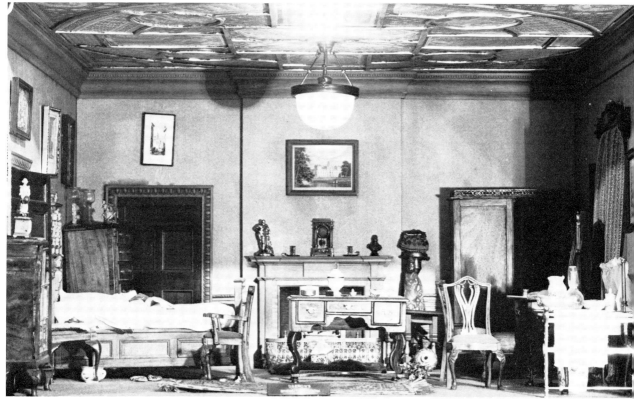

commode by A. Dunn & Co, dating to 1922. It is by this number of fully attributable and named pieces that the Palace is made particularly exciting, as few others, with the notable exception of Queen Mary's house, have any furnishings whose makers are recorded. Titania's boudoir contains many objects which Sir Neville mentions in his published stories that were set around the Palace, such as the Doria Lantern an ivory figure of Christ contained within a silver lantern which the characters in *The Grey Fairy* spend a great deal of time in finding. The Crystal Tear, which is also mentioned, is in the form of a gold octagonal stand inlaid with precious stones and supporting a rock-crystal teardrop. The back of this case is also inlaid with opals, and the piece is given a romantic aura by the story concerning babies who cry: 'Because someone has hurt them or because they are hungry and neglected, the first teardrop always disappears, you can never find it, because it goes straight to fairyland. It falls on the little golden stand.' Such tales are completely at discord with modern avoidance of sentimentality, but seen in the context of a period when the imagined behaviour of fairies was legitimate inspiration for works of art, the theme becomes less whimsical than descriptive of the climate of the age.

The remaining living-rooms are all decorated and equipped in the style of any wealthy Edwardian home, though the furnishings would have been too cluttered for the more progressive. The two Princesses of Fairyland share a room above Titania's boudoir and have a cupboard to store their spare wings. Although the Palace is not provided with a kitchen, the Princesses Iris and Ruby are sensibly given toothbrushes. The dining-room seems an unnecessary addition since there is no means of cooking, but the diners eat only fruit and do not require such items as cutlery. This room is furnished with several pieces of baronial-style oak and a few extremely graceful Chippendale-style chairs, made by Mr Metge. The chimneypiece is Connemara marble and surmounted by a bronze relief of St George. Miniature paintings of winter scenes, which hang above a high dado of gold canvas and probably originated in a Continental cabinet house, are believed to be the work of Claes Molinaer, who worked in the mid-seventeenth century. This functional room is provided with a number of interesting pieces, such as a seventeenth-century parcel-gilt goblet, Bristol and Nailsea glass and a number of ornamental items made of semi-precious stones, silver and gold, among which is a gold tabernacle containing an amethyst bust. The room is dominated by a satinwood serpentine-fronted sideboard of Sheraton design, made by Fred Early,which is given added impact by the fine Grecian-style knife-urns that stand on pedestals on either side.

Opposite above: The Royal Bedchamber. The ceiling is coffered and decorated with classical scenes. The Renaissance-style bedroom is painted. *Opposite below:* Oberon's dressing-room is typical of the period and has a 'Jacobean' bed carved by Uphill Jun. of Wilton.

Above: The morning room at the Palace is furnished in the idiom of the period. Some of the pieces, such as the red lacquered bureau, are made superbly. The ceiling is painted with a design of formal peacocks. The door-case is of carved Chinese ivory. *Opposite:* The bathroom in Titania's Palace, made completely in Edwardian style with painted mosaic decoration by Sir Neville. The floor was exhibited at the Royal Academy in 1927.

The day nursery contains a miniature copy of a particularly splendid doll's house built by Sir Neville in 1908 and first opened by Queen Alexandra with a golden key that is still kept in the hall. Sir Edwin Lutyens is thought to have derived inspiration on seeing this model for that ambitious project, Queen Mary's Doll's House. The miniature in the Palace nursery is well made and is painted to simulate faded red brick. Despite its very small size, the windows are glazed, and the proportions of a typical early eighteenth-century house, with recessed central columns and asymmetrical wings, are perfectly realized. As a miniature, the day nursery is one of the least satisfactory rooms, as the toys, made mainly of silver, are somewhat sparse, and it seems curious that use was not made of the small but well-made playthings that were available at the time.

Another graceful and completely Edwardian chamber is the morning room, with its chinoiserie lacquered furniture and, in contrast, comfortable if inelegant chairs with chintz loose covers. There are several good paintings and a splendid glazed bookcase, painted to imitate red lacquer with hinged and sliding doors, which was designed and painted by Sir Neville and made by Harry Hicks in 1927. The similarly made bureau-bookcase and matching chair have been claimed to be the very best pieces of miniature furniture ever made.

Though fairies do not need a kitchen, a splendid bathroom was obviously a

Top: The Prince's bedroom has a painted frieze and a carved ceiling. *Above:* A watercolour by Samuel Palmer, '*Now fades the glimmering landscape on the sight*'. Painted as a wedding present for Sir Neville's mother and later hung in the Palace. $2\frac{3}{4}$ inches by $6\frac{1}{4}$ inches.

necessity, and the dark green marble bath is flanked by Chinese carved ivory. In a rock-crystal basin the fairies can dye their wings. The furniture is typical of many homes of the period, but there are some fine additions, such as a nineteenth-century Amsterdam silver clothes-press.

In the private entrance hall of the Palace is kept the visitors' book, which includes the names of famous guests, such as W. B. Yeats. A mahogany door leads from the hall into Oberon's study, with its elaborate white and silver ceiling. The floor is made of rosewood and intarsia and forms a splendid foil for Fred Early's walnut bookcase and a cello and bow made by Mr Withers of Wardour Street. The contents of the room are carefully selected, so that we are in no doubt that Oberon's main interests are music and antique-collecting. His major collection is displayed in a private museum, though this is not as impressive as other rooms in the Palace, little effort being made to keep to any scale, and it is fairly obvious that the decoration was never completed. The showcases, of various sizes, contain a particularly complete selection of Bristol and Bohemian glass of nineteenth-century manufacture and a few fine Venetian pieces only very rarely found in this small size.

The treasures that lie, with quiet ostentation, around the Palace and the excellent craftsmanship of individual items arouse the admiration of all adult collectors, while children are fascinated by the books and characters that Sir Neville Wilkinson created for his own and their enjoyment. The very great importance of the Palace as a conception completely in tune with the literary and decorative movements of the period is almost invariably ignored, and it is often promoted as a cabinet of *objets d'art* and almost unmatchable craftsmanship. I would suggest that its importance, as an embodiment of the supernatural inspiration that was a phenomenon of the time, is far greater than this, and it seems tragic that this miniature exercise in the decorative arts could not have returned to Ireland or at least stayed in Britain when it was sold at Christie's in 1978. It is to be displayed far from the Irish mists that inspired its designer, in the brash atmosphere of 'Legoland', where, though it will no doubt be carefully preserved, it can never be fitted into the development of native arts or craftsmanship.

Titania's Palace is completely in the tradition of the art cabinets and is the forerunner of a number of adult-inspired constructions that attracted the attention of enthusiasts in the early twentieth century. A more sophisticated approach is also occasionally mirrored in children's houses, and in Diana Holman Hunt's reminiscences of life with her grandmother, wife of the famous painter, she tells of a tall, narrow house, made by her uncle, that stood in a corner. The ground floor was richly furnished with silver, a black velvet carpet and white lace curtains. Ordinary toy pieces assorted strangely with such elegance, and when she was given some conker chairs, she responded by throwing them on the fire, though she found postage-stamps perfectly acceptable as pictures. Her dolls were also deemed suitable: 'They uttered all

Above left: The simply made houses of working-class children rarely survive, making this small brick-painted model particularly interesting. The metal labels are of the type that could be punched out on railway stations. They read 'Babba's Villa' and 'From Uncle Willie Xmas 1904'. The house is front-opening and the interior is very crudely made. Height $23\frac{1}{2}$ inches.
Above right: The simplicity of this terrace house is reminiscent of the thousands of small houses built in towns all over Britain around 1900. It is typical of houses given to very ordinary children.

the time, and I moved them about. When I was falling asleep, they began to do things alone of their own accord; they behaved unsuitably, shouting and hitting each other and jumping out of the windows.'

Poorer children were encouraged, as in the mid-nineteenth century, to make their own toys, and craft and so called hand-work were often linked with dolls' houses. The encouragement of learning through play was promoted by some of the more progressive elementary schools after 1910, and doll's house furniture was included in the items made in craft periods. Girls were now included in such practical work and taught how to construct forms correctly. It was no longer surprising to see girls with saws and other carpentry tools – a trend that was obviously accelerated by the Great War when so many fathers were away from home. One girl, writing in 1916 of a handwork class she had attended, commented that among the projects was dolls' furniture for a friend. At home she was much more ambitious: 'I have made a basement for a doll gentleman's house, for the servants to live in; I papered it and made it look neat and tidy.'

R. and M. Polkinghorne of Streatham County School commented in a guide they produced for teachers that, through children's efforts to make toys, they became steadily more accurate and observant. Interestingly, one of the main aims of the classes they organized was to help children to use their leisure, a concept that we consider completely modern and which might have been considered somewhat out of place during the war years. The children began by making folded-paper toys, such as a wardrobe and a settee, with the paper chalked to represent wood or with a piece of silver paper glued to the back of a sideboard for a mirror. Some of the designs suggested for infants were extremely complex and involved accurate measuring, indicating either very different standards of achievement to the present or that the teacher gave a great deal of help. Once they were proficient with a saw, a whole range of furnishings was made, such as deckchairs and cradles. Some of the designs were highly pretentious and reminiscent of the drawings of the Arts and Craft movement, as they included copies of fourteenth-century designs made of cardboard or cigar-boxes. A fourteenth-century bed could be covered with coloured paper to give a good medieval effect, and the matchstick firedogs seem equally insubstantial. Fretsaws were among the most popular tools, and as blades sold from $1\frac{1}{2}$d to 3d a dozen, they were within the reach of the poorest people. Many patterns were available for adults who did not wish to create their own, and it is now often difficult to be sure whether particular sets that are found quite frequently were in fact home-made from patterns or produced commercially.

Craftsman-made toys were also becoming something of a cult before the war, encouraged by the Arts and Crafts associations. One particularly skilled maker was George Shergold, a Wiltshire shepherd, whose doll's house pieces included bureaux, gate-legged tables, sideboards and correctly made chests of drawers. He was encouraged in his work by frequent visits from the ladies of the Wiltshire Arts and Crafts Association who motored out to deliver seasoned wood and collect the finished toys.

Interest in novelty houses and furniture was also increasing in the years between 1900 and 1914. Perhaps children were growing a little tired of the substantial but commonplace models they had been offered for so long, and the manufacturers seem to have been eager to satisfy their demands. The Patent Office records show a very large selection of new designs registered before the war, though it seems doubtful if many were sold in really commercial quantity. There was particular interest in the use of card and paper, while folding houses inspired several designers. Manufacturers were becoming aware of the vast number of working-class children who had

The simplicity of both construction and furnishing reflects the taste of the 1920s. This model
was designed and furnished by a brother and sister and is known as the Russel house.

owned few toys in the past but who were now in better circumstances, and for
their small homes folding houses were an obvious solution. Several designers
utilized the box in which the model was contained as the base with the lid
forming a roof or a wall. Curtains, rugs and pictures were printed. In 1911 E.
Wintle registered a patent where a series of boxes and lids formed the rooms,
with separate pieces for the walls and chimneys. 'The whole or part of the
sides of the boxes are formed with hinged flaps to give access to the rooms
which are formed by division walls.' All the sections were fixed together by a
type of press-fastener.

In the following year L. G. Slocum designed a doll's flat, formed of a series of
suitably ornamented boards to represent the outside and inside of the rooms
and hinged at the vertical edges, 'Certain of the boards may have parts
adapted to form ceilings, either hinged to their top edges or adapted to be
unrolled from one of the edge boards.' The drawing showed a model with a

printed brick finish and attractive arched tops to each section. The methods for connecting the sections of folding houses were constantly being revised, as metal clips were soon lost and paper tabs soon broke away. F. Callcott suggested that items of furniture such as fireplaces should be used to lock together adjacent rooms, though even he was forced in some instances to resort to a metal shank.

In 1915 F. J. Sedgewick designed a more substantial folding model where the upper parts of the walls were hinged to lower fixed walls at different heights, so that the hinged portions, when folded, lie flat on each other. Parts of the walls are also independently hinged and open outwards to allow access to the interior. 'A floor, resting on ledges on the walls may also be provided.' He suggested that the house should be built up on a tray-type base that could be arranged in the form of a garden. In 1913 Currie Toys marketed a collapsible house that was claimed to be a scale model, made to the design of a well-known architect. The *Toy and Fancy Goods Trader* explained that the house could be supplied already made up but was of more interest to children if they were allowed to build it for themselves. Each section was provided with full directions and when completed formed a typical suburban villa. 'The building-materials are grooved lengths of wood with other lengths as uprights fitting into them with tongues. Pieces of uralite, cardboard, glass, wood or any other suitable material are slipped into the framework.' No nails or glue were needed, and it could be easily taken apart. Other models in the range included an Old English half-timbered house and a cottage.

The very complex folding house in my own collection was designed and built by J. C. Russley of Hull, who applied for a provisional patent in November 1921. The prototype is made with particular skill, and the attention to small detail is astonishing. When first seeing the house, there is no evidence to suggest that it is a collapsible structure, as it is a typical late-Victorian-style artisan's house with a large bay window and a neat porch. The roof tiles are made of leathercloth, as it has to fold back in several sections, but the walls are solidly made with grooved bricks painted cream at the front and with painted red bricks at the sides and back. The most attractive feature of the model is the front door and porch, perfectly made and supplied with brass furniture, which remains in position when the front of the house is opened. On lifting the roof, the details of the patent are found written in pencil, and there is also a list of detailed instructions for setting up the model:

Caution: When folding up this house, care should be taken
(1) To see that the small brass catch connecting the two parts of the curved portion of the staircase balustrade is released.
(2) That the flat straight part of the balustrade attached to the bedroom wall is lifted on the partition wall into a level position clear of the stairs. This will prevent damage to the balustrade and allow partition wall to fall flat to the bedroom floor.

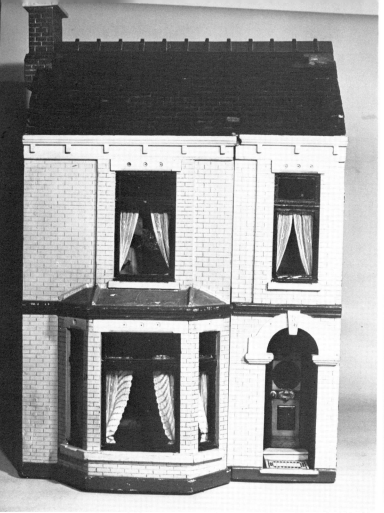
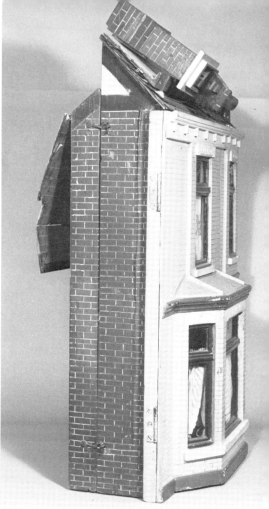

The folding house constructed by J. C.
Russley of Hull in 1921. *Opposite, far left:*
the façade. *Left and right:* Two views of the
complex folding process. *Opposite below:* A
stage in the folding showing how the
interior walls swing forward. *Below:* The
living-room contains fashionable Art Deco
furniture and a Japanese corner cabinet.
The curved staircase rises from the corner
of the room.

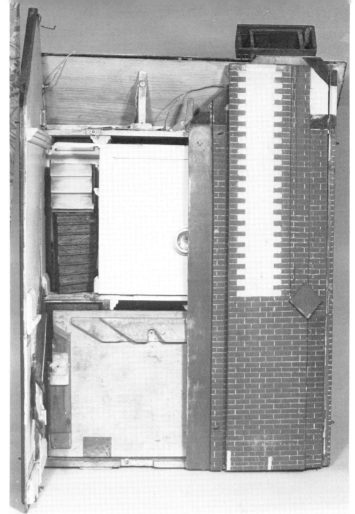

(3) See that the wooden button on the edge of the upper ceiling is clear of the latter when opening out house as it will prevent the ceiling parts coming together properly.

So concerned was this maker with packing the house into as small a space as possible that even the pots on the chimneys are hinged to be folded away.

The model contains one room up and one down, with a landing. The front door opens into the living-room, and the stairs also lead into this area. All the skirtings and cornices are correctly made, and there is a neat cupboard under the stairs. Particular skill was needed to design the curved staircase and balustrade, which collapse into a straight section, to lift to the upper landing. In order to fold away, the moulding of the upstairs door hinges from the wall, and the side walls, with the fireplaces, hinge forward. Amid all this activity the electric wiring remains in position, each fireplace having its own separately controlled switch. A note on the roof states that the house was restored in 1939, and the wallpapers would seem to be of that date as well as the upholstery-fabric carpets. It is difficult to imagine a house of such detail being made on a commercial scale, but certainly the principle could have been applied to a printed paper on wood structure to good effect.

Toy-making as a respectable craft was appealing to a far greater number of people in the twentieth century, as the progressive approach, begun in Germany before 1910, gained ground. British manufacturers were made shamefully aware of the shortcomings of the native industry during the war, when German imports ceased and the public saw, for the first time, only British-made toys in the shops. In 1916 an exhibition at the Whitechapel Gallery was arranged in order to survey the progress of toy manufacture during the war, though in the event it was mainly the artistic, especially made items that were displayed, as many British firms were reluctant to invest a great deal of money in special machinery, in case, at the end of the war, the Germans should unload huge surplus stocks. A few factories were set up in an attempt to copy German products, but the organizers were dismayed to discover that their workmen seemed to have little artistic flair and that much of the furniture produced was of poor quality. At the Whitechapel Exhibition, the work of the Noble brothers was shown, which included a windmill, 'The House that Jack Built' and a village school in retrospective style, with the teacher wearing nineteenth-century costume and a dunce with his cap. The *Toy Trader* reporter commented that, 'Perhaps the deepest pitfall some of the modern toy-makers have fallen into is to make their toys consciously picturesque or quaint by simulating a look of age. A doll's house, let us say, appears to have a leaky thatched roof, the walls are painted with cracks and broken plaster. This is quite beside the mark. In the ages of greatest art, when work was at its freshest, the notion of the picturesque was quite absent.' This writer would have disapproved of the work of Hugh Gee, who worked in the

A room assembled by Queen Mary that contains a splendid variety of ivory and bone furniture of German and Indian origin. Height $12\frac{1}{4}$ inches.

1920s from a Kensington studio and showed his models at various art exhibitions. One of his proudest achievements was 'The Sleeping Beauty's Castle' with a banqueting hall, throne room and chapel. There were a large number of rooms that were all lit by electricity, and there was a realistic garden. At the foot of the castle was a cave in which lived what was described in 1921 as 'a real dragon'.

The presence of such models in adult art exhibitions as well as dolls and miniature furniture encouraged intelligent interest in constructions of a similar kind. The furnishing of a cabinet-type model was again to the fore as a vehicle for the display of the best contemporary craftsmanship. Titania's Palace was the forerunner, but much more publicized was the model made for the woman who was christened Victoria Mary Augusta Louisa Olga Pauline Claudine Agnes. From birth, she, like so many other European princesses, was marked down as a pawn in the royal marriage game. Brought up and educated largely in Britain but with fine connections, this Princess was ideally suited for the throne, as she looked and behaved like an ideal British consort. When her fiancé, the heir to the throne, died, her affection, with expediency, was channelled towards the new heir, the Duke of York. She was greatly admired when she succeeded as George V's queen, as the new reign was regarded as a welcome change from the funereal excesses of Victoria and the worldly extravagance of Edward. The monarchy was treated much more favourably by the Press, and all Queen Mary's actions were reported with adulation. The sumptuous gift of a doll's house that would contain some of the

357

finest contemporary British craftsmanship was a tangible expression of this widespread affection.

The Queen's liking of miniature items was well known, and many of the fine pieces in the Bethnal Green Museum's collection were gifts from her own acquisitions; she also rescued many good pieces that related to the royal nursery, which can now be seen at the Museum of the City of London. Because of this great personal interest in toys and miniatures, it seems a pity that the Queen did not participate more completely in the arrangement of the model herself. A more personal involvement might have avoided the clinical perfection that is not apparent in the houses and model rooms she furnished. Despite the lack of atmosphere in the house, we cannot but delight in the fact that such a gift was considered appropriate. Today, if a similar scheme were to be envisaged, the legions of the Left would rise and point to needless expense and unnecessary work, and the mere suggestion would be concealed in embarrassment for fear of Press and Union censure and ridicule. The conception of the royal doll's house therefore stands as a lingering vestige of earlier centuries, when gifts were carried to the great, and has appeal simply because its spirit is so out of touch with the twentieth century.

The importance of the model as a chronicle of contemporary Court life cannot be over-emphasized, as it is the only cabinet that is catalogued with complete accuracy, from such items as a Fabergé mouse, presented by the Grand Duchess Xenia of Russia, to a box of Rowntrees' chocolates. Each manufacturer or individual donor was meticulously recorded, as was each object's position in the apartment, so that any loss or change would be obvious. The Queen's personal encouragement of British industry – in particular, silk, lace and china – was promoted, as virtually all the items came from native workshops, while the paintings and sheet music were the work of eminent British artists. In the years after the war, the nation was struggling to regain its commercial position, and this encouragement of manufacturing industry was completely in accord with the general atmosphere. It is as an exhibition in miniature of contemporary endeavour and life that this model is so illuminating: we find the style of fishing-rod a gentleman would have used, the design of a cocktail-shaker and the construction of a jewel-safe made by Chubb. All these items are of the quality used by the wealthier members of society and soon discarded when fashions changed, so that the model is the most perfect existing record of life in a rich household in the early 1920s. Though the fine eighteenth-century cabinets portray life with vigour, none encapsulates such a short period as this, and though collectors might carp at the lifelessness of the house in relation to toys of the type, its superiority as a factual record is unassailable.

Immured in its dimly lit chamber at Windsor Castle and gazed at through a plate-glass window, the model seems even more remote than the fine Dutch cabinets, as here we see a house that has never been added to, never depleted, never played with and not even re-arranged by a loving owner. The whole concept, with its exhibition of scientific skills and advances, is too perfect. We are not even given the relief of hinged fronts, as even the outer walls behave by divine command and waft upwards, to stand above the revealed interior. The contents of the house are now softened in appearance, and in some rooms the colour tone is very low and quite unlike the colour photographs with which collectors are familiar. Blues have faded to rich greys and yellows to cream, a reminder of the finer dyes used in the eighteenth century, as many of the Baby House textiles have retained their original effect.

The public showed immediate interest when the model was displayed at the British Empire Exhibition at Wembley. Perhaps they enjoyed a brief escape from the reality of life and the memories of brothers and sons who had died haplessly in the war. Despite the everyday problems of the working classes during this depressed period, the general attitude towards the house seems to have been one of mild amusement mixed with admiration for a well-executed project rather than the bitterness and envy that would be engendered today. The general popularity of the house is revealed by the large number of guides and postcards, and by the books that were sold, such as *Everybody's Book of the Queen's Doll's House*, which was purchased by many families including the unemployed. This somewhat fey account was an abridgement of a larger volume written by A. C. Benson and Sir Lawrence Weaver, who both seemed to consider that, when writing about a doll's house, it was necessary to imagine fairies and make-believe families, so that we are forcibly reminded of Titania's Palace, not by the doll's house itself but by the style of contemporary descriptions.

The first suggestion for the project was discussed in 1920 and was based, according to Benson, on 'a very natural human desire to sum up and express in an appropriate form, a deep and widespread emotion which has as much to do with affection as with respect and loyalty'. He went on to explain that the first thought in the minds of those who planned and made the house

was to express and symbolize in a gift which should represent in the highest degree the sense of personal regard and individual loyalty, not the mere outpouring of expensive trifles, but something which should evoke care and trouble, and labour which becomes pleasurable when it has in view the aim of giving pleasure! The house was therefore seen as a memorial to the art and craft, the design and manufacture of a short period in time that would otherwise be lost. It is dignified without being ostentatious; it is not a house to entertain many guests, nor is it adapted for profuse or sumptuous entertainments; it would give a reasonable degree of comfort and privacy. The approaching dinner hour would not be announced by an insistent smell of cookery, nor would the incense of the smoking-room be wafted into the children's schoolroom. The comfort of the domestics and the labour-saving apparatus are carefully provided for, the ventilation, lighting and warming are kept sensibly in mind, the sanitation is perfect; motor-cars for

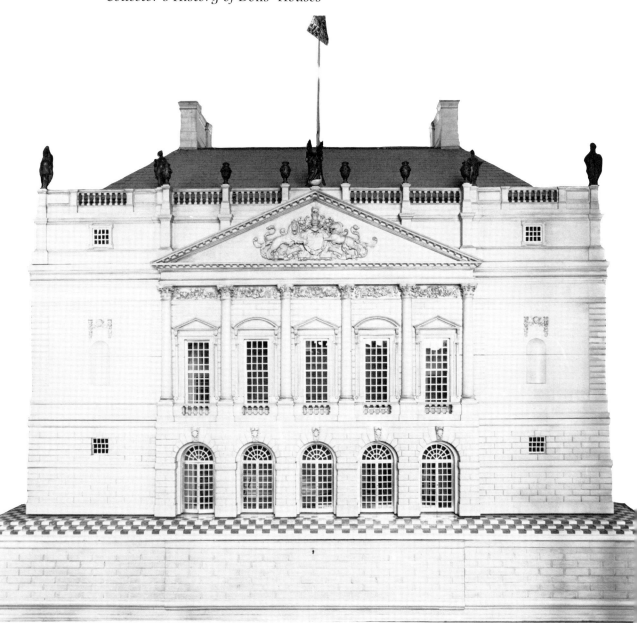

Sir Edwin Lutyens, who specialized in country house architecture, designed Queen Mary's Doll's House. The exterior was painted to resemble Portland stone.

daily use are not neglected, and the little garden is designed for recreation and contemplation.

What was envisaged was a complete model house rather than a 'doll's house', and it is this basic premise that is often misunderstood by its critics.

Despite the fact that the model was not peopled, except for the sentries and guardsmen made by Mr and Mrs Kennedy North, provision was originally made for the storage of dolls in the lower section of the base, which contains 208 interchangeable drawers, $11\frac{1}{2}$ inches long and $3\frac{1}{2}$ inches wide, in which they were to be kept. In the upper section of the base was all the mechanical equipment, including water-tanks and transformers. Presumably it was deemed to be impossible to make the dolls with realism comparable with that of the furniture, especially as the costume of the period was not flattering to dolls' legs.

The house was designed by Sir Edwin Lutyens, who specialized in country-house architecture and who in this case worked to a British impression of an Italian Renaissance design. The result was very much in the English eighteenth-century manner, with a *piano nobile*, pediment and massive royal coat-of-arms. The exterior is very perfectly constructed and is superior in basic workmanship to any other doll's house, as the detail is so perfectly proportioned. The complete structure was built by J. Parnell & Son of Oliver Street, Rugby. The painting, to represent Portland stone, was the work of Muntzer & Son, who also painted the interior. On the four corners of the parapet are found lead statues representing the saints of England, Scotland, Wales and Ireland, designed by Sir George Frampton RA. On the North Front stands an angel bearing the Queen's crown, made by Mallett & Son, and the four remaining figures are emblems of some of the Queen's names.

The visitor of today approaches the doll's house from the West Front, an approach that invariably disappoints as, to gain the impression of entering any model home, it is necessary to pass, as in real life, through the main hall. In this case the basic problem of moving a large number of people around the structure necessitates such an arrangement, but it seems a pity that the visitor is given such a delivery boy's view. The Queen's Dolls House, even from the West Side, is impressive, though it is to the arresting group of cars in the garage that the eye is drawn, as they epitomize the passing of time to a much greater extent than the conservative furnishings. The Rolls Royce, a correctly made model, supplied by the firm, stands imposingly in the foreground. There is a Daimler station bus, a Lanchester, Vauxhall, Sunbeam and motorcycle and sidecar by Rudge-Whitworth Ltd. All the petrol and grease-cans were supplied by Shell Mex, and the other pieces stored in the area, such as a baby-carriage, were made as special projects by firms who usually worked in full size.

The library, on the first floor, though less eye-catching to the toy-collector,

361

The library of Queen Mary's Doll's House – panelled in walnut by Parnell & Son. There are some seven hundred prints, drawings and watercolours contained in the cabinets.

is one of the most meticulously detailed apartments. This room was panelled in walnut by Parnell & Son, and the ceiling, with its fluted coving, was painted by William Walcot. The finished impression of the library is one of almost bare neatness, and it is hard to imagine that some seven hundred prints, drawings and watercolours are stored in the cabinets. They include the work of such eminent artists as John Nash, Russell Flint and Adrian Stokes, while the books contain verses and prose by Walter de la Mare, Rudyard Kipling, Hugh Walpole and Hilaire Belloc, all persuaded to contribute by Princess Marie Louise. Among the framed pictures is one of Queen Elizabeth I by William Nicholson. The rugs were made by the Gainsboro' Silk Weaving Company. An example of attention to small detail is an insurance policy of the Aviation and General Insurance Company that is kept in the safe. A Lloyds Bank cheque-book and cigars and matches made by Dunhill and Bryant & May also contribute to the atmosphere of a masculine room. For advice on journeys there is the inevitable Edwardian gentleman's friend, *Bradshaw's Guide*, augmented by an *ABC* Railway guide and a copy of *Whitaker's Almanack*. The concentrated desk-work, the inevitable lot of any twentieth-century monarch, is revealed by the presence of fourteen very realistic Dispatch Boxes. The King kept his guns, made by Nobels Explosive Company, in the library, as well as fishing-rods, fencing-foils, playing-cards and chess-sets. Not all the books are contemporary: there are several mid-nineteenth-century almanacs, old Bibles and a copy of Shakespeare's complete works. Photographic miniaturization processes made possible minute copies of the *Saturday Review*, *Punch*, *Country Life* and *Tit Bits*. Important royal dates could be checked on the Raphael Tuck calendar.

Immediately above the library is the austere King's bedroom, with red and gold silk damask hangings on the dominating antique-style bed made by the Royal School of Needlework. The burr walnut chests, armchairs and table are all in eighteenth-century style and were made by such firms as T. Collins, Langhorn & Field and Turner, Lord & Co. The masculinity of the room is somewhat softened by the wall-hangings of stylized birds in trees by George Plank, who was also responsible for the painted ceiling. The fine silver chandelier is a copy of one at Knole. Despite the apparent simplicity, there are many fine items, such as a Fabergé flowerpot, silver dishes and an effective practical reading-lamp made by Faraday & Son. Even the maker of a single candle is recorded and is a name still well-known today, Price's Patent Candle Company. The adjoining bathroom is sumptuous in a more Edwardian than 1920s manner, with wall panels of green African verdite marble and silver taps to the sarcophagus-like verdite bath, made by H. J. Jenkins & Son. Once again, the restrained general effect conceals a host of small details such as ivory collar-studs, nail- and toothbrushes and a fine selection of soaps, toothpaste and hair-wash. In case the King should feel the cold, there is a hot-water bottle. The bathroom is decorated with a group of *Punch* drawings and by the salutary *Expulsion from Paradise*, painted on the ceiling by Laurence Irving. Did the artist choose such a subject in order to create a sense of unease in the mind of the King as he soaked luxuriously in the comforting warm suds? His clothes are stored in another room on the opposite side of the bedchamber and are accompanied by a Field Marshal's sword, made by the Wilkinson Sword Company, and a fine variety of shooting- and walking-sticks. The mother-of-pearl light-fittings in both the King's Wardrobe and the bathroom were made by Noble & Co and contribute effectively to the period atmosphere.

The upper section of the West Front contains the more functional apartments, such as the night nursery, the maids' rooms, the Princess Royal's bedroom and the nursery bathroom, and it is in these more prosaic rooms that one finds the unmistakable atmosphere of the 1920s rather than in the formal State Rooms. The Princess Royal's bedroom might have been used by any daughter of well-to-do parents, as it is equipped quite simply with a chest of drawers, a wash-stand and a bed described as 'St Ursula style'. Prints and etchings were highly popular, as is shown by the presence of a set of *London Cries* that hang over the ivory looking-glass, which is accompanied by a pair of matching tall ivory candlesticks. A china toilet-set, complete with slop-pail, soap-dishes and beaker, was made at the Cauldon Potteries, and the brushes, as in the King's room, are mainly the work of Allen & Hanburys and Boot's, the Chemist's. A single fairytale touch was an especially grown miniature pea that Sir Edwin Lutyens arranged to be placed under the Princess Royal's mattress.

Between the room of the Princess Royal and the nursery apartments is the fanciful Queen's sitting-room, decorated in chinoiserie but with clouds, very much in the 1920s idiom, billowing across the painted walls. The furniture was made by Waring & Gillow and includes a delightful Coromandel screen, two vitrines on stands and a fine mirror in a lacquer frame. There is a strangely chosen eighteenth-century-style hob grate set into the corner chimneypiece, which contributes to the curious mixture of reproduction and modern. The Queen was presented with a large number of everyday modern items, such as a Kodak camera and a box of cigarettes, but the lavish effect of the apartment relies mainly on such treasures as carved amber ornaments, jade flowerpots and Egyptian amulets and scarabs, the majority of which were gifts from the Grand Duchess Xenia of Russia. Queen Mary was particularly fond of chinoiserie and surely delighted in this model with its cream and gold lacquer and the hand-woven Chien-Lung-style rug with 324 knots to the square inch. In order that the Queen should not be disturbed during the day, the night nursery is positioned alongside, with its imposing cradle made of applewood and inlaid and bound with silver. This piece was made by Amédée Joubert & Son and was highly praised, as the design was completely original. It now appears reminiscent of many Victorian designers such as William Burges but created a highly favourable impression when first exhibited. It is certainly an imposing item, with the hood surmounted by an ivory Prince of Wales coronet and feathers, and the interior also lined with ivory. In all other respects the night nursery is completely functional: there is a yew wheel-back high chair and an interesting selection of soaps, sponges and baby-food made by Allen & Hanbury. All the baby-clothes were supplied in detail and provided an accurate picture of the equipment needed by a wealthy child of the period. Even in his most tender years the child was to be made aware of his great heritage, for watching over the infants is a large portrait of their grandmother, Victoria.

Another room much to the taste of toy-collectors is the day nursery, a light, airy apartment, the walls decorated by Edmund Dulac with scenes from fairy stories. In the past the nurseries of even the wealthiest were often decorated with old furniture and drab hangings no longer needed in other rooms, but

AY NURSERY

The day nursery from Queen Mary's Doll's House with walls decorated by Edward Dulac. It provides a complete picture of the surroundings of well-to-do children in the early twentieth century.

here we see the completely modern approach of a designer who deliberately sets out to create a pleasant environment. The fairytale life of the children of kings and the prosaic needs of childhood are perfectly combined, where tins of Nestlé's Milk and Allenbury's rusks are seen in close proximity to a group of Chelsea porcelain figures. Some old nursery favourites still secure a place, such as the large rocking-horse which is a copy of the Duke of Clarence's horse at the London Museum, a Noah's Ark and a *Father Tuck's Annual*. Windsor & Newton created a miniature paintbox and Bassett Lowke a train and station that was described in one of the guide-books as 'a noble toy. Tickets please for India and the stars. Change at the Zoo and back to Nannie in five minutes.' A toy gramophone plays a tinny 'God Save the King' to end a performance of

Peter Pan in the electrically lit model theatre. The toy soldiers were made by William Britain's, and pieces such as a sedan chair, skipping-rope and roundabout were supplied by Pomona Toys. The miniature box of soldiers is a piece greatly coveted by all collectors of Britain's and is now on view in a display-area near the house so that visitors can examine in more detail the characteristic red box that spelled delight to so many generations. While the boys played with soldiers and a horse and shay, the girls could amuse themselves with the doll's room, a doll or a Swiss chalet. Their meals were taken at a walnut gate-legged table and eaten from Wedgwood breakfast- or Doulton dinnerware. Curiously, one the leading toy-firm, G. & J. Lines, supplied none of the nursery items, though Walter Lines presented several pieces of furniture for the maids' rooms, numbers two and three on the upper mezzanine floor. The furniture, made by Lines Brothers Ltd (Triang) consisted of a table, dressing-table, looking-glass, chest of drawers, washstand, towel-horse and two chairs. For maid's room number three, a bed and hanging cupboard were presented.

As in the eighteenth-century houses, the supply of household linen was stored near the nursery, and this room was arranged by Viscountess Cowdray, with an assortment of pieces from the Old Bleach Linen Company, a Singer sewing-machine and Coats threads. There are also a few retrospective touches, reminding us that this is a king's home, such as a lace-pillow and lengths of Limerick lace ready for use.

The Queen's bedroom, with its grey-blue silk-hung walls, is the most imposing apartment on this side of the house. The chimneypiece is in eighteenth-century style, and there is a painting of the Queen's mother, the Duchess of Teck, in the continued section. No expense was spared in the construction and furnishing of this room, which is given a somewhat turbulent atmosphere by the activity in the ceiling painting, the work of Glyn Philpot, RA. The bed is much more gracious in style than its flamboyant partner in the King's bedroom, though it retains the traditionally shaped brocade-covered top. The lavishness of this room is illustrated by the amboyna-veneered wardrobe with a green wood inlay, a dressing-table, *chaise-longue* and amboyna table, made by W. Turner Lord & Co, whose craftsmanship is so fine as to be silencing. The minutiae of the apartment are also impressive, and there are silver candle-sconces, a small silver chest of drawers, a porcelain tea-set, silver candlesticks, jewel-boxes, an ink-stand and several pieces of enamelled dressing-table equipment. The diamond-framed mirror on the dressing-table is a suitable accessory for a queen's toilet and was presented by Lady Sackville. The clocks and a barometer were made by Cartier, and basic items such as make-up were provided by Atkinson's, who also made the cold creams, bathsalts and eau de Cologne for the Queen's bathroom with its softly attractive mother-of-pearl floor and shagreen and ivory walls. The bathroom is much more contemporary in style than the

Part of a dinner service especially made for Queen Mary's Doll's House by Minton.

King's, and the ceiling much less oppressive, as it is decorated with a painting of mermaids in a pool by M. Greiffenhagen, ARA. The alabaster bath has silver taps and the chest of drawers a rich rhodonite top. Other luxurious touches include a Fabergé Japanese tree and a superb gilt clock. The work of contemporary glassmakers is represented by bottles, a water-jug and a basin made by James Powell & Sons.

The kitchen, beneath the Queen's bedroom, is disappointingly austere but completely in accord with contemporary insistence on hygiene. All is in absolute order, though the minute, and very perfect detail is often overlooked because of the lack of lively visual appeal. We hardly appreciate the 2,500 wood blocks on the floor or the strips of slate around the working-areas, while the minute brass locks on doors, each provided with a key, are so small as to be invisible. One longs for the colour and clutter of a room such as the kitchen of the Brighton Pavilion but cannot fail to note such details as the gold omelette dish, pattypans and jelly-mould made by Guy's Hospital Mechanics. The kitchen range made by Crittall's and a splendid set of scales and the jugs and storage-jars made by Doulton also impress with their realism. In true doll's house tradition there is a kitchen cat and a mousetrap. In the scullery are

Part of a dinner service made by Royal Doulton for Queen Mary's Doll's House.

deep, lead-lined sinks with hot and cold water, and in the butler's pantry glass-fronted cupboards, well stocked with china and containing several good cut-glass decanters. Some of this china is already in use in the dining-room, approached from both the butler's pantry and the kitchen by a service area.

In the dining-room the skill of contemporary British craftsmen, particularly in the fields of ceramics, linen, and silver, is seen to advantage. In pride of place over the fireplace hangs a portrait of Edward, Prince of Wales, by A. J. Munnings. A contemporary wrote that, 'It was easy to think, how, over the wine or the walnuts, or whatever may take their place in future years at the Royal table, there would be much discussion as to the accuracy of this portrait of this sporting young Prince Charming,' a prince whose character was later to bring much distress to the Queen herself. Carefully arranged on the other walls are paintings of the coronation of George V and Queen Mary, some interiors of Windsor Castle and an inevitable portrait of Victoria, in this case accompanied by Albert. On a large console table with a marble top lies a ravishing assortment of silver, including a candelabra and a soup tureen made by Garrard, who also made the cutlery, salts, pepper-boxes, mustard-pots and rose-bowls that are displayed on the long walnut table. The table, which extends from $5\frac{1}{4}$ inches to 20 inches, eighteen leather-upholstered matching chairs and a sideboard, were made by Turner, Lord & Co, who also made the exquisite console tables. The dining-table is set with silver and glass for a banquet that never took place.

This atmosphere of a lost event pervades, though to a lesser extent, the Throne Room or Saloon on the first floor. This impressive room, the largest in the house, has a painted ceiling with a somewhat out-of-character frieze of nude women in 1920s style, sporting above the picture-rail from a trellis-like background. The remaining decoration is completely in eighteenth-century tradition and reveals little of contemporary life. The walls are hung with rose-coloured silk, woven, like most of the other prestige silk in the house, by the Gainsboro' Silk Weaving Company. The patterns of foliage and flowers in gold provide a fine background for the perfectly made furniture, such as a black and gold lacquer cabinet with a red and gold interior, copied from a full-sized piece at Londonderry House and the Renaissance-style grand piano made by Broadwood, complete with sheet music from Novello & Co. The Empire-style chairs are finely embroidered in imitation of Aubusson tapestry, and there is a beautiful miniature clock with its own barometer, made by Cartier. The footstools, vitrines and Bergère chairs contribute to the formal atmosphere of this important room. The two thrones were designed by Sir Edwin Lutyens himself. The tonal effect of the room is now rather low, though impressive, and there seems little joy in the setting. We are aware of the Crown Jewels locked away in the strong room, just below the Saloon, comprising Queen Mary's Crown and the Imperial State Crown and regalia. A good silver-gilt dinner-service is also stored there for complete safety.

The entrance front of the house on the east side is strangely at variance with the State Rooms, as the painting of Adam and Eve, driven from the Garden of Eden, painted by William Nicholson, is so Rackham-like in effect that the viewer is immediately transported in atmosphere to the world of Titania's Palace and its legions of fairy presences. This painting, though exciting in its own right, is strangely out of character with the remainder of the house, which is so highly conservative. Despite this discordant note, the general atmosphere of the hall is cool and perfectly balances its abundance of marble with such necessary equipment as a hall porter's chair, two suits of armour, a few statues and a visitors' book.

The shining examples of Titania's Palace and Queen Mary's Doll's House encouraged a sudden spate of miniature house building among British adults who were in fact working almost in the eighteenth-century tradition. These structures were only very occasionally made to a high cabinet-maker's standard and were more usually put together for effect. Some very large adult-intentioned houses of the 1920s and 1930s were made mainly of plywood with only very slender strengthening supports, so that when they are moved or the doors opened they present a very unsubstantial and unpleasant feeling. This poor quality of basic construction is often compensated by the effective interior decoration, usually the province of the women of the family, who

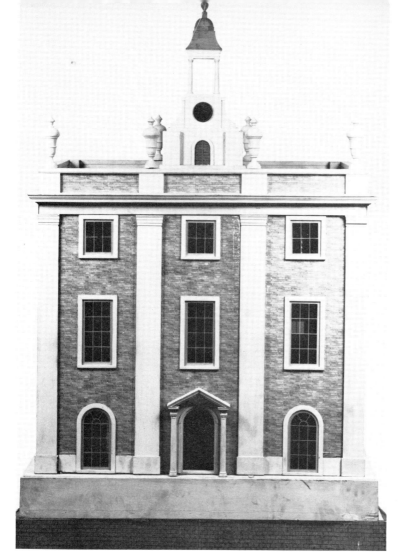

A painted wooden and printed paper-on-wood house designed by Sir Clough Williams Ellis. Opening at the back to reveal nine rooms, staircase and hall. The house was modelled on Orme Court, where Rupert Brooke was a frequent visitor. Height 40 inches.

Opposite: The suburban villa in stockbroker-Tudor style reflected the homes of many middle-class children in the 1930s, and a large number of dolls' houses in the style were made. This model, which is back-opening, has slates that are individually applied. Height 34 inches.

costumed the dolls, embroidered the cushions and sometimes sacrificed items of jewellery to provide wall plaques. Several firms were producing very acceptable furniture at this time, including Pit-a-Pat and Cartwright, though the pieces made by Elgin were among the best. Their nicely made wooden furniture is marked 'Elgin, Enfield' with the one large letter 'E' serving for the two words. The company was established in 1919 by Eric Elgin and his sisters and closed in 1926. The standard of their work was high for the period, which is probably why it went out of production within a fairly short time. Their better-quality antique-style pieces were intended as ornamental objects for arrangement in china-cabinets or bric-à-brac tables, and it is thought that the production was eventually sold to Lines. Furniture made by all these firms is sometimes found in the adult houses that were created probably at least partly as an escape from the bitterness of the war years, whose aftermath seems to have lasted emotionally far longer than that of the last war.

Children's play-houses in these between-the-wars years were disappoint-

ingly stereotyped, as the manufacturers seemed to think that every child's ideal home was in suburban Tudor style, and even the most expensive models were often just extensions of these small villa-like buildings. The British makers in these years were also supplying much more of the furniture themselves, and its construction, though very basic and often uninteresting, was usually strong and very durable, in complete accord with the British toy-makers' affection for 'strong toys'.

The Second World War resulted in a great shortage of all types of toys, and miniature dolls in particular completely disappeared from the market, though tenacious mothers often assembled small figures out of rag, bent wire and pipe-cleaners or, as a last resort, cardboard. A Liverpool woman recounted that, at Christmas 1941, with all the men in the family away in the services and only an elderly brother in the Home Guard at home, her daughter requested a doll's house for a present. Eventually an old birdcage was discovered which the Home Guard worked on between raids, making walls

Though the ground plan of this progressive house constructed in the late 1920s has complete realism, such functional designs rarely succeed as dolls' houses. The two views of this Southend-on-Sea-type house were given equal attention by the maker.

from pieces of cardboard and using an old office file for a roof. The floors were painted and a piece of hessian dyed red and fringed at the edges made a carpet. 'Never will I forget her face that dark Christmas morning as she saw those tables and chairs and the pictures made from cigarette-cards.'

From the standpoint of the historian, such models, despite their shortcomings, are of far greater interest than the dreary rows of suburban houses that had been offered to the children of the 1930s and which were again to re-appear in the 1950s. The fact that so few of the improvised war-time houses have survived is a great loss, as the privations suffered by people all over Europe in those hard years could hardly be more piercingly displayed than in the bleak interiors of models assembled from such unlikely materials.

For several years after the war ended there was little commercial production of houses, and the few that appeared on the market were so expensive that they were beyond the means of many people. My own house was made from sections of board that had been nailed over the windows of a local Home Guard hut and was constructed according to a set of instructions published in *Practical Handyman*. My father worked on the house late into the night for weeks before Christmas, finding it impossible to buy such necessary embellishments as slate and brick papers or miniature handles and window

frames, so that all the detail had to be improvised. The only available paint was an ugly brilliant red, left over from the repainting of the local buses, and this had to be used for both the roof and the walls. The house was concealed in the cellar of a neighbour's house while the furniture was constructed. Unfortunately something mysterious happened to the scale, and when the house was ready for arrangement on Christmas Eve, it was discovered that the country-style black-painted pieces were much too large for the rooms and had to be wrapped up and given to me as a gift for my dolls.

Few Christmas presents made as deep an impression as that home-made house. I was carried downstairs in a thick Welsh flannel shawl against the cold of the early morning, and there, in front of the big open fireplace with a chimney of more than adequate proportions for St Nicholas, stood the doll's house on two kitchen chairs. It was painted all over in a beautiful bright red shiny paint with startlingly white window frames and a fretwork front porch. Above the porch was a neat round window, resembling a porthole, which I found enchanting, as I had never before encountered a window of such a curious shape. Electric lights shone out from each room, and looking through the curtained windows, I was able to see all the opening doors and the neat strips of carpet. The furniture, whose scarcity had caused such heartache to

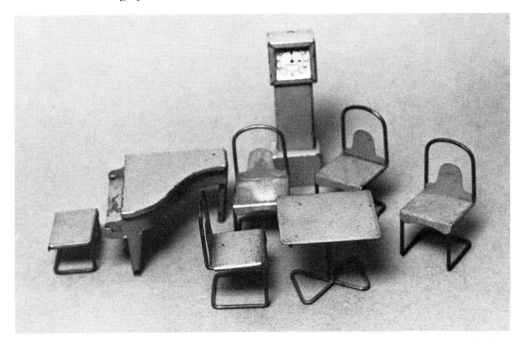

Red painted wire and metal furniture in progressive style by Holdfast. Only the clock is marked. 1930s.

my parents, I hardly remember, though there was a chintz-covered, padded three-piece suite made out of matchboxes by a neighbour. The shining red house looked so beautiful with its surface glinting in the firelight that I apparently stood quite speechless and seemed afraid even to open doors in case the vision should dissolve.

Such adulation is regrettably short-lived, and within a few months all my father's carefully decorated rooms had been repapered with sheets cut from a local ironmonger's old pattern-book. The doll's house soon ceased to be an object of touching delight to family and friends but became an excellent toy, strong enough to withstand extremely rough treatment. Each time my mother saw the heavy wallpaper pattern-book dragged out and was requested to provide yet another jar of flour-and-water paste, she groaned at her foolishness in ever allowing my father to build such an eyesore. With all the wiring, interconnecting doors and walls removed, I found the house gained another personality, and it became an ideal situation in which to sit and watch the world through my porthole. With the cat, a cushion and a tin of biscuits, nothing could compare with the secrecy of my snail-like hiding-place.

When I grew too large to inhabit the doll's house myself, my patient father re-instated the dividing walls, and until the age of eleven or twelve, on wet days I would again find sheets of wallpaper, figures cut from fashion magazines and strips of fabric and set about creating a perfectly decorated residence. The individual rooms were now furnished with sets of pink and green plastic furniture, the dining-room set in an almost Sheraton design and the bedrooms in a pink, mainly Edwardian idiom, all purchased on visits to Woolworth's in Swansea. One day, returning from school, I was informed casually that it had seemed better to give my house to some poor children, though in fact it is much more likely that the disreputable but still brightly shining house in fact met its end in a bonfire.

Fortunately for the collector, many children of earlier generations treated their toys with much more care, though my own early passion for decorating has never been dissipated, and a massive ruin or a disreputable doll's house immediately inspires a spate of papering and refurbishing, so that I find it very hard to understand why so many children of today find model houses uninteresting. Perhaps if they were much less perfect and the children were given sheets of paper, nails, paintbrushes and hammers instead of neat boxes of perfect plastic furniture, the doll's house could again exert its spell, not as a purely visual and imaginative object but as a practical, constructive plaything that encourages the child to express her own personality.

An effectively painted Bavarian doll's room possibly made as a souvenir-type item. An inscription reads 'Grüss Gott/Tritt ein/Bring Glück herein' ("Hello, step inside and bring luck with you").

376

SIX

German Houses and Rooms of the Nineteenth and Early Twentieth Centuries

The development of the European doll's house as related to Germany is concerned mainly with the good-quality miniatures that were produced in vast quantity and exported to all the European and American towns as well as to the colonial regions. In some cases, the small cradles, tea-sets and kitchen equipment were made on a traditional folk-type basis that changed little, even with the improved communications of the nineteenth century, so that individual families often made very similar items for several generations. These folk toys, of great interest to craft enthusiasts, are, in general, less liked by collectors than the more sophisticated, mass-produced items that originated mainly in the industrial towns and in whose designs contemporary fashion was more closely revealed.

In contrast to the number of surviving dolls' houses in Britain, there are comparatively few in Germany, so that we are presented with the paradox of a country that produced almost all the furniture, ceramics and metalware for other nations providing very few houses for its own children to enjoy. Instead, a number of model rooms were supplied that are often much more complex in structure than those sold in France and were ideal for the display of larger items of furniture. Wooden, tin and porcelain miniatures were assembled in the main towns by the great merchants, so much a feature of the early nineteenth-century German economy, and packaged in their own boxes, so that it is often possible to estimate only the date and the area of origin of individual pieces rather than the precise manufacturer. In certain areas, such as Bohemia, there were small factories dotted all over the countryside, often just a few hundred yards apart and employing only a handful of men. In this region, where glass-making was the main occupation, the humble factories appeared picturesque, but the faces of the workmen, as they filed past a journalist from *The House* in 1891, showed that the trade of the Bohemian glass-blower meant a weak chest and a reduced, if not ruined physique. The doll-industry workers at Waltershausen were damaged more by poverty and low wages than by difficult basic conditions, but the problems of all these workers serve to explain why German-made miniatures could be sold so cheaply.

The German economy at the end of the eighteenth century was the despair of 'rational' British visitors, who failed to understand the constant disagreements between neighbouring states and the lack of interest in a stable, central government that would encourage manufacturing industries. The character of the people was also a constant source of bewilderment, as the patriotic French and British travellers could not understand how loyalty could be accorded only to the state in which a person lived rather than to his country. In October 1795 the *Ladies' Magazine* commented:

> If only Germany could make itself one great people,- if it was united under one governor,- if the present interests of a single prince were not often in opposition to the good of the whole,- if all the members were so compacted into one body that the superfluous sap of the one could circulate and invigorate the rest,- what much greater steps towards civilization would the Empire then make! But then Germany would give laws to all Europe. How powerful, as things even now are, are the two Houses of Austria and Brandenburg, the greatness of whose strength consists in their German possessions, and who yet neither possess the half or even the best parts of the country. Conceive this country in such a situation that no burdensome excise should oppress the internal commerce of the different provinces,- no customs should prohibit the export of goods all over the world – in such a situation that the immense sums that it gives for outlandish commodities which itself can furnish should be spared – or that it could become a naval power . . . conceive this. What country in the world could then cope with Germany?

Although the problems facing a country of over a hundred dukedoms, Imperial Towns, principalities and independent monasteries that comprised the Holy Roman Empire of the German Nation were very apparent, unification was only gradually achieved, and until successive improvements eased their lot, the toymakers were forced to trade under extremely difficult conditions; it says much for the tenacity of the merchants that it was upon this unsatisfactory basis that world domination in this sphere ultimately depended. Duties levied by independent states were sometimes so crippling that the merchandise was viable only because of the pitifully low wages paid to the workers, especially those of Sonneberg and Waltershausen, where escapist drunkenness was a way of life among the men, who watched their small children being set to work in the factories and yet knew that they could not support their families themselves.

After the defeat of the Germans by Napoleon in 1806, the old principalities were regrouped and the power of the nobility was greatly diminished by reducing the number of smaller states by thirty-seven, which to some extent eased transport problems. This improvement was, however, fairly short-lived, though its long-term effect on the aspirations of the common people was considerable. After the Congress of Vienna in 1814–15 and the foundation of the German Confederation, individual nobles re-asserted their traditional customs and duties, and the management of the country again became very oppressive, despite the hopeful fact that a number of the smaller states were never resuscitated. The slight improvements in the area of commerce enjoyed under Napoleon's rule did serve to provide some impetus for re-organization, and in 1828 the South German Customs Union was formed, consisting of Bavaria, Württemberg and the Hohenzollern lands, as well as the Middle German Union of Trade that included the kingdom of Saxony, Nassau, the Saxon dukedoms, Hanover, Kurhessen and several other dependencies. In 1834 these two groups united, and in order to protect their interests, the German Customs Union, based on Prussia, was also founded, to provide its own free-trade area without burdensome tolls or a necessity for passports within the group. These changes resulted only gradually in an improvement in basic costs, and obviously any movement of goods across Prussian territory was still very expensive.

In addition to the heavy Customs duties, trade was also much hampered by the disgraceful state of the roads, as these were also the responsibility of individual states and dukedoms, though the Imperial Roads, under the care of the Emperor, were usually reasonably maintained. Much of the importance of Nuremberg as the toy-exporting centre of Germany depended on its position on the Imperial Road to Sonneberg and Gotha, and as it was itself a free Imperial Town, it retained many trading-privileges that encouraged its industries, among which one of the most respected was doll-making, recognized in the fifteenth century by the Nuremberg masters.

Having negotiated the difficult roads and paid all the state duties, the toy-merchants were still insecure, as their wagons were frequently attacked by highwaymen, who robbed the drivers of the money they had obtained at the various fairs. The *Kraxenträger*, the German pedlars who carried the wares from their own regions all over the country, were particularly vulnerable in this respect and, burdened with their heavy packs, known as *Krax*, must have been easy prey for such groups as the robber knights who hid away in the mountains around Sonneberg.

Though German wooden toys are purchased with affection by collectors of today all over the world, they were very lightly regarded in the mid-nineteenth century when William Hewitt, visiting the May Fair at Heidelberg, commented disdainfully on the quality of the goods offered to children: 'Every article was totally foreign and queer. There were trumpets and wooden horses and rattles and swords and such like, but they would have made the children of England stare at their oddity. The toys were very strange and very cheap

379

and of a primitive German air.' He attributed the poor quality of this merchandise to the bad state of the roads, which were often impassable by horse-drawn transport for long periods of the year. One of the first things a British visitor noted in the country at this time was the number of young handicraft men who travelled the roads with their packs on their backs and carrying stout sticks. It was necessary for young men, having finished their apprenticeship, to journey for three or more years and on their return home to display their mastery of the craft by creating their masterpiece in order to obtain permission to set up in business themselves. Ambitious young manufacturers were also much hindered by the guilds of ancient origin, whose rules stipulated that no person should be allowed to follow any skill until he had agreed to abide by all the guild regulations, no matter how inconvenient, expensive or restrictive. This system was still very strong in Germany though of hardly any force in Britain at the time, and for this reluctance to accept change, the people were castigated by Hewitt: 'They are full of power and will go on to eternity in the same track. They are like steam-engines set upon a line. They are full of power and will march on exerting it for ever on one course, unless some mighty influence from without breaks irresistibly upon them and throws them from the rail; as Buonaparte broke in and as steam-power is again breaking in, determined to produce far more wonderful changes than the fiery Corsican.'

Steam-power, the abolition of tariffs and the decline of the small rulers after the Unification of Germany in 1871, resulted in a rapid development of manufacturing industries not only in the traditional field of wooden toys but also in metal and *papier mâché*. In 1845 the line from Gotha to Eisenach was opened, and as it ran through Waltershausen, the importance of this area quickly became apparent, as the merchants were able to take advantage of the lower freight charges. Even in the sphere of railway development, it should be noted that change was not as rapid as in Britain, and many of the early versions were horse-powered, steam being generally introduced only by 1876. Despite some tardy development, the toy industry grew rapidly in the second half of the nineteenth century, and by 1910 the quality and quantity of German toys were the envy of Europe. The most enchanting nursery pictures, toys and decorations could all be purchased from a vast selection, the schools of craftsmanship, set up by the government, having participated in the development of much more interesting and artistic playthings. Almost every city just before the 1914–18 war had its own school of artists who encouraged the creation of well-made toys far superior in style to any that were available in Britain. Though many of these progressive toys were fine, they were not introduced at the expense of the traditional folk-type wares, and items such as the model towns and villages with trees made from wood-shavings were to be found in catalogues alongside the more sophisticated offerings.

380

A room (*circa* 1885) furnished in the style of the salon of a Munich home, decorated in almost rococo style. The furniture is partly carved and partly plaster decorated. The doll has a bisque head. Width $23\frac{1}{4}$ inches.

The German child was encouraged to play with toys of a domestic nature in order that she would eventually become a good housekeeper, wife and mother. The assortment of model laundries, kitchens, cooking-ranges and shops is therefore considerable, most of the major producers of toys offering at least a few items of this purely domestic type. The lot of the German female was much pitied by other Europeans, who considered that they were quite unnecessarily exploited. In country districts, the common woman was frequently little more than a beast of burden, expected to toil in the fields or in a small workshop as well as running a home and bearing many children. In consequence, both women and children were often untidy and dirty, and their living-conditions offended travellers with any degree of social conscience who were familiar with the somewhat more picturesque British agricultural workers. Even the young girls growing up in the castles and large town houses were often badly treated, as women were regarded as being of only

381

minimal importance. They were therefore only very occasionally presented with a gift as large and expensive as a doll's house, though domestic toil in miniature in the form of a model kitchen made a very appropriate gift and served as a preparation for the future.

W. H. Riehl published his very widely-read *Die Familie* in 1854, and his views appear to have remained generally acceptable in middle-class homes until the First World War. Basically, he stated that in Germany a woman was of little consideration simply because of her sex. The family was the most important feature of society, and the individual woman was therefore of little importance. No matter how hard she was required to work, ultimately this could not matter, as all her efforts were for the good of her family. Riehl disapproved of a woman entering any professions, as the position and the money she would earn might serve to make her independent of her family. Above all, he considered it unwise to allow a woman to pursue any of the arts and 'If she becomes an author, it is a sure sign that she is ugly, soured and bitter.' The woman should be kept strictly at home, and the husband should remain at all times the complete master of this home, with the exception of the kitchen, which was strictly a female province. The subservience of German women seemed absurd to other European women, who were used to husbands who carried their parcels and opened doors for them, and their lot was often compared with that of the German cow, expected both to provide milk and to pull heavily laden carts.

Despite this somewhat primitive approach to womenfolk, the German principle encouraged a deep love of home and of the finer aspects of domestic life, and there are many affectionate portrayals of family scenes in the form of boxed models, which can be considered as much more economical followers in the cabinet-house tradition. Some of these scenes were made up from commercially produced dolls and represent incidents of the most general kind, but others, of far greater interest, were composed as portrait groups of actual families. One of the most effective was constructed in 1810 by Johann Albani and can now be seen in the Stadt Museum at Munich. It represents the Seidle family in their comfortable drawing-room, which is viewed as through a window with lace curtains in the foreground. The characterization of the group is particularly effective, and the figures have painted eyes and inset hair to represent the actual characters. The most charming figure is the small daughter, who carries a parasol, presumably a newly received gift.

Another interesting and purely German form of model room was that contained in the front opening skirts of ladies or even monks. The lower sections of the figures were made as virtual boxes, and when the doors were opened, a fitted kitchen was found, with the shelves and hooks numbered for the utensils that hung from them. In another version the doors open to reveal a church with several ladies kneeling at prayer, models of this religious type apparently originating in the Berchtesgaden area. The kitchen dolls were made at a much later date in the Sonneberg region and were probably constructed in imitation of the old wooden religious toys, though *papier mâché* was now substituted for the wood. The Dubois foundry at Hanover in the mid-nineteenth century also produced small scenes that were to be arranged in cardboard rooms. These painted lead flats were particularly colourful, and one version represents an entertainment at the royal palace in the time of King Ernst August and measures some 17×20 inches. In this setting the metal flats, in Court dress, sit elegantly on sofas or walk around conversing with their friends. On the cardboard walls are paintings, various decorations and coats-of-arms. Other outdoor scenes, such as hunts and pleasure gardens, were also made by this company, but their interiors are particularly interesting, as they mirror the style of contemporary furniture and decoration so well.

During the nineteenth century, German manufacturers concentrated mainly on doll's house furnishings and inhabitants, as these small items could be easily exported. The number of surviving dolls' houses is therefore very small in relation to those found in Britain and America, where most middle-class children owned such a toy. Interest in nineteenth-century playthings has until recently been quite minimal (with the exception of the Toy Museums at Sonneberg and Nuremberg), and consequently few later models have been preserved and exhibited. German collectors now find much more difficulty in obtaining effective houses than do their British contemporaries, and their position is also hampered by the fact that dealers are often reluctant to carry such houses back on buying-trips, as they take up valuable space that could be used more profitably. The best selection of later houses and rooms can now be seen at the folklore museum in Kommern, but there are also several examples at the Toy Museums of Sonneberg and Nuremberg. The number of model rooms at each venue greatly exceeds that of houses, and we are left with the impression that the majority of German children played with model rooms and their furniture rather than the larger complete houses that appealed to British girls. This difference of emphasis is due at least partly to the fact that the urban middle classes frequently lived in flats, where a large model house would have become a nuisance. The children were not as strictly confined to the nursery area as in Britain, as the rooms in these apartments often led off one another and the segregation of the children was therefore much more difficult. The pattern of life in such flats is depicted with accuracy in some of the more complex rooms, whose basic structures are much more involved than those attempted by French makers.

Bedrooms and living-rooms, contained in a three-sided structure, were obviously popular, but the models to have survived in greatest quantity are the kitchens, which contained such an abundance of brass and copper that it seems probable that adults also found them quite irresistible. Such playthings fitted well into the adult approach to the upbringing of girls, whether the parents were influenced by the traditional Riehl or followed the much more progressive thinking of Friedrich Froebel (1782–1852). Froebel's influence on the lives of nineteenth- and twentieth-century German children was considerable, as, for more than half a century after his death, toy-manufacturers were claiming with pride that their products were the direct result of his thinking. The Froebel basket-maker, bead-stringer and embroidery set were commonplace in nurseries until the 1920s, and though the composition of many of these toys makes it obvious that the producers had very little understanding of his thinking, they do mark a more progressive and educational motivation in the commercial field.

Froebel opened his first Universal German Educational Institute in 1813, but the school did not become a success until his writings encouraged parents to demand others of the type, and he was eventually to found the first kindergarten in 1837 at Blankenburg, though he did not make use of this term himself until 1840. Froebel's influence was ultimately to lead to a much greater degree of freedom in the upbringing of German children, a freedom that was considered dangerous by the Prussian government and which led to the closing of his schools. He believed that we are all born with a tendency to create and work, so that the heavy hand of a teacher is not really necessary, and he certainly should not impose his own views on the child's mind. The soul should be allowed a high degree of freedom, and nature itself should be the main instructor. He believed that human nature has an inherent understanding of right and wrong, though modified and selected during the process of evolution. His basic views were more progressive in theory than in practice in the schools, but he was certainly eager to encourage the spirit of play and divided this activity into three sections comprising dramatic play, pure enjoyment of high spirits and another and much more serious sphere where the child was given a preparation for adult life. He therefore found it useful to allow girls to play with their dolls and to keep house, as these are both imitative pursuits, the girl wishing to keep her doll's house clean and neat, similarly to her mother's main task. In the small dolls with which the child peopled rooms or staged miniature scenes, he saw a natural expression of a basic symbolism that represented the foundation of family life. The serious-minded manufacturers who produced the superb and perfectly equipped model kitchens probably felt that they were giving substance to these respected ideals.

Of all the German rooms, it is these kitchens, often mistakenly described as 'Nuremberg kitchens', that leave the greatest impression. The Toy Museum at Nuremberg exhibits some particularly well made early examples, with the tin and brassware produced by skilled individual craftsmen who made saucepans and kettles that were quite suitable for actual use. There was also a vast production of much cheaper models with the side walls made of bent tin and the utensils representing the equipment of the very poorest homes. The most

A South German middle-class kitchen dating to around 1895. The exterior is wood-grained and the floor tiled in black and white. The doll is bisque. Width $39\frac{1}{2}$ inches.

splendid rooms included model water-tanks that supplied working taps at shallow sinks. Others offered working ranges to be heated by oil or charcoal, thus providing the girl with an early introduction to the problems of cooking on full-sized versions of the same equipment. The manufacturers who produced tin-plate toys, such as horses and carts for small boys, also made toy kitchenware, though in Germany as in Britain boys also occasionally found enjoyment in toys really intended for the other sex. Hewitt, writing in 1842, describes a scene in Saxony at Christmas: 'The prettiest sight of all was to see the stout little fellow of three years set out his gifts of kitchen utensils in the middle of the floor and, sitting down among them, forget all about him in arranging and rearranging them, pretending to cook and make coffee in true childish style until the wonders of the magic lantern called him away.'

385

A most unusual mid-nineteenth-century tin kitchen with built-in furniture. An actual fire could be lit on the canopied cooking-area. In front is a garden with a pond and garden furniture. Width $18\frac{7}{8}$ inches.

The true Nuremberg kitchens in the manner of those in the early *Dockenhäuser* were supplied with a hooded cooking-area, complete with a chimney, where the girl could pretend to cook on stands over the burning charcoal. The models were packed so tightly with plates, skimmers, saucepans and barrels that it is almost impossible to see any of the basic walls. Later versions, made in several other parts of Germany, contain ranges worked by methylated spirits or simply a candle. The young cooks were supplied with a small book entitled *First Instructions for cooking for girls. 8–14 years of age. Published by Joh. Phil. Rawsche.* On the cover of this now highly prized booklet we see one girl reading its instructions to her friend who is cooking at a toy range. In the background yet another fully-fitted model kitchen can be seen. Models and books of this type were given to girls of all social classes, as even the most wealthy German women in the nineteenth century were involved in the organization of their own kitchens, this being generally considered a part of every woman's duty. Foreign visitors found it strange to see the daughters of diplomats and minor nobility so at home in the kitchens, where they organized the maids, supervised the piles of monogrammed linen and worked pokerwork admonitory texts to hang on the store-room walls. This necessity for middle-class girls to be familiar with basic household tasks accounts for the number of very high-quality models of this type that are found in Germany itself, whereas those that were exported and sold in America and Britain seem in general to be of a much cheaper kind.

In Bestelmeier's catalogue, *circa* 1800, a very simple kitchen was offered, basically just a room with the usual round-paned metal windows. At the back was a stove, and there was also a heavy table and several chairs. The hand-coloured pattern-books distributed by this company are a very useful source of information on the more traditional German toys, as the line-drawings are surprisingly accurate in detail, though the wares were obtained from several regions. One of the better kitchens offered was supplied with running water and a small doll to represent the cook. Bestelmeier also offered 'a fully equipped laundry with a drying green'; presumably this model was not as popular, as no examples seem to have survived. These early nineteenth-century wooden kitchens often contained a chicken-coop, so much a feature of the early cabinet houses, and were in general quite lavishly equipped with both tin and turned wares. In comparison, those originating in the Erzgebirge seem much less splendid and were probably intended for the poorest section of the market. This was itself one of the least-developed regions of the country, with the centre of the toy-trade being located at Seiffen. The name of the region, meaning 'ore mountains', suggests its long history of tin-mining. The plentiful wood in the area supplied the raw material for the turners, and after the Seven Years' War, when mining activities ceased, this craft became the most important industry, so that by 1782 there were forty-one turners at work in Seiffen itself. The people were so poor in the early nineteenth century that they were unable even to purchase their own lathes, and these were leased to them by the merchants or landowners at a charge based very unfairly on their output. The toys that were produced by this cottage-type industry were of the simplest type and included very basic containers, barrels, water-carriers and almost abstract dolls with tiny waists that were sometimes assembled into cheaply produced but brightly coloured rooms. Later in the century much of the wood-turning for the busy Waltershausen manufacturers continued to be effected in this poor region, which in just one respect was quite progressive, as water-powered lathes were in use here from the late eighteenth century.

A catalogue dating to 1848 illustrates several miniature kitchens, including an extremely simple version consisting only of a fireplace and a shelf, which presumably the child and her mother were expected to furnish. Another contained a good dresser and a wooden bench, while the finest model was provided with a kitchen pump that worked from a tank situated outside, as well as a vast selection of cooking-pots and tools. Much of this turned wooden equipment, which is also found in actual dolls' houses furnished in Britain and America, originated in the Berchtesgaden region. Though few dolls' houses were exported from Germany, because of their uneconomical size, vast quantities of wooden miniatures were sent all over the world and often sold packaged together in the characteristic chipwood boxes also made primarily in this region. Kitchen tools on racks, tea-sets on neat round trays, small cradles, beds, kitchen dressers and benches all formed part of the vast output of the craftsmen of this southern area, concerned with such work since 1100. The monks of the Augustinian Priory, established in that year, brought with them many of the skills learned at the Rottenbuch monastery in Oberammergau. As the peasants of the region were concerned mainly with farm work, the woodwork at first formed an occupation only for the quiet periods of the year, and it was mainly items of a domestic nature that were made, though by the end of the fourteenth century the more skilled men were also making crèche figures. Gradually complete families became involved in the craft, with the children painting animals for arks and stencilling flower decoration on furniture for model rooms. The trade in the area gradually developed into specialist branches, such as the bone- and ivory-carvers, the trough-makers, box-makers and, eventually, the toy-makers. Their work was collected by merchants and taken to the docks at Laufen or Rosenheim and then by river to Vienna or along the old Salt Road to Munich.

This development of a large group of skilled woodcarvers in a relatively small area was not accidental but very consciously developed by the imposition of strict and often inhuman laws. In the sixteenth century the Prince Abbot issued a mandate to the effect that every man who was involved at the time in woodcarving was to remain with his craft and hand it on to his sons, so that the craft was said to 'lay on the house'. This strict rule served to encourage men to become really skilled in their own speciality, as they were aware that there was really no means of escape, and sometimes several generations carved the same group of items. It was felt by the rulers that complete specialization was absolutely necessary in order to maintain the variety of toys from the region that made their boxes of wares so attractive, as it was obviously a temptation for a poorly paid box-maker to attempt to raise his living-standards by becoming a woodcarver. One family is reputed to have broken its oath never to practise its craft away from the region and set themselves up as toy-makers in Nuremberg. Whether in fact the story is true or not, it serves to indicate the influence of the skilled men of one region on another, despite the very strict legislation. In the eighteenth century, for instance, Maria Theresa of Austria decided that similar wares could be made in her country, an ambition that was aided by the lifting of the strictest laws regarding the passing on of trades in the family. The advent of Napoleon completely disrupted the old system, especially in respect to the traditional distribution outlets such as Vienna and Amsterdam, and the peasants also lost their cheap allocation of timber from the Prince Abbots. Their brief prosperity, enjoyed at the end of the eighteenth century when the region became popular with tourists, was at an end as their skill in carving complete scenes from a cherry or apricot stone and their production of quaint toys had all become outdated and lacked sympathy with the new age.

The absence of a central organization, supplied in the eighteenth century by the Prince Abbots, meant that in the first half of the nineteenth century the workers again became reliant on the *Kraxenträger* and at the Folk Museum at Berchtesgaden is a contemporary carving of one of these important distributors with his well-stocked pack, including a number of miniatures and toys. In the mid-nineteenth century there were still 120 box-makers, 120 turners, sixty carvers and a few barrel- and trough-makers in the town, though box-making soon became the most productive section. The box-carvers included the manufacture of toys in their craft, often packing the small turned pieces intended for dolls' houses in the round or oval boxes that were sometimes also stencilled with flowers. The composition of the paint used in Berchtesgaden was considered completely unique, and the secret of its mixture with pigments and lime was above price, as it was mainly on the colourful decoration of their cheap pinewood toys that success depended. In order to encourage the local crafts, a technical school was founded in 1840, and in 1854 Berchtesgaden wares were given a Medal of Honour at the Munich Industry Exhibition. Some of the carvers worked so speedily that they were able to make as many as three hundred doll's house cradles in a single day. These cradles, with flat sides that themselves form the rockers, are perhaps the most frequently found doll's house pieces from this area, though a large number of cabinets and dressers, usually with the characteristic painted flower decoration, are also found. The tea- and dinner-services of wood in matchwood boxes often carry only a simple label describing the contents and rarely suggest their place of manufacture, as they were exported by the Nuremberg merchants. China services were also packed in these Berchtesgaden boxes at the distributors, so that items from several different regions were assembled together before sale. The beds and model rooms sometimes contained the simply turned swaddled dolls, again often flower-decorated, which are still made in the area, but as their form was somewhat primitive for the taste of town children, many of these original occupants were later replaced by the more acceptable bisque or china dolls. That the importance of the woodworkers of the area was generally recognized is indicated by the fact that at the Nuremberg Exhibition of 1882 the wares were awarded the Great Bronze Medal. After the last war, with the traditional industry in decline, various brotherhood-type organizations were set up in order to breathe life back into the craft of woodworking, and a new range of toys was designed. The architect Georg Zimmermann created a completely new series of models, such as candle angels and some new dolls' rooms, all of which are still very popular, though mainly as traditional Christmas decorations or as souvenirs of the area. Today, well-made kitchen tools, scoops, trays, tea-sets, barrels, platters and dolls can all be purchased, either painted or in plain white wood, in the town – items which, cleverly aged, often appear in antique-shops and markets described as being of nineteenth-century origin.

Though for ordinary children the importance of Berchtesgaden lay in its production of cheap wooden toys, some of the finest doll's house furnishings originating in this area were made of ivory and bone. Ivory is among the most suitable substances for the manufacture of miniatures, as, despite the most delicate carving, it will withstand very rough treatment and is also virtually unaffected by either water or fire. During the seventeenth and eighteenth centuries most of the European production of carved bone and ivory originated in Germany, entire families being concerned with the craft, such as the Zick family at Nuremberg. Many amateurs also practised the skill, including several German princes, so that it became in their country an art similar to wax portraiture in Britain, which was pursued both by professionals and by wealthy craftsmen, who enjoyed the activity as an amusing diversion. In Berchtesgaden this was a carefully protected craft, with the sons being told the deepest secrets only when their fathers lay on their deathbeds. It is said that the greatest of these family secrets lay in the method of making ivory as soft as wax so that it could be carved with complete ease. The bone and ivory carvers were traditionally much more highly regarded than the craftsmen in wood, as their work was intended mainly for the superior cabinets assembled by very rich patrons. Originally, the carvers of Berchtesgaden worked only in bone, but as imported ivory became more easily obtainable, it was used for the most prestigious pieces including some doll's house furniture. Several examples of local work are displayed at the Folk

Fine-quality carved ivory furniture with a small chess table in the foreground. Probably
South German. Late nineteenth century.

Part of a set of horn furniture in the Biedermeier style. German, *circa* 1830.

A particularly fine ivory dressing-table with opening drawers containing brushes, powder boxes, combs etc. South German, *circa* 1850.

Museum in Berchtesgaden, where it is seen to differ from Indian work, for instance, by its almost complete lack of filigree detail. In general, the local work relies for its effect mainly on skilful turning, seen particularly on the spinning-wheels and 'whatnots', where, though the detail lacks the delicacy of Indian or Chinese work, the basic designs are so strong that a very fine effect is still achieved. One whatnot displayed at the Folk Museum was carved complete with its arrangement of delicate decanters and wine glasses, and there is also an elegant dressing-table complete with an ivory-framed mirror. Very small-scale furniture obviously intended for cabinet display rather than for dolls' houses was also produced such as a tiny set of chairs and a table made from a mixture of white and stained black ivory. Miniature carafes and jugs, minute domino-sets and the most delicate individual glasses and steins were all produced in Berchtesgaden and eventually came to be included in some of the most perfectly equipped rooms and houses, such as those assembled by Queen Mary in the twentieth century.

Ivory and bone furnishings were not exclusively the province of Berchtesgaden; at the 1851 Exhibition in London it was the work of a Württemberg manufacturer, Wittich Kemmel & Co of Geisslingen, that

392

attracted most notice, culminating in the award of a Prize Medal for a display of more than two hundred small bone and ivory wares. The jury commented that the greater part of the collection consisted of very small and exquisite models of furniture that involved minute piercing and carving and showed the craftsmen's skill to advantage. This company specialized in a whole variety of bone and ivory wares, such as parasol handles and brooches, but the miniature furniture was exceptionally well made and apparently used at the time in Germany as chimney ornaments rather than doll's house equipment. It was probably adult toys of a similar type that were exhibited by F. Schmidt, though the simple table sets and ornaments that were used by the assemblers of model houses, involving a minimal degree of skill for their turning, would have formed a side-line for any company producing fancy goods.

One of the basic reasons for the success of German craftsmen in the manufacture of toys was their willingness to adapt their particular skills to various situations and festivals. Hewitt, in the course of his description of Saxony in the 1840s, relates that a man who all the rest of the year was a sieve-maker and seller of turnery ware, suddenly, before Christmas, filled his shop with every possible article in wood that could form a present.

> It was as if a magic spell had been exerted, and all his tubs and barrels, and sieves and spigots, were converted into dolls, wooden boxes full of toys, chess-boards and boards of other games. His tables were covered with boxes full of little household things, sets of kitchen utensils, little dinner-services, whips and hobbyhorses, carts, waggons, dolls without end, churches and other buildings in sections for children to put together and innumerable things of a like kind.

Below left: Part of a wooden tea-set with colourful birds and leaves on a cream ground. Gilt decoration. South German, *circa* 1830. *Below right:* An exquisitely painted wooden service of South German origin (*circa* 1810) decorated in shades of blue and grey.

A similar willingness to adapt production to market needs is seen in the folk art of regions such as Oberammergau and Grödnertal, as well as in the less important Grünhain area, again famed for its woodturning. The precise origins of the Oberammergau woodcarving industry are not recorded, but it is thought to have been connected with the monasteries at Rottenbuch and Ettal, and by 1563 a craft or guild constitution was awarded to the local craftsmen. It was only in the second half of the eighteenth century that the manufacture of toys assumed any real importance, and in general the emphasis was upon larger items, such as splendidly carved horses, model carriages and cleverly articulated puppets, but a few small dolls were also made that were similar in structure to those made in the Grödnertal, and there were also a few doll's house furnishings, such as beds in the so-called Empire style, with scrolled headboards, that were made in several sizes. The smaller, brightly painted swaddled dolls also occasionally found their way into the cradles of dolls' houses, as did some of the miniature models of animals which were used in the nurseries or in the hands of a child doll. Toy-making in both Grödnertal and Oberammergau declined in the nineteenth century, though some minimal production continued, and in the twentieth century there has been a revival, in accord with the greater interest in traditional skills and designs.

Many British and American dolls' houses, furnished in the first quarter of the nineteenth century, rely heavily for their effectiveness on the delicate, slim-waisted dolls made in the Grödnertal, and it is in the sphere of miniature inhabitants that the German makers exerted their greatest influence, as these figures were inexpensive to produce and weighed so little that the problems of exportation were readily solved. Mechanical lathes were used in this area in the late eighteenth century, and there was also a technical school to encourage the industry that operated on a traditional folk-type basis, with one family finding it possible to carve as many as eighteen hundred dolls in a year. The figures, often supplied with a carved comb, were made in many sizes from one inch upwards, so that a convenient height was available for almost any model house. The finest examples have more precisely carved faces, and there is occasionally some real characterization, though the majority have rather long, prim countenances. A few rare men were made with painted beards and moustaches, and I was recently shown an extremely unusual dark brown lady, perhaps originally intended for sale in America or one of the Colonies. Very occasionally some unusual additional detail was added which makes the figure much more desirable from the collector's angle, such as real hair or a plait made from heavily varnished string.

Miniature *papier-mâché*-headed dolls were made particularly in the Sonneberg region and rely for their effect on the detail accorded to the heads. The finest have intricate hairstyles either moulded in *papier mâché* or created by carefully braiding and arranging the hair in the most complex and

A silk-dressed Grödnertal representing a child with matching frock and pantalettes, *circa* 1820. Height 3 inches.

Below left: Grödnertal-type woodens with waxed heads are rare. This example (*circa* 1835) is undressed to show the construction. The plaited real hair is inset in the wax. *Below right:* A Grödnertal-type wooden with a *papier mâché* head. The bead-decorated red and black woollen costume is particularly effective. The man in the finely detailed military costume is also made of wood and a type of composition. The lady dates to 1845–50, the man to 1870.

Above left: An unusually small *papier mâché* lady (*circa* 1830), wearing the original mauve and yellow frock decorated with paper. The hands are *papier mâché*, but the remainder of the body is fabric. The stockings are knitted. *Above right:* Grödnertals are given additional interest by the variety of facial decoration. The child (*circa* 1820) is shown undressed to illustrate the typical construction. *Below:* Despite its small size of three inches, this Grödnertal (*circa* 1838–40) was supplied with a change of clothes.

Above left: Papier mâché boy, *circa* 1850, with wooden lower legs, the original costume of red and blue fine wool, and a press-type voice box in the stomach. *Above right:* A pink-tinted porcelain shoulder-head with moulded hair, plaited at the back. German, *circa* 1855. The Grödnertal-type man with an integral, part-moulded hat has a Brotteig-type head with moustache and side whiskers. *Below left:* A waxed composition lady, *circa* 1875, with glass eyes and a mohair wig, wearing the original lace and silk Court dress in pale green. *Below right:* A Simon & Halbig lady with a bisque-headed man marked "36 70 Germany". Both German, *circa* 1895.

fashionable styles. The bodies are usually made of white or pink leather, with carved wooden lower arms and legs, the joins being neatened by coloured bands. Despite the large number of these elegant ladies that were produced, the fragility of the heads has meant that comparatively few have survived in these smaller sizes. A few waxed *papier mâchés* with carefully plaited hair set into a slit in the scalp were also produced at this time, but the process must have proved too expensive, as these are even rarer than the coiffure heads. Waxed woodens, which seem by their basic construction to have originated in the Grödnertal region, are also very rare in miniature and probably represent somewhat short-lived experiments, as the technique soon fell into disuse.

The design of the Sonneberg *papier mâchés* was very gradually adapted as the century progressed, and by the 1840s their doll's house inhabitants were of the plump, round-faced type with pale pink faces rather than the attractive yellowed varnish of the earlier versions. These homely little figures are often encountered in doll's house kitchens because their original costume is often found to be that of the more remote regions, whose womenfolk were popular as servants in German town houses until the early twentieth century. In accord with the shape of the shoulder-heads, the bodies, now usually made completely of pink or white leather, are also much thicker, with the finer examples having small gussets at the knee and thigh, though the majority rely for their effect on the cutting of the basic shape. Both men and women were made in this way, and there are a few unusual examples, such as a boy with wooden arms and legs, whose cloth body contains a squeaker; others have much more complicated wigs or the most exquisite of fashionable costume, which adds to their interest from the collector's standpoint.

Sonneberg's geographical position encouraged its development as a manufacturing town, as it lay on the trading-route from Leipzig to Nuremberg at a crossing road from Coburg to Erfurt; another road led to Berlin. Its ideal situation was augmented by a plentiful supply of cheap labour and an abundance of raw material in the deeply wooded hills which surrounded it. In 1789 twenty-six merchants were given a *privilegium* by Duke Georg that granted the right to sell toys, a document that is considered to be the earliest relating to the Sonneberg toy-trade. Some toys had obviously been produced in the region before this time, and dolls are mentioned in 1735, but the great development came after Friedrich Müller and his brother developed a really commercial method of using *papier mâché* for dolls' heads, so that by 1818 pressure-moulding in sulphur matrices was possible. The subsidiary trades, such as box-making and woodturning that were practised in Seiffen, aided the doll-makers, as their output could be purchased very cheaply.

The Sonnebergers, with so many potential customers passing through the town or waiting for escorts to guard their wares on the journey through the robber-infested Thuringian mountains, had first begun to manufacture household items from the maple, beech and lime that grew so abundantly, though the real importance of the town as a craft centre was not to develop until after the Thirty Years' War. During the eighteenth century, the proportion of toys to domestic items was low, the output being sent to Nuremberg for sale. After 1740, when a dough-like material known as *Brotteig* began to be used for the modelling of figures, output of toys and ornamental wares increased, and Sonneberg merchants began to establish their own depots in all the European capitals, so that they were no longer dependent on Nuremberg: it is from this period that the great toy-trade rivalry between the two centres developed.

The demand for Sonneberg products grew steadily, and by 1800 the population of the small villages around the town had grown between three and six times, the workers being attracted from other parts of Germany by the lure of better wages. This initial abundance of labour was eventually to result in great poverty, as the merchants, also engaged in bitter rivalry with those of Neustadt, cut wages repeatedly, until many new machines were destroyed by workers in 1849 in an unsophisticated attempt to slow down the changes from folk output to mass production. It was upon these very poor wages that the success of the toy industry depended until the 1920s, and the region remains very poor to the present time.

During the eighteenth century, the joiners, woodworkers and turners formed themselves into guilds, though their toy production was centred mainly around utensils for model kitchens and the musical instruments for which the town was famed. The continual disputes between the *Brotteig*-moulders and painters led to a complete severing of relations in 1787, the modellers being deprived of their right to sell their wares independently, leaving the painters to become traders and merchants. There is a long tradition that the secret of manufacturing *papier mâché* was given to a Sonneberg landlord by a French soldier, though it seems more likely that it developed from examples seen in other countries by the merchants. Muller added kaolin to the paper pulp to make the substance much stronger, and it was upon this improvement that the real local development of the trade depended. The material could be pressed and moulded into shape and was ideal for small items, such as doll's house dolls, plates, food and even furniture, all a great improvement on the locally made wooden figures, chairs and tables that were of the very simplest folk type and not painted with the flair that enlivens the Oberammergau or Berchtesgaden work. It was no doubt the plainness of the round-faced *papier mâché* dolls that encouraged the dollmakers to experiment with other materials, and as porcelain was becoming much cheaper to produce, it was chosen as the substance of the future. At first, the glazed china heads were made in the same idiom as the *papier mâchés*, with glossy black hair and chalk-white complexions, but gradually a little more realism was introduced, and a pink tint was sometimes used or neat hair wigs were fixed to the bald-headed versions. Porcelain became really inexpensive only in the 1840s, and the doll's house dolls often continued to be made with the hairstyles of this period until the First World War. Of much more interest to collectors are those with moulded hats, ribbons, ear-rings or very ornate hairstyles, especially those that are lustre-decorated, a somewhat more expensive process. Heads of this type were made by the dozens of small potteries in the surrounding area, and the dolls were assembled and dressed mainly by outworkers, sometimes complete families who laboured together for some of the lowest wages in Germany.

Another type of miniature doll with a somewhat more realistic appearance began to be sold alongside the glazed heads in the 1860s and 1870s. These early bisque heads were untinted and are known to doll-collectors as 'Parians' because of their resemblance to the porcellaneous substance of this name. In concept, they are much more adventurous than the earlier heads, as much more complex hairstyles, frilled collars and even flowers were all possible in this material, which could be moulded so much more crisply. The most commonly found have fair hair, but others have black, auburn or light brown, sometimes decorated with a comb or ribbon. The somewhat unrealistic white finish was gradually replaced by pink flesh-tones, though some continued to be made in the earlier shade until the 1920s. One company to make doll's house dolls of this type was Kling, whose heads, sometimes with inset glass eyes, are usually marked with a bell. The material was ideally suited for doll's house figures, and long after it had passed out of general use for play-dolls, it was still adapted to current fashions, so that maids with the bobbed hairstyles of the 1920s are discovered in many houses made in a very outdated medium. Of particular appeal are the complete doll's house families made of bisque, which included white-haired grandparents, visiting gentlemen with side-whiskers and a wide assortment of pretty aunts and sisters. The small children are often made with great delicacy, and some have lustre boots to add to their appeal. These families were available from several makers and in different sizes, so that suitable inhabitants could be found easily for a large-scale room or the smallest lithographed cottage. Despite the realism of the heads, the bodies were all of the same basic construction, with small-scale lower arms and legs and tiny waists. The majority appear to have been costumed by their original owners, and some very complex outfits were attempted, such as those seen in the doll's house at the Holly Trees Museum, Colchester.

In order to give an atmosphere of complete realism to the doll's house interior, some of the men wore moulded soldiers' helmets or sailor caps, and at the Sonneberg Museum in particular we are given an impression of the great interest in military uniforms in the opening years of the twentieth century, as complete groups of shoulder-headed dolls wear slightly different helmets and

One of the finest quality bisque shoulder-heads ever produced is this Scottish man. The feathers are moulded and gilded, and even the leg sections were specially made with tartan socks and *skean-dhubh.* Very few bisque doll's house dolls have as much fine detail. The original Royal Stuart costume is worn. German, *circa* 1885.

well-made original uniforms representing all the regiments of the German army. Especially for the British market were the figures wearing plumed Scottish bearskins, a type of doll that is unusually well finished, as the socks are correctly painted with a plaid design: the hilt of the traditional knife can also be seen, indicating a much greater degree of attention to detail than is often found. Perhaps the most complete impression of the variety of doll's house dolls made of bisque is given in the Kämmer & Reinhardt catalogues, where in the 1928 issue we still find complete bisque-headed families.

The Kämmer & Reinhardt factory was situated some 50 miles from Sonneberg in Waltershausen, a small and unimportant town in the eighteenth century, whose workers were reluctant to switch from weaving to doll-making. The abolition of Customs duties and the development of the railway system both contributed to the growth of the doll-making industry, which relied very heavily on the child labour of Waltershausen. Upon this basis it was possible to manufacture dolls which, despite the high transport costs, could still be sold more cheaply than anything that could be made in France or Britain. A 1928 Kämmer & Reinhardt catalogue illustrates several different families of doll's house size. These consisted of six figures with bisque heads, mother, father, young son and daughter, and either two maids or a visiting lady and a maid. Elderly grandparents were obviously no longer an essential part of every household. Another set included a maid and a much more unusual chauffeur with a peaked cap and effectively made uniform. The dress of all these family characters is extremely well designed, and they provide a most instructive picture of a typical middle-class household of the period.

The firm of J. D. Kestner, established in Waltershausen from 1808, also made a large number of doll's house inhabitants that are often possible to attribute only by comparison with models illustrated in their catalogues. The very small size of the shoulder-heads of doll's house dolls made it difficult to mark the figures in the usual way, and the miniature Kämmer & Reinhardt families are equally difficult to identify. Some of the Kestner men have black curly hair and splendid moustaches, but others are much more in the idiom of the 1920s, with smooth brown or fair hair with side partings. All the male figures in the 1920s catalogues have dark-painted calf-high socks, and a figure with a moulded peaked cap also wears long dark gloves and was probably intended as a chauffeur. The majority of the ladies were made in the traditional manner, though they are brought up to date by their fashionable hairstyles, in a variety of painted colours. Of greater interest are those wearing actual mohair wigs and the much rarer examples where the shoulder-plate extends to just above waist-level. These ladies were an obvious improvement, as very low-necked dresses could be worn. The arms were made completely of bisque also and articulated at the shoulder, so that the popular sleeveless dresses could look effective. Many of these dolls were also sold fully dressed, together with a wide range of small all-bisques, a type of doll for which the company is especially revered. These all-bisque figures, unless of the very smallest size, do not fit as well in doll's house interiors as the shoulder-headed varieties, but in the 1920s a much more delicately constructed type was developed with thin, black-stockinged legs, which, when carefully balanced, looks extremely realistic. The babies and animals made of this material also work quite well, and a vast number of doll's house ornaments were also made by firms such as Kestner. The so-called stiff-necked all-bisques were produced in much greater number than those with neck-jointing and before the First World War were referred to in America as 'candy store dolls', as they were sold among the sweets and chocolates. The earlier examples, made of an almost white bisque, are sometimes very fine, as the lustred boots and delicately painted features give them a truly nineteenth-century appearance. The greatest number was produced around Sonneberg in the early-twentieth century, and there is a wide variety of painted and moulded hairstyles, those wearing actual wigs being particularly liked by collectors. A few of these figures are completely articulated, while others are jointed only at the tops of the arms. One unusual version, wearing the Kestner-type ribbed socks, is moulded in a seated position with the legs bent, a model that must have proved difficult and expensive to produce, as it is only occasionally found. Goebel, Limbach, Heubach, Stroebel & Wilkin, Kling and

Kestner all made figures completely of bisque, and these are frequently found in bathrooms and nurseries of dolls' houses. Those with moulded clothes were particularly suitable, though the most complex were obviously too large for inclusion in houses of average size.

The all-bisques were really the successors of the *Bäderkinder* or 'Frozen Charlottes', the very stiffly modelled figures that were made from the middle of the nineteenth century in sizes ranging from one inch to 14 or 15 inches. The slightly curled hair was almost invariably painted black, but there were a few fair-haired examples, and the hands were often modelled in a clenched position. The Toy Museum at Sonneberg displayed an extremely fine *Badkind* that lies in its own especially made porcelain cradle in a size that would have perfectly suited a model house. When a metal lever on the cradle's side is lifted, the *Badkind* can be made to sit up and then lie back on the pillows. Few figures of the type are as complex as this example, and the majority are found in bathrooms or standing in tin baths in the nursery. They were manufactured by many of the doll-making factories such as Bahr & Proschild, Kling and Eichorn. The black versions seem to have been intended mainly for the American market, as they are only occasionally found in Europe. Of particularly collectable interest are those *Bäderkinder* with moulded bonnets or more complex hairstyles, while examples such as those illustrated lying in baths in an 1850s catalogue are always great favourites. Exceptionally rare are those with a fabric inset which allowed for a squeaker in the stomach. The later versions were often dressed in striped bathing-costumes, and one particularly effective example is represented with the arms thrown back as though it is enjoying the fresh air. Though a few of the more complex models are quite expensive, the majority, made in simple two-part moulds, are still reasonably priced, as their original low cost meant that thousands have survived, especially those measuring about an inch that were used as good-luck charms in Christmas puddings but which often ended their days as a doll's house toy in the arms of some bisque-headed child.

The miniature furniture made in Waltershausen was as sophisticated as the bisque-headed dolls and formed a complete contrast to the robust peasant constructions of the Alpine regions. One of the most respected companies was that of Gebrüder Schneegass & Söhne, which was established in 1845 and which made some of the most perfectly proportioned items. Early twentieth-century toymen's catalogues illustrate many of the designs that this very prolific company was manufacturing at the time, and very up-to-date Art Nouveau long-case clocks, art pot-stands and attractive desks are seen in some number. In February 1910 the name of the firm was changed to 'United Toy Factories', and it was described as the most important firm for high-class single pieces. The furniture dating from this period is constructed from a pale, natural-coloured wood that is highly varnished but made very impressive by the extravagance of its detail, such as correctly made handles and especially

This imitation rosewood furniture was made with little change for some seventy years. The rosewood furniture was decorated with great skill and has stood the years well, as few pieces have cracked or warped.

cut marble tops for washstands and chests. A dark-stained version of this furniture is also occasionally discovered and seems to have been intended to represent rosewood, though the colour is somewhat hard. The Schneegass furniture was made in several sizes and, in very large scale, is sometimes encountered in model rooms.

The most popular doll's house furniture originating in Germany is that made in imitation rosewood and decorated with gilt transfers or painting. This furniture is sometimes claimed to date from the 1830s, as its basic style is often in sympathy with that period. In general, however, the pieces, now generally believed to have originated in Waltershausen, are made in the styles of the 1860s and 1870s, and it seems more than likely that they were in fact the first products of Schneegass, established in 1845. It is at present impossible to locate any early catalogues relating to this company, but both the character and the sophistication of the work seem to point to this source. The Biedermeier style, upon which many of the earlier designs are based, was itself very much the expression of German middle-class taste, and it was for the children of such homes that the miniatures were intended. The bourgeoisie, feeling their insecurity in a Germany that, after Napoleon, was a ferment of unrest, embraced this simple style with enthusiasm and clung to its simple fluid lines long after the most fashionable had deserted the idiom. This dark furniture, with its graceful basic lines, was felt to be in sympathy with the new-found atmosphere of German nationalism, which was also evidenced by a new love of the language, so that for instance it became used at the universities in preference to Latin. Throughout the unrest caused in the 1840s, the middle classes retained a low profile, so that the pattern of their lives should not be too disturbed by the repressive zeal of the princes, and the simple furniture exactly suited this mood.

404

One of the most important pieces in a room furnished in the Biedermeier style was the sofa, which was invariably situated behind a large table so that it could be used for seating at mealtimes. During the day a thick cloth was thrown over the table, and a few carefully selected books and a vase of artificial or real flowers were used as decoration. The proudest housekeepers used lavishly embroidered tablecloths for this purpose and finished the arrangement with a really fine coloured-glass oil-lamp. The sofa was always placed in the most important situation and was used only by adults, so that no young girl would ever have dared to settle herself in this prestigious situation. When the gilt-decorated sofas were exported to Britain, children placed them, in British-style, against the walls or near the fire in their model houses, and it is only in their country of origin that they were placed correctly behind the table.

The rosewood Waltershausen furniture is perhaps mainly remarkable for its strength of construction, as drawers and cupboards still open perfectly, and there is rarely any warping of the well-seasoned wood. At least three different scales were used, the largest, such as a set exhibited at Sonneberg, being of

A South German, late Biedermeier room (*circa* 1845–50) with very attractive painted walnut furniture. It also contains some later items such as the picture and birdcage. Width 81 centimetres.

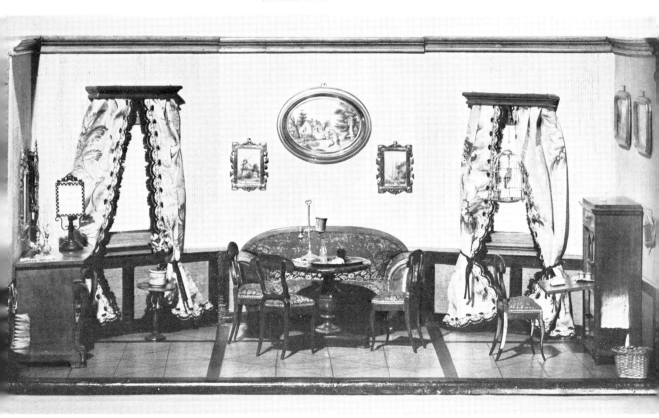

doll size and standing some 15 inches high, while there are some doll's house pieces where the chests stand only 3 inches from the ground. The earlier pieces are in the simpler classical idiom, but as the century progressed, furniture in the much more ornamented mid-nineteenth-century style was also made, such as splendid sideboards with turned-bone pillars and the most ornate glass-fronted display-cabinets, very much at home in the cluttered Victorian parlour settings, although furniture of this type in adult size was only very occasionally found in Britain, where much lighter mahogany was the most popular wood. In German rooms and interiors this dark furniture is completely at home, though the somewhat foreign look obviously had little effect on overseas sales, as pieces in the genre are found in models all over the world. A whole variety of furniture was produced by this company, ranging from hanging key-cupboards complete with tin keys to large Gothic-style hall cabinets, but no matter how small the item, the degree of craftsmanship was strictly maintained, despite the fact that some of the chests were sold in Britain for as little as sixpence. The most basic of this Waltershausen production is difficult to date precisely, as similar upholstery fabrics and decorative devices were used until around 1900, but some guidance is given by the larger sideboards and cupboards, where fashion seems to have been followed to some extent. There was also a lowering of the standard of the transfer-printing towards the end of production, and the gilding is much less crisp than on the earliest items. Earlier writers have sometimes suggested that the gold patterns were stencilled on the dark wood, but close examination reveals a complete absence of the ties that characterize work of this type, which would in any case have been virtually impossible on such a minute scale. It is possible that some method of screen-printing was used, but as the area already made use of a vast number of transfer prints in connexion with the production of inexpensive porcelain, it seems highly likely that this use was extended to the patterning of furniture. At the end of the nineteenth century many sets were made of printed paper applied to wood, and as the designs are virtually the same but without much of the complex finish within the basic detail that indicates the finest work of the firm, it seems probable that these were the most economical products.

The manufacture of such precisely made furniture indicates the presence of a highly skilled workforce, whose energy could be purchased at the lowest price. Several other companies, such as Louis Lindner & Söhne of Sonneberg, made furniture as well as dolls' houses, though the number of specialist factories seems to have been very much smaller than the number involved in tin toy- or doll-making. At Gossnitz was the factory of Carl Brandt junior, who specialized in miniature toys and included doll's house furniture in his range, and in Württemberg were Kindler & Briel of Boblingen, who were regular exhibitors at the Leipzig Fair and who produced miniatures in both metal and wood. Among their wooden furniture were washstands with turned legs and

A typical German town living-room (*circa* 1900) of simple basic construction but given added interest by the windows and the quality of the furniture.

fitted jugs and basins and a number of kitchen-type chairs, again with their characteristic delicate turning. Their tripod tables, a necessity in almost every possible situation in every Victorian and Edwardian home, are also encountered in some number and must have sold well at the London trade-fairs, where their work was also exhibited. Some much more lavishly produced furniture was the speciality of Ernst Goldmann of Neu Ulm, who used some of his plush, silk or leather-covered pieces to equip the model rooms which he also manufactured.

Though the names of the most famous of the furniture-making factories are recorded, it is virtually impossible to attribute individual pieces, as so few are marked, and we can only wonder as to the type of furniture shown at the 1851 London Exhibition by J. Hallers, Widow and Son-in-law, from Vienna, whose display of toys was the largest on view and who won a prize medal for pieces that included good miniature furniture. At the 1867 Paris Exhibition, M. Ousius displayed some noteworthy fretwork chairs, pianos and tables that caught the eye of the jury, while at the same exhibition H. Blumhardt & Co of Stuttgart showed furniture and dolls' houses that were both well made and

407

strong. The jury commented that the dolls' houses were filled with equipment but that the stoves were rather out of proportion to the rooms. This firm, like Rock & Grainer, apparently studied the overseas markets carefully so they could supply suitable items. Such a careful study of foreign taste was not particularly common among the makers of wooden toys, and it is possible that some pieces that are considered completely French or British in style could in fact have originated at the Blumhardt factory.

At the 1900 Paris Exhibition the Nuremberg toy industry mounted an impressive collective exhibit, a device that enabled small or poor companies to participate in what was, necessarily, an expensive venture. One of the exhibitors was C. Baudenbacher, established in Nuremberg since 1835. From this early period the company had produced a whole variety of small wooden goods and enjoyed extensive sales at home and abroad. So proud were they of such a long history that they informed the jury that they were the first manufacturers of wooden toys in Nuremberg itself. J. R. Baselsöder, who made both tin and wooden toys, was established some years later, in 1858, and their work seems a little more adventurous as they exhibited a high altar in addition to their wide range of dolls' furniture. Christian Hacker was also unusual in that he produced, in addition to the furnishings, complete dolls' houses, castles and shops, though, without access to a surviving catalogue, it is doubtful whether any of his structures could now be identified.

Despite great improvements in methods and marketing, at the time of the 1900 Exhibition a considerable amount of wooden doll's house furniture was still made on a home-industry basis. It is noticeable, however, that the production of wooden toys in comparison with metal and composition was becoming less important, as out of 207 establishments in Nuremberg and Furth, 148 were specialists in metal pieces.

The very general use of lithographic techniques in the last quarter of the nineteenth century made it possible to produce very effective furniture much more cheaply, as a simple basic design that needed only minimal skill for its assembly could be made eye-catching by the application of printed paper. Although furniture of this type was originally very cheap, it is very popular with collectors, as it is both colourful and lively. It also has the appeal of miniatures, with little relationship to full-sized pieces, as a completely fresh, purely doll's house idiom in the style was developed, where large pictures of playing children appear on the fronts of cupboards or where alphabet letters form the backs of fairly formal dining-chairs. The edges of the paper were often neatened with narrow embossed borders, which gave an extra richness to the general effect. The pieces with flower decoration are somewhat more realistic in manner than those where children or animals form the design and look much more at home in the conventional doll's house settings. Also of great appeal are the pieces in high-Victorian Gothic style, where the printing is often restrained to a rich yellow and black, and it is perhaps the structures of

Art Deco furniture was only occasionally made for dolls' houses. This set decorated in orange and blue is probably of German origin.

A lithographed paper-on-wood German group (*circa* 1875) in bright yellow and orange. The delicate turning of the legs and the attention to such detail as opening drawers and cupboards make such items highly collectable.

this type that most exactly portray the general concept of German nineteenth-century furnishings. Other fairly short-lived fashions are sometimes reflected in the lithographed work, so that the brief intellectual flirtation with oriental interiors in the 1870s and 1880s inspired one manufacturer to market a range of pieces decorated with panels of Chinese children at play, a comparatively unusual set, as chinoiserie is a taste that seems to have had only minimal effect on the builders and decorators of model rooms and houses.

A considerable amount of the German furniture that is available today and which can be seen to such effect in the gift shops in Nuremberg as well as at specialist suppliers in Britain, originates at the well-known factory of Babette Schweizer, which has produced metal filigree pieces since the first quarter of the nineteenth century. The fascinating history of this now well-respected firm was set out in a small booklet produced in 1930 and now in the possession of the family. Doctor Bruno Schweizer was obviously concerned much more with the firm's manufacture of religious items than with its toys but the firm's history, previously unrecorded in English, is interesting, as it must be typical of that of several other family firms who created the miniatures that could be marketed so cheaply in other countries.

Several craftsmen in tin were working in the parish of Diessen am Ammersee from the mid-eighteenth century, though their main concentration was on religious amulets and crosses for pilgrims, and around the Ammersee a small cottage industry developed to provide the many visitors to the monasteries with medals and amulets. There was also some production of sacred earthenware figures that were coloured in a primitive manner, again on a folk basis, with one person decorating a figure someone else had created. The industry seems to have been very loosely organized until Johann Baab, who was born in 1716, arrived in Diessen and went into partnership with the crucifix-maker Felix Riedel in St Georges near Ammersee. In 1743 he acquired the buildings of the Weinwirtschaft monastery and founded a very large industry, as he was possessed of that driving energy necessary for merchandizing local wares and was to become a very rich man on its proceeds. His main rival in the area was Schorn, and in 1773 they were still battling to become the leading merchant with all the small craftsmen of the cottage industry in their service. Eventually some six hundred people worked for Baab either in the small factories or from their own homes.

Johann Baptist Schorn, born in 1743, after serving the usual apprenticeship had worked for several German and Italian firms before returning to Nuremberg, where his father was a merchant, and he no doubt assisted him in setting up his own small workshop in Coburg. In 1764 he married Anna von Baab in Bayer-Diessen, and until 1782 the couple ran several businesses, especially those concerning outworkers. The Baab & Schorn wholesale business is first mentioned in the *History and Geography of Pfalzbaiern,* published in 1787, which describes a trade in miniature devices of a religious nature that were carried as far afield as Poland. A recession in trade around 1780 meant that several firms were encouraged to co-operate in the production of tin. Neumair, a ring- and bracelet-maker and the great-great-great-grandfather of Dr Bruno Schweizer, married one of the town councillors' daughters in 1780. The successful Schorn worked to a certain extent in co-operation with Neumair, and at the end of the eighteenth century the Schorn day-book suggests that the work was well paid and its craftsmen respected.

The finest tin used by these specialist makers was of British origin and was priced the same as silver. The method of weighing the substance is interesting, as a *Kreuzer* was placed in one scalepan and the same weight of tin in the other, and this set the price. Various improvements in the methods of casting were also introduced around 1800, though the processes were shrouded in great secrecy and carried out behind bolted doors and nailed-down windows in case they should be pirated by rivals. Adam Schweizer was so skilled in these new processes that he was eventually able to undercut his competitors so successfully that a rumour was soon in circulation to the effect that he was manufacturing counterfeit coins, and the firm was raided by the police. It soon transpired that the only coins produced were toy money, and a humorous verse was soon in circulation:

Adam Schweizer,	Adam Schweizer,
Mach' kleine Kreuzer,	Make a toy *Kreuzer*,
Mach' grosse Taler	Make a pile of money,
Bist ein guter Zahler.	But be a good payer.

Adam Schweizer's family had originally intended that he should become a cobbler, but he had completely refused to take up this work and had retreated to the chicken-house, crowing like a cockerel, until he was allowed to have his own way. He was apprenticed to the goldsmith Dieninger, in whose workshop he learned how to manufacture filigree work. In the evenings he worked secretly with his uncle Neumair, the ring- and rosary-maker, in order to know this craft also, and in 1796 he entered into a contract with his uncle to supply amulets and metal boxes. In 1812 Joseph Rathgeber, a man of considerable organizational ability, was taken into employment and eventually married Adam's sixteen-year-old daughter Helene, an energetic and highly disciplined businesswoman who was to be the main driving-force of the company, renamed Schweizer & Rathgeber, until 1875. This complete involvement of German women in commerce is a curious phenomenon in a country where females were thought to have been kept in completely menial positions and is similarly encountered in the history of the Märklin family, also producers of metal miniatures.

A catalogue of the Schweizer company, dating to 1821, showed the very wide variety of items made by the energetic Adam and his son Anton, who, though without any formal training in engraving, made all their own moulds. Though much of the work continued to be of a religious nature, doll's house items seem to have been included, though even in the sphere of toys the Church remained prominent, as miniature altar-sets were exported all over the world and either assembled in model chapels or used in devotional areas in room settings. The Schweizers never went heavily into the manufacture of soldiers, which might have seemed a logical progression of their castwork for amulets and religious ornaments, mainly because they felt that there was already too much competition, though limited numbers were made for the family's children, such as Bavarian dragoons and some foot soldiers. A shepherd with his flock, a hunt and a scene in Paradise, probably the Garden of Eden, were also made commercially and sold in an undecorated state, though a few were painted for special orders. An agreement with Schorn, dating to 1821, refers to doll's house equipment, such as baskets and bracket clocks, and an 1850 catalogue, still in the family's possession before the last war, gave an indication of the wide variety of filigree furniture that was made of this soft tin. The fact that the material bent out of shape easily if it was roughly handled made it unsuitable for larger pieces of furniture, so that when complete suites are encountered, they are usually of a fairly small size. The substance, though effective when used in the form of small tables and cupboards, was perhaps most successful when used for the smaller plenishments that add interest, colour and texture to the rooms, such as wall clocks, swinging cradles, light-fittings and later delightfully complex perambulators and even wheelchairs.

After the death of Adam Schweizer in 1821, the firm passed to his son Anton, whose energetic widow Babette was eventually to take over control of the company, together with their son Adam, who was sent to Munich to learn the art of engraving. It was in these years that the company's main production of doll's house furnishings flooded the European market, and in which the dozens of pieces, such as complete sets of cutlery, wall sconces, birdcages and table-lamps, which are still obtainable from the firm today, were first designed. The firm virtually stopped trading during the First World War but was resuscitated by Bruno and his brother in 1919 with the help of their sister Anni, who was also trained in Munich as an engraver but who was concerned mainly with the religious pieces. The old family concern is still very active today, and few miniaturists return from a visit to Germany without some of the pieces which are still produced in the old styles. The very fact that production of these traditional lines has continued serves to depress the value of the genuinely nineteenth-century pieces in the genre, and collectors are very much aware that more recent pieces can be 'antiqued' by the unscrupulous and passed off as old. The genuine pieces have often developed a

412

Known popularly as 'Nuremberg toys', such white metal sets (*circa* 1890) were made in several regions but packaged and exported by Nuremberg wholesalers.

pleasant soft, pewter-like patina which is effective in old dolls' houses, whereas pieces bought new are bright and metallic, though still very decorative. Filigree pieces are still made in other parts of Germany, and in Erfurt can be purchased small jugs and vases made in a similar style but of a much harder metal.

One of the oldest Württemberg toy factories, thought to have begun production in 1813, made tin furniture for dolls' houses as early as 1837. At the exhibitions and fairs that were such a feature of German commercial life in the nineteenth century, Rock & Grainer of Biberach were frequent exhibitors, and at the British Great Exhibition of 1851 they were also awarded a prize. Rock & Grainer was another small family firm, producing the toys from a small workshop behind their house and often continuing to use old and inefficient methods. They created bedroom, living-room and kitchen suites completely from tin, with the imitation cherrywood or mahogany finish being hand-painted on the surface. A company employee, writing of his old firm in the magazine *Puppen und Spielzeug*, commented that a variety of materials

413

were used for the doll's house furniture, including sheet zinc, galvanized sheet iron, brass, tinplate and copper. He also thought that some embossed silverware was made, though there seems to be some doubt of this. The production methods were very archaic, and all the pieces were shaped and decorated completely by hand, so that their toys were obviously uneconomical when in competition with the large companies such as Bing or Märklin. The company employee commented also that he had no recollection of any designers working for the firm, indicating that the workers either simply copied pieces they had seen elsewhere or worked from an example produced by a skilled tinworker. This small company was eventually taken over by Märklin, though it seems unlikely that their somewhat primitive designs were copied or needed by that firm. Though Rock & Grainer's manufacturing methods were old-fashioned, it seems that the quality of their work was very high, and they carried home a Prize Medal from the 1851 Exhibition in London for a collection that included kitchen utensils. A complete set of these pieces cost 6/8d, which the jury considered reasonable. At this period the firm was producing *papier mâché* as well as tinned plate, though their fame rested mainly on their fountains and other water toys, which were made with great skill. At the 1855 Paris Exhibition they received even greater acclaim, returning to Biberach with a "Mention for memory", a credit that was a stage above an honourable mention. This credit was awarded for a variety of varnished tin toys of the so-called watered or marbled effect, pieces similar to those in shades of brown popularly if erroneously labelled 'Orly'. The Rock & Grainer furniture was well made and offered at very advantageous prices, very necessary for the firm's considerable export trade in both tinplate and white metal. At the 1867 Universal Exhibition in Paris these Biberach toys were considered superior to any others manufactured, though the jury commented that the prices were much higher than those asked by Dessein in Paris. At this time Rock & Grainer were still making turned wooden wares in addition to their high-quality tinplate.

The metal-toy industry in Württemberg developed only towards the end of the nineteenth century, the real growth commencing with the founding of the German Empire in 1871 and the final granting of free trade. Metal, fabric and celluloid toys were all made in this state, whose commerce depended heavily on the railways, as the products were usually sold directly to the retailers, in contrast with the more traditional method of using merchants and wholesalers. The very seasonal demand for certain toys made it necessary for large numbers to be stockpiled, so that the capital investment at the end of the nineteenth century was high, especially as children were becoming more selective and demanded much more fashionable playthings.

One of the most famous Swabian makers of toy kitchenware and dolls' house equipment was Theodor Friedrich Märklin, born in 1817 and established in Goeppingen by 1840. After receiving his master's certificate as

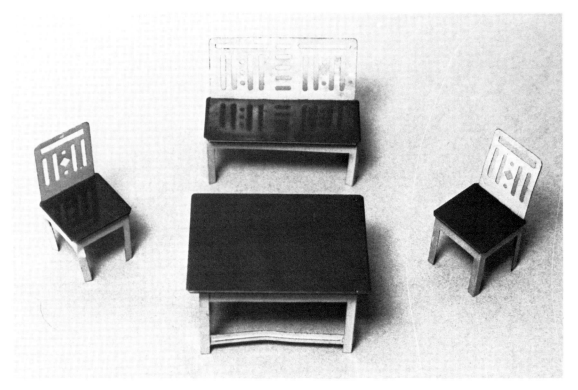

Tinplate furniture in progressive style marked 'J. L. Hess' of Nuremberg on table only. Painted in light and dark green.

a sheet-metal worker in 1856, he married Caroline Hettich and around 1859 decided to begin manufacturing items for dolls' kitchens. His wife was one of the most energetic sales-representatives in the toy trade and travelled all over the country promoting the name of Märklin. Their manufacture of miniatures in the early period is thought to have been mainly of the more basic type and probably in the larger scale needed for the model German kitchens and rooms. In 1888 their sons took over the firm and changed the name to 'Gebrüder Märklin', and in 1892 it was again changed to 'Gebrüder Märklin & Co', remaining under part control of the original family until 1935. Occasionally Märklin miniatures are found either with the firm's mark or contained in a marked box, and the date can frequently only tentatively be arrived at by the slight differences in title.

Their 1891 catalogue gives some indication of their vast production of doll's house equipment, and we find ornately designed pianos and organs made completely of tin and decorated with eagles. The bulk of their output was completely practical, such as several sets of water-pails with imitation oak graining and model ranges complete with all the necessary kettles, pans

415

A gazebo-like doll's house accessory probably made in Germany. Few of these fragile pieces for the doll's house garden have survived. Made completely of painted tinplate.

and coffee-pots. The small working fountains supplied with water from a wood-grained barrel must have looked highly effective in a doll's house garden, and there were also pumps and water-faucets in a wide assortment that could be used either in a kitchen or outside. Their range of small metal-ware is quite breathtaking and makes the modern reader very much aware of how poorly the child of today is supplied in comparison with those of the late nineteenth century, as the factories of today would find it impossible to manufacture a range a tenth of the size of that offered by Märklin. This wide assortment makes it very obvious that the furnishing and equipping of an effective doll's kitchen must have been easy, as a toyshop would have supplied all that could be considered necessary from one catalogue. Attractive moulds for jelly, mousse or even cakes came in shapes resembling pineapples, shells,

416

nuts and fish, and there were sets of twelve cake- or biscuit-tins and square baking-tins for sponges. Many of the toys could be obtained in copper, tin or nickel, so that a most colourful arrangement of hanging pans could be speedily assembled. The cutlery was obtainable in Britannia metal or German silver, some of the finest pieces being given bone handles and correctly nickelled knife-blades. This cutlery could be purchased loose, sewn onto cards, or boxed. The most expensive were laid out in perforated japanned knife-boxes. The firm's great attention to the most minute detail is indicated by their use of wood, ebony, bone or japanned metal for their knife-handles, so that the child played with accurate miniatures of objects used at home. There were spoons for all purposes, including the traditional soup-ladles and skimmers which seem to have been a necessity in any nineteenth-century kitchen. The dining-table was provided with matching sets of tin coffee- and milk-pots, and for the more progressive families there were tin filter-machines. The most exclusive homes could have a filter with its own specially made porcelain pot and cover. The brass coffee-machines with their spirit-lamps were completely accurate models, and all the pots in this complete range could be provided with matching cups and saucers.

Few of these perfect miniature kitchen pieces were ever marked, though reference to the original catalogues, which are now reprinted and sometimes available in Germany, makes it possible to authenticate individual items discovered in houses. The number of coffee-making toys illustrated in the catalogues gives some idea of the importance of the drinking of this beverage in late nineteenth-century Germany, and there are japanned coffee-tins, mills in several qualities and, only rarely seen in British kitchens, brass coffee-roasters with japanned stands. Some of these coffee-sets were sold standing on metal trays with blue- and pink-lined decoration.

For the laundry there were smoothing-irons of several different types, including one to be heated with charcoal. There were also neat trivets and ironing-boards, buckets, pans and baths in profusion, some fitted with metal mangles, though the traditional wooden mangles were also offered. For the bathroom there were japanned washstands complete with bowl and bucket, and baths with lion-paw feet and high backs. The poorest children could be given the most economical bath, a simple tin affair without feet and of the most basic shape that could be used in front of the fire. It is obvious from the catalogues that Märklin did not concentrate exclusively on metal wares but also marketed a number of wooden furnishings, such as cucumber-cutters, wooden barrels with neat supports, chopping-boards, spice-chests, cutting- and cake-boards and a good variety of kitchen chairs and benches. Their maple pantries were of the hanging type, so that meat and butter could be kept cool and protected from insects by a mesh door. The enthusiastic maid was offered sets of brushes, carpet-beaters, scrubbing-brushes and feather dusters, some of these being grouped together as sets on cards.

A German tin bathroom with a printed and applied border decoration. The bath and wash-basin are china and probably of a later date than the room itself, which dates to *circa* 1900.

The adult wishing to buy a child a really generous gift could purchase Märklin's rectangular kitchen, complete with brass and metal kettles, a Delft rack, wooden sink, table and bench; both floors and walls were tile-patterned. In order that the child should have every possible article in miniature, there was also a correctly produced cookery book, somewhat large in scale for the model kitchen but ideal for a child's hands.

By 1902, the Märklin output was somewhat more limited, presumably because their increasing use of mechanized processes made the production of some of the more unusual items uneconomical. Despite this slight change, many of the old designs were still sold, such as the hanging scales, the mincers and the flat hot-water bottles that are so deceptively eighteenth-century in

418

appearance. The kitchen water-tanks were now made in improved designs, and there was much greater emphasis on painted, brightly coloured trays and tea-sets. The babies' baths on turned wooden stands were particularly decorative, as they were embellished with swags of flowers and delicate lining. At the bottom, in imitation of full-sized models, there was a water-plug, beneath which stood a matching bucket, the more expensive models of this bath having a tap at the side. The somewhat more sophisticated child of the early twentieth century was offered a much greater range of doll's house furniture, such as metal chimneypieces, wrought-iron bedsteads, with resplendent brass knobs, and some pressed-tin beds in Art Nouveau style. For the most modern of houses there were ornate radiators and neat washing-machines. The chimneypieces for parlour and bedroom were still completely rococo in design, despite the progressiveness of the Art Nouveau beds, while the washstands with their china were rectangular and completely in the manner of small Edwardian homes. The lower-middle-class residence of the period was exactly suggested by the art pot-stands and the bentwood tables and simple dining-chairs. Many of Märklin's doll's house furnishings were sold in several sizes, so that a large-scale model room or a very modest house could be equipped. Their work is invariably of the highest quality and is frequently dated by collectors, because of this good workmanship, to a much earlier period than the actual date of manufacture, as it exhibits a degree of craftsmanship that it is difficult to equate with the twentieth century.

Several other German makers of metal toys are recorded in the lists of exhibitors and jury reports of the various nineteenth-century international events. At the 1851 London Exhibition M. G. Sohlke of Berlin was awarded a prize medal for a collection of pewter items that included several miniature tea and dinner services. A few years later, at the 1855 Universal Exhibition in Paris, their work included 'Little table services of gilded or silvered tin made with a great deal of taste'. This company manufactured a whole range of metal toys, including soldiers, and in Paris in 1867 their exhibit was described as 'An assortment of well-made metal toys, doll's house furniture, candlesticks, lamps, chairs, tables, stoves and English fireplaces'.

F. Buehrer, of Württemberg, at the 1851 Exhibition, showed boxes of miniature tools and kitchen utensils that were made of beautifully finished copper, suggesting a manufacturer of the very finest quality wares. Though copper and white metal pieces have continued to be included in rooms and kitchens to the present day, the new material in the 1860s was varnished tinplate that could be decorated in imitation of wood. At the 1862 London Exhibition H. Blumhardt & Co of Württemberg presented a vast number of small wares such as flower vases, baskets, trays, coffee mills, wash stands and clocks. The firm was apparently awarded an honourable mention at the 1851 London Exhibition and a Medal of Honour at Munich in 1854. At the 1862 event they again returned with an honourable mention. Their range included boxed sets of furniture, mirrors, grand pianos, tables with fish bowls, clocks and cages that included either an ordinary bird or a parrot, delicate items that make it obvious that they were continuing to use white metal as well as the more fashionable tinplate. Engler & Lutz, also of Württemberg, are recorded as winning an honourable mention for their japanned tin wares, while Ellwangen offered in their list of Württemberg products 'Nightstands, cradles, bedsteads, organs with action, flower stands, fine sets of furniture varnished *à médaillon*'. They also made 'Best-quality antique-style furniture' and some upholstered pieces. The varnished tinplate sets with silk or velvet upholstery are among the most attractive of the mid-nineteenth-century metal furniture as the delicate shapes capture the line of fashionable contemporary mahogany furniture so well.

In addition to their prolific output of wooden and metal miniatures, the German manufacturers also created an abundance of ceramic items, whose variety and artistry adds so much realism to the rooms and houses. The earliest reference to toy glassware is in a legend relating to St Elizabeth dating to the Middle Ages. The saint was returning from Eisenach, where she had purchased an assortment of small glass toys for the children at Wartburg Castle, but her horse unfortunately stumbled on the rocky path so that the toys fell from her robe into a stone-pit below. So great was her aura of sanctity that these fragile pieces remained whole and were eventually recovered for the delight of the children. The German glasshouses benefited from the skills perfected in Venice, with the main emphasis on coloured and decorated blown wares rather than on the cut glass that so attracted the British makers. The glassblowers often showed their skill at the great fairs and it was probably from this source that some of the pieces in the seventeenth- and eighteenth-century cabinets originated, though obviously miniatures could also be purchased from the so called toy-men's shops in the most fashionable streets. The apothecary's shop in the Princess Dorothea's town contains a very good variety of miniature bottles and jars which were most probably made locally, as the town of Erfurt has a long association with the glassblower's craft, and at the folk museum is a complete chemist's shop of similar construction, but in full size, which contains an assortment of very functional glassware made in Thuringia. The room devoted to locally-made toys includes a group of vessels made at Lauscha, and it seems likely that the fabulous chandeliers that were advertised in the Bestelmeier catalogues dating to the early nineteenth century were manufactured in this town. It was once fashionable to describe almost any item in blown coloured miniature glass as 'Bristol', even though its origin was much more likely to be German. At present the trend seems to run in the opposite direction, and virtually all small glassware is termed 'Lauscha', even though similar work was carried out over much of Thuringia as well as in areas of the Bohemian and Bavarian forests, so that the most the expert is able to do is attribute the piece according to the style of a particular

A group of
Thuringian glass
dating to the mid-
nineteenth century
and giving some idea
of the variety of pieces
made for dolls'
houses.

Delicate milk glass
with painted
decoration in red and
green. Thuringian.
Mid-nineteenth
century.

A complete set of
Thuringian glass on a
tray. The glasses have
gilded rims, and the
tray is edged with fine
yellow glass rod. The
original box reads
"Aug 6th 1878
Llaugharne treat. Aug
72."

area. The glassware itself was hardly ever marked in any way, and as large quantities were delivered from the glasshouses to the merchants for packaging, the containers rarely give any positive clue as to origin. During the first half of the nineteenth century, the glass was arranged in round or oval matchwood boxes, but later cardboard containers of similar basic shapes were used, sometimes with a somewhat idealized print of the contents on an applied label on the lid. In addition to the glass tableware, the Thuringian craftsmen also made groups similar in concept to the metal flats made by the tin-soldier makers and representing scenes such as stag hunts. Much more suitable for inclusion in miniature rooms, however, were the very lovely birds in glass cages and babies in cradles, the latter being found very rarely. The display of Thuringian miniature glass at Erfurt revealed the actual name of one manufacturer of such items, Carl Bohm Casper of Ernstthala Rennsteig, who in a nineteenth-century advertisement claimed to offer 'constant novelties in glass, Christmas tree ornaments, glass toys, art Christmas trees with miniature Christmas tree ornaments plated with genuine silver'. In general, the firm's output seems typical of that of several other Thuringian makers, though this company obviously specialized in Christmas decorations and offered a variety of bells. Their dolls' feeding-bottles were sold with or without a decorative picture, and their doll's house items were also obviously of the very ornate type with gilding and coloured motifs. Other firms that manufactured both toys and Christmas tree pieces included Adolf Eichorn, Engen Sohn, Kilian Müller, Müller-Hipper and Robert Adam, all of Lauscha, E. Reinhard of Rennweg and Rückert et Cie of Steinach, though, without comparison with catalogue illustrations, it is virtually impossible to differentiate between their products.

Frequently, in Thuringia, scientific glassmakers also produced a seasonal batch of miniatures, as the workforce was already skilled in the blowing of very detailed instruments. At Passau were manufactured a whole range of small jugs, spoons and figures and even model shops that sold items of glassware, much of which was made in the Venetian tradition, with lines, bands and finials. A large quantity of milk glass was also produced and often made even more attractive by coloured flower decoration. Tea- and coffee-sets seem to have been the more saleable, as dinner-services are only rarely encountered, but there were also dressing-table sets and the most complex candelabra, vases and decanters. Sometimes the tinmaker and the glassblower combined in their work to produce a group of tumblers in a filigree stand or a vase with metal mounts. The table-lamps made in this co-operative manner are particularly desirable, especially those where decorated coloured glass was used for the globe.

Doll's house china, of necessity cheaply produced, was also created mainly in Thuringia, particularly in the small towns around Sonneberg. The majority of the work is comparatively plain, and the firing is often crude, with

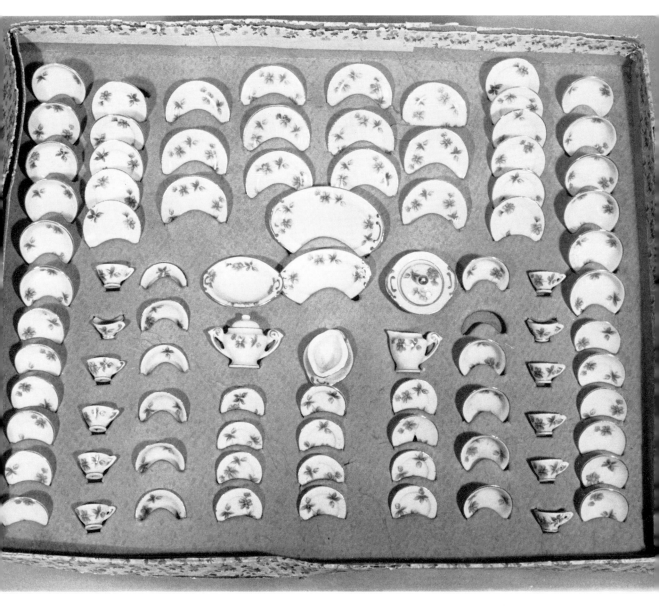

A remarkably complete porcelain doll's house dinner and tea-set with pink and green flower decoration. German, late nineteenth century. Despite its small size every piece is marked. Made by Kaempse & Heubach.

The complete dinner service still in its original box never fails to attract. This 'onion pattern' porcelain set dates from the last quarter of the nineteenth century. Probably Thuringian.

Opposite: Finely decorated porcelain furniture had a dual appeal to adults and children. This unmarked German set dates to around 1900.

many of the plates being very warped. Coloured or gilded bands or transfer-printed flowers, usually in only one colour, were the most popular subjects, those with a blue design loosely based on the traditional Meissen 'onion pattern' being the most frequently found. Dinner-, tea- and coffee-sets, jugs and basins and dressing-table sets were all made in this style, which seems to have been manufactured by several potteries, as the standard of workmanship varies so greatly. Individual pieces of this set are sometimes seen in antique-shops, at very inflated prices, described as 'Meissen', though the craftsmen of this famous firm would have blushed to acknowledge some of the mis-shapen, poorly produced wares. The firm of Huttensteinach was fond of the Meissen-based pattern for their toy dinner-services, as was Rauenstein, both of course being situated in Thuringia, though a marked doll's house size set has not to date been located. As in the case of the larger-scale toy services, it is often necessary to examine every single piece in a set to find the one marked plate that will establish the maker's name. Of much more relevance than attribution in this field is the basic quality of the china, and when paying the high price that is often demanded for these items, the collector should select those with well-shaped plates and crisp decoration, ignoring the often-heard dealers' claim that the crudity of construction indicates an early date. A complete set is also obviously of much greater value than odd cups and

424

saucers, though it should be remembered that the number of place-settings sold in a box often varied considerably, so that some contained only four, while others, such as that illustrated in its original box, supplied twelve dolls. In some dinner-services soup-bowls and tureen, fish-plates and serving-dishes, dinner-plates and central dishes, dessert-plates and bowls were all included, whereas in others, sometimes of identical pattern, there was a very rudimentary grouping of six dinner-plates, two tureens and two sauceboats. It is often possible to be sure that the set is complete only by reference to the illustration on the lid, and even then the information is sometimes incorrect, as large stacks of plates and dishes are seen when in fact the original contents were restricted to four or six.

The bedrooms as well as the dining-rooms of a nineteenth-century home necessitated many items of earthenware and porcelain, the chamber-pot being the item most frequently found. Not all the examples discovered were originally meant for dolls' houses, as a large number were intended as amusing gifts for adults such as those with a well-printed eye on the bottom or the phrase 'For me and my Girl' or 'Morning Exercise' written in gilt on the side. The majority of these adult gifts seem eventually to have found their way into the children's doll's house, where they appear completely at home, as chamber-pots of the type were so popular in the nineteenth and early twentieth centuries. Those originally intended for play were often included in a complete matching set of jug and basin, slop-bucket, soap-dish, vase and toothbrush-holder, those with lavish flower decoration being the most effective. Sometimes matching dressing-table sets of candlesticks, powder-bowls and a ring-holder on a tray were supplied, though the surviving examples indicate that the washstand sets were obviously considered much more necessary by the children.

Despite the fact that Britain, for instance, had many efficient potteries, it was not considered practicable to make many pieces of doll's house size in the second half of the nineteenth century, as those from Germany were sold so cheaply that it was impossible for the manufacturers in any other country to compete. This basic desire to retail pieces that were within the price-range of poorer people meant that by 1900 the quality of many of the sets was extremely low, with some of the individual pieces mis-shapen and decorated with minimal detail. In fact, it seems likely that some of these sets would have been almost unsaleable were it not for their attractive boxes, often showing scenes of children at play with a deceptively lovely tea-service. These very crudely potted sets can sometimes seem quite effective in the cluttered atmosphere of a doll's room, when their own lack of ornamentation is compensated for by the colour and refractive qualities of the other tableware, but few collectors of miniatures would choose to buy them for cabinet display. In contrast, some of the earlier and more expensive work, such as the set illustrated in its original box, is fine in its own right, and there are some very attractive highly glazed or lustred Art Nouveau sets on matching trays which hold their own among china of reasonable quality. Few of the best-quality German miniatures ever approach the standard achieved by Goss in Britain, whose toilet-sets, for instance, are both perfectly shaped and meticulously decorated as absolutely correct miniature items. The majority of these are found with a flower decoration, but perhaps best suited to the doll's house were those with amusing rabbits and delicately gilded crimped edges.

The busy German factories continued to manufacture many miniature sets for dolls' houses until the 1930s, often working in styles that were long outdated, so that it is often possible to suggest only the most approximate dates for unmarked items, which have to be evaluated on individual quality rather than origin. Alongside this traditional production of china there was also a considerable output of sets in the unbreakable substances that had so attracted the toymakers of Europe from the late 1880s, and pressed cardboard, celluloid, aluminium, printed tin and even bakelite were all used in turn, though rarely to the effect achieved by the potters or even the makers of the traditional wooden sets, such as those marketed by Wilhelm Mederer of Nuremberg around 1900. These turned sets decorated with painted flowers and blue ribbon are highly successful, as are the *papier mâché* sets that are often similarly patterned. The dollmakers also strove to provide children with

An amusing group of weighted celluloids decorated in pinks and blues. German, 1920s.

unbreakable figures, and some of those made of celluloid, especially in its early period, before 1905, rival the bisques for their precision of detail. The early celluloids were made completely in the idiom of the all-bisques, and as their colour has often changed to a soft ivory shade, they can look extremely effective in late nineteenth- and early twentieth-century settings, though the light weight of the medium often makes it extremely difficult to balance the dolls in suitable positions. Various composition substances were also used for miniature figures, in some cases the bodies being made of metal so that they could be bent into realistic positions. Kämmer & Reinhardt in their 1927 catalogue illustrated a rather strange series of figures that were intended, among other settings, for model kitchens and rooms, as they stood some 13 inches high. Described as 'highly original character dolls. Light as a feather, wire frame, felt cloth dresses and cloth faces', they are typical of the output of several German makers of the period. The K. & R. dolls were dressed to represent all professions and trades, and for especially large orders the company would make up figures representing either the trades or the soldiery of other countries. These figures would have been ideal in larger-scale rooms, as all the individual heads illustrated were modelled with real expression, and the clothes were very skilfully created. Judging from the catalogue photograph, it would seem that a few were also made in smaller, more conventional doll's house size. All the heads were made of what is described as 'a most durable material, fine dull varnished and well painted', and the bodies were movable as the limbs were wired. Several other companies made doll's house families of a similar substance, though the majority in more adventurous style were given composition-type heads. Of particular interest are the virtually unknown figures created by Käthe Krüse, memorable among

427

A model of two rooms with an opening door. Though some heavy furniture is still in evidence, the general atmosphere of the German home was much lighter by 1900. The fine soldier wearing a helmet reflects the fact that military service was a feature of family life.

toy-collectors for the very realistic baby and child dolls that she created with great artistry. A leaflet discovered in the archives of the toy-museum in Sonneberg revealed that this German craftswoman also made a series of dolls' rooms with their appropriate furniture, the chairs measuring 2 inches high. Around 1920 she also designed a 'modern family' with figures some 6 to 7 inches high, which she described as one-tenth life-size. She represented the family in a number of domestic scenes, such as the father reading the paper and the whole family out in a car, though those in model rooms are obviously of greatest interest to doll's house collectors. I was particularly fascinated by the Biedermeier families in their contemporary settings with both furniture and costumes in the style of about 1845. To work in this antique style seems almost a contradiction of the motivation that usually inspired this artist, who was striving to produce really modern dolls that fitted perfectly the desires and emotions of contemporary children, and it is curious that at that particular time she decided to work in such a derived and retrospective manner.

The dolls, glass and china produced by the hundreds of small German factories were mainly exported, so that the interiors of American, British, Dutch, French and Polish dolls' houses and rooms were all given a decidedly Germanic appearance. The tin-toy makers were very eager to design their products specifically for particular markets, but the manufacturers of doll's house pieces seem to have made little adaptation for the intended destination, except occasionally to translate the names on jars or other kitchen equipment. In consequence of this basic style of furniture that is mainly German in origin, the interiors present the viewer of today with a curious never-never land, purely the inspiration of the toymen and reflecting only in the most general way the home of the child who once owned it. German children seem themselves to have played only occasionally with dolls' houses, as the main concentration was on model rooms that were made in much greater variety than in France. The simplest were obviously those of the three-sided construction, common to all European countries, but the more expensive were made with a quite astonishing variety of interior plan and arrangement. A few included glass conservatories leading from the side windows and furnished with light, easily transportable furniture and jungle-like potted plants in wooden or glass flowerpots. The potted plants made entirely of glass are the most skilful arrangements, some of the flower heads being blown with extreme delicacy and showing the most authentic graduations of colour. The flower heads are wired to their stems and fixed into heavy glass bases, but other flowers were especially made for arrangement in groups in individual vases. The richest children were sometimes able to supply their conservatory with the exquisite porcelain potted plants that are now often collected in their own right and which were never as cheap as the glass versions. The china flowers, painted with complete

The massive turned pillars, stained glass and panelling combine to create the atmosphere of a middle-class Berlin home of the 1890s.

A bourgeois living-room in the 'old German style' dating to around 1870. It is constructed of pine and is especially interesting because of the alcove in the back wall.

assurance, are supported by ceramic stems and leaves and stand in elegantly decorated pots. It is thought that several of the leading German porcelain works made such miniatures, including Rauenstein, and though probably intended for adult china cabinets, they were often included in model rooms and settings. The conservatory or glass-roofed balcony was used much more in Germany than in Britain, as the Germans took advantage of every hour of fine weather to sit in these areas, which were really treated as part of the house rather than as very occasional sitting- or strolling-areas as in Britain.

One of the most impressively designed sets of rooms can be seen at the Folk Museum at Kommern, where a very heavily carved and ornamented natural-wood construction contains steps at the rear rising to a window area in which stands a heavy table. The windows are made of small panes of coloured glass,

430

cut with exactitude to provide a correct miniaturization of windows of the type seen in so many late nineteenth-century German homes. This museum contains the finest collection of model rooms and miniatures of German origin that has yet been assembled, and though the restoration has in many cases been somewhat unsympathetic, with the use of harshly coloured modern miniature wallpapers, the exhibition is an exciting portrayal of the arrangement and scope of such typically German toys. In some rooms there are archways through which we have a glimpse of another section or room; others have additional curtained areas, and others raised sections, all proving that the model room need not be the somewhat boringly plain structure that it is often claimed to be but which can, in its most complex forms, be as interesting structurally as very ornate doll's houses. The majority of the rooms at the museum are obviously of the simple divided type with interconnecting doors or curtained arches, a type that has to rely for its effect on the richness and complexity of the furniture and the lavish supply of bisque-headed dolls. One particularly complex example, with a fretwork veranda leading off the main bedroom, has a well-stocked windowbox fitted along one side. In the bedroom a pair of parian-type bisque-headed dolls sit on a sofa at the foot of twin beds with high headboards. There is also a very fine pale bisque shoulder-headed man with a moulded moustache and a small pointed beard, who wears a grey overcoat and is obviously visiting his friends. The family seems to consist largely of small children of similar age who sit obediently on the many chairs ranged around the living-room, which is heated by a white cylindrical stove. In an adjoining sitting-room, equipped with one of the most splendid wood and chrome wall-telephones encountered; the grandparents can be seen enjoying their peace and quiet away from the activity of the main reception-room. In one corner of this somewhat complex model, an extra section is added and its level raised by a fairly high step. This corner room has leaded windows and is furnished with the inevitable art pot-stand and several chairs. This set of rooms is made especially realistic by its nicely sewn draperies, all the interconnecting doors, for instance, having curtains that hang from poles and cover the wooden doors themselves during the evening, to be drawn back with heavy curtain-ties during the day. This complete interior exactly suggests the crowded activity of a German apartment of the late nineteenth century, whose atmosphere seemed so strange to British visitors, familiar with the segregation of family and servants in middle-class households, a segregation that was made possible in British homes by the number of passages and corridors found in even the smallest dwellings.

The exhibition at Kommern provides the doll's house enthusiast with a very concise picture of the various structures and construction methods of the craftsmen of the nineteenth century. The most effective have correctly made cornicing around the ceilings, turned pillars and ornately shaped outer

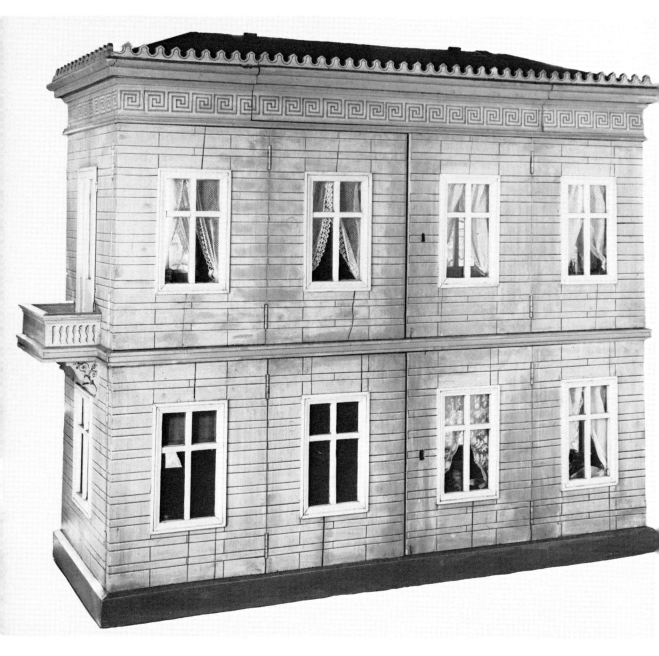

Above: A German doll's house decorated with a painted Greek key pattern. The roof is slightly pitched. The rooms are very light as there are windows on all sides. The front opens in eight sections that fold back at first-floor level. The walls are brick-painted.

Opposite above: A doll's house made in 1876 at Stüttgart. The veranda and balcony are typical German features, as on any warm days people take advantage of the fresh air.

Opposite below: A German kitchen and store-room dating to 1900 and showing the lighter furniture that was becoming popular.

432

The interior of the 'key pattern' house showing the sitting-room with fine tin furniture
including a grand piano and a marble-effect sofa table.

frames. One of the more arresting has decorative arches carved in the wide wooden panelling below the cornice and large pillared alcoves set at intervals in the walls for the display of white bisque statuary. The lower section of the walls is also wood panelled, and the heavy, carved furniture, made of the same lightly polished wood, was obviously especially selected for this completely integrated setting, where even the pelmets exactly match the tops of the alcoves in which the busts are displayed. On a gilt holder is a copy of the *Children's Newspaper*, which 'appears once a year in 500 copies only. Reproduction prohibited.'

With the availability of such complex structures, it is little wonder that the German child was completely satisfied with these models and was only occasionally supplied with a complete house. For the collector of today those in lightly polished natural wood with a lavish amount of carved and turned decoration are obviously the most interesting, as they perhaps most accurately reflect the interiors of the period. British and American collectors often express a dislike of the concept of a model room, but in many respects they are much better display items, as all the furniture and dolls that they contain can be clearly seen and as they take up so little space they can be accommodated in even the smallest flat. There is occasionally some problem in obtaining furniture in the correct scale, as the rooms often needed pieces much larger than the conventional doll's house size, though this can sometimes be turned to advantage, as the larger sets are often much cheaper, as are the plenishments of china and glass. The early twentieth-century rooms, still completely in Art Nouveau style, are also of some attraction, as the larger-scale furniture in the idiom can quite often be discovered, and a number of small tea- and coffee-sets are still generally available, as are the blue and green, somewhat elongated basalt vases, so that, with the addition of suitably dressed dolls, a high Art Nouveau interior can be presented. Few collectors, after visiting the exhibition at Kommern, could return home with any vestige of their traditional contempt for such constructions; rather, they will wonder why British children were not more generously supplied with such cleverly assembled playthings.

Despite the preponderance of rooms at Kommern, there are also a few dolls' houses, though one of these, the so-called Stüttgart House, with a large kitchen that runs across the complete width of the ground floor, is almost more in the nature of a model room as there are no staircases or passages. On the first floor is a living-room with an adjoining bedroom and an open balcony with several items of furniture. The most effective doll's house is painted cream and is decorated around the top with a Greek key pattern. As there are windows on all sides, the house is unusually light and cheerful in atmosphere. It is also very practical in general construction, as the front doors fold back separately in four sections, these sections themselves being divided at first-floor level, so that the rooms could be revealed consecutively from the centre

435

and so that the problems of the space needed for the opening of conventional large doors are also avoided.

Both the German houses and the rooms are noticeable for their lack of any significant laundry facilities, though a number of individual model washhouses and rooms were created. It seems probable that their omission is again due to the number of middle-class people who lived in flats, with a large attic that could be engaged by the individual households for certain periods. On washing-days, one servant, assisted by a laundrywoman who was hired especially, would wash and iron a complete month's supply of clothes, keeping the heat and steam well away from the household's living quarters, though the housewife would herself assist in the folding and ironing of the items.

At the Toy Museum in Sonneberg the very large 1890s doll's house is again more reminiscent of a frame containing a number of rooms than the architecturally inspired designs with which American and British children were more familiar. On one side of the model is a glass-sided conservatory, beneath which a very steep staircase rises. The main section contains two bedrooms and two living-rooms, each connected by very well-made doors. Most of the furniture is of the heavily constructed German type in light oak, but in the main sitting-room is a heavy sofa with a shelf along the top of the back, as well as a group of adult bisque-headed figures; a much earlier porcelain-headed lady stands in the downstairs hall. All the windows are hung with thick curtains with braided edges and a large number of potted plants and vases of flowers. It is noticeable that in neither the dolls' houses nor the rooms do we find any especial accommodation for the servants, and it appears that many German maids, even in the late nineteenth century, had no apartment of their own, as in France or Britain, but still slept in cupboard-like rooms, often without even a window. The German servant's status was itself very different to those in Britain, as she would undertake any duties that were required, rather than keeping to some special area of her own. This constant direction of the servants by the housewife was thought by British visitors to cause much of the indiscipline among servants, who were never encouraged to plan their own time but were constantly harangued by their mistresses.

The dolls' rooms in the collection of the Toy Museum in Nuremberg are all in very pleasing original condition and are effective, as the furnishings are completely in period. The mid-nineteenth-century room with its crudely printed wallpapers is a particularly lively period-piece, and among its generous furnishings are several infrequently encountered items of cream card decorated with gold paper, including a round stove and a delicate firescreen of printed paper with a floral design in the centre that is worked in beads and wool. Similarly constructed hanging wall-pockets also appear at intervals around the room, which, albeit hand-finished, are obviously commercial, though probably made in a limited number as they are not encountered in any other model. The metal filigree wheelchair in which reclines a wan, fair-haired boy, is also an unusual piece, making this room, with its silver tea-set and filigree rocking-horse, one of the most immediately desirable specimens.

The complete development of the German model room is revealed in this museum, as the earliest example is a three-roomed structure dating from the seventeenth century. In this model, the kitchen has the usual abundant supply of plates and cleaning equipment, and the living-room contains a large green-glazed earthenware stove. Such prestige stoves, which remained a feature of German interiors until the second half of the nineteenth century, were originally constructed in Austria, where the art reached its zenith in the Middle Ages. Those made in Germany during the rococo and Biedermeier periods were still very splendidly designed, with all the panels modelled individually, so that no two were identical. The chief towns associated with the manufacture of these prestige items were Salzburg, Steyr, Graz and St Florian, and the possession of such a piece of equipment was a matter of household pride, so that they were inevitably included in miniature settings. Many of the miniature stoves were not especially made for models but were intended as cabinet items to be displayed in their own right amid various items of interest.

In the living-room of the seventeenth-century model at the Nuremberg Museum, in addition to the good model stove, there are also several early Delftware plates, on the usual type of plate-shelf, and a very good inlaid table. The turned-legged chairs all have rich velvet seats. The bedroom, with its oak walls and finely detailed doors, contains a tin burner to perfume the apartment sweetly, and there is also a good brass barber's bowl hanging from one wall, reminiscent of the larger *Dockenhäuser*.

The twentieth century is represented by a series of pine rooms, made between 1913 and 1914, in which the bathroom is now seen to have some importance and is hung with Dutch type tiles. The washbasin, permanently fixed to the wall, has a water-tank, so that the equipment really worked. The lavatory is made of wood, and the dolls are supplied with neatly cut squares of newspaper. A modest curtain can be drawn across this area for privacy. The bedroom is also completely fashionable, with its white painted, simply constructed furniture given delicate gold-painted decoration. The pictures on the walls have scenes of children at play printed directly on the tin and are of a type only occasionally discovered. The dining-room, with a shelved sofa, is provided with a fine telephone and a grandfather clock. Large double doors lead to the next room. Behind a curtain at the rear we catch a glimpse of an extension room, in which can be seen baby dolls in their pram and high chair and a Christmas tree. Though this area is obviously given over to the children for the Christmas period, it cannot be compared with a British nursery, as in

Germany the arrangements for the care of children were quite different, and there were no special children's nurses in the majority of middle-class homes but simply a general servant who helped with the young when necessary. Very rich families hired either British women to look after the children or peasant girls, who wore their regional costumes in service. It was fashionable until the First World War to hire a girl from the Spreewald region if the family lived in Berlin or from the Black Forest if they lived in Baden. The Berlin streets were often colourful with the elaborate costumes of the nursemaids – costumes that were sometimes repeated in miniature toys, where the nurse pushes the child in its pram. Few peasant wet-nurses were employed by 1910, that figure, so typical of the earlier interiors, having been displaced by the sterilized milk that the progressive doctors ordered.

The small all-bisque doll's house dolls made and costumed in the years before the war are still frequently found wearing swaddling-clothes, as these were still used by families in remote parts of Germany. The babies in middle-class homes were kept warm in the *Steckkissen*, a long and frequently highly decorated and embroidered bag that fitted around the baby just below the arms and which was much copied by the doll-makers. As the bag was lined with wadding, it served both to protect the baby and to keep him warm for his first weeks.

German mothers of the early twentieth century were quite different in their attitudes both to their own position and to that of their children. The popular phrase among the more progressive women was 'Art in the Nursery', and these women, with a new spirit of adventurousness, showed tremendous concern for good design and were keenly interested in obtaining a good education for their daughters, as a woman without money had much less chance of marriage, despite good looks, than her British counterpart. So liberated were the ideas of many women that one of their aims was the realization of every German woman's right to motherhood, so that the subservient role that had amused women from other European countries for decades was fast changing, a progressiveness of spirit that is perhaps particularly suggested to toy-collectors by the very unrestricted life-style of Käthe Krüse.

The 1920s rooms at the Nuremberg Museum are constructed on an unusually large scale but are expertly made, as the marquetry-edged floors are obviously designed to complement the furniture exactly, and such a room must have proved completely satisfactory to the most artistic of parents. In some sections of these rooms, the scale is very strange, and in the bedroom for instance a very small man sleeps in a vast double bed under which is a large chamber-pot. In the dining-room is an impressive sofa with an integral shelf and mirror, and there is a good marquetry-panelled sideboard; maintaining the completely modern aspect of the room is the early wireless set, with earphones, that lies on a table.

438

A richly decorated town house with a façade that opens in two sections. On the ground floor there are two rooms divided by a hall. Note the similarity to the so-called 'French houses'. Though this example is the most perfectly finished yet encountered, there is a similar example at the Toy Museum in Nuremberg. Width 29½ inches.

The most effectively constructed commercially made doll's house on view is an ornate model dating to around 1880, with an elegantly proportioned façade, whose effect is heightened by a flower-and-leaf pattern on the pediment. The cream-painted house is decorated with pale red lithography, and there is a delicate metal balcony. The front opens separately for access to the first and second floors, and the complete house can also lift apart in two sections for ease in transportation. The basic design of this model is very similar to those usually thought to be of French origin, but this example is much more ornamental in effect, and it is possible that it was either made in imitation of the general construction of the successful French design or perhaps even especially made for sale in Germany. Inside there are the original printed floorpapers as well as a built-in dresser. One bedroom is situated on the ground floor, next to the kitchen, and the two living-rooms are upstairs.

In all the German rooms and houses displayed in the various museums, the quality of basic construction and workmanship is very high, and it is obvious that a nation that produced such exquisite miniature furniture, china and glass also thought it necessary to manufacture the rooms and very occasional houses to the highest specifications. Especially in the rooms, we are able to see the very real love of wood as a medium that underlies both the sophisticated and the folk-type work.

SEVEN

American Dolls' Houses

Traditional American dependence on the manufacturers, traditions and ideals of Europe was in rapid decline even in the last years of the eighteenth century. Though the Republicans were necessarily reliant on the old sources of luxury goods, it is obvious that there was a much greater willingness to manufacture items purely for the native market. The children of this new democracy were no longer expected to behave in a completely acquiescent manner, as the spirit of Revolution decreed that learning and conduct should be governed only by reason, and this greater freedom was allowed to colour the upbringing of the children of more radical parents. During the eighteenth century, American adults had feared the loss of their hard-won and often insecure civilization too much to allow any relaxation of strict paternal rule, but the nineteenth century was faced with much greater confidence, and young people were allowed to speak and behave with a freedom that often shocked European visitors.

Rousseau's educational theories had an obvious attraction for the Revolutionaries, but they were modified by ambitious parents so that hard work was seen as the most important feature of a child's upbringing, leading, hopefully, to a dutiful and successful adult life. In the most progressive homes a few amusing toys were allowed in the nursery, but the basic belief was that excesses of enjoyment or enthusiasm were not appropriate to the lives of young radicals. The Rational movement in children's toys, which was so passionately followed by Maria Edgeworth in Britain, was supported in America by writers such as Theodore Dwight, who believed that all games and toys should have a useful end. In his *Fathers' Book*, published in 1835, he despaired of toyshops ever attaining the production of completely rational items and suggested that fathers should make suitable pieces themselves and allow their sons to see various tradesmen at work so that they would gain

441

inspiration from watching true craftsmen producing fine objects. Sadly, his daughters were not as highly considered, and he believed that they should find their employment in work of a domestic nature. It is probable that this serious concern for rational, constructive play during childhood accounts for the great scarcity of early nineteenth-century American dolls' houses. In every country it was only the richer children who could own such an expensive toy, and as many of the leading American families were progressive thinkers, it is logical that frivolities such as Baby Houses would have been felt to savour too strongly of the empty-headed European nobility.

In 1809 Priscilla Wakefield commented on the industriousness of a group of little girls seated around a table. She thought that they were probably making dolls' clothes or perhaps 'the Baby House was to be furnished anew'; to her gratification, she discovered that they were making clothes for the poor and were not wasting their time on mere playthings. Obviously there were dolls' houses, but, being so lightly regarded by adults, they were presumably thrown away once the child's interest waned.

Fortunately a rather lighter note was gradually creeping into the lives of American children, mainly because of the influence of Clement Moore, a New York educationalist whose *'Twas the Night Before Christmas. A Visit from St Nicholas* was published in 1822. Moore believed that children would appreciate a happy, lively story that did not continually exhort them to do good things, and this thinking soon spread into all facets of nursery life in the better families, so that by the second half of the century these children were among the most indulged in the world, and toy-makers of all countries saw the American market as the most lucrative for their products. Doll's house furniture, miniature china, small dolls and a variety of metal kitchenware poured from Europe into the hands of eager children, whose parents enjoyed their obvious delight and who often continued to treasure the doll's house even after their daughters had left home, thus providing collectors of today with a wealth of material.

Despite the willingness of manufacturers in the early nineteenth century, it was many years before either dolls or dolls' houses were produced in any quantity for the home market, though tin model kitchens and small furnishings were still made. In 1837 the *Philadelphia Public Ledger* was advertising Christmas toys and New Year's presents that had just arrived from Europe, which included 'fine toys, wax dolls . . . and furniture for filling Baby Houses'. It is this furnishing of possibly home-produced models with pieces from Europe that makes it so difficult for the owners of old houses to be sure of their origin, especially as immigrant craftsmen from Germany or Britain would continue to make toys in their own native idiom for some years. It does seem unlikely, because of the large amount of space that they would occupy, that many European-made houses were imported, except for the richest of families, and we have therefore to assume that a number of houses

Some fine silver filigree pieces were made in South America around the turn of the century.
This set of complex design is decorated with tassel-like edging. Height of sofa 2 inches.

were produced in America, as there are frequent references in poems and
literature to this not-uncommon toy. The virtual disappearance of these
houses has perplexed collectors for many years, and the present writer can
only suggest that American love of new designs led to the destruction of
outdated dolls' houses, whereas in Britain, for instance, they might be stored
away and forgotten in a garden shed or attic. The search for these early, true
American houses is a continual challenge to serious collectors, and those that
are discovered are justifiably regarded as important landmarks in social
history.

One of the very few early nineteenth-century American houses to have
survived can be seen in the Independence National Park Collection and is
believed to have been originally made for Sarah Emlen Cresson, who was born
in 1806. This substantially constructed house has the simple proportions and
symmetrical solidity that is mainly associated with small British town houses
of the period, but it has the particularly American addition of a captain's or
widow's walk on the roof and unusual Green Tree Fire marks, indicating
cover by an insurance policy in a house of full adult size. It seems possible that
the marks are a somewhat later addition, as one is strangely positioned

443

The Cresson house bears the unusual addition of an insurance cover sign. The front door is mahogany, and there is a brass lock.

Opposite: Interior of the Cresson house with the remains of two fine beds. The simplicity of the interior is reminiscent of eighteenth-century play-houses. Height $42\frac{1}{2}$ inches.

against the lock, providing a lack of balance that would have upset the original craftsman. Probably the child owner insisted on their inclusion to make the model more closely resemble a house she knew well. The exterior of this well-made structure is completed by a neat, polished mahogany front door with a brass lock. The symmetry of the façade is maintained inside, as the ground floor is neatly divided by a narrow hall, and in each room, on either side of the chimneypiece, are either cupboards or shelves in almost eighteenth-century style. Sadly, little of the original furniture now remains, but there are two impressive four-poster beds of typical late eighteenth-century construction with the bed-rails pierced for the ropes that were stretched across to support the mattress. Originally the turned posts supported arched top pieces to hold the curtains in position, but in some ways this lack of drapery is beneficial, as the construction can be seen so clearly. Another particularly American feature of the house is the pattern, in imitation of carpet, painted on the floors. This floor decoration, often in highly imaginative and complex patterns, was a popular economical device in many

444

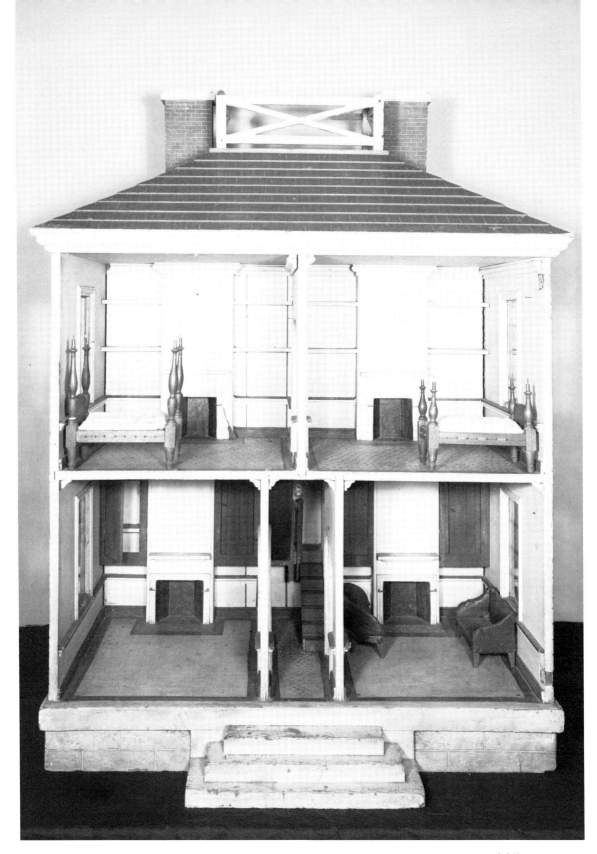

445

A rare early nineteenth-century American house (*circa* 1815) with the detail painted directly onto the wood. Note the 'framed' effect of the interior, reminiscent of some German houses.

actual houses, as genuine carpets were often a prohibitively expensive luxury even in middle-class surroundings.

The Shelburne Museum also owns a very effective early nineteenth-century house on which most of the detail of the façade is painted directly on the wood. Fanlight, curtains and windows are all nicely rendered, providing a strange, timeless effect, only a little spoiled by a rather oddly out-of-place round window. A device rather similar to that seen in early German houses, where an arch is fixed to the front ceiling of a room to mask the unrealistic effect, is used here to great advantage, as, in imitation of the earlier German houses, it is decorated with stylized flowers. It seems a pity that this method was not used more frequently in later models, as it does add greatly to the effect on the viewer. The house once contained both dolls and furnishings, which were protected by a lock, but only the painted chimneypieces now remain to suggest its old delights.

Chronologically, the next American doll's house of real interest was that made by a Philadelphia cabinet-maker and upholsterer in 1835. This structure is very much in the art-cabinet tradition as it stands a spectacular 8 feet high and is constructed and furnished to suit the very particular taste of an adult. Voegler's house has little in common with other children's houses of

446

The Voegler house with its fine detail and correctly made furniture is completely in the cabinet tradition and shows an 1835 interior.

the period, as it contains particularly fine Empire-style mahogany furniture and items such as a good long-case clock by Thomas Wagstaff, an eighteenth-century British clockmaker who worked almost exclusively for Quaker families in America. Voegler's house has an importance far above that of an antique toy, as it exactly mirrors the style of middle-class furnishing and life in the Philadelphia area, giving the house an exactness of period that is very rarely found in a plaything. Full-sized examples of most of the furniture and accessories can be seen in the collection of the Chester County Historical Society, giving this house a complete integration with its surroundings. Only in the doll's house can the visitor be given the complete atmosphere of the late 1830s and discover the exact arrangement of the more important rooms in a comfortable home. The scale of this model, being 2 inches to the foot, is unusually large and was probably necessitated by the fact that the maker wanted to put very correct detail into all the pieces and treat them as fine miniature objects rather than as doll's house fittings created only for basic effect.

The dining-room, with its landscape-painted walls, is reminiscent of Dutch houses and helps to create the atmosphere of a cabinet house. The larger pieces of furniture are made of mahogany-veneered pine, and some of the individual pieces, such as a four-poster bed and a very detailed corner cupboard, are examples of the very best American cabinet-maker's work. In this prestige house there is a tremendous air of organization and completely rational order, the kitchen, for instance, being free of the glorious clutter of equipment that characterizes European play-houses of the period, and it exactly mirrors the firm progressiveness of the age just before the deep-buttoned ornamented extravagance of the second half of the century. The carpets, polescreen and rugs are all worked in correct detail by a skilled needlewoman and exactly complement the correctness of the furniture. One of the great treasures that the house contains is a Tuckerware washstand-set, a miniature of considerable rarity from a factory that worked in Philadelphia between 1826 and 1838 and whose work, even in full size, is only occasionally found. The complete atmosphere of this house suggests that it was the delight of an adult rather than a child, and its obvious value and merit have meant that it has been preserved in perfect condition.

Another purely adult-inspired house is that now displayed at the Museum of the City of New York, which was made by the Rev. Dr Philip Milledoler Brett between 1838 and 1840. The exterior is visually somewhat unsatisfactory as it has nothing of the elegant symmetry that characterizes so many houses of the period in Europe. The central section of the model is constructed on two floors, and on either side is a wing of a single storey. The house is painted to simulate brick or sandstone and is surrounded by a substantial wall that encloses a green velvet lawn. This surrounding wall or fence was an indispensable feature of American houses and in the nineteenth century was

Though the exterior of the house made by Dr Philip Milledoler Brett between 1838 and 1840 is unexciting, the interior shows an abundance of calculated detail. Height 36 inches.

a surviving feature of earlier Colonial homes, considered safe only when surrounded by a barrier that was 'horse-high, bull-proof and pig-tight'. The inhabitants of Dr Brett's comfortably furnished house could have little association with such basic agricultural problems, but the early traditions remained even in the towns, where life was lived in comparative security. This model is the work of an ambitious and skilful man who was still in his early twenties, and the design reveals considerable ingenuity, such as the staircase hall at the back, which is lit by two graceful windows with arched fanlights, and a useful storage-cellar, a detail rarely found in nineteenth-century houses.

A Brett family portrait dominates the drawing-room, and this interest in ancestry is augmented by an impressive coat-of-arms on the centre wall. That the family is cultured and reveres learning is evidenced by the fine collection of miniature books and the lovely ebony and gold harp. The model is packed with literally hundreds of small treasures in silver, porcelain and glass and in atmosphere is perhaps more suggestive of the middle years of the century than its actual construction date, suggesting that Dr Brett and his family probably continued to add suitable pieces over the years.

In the 1840s one of New York's most eccentric bachelors, Peter Goelet, also created a model house which is generally considered to have been intended to represent his own home. The well-made structure was built of mahogany and contained eight rooms with a narrow staircase climbing steeply up the centre. Like the other early-nineteenth-century houses discussed, this also probably owes its survival to the fact that it was made to adult specifications, whereas toys were obviously soon destroyed.

Despite the scarcity of American early nineteenth-century play-houses, a number of companies were producing furnishings, mainly of the metal type, that suffered little in transit, and though primitive and frequently stripped of their original decoration, they are much prized by collectors. Wooden miniatures were occasionally made in the eighteenth century to special order, but there appears to have been no manufacture of this type of furniture in any quantity until the second half of the nineteenth century. After the Civil War, a much greater number of doll's house pieces were manufactured in New York, Connecticut and Philadelphia in particular, though obviously the majority were still imported from Europe.

The tin toys that were made in the eighteenth century are of considerable importance, as they mark the first traceable sphere of the native toy-trade and are therefore revered, even if particularly crude. Many of these miniatures began to be made as sidelines by craftsmen engaged in the manufacture of adult-sized equipment, often in imitation of the methods used in their own country of origin, so that it is often difficult for collectors to be absolutely sure that they are examining a genuine early-American toy. The very characteristic New England toys include painted pails, tea-pots and jugs that are decorated with bold, very stylized flowers and leaves, reminiscent of British bargeware or Berchtesgaden boxes. Louis H. Hertz suggests that an extensive tin-toy factory was operating in Philadelphia by 1838, and a number of decidedly primitive model kitchens are believed to date to this period. He disputes the often-claimed story that the tin-toy makers used up scrap metal in their work and believes that all the materials were properly selected. The models such factories produced were obviously popular with children, and the tin-toy industry developed with great rapidity after 1845.

Edward Patterson left Ireland around 1733, and his progress in business is typical of the very ambitious colonialist of the period. He set up a small factory in Berlin, Connecticut, to manufacture tinware from imported tinplate and was helped by other members of his family, who eagerly joined him in a potentially prosperous venture. At first, their products were hawked from traditional pedlars' packs, but soon wagons were used to carry their tinware, which included toys, all over the country. Many of the men that the Pattersons trained eventually set up their own firms, so that by the early

This mahogany house was made around 1845 by an eccentric New York bachelor, Peter Goelet. It contains eight rooms and a narrow staircase. Total height 60 inches.

nineteenth century there were several tinware factories in the lower Connecticut valley.

The Philadelphia Toy Manufacturing Company was established in 1838 and was owned by Francis, Field & Francis. This firm included toys 'superior to any imported' among their japanned wares, which they advertised in the *Philadelphia Directory* for 1848, in which were described tin chairs, clocks, bureaux and other doll's house pieces. Their 1853 advertisement offered the public 'clocks and other household pieces for the gentle girl to establish in her doll's house'. Toys were obviously beginning to sell well to families who were gradually living in much more comfort, and other firms, such as George W. Brown of Forestville, soon added their wares. In a catalogue of the 1860s they stated: 'To meet a want long felt, we have added to our list a number of tin toys expressly for girls.' The list included dustpans, coffee-pots, cannisters, silverware, plates with the alphabet embossed around the rim, watering-cans, baking-tins and sets of rosewood furniture for parlour or bedroom. This tin furniture, painted in imitation of wood, is very typically American, though

451

it was also made in both France and Germany. Some of the advertised furniture was painted to resemble the 'finest imitation rosewood with velvet upholstery', while that intended for less grand houses was 'oak grained'. The kitchen sounds very progressive, as it was supplied with a working water-pump, a stove and an ice-box.

Cast iron, a heavy metal that would appear to be completely unsuitable for toy-making, was a particular favourite of American companies, such as S.S. Stevens of Connecticut, who, in their 1868 catalogue, described their doll's house furnishings of this material. A wide variety was obviously sold: 'all in current adult styles and all in doll's house size . . . bureaux, wash-stands, cookstoves, laundry stoves, Franklin stoves, coal-hods with shovels, laundry tubs and washboards, sleds, rocking-chairs, cradles and dustpans'. Other firms also produced cast-iron furnishings, but mainly in the 1870s and 1880s, and it is extremely difficult to attribute them to particular makers, as the same models frequently appear in the catalogues of several. Flora Gill Jacobs, in her *History of American Dolls' Houses*, illustrates a group of iron chairs that appeared both in the 1869 catalogue of Ellis, Britton & Eaton and also in the 1872 catalogue of Stevens & Brown of Cromwell, Connecticut, thus underlining the difficulty of attributing these unmarked toys. One of the largest firms was Benjamin T. Roney's Tin and Sheet Iron Ware and Stove Manufactory of Attlebrough, Pennsylvania, which claimed to make 'everything in the tinware line that has ever been thought of'.

Pennsylvania was one of the richest of the toy-manufacturing states, but although the products were to give pleasure to the many children who received them as gifts, their low prices were made possible only by the labour of the less fortunate young. A manager of a large factory was quoted in *Children in Bondage*, published in America in 1914, as stating that, 'Much of the prosperity of Pennsylvania is owing to the fact that she has a lower age-limit for work than any of her neighbours. Tinkering with these existing conditions would drive the masters into other states.' This freedom from any real government restraint, even in the twentieth century, makes the reader forcefully aware of the exploitation of large groups to give joy to the few. The same book also describes how a master, going to Pennsylvania, from Patterson, New Jersey, where child labour was banned, said chortlingly, 'I save from 60 to 70 per cent in wages by the move, and I have twice as much labour as I need.' It is surprising to discover that, in a country founded on the liberty of the individual, only fifteen states had a fourteen-year age-limit for factory labour by 1914. Night-work for children under the age of sixteen was prohibited by only eight states, making British law of the time appear very advanced.

More fortunate American children, blissfully unaware of the grim lives of their fellows, could play joyfully with items made by firms such as Hull & Stafford, who included dolls' furniture among their toys after 1870. These pieces were very simply made in two halves joined by metal tabs, in the traditional German manner for cheap tin toys, and were made more attractive by painted decoration. Improbable materials such as velvet and silk were frequently imitated in pressed tin, but so skilfully made are many of these pieces that the effect, on such a small scale, was completely satisfactory. Stevens & Brown and I. F. Crocker of Rhode Island both made a substantial quantity of miniature furniture in this robust but curiously imitative manner, but it is again almost invariably unmarked. It is thought that this disinclination to put any trademark on products was due to the fact that distribution was largely in the hands of travelling salesmen, who obviously obtained goods from several sources and wished to keep their origin secret in case the shopkeepers might begin to order direct. As many small pieces of tin kitchenware, for instance, were often sold loose, by weight, there are not even boxes to give valuable clues as to origin. Edith Barenholz, in her book *The George Brown Sketchbook*, describes the practice among the larger toy-manufacturers of providing other firms with spare parts and points out an entry in the ledgers of the Union Manufacturing Company to the effect that both figures and horses in parts were supplied by them to George Brown of Stevens & Brown between 1851 and 1861. Both Stevens & Brown and Ellis, Britton & Eaton offered in their catalogues very similar sets of parlour furniture, in silk or velvet finish. Francis, Field & Francis and Hull & Stafford sold elaborate embossed and japanned furnishings, and, working only from catalogue information, it would be virtually impossible to distinguish between them. Although so few of these decorative and highly collectable pieces are marked, it seems probable that the exchange of parts extended into doll's house furniture as well as boys' toys. This traditional disinclination to mark work broke down gradually, and firms such as Crandall and Bliss found it very helpful to promote their own name on their products. Although few of the highly patterned and decorated tin pieces are attributable, they are popular, as they so exactly mirror the affluence of the middle years of the nineteenth century, when any surface without ornamentation was considered vulgar and when chairs and sofas as well as ladies were expected to be padded into beguiling but completely unnecessary shapes.

White metal, used to such good effect in the making of miniatures to the present time in Germany, was also favoured by American toy-makers, who were probably utilizing skills originally acquired in the Fatherland. A writer in *Harper's Weekly* claimed in 1900 that the pewter-toy industry had been introduced into America around 1850 by Italian craftsmen, but it is now generally considered that the metal was used at a much earlier date, the pewterer Robert Boyle of New York for instance advertising 'doll dishes, plates and platters' as early as 1781. The white metal usually used for children's toys was not the more costly true pewter but, because of its similar colour, was usually so described. This metal was very easily cut and moulded, so that the most complicated effects could be achieved with little difficulty. Even in 1900, American companies were still casting their models by hand from brass and steel moulds, and the assembled pieces were made even more alluring by their silk upholstery. The pieces came out of the moulds flat and were then passed into stamping-machines that produced, at a single stroke, a perfect rocking-chair or sofa. The *Toy Trader* commented in 1909 on the great skill of American designers, who would shape a piece of strawboard into a cushion by machine rather than by using a laborious filling as would the Europeans. One of the leading American makers was Peter F. Pia, who established his company in 1848 and was still in operation in 1950. Flora G. Jacobs illustrates a 1905 advertisement which shows a dining-room set by Pia in a square, decidedly simple shape that contrasts very clearly with the much more organic forms preferred by the Germans. Collectors face great problems in trying to decide whether acquisitions are of German or American origin, and it is only by the discovery of identical designs in catalogues or magazine illustrations of the period that sets can be conclusively attributed. A similar material was used by George H. Buck of New York who created 'Buck's Metallic Beds' and also produced an 'Oriental Cozy Corner' that was made of white metal but given a Venetian black finish and decorated with overwhelming lavishness. The advertisement detailed this embellishment and included 'spears, battle-axes, fairy lamps, oriental draperies and sofa cushions'.

Britannia metal, which was first used by James Dixon & Sons in Britain around 1800, was soon produced in America. It was a much harder metal than pewter and more suitable for pieces where strength was needed. It was at first used mainly for adult-sized pieces, but after 1860 a few miniatures were also made, as the process of manufacture became steadily cheaper. Many other American firms produced metal furnishings, such as Adrian Cooke of Chicago, Illinois, the New England Toy Company, I. F. Crocker of Valley Falls, Rhode Island, and the Toledo Metal Wheel Company, Ohio. Althof, Bergmann & Co of New York began as toy-importers in 1867 but soon began to advertise toys of their own manufacture, promising their customers that they went to great lengths to avoid all dangerous sharp edges and corners. Their 1874 catalogue shows pieces of an almost French Empire style, though some of their chests with painted decoration look very typically American. Among some of the more interesting furniture made in the early twentieth century was that produced by the Arcade Manufacturing Company of Illinois, who were producing cast-iron pieces and providing cardboard backgrounds and actual houses in which these items could be effectively displayed.

The rapid growth of the tin and metal toy industry was not matched by any great interest in the manufacture of wooden furniture, presumably because these small pieces were imported quite cheaply from Germany, as were most of the glass and china accessories which give such realism to the interiors of nineteenth-century houses. Despite the fact that miniature porcelain and earthenware were not made on any really large scale in America during the nineteenth century, there was a considerable production of both pressed and blown glass, and almost all these glasshouses created some smaller pieces, including some of doll's house size. This industry was one of the earliest to be established by the colonists, though the greatest expansion of manufacture took place between 1890 and 1900 when it increased by 52 per cent. The glasshouses were situated mainly in New Jersey, Vermont, New York and Pennsylvania, and it is thought that a few miniatures were produced from each of these areas. In particular, the Boston and Sandwich Glass Company produced decanters, pitchers, plates and candlesticks. Many of the most effective miniatures were made of pressed glass, though this technique was not very suitable for the smaller-scale pieces, and the majority of attributable examples, such as a punch-set, were made in the toy rather than doll's house size. It is often very difficult to decide whether pieces are of American or European origin as, in the creation of such small items, much of the design detail that usually characterizes the work of particular firms was lost, and we are left with the most basic of glassmakers' forms. Many of these cheaper toy pieces, to be purchased at fairs or from travelling salesmen, were made in Pennsylvania, where child employment in the glasshouses was a matter of concern as late as 1914 when it was felt that 'No other industry except the textile gathers so many children into its crater of death. Every motion is hurried; every boy is a darting automaton in his little rat-race of service. No halting, no lagging, no resting. Nothing waits.' The labour of small boys was chosen in preference to that of their fathers, as it could be bought so much more cheaply, but the result was that whole families were consequently dragged into the towns to be shamefully dependent on their employed children.

The commercial manufacture of dolls' houses, like that of furniture, was slow to become established, though many small local carpenters probably attained some skill in the manufacture of individual pieces for special orders. The number of actual surviving houses increases after 1870, and it is obvious that, because of their more settled life-style, many fathers were concerned to provide their daughters with a large and impressive toy. Regional architecture in America differs much more strongly, in both building materials and design, than, for instance, that of Britain, and it is therefore frequently possible for acquisitions to be attributed to individual states in a way that is quite impossible in European countries.

The Essex Institute, Salem, displays one of the few recorded mid-nineteenth-century American dolls' houses, which was commissioned by Annie Crowninshield Warren for her daughter in 1852. The model was made by a Salem cabinet-maker and, like some of the houses earlier, discussed, is one that an adult obviously enjoyed furnishing. With its tall, rather narrow rooms and gabled roof, something of the atmosphere of the Nuremberg cabinets is

given, though obviously the construction is much simpler. In common with many British dolls' houses of the first half of the century, the front door originally carried a brass plate on which was engraved the occupant's name, in this case 'Warren'. The interior is very simply arranged, with two rooms on each of the three floors; in the lower hall a staircase rises to ceiling level only. Among the furnishings of particular importance is a Pembroke table in the dining-room that is believed to have been captured from a British ship during the Revolutionary War of 1812. Mrs Warren and her four daughters obviously expended a great deal of time on the soft furnishings and linen, particularly on the sheets, pillowcases and table-napkins, which all carry well-embroidered monograms. Of particular charm are the curtained bookcases on either side of the chimneypiece in the library, which is believed to be a copy of one in the family house on Park Street, Boston, which was demolished in 1876.

Another doll's house constructed in the 1850s is now at the Milan Historical Museum, Ohio, and follows the same tall, narrow, basic plan of the Warren house, though without even a basic suggestion of a staircase. The detail of the façade is very simply painted, but, rather strangely, the side, less important windows are glazed, thus reversing the more usual convention of painted or printed windows at the sides. Of even greater fascination is the arched attic entrance, which is not even provided with a simple rail to protect the inhabitants from a dreadful fall to ground level past the brick-painted façade.

Doll's house enthusiasts of today frequently find it amusing to create a model in commemoration of some important event either in their own family life or in that of the nation. The Queen's Silver Jubilee inspired a large number of 'Jubilee' houses and cottages which were carefully furnished to mirror exactly the interiors of the year. Few European houses in the nineteenth century were constructed with comparable dedication, and the most one discovers is perhaps a 'Vittoria' cottage, commemorating the famous battle, or a rather stiffly titled 'Albert House'. American collections are, in comparison, much better endowed, though again it is wars rather than periods of tranquillity that seem to have inspired miniature building. In 1864 a particularly large model was constructed for display at the Philadelphia Sanitary Fair, where funds were being raised for the help of wounded Civil War soldiers. Dolls' houses were quite a feature at this fair, where, in the Children's Department, a whole row occupied one wall. Several stands in this section were kept supplied for the three weeks of the exhibition by G. A. Schwartz, who daily replenished the playthings which sold so quickly. The

This house was commissioned in 1852 by Annie Crowninshield Warren for her four daughters. It was made by Israel Fellows, a Salem cabinet-maker. Height 72 inches.

457

A house made for display at the Philadelphia Sanitary Fair. A silver nameplate on the door reads 'General Grant', and a date '1776' is carried on the fanlight. Note how the front of each room opens for easy viewing.

furnishers of dolls' houses were also able to purchase miniatures from the Bohemian glass-blowers, who contributed half their takings to the organizers.

The most famous house exhibited at the Sanitary Fair can now be viewed in the collection of the Delaware Historical Society. On its door is a silver name-plate that reads 'General Grant. 1776'. A good contemporary description of this model was included in a 'Memorial of the Great Central Fair' written by Charles J. Stille.

In every detail it is perfect, and the value – $1,000, which has been fixed for it –

The interior of the Sanitary Fair house. Of particular interest is the picture gallery with paintings by contemporary Philadelphia artists.

will not be deemed to be too extravagant in view of the amount of labour expended upon its construction and furnishing. Gentlemen who stand A.Number 1 in their respective departments were selected to build and furnish this miniature mansion. When we state that the marble chimney-piece in the parlour required three days of constant labour to bring it to its present perfect form, some idea may be gathered of the care bestowed on the building. An Italian artist performed the work. A placard informs visitors that the following gentlemen were concerned in the erection of the house:– Architects – Collis & Audenried, Builder – Michael Errickson, Marblework – E. Greble, Papering – Howell & Brothers, Painting – R. W.

Pegley, Arranging curtains – W. J. Ray, Divan, awnings and upholstery – W. H. Patton, Extension tables, bookcase and library – by Hochley.

This model has the assurance of a house that was designed expressly for exhibition, and each room has a complete wall that opens to reveal the contents, rather in the manner of the Uppark Baby House in Britain. The accommodation, divided into three storeys, is furnished with the substantial pieces so typical of the mid-nineteenth century such as a splendid round ottoman or 'conversation' which stands in the picture gallery. The Art Gallery was considered by Stille to be the crowning feature of the model, and he informs his readers that none of the paintings were more than five inches by three, and some even smaller, yet each would command a large sum of money as they were all the work of respected artists. At the door of the Art Gallery a catalogue of the exhibition of paintings could be seen, a catalogue whose title page and entries were of perfectly correct miniature proportion. Similar small-scale books could be seen in the library.

This model, which was contributed to the Fair by Miss Biddle, eventually brought $2,300 into the fund, while another doll's house, apparently of faultless proportions and finished with the same exquisite taste, presented by a Miss Wurts, was sold for $800. This doll's house sounds quite a dangerous toy as it was supplied with miniature gas fittings and lit to create a really eye-catching effect.

The Civil War years seem to have encouraged doll's house building, even among the soldiers themselves, such as the group of Connecticut volunteers who made a simple model while they were held prisoner by the Confederate army. Provisions were sent to the men by General Glover in wooden boxes which provided the basic material for the toy that they made as a present for his daughter, Deborah Anna. The model, though simple, was given extra appeal by the carved spray of flowers on the tympanum. A rather more elegant house was also made at the same time by a Confederate prisoner in a Federal prison, and as it was given as a gift to his own daughter, it has remained to the present time in the hands of the same family.

Dolls' houses such as those made during the Civil War were equipped with home-made or local craftsman-made furniture if the scale of imported German pieces was not suitable. Slowly, American manufacturers began to take an interest in wooden as well as metal furniture, though the output was never to rival that of Germany. The most interesting company to construct wooden miniatures was the Tower Guild of Hingham, Massachusetts, originally established as a co-operative venture in the late 1830s. Several craftsmen in various fields combined their work so that a good assortment of pieces could be offered to the public. The guild was founded by William S. Towers and initially traded under the name of 'the Tower Shop', later changed to the Tower Toy Company. William S. Towers was a carpenter who,

460

A group of characteristically well made furniture constructed by members of the Tower Guild of Hingham.

like many craftsmen of the period, made toys as a sideline. He saw the potential advantages of pooling the production of several Hingham workers, such as Jacob, Cushing, Litchfield and Wilder, until, at the highest period of the firm's success, some thirty local men were working for the Tower Toy Company. Joseph Jacob, one of the original founders, was mainly a hatchet-maker but made toy tools and novelty items as an interesting sideline, much as cabinet-makers created miniature chairs and bureaux. American toy-historians consider it likely that the organization of the guild was extremely fluid and that members contributed work when so inclined. Loring Cushing, one of the better-known members, joined in 1861, though it appears that his main production was of pieces in doll rather than doll's house size, including, in particular, dolls' beds and cradles. Cushing's name has been found on the label of a simple hooded cradle, and his own granddaughter was given a 10-inch bureau with four drawers. She remembered seeing the toy-makers at work in the shop, suggesting that the venture was not concerned entirely with marketing but that the men also occasionally worked together in almost Brotherhood style. Samuel Hersey was another founder member, and, in *American Dolls' Houses*, F. G. Jacobs illustrates a small card-table that carries his personal label. His apparent period of activity was between 1835 and 1880, and it seems probable that he supplied some pieces to his brother Caleb, who ran a retail toyshop in the 1860s.

Any item made by this interesting craftsmen's venture, so reminiscent of the later Arts and Crafts movement in Britain, is very highly collectable, while marked items are absolute treasures, as so few American toys of the period are fully attributable. Daniel Litchfield made some of the finest pieces, such as carved grandfather clocks with working watches set into the faces so that they appeared to work realistically, a device often used by Swiss makers of miniatures. Good-quality items were also made by Ralph T. Jones, whose Colonial-style doll's house furniture was praised in magazines such as *House Beautiful* in 1915.

During the Guild's most active period, from around 1855–85, their work was exhibited at events such as the 1878 Exposition Universelle in Paris. The painstaking work was highly regarded by the Minister of Commerce, though he saw little competition for French producers, who made similar items much more cheaply. During the early twentieth century, the Guild was run by the Griswold Company of New York, and it seems possible that, as the local aspect of the firm diminished, the Hingham craftsmen lost interest in an activity which could never have been very highly profitable. No other American-produced furniture of the mid-nineteenth century is of comparable interest to that produced by the Tower Guild, though items occasionally appear with a tradition that associates them with individual makers, and there were also, obviously, a number of small toy workshops that produced some miniatures which are completely unattributable as they are unmarked. The very famous firm of Bliss was established in 1832, but, sadly, there is no existing price-list or catalogue to give any idea of the type of goods produced until the appearance of their very characteristic lithographed paper-on-wood houses and furnishings at the end of the century.

The skill used in the design and construction of American houses varied considerably in the mid-nineteenth century, and examples range from large, heavily built mansions to simple, almost box-like structures with a single room up and down. One of the more splendid dolls' houses was that made for Fanny Hayes, daughter of President Rutherford B. Hayes, in 1878. The house was presented to the child's mother at a Methodist fund-raising fair and is of very special interest as the original maker's name, 'George C. Brown, Baltimore', was discovered during restoration in 1959. The model has a rather curious central tower which gives it great individuality, and it was possibly based on an actual house, as Brown was a carpenter and builder who worked on Saratoga Street.

San Francisco Bay, the Frederick area of Maryland and New Jersey are

A house made for Fanny Hayes, the President's daughter, in 1878. The maker was George C. Brown of Baltimore. The original furnishings are lost, and it now contains antique replacements. Height 57 inches.

among the regions carefully mirrored in doll's house architecture. Many of these houses are constructed with a much greater attention to very fine detail than is found in European houses of the period, and they reflect the way in which the decorative work on the exterior of many American town houses was painstakingly contrived to give eye-catching variety. American architects, in particular, made highly imaginative use of wood and cast iron, both of which offered the designer an unending series of curious combinations of balustrades, pillars, arcades and cupolas, all linked by further intricate sections. One of the most superb examples of an American doll's house in this highly decorative manner is now in the Smithsonian Institution, Washington, and was made in 1876 by Leonard Roth. The highly complex structure, possibly originally intended as some kind of architect's model, is approached by steps, flanked by impressive gas-lamps on tall columns. For many European collectors, this model epitomizes the best of individually made American houses, though lesser followers in the tradition are found in several museums, and the influence can even be seen in end-of-the-century mass-produced models.

The love of ornamentation also seen, for instance, in American-made dolls' prams, which are much more complex than those created in Europe, could not be extended into commercially produced dolls' houses, as the amount of time needed for assembly would have been too great. Instead, manufacturers of ingenuity sought for other methods of creating a lavishly decorated model and saw the tremendous possibilities of fancifully printed paper applied to fairly simple basic shapes. This method of manufacturing houses occurred simultaneously in both America and Europe, and it is not possible at present to know which country was the leader. Both the Germans and the French were fond of this technique for toys such as printed games, forts and constructional pieces, so that its extension into dolls' houses would seem only logical. It is thought probable that some of the American makers obtained their lithographed papers from Germany, though it must be remembered that there were several native printers more than capable of producing them. In fact, so effective were many of the American prints of the period that British firms, for instance, sometimes chose their work in preference to that produced in Germany.

The most famous firm to make extensive use of lithographed paper was R. Bliss, established at Pawtucket, Rhode Island, in 1832 and incorporated in 1873. Their first known range of paper-on-wood houses was introduced in 1889, though they are only recorded in a catalogue that illustrates a

This complex model was made in 1876 by Leonard Roth in a realistic combination of wood and metal. There is a double interior staircase. The model reflects fashionable Philadelphia houses of the period and has the additional feature of gas lights. Height 60 inches.

464

A detailed model (*circa* 1885) that is a copy of a chemist's house that once stood in Oakland. The interior is set out with the realism usually found only in architects' models. Height 22 inches.

Opposite: Possibly the most attractive of all American houses is this model built in 1873 for the daughter of F. Vogel. The amount of precise detail, such as the heads of the muses and the carved ornamentation, is remarkable and reflects the style of other Milwaukee buildings. Height 66 inches.

A paper-on-wood house marked 'R. Bliss' on the front door. Seven of the windows are mica with lace curtains. The top windows are lithographed paper. The hinged front opens to reveal two papered rooms. Made between 1895 and 1907. Height $26\frac{3}{4}$ inches to chimney-top.

collapsible model with the name 'The Fairy Doll's House' lithographed on the pediment. Made up, the model, which had no fronts, measured some 20×12 inches and was described as 'the best 50-cent house in the market'. Basically, the house took the form of a smaller box standing on a larger, which formed the ground floor, both sections being lithographed on the inside in a manner that was to characterize later Bliss models. The main range of lithographed houses was introduced in 1895, before this time the company having made wooden novelty pieces and more useful equipment such as tool chests in both adult and miniature sizes and some more general lithographed toys. The new range, which included stables, shops and cabins, was an instant success, as the bright colours and intricate detail held great appeal for children. The firm's name, R. Bliss, was proudly printed on doors, under gables, on floors and even on interior doors, thus making them instantly identifiable even by a child. The Bliss method of decoration meant that a very complex form could be suggested on models of the most modest size, which made them available to

468

A large lithographed paper house
(1895–1907) marked 'R. Bliss'
on the front of the first-floor door
and just under the peak of the roof.
Two triple and four single mica
windows with lace curtains. The
front hinges, and there are four
papered rooms. Height $25\frac{1}{2}$
inches to point of roof.

a much wider group of children. The usefulness of a doll's house that could be
accommodated in the smallest of homes is self-evident and the firm was
obviously aware of the changes in the social structure which resulted in
working-class families wishing to provide their children with attractive
playthings. Many of the original owners must have treasured these houses,
irrespective of size, as a surprisingly large number have survived, and a few
collectors have found it possible to assemble complete streets showing the
wide range of designs including apartment blocks and fire-stations.

Bliss described the houses in catalogues as 'true to nature in all respects'
and a few years later claimed that they were 'designed and modelled by a
practical architect'. Many toy-makers of the time found it appropriate to make
wild claims regarding both the educational and the artistic value of their
work, as to create mere playthings for a child's delight was obviously felt to be
too frivolous a motivation to appeal to parents. The gay fairytale architecture
which children saw in the models probably stimulated their imagination but

469

A lithographed paper-on-wood cottage (1895–1907) marked 'R. Bliss' on the interior connecting room doors. The downstairs windows and dormers are lithographed. Height $27\frac{3}{4}$ inches to chimney top.

could have held little educational impact, which is probably why they were so loved. One range of small cottages has round-arched trelliswork balconies incorporated in the main gable, while another housed a small tower-room in a completely improbable design. Most of the houses are characterized by metal or lithographed balconies and a wealth of bobbin-turning on pillars. The paper on the front doors was effectively grained; shutters were appropriately slatted and cast-iron verandas represented with even greater abandon than the most imaginative builder of actual houses could have attempted. Windows, complete with neat curtains, were usually printed, but at other times isinglass with lace curtains was substituted. The effective dormer sections on the roofs were not, as might be supposed, invariably made of wood, as the scale was sometimes so small that cardboard was much more suitable. Access was obtained to the rooms from either the front or the sides, and many stand on lithographed stone or brick bases, sometimes with wooden steps rising to the main door.

A lithographed paper-on-wood cottage, *circa* 1895–1907. It has two storeys with an attic, foundation, veranda and balcony. There are four single and two triple mica windows. The hinged sides open to reveal four papered rooms. The house is marked 'R. Bliss' on two doors and under the eaves on each side of the house. Height $29\frac{1}{4}$ inches to chimney top.

The imaginative efforts of the Bliss designers could not be restrained by the form of a basic house, and warehouses, shops, stables, mansions and blocks of flats were all made in this improbable style. Some of the models measure as little as 5×11 inches and are obviously popular with collectors as they can be displayed in a small cabinet. The number that have survived serves to commend the basic strength of the construction, which was alluded to in advertisements, where Bliss claimed to use only well-seasoned lumber that would not split. Their own splendidly made houses were compared proudly with imported models that were 'unsatisfactory in every way' as they soon warped and cracked. Bliss designers aimed to produce dolls' houses that would exactly 'suit the taste of American children', though in fact the models are so colourful and alive with pattern that they would have delighted almost any child, past or present.

Despite the proliferation of detail on the exteriors, the opened houses were slightly disappointing, as there was often only a single room up and down,

471

whereas the viewer would have expected an abundance of small rooms and staircases to match the printed detail. At first, the simple interiors, obviously designed with the careless hands of children in mind, were lithographed. Wallpapers, fireplaces, doors and windows were all firmly printed in position, making it necessary for the parent to provide only a minimal amount of furniture to create an effective interior. Later, ordinary wallpapers were substituted for the lithography, which obviously gives these models less appeal. The various designs were described in catalogues as 'elegant suburban residences or Modern City Residences', and the 1901 edition describes a twelve-storey skyscraper that stood only 5 × 17 inches and cost a mere 10 cents. Not all Bliss houses are marked, and unmarked pieces have to be attributed by catalogue comparison or with other, marked, attributable examples.

The firm's 1911 catalogue is of especial interest, as it featured folding houses, for which a patent had been applied. 'The line of folding doll houses that we are now offering will commend themselves at first glance to the buyer. They are made of heavy board, strongly hinged with cloth and made so simple and yet so rigid that they will stand more rough handling than the regular doll house. For people living in close quarters they are especially adapted, as they can be taken apart in less than one minute and packed in one quarter the space of the corresponding size of a regular doll house.' The design was obviously much less successful than the basic houses, as examples are very rare.

One of the finest collections of Bliss houses can be found in the Margaret Woodbury Strong Museum, Rochester, New York, where examples range from a $28\frac{1}{2}$-inch house with a romantic tower window in the bedroom and all the usual turned pillars, to a much simpler, $11\frac{1}{2}$-inch house with an almost completely flat façade, much more closely resembling the French houses of the period but clearly marked 'R. Bliss' above the door. The tower house was described in the 1901 catalogue as an unequalled doll mansion: 'Of all the attempts made in the designing and construction of dolls' houses, this house is the result of the most successful. A perfect beauty admired by both old and young. Many are the little girls who will become the happy possessors of one of these elegant homes for their dollies. Packed and set up in a good substantial box.' The Woodbury Strong Museum is an Aladdin's Cave for collectors of toys, as Mrs Strong left the museum some 300,000 uncatalogued items, including many dolls' houses, and when the very precise documentation is completed, the collection should be without parallel for the study of American toys.

Despite the fact that wooden furnishings had not previously formed an important section of the toy industry, Bliss found it appropriate to supply their fine houses with similarly decorated pieces. The basic designs of the rather limited range were quite simple but made attractive with the characteristic

A bedroom set attributed to Bliss and decorated with pictures of children playing at the seaside. The designs are coloured in shades of blue and highlighted with strong purple and gold tones with a pink stippled background. There is a lack of scale in the set as the bed is $8\frac{1}{2}$ inches long and out of proportion to the rest of the pieces.

Bliss lithography. These designs have little of the elegance seen in the house construction, with their towering gables and long, slim shapes, and some of the chairs are almost stunted, with thick turned legs and over-large backs and seats. Like many nineteenth-century games, these sets relied on their well-decorated boxes for much of their sales appeal, which showed idealized children playing neatly with their Bliss houses and furniture. The parlour or bedroom sets were attractively set out with gold and blue paper and must have provided a most delightful gift. The parlour set contained a small table, four dining-chairs, an upright sofa and a small family piano, all brilliantly coloured. The broad, flat areas on the backs and seats provided an ideal surface for the application of the Bliss papers, so that a footstool, which is also contained in the parlour set, really required only four bobbin-turned legs and a sheet of lithography to give a much more substantial effect. The printed designs range from prettily dressed children to the letters of the alphabet, popularly known as 'ABC furniture', which appears to have been introduced in 1901. It was originally described as 'adorned with beautiful lithographs

473

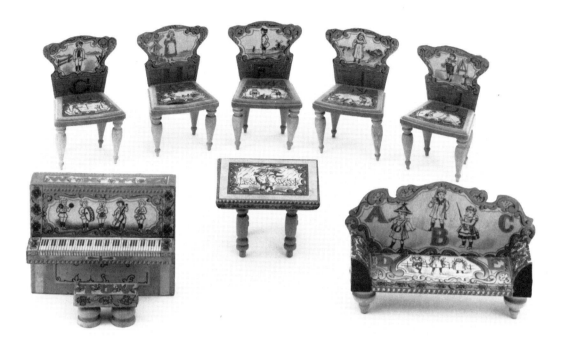

A set of Bliss-type alphabet living-room furniture that was sold as a unit. The letters, design and colour are all similar. The piano, sofa and stool are in inch-to-the-foot scale, while the table and chairs are in one-and-three-quarter-inch scale. Attributed to Bliss, *circa* 1897–1907.

and embellished with bronze'. The company registered patents for doll's house furniture from 1888, and it would appear that, almost from the first, the houses could be fitted by the company. Neither the alphabet nor the furniture decorated with children's heads seems to fit particularly well into the supposedly realistic houses, though the parlour pieces with square, late-Victorian shapes and the roll-armed sofa perhaps best suit the Bliss interiors. A boxed set of Bliss furniture is a collector's prize, and many would be content with just a few odd pieces to represent the work of this most popular company.

In 1907 the firm became associated with the Hardware and Woodenware Manufacturing Company of New York City, a co-operative sales organization, in effect a much more sophisticated version of the old Tower Guild. The membership included many of the leading toy-makers, and in the 1907 statement the Bliss sales totalled nearly $204,000, giving them the highest record for the year. It is interesting to note that the company did not only supply the home market but also exported work, a percentage being sent to

474

A small unmarked lithograph-on-wood house (*circa* 1916) with wooden pillars and base. The front is hinged and opens to reveal two rooms. Height 10¼ inches.

Britain. In 1914 the R. Bliss Manufacturing Company was taken over by Manson & Parker of Winchendon, Massachusetts, who continued to produce many of the traditional Bliss lines for some years.

Despite the attempts made by firms such as Bliss to export their toys, few could have competed with the very low-priced items that poured across Europe from Germany and, to a lesser extent, from France. A British journalist visiting New York in 1888 was overwhelmed by the high prices asked in the shops on Twenty-Third Street. She first visited a large and enticing toyshop where she found the high prices astounding: 'Tiny dressed dolls that in Regent Street would be 2 shillings are from 4 shillings upwards; a diminutive *couvre pied* for a doll's perambulator, 12 to 14 inches of plain woolwork, is 4 shillings; a doll's china tea-set of common pattern is 8 shillings, yet, even at these prices, there is no lack of purchasers.' These comparatively high prices were caused by a combination of higher wages and import costs, as a very high percentage of toys was still obtained from abroad, well into the twentieth

A lithograph-on-wood house made by Converse of Winchendon, Mass., *circa* 1913. It has wooden front steps, porch and pillars, roof and chimney. A boy in a sailor suit can be seen peering through the front door, and a cat and an old woman are pictured in the attic. The hinged front opens to reveal two rooms. Height $26\frac{3}{4}$ inches.

century. In 1909 the Bureau of Statistics of the Department of Commerce and Labour stated that over half the toys sold in America were of foreign origin, the value of imported toys reaching their peak in 1908. Something of a decline was begun in 1909, probably because of a substantial increase in capital investment in the industry, combined with a general depression of trade. Despite the high import levels, the marketing energy shown by firms such as Bliss was beginning to have an effect, and it was in the fields of metal and wooden toys that the development rate became most noticeable. The most important overseas markets for American toys were Great Britain, Canada, Australia and New Zealand, though, surprisingly, there were some exports even to Germany. The success of these ambitious firms depended on their way of adapting the old, cumbersome methods of creating toys into simplified yet attractive designs. Of particular interest among these progressive companies is the name of Morton E. Converse, who is said to have made Winchendon, Massachusetts, into 'the Nuremberg of America' and

This cottage (*circa* 1913) is one of the more basic of Converse structures. The hinged front opens to reveal a single room. Height $7\frac{1}{2}$ inches.

who included dolls' houses among his wide range of toys.

The early houses made by Converse were very economically lithographed directly onto the wood itself, so that a complete contrast in manufacturing method to that of Bliss is provided. The actual designs are also considerably more restrained and yet have all the charm that printed detail makes possible, such as a cat that sits staring out from an attic window in perpetuity, while two ladies peer at the world from their printed environment. The Converse decoration is at times almost austere and is reminiscent of the patterns seen on many nineteenth-century Noah's Arks of German origin, this similarity being even more noticeable in the stock-farms that the firm also produced.

The history of the company is very typical of the personal enterprise that characterized so many American undertakings of the nineteenth century. It was established by Morton E. Converse in 1878 for the manufacture of wooden strawberry- and fig-boxes but was diverted into simple toys after he had amused his sick daughter by making her a doll's tea-table from an old collar-box. His original commercial idea was for a collar-box containing four legs that could be used for its conversion into a doll's table, and towards this end a wooden tea-set was also to be included in the pack. It is not known whether this idea was particularly successful, but it served to give him inspiration for other children's toys in such number that his company eventually dominated Winchendon. The firm's name was changed several times from Mason & Converse before 1883 to Converse Wood and Toy Company in that year. There were several further changes before it became Morton E. Converse & Son in 1905.

The basic Converse house was extremely simple, composed of two columns, a veranda and windows that were printed on the hinged front. There are no balconies or eaves, and the most basic of bungalow-type homes of the period are represented. Printed furnishings give the interior colour, such as a chimneypiece with a blazing fire and a neat mantelpiece with a vase precisely positioned on either side. The effect is completed by a conventional picture that hangs over the fire, which would give even the poorest child an immediate point of identification with her own home. In many examples, the maker's name was printed on the border of the carpet that also formed part of the original design. These bungalows were described by Converse as 'perfect models, printed on wood by our new three-colour process'.

A few houses with a first floor and an attic (with a curious cat, tail erect, ready to spring at the world) were also made, though the bungalows are much more frequently found. These very basic structures could be obtained in five sizes, ranging from 9 to 17 inches. Flora Gill Jacobs discusses the similarities between Converse printed houses and those of Cass of Athol, Massachusetts, and points out that in later catalogues of both companies the same names appear, suggesting a considerable exchange of merchandise. Doll's house furniture was also provided for Converse houses and made its first recorded appearance in their 1885–6 catalogue, though it could not have enjoyed a great success as I know of no authenticated actual examples.

The Converse bungalow continued to be made for some twenty-five years with virtually no change, except for the substitution of square-sided pillars for the round ones by 1926. The stucco-finished houses, so popular in Britain, were among a few new designs, but their next notable invention was the 'Realy Truly Doll House' (*sic*), introduced in 1931, which was made of fibreboard and wood. The design was very typical of suburban architecture of the period but given a Georgian-style door and shuttered bow windows. The child could furnish the house with pieces from the Realy Truly range made of 'beautiful mahogany woods, gum and walnut'. This furniture must have been among the last toys produced by Converse, as the company ceased trading shortly after this time.

Though the basic Converse houses have a place in most American collections, the exotic, brightly coloured creations of McLoughlin have a much more international appeal, as they are so representative of the more attractive aspects of upper-middle-class life around the turn of the century. The McLoughlin company was already well established before their famous model house was offered to the public in 1896. According to an article in *Playthings* in 1905, J. McLoughlin had taken his brother Edward into partnership to establish the company in 1855. Previously, J. McLoughlin had worked for R. H. Elton & Co, and the new company is considered to have been a successor to this firm. The McClintocks, in their researches, commented that, as John McLoughlin was a printer by trade, he was naturally interested in developing this side of the concern, and certainly the work on the dolls' houses is characterized by its fine printing.

Marian Howard, a researcher on paper toys, described a McLoughlin house in an 1875–6 catalogue issued by the firm that was made in imitation brick and supplied with printed carpets and wall-coverings. This model was basically of the folding type and packed flat into a box with directions for assembly. The model was produced for over ten years, though unfortunately there are no surviving examples, and the majority of collectors associate the company with the simply-made folding house in which two lengths of card are slotted together to form an open-sided four-roomed apartment, a model that was first produced in January 1894 by a Baltimore woman. The rooms provide a wealth of information on the style of interior decoration, such as the use of a patterned border above the picture-rail and the disposition of furniture. In many actual dolls' houses, with three-dimensional furniture, this precise detail is lost, as each owner re-arranges the model, and new pieces are continually added. Here, in rich colour and adequate detail, can be seen the proper settings for the richly dressed ladies of the period, though a well-designed kitchen was also provided for complete realism. The advertisement claimed that the house was meant to be played with at a table so that a number of little girls could get around it to the best advantage. A dining-room, parlour, kitchen and bedroom were represented, and it was designed to be furnished with paper or other small-scale furniture and to be occupied by paper or small dolls. The 1896 catalogue described the model as 'new', and two richly dressed little girls were shown playing contentedly at a heavily carved table.

'Dolly's Play House' again exhibits the opulent interiors so loved by McLoughlin, but in this more conventional structure, a one-up and one-down plan without a front was followed. The effect was neatened by a decorated arched border. This model appeared on the market in 1903 and was a particularly ingenious construction as the parts were hinged together, lifted into position and retained by a wooden-backed cornice that slotted into place at the front. The parlour, with a tall, rococo mirror over the elegant chimneypiece and French-style panelled walls is of the most impressive appearance. The floor is equally lavish, with its expensive printed carpet, which is engagingly reflected in paler tones on the ceiling. The furnishing of the upper room is more restrained, and it could have served either as a lady's room or as a bedroom, as the pieces are less specific in intention. The interior of the house was shown in full splendour on the McLoughlin box cover, and there can be few European collectors who do not yearn for an example of one of these most successful of folding houses.

McLoughlin introduced another folding house, of completely different appearance, in 1903, in which they abandoned the tall, narrow line and developed a long and fairly low shape. The device of using pillars with a connecting arch to frame the two narrow rooms was again used, but the new house could also be closed. The front was hinged at ground level, and a long windowed house with a veranda was portrayed. When the front was lowered, the inside formed a neat garden. McLoughlin's advertising was as exaggerated as that of many German firms of the period, as the box lid showed a building of quite different construction in a symmetrical style.

Like Bliss houses, those made by McLoughlin are usually marked, so there is little problem in attribution. So perfect were many of the interiors that it is difficult to understand how even the most imaginative of children could have felt that their frequently out-of-scale furniture was satisfactory, and it is surprising that folding or cut-out pieces in the same style were not made.

The concept of a folding doll's house had an obvious appeal, and several patents were registered, such as that filed by Emily S. Russel of Plymouth, Massachusetts, in 1868. This involved 'a toy house made of two thin sheets of material secured together, the outer sheet having swinging doors and blinds concealing and disclosing representations of apartments on the inner sheet. The space between the sheets being adapted to the movement of a paper doll.' This construction was assembled by the designer and commercially printed by G. W. Cottrell of Boston. On the back wall are verses which tell the story of the cottage. Another maker of folding houses was Stirn & Lyon of New York, though their work was of a much heavier form, as the detail of the surface was pressure-printed on wood, and the sections were joined by dowel and tongued and grooved joints. Grimm & Leeds of New Jersey also produced a house packed in a box, with two rooms up and down and isinglass windows. In 1894 Montgomery Ward described a paper house that was printed in bright colours on 'extra quality board', and in 1909 another manufacturer brought out a wide range of folding houses that included hotels, bungalows and 'other handsome residences'.

Folding houses of American manufacture were also imported into Britain, though it is now extremely difficult to locate even a solitary example. The main importer was W. E. Peck & Co, who in June 1913 offered 'Betty's Bungalow', a house with a living-room and bedroom that was copyrighted in 1905 by the Bungalow Book and Toy Company of New York. This folding model was much larger than the usual houses of the type and was brightly coloured. When packed, it was only half an inch thick, but it could be opened into a two-storey house with chimney, fireplace, furniture and lawn enclosed by a hedge. The model was available in two styles, either with a living-room and bedroom or with a kitchen and bedroom. No glue was necessary for the assembly. This model, referred to in *The Toy Trader*, is of particular interest, as it was supplied complete with sheets of printed folding furniture and seems to be a logical development of, for instance, the McLoughlin houses.

'Letty Lane's house' of heavy-coated cardboard was also provided with its own furniture, which was printed on heavy board ready for cutting out. The

A two-roomed lithograph-on-wood house known as a 'Combination Doll House'. The box serves as a foundation for the house. Made by Stirn and Lyon, New York, *circa* 1881. Height $22\frac{7}{8}$ inches.

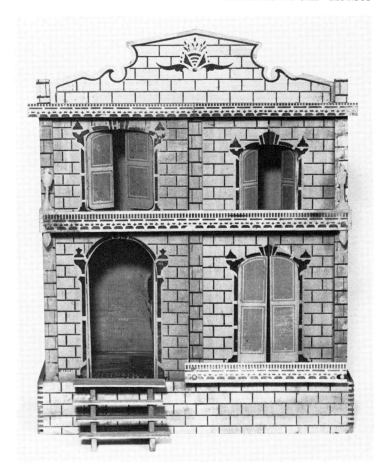

doll, of German bisque, known as 'Letty Lane', was sent with the house as a promotion for the *Ladies' Home Journal* between 1912 and 1913. The child received these gifts in return for three new yearly subscriptions and was encouraged in her efforts to obtain new readers by advertising of the most alluring type such as 'Every room is ready for doll housekeeping. Its little mistress bids you welcome.' Schoenhut in the 1930s added to their substantial list of toys 'toy apartment house rooms' that were hinged together for ease in storage.

The Schoenhut family had originated in Württemberg, where several generations had worked as toy-makers and carvers, so that the traditional skills of the German folk-type manufacturers were at their fingertips. At seventeen, Albert emigrated to America and in 1872 at the age of twenty-two, founded his own company. The original production was mainly of toy musical instruments, though the company is best known for the Humpty Dumpty Circus that was introduced in 1903. The first dolls' houses appear to

481

A simple Schoenhut cottage (*circa* 1918–25) painted grey to resemble stone. The hinged sides open to reveal two rooms which are represented by lithographed paper on wood. Marked 'A. Schoenhut Co.' on right side. Height 17 inches.

date from 1917 when 'attractive high-class dolls' houses, new styles and Modern Architecture' are mentioned in their catalogue. The wording seems to suggest that a series of more traditionally built houses was also available, but until an earlier catalogue is located, this can only be conjecture. The new houses were made of fibreboard and wood, to prevent warping, and were embossed to resemble stone walls and roofing-tiles. The construction method was obviously a feature of some importance, as a whole line of dolls' houses made in this new way was promised. Schoenhut informed his readers that these models would be less expensive than imported houses and would also be 'stronger, more beautiful and durable'. All were side-opening, so that the appearance of the front of the house was not spoiled during play, and, it was claimed, this method also gave the children easier access.

The interiors of the houses are reminiscent of the technique used by Bliss, as the walls were covered with lithographs to represent fancy wallpapers. There were no opening interconnecting doors, as these were simply printed in position to reveal 'a perspective view of another room inside of the doorway frame, producing the illusion of a house full of fine rooms'. Even the smallest Schoenhut houses give an illusion of space, as the child could see into non-existent rooms through cleverly half-opened doors. Like Bliss houses, these were made in a variety of sizes, the largest mansion containing eight rooms. Bungalows varied from a simple one-roomed model to another with four.

A very neat cottage made by Schoenhut between 1918 and 1925. The wood is painted grey to represent stone. The hinged side opens to reveal eight rooms. The interiors are represented by lithographed paper on wood. It has the original set of red painted living-room furniture. Marked 'A. Schoenhut Co.' on left side of house.

These were really more in the nature of small cottages with dormer windows and turned pillars on the verandas, which give them more charm than the Colonial-style bungalows that were so popular at the time. Both the houses and the bungalows stood on low bases that were embossed to resemble rough stone, and the roof section hinged upwards on a metal stay. Though of much less immediate appeal than the Bliss houses, the Schoenhuts have their place in any representative collection, as the device of the perspective rooms is so idiosyncratic. The models continued to be produced for several years, and it was not until the 1927 catalogue that another great change of structure is seen. To the collector, the advances of the 1920s were depressing, as the decorative styles were abandoned and a much more functional idiom moved to the foreground, with little of the Victorian charm that was still evident in the 1917 catalogue. The beguiling perspective interiors were dispensed with and very basic wallpapers substituted. Though the new styles included windowboxes and shutters, they could not compete with the attractiveness of the older versions. They were in new 'Colonial style' with mock fanlights over the doors and the conventional shutters on all the windows. The two-storey models and bungalows were provided with a garden containing a shrubbery and trees as well as a garage. A special car could be provided at a small extra cost. If required, Schoenhut could also supply the especially made furniture, a line that was begun in 1928.

The interest of the Schoenhut company extended far beyond dolls' houses into the area of the constructional toys that were always claimed to aid a child's development. The educational theme was of paramount importance in toy-advertising after 1900, Charles M. Crandall having begun the fashion for

Waxed compositions of doll's house size are comparatively rare, making this family of six something of a treasure. They all wear original costumes and have glass eyes and mohair wigs. Probably German, *circa* 1885. The adults are 19 centimetres high.

dolls' houses of the type in 1867, when he suggested that his building-bricks could be used in the construction of accurate models such as one in high Gothick style. A log cabin construction-toy carries the label of French & Wheat of Ann Street, New York City, who worked between 1859 and 1866, suggesting that interest in such models was well founded even before it became fashionable advertising-copy. A few houses were themselves produced as an advertising device, such as that made in the 1890s by 'Durnham's Cocoanut' – in fact, just the crate in which the product was contained. The inside walls were papered to represent interiors, and in return for tokens pieces of furniture could be obtained.

Few American companies made doll's house inhabitants, as the German imports were of such a high standard and sold so cheaply that competition was pointless. As in Britain, there were some producers of fabric and celluloid figures on a fairly limited scale in the early twentieth century, but most children relied on the imports of firms such as Schwartz, from whose shelves complete families of well-made figures could be purchased. Several small all-bisques were made in Germany to specific American designs, but the stiff shapes of most of these dolls made them unsuitable as doll's house

484

Bisque shoulder-headed dolls of German manufacture. *Above left:* A doll's house man (*circa* 1890) with blue painted eyes, moulded brown hair, handlebar moustache and goatee beard. The hands and feet are bisque. Original woollen costume. Height $7\frac{1}{8}$ inches. *Above right:* An elderly gentleman (*circa* 1900) wearing the original black suit. He has blue painted eyes and grey hair and beard. The body is fabric with bisque arms and feet. Height $7\frac{1}{2}$ inches. *Below left:* A lady (*circa* 1890) with painted eyes and a blonde mohair wig, wearing the original silk-painted dress. Height $6\frac{3}{4}$ inches. *Below right:* A lady (*circa* 1920) with brown glass eyes and a closed mouth. Bisque lower arms and legs, stuffed fabric body, moulded white shoes; wearing the original cotton frock. Height $6\frac{3}{4}$ inches.

Betty Bonnet's Household Servants

By Sheila Young

NOTE—If the whole page is mounted on muslin or linen before the figures are cut out the different parts will last longer and the tabs will not tear so easily. By pasting an inch-wide strip of cardboard at the waistline, slightly bent to form an easel, the doll can be made to stand.

Paper dolls made ideal doll's house inhabitants. This example from the *Ladies' Home Journal* was published in 1918 and gives an exact picture of the costumes of servants in a rich American household.

A set of doll's house dolls representing an American family from infants to grandparents. Designed by Grace Story Putnam around 1945 but not produced commercially. They have unusual realism for doll's house figures.

This most complex house carries a silver shield on the front door: "Doomville House Built in 1899 by Percy Doomville for his daughter Mary Percy." Mary was only three when the house was built. With its twelve rooms and height of 46 inches, it must have overwhelmed such a small child. *Opposite:* Another view of the Canadian house built by Percy Doomville. All the original furnishings have been lost, but it was refurbished by the original owner before she presented it to the museum in 1968. It is some 70 inches wide when opened.

inhabitants. One interesting exception lies in the figures designed by Grace Story Putnam, designer of the world-famous 'Bye-lo Baby', who, just before the Second World War, designed an American family of dolls showing all ages from infant to grandparent. These dolls were exhibited in California, but it appears that they were never produced commercially. Today a large number of dedicated enthusiasts create a large range of doll's house inhabitants in a variety of materials that represent all sorts of characters, and America has moved from offering the smallest selection of home-produced dolls to having a much larger selection than any seen in Europe.

A large number of very basic dolls' houses were produced both by local carpenters and by small companies in the early twentieth century, but, like the majority of those made in Britain, they are frequently of much too basic and uninteresting a construction to be of any lasting interest to collectors,

though individual pieces of merit do sometimes appear. These cheap, substantial houses, which were available to a wide range of children, probably made ideal toys, as they could be handled roughly and redecorated at will. Those models that hit the headlines were of the grandest type, such as one mentioned in the *Winnipeg Tribune* in 1909. This article listed the many presents bought by a Western man and paid particular attention to a doll's house which, owing to its vast size, had to be taken to the nursery of his mansion in sections and fitted together again there. The reporter described it as 'a wonderful affair' with its garage that contained two cars, and stables with a finely modelled carriage and pair. The house was a six-roomed model and was occupied by a lady, gentleman and servant, each provided with a complete wardrobe. The lady of the house had twelve different changes of clothes and must surely have been among the best-equipped doll's house inhabitants ever made.

Though the structure of this house, made around 1900 for Elizabeth Jennings of Fairfield, is simple, the contents, well set off by the original wallpapers, give the piece great interest. The carpets and curtains were made by her mother. The furniture is mainly commercial and of German origin. Height 32 inches.

While the wealthiest of children played with houses of such extravagance that they were reported in British newspapers, a vast army of exploited and unhappy boys and girls slaved throughout the year on the production and packaging of such items. Small girls were particularly welcome in the gift-box factories as they were 'good workers who asked for nothing and objected to nothing. They do not complain when their fingers are caught and crushed in the machines . . . they are quick to go to the hospital with their bloody fingers, anxious not to offend the overseer with any bloodstains on the boxes.' These uncomplaining little girls were perfect food for the profitmongers, as they were so content with the station in life to which they believed God had called them, complained the authors of *Children in Bondage*. There must be long preparation for 'the bulging paper sack and the swollen tarlatan bag of the Christmas Tree, for the bottle of striated sticks and the pudgy sucker . . . one

490

band of little children wasting their bodies and souls to make a little joy for the rest. That lovely heart-shaped box, wreathed with holly and marked "All Christmas Joys be Thine", came perchance from such tired fingers.'

American children's books and prints of the early twentieth century suggest a much happier life surrounded with an abundance of fine toys. Because the general standard of living had increased so rapidly, many firms were producing toys for children of quite poor parents, but it is very easy to exaggerate general American standards and forget that a large group of the very poorest and most uncared-for were exploited to a much later date in the twentieth century than those in the more socially progressive European countries. Fortunately, much of the old order was changing because of the publicity given to the most terrible conditions, and there was a great levelling out in the variety of toys made for general sale in the years after the First World War. After this time, though toys are less romantic and made with much less attention to detail, they are free of the taint of exploited child labour and made for the enjoyment of the masses. Dolls' houses, because of this basic change, became, in the eyes of collectors, too utilitarian and unadorned to be objects for display, and though they are sometimes included in the most representative settings, they are generally lightly regarded.

During the 1920s dolls' houses became, for a short while, the pre-occupation of fashionable women in both Europe and America. Of those created in the United States, that exhibited in the museum of the City of New York is probably the most famous. This two-storeyed house was the work of Carrie Walter Stettheimer, a member of a fashionable intellectual family that reigned over one of the most highly regarded New York salons. The house is of great interest, as it so closely mirrors the progressive interiors of the period and exudes an atmosphere of extravagant decadence that characterizes a period when new materials were eagerly seized by decorators and when the exact arrangement of a room could mean so much to a fashionable hostess.

Ettie Stettheimer, sister of the creator of the model, presented it to the museum in 1945 and personally supervised the re-arrangement of the rooms. The interior decoration is heavy with the self-conscious daring so evocative of the fun-loving 1920s, which this model perfectly encapsulates. In the introduction to the doll's house that Ettie wrote in 1947, she describes how her sister became fascinated by model houses during the summer of 1916 when the family was staying on Lower Saranac Lake. In connexion with a bazaar that the ladies were organizing, Carrie Stettheimer made a doll's house from some wooden packing-cases that she obtained from a grocer and which she decorated so well that a substantial sum was raised for charity. The concept of creating an effective model from scrap materials used imaginatively is one that has appealed to adults of several generations, and she was to work intermittently on the project throughout the 1920s. Her enthusiasm obviously infected others, as the art gallery, for instance, is hung with

Part of the Stettheimer house, built in the 1920s by Carrie Walter Stettheimer, a model that closely mirrors the adventurous spirit of the period.

These dolls in the idiom of the 1920s were recently constructed to give added zest to the interior of the Stettheimer house.

miniature paintings by some of the leading New York artists, such as Marcel Duchamp. Neither of her sisters was in any way involved with the model, so that the finished work was a complete reflection of her own personality, recreating the life-style of one small group of fashionable society in a way that no mere play-house can approach. Her personal touch is evident in such details as the decoration of the blue and white kitchen that would have pleased the most discriminating adult and which forms a direct contrast with the rather austere work-places that were found in most dolls' houses of this time, when functionalism was taking so much charm away from the traditional and cluttered interiors. The nursery has an adventurous rich black carpet and is colourfully decorated specifically for the needs of active children, who are also supplied with their own gramophone. The library, with its Chinese-style adornments, is also of interest as it indicates the fascination of chinoiserie that has continued among doll's house decorators for several centuries. This room shows the taste in its purely twentieth-century expression, with hanging lanterns of Chinese restaurant type and an assortment of bric-à-brac culled from small gift-shops. Jewelled bonsai trees and bright, lacquered furniture give an effect of great richness, which is augmented by the gilded glass dragons that hang from the walls. The intellectual aspect of Carrie Stettheimer is emphasized by the types of books she chose for her library, including works by Henri Waste and Theodore Dreiser. The master bedroom, in blues and pink, with a grey carpet, is supplied with blue-painted furniture with extravagantly gilded low-relief decoration in the free manner of the period.

As the Stettheimers presided over the most fashionable salon of the period, it is inevitable that great attention should have been lavished on this room in the doll's house, with its walls of cream, gold and white that perfectly complement the soft colours of the needlepoint carpet. The pastoral scenes painted by Albert Sterner give the room further prestige and underline the almost art-cabinet aspect of the undertaking. Sadly, the actual furniture defies description and can only be termed 'Rustic French Empire', a style that accords strangely with the dominating Gothick chimneypiece.

A chimneypiece of Italian Renaissance style dominates the ballroom, which was still incomplete when Carrie died and which was later hung with paintings and drawings to form the art gallery, though this was not her own intention. Many of the paintings are in the most progressive style and help to set this construction quite apart from the basic, conventional models of the time, which are often disappointingly retrospective rather than *avant garde*. Part of the model's appeal lies in its basic realistic planning, as it has rooms on all sides and interesting staircases, including one of the spiral type that leads to the musicians' gallery in the original ballroom. Although rich ladies of the period luxuriated in the most opulent of bathrooms, that in the Stettheimer house is something of a disappointment as it is so completely basic and of the type that could be obtained from ordinary toyshops. A great deal of the general construction is also fairly crude, as is some of the ornamentation, but the completed effect achieves absolute success because of its perfect reflection both of the period and of the character of the people who would have inhabited it.

A doll's house family had formed part of the original plan, and its group portrait was to have occupied a position of importance over the ballroom chimneypiece. This painting was to have been the work of Florine Stettheimer, a set- and costume-designer who, it is thought, also intended to make the actual dolls. Sadly, this original project remained incomplete, though dolls carefully created in the idiom of the 1920s have recently given the model fresh life.

While a few very elegant adults were delighting in the creation of minor

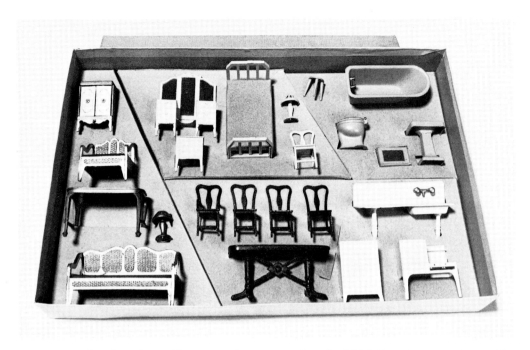

A very complete boxed set of furniture that appeared in the 1933 Tootsietoy catalogue. The pieces are diecast lead or similar metal. The parlour furniture is painted gold with red seats; the bedroom set is pink, the bathroom orchid and the dining-room set walnut. The kitchen is white. Tootsietoy was made by Dowst Manufacturing Co., Chicago.

works of art, their children played with dolls' houses and furniture that were much plainer and which had considerably less charm than those enjoyed by their grandparents in the nineteenth century. The First World War had broken the complete German ascendancy in the toy-industry, and home-produced toys were now readily available. These new factories saw little point in continuing to produce retrospective work, such as had satisfied the German producers, and they deliberately set out to provide American children with wares that exactly mirrored their own homes. Ice-boxes, electric cookers, vacuum cleaners, radios and twin beds replaced the 'Edwardian Renaissance' style as a new and forward-thinking group of designers developed a native industry.

One of the best-known American brand names in doll's house furniture in the 1920s was Tootsietoy, manufactured by Dowst Brothers Co of Chicago, Illinois, which first began to market this particular range in 1923. Their furniture was made completely of metal and carried the advertising slogan, 'All the Strength of Metal. All the Beauty of Wood.' The designs were fairly accurate miniaturizations of full-sized fashionable furniture and were sold in boxed room settings. The first Tootsietoy dolls' houses were made in 1925, and among the most attractive was a 'Spanish Mansion', made of heavy bookboard that cost a very economical $5. Small accessories to give complete

495

Fordham Briggs built his Colonial Revival house in the 1930s, during lunch hours when he was working at the Museum of the City of New York. He gave the house a fashionable Art Deco bedroom.

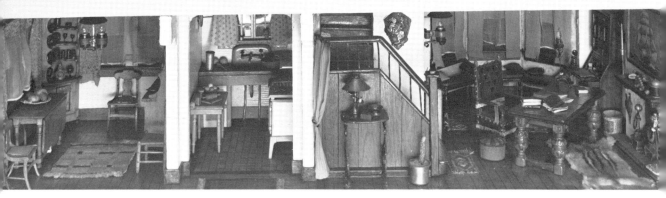

Henry Hammond Taylor, an authority on Colonial furniture, built this house for his granddaughter *circa* 1930. It is a model of unusual realism with mortar between the clapboard and the interior panelling. He made the furniture himself. Height 41 inches.

realism to the interiors were also available in the 1930s, all at very low prices, so that poorer children, who were now forming the mass market, could afford to purchase items themselves from their pocket money.

The very similarly named Tynietoy furniture was first created in 1920 by Marion I. Perkins and Amy Vernon, who both admired Colonial styles and sought to reproduce some of the finest designs in doll's house size. They opened a shop in Providence, Rhode Island, from which 'high post beds, chests of drawers and rush-bottom colonial chairs' were supplied. Although the name of the two companies is so similar, the intention could not have been more diverse, as Tynietoy was attempting to stand back from basic progress and recreate the atmosphere of the past, in suites of Hepplewhite, Sheraton or general Victorian style. Despite the very high-quality finish, sometimes with brass detail, the prices asked were surprisingly low, even when production ceased in 1950. Special reproductions, such as George Washington's bed, were undertaken to order, and at one point some fifty craftsmen were working for the firm. Part of the attractiveness of the furniture lies in its variety, from unpainted wood to highly polished pieces. Metal accessories, such as well-made telephones, were also offered, though it is thought that these were obtained from other suppliers. The dolls' houses, sturdily built in a vaguely Georgian style, were much more expensive, such as a mansion that was more than 6 feet wide and cost $145 in 1930. It contained nine rooms and a pantry, and the rooms were properly finished with cornices and skirting-boards: the music room, in eighteenth-century style, was also provided with a chair-rail. A cheaper range of houses included a cottage and a four-roomed village house, all of which could be furnished attractively but economically. Doll's house dolls of both the cloth-wired and wooden peg type were offered and, though less than realistic, were competition to the traditional German types. In general, the furniture made by Tynietoy is of more interest to collectors than their dolls' houses, as the designs are so varied and the pieces are of such good quality that it is difficult to understand how they could be produced so cheaply.

Collectable metal doll's house furniture was also made in the 1920s and early 1930s by the Arcade Manufacturing Company, Freeport, Illinois, known as 'Arcade'. This company realized the importance of offering children models that were as realistic as possible, and name brands of particular firms were marketed, such as Hotpoint cookers and bathroom fixtures with the Crane label. In order to display the pieces correctly, Arcade manufactured both houses and cardboard backgrounds, a similar idea being used in 1965 by the Ideal Toy Company to display 'Petite Princess Fantasy Furniture'. The 'Dolly Dear' company is also particularly connected with the period between the wars and was founded in 1928 by A. E. Kirkland. A particularly wide range of furnishings was made, though pieces are of less interest than those manufactured by, for instance, Lynnfield. This firm was established in the early 1930s by a woodworker, Chester H. Waite in Lynnfield, Massachusetts. The range of rather basic furniture was redesigned by Henry Messerschmitt, and he eventually took over its manufacture. As the toys were distributed by Block House Inc, the pieces are often referred to as 'Block House furniture'. In the 1940s a range of accessories was added to the furniture that was offered in a variety of finishes from mahogany and fruitwood to painted or light finished. In 1965, the company moved to Colombia, and the name was changed to Andi Imports.

Though the character of dolls' houses and furniture was almost austere in the 1920s and 1930s, this economy of style seems one that was confined mainly to actual children's toys: once an adult becomes involved, the atmosphere changes almost instantly, and buildings of an extravagance not attempted in the nineteenth century are discovered. The Stettheimer model presented a picture of the racy Charleston days when brash colours and abstract art dominated the scene. Other enthusiasts commissioned leading cabinet-makers to create almost perfect models in miniature to represent perhaps an artist's studio or, as in the case of the Thorn Rooms, interiors in correct period style. Even the lure of fairyland was evidenced, though in a somewhat Walt Disney idiom, by a young Hollywood actress.

That Colleen Moore's Castle, despite its hard glitter and lack of true scale, is so successful, is due to the skill of Horace Jackson, a designer of sets at the First National Studios in Hollywood who, together with her father, Charles Morrison, planned its execution with a professional skill. In this respect there is some similarity between Titania's Palace and Colleen Moore's Castle, as both were originally planned in true architectural style, and a complete effect was aimed at from inception, rather than, as so often happened in home-made projects, the design being allowed to develop as the work progressed. It is this absolute cohesion that gives both houses their considerable, though completely different, appeal and makes them of importance in their own period, equal to that of the finest eighteenth-century cabinet houses.

Inspiration for the construction of the Castle is said to have come to the young actress, once described as 'the quixotic pixie of motion pictures', while she lay on the grass at sunset gazing at the exciting cloud formations. She dreamed of a splendid palace with furniture of gold and silver, inhabited by a fairy princess. 'The chandeliers were hung with diamonds. A great hall was filled with treasures that belonged to the fairy folk'; then, in true cartoon fairy style, 'The floor of the drawing room was made of strawberry ice-cream'. This amusing contrast between high-flown and sometimes tasteful ideas and the worst of Hollywood kitsch is seen to run throughout the complete equipping of the castle and creates a vivid picture of the unregulated taste particularly associated with the period.

The exterior of the Castle, rising to over 12 feet, is pure storybook and everything a child imagines such a building should be, with turrets and gables

Colleen Moore seen examining Cinderella's coach in the courtyard of the castle that her father built for her when she was a girl.

creating a really romantic effect. Constructed of aluminium and copper, the model is some 9 feet square at the base and is reminiscent of Titania's Palace in that it can be disassembled for transportation. The utilization of light-weight aluminium was highly practical and is typical of the way in which its designers were not shackled to any traditional ideas or materials. Charles Morrison obviously provided much of the impetus and had previously shown great interest in dolls' houses, as he had presented his daughter with seven different models during her childhood, beginning when she was only two. Good miniature items were continually supplied by this eager father, until Colleen owned a considerable collection that itself needed some means of display and was eventually to form part of the Castle's furnishings. Visually, the Castle is much more dazzling than Titania's Palace and must closely rival it in basic value, as it contains items such as a specially commissioned gold box decorated with diamonds in which a fairy-sized wedding-ring is contained. While the Castle was in process of construction, father and daughter combed the studios and workshops of craftsmen as well as antique-shops, in their determination to find pieces that were exactly right for each setting. Unlike Sir Neville Wilkinson, Charles Morrison did not plan the architecture and engineering of his project unaided; he was assisted by Harold Grieve, an interior decorator who had worked on some of the most fashionable Hollywood homes, and Jerry Rouleau, who gave technical advice. Many other well-known painters, designers and craftsmen added their skills, so that the Castle gives as clear a picture of the artistic mood of Hollywood in the 1920s and 1930s as Titania's Palace gives of fine Irish craftsmanship in the earlier decade. The Castle abounds with lively touches of contemporary Hollywood, such as a pair of silver-armoured knights, once the property of Rudolph Valentino, paintings of famous film stars and, inevitably, Mickey Mouse. This atmosphere is aided by the lustrous and glittering materials used for decoration and by the amount of water that gives life to the rooms and gardens, as it runs and splashes into baths and spouts gracefully from garden fountains.

Colleen Moore was obviously much less interested than Sir Neville in discovering truly antique pieces and was perfectly happy to commission contemporary craftsmen, so that the completely modern effect of the rooms was maintained. She sometimes went to great lengths in order to create a specific effect and on one occasion surrendered several pieces of her personal jewellery in order that a really magnificent chandelier could be made. In some cases the use of special effects was pushed to such extremes that they become over-sentimental and even unpleasant, such as a weeping willow that drips real tears and a 'Rock-a-Bye baby' whose cradle swings in a conveniently situated breeze.

The Castle, whose first castings were made in 1928, contains eleven rooms and the Great Hall, with its ivory floor and golden pillars, which is the highest of the State Rooms. Proportionally, the Great Hall is extremely elegant, with a slender flying staircase which cleverly accentuates the unreality of the construction. Classical statuary, saints and armoured figures decorate this colourful room, which is dominated by a towering etched, stained-glass window that overlooks the garden and illustrates fairy stories. This theme is continued in many of the paintings, such as those of Snow White and other characters familiar to American children of the time through their comics and films, including 'Jiggs' in the costume of Old King Cole, painted especially for the house by his creator, George McManus, and 'Skippy' in a suit of armour painted by Percy Croaby. Walt Disney supplied a watercolour of Mickey and

Minnie Mouse in the costume of the King and Queen of Hearts. This attempt by Miss Moore and her father to relate the house to the characters known to contemporary children was a completely new venture in doll's house building, as the theme was usually completely traditional. The young actress herself was shown in several of the paintings in the Great Hall, such as in her 'Alice Blue Gown' from *Irene*, painted by Leon Gordon. Many of the prestige items discovered by father and daughter are displayed in the hall, such as a carved ivory table on which lies a pair of working duelling-pistols with silver bullets, an ivory cabinet that displays a collection of snuff-bottles, an alabaster jar from the Tomb of the Kings in the Nile Valley and a thousand-year-old Thailand urn. 'The Goose that laid the Golden Eggs' sits on a gold and enamel table, accompanied by a gold-mesh basket containing golden eggs; a glass bell protects the chairs of the Three Bears, each resting on a pin head, the largest weighing only one-150,000th of an ounce. Cinderella's glass slippers were very skilfully blown completely hollow, at Colleen Moore's insistence, by E. H. Rohl of Jackson, Michigan.

From the Great Hall, an archway leads to the lower drawing-room, decorated in a curious mixture of Baronial and French Empire and dominated by the famous chandelier that was made by H. B. Crouch, known both as a jeweller and as an authority on antiques. This room is equipped with silver furniture, though the grand piano is rosewood, and the chess-table, with its accompanying men, is ivory. The emerald, diamond and pearl chandelier, in conjunction with the silver furniture, is reflected in the rose-quartz floor with a jade border, which was made in China. The walls are decorated with murals, painted by George Townsend Cole, that tell the story of Cinderella. The sheets of music rival anything in Queen Mary's Doll's House, as they were also written by living composers, Rachmaninoff contributing his 'Prelude', Stravinsky his 'Firebird Suite', and Irving Berlin, 'Alexander's Ragtime Band'. The drawing-room has some importance in the documentation of the Castle as over the entrance hangs a shield with the date of the first castings.

'King Arthur's Dining-Room' is one of the Castle's most photographed rooms, possibly because its furnishings are in such contrast to the other apartments, being totally in film-set Baronial style, with marble walls and an inlaid wooden floor. The strangely designed Round Table and its accompanying chairs, with their rather crudely decorated shields, seem more appropriate for the filming of Robin Hood than to the Arthurian legends. The wall-hangings are in a much higher tone and were especially made in Venice, in late-nineteenth-century style to represent Arthur's adventures. The table is

The Great Hall with its many paintings as well as treasures from Fairyland such as the singing harp that Jack stole from the giant up the beanstalk. Tall etched glass windows overlook the garden.

The library of Colleen Moore's Castle, dominated by a splendid chimneypiece in copper and bronze, representing Neptune and two mermaids caught in a net. The average size of the books is an inch square.

supplied with a solid gold service and cutlery with monogrammed handles. On a walnut dresser is displayed an ivory chocolate-set and a collection of gold teapots. Unlike Sir Neville, Colleen provided her dining-room with a kitchen, though it has little of the charm found in the haphazard contents of children's play-houses and is furnished with great control. There are some interesting individual pieces, such as a copper stove on which hums a kettle, a cookery book holding the recipes of America's greatest cooks and, in a store-room, some pieces of old Mexican earthenware. One of the Royal Doulton dinner-services made as copies of that supplied for Queen Mary's house stands on the table, and over a ledge on the kitchen range is a completely American novelty in the form of a set of pewter mugs made by Thomas F. Owens, which are copies of early pieces and have wooden handles carved from wood recovered after the bombing of Westminster Abbey in the last war. This kitchen is the domain of Mother Goose, and the walls are decorated with nursery-rhyme characters, painted by Alice O'Neill.

The library is one of the Castle's most impressive rooms, though its supply of bookcases is somewhat meagre in contrast to the other furnishings. The room is completely dominated by a massive and totally improbable chimneypiece made of copper and bronze representing a fishing-net that has captured Neptune and two mermaids. Disconcertingly, Neptune was provided with the features of the actor Wallace Beery. Above the net stands Captain Kidd, with arms folded as he surveys his treasure-chests. This nautical theme was continued in high relief over the arched doorways to Aladdin's Garden and represents on one side Gulliver with the Lilliputian navy and Robinson Crusoe with Man Friday. A sofa is made of a copper shell supported by sea-horses, and other small chairs are based on shells. The bookcases are stocked, in the manner of Queen Mary's house, with a number of plain volumes that were then inscribed with short stories or a few sentences by well-known writers whose names are embossed on the leather bindings and who include Elinor Glyn, F. Scott Fitzgerald and Sinclair Lewis. *The Enchanted Castle* was written by Colleen herself. The antique books date from 1820 to 1900, and there is an interesting autograph album with signatures as divergent as Paderewski and the Duke and Duchess of Windsor.

The bedrooms of the Prince and Princess are in a completely spectacular idiom, and in comparison, Wilkinson's rooms for Oberon and Titania appear very dreary. The Princess' bedroom has a gold-bordered mother-of-pearl floor and a boat-shaped canopied bed with a golden 'spider web' counterpane. A particularly effective toilet-set, the work of a well-known Boston jeweller, Guglielmo Cini, stands on an ivory table, while another jeweller supplied the misguided advice to Colleen that she should convert a pair of diamond and emerald dress-clips into chairbacks – a piece of conversion that is even more glaringly unsuccessful than the use of a brooch in the throne in Titania's Palace.

The bedroom of the Princess with a mother-of-pearl floor and a canopied bed of gold with a gold spider-web coverlet. It belonged to the Sleeping Beauty. Nearby is an ivory spinet. The ivory dressing-table has gold plenishments.

The Princess' bathroom is all a modern Cleopatra could desire, as it is constructed of crystal and jade, with etched walls representing the story of Undine. Soaring butterflies and birds form the decoration of the glass ceiling, and into the reflected bath, water continually runs from the mouths of silver sea-horses, In contrast, the Prince's bathroom is fashioned in alabaster and has a distinctly masculine, if somewhat decadent atmosphere, with its golden lavatory and cabinet and guarding mermaids. His bedroom contains that piece of decoration so typical of almost every doll's house furnished between 1920 and 1938, namely the bearskin rug. This example is very fine and quite unlike the moth-eaten scraps of fur-fabric usually encountered, as the taxidermist that Miss Moore consulted used ermine and obtained the truly ferocious teeth from a mouse he captured. The Prince's bed, like his bathroom, is less comfortable than pretentious and has posts at the foot representing the witch in a Russian fairy tale who turned the arms and legs of a boy prince to silver. From this distinctly draughty apartment, an uncurtained arch leads to a balcony that overlooks the great hall. The Prince was well supplied for war, with a collection of swords that includes Excalibur, and a gold cannon. While preparing for battle, he could kneel at his own *prie-dieu*, which stood before a painting of the Virgin of Guadalupe, painted by a Mexican artist, Ramos Martinez.

The Prince and Princess are intended to worship together in the fairyland chapel, whose ceiling was inspired by the Book of Kells and whose floor is inlaid with biblical symbols. The flamboyant realism of this chapel is somewhat marred by its stained-glass window, unfortunately reminiscent of many cartoons, with a scene from David and Goliath. This blends very strangely with the lavish religious decorations that include a jewelled icon, illuminated by a gold vigil-light, set with a huge diamond, sapphires and rubies, and lit by six candles on either side. There are several other paintings and, another curious souvenir of bombed London, a piece of stained glass from Lambeth Palace. The Castle is quite unique among dolls' houses, as its sound-effects were planned from the beginning, so, at each quarter hour, the bells chime and the chapel organ plays continually. Another constant sound comes from the Palace garden and is that of the nightingale, introduced in 1935. It was in that year that the Castle's gold cornerstone was laid by the mother of President Roosevelt, indicating the great interest that was taken in the house by famous people and again paralleling Titania's Palace.

It is almost too easy to be supercilious when discussing Colleen Moore's Fairy Castle and to attach labels such as 'brash' and 'vulgar' to the concept, but the model has its own unique attraction in its complete truthfulness, both to period and as a vehicle of expression for the characters who were involved in its decoration, so that the viewer of today is provided with a picture of the flights of fancy that particularly represent Hollywood. Though adults might scorn, children are constantly fascinated by scenes such as Father Christmas flying

507

towards the Palace in his sleigh, Cinderella's coach-horses pausing for a drink, or a representation of the Wizard of Oz. Colleen Moore's intention, above all, was to create a model where children could meet the characters they knew, in settings which they could only imagine, and so escape into a charming make-believe world in which items from all periods and a variety of sources were assembled purely for a Hollywood nursery-rhyme effect.

EIGHT

Continental Houses

French affection for miniature scenes that are contained in small frames or display-cases has been obvious for several centuries, but curiously there is little traditional manufacture of complete model houses. Like the Germans, the urban French often lived in flats, so that models representing individual rooms would have provided the child with a much more understandable picture of actual life than the houses favoured by British and American manufacturers. The French girl in the nineteenth century was as closely guarded by her parents as a family treasure and rarely allowed out alone, so that she continued to amuse herself indoors with the exquisite costuming of dolls and the arrangement of rooms until she left the schoolroom, the needlework involved in such projects often being seen as a preparation for adult life. After a few years in a convent school, girls spent most of their time in their mothers' care, as all the emphasis was upon creating attractive young women with a knowledge of the useful social arts, such as letter-writing and embroidery, and several of the lavishly equipped rooms with carefully stitched carpets and fringed curtains serve as reminders of the long hours which mothers and daughters often expended on such activity. Prints and trade-cards dating to the last quarter of the nineteenth century show beautifully dressed children playing with their elegantly costumed dolls and colourfully furnished rooms in the setting of the drawing-room and rarely in the nursery, and we are reminded that these girls were not as completely segregated from their parents during the day as those of a similar class in Britain, who were expected to amuse themselves in the nursery, a room with plenty of space for the larger toys such as rocking-horses and dolls' houses. It is this very basic difference in the life-style of French children that most probably accounts for the scarcity of model houses, as few adults would have liked their reception rooms continually filled with large models, whereas a room, sometimes with folding sides, could be easily moved out of sight.

Few French collectors possess any authenticated examples of dolls' houses made before 1850, and it was not until the last quarter of the century that such models were commercially made, though rooms, often of the most basic construction, were produced in some number. Representations of the salon, that most peculiarly French institution, have remained the most popular, the art of conversation being cultivated and elaborated into a virtual art-form, mastery of which was obviously of great social benefit to any ambitious woman, as the memory of the *salonnières* of the eighteenth century, exercising power over men of great influence was still strong, and the cultivation of conversation of the most exquisite and delicate form remained a great ideal. Though the perfection of the eighteenth century salon became debased in the nineteenth century, some of the old atmosphere seems to have lingered, and the apartment has an air of cultured refinement quite unlike that of the somewhat staid British drawing-room. It was consequently little wonder that children so enjoyed assembling the salons and peopling them with nicely dressed figures, in imitation of their mothers' attitude to this most important room.

Parisian children were particularly fortunate, as they could select furniture and accessories from many specialist toyshops that closed on only one day of the year and remained open from eight in the morning until eight-thirty at night. Their stock of beautifully made miniatures of ivory, silver and porcelain were almost as much a treat for the adults who escorted the children and who were able to appreciate the skill involved in creating effective items from the cheapest and most basic materials. In the second half of the century there was also a number of magazines aimed at the young girl and her dolls, which, among the patterns and instructions for miniature clothes, also included many designs for furniture for model rooms. In some instances, the child was expected to enlarge the design herself, but at other times the printed outlines could be glued to card and then scored and bent into shape. Pot-stands, chairs, chimneypieces and tables could all be made in this way and decorated with silk, gold-bordered papers and fringes to give a much more substantial effect.

In 1864 *Poupée Modèle*, at this time still being printed on the large early sheets, offered its readers very detailed sewing-instructions for a 'toilette', in fact a fairly conventional dressing-table, whose base was to be constructed from an oval cylinder of card. After fixing a small mirror to the wall, lace was draped from the top, decorated with a bow, down to the ground. The base of the table itself was also covered with an apron-like front. A narrow frill was fixed to form an oval shape round the mirror, making a very French piece of furniture that a restorer lacking genuine furniture could easily re-create. Other items such as a chinoiserie pot-stand were also included in this magazine, which, among its patterns for embroidery and Berlin woolwork in 1868, suggested a boulle-type clock, which, when assembled, stood some 2 inches high. In August of the same year, when the publication was situated at

No 1 Boulevard des Italiens, a most elegant Empire-style chair must have inspired many young readers. All these designs were to be mounted on thin card and then scored and folded into shape after painting. In this instance, a working pattern for a needle-embroidered chair seat was also suggested. Many of the drawings were heavily reliant on somewhat florid curves but when complete must have seemed very effective, such as a splendid fender decorated at the sides with scrolls and cornucopia, and a *console terminée* with cabriole-style legs. In May there was an impressive piano, on which almost every surface was heavily decorated, the lower panel bearing a composition based on musical instruments. Music-stands, piano-stools, candelabra and dining-chairs were all to be made from folded paper, and typically French is the fact that the young girls were expected to spend hours embroidering seats and backs for such ephemeral items. An egg-shell cradle mentioned in the August 1869 issue, after being decorated with paper and painted, was to be supplied with a small fabric doll that was costumed in detail and then covered with fine blankets and a neat cover, accurately quilted and suggesting a readership that was much more meticulous and patient in its approach than its contemporaries in Britain, where eggshell cradles were usually much more rudimentary.

This very ephemeral quality of French work seems to have extended even into commercially produced furniture and is at once alluring and irritating, as so many charming pieces were easily broken or damaged. The commercially made items were often decorated with embossed or gilded paper, almost impossible to restore when damaged, so that while we admire an art-form that could create such extravagant objects from the most trumpery basic materials, we sigh for the many colourful plenishments long since destroyed. Even in the eighteenth century, according to d'Allemagne, manufacturers were already making an ingenious use of cheap materials to represent other finer substances, so that the late-nineteenth-century furniture makers who glued on oak-grained or satin-finished paper were working in an almost traditional native idiom for inexpensive but eye-catching items of this kind. French children would have despised the 'Strong Toys' of which the British makers were so proud and would have considered them both ill-designed and crudely constructed. Their own light, insubstantial miniatures exactly matched their silk- and lace-decorated frocks and their lavishly costumed dolls, while the much plainer dress of British and American children suited the sensible furniture of solid wood, made to withstand much rougher play.

One of the earliest French houses has been described in turn by Leo Clarétie, Fournier and Calmettes, and though their accounts differ in detail, it would appear that the model was still in original condition and in the collection of Monsieur Ehrman in 1900. The model, which represented middle-class life, stood $78\frac{1}{2}$ inches wide and $39\frac{1}{4}$ inches high and contained four rooms. Its doll inhabitants were not the patrician figures usually associated with cabinet models but somewhat coarse peasant types, whose womenfolk wore pointed black felt hats and tight bodices with padded sleeves. Over the main door was the date '1680', the entrance itself containing a shuttered window so that visitors ringing the bell could be examined before gaining admittance. It is thought that the model belonged originally to a Strasbourg family, and it seems to resemble others made at the time, as it included a courtyard with an apiary, sundial and poultry yard. The low-ceilinged main room was furnished with a buffet, dresser, clock and large armoire. The kitchen and bedroom were on the first floor, the former apartment being particularly effective because of the vast array of equipment that stood on every shelf and ledge. It seems strange that such a well-considered model could have disappeared so completely after the First War, and its description remains to tantalize collectors with the hope that it might one day be rediscovered.

Leo Clarétie also refers to a model which he claims was owned by Marie Antoinette and which contained a 'delicate little bust of crystal'. He also mentions a fine glass chandelier thought to have come from a house which she assembled for her children. There is a tradition that her husband, Louis XVI, made working locks for his children's dolls' houses, as he took great pride in this craft. Though attractive, several of these stories seem to have no positive basis, and it seems highly probable that they have accumulated around the romantic tragedy of this ill-fated royal family. The earlier French models that have survived are almost invariably those of adult intention, such as the exquisite example of Nevers glass dating to the eighteenth century that is at the Musée des Arts Decoratifs, Paris. In Alsace that ever-popular subject, the lying-in room, was often made completely of gum tragacanth, which was brightly coloured and whose appearance resembles painted wax models, a few rare miniature figures of this substance being displayed at the Kirschgarten in Basle. Other edible settings were created by the leading confectioners, who assembled houses, castles and rooms inhabited by skilfully made figures and representations of furniture. The very splendid settings of this type were created for great banquets, but on a lesser scale they were also used for family events such as baptisms, in which miniatures of glass, porcelain and metal were incorporated, so that many of the items that we now place in the context of dolls' houses and rooms were in fact made originally for use as ornaments on edible structures.

Various chroniclers offer tantalizing descriptions of the early French production of models, Heroard, personal physician to the Dauphin, later Louis XIII, making several mentions of miniatures that the young prince owned and in particular describing several model rooms that belonged to the Dauphin's sister, such as a somewhat ghoulish setting that showed Judith killing Holofernes. Madame de Maintenon, mistress of Louis XIV, also possessed a very sumptuously equipped model room which she later converted to a penitent's closet with a *prie-dieu* and a bed of bast as an outward sign of her

512

own repentance for her past life. There is also an eighteenth-century convent room at the Musée des Arts Decoratifs, furnished with cleverly contrived straw-work pieces. The nun represented is obviously a rich woman who has taken the veil, as her cell is quite luxuriously furnished, with a four-poster bed hung with curtains to protect her from draughts. The wax-headed nun sits reading a devotional book surrounded by religious emblems. Such rooms were in themselves devotional tableaux, and a few in light vein found their way into children's rooms, where their presence was expected to act as a spiritual curb on a headstrong child. In secular mood, at the house of Madame de Sévigné in Paris is a miniature room in which the figure of Voltaire stands.

The assembling of miniatures, though never as popular in France as in Holland, attracted many of the nobility, and Louis XIV, following his father's example, delighted in such items. Among the royal collection was a ménage consisting of a brazier with eight dishes, a small basket made to resemble wickerwork, four torches, five chairs, an armchair and a table, all made from silver, enamel and gold. There were also several figures to serve in the ménage. He possessed a market scene of the same type, with nine stalls and figures made of enamel. A *ménage*, usually a box or some form of container filled with small objects, such as tea-sets or cooking-pots, is a peculiarly French toy and was made in a variety of substances to suit the pockets of all classes of people. The boxes given to Louis XIII when a child and catalogued by Heroard contained pewter objects, dinner-services and fine Nevers glass. D'Allemagne, in his discussion of the 1849 and 1855 Exhibitions, groups together kitchens and *ménages*, as by that time their manufacture was in the hands of the toymen who were creating pieces for the enjoyment of children rather than adults. He mentions Monsieur Collin of 10 rue d'Anjou who was particularly well known in this field and who exhibited a kitchen that looked so effective that it aroused general acclaim. At the 1849 Exhibition this manufacturer showed models of kitchens and workshops as well as the grocers' and novelty shops that were then fashionable, and he obviously specialized in the making of a whole variety of miniatures.

Some of the commercially produced *ménages*, apparently made of porcelain, faience and earthenware were made in the Departments of Seine-et-Oise, Moselle and Haut-Rhin but decorated in Paris. A reporter at the 1855 Exhibition described the stand of Monsieur Larbaud, who showed a workshop for the making of the *ménage* and *batterie de cuisine* that he sold in some quantity. The reporter was surprised by the care that was taken to make these small items as perfect as possible. M. C. Larbaud made these *batterie du cuisine* and ménages of copper, tin and white metal and was awarded a second-class medal for his entry. Small pieces of tableware were also made in the mid-nineteenth century at the shop of Monsieur Sohlke and were apparently of a good standard. At the 1867 Universal Exhibition it was obvious that the vast majority of toys were manufactured in Paris and its suburbs though Limoges apparently supplied the china services which were actually decorated in Paris. At Nevers and Sarreguemines similar sets were made in earthenware, while the very cheap wooden tea-sets and ménages were obtained from Liesse Aisne. Most of the ménages, of either metal or ceramic substances, were the products of very small workshops, such as those in Paris where few employed more than twenty people, the men serving in the shops and marketing the pieces which were manufactured mainly by women. Interestingly, there was little child labour, the small items often being too difficult for children to handle. One of the cheapest sources of miniature kitchen utensils was D. Dessein of 13 rue de Chapon in Paris, though the larger exhibit at the 1867 Exhibition was that of A. Dehors of 8 rue des Vieilles, Haudriettes, Paris, who made both metal and china pieces. The jury commented: 'Knives, forks, dinner services, and every description of dolls plate both in metal and china are to be seen on his stand. Several of the specimens are in aluminium bronze and these, from the beauty and gold-like appearance of the metal are most attractive. They also exhibited some of the moulds. The little toilet services have great charm for children, they are so nicely made and though superior to most are not quite as elaborate as some in neighboring cases.'

At the Antwerp Exhibition, in 1885, in a report on the French toy industry, it was suggested that the makers were well paid in contrast with those in other countries, men earning between 5 to 8 francs a day and women between 2.50 and 3.50. The toys exhibited had often passed through the hands of several small factories for additions and decorations before they were sold, and they relied for their appeal mainly on their visual attractiveness and style. From 1845 a number of new firms had been established in France to specialize in the manufacture of the metal toys that before that time had been the monopoly of the German makers. From the mid-nineteenth century the older established companies had also been encouraged to improve their work, and great efforts were made to sell abroad, even in Germany though the 1870–71 Franco-Prussian War, with its resulting heavy taxes on France, intervened.

At the Antwerp Exhibition, the Union of the Makers of Toys, a syndicate of more than fifty makers, set up an impressive display to show how such associations could aid the marketing of French goods. It was obvious that the most important speciality was metal toys that included tinplate, white iron, copper and tin, all of course ideal for the manufacture of ménages, and in this particular area France exported more than she consumed.

Many of these toys were made in the rooms and slums of the Marais and Menilmontant, where the shadowy out-workers employed by the larger companies lived. These workers were supplied by the factory owners with lengths of wire and scraps of wood and metal which they soldered together to make into attractive objects which they delivered in huge baskets once a week, reluctant even to give their names, as they lived in constant fear of the authorities and the police.

At the 1900 Exhibition was displayed a *batterie de cuisine* dating to the period of Louis XVI and made in Flemish style, each individual item being marked with a royal crown used only by this particular maker. Girls were much encouraged to play with such toys, so that by the mid-nineteenth century there were many manufacturers, including Monsieur Collin at 10 rue d'Anjou, established *circa* 1830, who was particularly skilled in the manufacture of copper miniatures. In *La Femme*, Nichelet wrote: 'If you give a little girl the choice between toys, she will certainly choose miniature kitchen and household utensils. It is a natural instinct and the presentiment of a duty that women must fulfil. Woman must look after man.' It was no doubt with such an aim in mind that fathers and uncles presented girls at New Year and Easter with so many toys of this type, so that the industry grew continually until the end of the nineteenth century.

The Nevers glass miniatures are obviously of a very different quality, and though a few pieces were given to very rich children they were generally more in the nature of adult toys to be displayed in cabinets. This particular skill was introduced to France as a result of the marriage between Ludovico Gonzaga and Henriette de Clèves, which made Ludovico Duke of Nevers. Italian glassmakers were brought from L'Altare to settle in Nevers, where glass continued to be made in the Italian manner well into the eighteenth century. The small figures that so delighted the Dauphin were made of blown and manipulated portions of deeply coloured glass rod. Obviously this technique was not practised only at Nevers, but all figures made in the manner tend to be so classified. The very delicate threads were wired with copper, but in a few instances, where the model was particularly fine, it remained unsupported. The animal shapes are often hollow-blown, and their delicate, thin, glass-threaded decoration, known as '*verre frise*', is a particular characteristic. This particular technique is more in the nature of lamp-working, as the rods of different-coloured glass were softened and then wound over a metal armature. When the glass was sufficiently soft, it was reheated and then modelled to shape. This technique, almost a free artistic expression, meant that a whole variety of items ranging from crèche scenes to model rooms and intricate individual figures could be achieved.

The majority of contemporary reports regarding French manufacture concentrate mainly upon ménages, but a few of the furniture-makers were also acknowledged, such as the Widow Fialont of 16 rue de Choiseul and Mademoiselle J. L. Bereux of 21 rue de Hanovre, both of Paris. At the Antwerp Exhibition of 1885 it was commented that a large number of miniature white-wood pieces were made in the Forest of Compiègne in the Department of L'Aisne, whose products competed to some extent with those of St Cloud, though made with less finesse.

The most authoritative account of French rooms and their furnishings was provided by Henri d'Allemagne in his account of the Paris Exhibition of 1900, at which he and a group of enthusiastic early collectors had assembled the exhibit. In general his information, except that relating to Duke Albrecht's house, which he thought was still in existence, is reasonably accurate, but as so many of the pieces that he describes were sold or lost after the exhibition, it is difficult to be categorical, especially as there was already a substantial trade in forged items. With a collector's inherent mistrust of items that appear to be completely unique, one cannot help but wonder whether all the items referred to were in fact authentic. Certainly a number of the settings were especially constructed for the exhibition in order to display more exactly pieces in their correct time-scale, and as our knowledge of the items is derived from contemporary illustrations, it is inevitable that there should be some disquiet. Be this as it may, d'Allemagne's account is a useful source of information on the early development of French rooms and miniatures, and as so few actual examples exist, we are forced back on his observations, which were themselves based on the researches of Alfred Franklin, published in the series *La Vie Privée d'Autrefois*.

With typical French chauvinism, he comments that the French model rooms seem greatly superior to examples made abroad, as 'real' artists had applied themselves to their manufacture, the memory of these curious constructions being handed down to us by Tallemant des Reaux, who told how in 1630 Cardinal Richelieu presented the Duchess of Enghien with a small room in which there were six dolls. The mother doll lay in bed, her baby having been just delivered, and the wet-nurse with her breast bared awaited his first demands. Also in the room were a midwife, the grandmother, a maid and a small child. The children were delighted with their lying-in room, and the dolls were undressed and put to bed every evening; they were also made to eat and take medicine. One day Madame wished to bathe her dolls, and great difficulty was encountered in preventing her ruining them in this way. Though the subject of this setting might therefore have suggested an adult toy, it was in fact intended as a child's plaything, though obviously on a princely scale.

In 1675 de Thianges presented the young Duc du Maine with a model room of his own, and shortly afterwards he received another room of a similar type as a New Year's gift, indicating that such settings were as much liked by seventeenth-century boys as girls. His New Year's gift was described as a gilded chamber as large as a table, with the words '*Chambre du Sublime*' written above the entrance. Inside was a bed and a dais, and in a large armchair sat a portrait model in wax of the young Duke himself. Near him stood Monsieur de la Rochefoucauld, who was reading poetry, and grouped around the armchair were Messieurs de Marcillac and Bossuet. At the other side of the room and also reading poetry were Madame de Thianges and Madame de la Fayette. Beyond the dais was Despreaux, who was represented beckoning to La Fontaine. All these figures were in the form of wax portraits and were presented to the young Duke by the people they represented.

516

At the 1900 Exhibition, a particularly splendid lying-in room was shown by Monsieur Bernard, which contained furniture apparently made for the Princess of Nassau. This scene is a good example of the adaptations resorted to by this early group of collectors, as figures originally from a nativity scene were arranged as a lying-in. 'The principal personage is lying in a sumptuous bed with four columns surmounted by eagles in gilded bronze. The curtains and the baldachin are made of green serge, smothered with braid that forms rich arabesques. Not far from there, nearly in the fireplace, a nurse is sitting near a baby's cradle that she rocks by means of a length of cloth.' Their other reconstructions included a seventeenth-century toyshop. All these settings were quite openly fabricated and arranged in order either to present a social or historical background or to display objects in a more interesting context. In some cases it is difficult to be sure whether the line-drawings or his descriptions relate to completely genuine settings.

He also mentions the small enamel figures that were especially made for display and comments that interiors including such items were still made in the mid-eighteenth century for the appreciation of adults. In 1745 Raux le Fils, a jewellery dealer of rue du Petit Lion, advertised in the *Mercure* small *papier mâché* cabinets in chinoiserie style that were peopled by enamel figures representing men and women, actors and musicians. He also offered some little houses of the same material with very pretty rooms in which 'interesting events are taking place'.

Many of the settings arranged for the exhibition were composed of groups of miniature furniture that were probably originally made as cabinet-makers' pieces, created with great skill for display in the salon on a bureau or side table and representing fashionable full-sized furniture of the period. One of the most splendid interiors was a mahogany room enriched with ormolu, part of the collection of Monsieur Michon.

> Perhaps the most delicious in effect is a little day-bed covered in red silk and decorated with cornucopias. The bed, commode and console table are all in the same style. Each one of these pieces of furniture has such fine, well-proportioned decoration that one could have said that the bronzes were made in the country of Lilliput as they all harmonise so well together. The principal clock, placed, as usual, on the commode, is of light pressed copper surmounted by a crown of artificial flowers, the taste of which is a little problematic, but we must remember we are looking at a doll's room and not be too strict . . . in the foreground a soldier in a brilliantly coloured uniform appears to be preparing to dance a minuet with the beautiful lady, whose simple robe conforms well with the furnishings.

The writer was obviously much taken by this chamber and describes it as one of the most curious relics of the past he had discovered.

In another room, the Directoire period was represented, with a doll lying in a gold-embellished bed lit by a green paper-shaded lamp. A small child is seen visiting his mother in this richly furnished interior, apparently created not as an adult's model but as a toy to amuse children. The majority of the dolls which one can see in the foreground of this charming interior must have been dressed by the children themselves, for their cut and their sewing have a touching naïveté. From the point of view of the cabinet-maker, the manufacture is very simple. It is of whitewood, simply glued and decorated in a rather summary manner. It is painted all in green with little ornaments or a mixture of gold paint intended to represent bronze mounts. In a corner of the room one can see a little round stove standing on three feet, whose chimney goes out through the panelling. On the *armoire* at the back of the room are some fine silver vessels, a coffee-pot, sugar-basin, milk-jug and chocolate-pot, all a little large for the dolls in the foreground – or is it profitable to imagine that these were used by children as toy sets rather than for the room?

D'Allemagne goes on to review the dolls' rooms that had appeared in previous exhibitions and describes the model of a dining-room that M. Kopp of 56 rue du Temple had exhibited on his stand. The proportions were exactly studied, and all the correct furniture was provided. Worthy of particular note was a *dressoir* furnished with its vessels and a miniscule dining-table, complete with every glass and plate. At the 1867 Exhibition a magnificent salon was shown in contemporary taste with ostentatiously lavish furniture. A group of dolls in gala dress, with trained robes and bare shoulders, was surrounded by men dolls representing senators, marshals, councillors of state and prefects, creating a most highly impressive scene. British visitors, somewhat to the writer's surprise, preferred a model family house in which a simply costumed mother and father admired their baby, who was dressed to be taken out.

Of particular interest are d'Allemagne's comments on the tricks resorted to by the manufacturers of miniatures, such as using gilded paper or heavy paint to represent bronze mounts. Wooden furniture was frequently made from the thinnest wood, such as beech, not properly jointed but fastened together with nails. Painted paper was often used to represent wood, and the fine brass-mounted key escutcheon was most probably simply gold paper. Many items were given handles of copper wire, and doors were provided with the cheapest knobs. Some furniture, highly complex in appearance, was made completely of painted *papier mâché*, while others were made of a mosaic of straw-work, perhaps deserving d'Allemagne's contempt but now arousing only admiration for the intrinsic skill that enabled the French craftsmen to create beautiful objects from the most tawdry of basic materials.

The term '*bijouterie de St Claude*' was used in the nineteenth century to describe a whole range of miniature light wooden toys, with a particular emphasis on pieces intended for model settings. In 1799 the town of St Claude was destroyed by fire, and the inhabitants, in an effort to re-establish some basic industry, turned to the manufacture of cheap wooden toys in imitation

A middle-class American house. *c.* 1900

An American lithograph-on-wood house, *c.* 1916

A McLoughlin folding house, *c.* 1897

A two-storey lithograph-on-wood house
from Massachusetts, *c.* 1913

A lithograph-on-wood cottage
from Massachusetts, *c.* 1913

Mid-nineteenth-century porcelain-headed dolls with fabric bodies

A German lithograph-on-wood house, late nineteenth century

Interior of the German Muller-type house

The Deauville-House, late nineteenth century

A collection of doll's house dolls of the 1860s

Above left: An unusual waxed composition doll's house doll and one with a bisque head;
both wear mohair wigs. *Above right*: Poured wax dolls of English origin,
mid-nineteenth century

Below: A British-made house with German furniture, *c.* 1900

Above: The Danish 'Bay Room', *c.* 1880

A German house of lithographed paper on wood, *c.* 1871

Rare German porcelain dolls, *c.* 1840

From the Gardner House: *Above left*: A German *papier mâché* doll with onion-pattern service, *c.* 1835–40.
Above right: A doll's house pedlar

German dolls probably
costumed in America,
c. 1885

of those which had previously been imported from Germany. (This turning towards the manufacture of toys after major calamities is a strange feature of European life, so that we later find the war-wounded and people in flight from the enemy in the twentieth century deciding that there might be some outlet for their skills in this field.) Such experimental craft-activity was usually fairly short-lived, but the St Claude industry seems to have prospered, though the original output was in almost complete imitation of that previously obtained from Germany, and the Parisian toy-makers, becoming envious, increased their own production, many items being displayed at the 1849 Exhibition. The majority of the miniature beds, armchairs and tables originated in small workshops in the Temple Quarter in the Faubourg St Antoine, from where they were sent all over France and also exported. In contrast to such cheap items made for the poorest children, it was felt necessary at the 1900 Exhibition to show some of the finest French toys ever made, and of particular interest was an oak dresser of the Louis XIII period, supplied with a faience service, the central piece being decorated in Nevers blue with a basket of flowers and fruit; other miniatures on the dresser were made of Strasbourg polychrome faience. At the same exhibition a provincial maker of dolls' houses showed a turreted house with a bell-tower, balconies and flights of steps. This effective model was inhabited by a family of dolls, and another group played croquet on the lawn.

A report of the toys shown at the 1900 Exposition was also supplied by Leo Clarétie, who commented on the large doll's house described by d'Allemagne that was shown by the manufacturer from the eastern provinces, but adds that it was constructed in the German style. He goes on to observe that two makers in particular showed children's and dolls' furniture and displayed several interiors furnished with great ostentation. Possibly the most admired was a bedroom with white lacquer furniture that included a bed draped with mauve silk and lace, the baldachin delicately arranged and the armoire having a mirror. The dressing-table was arranged asymmetrically in Art Nouveau taste, a style that Clarétie hated almost to the point of the ridiculous, constantly castigating its emergence in the field of furniture design. He felt that, in general, dolls were of too conservative a nature to appreciate such adventurous design and adds that the pieces that were most popular came from the Faubourg St Antoine. 'However certain more advanced dolls demand to be kept in more fashionable style and it is for them that some makers, the minority, have made furniture such as the art nouveau armoire which in full size would rejoice the heart of an aesthete.'

Clarétie is completely in favour of toys in the well-tried traditional style and was pleased that extravagant, very modern pieces were quite rare, the manufacturers in general remaining hostile to the innovations of Art Nouveau, which he felt achieved success only among the frivolous and curious and had not reached or interested the masses. He must have found it distressing a few years later when the majority of doll's house furniture-makers were also making items in this new style whose influence continued to be felt well into the 1920s.

The manufacture of doll's house dolls was never as great an industry in France as in Germany and in fact remarkably few examples that can be positively attributed to a French source have survived. It is thought that most of the great French makers created some dolls of this type, but as their size was so small, they were not fully marked on the head, as were the larger versions, though originally many were sold in marked boxes or arranged in groups on manufacturers' display-boards. It is usually thought that the small all-bisque figures with stringing-loops moulded in one with the head are of French origin, and certainly their cleverly contrived costumes seem to exude the atmosphere of Paris, with its skilled dressmakers whose skill could be purchased at a sufficiently low cost for such trifles. It should be remembered, however, that such integral loops were also used by German makers such as Heubach, and it was not unknown for undressed German dolls, imported in vast quantity to France despite restrictive tariffs, to appear a few weeks later costumed in the French taste and sporting a French label suggesting that the complete object was of native manufacture. The French doll-makers were never as skilled as the Germans in creating effective yet very cheap dolls, though a few all-bisques have been discovered marked 'Bte' for *Breveté* on the back of the torso. Others have to be attributed to a French source because of their facial similarity to other, larger, marked examples, though again it must be remembered that German firms were sometimes commissioned to manufacture heads to exact French specifications, so that for instance 'Jumeaux' made by Simon and Halbig, Schoenau & Hofmeister and Heubach have been found. Any unmarked doll can therefore at best be termed 'probably French', though this seems adequate for most collectors, who seem to pay a much higher price for such dolls, irrespective of quality, simply because of the probable origin.

Round-faced all-bisque doll's house dolls similar to play-dolls made by Huret have been discovered, and a considerable number have heads obviously made by the same manufacturers who produced the elegant Parisiennes. Several of these figures closely resemble marked 'FG' moulds and have the large eyes and quite brightly painted closed mouths associated with that manufacturer. The figures marked 'Liane' with an anchor are usually too heavy in proportion to be included in a conventional doll's house, even though they are sometimes only 6 inches tall, and they are made of the coarse bisque and inferior general quality associated with the Limoges area where, despite considerable skill in manufacturing miniature porcelain, the dolls' heads never reached a very acceptable standard. The most popular French-type doll's house figures are those with large glass eyes and tightly curled mohair wigs that seem usually to have been sold as complementary pairs, one

A lithographed paper-on-wood house containing four rooms, hall and staircase, *circa* 1905. Probably French.

often being costumed as a boy. The costume is invariably good whether intended to represent that of the provinces or the best turned-out of Parisian children, and the use of narrow braids, fringe, gilded embossed paper and the most delicate machine-made lace is reminiscent of the skill and utilization of materials evident in the doll's house furniture.

French museums offer the researcher few examples of either dolls' houses or doll's house dolls for serious study, though many rooms are displayed that are sometimes peopled with figures that would perhaps not normally be associated with miniature living, such as the fairly substantial composition-bodied dolls marked 'Unis France' at the back of the bisque heads. Like the miniature all-bisques, these dolls are often costumed with flair, though as they were made until the 1930s, some wear the cheaper fabrics and exhibit the rough machining of the period. When asked for information regarding dolls' houses in France, both dealers and museum curators usually direct the curious towards the lithographed paper houses that were made at the end of the nineteenth century. These models, known in France as 'the Deauville type' have idiosyncratic cardboard balconies cut in imitation of cast ironwork and usually painted red. The models were made in several sizes and in several colour combinations and stand almost invariably on a marbled paper covered

521

A paper-on-wood French-type house in effective original condition with the typical blue painted roof. The interiors are usually plain and have either two or four rooms without a staircase.

Opposite: A complex French doll's house advertised in *Grands Magasins de la Ville de Saint Denis.* The balcony would have been made from card and wood. On the left was a lift. This was probably the largest Deauville type, *circa* 1905.

base, sometimes with wooden steps leading to the front door. In some cases there is a blue-painted steeple-like section to one side of the main roof, while others have a low gable with a semicircular printed window. In the larger sizes the windows were cut out and inserted, but the smaller were obviously more realistic, with printed windows and neat curtains. The wood from which these models were made is very light, and they are therefore easily transportable, which ensures their popularity with collectors. The interiors are remarkably plain in comparison with the colourful lithography of the façades, though the more expensive versions sometimes contain a working lift and were wired for electricity. Though these very recognizable models appear in many French catalogues until around 1912, they are at present completely unattributable, as no marked examples have been discovered.

Another model found in a number of variations is made in a more substantial manner but is also very much in the French idiom and again made from the curiously lightweight timber. These models were almost invariably

Nº 19052.

CHALET MEUBLÉ

pour poupée, **bois peint** décoré.

	0ᵐ72	0ᵐ76	0ᵐ82	0ᵐ88
	11.75	16.75	21.	25.
Le même, avec éclairage électrique.	17.50	22.	27.	31.

523

The French mansard-roofed houses are rarely found in such fine original condition as this example with a roof that lifts to reveal the attic rooms. The front opens and there are six rooms with a staircase and the fireplace and dresser characteristic of this manufacturer's work.

An almost identical French house that has been repainted though its good basic lines remain. The decorative pillars that finish the sides are particularly effective.

524

This mansard-type house varies from the example opposite, above, only in that the attic windows have arched tops. In the kitchen can be seen the fitted dresser and fireplace. The wallpapers are original, and the furniture is typically French.

provided with a mansard roof that lifts away at one side so that the roof space could be used for storage. The windows are often given importance by their rectangular or arched pediments made of especially cut moulding. A variety of surface decoration was used, ranging from lithographed paper to a simple painted effect with neat lining around the important features. Some open at the back, but the majority are front-opening, the most attractive being further embellished with colourful scraps or printed architectural motifs, one of the most effective examples of this maker's work being displayed at the Toy Museum in Nuremberg. The general finish of these models is usually good, and they seem to have continued in production until the First World War, though again the name of the manufacturer is unknown. Like the Deauville type, the interiors are fairly plain, though a few have extremely effective wallpaper neatened with especially made borders. The kitchens nearly always contain a large arched fireplace edged with orange or dark blue lines and a somewhat strangely large-scale matching dresser, both usually being painted in a cream colour that has faded to yellow. A flight of stairs ending at ceiling-level is seen in the larger models; this was a necessary economy, as the houses

Opposite : A French-style house with a mansard roof that lifts off for access to the attic rooms. This version does not separate at first-floor level. Known as the Wachter House. *Above:* The interior of the Wachter House showing the fitted dresser and range that were standard features on houses of this type. Late nineteenth century.

527

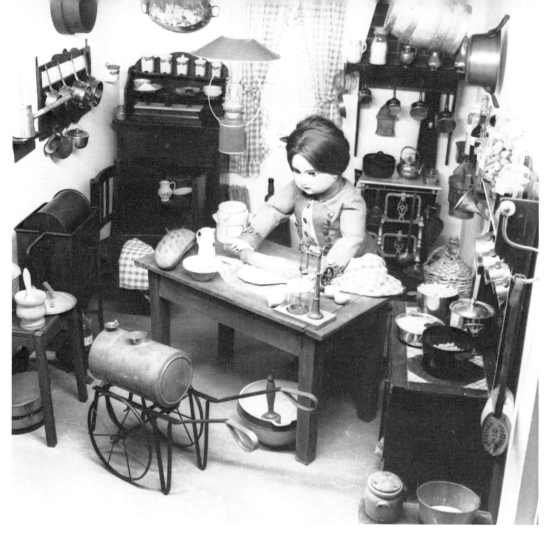

The kitchen from a huge doll's house 24 feet long by 6½ feet deep. It is filled with items dating from between 1880 and 1910, arranged under the direction of Jac Remise.

often came apart at first-floor level, presumably for ease of transportation. In some examples the attic area also lifts away, making it possible for the house to be moved even by a child.

It is noticeable that many French houses, even those made just before the First World War, do not contain bathrooms, though they are lit by electricity. It seems possible that this omission was due to the townswoman's custom of hiring baths, which were carried, together with hot water in buckets, up to her flat. These baths were lined with a white cotton sheet so that contact with the metal was avoided and the family was saved the bother of storing such a large item in their often confined space. Laundry facilities are also noticeably lacking in these model houses, again mainly because in France a townswoman's laundry was usually sent out and because the Frenchwoman, like the Dutch, took great pride in the fact that her cupboards were so well

528

The salon, centre of every fashionable French household, was decorated without the economy that often characterized other rooms. This 1840s interior contains a number of fine miniatures including the lamp and chandelier.

stocked that this process was necessary only once a month. Her linen was of the highest quality and often monogrammed, as no respectable French housewife would have considered the expense of laundering cotton items worthwhile.

The lack of utilitarian features such as were found in most British dolls' houses of the period gives the French models an almost frivolous appearance, as even their model kitchens are without the great assortment of equipment that a Dutch or German child would have considered necessary. The main decorative emphasis in these houses and the much more common rooms, is on the elegant living-rooms and the prettily arranged bedrooms with their silk-decorated windows and draped beds. The French bedroom in the late-nineteenth century was still considered suitable for the reception of guests, so that when a young girl invited her schoolfriends home, it was in her bedroom

A mid-nineteenth-century French house of heavy construction yet retaining a lightness of effect. The ground-floor windows had protective bars. The large double doors and the arched windows contribute to the effect of a substantial middle-class home.

Opposite: This early nineteenth-century Spanish or Portuguese doll's house, with its chinoiserie lantern on the roof, is more of a cabinet-type structure than a play-house, and both the atmosphere and the decoration are in adult taste.

that they talked and played. In a similar manner, when space was restricted, the bedrooms would be used as extra rooms for sitting and talking when there were a number of visitors, and consequently the beds were covered with ornamental drapery and made as elegant as possible. There were no washing-facilities in these rooms, as it was necessary that they should appear perfect on all occasions, though there were usually side rooms where, for instance, several sisters might share a washstand. Conditions in country areas were obviously different, but the models seem to reflect mainly urban middle-class life.

The Musée des Arts Decoratifs, in response to the many requests of collectors, now has a section devoted to antique toys, and the display includes a substantial mid-nineteenth-century town house, the Nevers room already mentioned and the very curious early-nineteenth century Spanish or Portuguese model more in the nature of an adult's cabinet than a child's toy. This model, basically a large rectangular salon set above a larger separate rectangle divided into three, is one of the strangest encountered, as its somewhat sinister atmosphere and rich dark colours are without parallel. On the roof is a curiously styled chinoiserie lantern that contributes greatly to its air of mystery. This museum has long been suspected, by both American and European researchers, of hiding away many toys in bottomless cellars and dusty store-rooms, impossible to penetrate. The museum's new-found enthusiasm for toys and the display now arranged by an energetic curator of the department completely disprove these old suspicions regarding dolls' houses never being allowed in the light of day, as those in charge are only too

Model rooms were much more popular with French children than complete houses. The rich colours of this salon, the fringed curtains and the all-bisque dolls contribute to the unmistakably Parisian effect.

delighted to display all that the museum possesses. In some respects this is something of an anticlimax, as the very whisper of unrevealed treasures made collectors anticipate the time when an abundance of rare items would be revealed. Sadly, until very recently French interest in toys has been minimal, and many museums are now attempting to purchase important representative items before they are exported or pass into unknown collections.

Another recently arranged display of antique toys is to be found at Poissy, where a museum was opened in 1976 with the intention of illustrating the development of playthings. Its curator, in common with collectors, soon discovered a complete dearth of native model houses, though there is an example of a Deauville house with a lift. The museum does show a number of

A large-scale doll's house flat (*circa* 1905) with windows on three sides through which can be viewed the typically French rooms.

model rooms, and the visitor is made very aware of the delight that was taken by French children in their model rooms and *petit ménage*. There was certainly no shortage of home-produced glass and china, though its scale is usually more suitable for the model rooms and kitchens than houses. Among the most recent acquisitions is a very large one-storey flat-roofed apartment with effective balustrading and large windows on three sides, through which glimpses of the very large-scale rooms can be seen. The model is richly furnished and has the heavy curtains and upholstered furniture encountered in the much smaller-scale rooms. There is also a charming room representing a salon, complete with an attractive group of all-bisque dolls and that lightness of decoration that yet contains a wealth of precise detail so typical of

533

A room setting showing a bride and groom *circa* 1870. The curious furniture is made from pine twigs. The dolls have bisque heads.

late-nineteenth-century French toy-makers.

One of the most attractive rooms at Poissy is arranged in a small glazed case and presents a bride and groom surrounded by very unusual furniture made from the delicate twigs of pine trees, giving an effect somewhat similar to that of the feather furniture of Britain. The walls of this small room, which dates to the 1870s, are hung with a series of engravings, and the general atmosphere of the setting, with some of the furniture made of grained paper, is both light and delicate. The model has added interest in that it seems to be set amid country rather than among town folk, though the number of religious accessories such as a *prie-dieu* and a missal suggests that there might have been some moralistic interpretation of the scene.

The attractiveness of the rooms supplied by French printers is obvious, as here were toys that the child could enjoy constructing from the brightly coloured sheets that were sold from the baskets of hawkers and from small shops all over the country. These rooms have usually survived only in uncut form as, once assembled, the furniture was extremely fragile and soon discarded. The uncut sheets provide a very complete picture of mid-nineteenth-century French middle-class life, as we see the exact arrangement of drapery and the types of decoration and wall-coverings most favoured. As well as the well-known Pellerin, a number of other firms produced such rooms, and at Poissy is an effective chromolithograph of a child watering a garden in front of a yellow house, as well as several of the more conventional uncut prints.

The most famous of the printers was the firm of Pellerin, which worked in Epinal in the Vosges. The company was founded by Nicholas Pellerin, who was a merchant in the town at the beginning of the eighteenth century. His initial interest seems to have been with card-games and the broad sheets that are known in France as '*canards*', though the firm also printed religious tracts and stories. The prints made during the lifetime of Jean Claude Pellerin (1756–1836) are of the greatest interest to collectors, though he was mainly the distributor of the work. At its height the factory employed five engravers, François Georgin, Reveille, Charles Pinot, Canivet and Verneuil. The model rooms are usually in the Empire style, but there are a few settings that reflect very late-nineteenth-century taste and which are printed in chromolithography, less popular with collectors than the hand-stencilled earlier items. Some of the designs marketed by Pellerin were in fact produced by other printers, such as those of Caen, Troyes, Cambrai and Orleans, so that the words 'Epinal Prints' and 'Pellerin' can only be taken as an indication of type. A museum of Popular Imagery was recently opened in Epinal, and traditional examples of the firm's work are again being produced to delight children of today, who still find great pleasure in cutting these wonderfully coloured sheets.

The French manufacture of houses, furniture, accessories and dolls reached its peak in the early years of the twentieth century, and catalogues dating to the years just before the war illustrate a wide assortment of effectively constructed items, especially noteworthy being the well-furnished rooms. The girls of this period were likely to leave their mothers' personal care at a much earlier time, as they were educated in the state *lycée*, and the toys are therefore intended for a much younger age-group. The individual pieces of furniture were still quite effective, such as dressers in Renaissance style made of natural wood and provided with opening doors and drawers at 21 francs 50 centimes. This particular model, with glazed upper doors, came complete with a four-piece metal tea-set. Other makers offered bedrooms in pitch pine and bamboo, where the bed was decorated with a satin cover and the curtains and drapery were festooned with lace and ribbon. Louis XVI-style rooms were also available and were furnished with fashionable white-enamelled furniture, the complete settings costing around 70 francs. A model kitchen contained an oven, a proper working water-tank with a tap, and twenty-four pieces of cooking equipment suitable for the most discriminating housewife. This model was available in two widths, 10 or $25\frac{1}{2}$ inches. There was also a good variety of miniature tableware, the cheapest being of metal with between two and six covers. There were several thirty-two-piece faience sets, but the most desirable were those of porcelain 'decorated in Saxon style'. In order to equip the model room completely, there were extra items, such as grand pianos and well-dressed dolls and an especially good variety of more basic items, such as lace curtains.

The First World War completely disrupted the traditional manufacture of inexpensive toys, and many items seem to have disappeared completely from the toyshops after the war. Writing in 1924, Pierre Calmettes commented that dolls' houses were no longer fashionable and could be seen only in large shops or in illustrated catalogues. He considered that the sheer bulk of model houses had led to their abandonment, in combination with the mania for cleanliness and dust-free rooms that seemed to affect every mother of the period. Though the continual reduction of living-space was ending in the loss of rooms and houses, there was still a considerable production of furniture, especially by the war-wounded. The pieces made by these men were painted in very bright colours, and the dressers were supplied with faience plates. Of great interest are Calmettes' comments regarding the price-rises in relation to toys in the years after the war, prices that were in themselves probably causing the demise of the larger rooms, as they rose by an astonishing 300 per cent. Before the war, many of the doll's house furnishings had been imported from Germany, but now 'only a treacherous few' were prepared to stock German-made pieces. Miniatures for dolls' houses were therefore extremely difficult to obtain and were in some cases more expensive than full-sized furniture of the same type. Calmettes compares the price of a tiny bed at 70 francs with an adult's double bed that could be purchased for 60 francs and

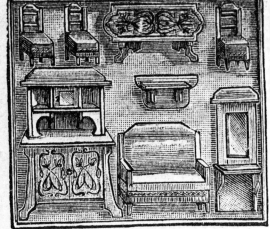

Z — 196. **SALON DE MA POUPÉE**, bois verni et décoré, chaises et canapé rembourrés. *Prix* **3.50**

Z — 195. **MAISON DE POUPÉE** meublée, salon et chambre à coucher, en bois richement décoré. Hauteur 0ᵐ42. . . **6.50**

This two-roomed house has a much simpler façade than that usually associated with houses of French origin. The boxed set of furniture would, presumably, have fitted the house. Advertised in the catalogue of *Grands Magasins de la Ville de Saint Denis, circa 1905.*

MAISON DE POUPÉE meublée, salon et chambre, avec ascenseur, Hauteurs. 0ᵐ51 0ᵐ56
A la Samaritaine. . **12.50 17.50**

Les Grands Magasins de la Samaritaine sold this two-roomed house with a lift in 1906.

goes on to observe that, in order to show their daughters a true and traditional *ménage*, mothers would have to 'spend such sums as will suffice to furnish a house for real people', a statement that remains true today in relation to antique miniatures. In more encouraging mood, he adds that bronzed lead items, frequently originating in North America, were still readily available and could be found displayed on the pavements of Paris, though the makers made no attempt to provide any scale objects, as the cooking-ovens and cars, for instance, were often of the same size, which would have meant that the majority were of little use in model rooms.

The term 'art in the nursery' never gained as general an appeal in France as in Germany, where doll-makers in particular were working in this new idiom from around 1908. Though some imitative dolls were made in France, it was not until after the First World War that much more adventurous models and furniture began to appear on the market. *The Studio* commented that, despite the traditional French manufacturing methods of creating toys from scrap metal and on a folk-type basis, from inexpensive wood, every type of toy had been recently improved and adapted to the real needs of children. Toy villages, medieval monasteries and well-made construction sets featured among the superior work made by 'Le Jouet de France'. This co-operative venture was set up when a group of makers saw the advantages of pooling their resources and arranging displays and exhibitions of their work. Among the group's leading designers were Le Borgeois, Rapin and Francis Jourdain, the latter being particularly interested in the creation of complete nursery schemes. Jourdain's creations for Le Jouet de France were particularly adventurous, as the children could construct their own model cottages that could stare and grin, roll their eyes and show their teeth. Simple, beautifully decorated miniature furniture was also made by these artists, 'far more satisfactory from every point of view than the elaborate, costly reproductions of current types of furniture that not long ago were the only substitute for even more coarsely adjusted rubbish'.

A more artistic approach to toy-making was also the aim of various groups of disabled and war-wounded men who were encouraged to manufacture toys almost as a form of therapy. 'Le Jouet Belge' was a co-operative organization for the distribution of the work of disabled Belgian soldiers and appears to have operated between 1916 and 1922. Contemporary descriptions of their creations in British magazines shower them with praise for the inventiveness of their designs, though I have to date encountered none of the model houses they manufactured. The individual models of old houses of various types were apparently both accurate and effective, and replicas of groups of habitations were also made, such as the Grand Place at Furnes and the Béguinage at Dixmunde. In common with the men who worked at the Lord Roberts workshops in Britain, their main concentration was upon small model animals and figures which were used to good effect in the Flemish

Both Swiss and German toy kitchens were becoming more practical by 1900. This model was made in Basle for a Miss Schweiger when she was ten years old. Its simplicity contrasts with the crowded German interiors of the same period.

farmhouses that were very adequately stocked. Of particular interest was an 'Old House in Ypres', which had been destroyed in the war and which was of the typical Dutch stepped-front construction, giving a great appearance of antiquity. The doll's house opened at the back in two sections and contained a single room on each of the two floors. In the bedroom was a large four-poster and in the lower section a very wide assortment of plates and kitchen equipment. The majority of the models were constructed from designs supplied to them by Madame Meunier Gaudron, Mademoiselle Leo Jo and Madame Franchomme van Halteren. Despite this fairly short-lived spate of model-building in the early twentieth century, the Belgian contribution to the development of dolls' houses is slight, partly because of the difficulty of making precise attributions to models that show no particular national characteristics, as the French and Dutch influence was so great. At a very representative exhibition of antique toys held at the open-air museum in Bokrijk in 1976, there were several good examples of both French and German houses, but the absence of any native pieces was very obvious.

Middle-class Swiss children seem to have been provided with much more play-space than was allowed in either French or Belgian homes, as a number of model rooms and houses have survived. An extremely comprehensive selection of models that belonged to Swiss children can be seen in the attic rooms at the Kirschgarten at Basle, a most elegant house that was once the home of Madame du Barry. After walking around the beautifully arranged rooms, still containing fine period furniture, the visitor climbs the stairs to the old servants' quarters, where an impressive collection of toys is displayed.

Though not by any means the finest model in the collection, that made by *Kunstmaler* Ludwig Kelterborn and known as the '*Dorggetekansterli*' is particularly interesting. Kelterborn, an artist who lived in Basle, constructed this highly complex model in 1850, with its balconies, attics and cellars as well as a charming sun-room, providing a construction very much in the idiom of the traditional German cabinet houses, more accurate models than children's playthings. Its creator was born in Hanover in 1811 and, though working in an almost traditional German manner, was in fact supplying a toy for his three daughters, Elise, Emma and Lina. Two of the bells on the front door, which is set back in a pillared porch, are labelled 'Lina' and 'Emma', and the contents are obviously commercial items of the period rather than the especially constructed pieces one might expect in a cabinet-type model. The front of the dolls' house commands attention, as it is so completely different from any conventional arrangement and is painted mainly in soft yellow and white with pink and green detail, giving a somewhat French atmosphere that is accentuated by the gay green and white striped awnings over the sun-room and the central balcony. This main balcony is one of the more formal areas, and there are potted plants arranged behind the railings, which show up well against the red-painted walls decorated with several border friezes of the type that were popularly in use in the 1870s. From the balcony, French windows and a door lead into a landing-room that is also well supplied with plants. The sun-room has green and white painted Gothic arches, and the whole front of this section lifts up for easy access to the potted plants and the sunbathing dolls. Large double windows lead through to a very well-furnished sitting-room, given added interest because of its corner stove with a very complex twisted chimney. Similar white stoves can be seen in many of the rooms, but this example is particularly ornate.

The top floor has an impressive balcony with four large arches and a fretted balustrade, in front of which the washing hangs from a wooden clothes-line. The attic area is also of note, as there is a pulley for lifting goods up to the store-room from street level, a correctly working device enabling the children to haul up provisions and laundry equipment from the other utility area on the ground floor, where, in the kitchen, a bisque shoulder-headed doll can be

Part of the exterior of the house known as the 'Dorggetekansterli' and made by Ludwig Kelterborn, a Basle artist, in 1850 for his three daughters.

seen at work in front of a wooden German-style stove. On the right-hand side of the ground floor there is yet another area intended mainly for laundry, with a huge canopied copper in one corner and a matched set of wooden tubs standing on a bench. In the dark, arched cellars, painted in realistic grey and approached by a spiral staircase, are stored many barrels, so much a feature of many Continental houses.

The exterior of this complicated model is unusual because of its complete lack of symmetry, and it obviously poses the question as to whether it was in fact intended as a copy of an actual building with the additions and adaptations of various occupiers, all carefully recorded by the artist builder. The interior is much less exciting, and Kelterborn's lack of professional carpentry skill is very obvious, though the completed effect is still both accurate and arresting. The rooms, in comparison with those in both British and German houses, are particularly light, as there are seven additional side windows at each end of the model. In the much darker attics worked the maids in the laundry room with its clothes-lines and sturdy ironing-table. The centre section is boxed off to make a somewhat gloomy maids' bedroom, and lying around in other parts of the large attic are an old Christmas tree, a sledge and a heap of wood with a chopper, all indicating that winter is still some time away.

Almost complete realism is attained in the central section of the house, where the steep staircase is predictably supplied with potted plants on each landing. All the doors have neat metal handles, and the floors are covered with paper which is painted to resemble tiles. On the ground floor, a trap, of the same size and proportions as the vertical doors, leads to the cellar stairs. All the rooms are somewhat sparsely furnished, and obviously some items have been lost over the years, so that what remains, with the exception of the fittings in the attics and cellars, is very basic. The curtains, of spotted nets and muslins, are all held in place with that completely international doll's house device, the ornamental upholstery tack that imitates quite successfully the brass cord-retainers used in so many nineteenth-century homes.

One of the finest dolls in the *Dorggetekansterli* is a bisque-headed, moustached man of German manufacture who wears a grey silk dressing-gown and a smoking-cap and sits at a writing-stand of painted wood, lit by a candle. The other inhabitants are of the basic shoulder-headed type with moulded hair, though they are all effectively costumed to represent characters in a typical Swiss home of the period, which gives this model particular importance, as the majority of children in the nineteenth century

The interior of the house made by Kelterborn viewed from the back to show the realism of his plan that must have imitated a style of building he knew well. Note the fine model stoves in several of the rooms.

played mainly with the toys that were imported from France and Germany. There was consequently little commercial production of either dolls or dolls' houses and their furniture until the last quarter of the century, when some, mainly of a folk type, began to be made for the ever-growing number of tourists who delighted in returning home with brightly painted cradles and dining-room sets made in the Alpine regions.

The almost complete dependence on imported miniatures can be seen very clearly in the contents of the mainly cupboard-type model houses at the Kirschgarten, which display many fine pieces of wood and metal that are almost exclusively of German manufacture. All these models are obviously children's toys and are constructed on a fairly small scale, with the notable exception of a large walnut cabinet house dating to around 1700, which still retains its original massive hinges and locks. This cabinet, known as 'the Wengen house', as it once belonged to a Basle family of that name, stands just under 6 feet high, somewhat lower than the German and Dutch examples but bearing a strong resemblance to the two-roomed structure at the Nuremberg Museum, though this example is much lighter in atmosphere, as both the cabinet and the interior decoration are made of paler wood. The upper room, panelled in green, is given added attraction by a painted formal frieze above the panelling. The fine cupboard, with barley-twist carving on the columns which terminate in angels' heads, is a superb item of miniature craftsmanship obviously intended for the appreciation of adults. The green-glazed stove, of quite different proportions, is also a display-piece and is given added effectiveness by the steps at the side. Yet another fine stove stands in the central room, but this is much more correctly proportioned for the cabinet and is provided with several raised sections where kettles and pots could be almost separately heated and is obviously a refinement of those seen in the Nuremberg houses. A similar full-sized stove can be seen in the kitchen of the Kirschgarten itself, enabling the visitor to relate the models to the functional, adult-sized versions. (In the room where the Wengen cabinet is displayed can also be seen a glazed full-sized earthenware stove so that the comparison between those intended for actual interiors and those for models is clear.) A few pieces in the central room of the cabinet were added in the nineteenth century, though the authentic effect was maintained: a cooking-stove that was added at this time was replaced by the eighteenth-century piece with its shelved heating-areas already mentioned. One of the finest pieces in the cabinet is, without doubt, the silver dish that was made by the Basle goldsmith Peter Biermann and which is dated to 1709. The cellars in this model are used

A walnut cabinet house (*circa* 1700) that was once owned by the Wengen family of Basle. The pale wood of the structure and the bright green of the earthenware stove give a much lighter effect than the German cabinets.

purely for the storage of kegs of wine and beer, which were given added protection by a high red-painted fence, indicating the degree of protection that stores required to keep them from the thieving hands of the many servants.

Another, much later cabinet house is made of oak-grained pine and dates from between 1860 and 1865. The construction is very basic, consisting of four rooms that retain their original wallpapers and which have effective gilded-paper borders, which give the interior a much richer effect than that of the Kelterborn house. This effect is accentuated by the opulence of the black and gold Waltershausen furniture and rich, individual detail, such as the bearskin rug on the bedroom floor. There is a drawing-room, kitchen and dining-room besides the bedroom already mentioned, the drawing-room, on the first floor, being furnished with blue velvet upholstery that looks very effective against the brown sprigged wallpaper. The doll inhabitants are again mainly of the German shoulder-headed type.

Much more unusual, though without the opulence of the well-furnished cabinet, is a most effective house and shop built on completely classical lines with a turned pillared balustrade running around the flat top. Despite its early nineteenth-century effect, the model was made around 1870 in imitation of the more formal stores of the period. All the windows are arched, and the shop has two effective bow windows that continue the almost Georgian effect. Though it has not seemed appropriate to include shops in a book on dolls' houses, this particular example, with its generous living-accommodation, approaches the spirit of a model house so closely that it seems impossible to ignore its claim for inclusion. Over the shop windows '*Porzelain Glaswaaren*' is painted, though the interior shelves exhibit a somewhat depleted stock, including miniature Chinese figures, porcelain and glassware as well as several tin votive-pieces, all watched over by the shopkeeper, a carved wooden man who wears Swiss costume. Alongside the main shop is another area of somewhat doubtful intention, where there are several roughly made kitchen fittings, and adjoining this is the main front door to the flat, which is on the first floor. In the sitting-room three bisque-headed lady dolls sit on well-upholstered chairs, listening to the ticking of a porcelain clock that is protected by a glass shade.

The four remaining houses displayed at the Kirschgarten are all of the nineteenth-century cupboard type, though given individuality by certain details: one has a delightfully cluttered attic room and a very rare Waltershausen shaving-mirror with the original fitted tin candleholders on

A mid-nineteenth-century cupboard-type house that has retained its original wallpapers as well as a variety of commercially made furniture, mainly of German origin.

547

either side; another has an unusual kitchen, curiously situated on the top floor, and is also supplied with a useful storage-drawer in the base. A particularly fine extending circular pedestal table with a drop-in leaf that extends by the division of the pedestal itself is extremely rare, as it is again made of the imitation rosewood associated with the Waltershausen area. The same house contains a very small *papier mâché* doll, some 2 inches high and conventionally constructed, which sits in the kitchen. One of the other houses is also of interest, mainly because of its good selection of German *papier mâché* inhabitants, among which is a very fine, rare, genuine man of the type with painted hair, who is represented lying in bed in a room in which we also see some exquisitely made bonnets on a table.

A curious mechanical house can also be seen at the Kirschgarten and is believed to have been constructed by an amateur. On one of the towers is a sundial, and in both size and appearance the model is completely in the manner of a doll's house, though a sandwheel is concealed within to activate the groups of figures which stand on balconies and near the waterwheel. In a charming vignette under a porch we see a maid making pats of butter while a lady is spinning; on an upper balcony two lovers bid each other goodbye; two coopers work near the waterwheel. A very similar toy, made at the same period and suggesting that the models were in fact commercial rather than amateur items, can be seen in France at the Museum of History and Education. In the French example, the waterwheel is situated in front of the central tower of the house, and there is a greater number of single figures, so that when it is in operation, the effect is much less complex.

One of the most elegant paper models is also on display in this museum, though its impact is perhaps less when seen than when arranged for a photograph, when all the colours take an added brilliance and the basic perspective becomes more precise than when it is examined in a display-case. In the background is a very formal garden with clipped, shaped trees and hedges, in the midst of which is set a garden pavilion with Gothic-inspired windows set in a mainly Palladian façade. The individual figures were drawn and painted by Johann Jacob Uebelin, who was born in Basle in 1793 and who was a private tutor to the Fischer von Reichenbach household. The 'Palace Garden' was created as a gift from a tutor to his pupil and represents the Prince August von Hohenlohe-Kirchberg with his family, members of his Court and his household in the grounds of his palace. In concept the model can perhaps be compared with Mon Plaisir, as the figures in the garden were all known personally to Uebelin and were drawn as portraits. This attractive gift was accompanied by a very precise plan, which showed how the forty-seven figures and thirty-seven pieces of scenery were to be arranged and which now makes identification of all the characters possible. Though a pavilion in a lovely garden made of paper cannot be precisely classed as a doll's house, it forms an interesting nineteenth-century parallel with the

A late eighteenth-century mechanical house containing a sand-wheel which activates the groups of figures seen on the balcony and near the water-wheel.

This 'Palace Garden' was painted by Johann Jacob Uebelin and represents the Prince August von Hohenlohe-Kirchberg with his family and Court. It was made *circa* 1820 but in eighteenth-century style.

Princess Dorothea's Mon Plaisir, a project that would have held even greater importance had she possessed the foresight to list and identify all the wax characters her craftsmen created. This paper setting, with its elegantly designed gateway surmounted by the family coat-of-arms, its proud sentries in their striped boxes, its finely dressed figures in very retrospective Court dress and general air of precise order, makes this Palace Garden one of the more effective early nineteenth-century toys, though it is curious that the tutor, working in the 1820s, chose to illustrate the noble family so completely in eighteenth-century style.

Similar scenes made of painted tin were also made in Germany at this time and included formal trees, potted plants and shrubs and attractive buildings.

The makers of metal flats obviously enjoyed the amount of detail that was necessary to describe fashionable women's dress, and there are figures eating and drinking at tables, strolling in the gardens and walking near the arches. These brightly coloured settings were often enclosed within ornamental railings, and there was almost invariably one large central building similar to the pavilion created by Uebelin.

Like the Swiss, who were quite happy to encourage their woodcarvers to create items for the tourist market in the late nineteenth and early twentieth centuries, the Russians manufactured simple peasant-like figures and items of furniture that were gaudily painted and bear only the slightest resemblance to pieces actually used at home. Few examples of the toys loved by richer Russian children survived the Revolution, and the museums are much more interested in the folk-type pieces, despite the fact that they were often made for export, rather than the elegant toys with which the more privileged children played. It used to be thought in the toy-trade that a number of the pale wooden sets with marble-topped tables and washstands originated in Russia, but there is no real proof to this effect, and in fact it seems more likely that such pieces were made in Germany.

The Russian contribution to the history of dolls' houses relies mainly on a curious nineteenth-century model created by Pavel Voinovich Nachtchokine (1801–54). Though it is quite common for men of today to construct model houses, late eighteenth-and early nineteenth-century gentlemen seem to have kept themselves aloof from what was obviously considered a somewhat frivolous pursuit. Nachtchokine created a model of such precision and correctness that from the time of its manufacture it was regarded as an important work. This importance is much enhanced by the connexion of the doll's house with the poet Pushkin, who was a close friend of Nachtchokine and often stayed at his Moscow home. It is at least partly due to this friendship that Nachtchokine was held in high esteem by academics and people concerned with the arts, and it was possibly to retain their good opinion that he commissioned a portrait of Pushkin, after his death in a duel in 1837, by the sculptor Vitali.

It is difficult to imagine why, at the beginning of the 1830s, the poet Nachtchokine decided that it was necessary to create a miniature of the interior of his home, though, as he was to move house some five times before 1837, he perhaps felt some desire for a permanent record of happy times. The visits of Pushkin were obviously highlights in his life, and the room which the poet frequently occupied is included. The other apartments included a study, kitchen, billiard-room, salon, dining-room, office and bedroom. These were arranged on two floors with a basement and could be viewed through opening windows. It is obvious from enthusiastic contemporary reports that the skill of the assembler was greatly admired, especially with regard to the care he expended on the acquisition of absolutely correct miniatures. 'It is a precious thing both as a monument of the past and as a work of art of a grand miniaturist,' wrote Kouprin.

Pushkin obviously took a great interest in the somewhat eccentric pursuit of his friend and wrote home to his wife in 1831 with the comment that 'The little house of Nachtchokine is entirely finished. He has ordered a piano on which you could play a tune.' Nachtchokine's wife, Vera Alexandrovna, did in fact play tunes with her knitting-needles on its keys, which were made of ivory. This superb model was made in the Moscow workshops of F. Fischer and cost 1,500 roubles, a high price, as it was made with absolute precision, and the weak notes could be amplified by the pedals. This grand piano of $7\frac{1}{2}$ octaves stands on correctly turned legs, and there is an elegantly carved music-rest that can be lifted into position. Despite the information contained in Pushkin's letter, the work on the house was not in fact complete, as, in 1836, he again commented that the model was at last realized to perfection and all that was now needed was little living people – a refinement that was never adequately realized, probably because the available dolls were not considered sufficiently realistic.

The more impressive items of furniture reflect in particular the pastimes of men of the period and range from music and letter-writing to cards, billiards and, ominously, duelling. The equipment that relates to the game of billiards is truly remarkable, as it is precisely constructed and the complete billiard-room is still in a good general state. The billiard balls are made of ivory, and there are two types of cues in their special rack, where the end of each cue rests in an ivory cup, and the complete structure ends in a carved ivory ornamental flame. The players were also given a rack for holding the balls and a scoreboard. Various card-games were played on a folding-top card-table with a pedestal base resting on three massive carved lions' paws. As in full-sized versions of this piece, the surface is covered with green baize for protection from the players' hands and from the small counters kept in a mother-of-pearl box.

The great interest of '*La Petite Maison de Nachtchokine*' lies, however, not so much in its miniature size as in the fact that it contains the work of so many recorded craftsmen, all contributing to a representation in miniature of the most skilled Russian work of this type. In this context the dinner-service and china from the porcelain factory of A. Popov is particularly notable, as this factory made some of the very finest porcelain and is regarded with great respect by ceramic collectors. All these miniature items are completely attributable to Popov, as they carry the firm's blue mark. The cabinet-maker Hambs provided much of the best furniture, while the silver bears the marks of various Moscow silversmiths, some of whom would be completely unrecorded without the evidence in this model. The cutlery was supplied by the cutlers of Toula. Despite the fact that many of the original pieces from the house were lost, the museum still retains over three hundred miniatures, all made as

Above left: This ornate French Empire-style clock gives some concept of the extravagance of Nachtchokine's model assembled in the 1830s. *Above right:* The billiard room contains several perfectly made items such as these ebony and ivory cues with their stand.

precise copies, so that tables, writing-boxes and cupboards all open properly, and all the utensils could be used for the purposes for which they were intended; there is even a correctly made folding bed.

The large dining-table with twenty baluster legs was of the extending type known in Russia as a 'thousand feet dining-table'. The matching chairs have caned seats and are typical of the lighter type of furniture that became popular all over Europe around 1830. When laid with the Popov porcelain and exquisite glassware and cutlery, this table must have presented a scene of great realism and grandeur, though Nachtchokine added a somewhat gruesome touch in the form of a dead mouse, covered in jelly to resemble a sucking pig. It appears that he quite frequently staged mock receptions in the model, and in one letter to his wife Pushkin commented that a ball had been held in the little house. Typically Russian is the generous supply of samovars, including four very small examples in silver that formed part of a silver table-service, which consists of a delicately gilded sugar-bowl, teapot, slop-basin

553

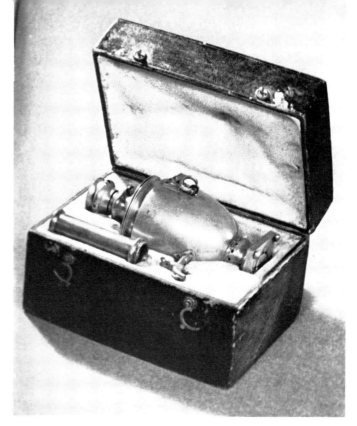

Articles from Nachtchokine's house. *Above left:* One of several silver samovars found in the house. The matching driptray makes this example unusually complete. *Above right:* A travelling samovar made of copper and contained in a correctly made case. *Below left:* A fine candle-snuffer and stand decorated in blue and gold, made by Toula craftsmen for Nachtchokine *circa* 1835. *Below right:* The furniture in Nachtchokine's house was in perfect scale, and most of the porcelain came from the Popov factory.

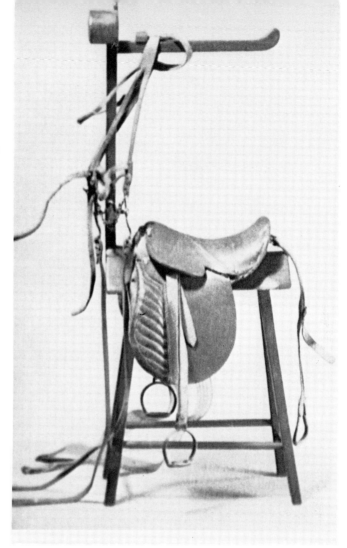

All the sports equipment in the Nachtchokine house was perfectly made by specialist craftsmen, such as this harness on its own stand.

and cake-basket. A much larger travelling samovar in its own box is made of copper. The dining-table was lit by massive gilt candlesticks, and the cutlery when not in use was stored in the appropriate sections of a box marked in mother-of-pearl.

The kitchen was able to supply all that was needed at a banquet, as its equipment was very complete and included cake- and fish-moulds, coffee-makers, mortars and even a very rarely found napkin-press and a large guillotine-like tool made for cutting the sugar loaves for guests. After dinner, all the visitors sat in the impressive salon lit by a massive and quite splendid chandelier suspended from intricately worked chains. Additional lighting was provided by candles in charming bronze sconces, ornamented with cherubs' heads, and by completely up-to-date oil-lamps, all made with great precision. Among the smaller items in this room which particularly attract is a candle-snuffer with a matching tray made by a Toula craftsman and decorated in blue and gilt with a country scene, the border of the snuffer being echoed on the edge of the tray.

Having eaten, played cards and listened to music, the gentlemen were expected the following morning to turn to more serious matters, such as hunting and shooting. Documents relating to the house mention an arsenal, but now only a single but exquisite pair of travelling-pistols survive in a blue silk and velvet-lined box marked 'P. H. Huberty à Liege'. These pistols are made of steel and bronze and are accompanied by a lead bullet-mould. Individual items, such as the pistols and the billiard equipment, make this model particularly interesting, as it forms such a direct contrast to the majority of other examples with their emphasis on womanly concerns, such as nursery furniture and sewing-rooms. In Nachtchokine's house are discovered such unusually masculine items as an extremely wide selection of riding-boots, shoes and outdoor boots, as well as a complete and very accurate harness arranged on a horse-stand. All the well-made boots have their own silver-mounted trees, which were supplied by Pelle, the fashionable St Petersburg boot-maker, while well-known hatters supplied the varied but fashionable headgear that is also found in profusion. The gentlemen obviously had need of a number of walking-sticks, and these all have carved ivory handles and are again absolutely correct miniatures.

Like so many of the other fine cabinet houses, Nachtchokine's creation passed through the hands of several collectors, many of its furnishings being owned at the beginning of the twentieth century by P. Chtchoukine, who presented them to the Historical Museum in Moscow. In 1918 the house was also acquired by the museum. Eventually, because of the connection of the model with the life of Pushkin, it was exhibited in the Pushkin Museum in Leningrad, where attempts are still being made to recover many of the dispersed items so that it can be seen exactly as it was displayed when Pushkin admired its craftsmanship. Originally Nachtchokine had willed this doll's house to the poet's wife who had followed its progress so avidly in her husband's letters, but sadly, in 1840, because of the loss of all his money, its assembler was forced to pawn the model and could not afford to redeem it, even though he wished to give it to such a dear friend. 'La Petite Maison' was consequently dispersed, certain valuable and interesting pieces disappearing in the course of each transaction. It is thought that in Pushkin's time the model consisted of a rectangular mahogany cabinet some $98\frac{1}{2}$ inches by $78\frac{1}{2}$ inches, with opening windows that allowed the visitor to view the interior. It originally comprised two floors and a basement. Though so many of the furnishings have been re-assembled and the British clock has been re-stored, the viewer inevitably sighs over the lost pieces, such as the copies of Nachtchokine's house-slippers that gave this model such a completely personal appeal.

Although adult-inspired dolls' houses are comparatively rare in Northern Europe, the cold, long winters formed ideal periods for the construction of play-houses that would keep the children happily employed indoors. The southern parts of Europe, such as Spain and Italy, have few model houses, with the exception of the exquisite little model at the Museum of Industrial Art in Bologna, which is completely in the idiom of a princely toy, and it seems highly probable that this lack of an essentially indoor toy is due mainly to the fact that children were not confined to the house for such long periods. The children of Norway, Sweden and Denmark have, in comparison, a large number of houses, the Nordiska Museum in Stockholm, for instance, displaying some thirty examples, among which are several cabinet houses, though made much less completely than those of Germany and Holland. The most elegant is in the form of a light eighteenth-century drawing-room cabinet that stands on very delicate legs; the rooms are simply arranged on open shelves and include a dancing-chamber. Another but much later model was made around 1925 as a copy of the Hersbyholm Manor at Lidingo near Stockholm. This construction is completely functional and stands on a simple base, though it is given considerable importance by the heavy double doors. In one room we see the presents laid out all around the Christmas tree.

Another curious model at this museum dates to around 1840 and is made completely of cardboard. Despite its many heavily ornamented windows at the sides and front, the house contains only a single room, furnished with a table, chairs and sofa. The Nordiska Museum also displays the very well-designed house made by the chemist C. D. L. Carlson of Skinnskattenberg between 1900 and 1905. Its designer was obviously very much in tune with the most modern work in architecture and furniture, and the model is very progressive in atmosphere, with open-plan staircase and simple woven rugs.

Possibly the most interesting Finnish house at the National Museum, Helsinki, was once owned by the daughter of State Councillor M. Hallberg and dates to the 1890s. This structure is of particular interest, as it contains a quantity of furniture made at M. Nordensvan's toy-factory at Kuopio, which is of an exceptionally high standard. These pieces are made of blond-coloured wood with highly effective and correctly scaled turning on the legs and chair-backs and is similar to, though much more complicated than, some of the smaller-scale furniture made at the same time in Germany. Many of the other northern houses contain plenishments from France, Germany and even Russia, and it is this complete interdependence of nations within the confines of these small rooms that makes their examination so absorbing.

A group of three modern houses made to suit the requirements of the collector of today who places great emphasis on correct detail and carefully scaled furniture. The East Anglian cottage (centre) opens at back and front and can be furnished with 1:12 scale furniture. The Victorian weatherboard cottage (bottom) is front opening. The London house (top) is based on an actual Victorian building.

NINE

Collecting and Restoration

Possibly the most refreshing aspect of doll's house collecting is that this is the one area where there is no segregation of either age or sex among the enthusiasts: dolls tend to be mainly the province of women, and soldiers and trains that of men and boys, but in the miniature house or room the interests converge, and many a model is seen to profit from a complete family's enthusiasm and skills. The purchase of a reasonably old house is not prohibitively expensive in relation to the price of other antique toys. Houses have not escalated as rapidly in price as dolls during the last ten years, and very attractive nineteenth-century models can still be bought for less than a single, very common doll. The relative stability of prices in this sphere is due mainly to the fact that the sheer size makes it difficult and expensive for dealers to transport them to America and Europe, and they are often not as immediately saleable as a small doll or a tin toy because they consume much-needed space in a modern home. For these reasons a miniature doll's house or one that is small enough to stand on a shelf or side table will often command a price completely out of line with the workmanship involved in its construction, while a huge model that is well detailed will sell quite cheaply.

Though it is usually possible to suggest some price guidelines for dolls, the houses are much more unpredictable, as some will pass through the specialist sales with scarcely a bid, while on another day a model of exactly the same type will arouse feverish competition and a high realization. As with doll's house dolls, the best advice is to acquire the finest example you can afford at the time and, above all, purchase only what really appeals, as it may take several years before the item can be re-sold at a profit. Fashion always plays a considerable part in collecting of all kinds, and it is possible that, as in the area of certain dolls, the house might possibly be worth less in two years time than when it was acquired. At the time of writing, such models are enjoying a burst of popularity, but it should in fairness be pointed out that dolls' houses are not really within the scope of the pure investor, partly because it is virtually impossible to realize the full market value of the object after it has been restored and furnished, as the individual plenishments are now so very expensive. We must therefore regard the doll's house not with the eye of the profiteer but with the enthusiastic devotion of the true collector, who delights in an item for its own sake rather than for vulgar monetary value.

Dolls' houses suffer much more radically than dolls at the hands of amateur restorers who smother them with modern plastic paints, nylon carpets and harshly coloured wallpapers, having stripped out all that was faded, original and beautiful. It is very easy to understand how such vandalism occurs: the scratched, battered and roughly furnished model almost begs to be improved, and unfortunately this is what generations of eager children and their parents have proceeded to do. A fragile doll might be redressed, but its wax or china face is unlikely to be repainted, whereas the doll's house façade seems to beg every person able to hold a paintbrush to set to work. Frequently, lovely models are found covered with layers of paint, papers, lithographed scraps, cellotape, resin-type glues and plastic decorations. Faced with such an accumulation, the only solution open to the restorer is to strip down the model to as near its original condition as possible. The great temptation to which we all succumb at times is to arrive home in triumph with a purchase and at once begin to pull away the new papers and scratch at the paintwork in order to achieve an immediate improvement. The more sensible and rewarding course is instead quietly to study the house from all angles to discover any clues that might help to trace the original owner, such as fragments of old letters used to level a floor or pushed into firebaskets, or even an old removal man's label. Some children wrote their names on the back of the house or on pieces of furniture, and this information might also forge a chain in a link that will lead you back to the last owner. Auction houses are now very reluctant to disclose the name of the vendor to purchasers and, more culpably, also frequently lose the original documentation that accompanied the houses, so that I have known collectors take several years to re-discover information that should have been sold together with the house and which might also have resulted in a higher realization had it been made known. Such essential information is too easily lost through a hasty cleaning of the doll's house, when what appears to be rubbish is thrown indiscriminately into the dustbin.

Having removed any actual rubbish from the model and laid aside any pieces of possible use or information, clean out the rooms thoroughly, using a paintbrush and a toothbrush to loosen the dust from corners and difficult areas such as stairwells. I find that this method, in combination with the nozzle of a vacuum cleaner, is most effective, but do watch for any woodworm dust that will sometimes trickle down from a ceiling-join and which is perhaps

One of the first do-it-yourself kits for dollmakers was the series of fretwork designs available from magazines such as *Hobbies*. Sometimes not only the patterns but the wood, furniture and wallpapers could be obtained from the one source. In this small example (*circa* 1900) the front, brick papered in red, opens in two sections to reveal a four-roomed interior.

the only clue given to the fact that worm is active in the upper section of the roof. Treat any suspicious sections immediately with killer so that there is no possibility of the infestation spreading. Worm is most active in the spring, so no model purchased at that time of year should be left untreated for any time, as it can spread quickly, especially through plywood. The proprietary brands of worm-killer were once supplied with metal injectors that enabled the holes to be penetrated sharply, but progress has now replaced these useful devices with plastic nozzles, much too wide for use on antique pieces, and I would therefore advise the purchase of a metal oil-can with a very narrow injector, so that the liquid can be forced into the wormholes without spreading them any wider than is necessary. If the house has been completely repainted and papered, then the killer can be applied very generously and allowed to dry out in an outhouse or even out of doors, otherwise the smell will permeate everything around. If the model with worm is otherwise in original condition, apply the solution sparingly and test a few sections on the back or sides before attempting to treat the front, as some surfaces can change colour slightly. Paper-covered models are particularly vulnerable, as they were so often made of plywood, but even considerable infestation can be halted, and it seems a pity to avoid buying a house simply because of some worm. As lithographed paper will mark if spotted with the liquid, I find it safer to paint the whole surface of the paper inside and out, after the individual injection, in order to even the tone, which is bound to change slightly, despite makers' claims to the effect that their solution will not mark in any way. Again, before attempting to brush the surface with the solution, try a small section and allow it to dry out completely before continuing, as it is possible for the paper to dry unevenly or come away from the wood so that the whole process must be one of trial before application.

Original or old wallpapers, even if badly stained, should be left in place, as a badly marked but original paper is preferable to the finest replacement. A purely cosmetic improvement can be effected by the judicious hanging of pictures, or the placing of a screen or a wall-hanging. If one section is missing completely, then it might be possible to paint a small panel and fix this over the offending area. The removal of layers of new paper is often a hazardous exercise, as it is easy to apply the wrong pressure and pull away some of the original also. If an old adhesive, which has become granular with age, was used, then it is sometimes possible to separate the layers without wetting. In other cases, warm water, brushed on the surface, will loosen the glue sufficiently for a layer to be removed. Fortunately the lower layer is usually fixed very firmly to the wood and will stand a surprising amount of hard treatment. If the paper is very reluctant to come away, then a proprietary stripper can be used, though again, use sparingly and attempt to salvage any of the bottom layer. Often during this stripping process one becomes very disillusioned, as so many sections of the original paper are found to be missing. My advice is, do not despair but continue resolutely and finish the room to the best of your ability and then examine what remains. Sometimes, two walls, for instance, will be only slightly damaged while the remainder is ruinous, and in this case it seems legitimate to remove the few pieces from the worst wall and use them to fill the gaps in the better sections, so preserving most of the original covering and leaving the bare wall free for a decorative panel, a cleverly copied pattern, or a large piece of furniture. Damage at ground-level in a late-Victorian or Edwardian room can be covered by a mock lincrusta frieze, while just below ceiling-level it was fashionable to use an ornamental patterned frieze paper which would be useful in covering tears. Obviously such additions alter the character of a room to some degree, but this seems better than completely replacing the whole covering. Some of the late-Victorian friezes were very ornate, and if the restorer has any artistic skill, it should be possible to copy an original design. A number of reprinted books on Victorian ornament are now available, and for those with less skill, these could be traced and painted. When fixing any water-coloured sections in place, remember that the paste is likely to lift the colour or make it run, so use very sparingly, otherwise hours of patient colouring can be lost with one sweep of a cloth. Nursery friezes can look particularly effective and could be derived either from those created by Kate Greenaway or by copying contemporary designs seen in old photographs.

Very marked wallpaper is sometimes recoverable if the individual motifs are carefully repainted in meticulously matched colours. Though this process is both difficult and slow, it is very worthwhile, as an almost original effect is regained. If a complete section is missing, then tear a patch roughly from a piece of paper of similar texture and weight and press it firmly in position so that the roughly torn edges blend with the original; when dry and painted, the repair should be unobtrusive. Modern poster-type paints often lack the subtlety of colour necessary for such work, and I find the old-style artists' watercolour boxes, such as those sold by Windsor & Newton, much more sympathetic. When sketching in the missing sections of pattern, work in a very pale grey or blue with a fine sable; the expense of a good brush is more than worthwhile, because the bristles do not separate at that critical moment and ruin hours of work. It is also much easier to work in such a confined space if the handle of the brush is cut short, so that it is not continually catching on the ceiling or opposite wall.

Many of the old embossed papers that were used as borders in dolls' houses are no longer available, though old-fashioned ironmongers occasionally have some rolls that can be cut into narrower sections. If such an old supply is discovered, it is advisable to purchase more than is immediately required, as items of this type can often be swopped for other useful pieces with fellow enthusiasts, as few shops are now able to obtain such out-of-date materials. The metal foils used for cake-decoration can sometimes be adapted for use by

A modern doll's house (1975) in Victorian Gothic style designed for easy access to the rooms. The exterior is an effective scale model.

painting with gloss paint to give the appearance of old-fashioned heavily varnished dados. The obvious source of genuinely old wallpaper is house-sales, as people almost invariably order a spare roll when decorating a room in case of future damage. Sometimes, if a family has lived in a house for a long time, the whole development of interior decoration can be seen in the odd lengths stored away in old suitcases. Auctioneers think it hardly worth putting such rubbish into a sale, so it is sometimes useful to discover where the real junk is stored away. When redecorating old family houses it is also sometimes possible to remove quite long strips of Victorian and Georgian paper and, with some careful matching, re-use this in a doll's house, as it was quite usual for vcry large-scale papers to be used in early models. Occasionally old papers have striped designs of various kinds, and it is possible to cut out the narrower sections and carefully join them together to make a convincing smaller pattern. The larger pieces can perhaps form panels in other rooms edged with wooden moulding or small borders: never throw away even the smallest pieces of old paper, as they can be useful for lining wardrobes or drawers or even for wrapping up small blocks of wood to serve as presents around the Christmas tree.

If no suitable old papers can be found, then modern book-end papers are sometimes useful, those with a marbled design being very suitable for halls and dining-rooms of the late Victorian period. If just the right colour is unobtainable, then it is quite a simple process to marble your own by following the instructions in a craft book or in a leaflet such as those produced by Dryad. Instructions for wood-block, screen-printing and lithographic and etching processes are all set out clearly in such leaflets, so that the beginner should have no difficulty in understanding the basic principles, though ultimate success in producing really effective designs obviously comes only with practice and a complete familiarity with the medium. Original designs in the manner of the period are not easy for the amateur to create, and it is more encouraging to reproduce simplified original designs. If, after experimenting, the patience necessary for creating sheets of small repeat patterns is not available, then more success might be obtained by painting soft monochrome panels to decorate a room in a manner similar to that used in the Tate house. For an eighteenth-century house the most artistic might enjoy painting a chinoiserie paper in imitation of the expensive panels that can be seen in museums and in the more lavishly produced books on the history of wallpaper. When using any kind of hand-painted wallpaper, do not attempt to paint the design *in situ*, as this is virtually impossible. All the pattern must be completed before the paper is fixed in place, though some hand-finishing can sometimes be effected if the room is not too small.

During the eighteenth century, a print room formed an amusing occupation for the ladies, and as bundles of old damaged pages cut from books of the period are still very cheap, a room that has completely lost its original wall-coverings could be decorated in this way. The prints in an actual house, such as at Heveningham Hall in Norfolk, were outlined with a band of colour after they were glued in position, so that the separate scenes were linked and some unity was given to the arrangement. In some cases delicate linking patterns were also used, and the restorer is advised to study actual examples to find a room in the same style. Landscapes and portraits were often used together, so that the possibilities of this type of treatment are infinite, though of course it should be used only when the room is without any original features. Other eighteenth-century doll's house furnishers sometimes fixed a large print edged with wooden moulding or even braid to form a mock painting or wall-hanging, and these were coloured to look more realistic. In

'Mon Plaisir', small cut-out figures from prints were glued to the walls to form a type of *decoupage* and, when dry, lightly varnished to give an even texture. The Princess Dorothea was particularly fond of creating wall-decorations from such cut-out sections, and as this style of decoration continued until the 1830s, it can be usefully adapted for early models.

If you have no artistic skill and can find no genuine papers, as a last resort we turn to modern wallpapers and wrapping-papers. The latter are generally more useful, as they are printed on thin paper, which is much easier to handle in a small space. One collector, in her determination to obtain a really antique appearance, first boiled a sheet of paper and then ironed it flat to give a suitably aged appearance. Others leave the paper out in the weather for a few days or lay it on a sunny windowsill to fade convincingly. As a last resort, it can be rubbed down with light brown paint or even coffee. The great disadvantage of the modern papers is that there is always someone who recognizes the design, and there is nothing more infuriating than having a fellow collector comment that she too has found that particular paper effective! Far better to create something that is, if not absolutely perfect, at least unique.

Reproduction doll's house papers that are available in some number today seem to suffer from the same fault, though they are excellent for modern houses. Reproduction furniture seems to suffer the same drawback also; though it is a temptation to include for instance a four-poster bed, because an antique cannot be found, it is rarely satisfactory, as even if the viewer is deceived, you are aware that the object is new and should not really be in the setting. This is obviously a personal and somewhat purist view, and many collectors are perfectly happy to mix old and new, but in these circumstances I find that the atmosphere is lost, as so much of the enjoyment comes from handling the small objects that have passed through so many other hands. Many creators of reproduction furniture claim that their work is superior to that commercially produced in the eighteenth and nineteenth centuries, and it has to be agreed that the finish is often of a very high quality. What these pieces lack is the atmosphere of age, the quality that furniture acquires only after passing through the lives of many people, an atmosphere of the past that is completely spellbinding and which the new piece cannot hope to emulate. Old furniture was made in imitation of pieces in current use in its country of manufacture and has an importance that is both historical and social, whereas the modern item, made completely for the appreciation of contemporary collectors, has no historical relevance and can stand in the future only as an example of the taste of the collectors of today. A few might well prove to have been sound investment-pieces, but many will never rise in value above what was originally paid, despite all the lavish claims of limited editions and investment-pieces. The collector is therefore advised to purchase modern items with his eyes completely open, to accept the fact that he is

The interior of a modern house in Tudor style opening in four sections. All the rooms are furnished with pieces made by the woman who created the house. Height 168 centimetres.

buying purely on a personal basis and that it is very possible that there will be no further appreciation. Recently a set of furniture made by Fred Early, who worked on some of the pieces in Titania's Palace, was auctioned and realized very substantial figures from Continental buyers, who appreciated the finely made knife-boxes, sideboards and cabinets, despite the fact that they were originally made as retrospective objects. This single instance serves to illustrate the point that in individual cases a substantial investment might be possible when purchasing a reproduction, but it should be remembered that these pieces did have an association with a famous doll's house and that, when this craftsman was working, there were relatively few others creating miniatures, whereas today a number produce really excellent work. In general, my own inclination is to avoid reproductions, as they have no truth of period, though it is easy so imagine the enjoyment that could be derived

A model of a room in Windsor Castle (once owned by Queen Mary) with imitation lacquered furniture and painted curtains. The front wall of the room has been removed. Height 9 inches. *Opposite:* An early twentieth-century cabinet containing two rooms made by David Allan, Tapissier to George V at Buckingham Palace. The contents were assembled by Queen Mary. There is a fine ivory clock on the mantelpiece. On the writing desk is an unusual pair of spectacles with emeralds instead of lenses.

from buying an impressive reproduction mansion and fitting it with the finest of modern items.

The great scarcity of dolls' houses with original furniture is due at least partly to the vandalism of dealers, who were quick to realize that their profit on an individual house would be much increased if they sold all the items separately. This attitude reflects great discredit on a trade whose members often belong to dealers' associations that profess to wish to protect objects of interest, though in fairness it should be stated that, as many houses contain pieces added over the years, complete originality is something only very occasionally found. Few houses reflect a precise period or the character of the original assembler, though a few constructed in the aftermath of the unveiling of Queen Mary's house, and very much adult pastimes, do provide a precise impression of middle-class British life in the 1920s and 1930s, when there were still many servants and even the occasional butler. Queen Mary was herself responsible for the rescue of several dolls' houses, and she enjoyed equipping model rooms, such as the elegant example furnished with delicate carved ivory. She was not particularly concerned with authenticity and often mixed modern items, such as those marketed by Triang, with fine old tables

The eighteenth-century doll's house that Denton Welch restored in the 1940s. He was particularly pleased with the fan-light, which he constructed from matches.

and bureaux. Her enthusiastic restoration did much to encourage an interest in the subject, and the results of her work can be seen at the Bethnal Green and London Museums.

Possibly the best-documented piece of doll's house restoration concerned the house that was rescued during the last war by the ailing writer and artist Denton Welch, who died at the age of thirty-three in 1948. Welch derived a curious invalid's enjoyment from all the simple pleasures of the life that he shared with his male companions and which he detailed, often with almost embarrassing intensity, in his journals and books. His imagination was stirred when, by the light of a torch, he saw a dilapidated doll's house in a friend's cellar. Its owner, Mrs Bosanquet, explained that it had belonged to her mother's family, the Littledales of Yorkshire, and when the doors were opened, he saw the detail of the chimneypieces with their perfect mouldings and the properly carved panels of the doors. The house was in a sad state as it was daubed and coated with thick paint and hung with moth-eaten curtains, and he obviously longed to care for it. Eventually it passed into his keeping, because the cellar was needed as an air-raid shelter, and its owner was glad to be rid of the responsibility.

No other account of the restoration of a doll's house brings so vividly to life the mixture of acquisitiveness and responsible improvement that underlies all restoration. The writer's enthusiasm for the project was so great that on his birthday his friends delighted him with presents for the house, including a fretsaw, wooden mouldings, glue and a vice, all items difficult to obtain at the time. In a small whitewood box was a set of 'Bristol' glasses, 'four clear tall champagne-glasses, two bulging wine-glasses on stems, three beakers, one dark blue, two dark purple, four little white cups and saucers, a perfect jug and cover, a damaged one and a fruit-dish and plate. Even the champagne-glasses are less than an inch high.' This loving itemizing of each article, so familiar to every enthusiast, makes the restoration of the house seem as though it were taking place at the present time and not among the problems and difficulties of wartime Britain.

While scraping the paint away from a block of wood to the right of the kitchen fireplace, Welch discovered the initials 'MJD', with the date 1783 painted in shades of grey and black, suggesting perhaps that the Littledales had inherited the house from another family. Few houses are known by the name of their restorer rather than their family, though the quality of the restoration was exceptionally high, as can be seen from an examination of the model, which is now at the Bethnal Green Museum and which can be studied with a knowledge of the work that the writer carried out. Like every collector of today, he plunged into the restoration of the model as soon as it was delivered, and after tearing out the dirty curtains and emptying every room of its later, Edwardian furniture, he found only three useful and possibly original items, a dark mahogany Pembroke table with two missing legs and a flap, which he later mended, a small chest in dark mahogany and an oak kitchen stool. There was also an old brass saucepan, two pewter platters and a few Victorian dishcovers.

Generations of children had covered the mouldings with pink and green enamel, and the old leather hinges on the cupboards had been replaced with brass hinges; virtually nothing was left of the bannisters. By a great stroke of good fortune, the classical pediment that was missing from the arched central window was discovered in one of the drawers of the stand, 'with its straight little Chippendale legs' and brass drop-handle. The stand was decorated with a Chinese Chippendale fret-design in ochre and white, which he carefully painted in to preserve the pattern that had almost faded from sight. Under the battleship grey of the house itself, he saw a lighter fawn paint on which bricks were outlined in black. Under these were two further coats of yellow, larger bricks with white outlines and, right at the bottom, the original coat with tiny red bricks. Sadly, it was impossible, without ruining the house, to scrape through all these layers, so he contented himself with the first beige bricks that seemed to date from the early-nineteenth century. Even these were revealed only after months of industry between bouts of illness and feverish writing.

Originally, each room was papered in a different pattern, and he found a fragment in the hall that was based on a somewhat stiff tulip motif. Under the enamel paint, every room was also painted in a different colour, the dining-room white, the drawing-room pink, the bedroom blue and the kitchen white and ochre. The doors were made of polished mahogany with white cases. The restoration of the house was halted between 1942 and 1945, as Welch was forced to move house, and he was not able to begin his carpentry repairs until 1945. 'I mended the stand fairly well, then one of the big doors, which was in three pieces. Gradually I turned to the more intricate things, making the missing tapering legs of the Pembroke table, supplying two missing windowsills, the front-door steps and the pediment and tops of the columns. The fanlight I made all of matches and putty, and it was good.' Encouraged by such achievements, he proceeded to the interior: 'I made little leather hinges, just like the originals, for the doors, and I began on the staircase, doing the chief newelposts in colour, attempting to match the three originals left. . . . I have now nearly made one of the two chimneys and am about to begin on the balustrade, which runs along the top of the house, linking up the pediment above the deep cornice'.

On a trip into Tonbridge with his companion, Eric, he found 'two awful Turkish brackets with just the right balustrading on them . . . tomorrow I am going to dismember them and put the balustrade on the doll's house. Nothing will look grander than the doll's house with its perfect classical door, window proportions, heavy Palladian coigning, cornice and then the pediment and the reconstructed balustrade, all standing on the stand with its fret patterns revived'. He worked on the house for several months that summer, his delight culminating in the birthday gift of the coloured glass. After this, his excitement and interest seem to have waned, perhaps because of his constant ill-health or because of the great difficulty in obtaining any more furniture for the model. He does tell of a visit to an antique-shop near the gate at Rye in October 1946, giving a vivid impression of the problems encountered by collectors of that period. At the back of the shop was an old doll's house, 'early-nineteenth century, clumsy and formless'; but when he opened the doors he saw that things had been collected with care for each room. Its owner explained that the furniture had been purchased in the company of his brother, and had cost more than £40, an astonishingly high figure for the period and an indication of how difficult it was for these early enthusiasts to obtain pieces. Collectors always tend to think that, if only they had been interested in the subject ten or forty years ago, they would have been able to purchase items very cheaply, but this anecdote illustrates the difficulty of collecting at a time when there were few other enthusiasts and should serve to encourage those of us who sometimes despair of ever acquiring particular objects.

For the majority of collectors without the natural skill of Denton Welch, repairs to the basic woodwork of a doll's house are probably better left to a good carpenter or cabinet-maker, though it is inadvisable to allow him to work on the model without very close supervision, as many very skilled men find difficulty in working in the antique manner. The sections needing actual repair or replacement should be carefully stipulated, as it is too easy for an over-enthusiastic craftsman to remove complete sections that he considers a little shabby or capable of improvement. Insist that any new sections should be jointed into the structure to replace missing sections rather than lose an inch of the original woodwork unnecessarily, though it is obviously much easier to replace a complete section of pediment than to fix in a small piece from a corner. Above all, do not replace wood-wormed sections, as these, once treated, are simply the honourable marks of age and do not detract in any way, as they are also very visible in some of the most expensive and superb furniture.

In certain cases it is advisable to use a woodfiller to make good a very small damaged section, as it is easier to obtain a completely smooth join. Eighteenth-century decorators frequently resorted to the use of putty to fill small sections and knots in the wood, so that this material would be quite appropriate in an eighteenth-century model. Even in the Edwardian period, putty was still in general use as a filler, and in that textbook of the Socialist movement, *The Ragged-Trousered Philanthropist*, the reader is frequently reminded of the high incidence of its use, though it should be added that it is a filler that is often extremely difficult to remove, and restorers of pine furniture in particular rue the fact that it was once in such general use. It is rarely used today by woodworkers, having been replaced by various proprietary fillers, but it can be useful for early houses on sections that need to be repainted.

Very complex sections of moulding are a great problem, and the restorer is advised to haunt demolition- and junk-yards in the hope of finding pieces than can be utilized. In this area of restoration every problem has to be separately assessed, and the complete amateur is advised to enlist the advice of an experienced carpenter, as it is often better to pay a fee for help rather than make some unfortunate mistake. The too hasty replacing of a missing piece with a modern section should also be avoided, as it is much better to search and wait for an ideal solution than to rush into an unsatisfactory compromise. Missing doors are invariably a great problem, as it is extremely difficult for the amateur to create a correct miniature with inset panels, so that again it is better to seek the advice of a competent craftsman, who will often take great interest in such comparatively unusual work. Several wood-workers now specialize in miniature restoration of this kind and advertise their services in specialist magazines, so that it is possible to obtain minute turned legs, columns or stair-rails as well as specially made small-scale mouldings. Later houses were usually supplied with much plainer doors, sometimes with the detail painted or lithographed to seem more interesting, and these can often be copied by the amateur without too much trouble. Good bone and ivory door-knobs are available from the specialist makers of fittings, but antique versions can be found on broken dressing-tables or small boxes, and the enthusiast is also advised to remove any old hinges and locks from pieces past repair for future use. Many houses were originally supplied with quite crude leather hinges, and I have known many collectors who have been unable to resist the temptation to replace these with bright modern ornamental substitutes. In general, no matter how large or clumsy the original hinges might be, they are far more in sympathy with the house than the most beautifully scaled modern version could possibly be.

Missing window-glass is not too great a problem, as broken prints and pictures in their original frames often appear in miscellaneous lots in auction sales and after a little practice can be cut down to size without too much trouble, so that glass of the appropriate period can be used. The windows can be fixed in place with old-style carpenter's glue or putty, and a paper border can sometimes be used to neaten the edge. The French-style houses in particular have most attractive flowered borders around the windows, and though such perfectly designed patterns are no longer available, these could be wood-block-printed or stencilled and finished by painting the delicate detail. The slender glazing-bars of eighteenth- and early nineteenth-century houses are sometimes difficult, as such detailed work needs the finest carpenter's skill, especially if the windows have to open correctly. Fortunately many early models, even of the most splendid type, were given simple, straight dividers, almost like matchsticks, while in other cases the bars were

574

simply painted in place, and the restorer can use either thickly mixed poster-colour or ordinary undercoat.

Throughout the whole process of restoration, use materials that are compatible with those available when the house was made, so that modern glue and paint should be avoided wherever possible. Modern paint is particularly flat in appearance, as it is mechanically mixed, and much better effects can be obtained with artists' colours or even powder paints. If a glazed surface is required, then artists' varnish used over the base colours will give a much more authentic effect. In some cases a good-quality wax polish applied over a painted section will give a charming, lightly polished surface, but care should be taken as polish will sometimes remove the paint completely, so a trial section should be first attempted. The mixing of matching colours for chipped or flaking paintwork is a long and sometimes almost impossible process, as when the model is viewed in a different light, the repair that looked so perfect in a north light is seen to look quite wrong. The best advice is, to avoid working in artificial or very bright light, and not to attempt to hurry the process but sit down with a wide assortment of paints and be prepared to spend several days if necessary in making up just the right colour. The work is often made easier if the damaged section is first built up with gesso to the level of the sound paintwork, so that there is a smooth basic surface. It is obviously much easier to match in a complete section than a small chip, but as the basic aim must be to keep the object as original as possible, it is better to work patiently. Sometimes an absolute match is quite impossible because of the degree of fading of the original colour, and at such times it will be possible to effect only a partially successful restoration.

If the original paintwork is so damaged that the model needs complete stripping, then repaint with as thin a layer of paint as practicable, and again use original or old materials if at all possible. Cheap undercoat mixed with powder colours is also sometimes effective, especially if several colours are mixed together to give an interesting shade. Nineteenth-century paints were much less flat than those of today and the slight graduations of colour that will be achieved by this hand-mixing will provide a surface much more in sympathy with the original effect. Old paint of the gloss types can occasionally be found in worksheds and attics and can sometimes be thinned down sufficiently for re-use, though it should be remembered that such old colours are often very difficult to dry, and sometimes the model has to be left for several days.

A number of books dealing with the making of miniature furniture is now available, and the methods suggested can often be adapted for the repair of old pieces. As on the exterior of the house itself, as little restoration as possible should be carried out, and damaged upholstery, bedcovers and curtains should all be replaced with materials of the same weight and date. Unless fabric is quite literally hanging in shreds, I would avoid replacing it in any way, as the shabby fabrics often add to the mellowed atmosphere of a

A substantial early twentieth-century brick-painted house opening at front and back to reveal a staircase and nine rooms in Georgian style.

genuinely old interior. Professional textile-restoration is sometimes advisable in very interesting or valuable houses, but this is often expensive, and most collectors have to be content with a cosmetic improvement. Though cottons and linens can often be washed successfully, it is inadvisable to wet silk and satin, as these materials will sometimes fall apart if washed roughly. There are several textile conservation centres attached to museums, and if faced with particularly difficult problems, the collector is advised to seek professional help on the days set aside for dealing with questions from the public.

When a doll's house has lost its original soft furnishings, the collector is able to indulge his own taste in creating effects that contribute to the atmosphere of the period. There are many excellent National Trust guidebooks to important houses, and the illustrations can be studied for decorative detail, as can the many general books on this subject. The reprinted eighteenth- and nineteenth-century decorators' catalogues are also a great help in deciding on window treatments and the arrangement of furniture in a room, and almost as much pleasure can be derived in discovering the precise details of daily life at a particular time as in the final arrangement of the house. The late nineteenth and early twentieth century saw a great increase in the number of magazines dealing with the subject of decoration, and there is an abundance of photographs of all types of houses, ranging from splendid, ostentatious mansions to country retreats. It is not necessary to buy these journals, as many museums and libraries have sets that are available to read on the premises.

Enthusiastic doll and doll's house collectors usually save pieces of old fabrics, buttons, jewellery, lace, screws, hinges and papers so that, when a new acquisition has to be restored, they have a wide choice of suitable materials. The magpie instinct develops very quickly if you are aware that several rooms are standing bare, awaiting papers and carpets, and junk-shops, jumble sales and market stalls are scoured for fragments of printed velvet for carpets or soft silks for curtains. This aspect of collecting can be enjoyable, as frequently a tour around the shops can reveal a good early brass knob, some old beadwork that will cover a stool or make a wall-hanging, or some minute prints that will look well in frames. Old reels of cotton also frequently appear in the boxes of odds and ends that house-clearers put outside their shops, all of which can be stored away for a meticulously correct exercise in restoration.

The acquisition of figures for a doll's house has become much more difficult because of the number of people who now collect miniature dolls in their own right. These small dolls have recently enjoyed a surge in popularity and often command prices much higher than dolls of the same quality but of a much larger size. The all-bisques with stringing loops at the base of the neck, usually thought to be of French origin, are by far the most popular and most expensive, followed by the shoulder-head-type characters that represent

577

A fashionable house designed by Ira Grandberg, a New York architect for *Woman's Day* magazine in 1976. The model comes apart in sections for easy access and reflects interiors of the period.

adults. As in any field of collecting, it is advisable to purchase items in as good a condition as possible and of the best quality. Even in dolls as small as those needed for model rooms and houses, the quality of both moulding and decoration varies considerably, and the price should be so adjusted, though a particularly ugly example is often very suitable for a cook or maid, as the original assemblers frequently used the worst of their assortment of figures for this purpose. Only rarely do we find the most beautiful doll wearing a maid's cap and forming a snare for the master and the blond-haired young soldiers with their moulded moustaches. In general, maids were plump and ugly and kept firmly in their place.

578

The very basic porcelain-headed doll's house dolls with black glazed hair have not risen very much in price, as they were made in such large numbers, but their bland faces are highly adaptable and will fit into almost any situation, from a splendid butler to a bed-ridden aunt in the last stages of consumption. The porcelains were also made in a wide variety of sizes, so that some can be costumed as children. The better examples of this type with moulded headdresses or complicated hair-styles are obviously much more expensive, those in original costumes being the most sought-after. The stiff-legged dolls known as '*Bäderkinder*' or 'Frozen Charlottes' are not at present very popular because of the large number of reproductions, though some, especially those in seated positions with a soft pink lustre finish are ideal as bathroom or nursery occupants. Japanese doll's house dolls are also unpopular, though a few were of acceptable quality and can look very effective in houses made in the 1920s and 1930s.

Many of the reproduction figures made in both Europe and America are of the highest quality and fit perfectly into the best of the reproduction houses. Miniature waxes, resin-headed characters, porcelain- and bisque-headed figures are all made by a group of enthusiasts who finish their work with much more care than the German producers of the late nineteenth century, whose costuming, for instance, was sometimes of the most basic kind. These modern miniatures are often available at doll and toy fairs in Britain and at the regional doll club conventions in the States, but they are also stocked by specialist shops or can be ordered from catalogues issued by the makers and advertised in collectors' magazines. These reproduction dolls, like the furniture and ceramics, though made to the highest specifications, are really best suited to modern period houses, as they create an unharmonious atmosphere in an antique model. A somewhat bare nineteenth-century house looks much more effective than another that is cluttered with modern pieces quite out of natural accord with the other plenishments.

The modern movement towards the collecting of frequently very expensive miniatures is an almost certain result of our affluent society, within which people have a reasonable degree of leisure for personal hobbies and pursuits. Many of the houses, made with great skill and charm, represent all the changes of fashion in British and American history, presenting sugary Gothick villas and neat Regency town houses. Some of these structures are neatly papered and painted, but others are left quite plain so that the buyer can give the model its own very individual character. A few of these modern houses are made to special order by one-man concerns, while others are made more commercially but the majority are finished with care and are very acceptable items of furniture. This manufacture of modern miniatures is an industry that caters almost exclusively for adults, so that we seem to have turned full circle and returned to the eighteenth-century concept of cabinet-type houses, decorated with good textiles and fitted with expensive furniture.

Strangely, children's dolls' houses seem to arouse comparatively little thought and ingenuity, and only rarely does the enthusiast encounter a modern play-house that engenders any great interest. Perhaps, as a small girl's future role is no longer necessarily that of wife and mother, these essentially domestic teaching-toys are of less relevance to her life. Even the leading toyshops have only a few models on display.

As children have gradually lost their interest in dolls' houses, that of adults has steadily increased, and the cabinet of miniatures has again become quite an accepted feature of an elegant living-room.

Bibliography

Ackland, Eleanor. *Good-Bye for the Present* (Hodder & Stoughton, 1935)

Allison, J. Murray, editor. *Official Catalogue of the Queen's Doll's House* (Fleetway Press Ltd, 1924)

Angione, Genevieve. *All-Bisque and Half-Bisque Dolls* (Thomas Nelson & Sons, New Jersey, 1969)

Anka, Georgine, and Ursula Gauda. *Die Deutsche Puppenindustrie, 1815–1940* (Puppen & Spielzeug, Stuttgart, 1978)

Ariès, Philippe. *Centuries of Childhood* (Jonathan Cape, 1962)

Benson, A. C. and Weaver, Sir Laurence. *Everybody's Book of the Queen's Doll's House* (*Daily Telegraph* and Methuen, 1924)

Boehn, Max von. *Puppets and Automata* (originally published 1929; Dover Reprint, 1972)

Bradley, R. M. *The English Housewife in the Seventeenth and Eighteenth Centuries* (Edward Arnold, 1912)

Calmettes, P. *Les Joujoux* (Librairie Octave, Paris, 1924)

Centraal Museum, Utrecht. *Het Utrechts Poppenhuis* (1977)

Crump, Lucy. *The Story of the Dauphin of France. Nursery Life 300 Years Ago* (Routledge, 1929)

d'Allemagne, Henri. *Musée Retrospectif de la Classe 100. Jouets* (L'Exposition Universelle Internationale, Paris, 1900)

——*Histoire des Jouets* (Hachette, Paris, 1902)

De la Mare, Walter. *Early One Morning* (Faber & Faber, 1935)

Denton Welch Journals, edited by Jocelyn Brooke (Hamish Hamilton, 1952)

Dickens, Charles. *The Cricket on the Hearth*

Earle, Alice Morse. *Child Life in Colonial Days* (Macmillan Co, New York, 1899)

Franklin, Alfred, *La Vie Privée d'Autrefois* (E. Plon, Nourit et Cie, Paris, 1896)

Gröber, Karl. *Children's Toys of Bygone Days* (Batsford, 1928)

——*Die Puppenstadt* (Karl Robert Langewiesche, Königstein im Taunus, undated)

Haags Gemeentemuseum. *Een rondgang door het poppenhuis* (Undated)

Hansmann, Claus von, and Juliane Roh. *Altes Spielzeug* (F. Bruckmann, Munich, 1958)

Heal, Sir Ambrose. *London Goldsmiths* (1935)

Hewitt, William. *Rural and Domestic Life of Germany* (Longman, Brown, Green & Longmans, 1842)

Himmelheber, Georg. *Kleine Möbel* (Deutscher Kunstverlag, Munich, 1979)

His, H. P. *Altes Spielzeug aus Basel* (Historisches Museum, Basel, 1973)

Hobbies Catalogues, 1939, 1940

Holme, C. Geoffrey, editor *Children's Toys of Yesterday* (*The Studio,* 1932)

Hughes, Bernard. *Antique Sheffield Plate* (Batsford, 1970)

—— *Small Antique Silver* (Batsford, 1957)

—— *Collecting Miniature Antiques* (Heinemann, 1973)

Jacobs, Flora Gill. *Dolls' Houses in America* (Scribner, 1974)

Jourdain, M. J. *English Interiors in Smaller Houses. Restoration to Regency* (Batsford, 1923)

Kiefer, Monica. *American Children through their Books, 1700–1835* (University of Pennsylvania Press, 1948)

King, Constance E. *The Collector's History of Dolls* (Robert Hale, 1977)

—— *Dolls and Dollshouses* (Hamlyn, 1977)

King-Hall, Magdalen. *The Story of the Nursery* (Routledge & Kegan Paul, 1958)

Lane, Margaret. *The Tale of Beatrix Potter* (Warne & Co, 1946)

Latham, Jean. *Dolls' Houses: A Personal Choice* (A. & C. Black, 1969)

Leber, Wolfgang. *Die Puppenstadt Mon Plaisir* (Museender Stadt, Arnstadt, 1975)

Lewis, Frank. *English Chintz* (F. Lewis Publishers, Leigh-on-Sea, Essex, 1935)

Lines Brothers Ltd. *Looking Backwards, Looking Forwards* (1958)

Locke, John. *Some Thoughts Concerning Education*

Low, Frances H. *Queen Victoria's Dolls* (Newnes Ltd, 1894)

Mace, L. H. & Co. *Toy Catalogue*, 1907 (New York)

McClinton, Katherine. *Antiques in Miniature* (Scribner, New York, 1970)

Malvery, Olive Christian. *Baby Toilers* (Hutchinson, 1911)

Markham, E. B. B. Lindsey and George Creel. *Children in Bondage* (Hearst's International Library, New York, 1914)

Mayhew, H. *German Life and Manners as seen in Saxony* (William Allen & Co, 1865)

Molodovsky, Nikolai and Erica Schwarz. *Berchtesgadener Handwerkskunst* (Pannonia, 1977)

National Trust. *Nostell Priory. Guide to main house* (1973)

—— *Uppark. Guide to House* (1976)

Nazarova, G. I. *Naschokinskii domik* (Editions d'Art, Aurore, Leningrad, 1971)

Niesser, C. *Toy Catalogue* (Vienna, *circa* 1910)

Noble, John. *A Fabulous Doll House of the Twenties* (Dover, 1976)

Ortmann, Erwin. *The Collector's Guide to Model Tin Figures* (Studio Vista, 1974)

Pettit, Sheila, *The Wallington Collection of Dolls' Houses* (National Trust, 1975)

Pijzel-Dommisse, Jet. *'t is poppe goet en anders niet.* (D. Haan, Haarlem, 1980)

Pinchbeck, M. & Hewitt, *Children in English Society* (Routledge & Kegan Paul, 1967)

Pinto, Edward H. and Eva R. *Tunbridge and Scottish Souvenir Woodware* (Bell, 1970)

Polkinghorne, R. K. and M.I.R. *Toy-Making in School and Home* (Harrap, 1916)

Powell, Rosamund Bayne. *Housekeeping in the Eighteenth Century* (John Murray, 1939)

Rijksmuseum, Amsterdam. *Poppenhuizen* (1967)

Ritz, J. M. *Oberammergau. Guide to Folk Museum* (Community Oberammergau, 1963)

Schweizer, Dr Bruno. *Die Geschichte der Kleinzinngeisserei in Diessen am Ammersee* (Im Verlag der Zinnspielwarenfabrik B. Schweizer, Diessen am Ammersee, 1930)

Schiffer and Schiffer. *Miniature Antique Furniture* (Livingston, New York, 1972)

Science and Industry, Museum of, *Colleen Moore's Fairy Castle* (Chicago, 1964)

Sidgwick, Mrs Alfred. *Home Life in Germany* (Methuen, 1908)

Stille, Eva, *Christbaumschmuck* (Verlag Hans Carl, Nürnberg, 1979)

Sully, James. *Children's Ways* (Longmans, 1897)

Vuillier, Gaston. *Plaisirs et Jeux* (Rothschild, Paris, 1900)

Whatman, Susanna. *Housekeeping Book* (Geoffrey Bles, London, 1956)

Wilkens, L. von. *Das Puppenhaus* (Georg D. W. Callwey, Munich, 1978)

Wilkinson, Sir Neville. *To All and Singular* (Nisbet & Co, 1925)

—— *Grey Fairy and Titania's Palace* (Oxford University Press, 1922)

—— *Yvette in Italy and Titania's Palace* (Oxford University Press, 1922)

Index